D1067492

THE CONSUMER PRODUCT SAFETY ACT

Text

Analysis

Legislative History

Prepared by the Editorial Staff of
The Bureau of National Affairs, Inc.

THE BUREAU OF NATIONAL AFFAIRS, INC.
WASHINGTON, D.C.

Printed in the United States of America
Library of Congress Catalog Card Number: 72-95897
International Standard Book Number: 0-87179-184-6

TABLE OF CONTENTS

INTRODUCTION

Until only a few years ago, most corporate executives considered problems of product liability to be primarily within the domain of house counsel, as matters involving litigation, negotiated settlements, and/or insurance. Production costs, competitive pressures, and consumer apathy combined to make product safety a secondary consideration in the production and marketing of consumer products.

More recently, however, there has been a growing realization that product safety—or, more precisely, the prevention of product liability—originates not with the company's legal department, but with the personnel involved in product design, engineering, quality control, production, packaging, labeling, and distribution of the product.

This change of attitude derives from a variety of causes—including the proliferation of personal injury suits and the mushrooming judgments or settlements resulting from them; recent federal legislation dealing with specific hazards in individual industries, such as flammable fabrics, motor vehicles, toys, chemical packaging, and radiation; the increasing activities of the liability insurance industry in seeking to eliminate or minimize product-caused injuries; and the social and political forces behind the so-called "era of consumerism."

These various elements have now been crystallized in the Consumer Product Safety Act, effective December 26, 1972, which opens a new era in Government-business relationships. For the first time, an independent federal agency has been given regulatory authority over the production and distribution of virtually all consumer products for the purpose of preventing or minimizing product-caused injury, illness, or death. At the same time, the new Consumer Product Safety Commission will be gathering and disseminating hitherto unavailable information on product hazards, for the use of both businessmen and consumers in their production, selling, or buying decisions.

In addition to its basic authority over mandatory safety standards and consumer education, the Commission has been given the power to inspect all industrial and commercial premises dealing with consumer products, impose strict recordkeeping requirements, subpoena all pertinent business documents, establish testing standards, prescribe remedial action, remove imminently hazardous products from the market, ban all nonconforming imports, and seek substantial civil or criminal penalties for safety violations.

The impact of this new legislation on manufacturers, importers, and distributors of consumer products has been analyzed by the editorial staff of The Bureau of National Affairs, Inc., with extensive references to the background and legislative history of the new law. This analysis was prepared under the direction of Wm. J. Barnhard, Managing Editor, and Patricia R. Westlein, Assistant Managing Editor, of BNA's PRODUCT SAFETY & LIABILITY REPORTER, with the assistance of Cynthia J. Bolbach, Roger E. Copland, Jean Culler, John A. Jenkins, Jennifer McMurray, Jeffrey L. Nesvet, and Judith Springberg, and was indexed by Oscar L. Noblejas, Chief Index Editor.

CHAPTER I
THE LAW IN BRIEF

The Consumer Product Safety Act of 1972, approved by the Congress in the closing days of the 92nd Congress as S. 3419, was signed by the President on October 27, 1972, to become Public Law 92-573. (The full text of the Act appears in Appendix A.)

The new law, hailed by the President as "the most significant consumer protection legislation" of the 92nd Congress, creates an independent regulatory agency—the Consumer Product Safety Commission—with five members to be appointed by the President for staggered seven-year terms. One of the members will be appointed as Chairman, and is to continue to serve in that capacity for the full period of his term. No Commission member may be employed by or hold any official position in a company producing or selling consumer products, or have any substantial financial interest in such a company, as stockholder, bondholder, supplier, or otherwise. No more than three of the five Commissioners may be affiliated with the same political party.

A Product Safety Advisory Council is also established by the new law, to be composed of 15 members experienced in the field of product safety—five each from governmental bodies, including federal, state, and local governments; from consumer product industries, including at least one representative of small business; and from among consumer organizations, community organizations, and "recognized consumer leaders." The members of the Advisory Council are appointed by the Commission, and will meet at the call of the Commission, but not less than four times a year. The Council may propose consumer product safety rules for consideration by the Commission and may be consulted by the Commission on any action to be taken.

A. WHAT THE LAW SEEKS TO DO

There is no doubt that the new Commission has unprecedented authority to impose safety standards and other rules that can have devastating impact on all manufacturing and commercial operations related to consumer products. It has been given authority to identify and regulate safety hazards in all products sold to, or used by, the consuming public, with only a few named exceptions already subject to safety regulation by other federal agencies. Its authority extends to new consumer products, as well as those already in the market; it covers imported consumer products, as well as those manufactured in the United States; and it applies to all consumer products that "affect" interstate or foreign commerce, as well as those that actually move across state lines.

The language of the Act, as well as its legislative history, however, makes it clear that the congressional intent, while strongly pro-consumer, was not anti-business. The pattern of regulation established by the Act is one of cooperation and coordination through the active participation of Government, business, consumers, and technicians. The starting point for mandatory safety standards is to be the long list of voluntary standards already adopted by industry. The devising of new standards, where they are found to be necessary, will be initially in the hands of professional organizations of technicians, most of them already involved in the formulation of the voluntary industry standards. In the gathering and dissemination of product or injury information, safeguards are provided for trade secrets and other significant economic information. Judicial review and enforcement of product safety rules and other orders of the Commission is provided for both business and consumer interests. And, at least for the foreseeable future, the bulk of the research and testing activities will be conducted at existing facilities, both private and public.

What's more, creation of the Consumer Product Safety Commission with power to establish and enforce mandatory federal safety standards does not mean the end of voluntary industry standards. In the Final Report of the National Commission on Product Safety, as in much of the congressional debate and testimony, it was emphasized that the mere existence of mandatory governmental authority "often motivates an industry to reduce risks to consumers." One factor in the Commission's determination of priorities among the thousands of consumer products falling within its jurisdiction may well be the extent to which industry groups take voluntary action to increase the level of safety standards.

The Commission's Basic Functions

In order to achieve its ultimate objective of reducing the incidence of product-related injuries, deaths, or serious illnesses, the Consumer Product Safety Commission has been given two basic functions: (1) the gathering and dissemination of information relating to product hazards and the injuries caused by them; and (2) the creation and enforcement of safety standards designed to eliminate or reduce product hazards.

Which of these two functions will have the greater impact on the reduction of product-caused injuries is a matter of some dispute, as the legislative history of the Act demonstrates. The starting point for any evaluation of benefits to the consumer has almost invariably been the 1969 estimate by the Department of Health, Education and Welfare that household accidents, most of them associated with products, account annually for 30,000 deaths, 110,000 permanently disabling injuries, and 20,000,000 injuries serious enough to require medical treatment. How many of these accidents are *caused* by unsafe products—rather than by carelessness, neglect, or misuse by the consumer—is not clear. The Chairman of the National Commission estimated that perhaps 20 percent of the total could be eliminated by mandatory safety standards, while the president of Underwriters' Laboratories believes that only a five percent reduction could be achieved in this manner, with even greater results possible through a program of consumer education. The Consumer Product Safety Commission has been directed and authorized to move in both directions, with questions of emphasis and priorities left to the Commission's discretion.

In the development and promulgation of product safety standards, the banning of hazardous products, and the enforcement of Commission rules and regulations, the Act goes far beyond existing legislation to guarantee the maximum participation of all affected members of society. Business and its trade associations, consumers and consumer organizations, professional and academic groups, state and local governments, are all offered an opportunity to participate at every level of the Commission's activities in seeking to reduce or eliminate the incidence of product-related injuries. The Commission's procedures call for more than the minimum rulemaking requirements of the Administrative Procedure Act; maximum emphasis is placed on non-Commission activities in the formulation of product safety rules; private initiation of Commission action, as well as private enforcement of Commission rules, is made a basic part of the safety program; federal-state cooperation in the safety program is guaranteed; and full resort to the federal courts is reserved for both business and the consumer.

The history of consumer product safety regulation will depend in large part on the extent to which these many involved groups comprehend their rights and their responsibilities under this unique legislation, and the extent to which the various diverse interests, both private and public, can cooperate between and among themselves.

B. WHAT PRODUCTS ARE COVERED

For the first time in the brief history of federal product safety legislation, the Consumer Product Safety Act provides all-inclusive coverage of consumer products, with only certain specific exemptions. Every consumer product that is now on the market or may enter the market in the future is included within the regulatory authority of the Consumer Product Safety Commission, unless it specifically falls within one of the exempted categories.

The basic definition of Section 3(a)(1) of the Act provides that the term "consumer product" includes any article produced or distributed for sale to, or use by, a consumer in or around a permanent or temporary household or residence, a school, in recreation, or otherwise. Thus, there is no requirement that the goods be "sold" to a consumer; the law is applicable to distributed samples, "free" product gifts, leased commodities, and a variety of products sold to others but used by consumers—for example, glass patio doors and household appliances that are sold to construction companies but are used by the home purchasers.

The first requirement for coverage is that the products be "customarily" produced or distributed for sale to, or use by, a consumer. Occasional use of an industrial product by a do-it-yourselfer, for example, would not bring the product within the Commission's jurisdiction, but increasing private use of such products, particularly when accompanied by industry efforts to foster its use by consumers, could quickly remove a product from its initial exempt status.

The explicit exemptions specified in the Act fall into three categories:

1. Products already subject to safety regulation by other agencies under

other federal laws. These include motor vehicles, food, drugs, cosmetics, medical devices, aircraft, boats, and economic poisons.

2. Products that the Congress decided should not at this time be subjected to the safety-regulating authority of the Commission. These are tobacco and tobacco products, firearms and ammunition, and, specifically, meat, poultry, and eggs.

3. Product hazards that can be adequately controlled by other agencies under the Occupational Safety and Health Act, the Atomic Energy Act, the Clean Air Act, or the Radiation Control for Health and Safety Act. This exemption relates to particular hazards, not to the products themselves—for example, existing regulations to protect consumers from radiation emanating from microwave ovens would not remove such ovens from the new Commission's jurisdiction so far as fire and explosion hazards are concerned.

The legislative history of the Act makes it clear that Congress did not intend the Commission's authority to extend to the basic structure of mobile homes, although it does have authority to regulate components, equipment, or appliances sold with, or used in or around, a mobile home (see Appendix G, p. 218).

With these few exceptions, the new Act is to cover virtually all consumer products that may be available to the buying public. In addition, specific provision is made for information to be provided to the Commission on all new consumer products, *before* they enter the market for distribution to the public.

In many cases, where dual regulatory authority may exist, it will take cooperative efforts by the agencies involved, and perhaps court decisions, to resolve the issue of Commission jurisdiction. For example, OSHA regulates power lawnmowers, fire extinguishers, and power tools that are used in commercial establishments, yet these are obviously products that are customarily used by consumers. The Clean Air Act, for another example, permits states to establish standards over home furnaces and fireplaces, to meet federal pollution standards, yet factory-built fireplaces and home furnaces are clearly household items regularly used by consumers and having a potential for product-related injuries. Although both boats and boating accessories are exempt from Commission control, it may be that flotation devices sold as beach toys are covered, even though their use for boating safety purposes is regulated by the Coast Guard. These are only some examples of particular decisions that will have to await Commission action, inter-agency cooperation, and perhaps court action before the exact dimensions of the new Commission's vast authority can be precisely defined.

C. HOW IT AFFECTS MANUFACTURERS

The most direct and most extensive impact of the Consumer Product Safety Act is on the manufacturers of the consumer products that are subject to the jurisdiction of the Consumer Product Safety Commission.

The definition of "manufacturer" in Section 3(a)(4) of the Act states only that the term applies to importers of foreign-made consumer products, as well as to domestic producers of such products. Section 3(a)(8) makes it clear that the term also encompasses assemblers, as well as actual producers. In addition, the definition of "consumer product" in Section 3(a)(1) provides that the term includes not only finished products but also any "component part thereof." Thus, in the case of certain electronic products, for example, where different companies may produce or import various component parts for assembly by still another company, there may be three or four—or even more—manufacturers of the same end product, each of them subject to all the statutory provisions as well as the Commission's rules and regulations dealing with manufacturers. Moreover, private labelers will also be treated as "manufacturers" for certain purposes of the Act, even though they perform no manufacturing or assembling functions (see succeeding section of this Chapter).

Like the basic functions of the Commission, a manufacturer's responsibilities under the Act fall into two major categories—first, accumulating necessary information and providing it to the public, to customers, or to the Commission; and, second, complying with product safety rules. In each of these areas, substantial new demands will be made on all persons who fall within the definition of "manufacturer."

Information Programs

In the broad area of information gathering and dissemination, the Commission has authority to require manufacturers to:

- Establish and maintain such records and reports as may be prescribed, dealing with customers, production processes, testing methods, or other matters—all of them to be subject to Commission inspection or to its subpoena powers;
- Permit inspection of the manufacturer's premises, including areas where the products are produced, stored, or transported;
- Submit to the Commission, and possibly to purchasers, technical data related to the performance and safety of the products;
- Notify the Commission whenever it learns that a product is defective or fails to comply with an applicable standard;
- Provide the Commission with notice, including a description, of any new product being offered on the market;
- Accompany the product with a certification of compliance or appropriate labeling instructions;
- Notify the general public, commercial handlers, or known purchasers whenever it is found that a product is defective or is not in compliance with a safety rule; and
- For the purposes of the Commission's own testing or other informational functions, require the manufacturer to sell his product to the Commission at cost.

In authorizing these vast informational activities of the Consumer Product Safety Commission, the Act provides certain safeguards for manufacturers subject to its terms. Section 6(a) prohibits the disclosure by the Commission of trade secrets and other sensitive economic information, while Section 6(b) requires advance notice to the manufacturer of any product-related information that could identify the particular brand of merchandise.

Product Safety Rules

With regard to safety standards or other product safety rules issued by the Commission, the manufacturer's minimum responsibility is to make such changes in his manufacturing processes, packaging, labeling, and testing activities as may be required by the Commission's mandatory rules. In many industries, a new emphasis will be essential on safety aspects of design engineering, quality control, production techniques, and product testing in order to avoid the potentially severe civil and criminal penalties of the new law. Corporate planners will be required to devote increased attention to the *prevention* of product liability, instead of relying chiefly on their counsel and their insurers to handle the consequences of having produced relatively unsafe products.

Manufacturers will have the opportunity to participate in the formulation of product safety standards, through their trade associations, other industry groups, and sometimes even individually; the Nelson amendment to the Senate product safety bill, which would have barred such participation, was eliminated in the final enactment. More significantly, the starting point for mandatory safety standards to be issued by the Commission will be existing voluntary standards to which manufacturers have generally adhered; and even when the Commission has determined that existing consensus standards are inadequate, the first opportunity to develop new standards will generally be provided to private organizations, principally those groups that have previously been involved in the formulation of the voluntary industry standards. The Act specifies that any organization developing a proposed safety standard is to offer all interested persons, including manufacturers, an opportunity to offer their views.

Throughout the legislative history of the Act, the hope was expressed that the mere existence of the Commission with its authority to issue mandatory standards, plus the increased information available to industry on the nature and frequency of product-related injuries, would provide an incentive and an opportunity to individual manufacturers and their industry associations to take voluntary steps to remove injury-causing features of their products, and thus avoid the necessity for Government-imposed standards.

After the Commission has issued a safety standard or other product safety rule, any affected manufacturer, as well as any consumer organization, has the right to seek judicial review of the Commission's action, to determine whether the need for and the validity of the rule is supported by substantial evidence.

Once the rule becomes effective, a variety of enforcement actions are prescribed in the law to effect compliance—including private as well as public actions, civil as well as criminal penalties, and, where appropriate, injunctive relief or condemnation of the merchandise whenever a substantial hazard is presented. Except where the severity of the hazard requires the product's removal from the market, the remedies imposed upon a noncomplying manufacturer may include notification to the consuming public, repair or replacement of the product, and/or refund of the purchase price. The manufacturer is given authority to determine the most appropriate remedy, subject to the approval of the Commission.

The civil penalties authorized by Section 20 of the Act—$2,000 for each violation, up to a maximum of $500,000—may be applied to each product involved in a violation of a product safety rule, a stockpiling regulation, a remedial order, or a failure to furnish required information, certification, or labeling. Any violation of the inspection requirements of the Act or the provisions giving the Commission access to a manufacturer's records, if a continuing act, shall constitute a separate violation for each day.

To prevent retroactive application, the Act specifically provides that no product safety rule may be made applicable to any product manufactured prior to its effective date, which ordinarily would be at least 30 days after the rule is promulgated (this limitation does not apply to hazardous products banned from the market). However, in order to prevent frustration of any safety standards, the Commission is given authority to issue regulations barring any "stockpiling" of consumer products through drastically increased production between the time a new rule is promulgated and the date it is to become effective. There is no authority given to the Commission to limit manufacturing levels prior to the promulgation of a new rule—for example, after notice has been given that a new standard is to be developed, or after the new standard has been proposed. It is anticipated, also, that any Commission regulations on stockpiling will make some provision for special circumstances, such as the varying production levels for seasonal products.

Advantages to Manufacturers

Although companies manufacturing consumer products will be faced with a plethora of new federal regulations affecting their record-keeping, production, and distribution operations, the legislative history of the new Act evidences widespread support among industry spokesmen for the basic pattern of the Act. For one thing, corporate officials are as interested in avoiding unnecessary product-caused injuries as any other citizens—a natural attitude reinforced in recent years by the dimensions of awards and settlements in products liability litigation. For another, many industries were finding themselves faced with a baffling and often contradictory array of state and local safety requirements that militated against the establishment or maintenance of a national market for many products. Third, many companies found that, in the absence of unanimity among the members of their industry, competitive pressures kept them from adding safety features they deemed helpful or essential. And, finally, in industries dominated by one or a few individual manufacturers, any pressure by the leading producer or producers to force certain safety features on smaller members of the industry could have run headlong into the antitrust laws.

Manufacturers' representatives have expressed the hope that many of these problems may be eliminated or reduced through effective implementation of the Consumer Product Safety Act.

D. HOW IT AFFECTS PRIVATE LABELERS

Private labelers who sell or distribute consumer products under their own name, although they are neither the manufacturers nor the assemblers of the product, are to be treated as manufacturers for only certain purposes of the Consumer Product Safety Act.

According to Section 3(a) (7) of the Act, a privately labeled product is one that carries the brand or trademark of a person other than the manufacturer in lieu of the manufacturer's own name or mark. In most instances, a private labeler will also be a retailer or distributor of the products he sells under his own name, and as such he will be subject to the rules and regulations affecting retailers and distributors (see succeeding sections of this Chapter). Thus, a mail order house or supermarket or drug chain that uses its own brand on products sold to consumers, without revealing the name of the actual manufacturer, would be considered a "retailer," while a cooperative organization using its own brand on products sold to the public through independent but affiliated retail outlets would probably be considered a "distributor" under the Act. Similarly, a manufacturer who adds to his own brand name products a line of consumer goods manufactured by another company—for example, an oil company that sells another company's tires and batteries under its own name, in addition to its petroleum products—would be considered a private labeler for the products it does not manufacture, in addition to any other classification that may apply with respect to the goods it does manufacture and sell.

The basis of the additional responsibilities imposed on private labelers is the congressional belief that "if a person holds himself out as manufacturing a product and as standing behind the product's quality or performance, it is reasonable to ask him to assume certain responsibilities for that product" (see Appendix G, p. 219).

Therefore, in addition to the generally applicable provisions of the Act that affect all industrial and commercial handlers of consumer products—for example, the prohibition against the distribution or sale of noncomplying or banned products, and the Commission's right to enter and inspect any commercial premises where consumer products may be held—the private labelers are subject to certain additional sections of the law.

The requirement imposed on manufacturers by Section 14 of the Act with regard to product certification and labeling is equally applicable to private labelers. Like the manufacturers, the private labeler will be required to test the products, or have them tested, in accordance with procedures and criteria to be established by the Commission, and to provide the requisite certification or labeling. Where there is more than one private labeler of a product, the Commission may specify by rule which of them is to issue the required certificate. The requirement that a label identify the manufacturer of the product is waived in the case of privately labeled goods, provided the label contains a code mark that will allow the seller to identify the actual manufacturer upon request by a purchaser. Other information, such as the date and place of manufacture, may also be coded, with the approval of the Commission, although such permission may carry with it added responsibilities to assure adequate notice in the event recall, replacement, or refunds should be ordered.

Private labelers are also specifically made subject to the record-keeping provisions of Section 16(b), which require establishment and maintenance of such records and reports as the Commission may prescribe and authorize Commission access to all appropriate books, records, and papers. The required records may relate to customer lists, compliance procedures, and any other reports that may be prescribed by the Commission. While retailers are exempt from the record-keeping requirements, the House Committee Report (Appendix G, p. 234) makes it clear that the exemption applies only to retailers who are not also manufacturers, private labelers, or distributors.

E. HOW IT AFFECTS DISTRIBUTORS

Section 3(a) (5) of the Act defines a "distributor" as any person to whom a consumer product is delivered or sold for purposes of distribution in commerce, unless that person is a manufacturer or retailer. At a minimum, the term includes wholesalers, jobbers, and other middlemen in the stream of commerce, and may include warehousemen and centralized cooperatives that distribute to affiliated retail outlets. Excluded from the definition of "distributor" by Section 3(b) of the Act are common carriers, contract carriers, and freight forwarders, if their only function is the receipt and transportation of a consumer product in the ordinary course of their business.

Except for the product safety standards that relate to the actual production of consumer products, distributors are subject to most of the requirements applicable to manufacturers. Like all handlers of consumer products, they may not distribute nonconforming or banned products, they may be subject to injunctive or condemnation orders applicable to hazardous products, and they must allow Commission inspection of their premises. In addition, they are subject to such record-keeping regulations as the Commission may prescribe, they are required to inform the Commission of any product defects or any noncomplying products they observe, and they may be ordered to provide public notice of product hazards and appropriate remedies.

Civil penalties applicable to distributors are the same as those for manufacturers, calling for not more than $2,000 for each violation, up to a maximum of $500,000, with provision for multiple penalties for each product involved. While civil penalties are applicable only when there has been a "knowing" violation, Section 20 defines the requisite knowledge as including not only "actual knowledge" but also knowledge presumed to be possessed by a reasonable man acting in the circumstances upon the exercise of due care.

Unless a distributor is also a manufacturer or private labeler, he is not subject to the Act's requirements involving certification and labeling.

F. HOW IT AFFECTS RETAILERS

The term "retailer" is defined in Section 3(a) (6) as meaning a person to whom a consumer product is delivered or sold for purposes of sale or distribution to a consumer. This includes not only the traditional independent or chain retail outlets and mail order houses, but also door-to-door selling operations and all others having direct relations with the buying public, whether the products are sold, rented, or distributed as "free" samples.

Retailers are subject to all the generally applicable provisions of the Act, dealing with the distribution of nonconforming or banned products, the seizure of hazardous products, and the right of Commission personnel to inspect the premises. They are not subject to the provisions affecting certification and labeling, but they are required to inform the Commission whenever they obtain information that a consumer product fails to comply with an applicable safety rule or contains a substantial product hazard.

The two major exceptions applicable to retailers deal with record-keeping and civil penalties. In order to relieve retailers of the onerous task of keeping records of all sales of all consumer products, the record-keeping provisions of Section 16(b) were made inapplicable to retailers who are not also manufacturers, importers, private labelers, or distributors. In the event of noncompliance, the Commission may require retailers to provide the necessary public notice, but it cannot require individual notification to any but known customers. The Commission has authority to prescribe use of a warranty or registration card that will advise the manufacturer or distributor of the purchaser's name and address, but the major burden of any such record-keeping program would not fall upon the retailer.

With regard to civil penalties for the distribution or sale of nonconforming or banned products, the provision for "multiple penalties" that can be imposed on manufacturers, private labelers, and distributors is not applicable to retailers, if they did not have either actual knowledge of the violation or notice from the Commission that the distribution or sale of the product would constitute a violation. Multiple penalties would be applicable to retailers for any refusal to permit inspections of premises or books, failure to furnish required information, or failure to comply with an order for notification, repair, replacement, or refunds.

G. HOW IT AFFECTS FOREIGN TRADE

The Consumer Product Safety Commission is given substantial, and in some cases unprecedented, powers to regulate the safety of consumer products imported into the United States. However, with only one limited exception, it does not have authority to regulate consumer products that are exported from this country.

U.S. Exports

Section 18 specifically provides that the Act shall not apply to any consumer product that is manufactured, sold, or held for sale for export from the United States, and is so stamped or labeled. Included within this provision are products that are imported for reexport. The sole exception relates to products that are destined for "any installation of the United States located outside the United States"—such as military commissaries, diplomatic missions, and similar establishments.

The Senate and House versions of the product safety bill contained almost identical language with regard to exports (Sec. 318 of the Senate bill, Appendix F, and Sec. 18 of the House version, Appendix I). Both differed markedly from the recommendation of the National Commission on Product Safety, which would have made the Act applicable to exports, unless the U.S. manufacturer filed with the Commission a certification by the responsible official of the importing country waiving the safety regulations (Sec. 22, Appendix B). The Final Report of the NCPS, in its recommendations on "World Responsibility" with regard to consumer safety, urged Government support for international safety standards development as well as the application of safety standards to exported products. "In good conscience," the Report stated, "we must extend to all the protection we expect at home."

Similar sentiments were expressed during congressional debate on the bill (see, e.g., Appendix H, p. 293), but were countered by statements that consumer safety within any importing country is an internal matter for resolution by that country's government, and that the application to American products of safety standards not applicable to products of other countries could make U.S. consumer goods noncompetitive in world markets.

U.S. Imports

All United States imports of consumer products are subject to the provisions of the Consumer Product Safety Act, and the most immediate and controversial impact of the new statute may well be on U.S. importers, their customs brokers, their overseas suppliers, and the U.S. Customs Bureau.

By definition, the owners or consignors of imported consumer products are subject to all the rules and regulations applicable to U.S. manufacturers. Thus, they may not import, distribute, or sell any nonconforming or banned product; their offices and warehouses are subject to Commission inspection; they are required to keep such records as the Commission may specify; they are prohibited from "stockpiling" consumer products between the time a product safety rule is promulgated and its effective date; they are subject to the certification and labeling requirements of the Act; they are required to notify the Commission of "new products" before their introduction into commerce; and they are subject to the many enforcement provisions of the Act, including injunction, seizure, civil and criminal penalties, and orders for notification, repair, replacement, or refunds.

In addition, U.S. imports of consumer products face a number of unusual problems under the Act. First, during the period in which tests are being run to determine whether an imported product complies with the requirements of a product safety rule, the merchandise being tested may *not* be entered under bond, as imports ordinarily are while their compliance with U.S. tariff or other statutes is being determined. Second, even imports that meet all safety standards promulgated by the Commission may be denied entry into the United States if the overseas supplier of the merchandise has not complied with the inspection and recordkeeping regulations prescribed by the Commission. Third, although no product safety rule is meant to be applied to any product manufactured before the rule's effective date, there is some question as to how that provision of the law is to be applied to foreign-made products. Fourth, the certification provisions of the Act, which require the overseas manufacturer and/or the U.S. importer to test their products, or have them tested by qualified third parties, appear to require Commission approval of overseas testing facilities and procedures, whether those of the manufacturer or of an independent testing laboratory. And, finally, in the case of imported products that are ordered weeks or months before their actual importation, the anti-stockpiling regulations to be issued by the Commission will have special impact and could have drastic results.

(For a more detailed discussion of these problems, see CHAPTER IX.)

H. HOW IT AFFECTS CONSUMERS

The ultimate beneficiary of the programs instituted under the Consumer Product Safety Act is, of course, the United States consumer. It is he whom the Act is designed to protect against unreasonable hazards associated with consumer products.

Aside from this passive role as beneficiary, however, the consumer is given a variety of opportunities for affirmative action under the Act's provisions. Perhaps most important, from the viewpoint of eliminating or reducing product-related injuries, is the information that will be made available to the consuming public on the cause and nature of product-related injuries, the recognition of unavoidable hazards, the identity of products causing frequent or serious injuries, and other such information to be provided not only by the Consumer Product Safety Commission but also, it is anticipated, in ever increasing volume by industry itself. One of the major purposes of the Act—one which the legislative history indicates may be even more beneficial than the devising and enforcement of product safety standards—is "to assist consumers in evaluating the comparative safety of consumer products."

Other avenues of participation open to the consumer or his representatives include:

- The right to participate in the formulation of a product safety standard or other rule, at the initial stage when a proposed rule is being developed, during the actual formulation of the proposed rule, at hearings on the proposal, and even, if technically qualified, taking over primary responsibility for the development of a rule.
- The power to seek a court order requiring the Commission to initiate rulemaking procedures (but not until the Act has been in effect for a period of three years).
- The right to seek judicial review of any consumer product safety rule promulgated by the Commission.
- The right to institute court action to enforce a safety rule or other Commission order, through injunctive action, after appropriate notice to the Commission.
- The right to sue in federal court for any injuries sustained by reason of a knowing violation of a product safety rule, provided the $10,000 jurisdictional test of the Judicial Code is met.

The new Act specifically provides that its provisions shall not affect any existing rights or remedies available to consumers under common law or statute. Thus, the remedies now available in personal injury cases will continue as before, with only minimal changes as a result of the new legislation. Typical products liability litigation will henceforth involve an additional fact that may be argued to the judge or jury—that is, the defendant's compliance or noncompliance with an applicable federal standard—and may assist plaintiffs or defendants in acquiring more information on the extent and nature of injuries caused by similar products. But, so far as the legal issues are concerned, traditional personal injury cases will be little affected—except for a hoped-for decline in their number.

(For a more detailed discussion of this subject, see CHAPTER VI.)

I. WHAT IT MEANS TO PRODUCT STANDARDS

One of the most significant aspects of the Consumer Product Safety Act will be the substitution of uniform mandatory federal product safety standards for the voluntary standards already adopted by most industries and the varying standards previously enforced by state and local governments. How quickly that substitution will be made, and on which products, is a matter addressed solely to the discretion of the Consumer Product Safety Commission.

Until the Commission has acted on a particular hazard associated with a particular product, existing standards—whether issued by industry groups or by state and local governments—are to remain in effect. Once a Commission standard has become effective, however, the voluntary industry rules will be completely ousted so far as the pertinent hazard is concerned, while state and local rules will have to conform to the exact requirements of the federal rule, with only two limited exceptions (see CHAPTER X). Compliance with the federal standard will then become subject to all the private and public enforcement procedures specified in the statute.

The Commission has been given specific authority to adopt existing voluntary standards when it determines they provide adequate protection to the consumer. If it determines that additional safeguards are needed, existing professional and industry organizations—both private and public—will be given an opportunity to develop new standards to meet the Commission's stated objectives. Only if there is no satisfactory progress in meeting those objectives through non-Commission procedures will the Commission itself proceed to develop what it considers to be an adequate safety standard.

In the development of safety standards, whether by the Commission or by other private or public organizations, adequate opportunities will have to be provided for full participation by all interested persons, whether in industry, commerce, government, or the consuming public. What changes will be required in previous standards-setting procedures to meet this test of participation will be spelled out in early Commission regulations.

With thousands of consumer products subject to its regulatory powers, the Commission will clearly have to establish its own priorities in acting on particular products and hazards. In making such decisions, the Commission will certainly consider the Final Report of the National Commission on Product Safety, the products that were investigated in depth by that temporary organization, and the revised list of largely unregulated products it included in its Final Report (Appendix N herein). The legislative history of the Act indicates also that industry's reaction to the new regulatory authority may also play a major role in determining the Commission's priorities, since voluntary action by industrial groups to enhance the safety features of their products could induce the Commission to concentrate on other products presenting greater hazards.

In order to give the Commission time to study the vast problems presented to it and to establish some sort of priority list, the Act specifically prohibits any consumer initiation of standards-setting procedures for a period of three years. Thereafter, if there is no change in the statutory provision, priorities may be established in large part by court orders resulting from consumer action.

J. HOW IT AFFECTS THE STATES

As the Consumer Product Safety Commission develops its own standards of safety for consumer products, states and their political subdivisions will play a gradually decreasing role in the development of product safety rules. However, by adopting safety standards identical to those promulgated by the Commission, they may play an increasing role in the enforcement of those standards in state and local courts. In addition, the federal law contains provisions for the use of state and local officials for inspection and other investigatory purposes, as well as provisions for the training of non-federal personnel in product safety enforcement.

The language of the Act, as well as its legislative history, clearly contemplates a maximum of cooperation between states, counties, and cities that seek to play a role in consumer safety and the new Consumer Product Safety Commission.

States and their political subdivisions may petition the Commission for authority to impose safety standards stricter than those promulgated under the federal law, if they are required by compelling local circumstances and do not unduly burden interstate commerce.

(For further discussion, see CHAPTER X.)

K. HOW IT AFFECTS THE COURTS

The Consumer Product Safety Act creates many new types of federal actions, but the Congress was in most instances careful to include limiting provisions designed to prevent any "flooding" of the already overburdened federal courts.

Section 10 of the Act provides for petitions by any consumer or consumer organization seeking a court order that would force the Consumer Product Safety Commission to institute rulemaking procedures. However, this new source of citizen action in the courts will not become effective until October 27, 1975.

The Act also opens the federal courts to suits by consumers who have been injured as the result of a safety rule violation. However, the original plan to make the federal courts available to all injured persons was amended during debate on the floor of the House (see Appendix H, p. 281) to include the Judicial Code provision requiring a minimum amount of $10,000 to be involved. Moreover, the requirement that the federal action involve a "knowing" violation by the defendant is expected to limit the number of federal suits filed in preference to the traditional products liability litigation in state and local courts. The original proposal for treble-damage actions in cases of knowing violations resulting in injury, as recommended by the temporary National Commission on Product Safety, was also eliminated from the legislation.

A unique aspect of the new law going beyond the question of product defects is the provision in Section 23 that authorizes damage actions not only for injuries sustained by reason of a defendant's noncompliance with a promulgated safety standard but also for defendant's failure to comply with a Commission order requiring notification, repair, replacement, or refund, where such failure has resulted in injury, illness, or death.

In cases where many actions involving the same or similar products have been instituted, the Act provides for consolidation of the cases in conformity with the rules on multi-district litigation.

Judicial review of a product safety rule, which can be sought by any affected person or by any consumer or consumer organization, will involve the reviewing court in a more extensive review of the agency's decisions than is customary, since the statutory test is not whether the Commission's action was arbitrary or capricious, but whether its rule is supported by "substantial evidence."

The federal courts will also be involved in actions by the Commission to enjoin distribution or sale of an imminently hazardous product and/or the seizure of such products. In such cases, the Commission may sue in federal court through its own attorneys and without regard to the existence of a product safety rule covering the challenged product.

The courts may also be involved in consumer actions seeking to enforce an effective product safety rule through injunctive or other appropriate relief, although the provision that a consumer contemplating such action must give the Commission at least 30 days' notice before filing his suit could minimize the number of such private suits.

Class actions under Rule 23 of the Federal Rules of Civil Procedure are not expected to be a major factor in product safety litigation, despite the new Act's provision opening the federal courts to certain personal injury cases. In other fields of consumer protection, such actions are playing an increasingly important role in the resolution of private damage claims affecting many members of the public. In product safety, however, several factors appear to limits its usefulness. For one thing, consumer actions to initiate rulemaking proceedings, review Commission action, or enforce product safety rules may be instituted by individual consumers or consumer organizations, and do not require action by a class. For another, personal injury cases do not ordinarily lend themselves to class determinations, in view of the variety of circumstances affecting each determination—involving the plaintiff's use or misuse of the product, the conditions under which the product was used, the servicing it received, and other variables. It is possible that the class action device may be available in cases where an alleged defect appears to be common to many individual injury claims—for example, a defect in the basic design of a product. Whether the plaintiffs' bar will seek to utilize Rule 23 in such cases—and, indeed, whether the defense bar will encourage such procedures in order to gain the protection against multiple litigation afforded to defendants by Rule 23—only time will tell.

L. HOW IT AFFECTS OTHER FEDERAL AGENCIES

The federal agencies most directly affected by enactment of the Consumer Product Safety Act and creation of the Consumer Product Safety Commission are those whose product safety functions are transferred to the new Commission. These include the functions of the Department of Health, Education and Welfare under the Federal Hazardous Substances Act; of the Environmental Protection Agency and HEW under the Poison Prevention Packaging Act; of the Department of Commerce, HEW, and the Federal Trade Commission under the Flammable Fabrics Act; and of the Commerce Department under the Refrigerator Safety Act (the statutory transfer of FTC functions dealing with refrigerators appears to be in error, since the FTC has no authority under that 1956 statute).

The Consumer Product Safety Act's provisions concerning "limitation on jurisdiction" (Section 31) will involve some interplay of regulatory powers and functions with other federal agencies. As explained earlier, the limitations imposed on the Consumer Product Safety Commission by this section deal with specific hazards, not with particular products. The Commission has no authority over products regulated under the Occupational Safety and Health Act, the Atomic Energy Act, the Clean Air Act, or the Radiation Control for Health and Safety Act, to the extent that existing agencies *can* eliminate or reduce risks of injury under the statutes they enforce. Existing authority to protect consumers from the radiation hazards of TV sets, for example, would not oust the Consumer Product Safety Commission from its authority to prescribe safety standards for TV sets involving fire or explosion hazards. Since the limitations on the new Commission's authority depend not on what other agencies *have* regulated, but rather on risks that "could be eliminated or reduced" or on risks that "may be subjected to regulation" under preexisting statutes, it is clear that close coordination will be essential between the various agencies involved with such products.

Coordination will be essential also in the promulgation of standards under these various statutes. For example, at the time the Consumer Product Safety Act was signed into law, OSHA had in effect a safety standard dealing with power lawn mowers—a product which, in its commercial uses, is subject to OSHA regulation but, in its consumer uses, will clearly be subject also to CPSC control. The OSHA standard for powered lawn mowers (Sec. 1910.243(e)) adopts the design specifications of the American National Standards Institute for "power lawnmowers of the walk-behind, riding-rotary, and reel power lawnmowers designed for sale to the general public * * *." Aside from any jurisdictional conflict over products "designed for sale to the general public," it is clear that manufacturers of such products would be subjected to difficult and perhaps irreconcilable regulations if the Consumer Product Safety Commission should decide that the OSHA standards do not adequately protect the general public. Similar problems of reconciliation may be involved in a whole array of products that appear to be within the jurisdiction of both OSHA and the CPSC—for example, fire extinguishers, power tools, chain saws, and many others.

With other federal agencies regulating the safety of products over which the CPSC has no jurisdiction—motor vehicles, economic poisons, aircraft, boats, food, drugs, cosmetics, and medical devices—there will be less compulsion for the coordination of policies and rules, but some congressional sources anticipate that on such matters as the certification of testing laboratories, the regulating of standards-setting procedures, and similar general safety considerations, a mechanism may be developed for coordination.

Other federal agencies will inevitably function in fields of economic activity related to the jurisdiction of the CPSC. The Federal Trade Commission, for example, while losing its operating and enforcement authority under the Flammable Fabrics Act, will still have authority to operate in the product safety field through its power to regulate advertising. For example, just prior to enactment of the Consumer Product Safety Act, an FTC suit under the Flammable Fabrics Act against an importer of berets was dismissed by a federal court on the ground that such "hats" were excluded from the provisions of the Act. Soon thereafter, the FTC moved against the same importer under the provisions of the Federal Trade Commission Act, alleging that the importer's *advertising* of the berets was misleading and deceptive. Since the FTC will clearly retain its authority over consumer product advertising, including ads that relate to safety, coordination between the CPSC, which regulates product safety, and the FTC, which regulates product safety advertising, will obviously be essential.

Early versions of the product safety legislation contained specific provisions authorizing the CPSC to initiate proceedings before other regulatory agencies, whenever it determined that existing safety regulations of the administering bodies were insufficient to protect the consuming public. As finally enacted, the law contains no such provision—in part, apparently, because at the time of its final consideration the Congress was still debating the merits of creating a Consumer Protection Agency whose advocacy functions would include such authority. That bill was not enacted by the 92nd Congress.

Section 29(c) of the Act authorizes the Commission to obtain from any federal department or agency such statistics, data, program reports, and other materials as it may deem necessary to carry out its functions, and directs all governmental bodies to cooperate and consult with the Commission, to the maximum extent practicable, in order to insure fully coordinated efforts.

CHAPTER II
BACKGROUND AND LEGISLATIVE HISTORY

Over the two decades preceding enactment of the Consumer Product Safety Act of 1972, Congress adopted a piecemeal approach to product safety legislation, usually reacting to public outrage over specific hazards identified with a narrow range of consumer products. This was the stimulus for the Flammable Fabrics Act of 1953, the Hazardous Products Labeling Act (later to become the Hazardous Substances Act), the Child Protection and Toy Safety Act, the Refrigerator Safety Act, the Poison Prevention Packaging Act, the Caustic Poison Act, the Radiation Control for Health and Safety Act, and the National Traffic and Motor Vehicle Safety Act.

"While each of these acts is meritorious in its own right and deserving of enactment," states the House Commerce Committee Report (see Appendix G), "this legislative program has resulted in a patchwork pattern of laws which, in combination, extend to only a small portion of the multitude of products produced for consumers."

Not until the mid-1960s did the Congress turn its attention to the possibility of broad, all-encompassing legislation that would give the Federal Government a major role in protecting consumers from unreasonable risks from any consumer product. During that same period, the concern of some industries over this type of federal regulation was being substantially diminished by the proliferation of State and local safety standards that posed substantial problems for the production and distribution of consumer products on any national scale.

The result was the creation of the National Commission on Product Safety, whose two-year study and Final Report constitute the starting point for the legislation that eventuated in the Consumer Product Safety Act of 1972.

A. THE NATIONAL COMMISSION ON PRODUCT SAFETY

The National Commission on Product Safety was established by law in November 1967 (Public Law 90-146). The seven-member bipartisan commission was appointed in March of 1968, chaired by New York City Attorney Arnold B. Elkind. The other members were Emory J. Crofoot, Attorney, Portland, Ore.; Henry Aaron Hill, president of Riverside Research Laboratory, Haverhill, Mass.; Sidney Margolius, syndicated columnist, New York City; Michael Pertschuk, chief counsel of the Senate Commerce Committee; Hugh L. Ray, director of the Merchandise Development and Testing Laboratory of Sears, Roebuck and Company, Chicago, Ill.; and Dana Young, senior vice president of the Southwest Research Institute, San Antonio, Tex.

A national commission to survey product safety was first proposed by Senators Warren G. Magnuson (D-Wash) and Norris Cotton (R-NH) on May 12, 1966. While their proposal failed of enactment that year, it was reintroduced in February 1967, and signed into law on November 20, 1967.

In urging approval of the measure authorizing a commission to study unreasonable risks of injury from household products and to recommend remedial action, Senator Magnuson said: "There exists today no definitive study of the extent to which these hazards constitute a major public health problem. There has never been a significant effort to examine the workings and interrelationships of the present systems of voluntary self-regulation, common law product liability, state and federal regulatory legislation, and municipal ordinances."

The NCPS had been directed to transmit its final report and recommendations to the President and Congress in two years. Because of funding delays, the tenure of the group was extended (Public Law 91-51), and the Final Report was filed on June 30, 1970.

In formulating its recommendations, the Commission followed a basic premise that protection against unreasonably hazardous consumer products should begin at the design stage before the products are on the market, and that product safety is a joint responsibility of private enterprise, public agencies, and the consumer.

In its investigations, the "consumer products" studied by the Commission were defined to include all retail products used by consumers in or around the household, except foods, drugs, cosmetics, motor vehicles, insecticides, firearms, cigarettes, radiological hazards, and certain flammable fabrics.

While conceding that no completely satisfactory definition of "unreasonable hazards" is possible, the Commission assessed individual hazards by studying data relating frequency, severity, duration, and sequelae of injury to the frequency and degree of exposure to the product. The group also considered the degree of inherent risk, the essentiality of the product, and the feasibility and approximate cost of safety improvements.

The Commission considered whether there were acceptable alternatives for a hazardous product; effects on the product of aging and wear; the contribution to hazards of defective maintenance and repair; exposure to instructions or warnings; influence of product advertising on behavior; the extent and forms of abnormal uses of the product; effects of storage, distribution, and disposal; and characteristics of the persons injured, including age, sex, skills, training, and experience.

Products List

The Commission had the whole range of consumer products to consider, and compiled a list of over 200 items that was published in the Federal Register. That original product list later was refined to include approximately 350 largely unregulated product categories, including general household and kitchen appliances, space heating and ventilating appliances, housewares, home communications and entertainment appliances, home furnishings and fixtures, home alarm and protection devices, home workshop apparatus and tools, home and family maintenance products, some farm equipment, household product packaging and containers, sports and recreational equipment, toys, yard and garden equipment, child nursery equipment and supplies, personal use items, home structures and construction materials, and other products such as Christmas decorations, mobile homes and equipment, wheelchairs, and home first-aid and health equipment (see Appendix N).

However, rather than considering the total list of consumer products, the Commission chose to study a number of household product hazards in depth. The 16 products selected for this comprehensive investigation were:

- Architectural glass
- Color television sets
- Fireworks
- Floor furnaces
- Glass bottles
- High-rise bicycles
- Hot-water vaporizers
- Household chemicals
- Infant furniture
- Ladders
- Power tools
- Protective headgear
- Rotary lawn mowers
- Toys
- Unvented gas heaters
- Wringer washing machines

Cases of deaths or injuries, and other statistics on the hazards of these products were compiled. The Commission concluded that "product safety is an open-ended affair," with periodic restudy required for familiar products and safety guidelines required for new products.

The Commission reported that 20 million Americans are injured each year in the home as a result of incidents connected with consumer products and that, of this total, 110,000 are permanently disabled and 30,000 are killed. The group concluded that the annual cost to the nation of product-related injuries may exceed $5.5 billion.

In testimony before the House Commerce Subcommittee on Commerce and Finance in November 1971, Commission Chairman Elkind declared that "the laissez-faire approach to consumer products costs the American public about 20 percent of the overall toll that the public pays in injuries or deaths for the privileges of enjoying consumer products."

While most of the casualties cited by the Commission were found to be associated with consumer products, the group explained that the role of specific products was difficult to define. In fact, the Commission reported that it encountered from the beginning considerable difficulty in obtaining valid statistical information on product-related injuries.

The Commission declared: "Ideally, a rational approach to the system of reducing unreasonable risks in consumer products would be based on data covering injuries, product usage and performance, costs and techniques of manufacture, exposure, and utility."

Citing the principle that no product should be marketed with an unreasonable hazard, the Commission added that the decision on what is unreasonable would benefit from detailed information on the product, together with injury data.

While parts of an injury information system are in existence, the Commission found that "critical elements are barely operative." In its recommendations, the group called for creation of an Injury Information Clearinghouse within the proposed Consumer Product Safety Commission, with responsibility to collect and analyze data on product injuries and to assure widespread distribution of information about defective products, the degree of hazard, and the nature of proposed remedies.

The NCPS explained that the consumer would benefit from information about the products, but emphasized that information is "properly a guide and supplement, not a substitute for regulatory action."

Safety Responsibility

During its deliberations, the Commission considered the very basic question of how to achieve safety in the use of consumer products. Is the consumer responsible for using the products in a safe manner, should the home be so constructed as to provide a safe environment, or should product safety be solely the responsibility of the factory, with regard to design, construction, hazard analysis, and quality control?

The Commission concluded that the answer is neither an unqualified "yes" nor an unqualified "no" to any of these questions. The group pointed out that no safety programs on the manufacturer's level can eliminate all household hazards, since "a society which uses energy in the volume and variety of forms prevalent in ours is certain to see traces of that energy go astray." In addition, the Commission said, many persons like to participate in "dangerous" activities and are conscious of the hazards but take care to control them. However, it was noted, everyone at one time or another suffers from complacency and in that moment disaster can strike. As for the environment, the Commission declared that the majority of American homes contain certain potential hazards such as electrical fire and shock, dim lighting, uneven floors, irregular steps, slippery surfaces, obstacles, steep inclines, poor drainage, or faulty ventilation.

However, the Commission explained, a sound strategy for a safety program is "to seek the weak link in a chain of events leading to injury and to break the chain at that point," and concluded that the greatest promise for reducing product risks "resides in energizing the manufacturer's ingenuity."

The Commission promptly added that the manufacturers should not be expected to act by themselves, but that "with government stimulation they can accomplish more for safety with less effort and expense than any other body—more than educators, the courts, regulatory agencies, or individual consumers."

The NCPS said manufacturers have the power to design, build, and market products in ways that will reduce, if not eliminate, most unreasonable and unnecessary hazards. The Commission stated that there is an implied representation of reasonable safety in the sale of a consumer product, but found, as Chairman Elkind told the House hearing in November 1971, "that the competitive marketing imperatives are eye appeal and cost as opposed to safety."

Regulation by Industry

After studying the record of industry regulation of product safety, the Commission concluded that, with few exceptions, self-regulation by the producers cannot be regarded as adequate. More than 1,000 industry standards are applicable to safety characteristics of the 350 product categories listed by the

Commission. However, the group found these standards "chronically inadequate, both in scope and permissible levels of risk."

"The past effectiveness, or lack of it, of voluntary groups and their standards may be judged—apart from the adequacy of select standards and degree of manufacturer compliance—by the record of injuries associated with consumer products," the Commission declared.

Many of the existing product safety standards were found to be out of date, and consumers were found to have had no substantial voice in the standards procedure. The Commission charged that safety has been "a secondary consideration" in the usual process of developing voluntary standards and that the need for a consensus usually dilutes a proposed standard until it is little more than an affirmation of the status quo.

The Commission concluded: "Dependence on industry financing and technical experts who are paid by industry as regular employees, consultants, or contractors tends to subordinate national interest to private ends. Compliance with voluntary safety standards consists in large part of an honor system which has proven on occasion to be less than honorable. At the same time, voluntary safety programs, with due regard for the public interest, need and warrant federal technical and financial assistance and oversight."

In addition, the Commission said, manufacturers must take all practical steps to prevent foreseeable misuse of products, and should "build safety" into the design and construction of their products.

The group said the measure of voluntary consumer protection provided by the certification programs of independent laboratories is substantial, but is "theoretically flawed" by the laboratory's economic dependence on the goodwill of the manufacturer, even if the lab is nonprofit.

As for the various seals of approval on consumer products, the Commission warned that the protection thus provided is no better than the technical competence, product-testing protocols, and independence of a certifier. In addition, the group warned that such seals may convey a deceptive implication of third-party independence when an industry association awards the seal or when it is awarded in return for paid advertising.

Inadequate Laws

As for existing laws—federal, state and local, and common—concerning consumer product safety, the Commission found the current situations to be piecemeal or "hodgepodge," but consistently inadequate to afford protection to the U.S. consumer.

On the question of federal laws, the group noted that consumers assume that the Federal Government exercises broad regulatory authority in the interests of their safety, while in reality federal authority to curb consumer product hazards is "virtually nonexistent."

While there are various laws treating specific hazards in specific product categories, no federal agency possesses general authority to ban products which harbor unreasonable risks or to require that consumer products conform to minimum safety standards.

The limited federal authority which does exist is scattered among many agencies and the Commission found existing product safety regulation burdened by "unnecessary procedural obstacles, circumscribed investigative powers, inadequate and ill-fitting sanctions, bureaucratic lassitude, timid administration, bargain-basement budgets, distorted priorities, and misdirected technical resources."

On the other hand, the Commission said, in the rare instance when there was adequate authority and administrative support, federal safety programs have succeeded in substantially upgrading industry safety practices.

As for state and local regulations, the study showed a mixture of "tragedy-inspired" responses weakened by diffuse jurisdiction, minuscule budgets, absence of enforcement, mild sanctions, and casual administration. In addition, the Commission charged that in many instances state laws for consumer product safety may be worse than none, since the laws provide only "an illusion rather than the reality of protection." However, the Commission declared that state and local governments have a significant contribution to make in governing installations and repairs, in assembling and disseminating information, and in assuring compliance with safety regulations. While recommending primary federal responsibility for administration and regulatory actions dealing with hazards associated with composition, design, and packaging of products, the Commission therefore deferred to the states for regulations concerning product installation and use. Furthermore, the Commission proposed several methods of federal-state cooperation, including grants, technical assistance, and the deputizing of state and local officials to assist in inspection and enforcement.

Common law has reflected the changing social philosophy toward consumer safety responsibilities over the years, the Commission said, and its ability and freedom to innovate should be preserved. While this does not negate the need for built-in product safety through product design and effective standards, the study showed that some outdated rules which have frustrated the injured consumer may disappear soon, as the result of a combination of legislation and judicial decision.

However, the Commission said, common law has not been primarily concerned with prospective enforcement of product safety but with postinjury remedies. There were no reports of consumers successfully restraining the marketing of potentially hazardous products, and the Commission concluded that the common law puts no reliable restraint upon product hazards.

Basic Conclusions

Commission principles thus included:

1. Consumers have a right to safe products;
2. A manufacturer's offer of a product implies a warranty that the item is not unreasonably hazardous;
3. Consumer products hazards have been found to be excessive;
4. Industry efforts, the common law, and existing federal programs have been found inadequate to protect the public;
5. State, local, and voluntary agencies lack authority to issue uniform regulations and mandatory standards nationwide and have few resources to gather and distribute basic information about product hazards.

Therefore, the Commission concluded, broad responsibility for the safety of consumer products should be vested in a "conspicuously" independent federal regulatory agency given extensive authority to issue regulations and develop mandatory safety standards, and a Consumer Safety Advocate should be appointed by the President to the Consumer Product Safety Commission staff to serve as the consumer representative.

Independent Agency

In calling for an independent federal authority over product safety, the Commission reiterated its findings on the weaknesses of existing programs on specific products, and said reasons for the inadequacies include lack of substantial funding and staffing because of competition with other programs within an agency, lack of vigor in enforcing the law, and a low priority assigned to programs of low visibility.

While conceding that there have been exceptions to these problems, the Commission concluded that a federal agency needs independent status when it must take up substantial and controversial issues of consumer safety and economics. In addition, the group said, independence can be furthered by appointment of commissioners on a nonpartisan basis, for staggered fixed terms subject to removal only for cause, and by designation of a permanent chairman to serve an entire term in that capacity.

From its own experience, the Commission reported that the mere existence of a government-authorized group studying and raising issues of product safety has resulted in some significant safety innovations.

The Commission explained that the Government's role in product safety would initially be to motivate businessmen to reduce product hazards, while assuring fair treatment of competing interests, and secondarily to promulgate and enforce safety regulations where voluntary efforts fail. While concluding that the forces of competition and the profit motive are neither inherently conducive to, nor inimical to, consumer protection, the Commission added that with Government support these forces can be channeled to assure compliance with safety standards to reduce unreasonable hazards.

Commission Recommendations

The recommendations of the National Commission on Product Safety were incorporated in the proposed Consumer Product Safety Act, which included specific proposals for an independent federal product safety agency, with the power to develop and set mandatory product safety standards, authority to seek a court order to enjoin the marketing of specific products creating an unreasonable risk, sanctions to secure compliance, and authority to conduct hearings requiring witnesses to testify or provide pertinent documents (see Appendix B).

In addition to calling for establishment of an independent product safety agency and a consumer safety advocate, specific recommendations of the National Commission on Product Safety in the June 1970 report included the following:

1. Establish an Injury Information Clearinghouse;
2. Authorize the Consumer Product Safety Commission to accredit private

laboratories to test and certify compliance with specific product safety standards;

3. Rigorously apply and/or expand the authority of the Federal Trade Commission to any certification program which misleads or deceives the consumer, and apply the FTC powers where appropriate to the advertising of consumer products to assure disclosure of substantial hazards;

4. Expand existing programs of the Small Business Administration to authorize granting long-term, low-interest loans to assist small businesses in meeting requirements of product safety standards;

5. Establish a laboratory facility within the commission to conduct safety research, to cooperate with other federal agencies in supporting safety research, and to develop technical information for use by manufacturers and standard-making groups;

6. Authorize injured consumers to file claims for treble damages, as well as class actions, in the district courts against manufacturers who knowingly or willfully violate federal consumer product safety standards;

7. Apply uniformly the doctrine of strict tort liability in state and federal courts to enable a consumer injured by a product in defective condition to obtain fair compensation; and seek modification by state legislatures of obsolete statutory provisions which unduly impinge on the consumer's right of redress for injury;

8. Authorize the commission to support states and localities in product safety activities or projects in surveillance, injury reporting, hazard reduction, research, and training;

9. Preempt any state or local standard by a mandatory federal safety standard, with appropriate provision for exemption where clear and compelling conditions in the state make it necessary;

10. Require that consumer products imported for sale into the U.S. be denied entry if they violate federal consumer product safety standards or regulations or are deemed to be unreasonably hazardous; and

11. Have the Government close the gap in legislative authority existing between the U.S. and other industrial countries, support international safety standards development, and prohibit the export of hazardous products to other countries.

B. HOW THE LAW EVOLVED

As soon as the final report of the National Commission on Product Safety was made public in June 1970, there was a flurry of activity on both sides of Capitol Hill as Senators and Representatives introduced measures designed to carry out the recommendations of the Commission.

On June 24, the Senate Commerce Committee met with members of the National Commission on Product Safety to receive a verbal explanation of the recommendations. Committee Chairman Warren Magnuson (D-Wash) said the Commission's report "makes a sound case for strong, innovative omnibus product safety legislation," and Chairman Frank E. Moss (D-Utah) of the Commerce Consumer Subcommittee pledged to work "vigorously" for enactment of legislation to carry out the recommendations.

Commission Chairman Elkind pointed out that his group's proposed Consumer Product Safety Act would establish an independent, bipartisan consumer product safety commission with authority "to police and punish" manufacturers "who unreasonably violate their duty to produce safe products." In addition, he noted that a consumer advocate, as proposed to be appointed in the new agency, would be free to criticize or offer suggestions on areas the commission should cover.

Commission Proposal

While the Commission's final report was dated June 30, 1970, the first product safety bill patterned after the panel's legislative recommendations was introduced in the House on June 24 by Rep. James G. O'Hara (D-Mich), and referred to the House Commerce Committee (H.R. 18208, 91st Congress). In the following three months, seven identical product safety bills were introduced in the House.

On the Senate side, Senators Magnuson and Moss introduced the consumer product safety measure (S.4054, 91st Congress) on July 1, 1970, just one day after the formal publication date of the Commission report. That bill, like those introduced in the House, followed the recommendations of the panel for an independent federal product safety commission composed of five commissioners, with power to set safety standards for consumer products, to establish an injury information clearinghouse, and to conduct investigations into the safety of existing products. The measures also provided for appointment of an independent "safety advocate" to represent consumer interests before the proposed commission.

Little of substance on a consumer product safety agency was accomplished during the remainder of the Second Session of the 91st Congress. No committee action was taken and therefore no product safety agency bill made it to either floor of Congress. It was explained at the time that the release of the National Commission's report and its legislative recommendations so late in the session left little time for congressional action on such a complex and controversial issue. In addition, 1970 was a congressional election year and both House and Senate spent several weeks in recess in the late summer and early autumn of the year.

With the opening of the 92nd Congress in January 1971, however, consideration of consumer product safety commission measures began again. Rep. John Murphy (D-NY) reintroduced the NCPS-proposed Consumer Product Safety Act (H.R. 260) in the House on January 22, 1971, and Senator Magnuson reintroduced it in the Senate (S.983) on February 25, 1971. Rep. John E. Moss (D-Calif), Chairman of the House Commerce Subcommittee on Commerce and Finance, on May 6, 1971, introduced a bill (H.R. 8157) similar to the Murphy measure and based on the National Commission's recommendations.

Administration Bill

The Nixon Administration also made proposals for consumer protection legislation in 1971, including strong recommendations for establishing a consumer product safety program within the Department of Health, Education, and Welfare. That proposal was introduced in the Senate by Senator Magnuson, by request, as S. 1797, and in the House by House Commerce Committee Chairman Harley Staggers (D-WVa), by request, as H.R. 8110 in May 1971.

As congressional debate began on a consumer product safety agency, the four measures surfacing as the most important in this area were S. 983 and H.R. 8157, based on the recommendations of the National Commission on Product Safety; and S. 1797 and H.R. 8110, the Administration proposals giving product safety authority to HEW.

Senate Commerce Committee hearings on the bills began in July 1971, and it became apparent that these four bills would form the basis for the product safety legislation coming out of Congress. The major issue then wasn't whether there should be a product safety agency, but rather what powers it should have and whether it should operate as an independent agency or as part of a Cabinet-level department.

As the Senate hearings began, President Nixon sent a letter to the committee urging approval of the Administration plan to set up a Consumer Safety Administration within HEW. Mr. Nixon called this a "strong," satisfactory plan, and explained that the new office would expand work done by the Food and Drug Administration and would provide "the facilities, the personnel, and the organizational prominence that will ensure an effective, efficient, and responsible product safety program."

However, Elkind told the Senate panel that the Administration's proposal was nothing more than a "paper tiger," and said his opposition to that plan "is not arbitrary nor political but is grounded on the lessons which the Commission learned in the course of its work." In urging approval instead of the Commission's proposals as provided in S. 983 and H.R. 8157, Elkind warned that if the Administration bill were enacted "it would be as though the Government were to fashion, like Dr. Frankenstein, a man with beautiful sinews, long arms, and piercing eyes, with just one weakness—an inability to hear from the consumer and respond to its needs."

After the Senate committee concluded 10 days of hearings, the staff members began writing a revised or "clean" bill for committee consideration when Congress returned from its summer recess.

The House Commerce Subcommittee on Commerce and Finance began its hearings on the consumer product safety proposals on November 1, 1971, and conducted them at intervals through February 3, 1972. As was the case during the Senate hearings, Administration and business officials generally endorsed the plan placing product safety authority in HEW, while consumers representatives, including Ralph Nader and representatives of Consumers Union and the Consumer Federation of America, backed the independent agency approach.

Senate Unit Action

Meanwhile, the Senate Commerce Committee was moving toward final approval of its own product safety bill, and on March 24, 1972—almost two years after the National Commission on Product Safety issued its final report—voted out a revised version of the legislation by an overwhelming margin. As expected, the Senate committee approved a "clean" bill introduced as S. 3419, rather than amending the bills already before it (see Appendix C).

The measure that finally made it out of the Senate Commerce Committee bore the markings of Senator Magnuson's handiwork—it would establish an independent Consumer Safety Agency with authority over virtually all consumer goods, including food, drugs, and cosmetics. Since the bill would alter the government regulatory process and affect the lives of every American, the Commerce Committee sent the bill to the Senate Government Operations Committee and to the Senate Labor and Public Welfare Committee for further consideration. A subcommittee of the Government Operations Committee held hearings on the measure, and the Senate Labor Committee recommended numerous amendments in which the Government Operations unit concurred. These changes were incorporated into the measure and the resultant proposal was for establishment of a Food, Drug, and Consumer Product Safety Agency (see Appendix D).

The measure provided for transfer of Agriculture Department authority under meat, poultry, egg, and other agricultural product inspection laws to the Product Safety Agency, and for transfer to the new agency of the authority under the Hazardous Substances Act, Flammable Fabrics Act, Radiation Control for Health and Safety Act, Poison Prevention Packaging Act, Refrigerator Safety Act, and Food, Drug, and Cosmetic Act.

Thus, Senate committee action on the consumer product safety bill was completed by early June 1972, with the way clear for Senate floor consideration of the proposal before a two-week recess in July for the Democratic National Convention.

House Measure

While all this was going on in the Senate, the House Commerce Subcommittee was meeting in an attempt to work out a bill acceptable to supporters of the independent agency approach as well as to staunch Administration allies. In late May 1972, the House subcommittee approved a "clean" bill, H.R. 15003, to establish an independent product safety commission with authority over all consumer products except tobacco, economic poisons, motor vehicles and equipment, firearms and ammunition, food, drugs, medical devices, and cosmetics. That bill gained full House Commerce Committee approval in early June (see appendix G).

While the recommendation of the National Commission on Product Safety for establishment of an independent federal authority over product safety was included in both Senate and House measure (S. 3419 and H.R. 15003), albeit in significantly different forms, one potentially controversial recommendation of that Commission was left out of the bills approved by the congressional committees. This was the proposal for appointment of a Consumer Safety Advocate to represent consumers before the proposed new agency.

The bill (S. 3419) originally approved by the Senate Commerce Committee had included provision for appointment of a consumer counsel to represent the consumer interests in any rulemaking proceedings undertaken by the agency. However, the committee explained that if a separate consumer advocacy agency were created, as proposed in other pending legislation, it was the intent that reliance be placed upon an advocate furnished by that agency for representation of the consumer interests. When the Senate Labor Committee considered the bill, however, all provision for consumer representative appointment was dropped. The House Commerce Subcommittee dropped the provision for a consumer advocate within the product safety commission during its drafting sessions on the bill, explaining that the consumer representation question was being taken care of in separate legislation.

But the plan for a separate Consumer Protection Agency or consumers "ombudsman" died in Congress late in the 1972 session. While the House had passed its version of that legislation in October 1971, the Senate deadlocked on its bill late in September 1972 and the measure was lost in the 92nd Congress adjournment procedures.

Bill Amended

In the consumer product safety area, Senate passage of S. 3419 came on June 21, 1972, on a 69 to 10 vote, with only a few changes made on the floor (see Appendix E and Appendix F). Most importantly, the Senate rejected by a vote of 32 to 51 a proposal by Senator Norris Cotton (R-NH) to establish the product safety office within HEW. Another key vote was the 39-to-41 rejection of Senator Cotton's proposal to eliminate criminal penalties from the measure. Senator Edward R. Gurney (R-Fla) was unsuccessful on his amendment to delete authority for the product safety agency to prosecute its own cases; the amendment lost by a vote of 31 to 51.

The Senate approved by voice vote an amendment by Senator Moss to leave meat and poultry inspection authority within the Agriculture Department, and also agreed to an amendment by Senator Herman Talmadge (D-Ga) to provide that a manufacturer may be awarded actual damages suffered by him as a result of any order banning a product as a hazardous substance determined by a federal court to constitute an abuse of the discretion granted by the Commissioner. Under the Talmadge amendment, if a federal court finds that a product which was banned should not have been banned, the court would determine whether the decision to ban the product constituted an abuse of discretion. If such an abuse was found, then a special master would be appointed to assess the manufacturer's actual damages and refund them to him from the public treasury, along with the payment of the legal rate of interest on this sum computed since the order to ban was issued.

Another amendment successfully proposed by Senator Talmadge was designed to give a manufacturer an option whereby he may be protected on repurchase requirements. The provision gave the manufacturer of a banned hazardous consumer product an opportunity to notify distributors and retail dealers of the ban and thereby limit liability to the price paid for the product by the distributor or retail dealer.

A proposal by Senator Gaylord Nelson (D-Wis) dealing with development of suggested consumer product safety standards also was approved by the Senate. That amendment provided that consumers could participate in an offeror's development of a standard, but that the offeror could not be a manufacturer, distributor, or retailer of a consumer product to be included in the standard.

Other amendments approved by the Senate provided for registration of toxic or corrosive products, for protection of businessmen against unwarranted dissemination of business information, for inclusion of a separate function of veterinary medicine, and for making the bill applicable to defects in design as well as manufacturer's defects.

For the Senate, the 69 to 10 approval of the amended bill marked the end of another legislative chore, and the next step was up to the House. However, that step was slow in coming. Recesses for the Democratic and Republican National Conventions precluded a vote on the bill throughout the summer, and as September rolled around the House Rules Committee—the panel that sets the terms of floor debate—hadn't yet granted a rule to send the measure to the House floor. The Consumer Federation of America accused the Rules Committee of attempting to "bushwhack" the product safety bill by leaving it off the meeting agenda. On September 13, the Rules panel voted 10 to 4 to send the measure to the House floor.

When the House action finally came—on September 20, 1972—the result was a lopsided victory for supporters of the bill. The House passed the measure on a roll-call vote of 318 to 50, accepting the Senate number, S. 3419, but incorporating the language of H.R. 15003, a usual parliamentary procedure on a bill that has passed in the other body first (see Appendix I).

During House debate on product safety, some rather significant amendments were approved (see Appendix H). These included a proposal by Rep. David Dennis (R-Ind) providing that product injury suits may be brought in the federal courts only if the amount in controversy is $10,000 or more. House Commerce Committee Chairman Staggers successfully proposed an amendment providing that the effective date of a consumer product safety standard would be set at a date at least 30 days after the date of promulgation, unless the commission determines that an earlier effective date is in the public interest, and another providing for coded dating rather than open dating on certain noncompetitive products. The House also approved amendments proposed by Rep. Moss to authorize the commission to utilize the resources of the National Bureau of Standards on a reimbursable basis on research and analysis of product hazards, and to provide that no one would be liable to damages for responding to a commission request for information on a product.

The House rejected proposals to provide for coverage of firearms by the product safety commission, and to transfer to the new commission authority over electronic product radiation.

Since neither version of the bill was completely acceptable to the other House of Congress, a Senate-House Conference Committee then was set up to work out a product safety bill that could be approved by both sides of Congress.

C. THE FINAL AGREEMENT

After Senate and House conferees met several times in late September and early October 1972 on the very significant differences between their two bills, the measure which resulted strongly resembled the House-passed version, with

Senate provisions prevailing in few cases, and with substitute language added in others (see Appendix J).

The final measure—the conference agreement—was approved by the House October 13 and by the Senate October 14, and the President signed it October 27.

It is general practice with congressional conferences for each side to give up something in order to gain approval of something else, but with the consumer product safety bill, the Senate came out with very little of its bill intact.

The major hurdle for House acceptance was the Senate's inclusion of broad regulatory authority over almost all consumer products, including food, drugs, cosmetics, medical devices, and veterinary medicine. There were general negotiations early in the conference for the Senate to delete the extensive coverage if the House then would agree to numerous refining amendments to bring the two versions closer. Since time for the 92nd Congress was rapidly running out, and since most of the conferees wanted a product safety bill in 1972, the Senate negotiators agreed to drop the controversial language.

Conferees Agree

Thereafter, the House conferees agreed to some revisions in their bill and to some substitute provisions, but the final measure retains little of the Senate-proposed language. Rather, the measure more closely resembles the recommendations of the National Commission on Product Safety, at least in its broad patterns.

The final measure provides for transfer to the Commission of the functions under the Federal Hazardous Substances Act, the Poison Prevention Packaging Act, the Flammable Fabrics Act, and the Refrigerator Safety Act. The conference version does stipulate that a risk of injury associated with consumer products which could be eliminated or reduced to a sufficient extent by action under the Federal Hazardous Substances Act, the Poison Prevention Packaging Act, or the Flammable Fabrics Act may be regulated by the new Commission only in accordance with provisions of those Acts. On refrigerator safety, the conferees set no such restrictions.

One significant Senate proposal on development of a product safety standard was lost in conference. The Senate-passed bill had permitted the product safety agency to proceed with development of a proposed standard even while a standard on the product was being developed by an outside offeror. The House version had prohibited the commission from publishing a proposed rule or developing proposals for a standard during the development period of an offeror, unless no offeror was making satisfactory progress.

As a compromise, the conferees wrote a substitute provision allowing the Commission to proceed independently to develop proposals for a standard only when the sole offeror working on the standard is a manufacturer, distributor, or retailer of the product proposed to be regulated.

However, the conferees cautioned that the provision should not be interpreted "as preventing the Commission or its staff—while awaiting the submission of recommended standards—from developing or acquiring the technical capability necessary to properly evaluate the standards recommended to it."

The Senate bill also had included requirements that interested persons be given an opportunity to participate in the development of the standard "in accordance with accepted standards of due process" but the House measure had included no comparable provision and the Senate language was dropped in conference.

On stockpiling a product during the period from issuance to effective date of a standard, however, the Senate was more successful. The House had no comparable provision, but the Senate bill had prohibited any manufacturer or importer, in an effort to stockpile a consumer product, from producing or importing the product during the time between issuance of a final order establishing a standard and the effective date. The conferees revised the provision to authorize the commission by rule to prohibit manufacturers, including importers, from stockpiling the product, with "stockpiling" defined as manufacturing or importing, between date of promulgation of the consumer product safety rule and its effective date, at a rate which is significantly greater than the rate at which the product was produced or imported during a base period. There is no provision affecting any increased marketing between the date the standard is proposed and the date of promulgation.

On product certification, the final bill includes the House provision that the requirement to provide certification applies only to manufacturers and private labelers, and does not apply to distributors or retailers. On banned hazardous products, the Senate provision requiring manufacturers to repurchase noncomplying products was eliminated in favor of the House provision giving the Commission authority to issue rules on repurchases. Both bills had given the new agency administrative authority to ban a consumer product if no feasible standard would adequately protect the public. The Senate had included a requirement for a person in the distribution chain to repurchase any product sold by him after a proposed rule banning a product was published. This provision was taken out by the conferees.

In the final bill, commission authority to order reimbursement to purchasers of unsafe products may be extended not only to consumers, but also to purchasers who are themselves manufacturers, distributors, or retailers. In addition, the Commission has authority to determine whether the manufacturer, distributor, or retailer of the product is responsible for the reimbursement. The compromise version also eliminates the Senate bill's provision authorizing a court, in its review of an order banning a hazardous product from the market, to award the manufacturer damages, costs, and attorneys' fees if it should be determined that the Commission had exceeded its authority in banning the product.

On imported products, the conferees rejected the Senate provision allowing noncomplying imports to be entered under bond, and adopted instead the House provision for an outright ban on noncomplying entries.

The Senate provision for civil penalties of $10,000 "for each act" in violation was dropped in favor of the House provision for $2,000 for each act up to a maximum of $500,000, and the Senate provision for criminal penalties of one year in jail or $10,000 for each act gave way to the House provision for a fine of $50,000 or one year in jail.

Suits to compel compliance with product safety rules or to enjoin violations may be brought by commission attorneys, but only with the concurrence of the Attorney General. The final measure authorizes private suits for enforcement of consumer product safety, but the conferees dropped the House bill's provision allowing private litigants to have free access to accident and investigative reports compiled by the Consumer Product Safety Commission and to have Commission investigators testify in the private suits.

CHAPTER III
ADMINISTRATION

A. CONSUMER PRODUCT SAFETY COMMISSION

The Consumer Product Safety Commission is designed in the image of other regulatory commissions, such as those established to regulate rail and air transportation, oil and gas production, communications, and the securities markets. However, while the Act includes the usual mechanisms for organization of independent agencies, it also involves certain departures from traditional practice in this area.

In its report, the House Commerce Committee emphasized that it intended "that the agency be independent of the executive department and to be removed as far as possible from the influence of partisan politics or political control." The House unit said it intended the Commission to be designed in the image of other regulatory commissions and subject to traditional requirements relating to appointment and organization, but with certain revisions designed to improve upon traditional practice (see Appendix G).

Personnel

Some of the "departures" from traditional practice are evident in the law's provisions for appointment of the members of the Commission. The President is to appoint, with the advice and consent of the Senate, five Commissioners, with not more than three from the same political party. The first five Commissioners are to be appointed for terms ending three, four, five, six, and seven years, respectively, after the October 27, 1972, date of enactment of the Act. Each of their successors is to be appointed for a term of seven years from the expiration of the term for which his predecessor was appointed, thereby providing for seven-year staggered terms.

The President is to designate one of the five Commissioners as Chairman, and it is from here that the Act begins to depart from tradition. The Chairman is to continue in that office until the expiration of his term as a member of the Commission. The House Commerce Committee said that, because the Chairman is designated as the principal executive officer and assigned special powers to control the operation of the agency, the Chairman should not serve "at the pleasure of the President." Thus, the President will not be empowered to designate some other Commissioner to serve as Chairman within the Chairman's term of office on the Commission. Also, if the Chairman's term of office runs into another Administration, the incumbent President would not be able to remove the Chairman and replace him with his own designee.

The Act stipulates that members of the Commission may be removed only for neglect of duty or malfeasance in office, and for no other cause. This is designed to "properly isolate members of the Commission from removal from office at the whim of the executive," the House Committee explained, and, "by delineating the bases for removal, your committee intends to restrict the President's power to remove from office to these grounds alone."

A Commissioner appointed to fill a vacancy occurring before the expiration of a predecessor's term will serve only for the remainder of that term. A Commissioner may continue to serve after his term expires until a successor has taken office, but he may not continue to serve "more than one year after the date on which his term would otherwise expire."

The Act includes some strict and unusual restrictions on those appointed as a Commissioner. No person may be a Commissioner who is employed by, or holds any official relation to, anyone selling or manufacturing consumer products. Commissioners also are prohibited from owning stocks or bonds of substantial value in those so engaged, and from having any pecuniary interest in such a person or in a substantial supplier of such a person. In addition, the law specifies that the Commissioners may not be engaged in any other business, vocation, or employment. The House Committee, recognizing that these restrictions are "severe," said it intended "to create a standard for members of the Commission which will assure that they are their own masters and are known to be such."

In another provision designed to assure that Commissioners and principal agency employees carry out their responsibilities "vigorously and without compromise," the Act stipulates that no full-time officer or employee of the Commission who received compensation in excess of the GS-14 rate at any time during the 12 months preceding termination of his employment may accept employment or compensation from any manufacturer subject to the Act for a period of 12 months following his employment with the Commission. The House unit said this restriction "is intended to assure that persons will not seek employment with the agency or use their federal office as a means of subsequently gaining employment in the regulated industry or as a means of acquiring members of industry as future clients."

A Vice Chairman is to be elected annually by the Commission to act in the absence or disability of the Chairman, or in case of a vacancy in the office of Chairman. Three members of the Commission are to constitute a quorum for the transaction of business, and no vacancy is to interfere with the right of the remaining members to exercise all the powers of the Commission. The Commission will have an official seal, and a principal office and such field offices as it deems necessary, but may meet and exercise any of its powers at any place.

As principal executive officer of the Commission, the Chairman will exercise all of its executive and administrative functions, subject to the Commission's general policies, regulatory decisions, findings, and determinations. He will appoint, supervise, and distribute business among the Commission personnel other than those employed regularly and full time in the immediate offices of the other Commissioners. He also will distribute business among administrative units of the Commission and administer the use and expenditure of funds. The Chairman may employ other officers and employees, including attorneys, needed to carry out Commission functions.

An Executive Director, General Counsel, Director of Engineering Sciences, Director of Epidemiology, and Director of Information will be appointed by the Chairman, subject to Commission approval. The Act stipulates that the rate of pay for these officials may not exceed grade GS-18 of the General Schedule. In the bill approved by the House Commerce Committee, this provision (Section 4(g)(1)) would have provided that these five appointments could be made without regard to competitive civil service, classification of positions, or the General Schedule rates of pay up to GS-18. Rep. David N. Henderson (D-NC) proposed an amendment during the House debate to delete these exemptions, explaining that the "provisions have the effect of authorizing five additional supergrades which may be filled by political appointees." (see Appendix H, p. 283). The amendment to delete the exemption was approved, and was retained in the final version of the law.

The Chairman of the Commission will be compensated at Level III of the Executive Schedule—$40,000 per year—and the members of the Commission will be at Level IV of the Schedule—$38,000 per year.

Additional Functions of the Commission

In addition to its basic regulatory authority, the new Commission is directed to report to the President and Congress each year, and also is given authority to conduct hearings, subpena witnesses and information, initiate and prosecute court actions, and enter into contracts with other agencies, private organizations, or individuals.

In another significant departure from tradition, the new Commission is to submit its budget estimates and requests to Congress at the same time the estimate or request is sent to the President or the Office of Management and Budget. In addition, whenever the Commission submits legislative recommendations, testimony, or comments on legislation to the President or the OMB, it shall concurrently transmit a copy of it to Congress. The law specifies that no officer or agency shall have any authority to require the Commission to submit its legislative recommendations, testimony, or comments for prior approval, comments, or review.

These provisions were strongly opposed by the Office of Management and Budget, which urged President Nixon to veto the consumer product safety bill. While he signed the measure, President Nixon said the provisions "will tend to weaken budget control—and a coordinated, unified budget is the consumer's ally in keeping inflation and taxes down." The President declared that the provisions are "unfortunate," and warned that they should not be regarded as precedent for future legislation (see Appendix M).

In discussing similar provisions in the Senate bill during debate on that measure in June (see Appendix E), Senator Edward Kennedy (D-Mass) said: "If the Agency is to be effective, the Administrator must be capable of informing Congress, directly and without interference, exactly what he and his Agency believe to be the facts about the matters before it. The inevitable compromise softening of approach and delays achieved through a review process, which often includes several departments and agencies, is inconsistent with the type of strong new Agency envisioned by this bill. Similarly, it is important that the Administrator establish his own personnel policies in a manner suited to the regulatory mission of the new Agency, rather than the judgment of some official outside the Agency."

Annual Report

A comprehensive report on the administration of the Act for the preceding fiscal year is to be prepared by the Commission and submitted to the President and Congress on or before October 1 of each year. In his November 1971 testimony at the House hearings, National Commission Chairman Elkind said the annual report "is designed to present to Congress and to the President a graphic picture of whether or not this organization or this Commission has something to do, is doing it, whether it is worthwhile . . ."

The annual report of the Commission must include:

1. A thorough appraisal of the incidence of injury and effects to the population resulting from consumer products, with a breakdown among the various sources of the injuries;
2. A list of consumer product safety rules prescribed or in effect during the year;
3. An evaluation of the degree of observance of the rules, including a list of enforcement actions, court decisions, and compromises of alleged violations, by location and company name;
4. A summary of outstanding problems with administration of the new law, in order of priority;
5. An analysis and evaluation of public and private consumer product safety research activities;
6. A list of completed or pending judicial actions;
7. The extent to which technical information was disseminated to the scientific and commercial communities, and consumer information was made available to the public;
8. The extent of cooperation between Commission officials and representatives of industry and other interested parties, including a log or summary of meetings;
9. An appraisal of significant actions of state and local governments relating to responsibilities of the Commission; and
10. Recommendations for additional legislation considered necessary to carry out the purposes of the Act.

Although neither the requirements for the annual report nor any other section of the Act makes mention of the duration of the Commission's existence, it is interesting to note that Chairman Elkind of the National Commission on Product Safety regarded it as containing the elements of self-destruction. In testimony before the House Commerce Subcommittee in November 1971, he suggested that when "standards have been established and the job has been done, this governmental function can be substantially reduced and a continuing program of monitoring could then readily be transferred to some existing agency. * * * What is needed is a highly visible task force that will obtain the necessary money to do its job—that will render regular accountings directly to the Congress of its stewardship of the problem, and that will in effect self-destruct when its mission has been accomplished." He added that the annual report required of the Commission could function as an indicator of the continued need for its existence.

Hearings

Hearings or other inquiries may be conducted anywhere in the United States by the Commission, its members, or its designated agent or agency. Participation in a hearing or inquiry will not disqualify a Commissioner from subsequently participating in a Commission decision on the matter. Notices of hearings will be published in the Federal Register, and interested persons given an opportunity to participate.

The Commission also has the power to require written reports and answers to questions, within a reasonable period, and under oath or not. It may administer oaths, require by subpena the attendance and testimony of witnesses and the production of documentary evidence, and order testimony to be taken by deposition before any person it designates who has the power to administer oaths. Except for the power to issue subpenas, any function or power of the Commission may be delegated to any of its officers or employees.

The Commission can pay witnesses the same fees and mileage paid by the courts of the United States in similar circumstances. It also can accept gifts, and voluntary and uncompensated services. No person who discloses information at the Commission's request shall be civilly liable to any person, other than the Commission or the United States.

The Commission may initiate, prosecute, defend, or appeal any court action to enforce laws subject to its jurisdiction through its own legal representative, with the concurrence of the Attorney General, or through the Attorney General. (See also Chapter VI, Enforcement.)

In case of refusal to obey a subpena or order issued pursuant to these powers of the Commission, any United States district court within the jurisdiction of an inquiry can require compliance, upon petition by the Commission, with the concurrence of the Attorney General, or by the Attorney General. Failure to obey such court orders may be punished as contempt of court.

Technical Data

The law provides that the Commission may, by rule, require any manufacturer of a consumer product to provide it with performance and technical data. It may also require that notification of performance and technical data be given at the time of original purchase to prospective purchasers and to the first purchaser of the product for purposes other than resale. However, the conference report (see Appendix J) treats the requirement pertaining to first purchasers differently, stating that the Commission has the power to "require manufacturers of consumer products to provide performance and other technical data to the Commission and to retail purchasers." What weight the Commission might give to the conference committee's interpretation of this section, requiring manufacturers to provide the data rather than mere notification to retail purchasers, remains to be seen.

The Commission may purchase any consumer product, and may require the manufacturer, distributor, or retailer, to sell the product to it at cost.

Commission planning, construction, and operation of facilities for research, development, and testing of consumer products also is authorized in Section 32(b), which provides that no appropriations for planning or construction involving more than $100,000 can be made without prior approval of the House and Senate Commerce Committees. To obtain this approval, the Commission must submit to Congress a prospectus including a brief description of the facility, its location, an estimate of the maximum cost, a statement of those private and public agencies which will use it and the contribution toward the cost to be made by each, and a statement of justification of the need for the facility. The Commission may increase the estimated maximum cost of any approved facility by the amount equal to the percentage increase, if any, in construction costs from the date of transmittal of the prospectus to Congress, up to 10 percent of the estimated maximum cost.

The Commission has authority to enter into contracts, and shall require recipients of assistance from grants or contracts entered into other than competitive bidding procedures to keep whatever records it may prescribe, including records disclosing the amount and disposition of proceeds, the total cost of the project undertaken in connection with the assistance, the amount of that portion of the project's cost supplied by other sources, and whatever other records are needed to facilitate an effective audit. Pertinent books, documents, papers, and records are to be made accessible for audit and examination by the Commission and the Comptroller General.

B. PRODUCT SAFETY ADVISORY COUNCIL

The Consumer Product Safety Commission is directed to establish a 15-member advisory council which it may consult before prescribing consumer product safety rules or before taking any other action (Section 28).

The need for a Product Safety Advisory Council was both questioned and endorsed by industry representatives during the House hearings. George P. Lamb, General Counsel of the Association of Home Appliance Manufacturers (AHAM), told the House unit on February 1, 1972, that establishment of an advisory council would not necessarily contribute to a product safety program. "Its existence and the time taken to negotiate with it would divert the agency from its primary task of promulgating mandatory performance safety standards for consumer products," he said.

On the other hand, F. Donald Hart, president of the American Gas Association, told the House group on December 1, 1971: "Such a Council should be more than just a group the Secretary can consult if he so desires. The Secretary should be required to submit all proposed safety standards and regulations to the Council and should be required to publish the reasons for any disagreement he might have with the Council on such proposals. Such a provision was put in the Natural Gas Pipeline Safety Act of 1968 and as a result, the Technical Pipeline Safety Committee which was created has been able to operate as an effective liaison between the Office of Pipeline Safety and experts in the field from industry, Government, and the public."

Council Members

The members of the Product Safety Advisory Council are to be appointed by the Commission, with each member to be qualified by training and experience in one or more of the fields applicable to the safety of products covered by the Act. The Council is to include five members selected from government agencies, including federal, state and local governments; five members from consumer product industries, including at least one representative of small business; and five members from among consumer organizations, community organizations, and recognized consumer leaders.

The Council, which may propose consumer product safety rules to the Commission, is to meet at least four times a year, and also at the request of the Commission. All proceedings of the Council are to be public, and a record of the proceedings made available for public inspection.

Compensation for those Council members who are not federal employees may be fixed by the Commission for the time spent in Council business at a rate not to exceed the daily equivalent for grade GS-18 of the General Schedule. Travel expenses, including per diem in lieu of subsistence, also is authorized. The Act specifies that these payments will not render members of the Council officers or employees of the United States for any purpose (Section 28(d)).

The Advisory Council provisions in the law follow the provisions of the bill approved by the House of Representatives. The counterpart bill in the Senate merely provided general authority for the Commission to establish advisory committees within its own discretion.

CHAPTER IV
INFORMATION AND RESEARCH

Although the greatest attention has been given to the standard-setting authority of the Consumer Product Safety Commission and its impact on the manufacture, labeling, and packaging of consumer products, the broad authority given to the Commission in the fields of information and research may prove to be at least equally effective in reducing the incidence of product-caused injuries, deaths, and illnesses.

Section 5 of the Consumer Product Safety Act:

1. Directs the Commission to maintain an Injury Information Clearinghouse, conduct continuing investigation of injuries involving consumer products, and disseminate product safety information to the public;
2. Authorizes the Commission to conduct research and investigations, test products, develop testing methods, and train others in product safety investigation; and
3. Authorizes grants and contracts for information and research purposes.

The Commission's information-gathering, research, and testing activities will be of prime importance in effective operation of its standards-setting authority, for the establishment of meaningful priorities among the thousands of consumer products subject to its jurisdiction can be accomplished only by engineering analysis or by an evaluation of injury statistics.

Perhaps even more important, the information collected or developed by the Commission on the causes and prevention of product-related injuries is to be disseminated to the public—forming the basis for a consumer education program that, according to many witnesses during hearings on the product safety legislation, could do more to prevent product-related injuries than any product safety standards. A primary purpose of the Act, according to Section 2(b), is "to assist consumers in evaluating the comparative safety of consumer products."

A. INJURY INFORMATION CLEARINGHOUSE

The Final Report of the National Commission on Product Safety, which included among its recommendations the establishment of an Injury Information Clearinghouse, noted that its investigators had encountered "considerable difficulty in obtaining statistical information on product-related injuries."

The NCPS stated: "While the literature of accident prevention contains thousands of studies, the individual papers do not provide data consistently in forms needed to build up a national bank of information. For purposes of comparison, biometricians have yet to develop suitable baselines or standard nomenclature or definitions. Even categories of products and levels of severity of injury are usually framed according to the judgment of individual investigators, not in the context of a national system. We stress the importance of gathering useful data about injuries linked to consumer products. Individual manufacturers and entire industries have requested that the Federal Government assume responsibility for gathering comparable data and processing it through a clearinghouse for product safety information."

The NCPS during its two-year lifetime conducted several experiments in information-gathering techniques, including electronic data processing of hospital reports, surveys of product liability claims closed by insurance companies, questionnaires sent to physicians, and analysis of consumer complaints. Its recommendation for creation of a clearinghouse of information did not specify the type of data-gathering mechanism to be employed, but its reports indicated the advantages of a broadly based computerized system, reinforced by "intense field studies of specific injuries." The National Commission determined that a statistically valid sample for a national surveillance network can be based on 200 hospitals and 200 physicians, utilizing remote consoles for electronic data processing.

The NEISS System

A system following the broad outlines of the NCPS recommendations was made operational by the Food and Drug Administration's Bureau of Product Safety prior to the enactment of the Consumer Product Safety Act, and will be transferred to the new Consumer Product Safety Commission. The National Electronic Injury Surveillance System (NEISS) is expected to form the nucleus of the Commission's injury information system. As of November 1972, NEISS connected 119 hospital emergency rooms in 30 states with a computer in Washington, D.C., to provide statistically valid figures on product-related injuries that receive emergency treatment. However, as the NCPS reported as a result of its pilot operations, the NEISS reports indicate only that a product was involved in an accident, but not necessarily that the product was the *cause* of the accident or injury. NEISS relies on selective follow-up investigations to determine precise circumstances surrounding a product-related injury.

A major problem to which the Commission's attention will be directed in its information-gathering activities will be the standardization of information to be provided by the reporting agencies. NEISS has made a start in that direction through its coding system, but further refinement will clearly be necessary to augment the value of the information for both standard-setting purposes and consumer education. In announcing its NEISS system, FDA also noted that "the system may eventually be expanded to include data from private physicians' offices, hospital in-patient admissions, community clinics, household surveys, and death certificate records for fatal injuries in all 50 states."

Need for Injury Data

The need for precise and detailed injury data has been universally recognized, by industry spokesmen as well as by the National Commission, the Congress, and consumer representatives. The absence of a central facility for the systematic collection of such data, said the House Commerce Committee report, makes it "impossible to measure the true magnitude of product-related injuries or to determine with confidence what portion of the annual toll of 30,000 deaths or 20 million injuries which are estimated to occur around the American home are actually caused by unsafe products."

NCPS Chairman Arnold Elkind told the House committee that his "gut estimate" was that 20 percent of these deaths and injuries could be avoided by more effective product safety standards. Baron Whitaker, president of Underwriters' Laboratories, however, provided the committee with extensive data indicating that only 5 percent of the accidents would have been prevented by revisions in product design or manufacture.

He testified: "We cannot emphasize too strongly the need for in-depth analysis of accident data as the only sensible basis for generation of injury reduction measures. Calling attention to a seemingly large number of injuries without supporting information as to causes will not provide the information essential to increasing safety with minimal decreases in utility, minimal decreases in availability of choices, or minimal increase in cost which the consumer has the right to expect from a federal consumer safety program."

The importance of such information to manufactureres as well as consumers was emphasized by the NCPS in its report: This information can tell which hazards warrant remedial actions, such as design change, consumer education, industry standards, or Government regulations," the NCPS said. "It can help set priorities for action and to evaluate the relative efficacy of various methods of preventing injury * * * Manufacturers will benefit from the technical advice to be furnished through the center by Government scientists and engineers. Injury information will help define areas where safety standards are needed and will furnish guidelines for product instructions and warnings. The consumer will benefit from information about selecting, using, and maintaining consumer products with minimal risk. Rarely do consumers seek safety information; usually they are unaware of risks which are not well publicized. * * * The Government will benefit internally because the Center will facilitate exchange of information among more than 30 federal agencies which now conduct more than 200 programs bearing on product safety. In fact, the entire economy can be expected to gain from improvements in design and reduction of risks to the extent that useful information is relayed to manufacturers and consumers."

The National Commission emphasized, however, that information on product safety "is properly a guide and supplement, not a substitute for regulatory action."

The House Commerce Committee said in its report (see Appendix G, p. 221): "It is recognized, of course, that the powers given the Commission to collect and analyze injury data far exceed the abilities of any single manufacturer or industry association to acquire information concerning the accident experience associated with their products. Private industry however, should not rely totally on the Government to discover product hazards. Each manufacturer has today and should continue to have the responsibility to assure through testing and other independent means that his products are free from defect or hazard and are properly designed for the use for which they are intended or applied."

B. RESEARCH-TESTING-TRAINING

The Act also authorizes the Commission to conduct research, studies, and investigations on the safety of consumer products; to test products and to develop safety testing methods and testing devices; to offer training in product safety investigation; and to assist others in the development of safety standards and test procedures (Section 5(b)).

"This authority is designed to give the Commission the means of identifying hazards before consumers are exposed to them," the House Commerce Committee explained. "The application of modern technology makes possible sophisticated analysis of product design and testing for product degradation so that potential accidents may be foreseen and avoided. Such analyses may well provide a proper basis for regulatory action without awaiting an accumulation of accident statistics of the maimed and injured."

As enacted, the law contains no reference to the "risk-based analysis" provided for in the Senate-approved bill. In authorizing the Commission to undertake such analyses, the Senate Commerce Committee had described the authorization as a new approach to product safety legislation—"an approach which identifies hazardous elements, conditions and potential accidents, determines the significance of their potential effect, and provides * * * an analytical basis for design and procedural safety requirements to eliminate or control hazards *prior to the time* that these hazards produce actual injury or death" (see Appendix C, p. 75). The conference committee, however, decided not to include these provisions of the Senate bill, in view of the broad provisions dealing with the Commission's research and test capabilities (see Appendix J, p. 314).

The Commission is given broad authority to make grants and enter into contracts with anyone, including a governmental entity, to conduct any of these research, testing, and training activities. Whenever a person other than the Commission carries out any information, research, or development activity under contract or with the aid of a grant from the Commission, provision is to be made for the availability to the public of the rights to information, uses, processes, patents, and other developments resulting from that activity free of charge and on a nonexclusive basis.

However, the provision stipulates that this is not to be construed to deprive any person of any right which he may have had to any patent, patent application, or invention prior to entering into the arrangement with the Commission.

The Commission is directed by Section 29(d) of the Act to utilize, to the maximum extent possible, the resources and facilities of the National Bureau of Standards to perform analysis and research related to risks of injury associated with consumer products, to develop test methods, and to provide technical advice and assistance to the Commission. All such activities by the NBS are to be on a reimbursable basis. Although the administration of the Flammable Fabrics Act is transferred to the Commission, however, the personnel, property, and obligations of the NBS related to the development of fire and flammability standards are to remain with the Bureau, instead of being transferred to the Commission (Section 30(e)).

C. DISCLOSURE OF INFORMATION

Trade secrets or other sensitive cost and competitive information are protected from public disclosure under provisions of Section 6 of the new law. The legislators concluded that the Commission must have complete and full access to information relevant to its statutory responsibilities and provided the new agency with broad information-gathering powers.

However, Congress also recognized that in so doing it provided the Commission the means of gaining access to a great deal of information which would not otherwise be available to the public or to Government. Therefore, the Act provides detailed requirements and limitations relating to the Commission's authority to disclose the information it acquires.

Information obtained by the Commission which contains or relates to a trade secret or other matter referred to in section 1905, title 18, United States Code, cannot be publicly disclosed (Section 6(a)(2)). However, such information can be disclosed to agency officers or employees carrying out the provisions of the Act or, when relevant, in any proceeding under the Act.

In its report, the House Commerce Committee (see Appendix G, p. 222) said the term "trade secrets" is to be given the same judicial construction as that term has acquired under 18 U.S.C. 1905. Therefore, for the purposes of Section 6 of the Act, a trade secret means "an unpatented, secret, commercially valuable plan, appliance, formula, or process, which is used for the making, preparing, compounding, treating, or processing of articles or materials which are trade commodities."

Debate on Trade Secrets

Disclosure of information without adequate protection of trade secrets and other sensitive material was a question widely discussed at the congressional hearings. Several witnesses warned that lack of protection for trade secrets could jeopardize government-industry cooperation and economic success in competition between manufacturers.

HEW Secretary Elliot L. Richardson criticized the National Commission proposals as embodied in H.R. 8157 that would have allowed disclosure of trade secrets if the new agency determined that disclosure was necessary. The Administration bill, H.R. 8110, included provision for the full protection of trade secrets afforded by 18 U.S.C. 1905.

Secretary Richardson said: "We question the premise of the Commission bill that revelation to the public of these secrets or of similar confidential commercial data would be much aid in administering either that bill or our own. To the extent that either bill relies for its effectiveness upon educating the public to the dangers of a product, the detailed technical information embodied in trade secrets would be of little use.

"In fact, however, both bills are regulatory measures which rely less upon public awareness of product hazards than upon mechanisms to reduce these hazards. The adoption of the Commission provision would therefore add little to the regulatory power under either bill but might well dampen the willingness of responsible manufacturers to cooperate with the Government in increasing the safety of the marketplace. In a bill that seeks, as ours does, to use the expert knowledge and resources of industry, in aid of the resources of Government, this cooperation is indispensable. We believe that manufacturers must have the assurance that their cooperation will not place them at a competitive disadvantage."

Walter S. Lewis, Jr., testifying on behalf of the Gas Appliance Manufacturers Association, also emphasized the need for protection against "unfair or unwarranted release" of proprietary information.

He said: "Trade secrets, formulae, processes, product costs, methods of doing business, competitive information, and intellectual properties are of great importance to industry and should be protected wherever feasible. Product safety legislation should not require the release of any such information without a clear demonstration that such disclosure is required in the public interest. In no event should release of information be made relative to specific occurrences or specific parties."

National Commission Chairman Elkind, on the other hand, declared that if a manufacturer's processes, formula, or cost differential results in inadequate safety of the product, information on those factors is a matter of great public interest and concern.

"I think the public has learned to disrespect the labels that one puts on information," Elkind said. "It is essential to our society that we have access to the information that affects us in our everyday lives. If a product represents a danger to the consumer, the public has a right to be told about it by the Government, and the Government should not be permitted to conceal that information from the public because it has been labeled 'trade secret, or a formula, or a process, or a method of doing business.' Only by being informed can the public make intelligent and informed choices in the marketplace."

Balance of Need and Right

Provisions for disclosure of information were those of the House bill, and reflect the intent of the House Commerce Committee to provide a balance between the needs and rights of the public to information concerning their welfare, and the needs and rights of manufacturers, private labelers, distributors, and retailers regarding economic interests invested in a particular product.

The committee said it wanted to assure that public disclosure of information would not be unnecessarily restricted, but that trade secrets would be protected, information would be fairly and accurately disclosed, and, in the event of inaccuracy, a retraction would be made.

With one exception, the new law specifies (Section 6(a)(1)) that nothing in the Act shall be deemed to compel the Commission to disclose information which would not otherwise be available to the public under the Freedom of Information Act (5 U.S.C. 552(b)). That Act would not require a federal agency to permit public access to investigatory files compiled for law enforcement purposes, but Section 25(c) of the Consumer Product Safety Act qualifies the Commission's authority to deny access to investigatory files by making accident investigations specifically available to the public so long as they do not identify injured parties or attending physicians.

Section 6(a)(2) provides that nothing in the Act is to authorize the withholding of information by the Commission from any duly authorized congressional committees.

Prior Notice

Before disseminating any information identifying the manufacturer or private labeler of a product, the Commission is directed to give the manufacturer 30 days in which to comment on the proposed disclosure of information (Section 6(b)(1)). This 30-day period may be shortened if the Commission determines that the public health and safety requires a lesser period of notice. According to the House Commerce Committee, the period of notice is designed to "permit the manufacturer or private labeler an opportunity to come forward with explanatory data or other relevant information for the Commission's consideration." However, the committee emphasized that it did not intend that the Commission be required to include such explanation in the materials to be disseminated.

The Act specifically directs that, prior to public disclosure of the information, the Commission "take reasonable steps" to assure that the information is accurate, and that the disclosure is fair in the circumstances and "reasonably related" to carrying out the new law.

If the Commission finds that it has made public disclosure of inaccurate or misleading information reflecting adversely upon the safety of a product or the practices of any manufacturer, private labeler, distributor, or retailer of consumer products, it must publish a retraction in a manner similar to that in which the disclosure was made.

"It is intended that a retraction receive at least the same notoriety as the original disclosure," the House Committee said (see Appendix G, p. 222). "Accordingly, if the Commission had publicly released information to the news media which was inaccurate or misleading, the retraction must also be released to the news media and not simply placed in the Federal Register. By requiring that the Commission publish its retraction in a manner similar to that in which the original disclosure was made, the committee does not intend to limit the Commission to these means. There may be circumstances where equity requires fuller disclosure of the Commission's mistakes in order to repair the damage to any manufacturer, distributor, or retailer of the product which may have resulted from publication of the inaccurate information."

The Commission is not required to give prior notification to manufacturers of any information which may be disclosed with respect to a product for which an action has been brought under provisions relating to imminently hazardous products, or a product which the Commission has reasonable cause to believe is in violation of the provisions relating to prohibited acts. The Commission also need not notify manufacturers and await a 30-day period prior to disclosure of information regarding an administrative or judicial proceeding (Section 6(b)(2)).

The Commission is required to communicate to each manufacturer of a consumer product information as to any significant risk of injury associated with the product (Section 6(c)).

CHAPTER V
PRODUCT SAFETY RULES

The heart of the consumer safety program established by the Consumer Product Safety Act lies in the issuance and enforcement of mandatory product safety rules by the Consumer Product Safety Commission.

Product safety rules will be of two distinct types: (1) Consumer product safety standards applicable to products that are in or may enter commerce, and (2) Rules banning certain "hazardous products" from the marketplace.

Consumer product safety standards are further broken down into two types: (1) Requirements as to the performance, composition, contents, design, construction, finish, or packaging of a consumer product; and (2) Requirements for cautionary labeling or marking.

The broad authority granted to the Consumer Product Safety Commission to issue and enforce such rules across the whole range of products used by the consuming public—at home, in school, for recreation, or otherwise—represents a synthesis of more limited powers previously granted by Congress in certain specialized fields. It incorporates the standard-setting authority utilized under the Flammable Fabrics Act and parallels the National Traffic and Motor Vehicle Safety Act; the cautionary labeling requirements that have dominated enforcement of the Hazardous Substances Act and Caustic Poisons Act; the power to ban dangerous products from the market, as in the Child Protection and Toy Safety Act; and the authority to issue standards for new products not yet on the market, although it does *not* incorporate the pre-market testing procedures of the Food, Drug and Cosmetic Act.

For the first time, this wide-ranging power has been vested in an independent federal agency having complete discretion to determine which industries and which products require regulation to protect the consumer from product-caused injuries.

A. CONSUMER PRODUCT SAFETY STANDARDS

The new Act and its legislative history indicate clearly the congressional intent that the starting point for the mandatory standards to be promulgated by the Commission will be the voluntary standards already adopted by industry through its self-regulatory processes. Moreover, the expertise required to develop adequate product safety standards will be provided in most instances by private organizations with demonstrated technical competence.

Of the approximately 400 organizations in the United States that develop or sponsor commercial standards, however, only a small fraction have dealt with safety problems involving consumer products. The Final Report of the National Commission on Product Safety stated that the more than 1,000 industry standards applicable in some way to the safety characteristics of the 350 consumer products listed by the Commission (reproduced herein as Appendix N) represent the efforts of only 48 standard-making organizations, while Deputy Assistant Secretary of Commerce Richard O. Simpson told the House Commerce Committee that "only about 15" of the 400 organizations are active in writing consumer product standards.

It must be remembered also that of the countless thousands of voluntary industry product standards, only a small proportion relate specifically to product safety. Most of the specified requirements deal with nomenclature, interchangeability, materials, sizes and weights, methods of rating, and other factors that have little or no relation to prevention of injury. From the voluminous literature provided by industry self-regulation the new Commission will have to cull only those performance or descriptive specifications that relate exclusively or primarily to safety.

It is in this context that the standard-setting provisions of the Consumer Product Safety Act must be considered.

Performance and Descriptive Standards

Under Section 7(a) of the bill, the Commission is authorized to promulgate mandatory safety standards for particular products where it finds such standards "reasonably necessary to prevent or reduce an unreasonable risk of injury associated with [a particular] product." Although the Commission has authority to prescribe the composition, contents, design, construction, finish, or packaging of a consumer product, the law stresses that safety standards will be expressed in terms of performance requirements whenever feasible, rather than employing descriptive criteria. The legislation attempts, whenever possible, to avoid adopting descriptive standards, since such standards tend to lead to product uniformity and limit the product manufacturer's freedom to develop or innovate superior products. Performance standards dictate what a consumer can minimally expect from a product without limiting the manufacturer to using certain materials or designs. The conference committee expressed a strong preference for performance standards, "in the recognition that such standards permit industry to make the fullest use of its technological resources in meeting safety requirements." The objective is to give manufacturers the widest possible latitude, while giving consumers some assurance that they will be able to use the products they buy without risking physical injury. Performance standards will mitigate against product similarity and any resultant anticompetitive effects for, as the committee recognized, "mandatory standards which prescribe performance requirements can often be expected to foster rather than stifle competition."

Nevertheless, there will, of course, be safety standards for numerous products that will require specific descriptive characteristics so as to prevent or reduce risk of injury. For example, the Commission may decide that it cannot adopt safety standards for infants' cribs without requiring specific design or construction criteria minimizing or negating the possibility that the infant might fall out of the crib or trap a part of its body between the side slats. However, safety standards for materials would not ordinarily dictate what could or could not be used, but would require that any materials used in construction meet certain performance criteria, such as bearing a certain load without breaking, splintering, chipping, or cracking for a specified period of time. Therefore, it is safe to assume that in many instances a combination of descriptive and performance requirements will be necessary reasonably and adequately to protect the consumer.

Labeling Standards

In cases where the risk of injury cannot be sufficiently removed or reduced through performance or descriptive standards; the Commission is directed to adopt requirements that "a consumer product be marked with or accompanied by clear and adequate warnings or instructions, or requirements respecting the form of warning or instructions."

As in the case of performance or descriptive standards, the Commission must determine that its labeling requirements are reasonably necessary to prevent or reduce an unreasonable risk of injury associated with a consumer product.

B. HAZARDOUS PRODUCT BANS

In addition to consumer product safety standards, the Commission may issue another form of product safety rule in the form of an order banning any hazardous product from the market. Whenever the Commission finds that a consumer product presents an unreasonable risk of injury and that no feasible product safety standard would adequately protect the public from that risk, it may propose and, after appropriate administrative procedures, promulgate a rule banning such product from the market.

There is no requirement in Section 8 of the Act that the Commission must first develop a product safety standard before it proceeds directly to adopt a rule banning the product. In the case of an "imminent hazard," the Commission may completely bypass administrative proceedings and go directly into a district court for an order enjoining the distribution of the product or authorizing its seizure (see Chapter VII, infra).

C. DEVELOPMENT OF PRODUCT SAFETY RULE

The Commission will commence a proceeding for the development of a consumer product safety standard by publishing a notice in the Federal Register. This notice will (1) identify the product and the nature of the injury associated with it; (2) state the Commission's determination that the adoption of a safety standard for the product is necessary adequately to protect consumers; (3) note what relevant information regarding a pre-existing standard is known to the Commission; and (4) invite the submission by interested parties within 30 days of either an existing voluntary standard or an offer to develop a product safety standard.

Noting the scores of existing voluntary standards relating to product safety, the conference committee recognized that many of these standards may be perfectly adequate to protect the consumer if they could gain industry-wide adherence to their terms through the force of law. Therefore, the Act enables the Commission to adopt an existing voluntary standard which it finds would prevent or reduce the hazardous consequences related to a product if promulgated as a federal mandatory standard.

Offers to Develop

Where such a standard is determined not to exist, the Commission is required to accept one or more offers to develop a viable safety standard, if it finds the offeror technically competent, likely to develop an "appropriate" standard within the prescribed time period (150 days from the publication of the notice, unless otherwise provided), and willing to comply with Commission regulations relating to developmental procedures.

The prescription for technical competence envisions a demonstration by the offeror of his expertise and capability to carry out the development in a successful manner. Experience in developing standards is not necessary and the Congress has indicated that universities and research laboratories with the requisite technical competence should be able to participate despite a lack of previous experience in the field. Once it accepts an offer for the development of a safety standard, the Commission may agree to contribute to the offeror's costs.

The conference committee contemplated that controls over cost contribution would assure "adequate participation by public representatives in the development process" when an offer from a technical committee or standard-writing organization is accepted. The Commission, upon accepting an offer, is directed to issue regulations itemizing the costs to which it may contribute, but may not dispense any funds for the acquisition of land or buildings.

Section 7(d) (3) directs the Commission to prescribe regulations governing the development of standards by those parties whose offers have been accepted. Substantially paralleling the Administrative Procedure Act, 5 U.S.C. 551, the regulations will require that the development of the standards be supported by test data and other appropriate substantiation and contain test methods to determine compliance and that the offeror (1) provide notice and opportunity for interested persons to participate in the development; (2) maintain and make available public records disclosing the courses of development as well as comments and other information submitted by persons interested in the standard development; and (3) make available to the Commission and the Comptroller General any books, documents, papers, or records relevant to development of the proposed standards or to expenditure of Commission funds.

Neither the conference committee report nor the law makes clear how interested parties will receive their notice and opportunity to participate in the developmental process once an offer has been accepted. Furthermore, the Act does not establish any qualifications or criteria to determine what credentials interested parties shall have to participate in the development of standards or what interests they may represent.

Commission Development

Pursuant to Section 7(e)(1), the Commission may develop a proposed safety standard if it has not received an offer within 30 days after publication of the notice. However, once the Commission accepts an offer to develop a standard, it may not, during the specified development period (1) publish a proposed rule applicable to the same risk of injury assocated with the product, (2) develop a proposed rule itself, or (3) contract with third parties for such development, unless the Commission determines that *no* offeror whose offer has been accepted is making satisfactory progress.

The one exception to this restriction represents a compromise of two provisions originally contained in the Senate version of the product safety legislation. The Nelson amendment (see Appendix E, p. 181) would have prohibited manufacturers or handlers of any product, or anyone closely affiliated with them, from participating in a rulemaking proceeding involving that product. The Senate bill (Appendix F, p. 202) also contained a provision permitting the Commission to proceed with its own development of a product safety rule while an offeror was working on the same rule. In the compromise that is reflected in the Act as finally approved, the prohibition against industry participation is completely removed. However, when the sole offeror is the manufacturer, distributor, or retailer of the consumer product proposed to be regulated, the Commission may proceed independently to develop its own proposals for a safety rule.

Supporters of the Senate version of the legislation regard the limitations on the Commission's authority to develop proposed standards independently as one of the greatest weaknesses in the final enactment. However, the report of the conference committee made it clear that the limitation on development "should not be interpreted as preventing the Commission or its staff from developing or acquiring the technical capability necessary to properly evaluate the standards recommended to it."

The qualification that the Commission, upon finding a lack of satisfactory progress by offerors, may independently, or by contract with third parties, develop a product safety standard, is intended to stimulate development within the specified time period. If the Commission determines that no offeror can adequately develop a standard, it may terminate the development period and immediately publish a proposed safety standard applicable to the product hazard with which the standard was to have dealt, or, if appropriate, declare the product a banned hazardous product.

The Commission has 210 days after publication of the proceeding notice to publish in the Federal Register a proposed rule which either proposes a product safety standard or proposes a banned hazardous product. The 210-day period may be extended by the Commission by a notice published in the Register which will expound the reasons for the extension. Should the Commission neither propose a safety standard or banned hazardous product, it must publish in the Register a notice withdrawing the notice of proceeding.

Individual Petitions

Section 10 of the Act provides that "any interested person, including a consumer or consumer organization," may petition the Commission to initiate an agency proceeding for the purpose of issuing, amending, or revoking any product safety rule. The Commission shall act on such petition within 120 days, with or without public hearings. If it agrees, it must promptly commence a proceeding under Sections 7 or 8 of the Act. If it disagrees, or takes no action within the prescribed time, the petitioner may file an action in the federal courts. If the court finds that the particular consumer product presents an unreasonable hazard, it may order the Commission to initiate appropriate proceedings, but it will have no authority to predetermine the outcome of those proceedings.

In order to give the Commission time to establish its own priorities and make its own initial determinations, the provision for private action to force Committee consideration of a safety standard or a product ban is not to become effective for a period of three years—that is, until December 27, 1975. Senate provisions that would have extended this authority to any form of Commission action were deleted by the conference committee (see Appendix J, p. 326), thus limiting private initiative to the categories of product safety standards and hazardous product bans.

D. ADMINISTRATIVE PROCEDURE

The Act establishes certain procedures which must be followed by the Commission before a proposed consumer product safety standard can become a final rule applicable to manufacturers or before the Commission can ban a product deemed to be hazardous.

Section 9(a) (1) establishes a time limit within which the Commission must act upon proposed standards. After the Commission publishes notice of a proposed standard or ban in the Federal Register, it then must either accept or reject that proposed standard or ban within 60 days. The Commission, however, may extend this period if it finds an extension of time to be in the public interest, and if it publishes a notice in the Federal Register which explains the reasons for such extension. If the Commission does not either promulgate a final standard or request an extension within 60 days, the proposed rule must be withdrawn from Commission consideration.

Before a proposed standard or ban becomes final, the Commission is required under the Act to follow procedures designed to insure that manufacturers and other interested parties will have some input into the Commission's deliberations concerning that standard.

Section 9(a) (2) mandates that the Commission follow, with one significant exception, the rulemaking procedure contained in Section 553 of the Administrative Procedure Act.The exception is significant in that it serves to expand the opportunities available for interested parties to appear before the Commission. The APA decrees only that an agency *may* provide the opportunity for oral presentation of views. Section 9(a) (2) *requires* the Commission to allow "interested persons" the opportunity to present *orally* "data, views, or arguments" concerning a standard or ban as well as allowing such persons to submit written views or comments. In addition, the Commission must keep a transcript of any oral proceedings that are held, and this transcript becomes a part of the final record and is available to the court if judicial review of a rule is sought.

Thus, the Act seeks to establish a middle ground between the non-adversary rule-making procedures of Section 553 of the APA and the formal adjudicatory procedures codified in Sections 556 and 557 of the APA, under which a full trial-type, adversary hearing is required. The House committee report on the bill notes that the compromise between the two extremes of the APA "will maximize opportunities to participate in the rule-making proceeding without unduly entangling the commission in trial type procedures."

Other requirements of the APA which the Commission must follow include publication in the Federal Register of notice of the Commission's intention to promulgate a rule, setting out the time, place, and nature of the proposed proceeding, the legal authority under which the Commission is proposing to issue the rule, and either the substance of the proposed rule or a description of the subjects and issues involved in the rule's issuance. Such notice must be published more than 30 days before the final rule-making is to occur.

What type of presentation or evidence should be submitted by manufacturers or others interested in influencing the course of a proposed standard? Sections 9(b) and (c) provide some guidance as to the type of evidence that should be submitted.

Section 9(b) requires the Commission to consider "relevant available product data." Such data include the results of research, development, testing, and other investigatory activities.

Section 9(c) directs the Commission to include in its deliberations four distinct considerations: (1) the degree and nature of the risk of injury the rule is designed to eliminate or reduce; (2) the appropriate number of products that would be subject to the rule; (3) the public's need for the products that would be covered by the rule; and (4) whether there are means available to minimize the rule's adverse effects on competition and manufacturing while still achieving the rule's objectives. Thus, evidence directed toward these considerations would be pertinent to the Commission's deliberations.

Prior Findings

The Commission satisfies Section 9(c) (1) by considering the four stated objectives and including its findings in the rule. It conceivably could promulgate a rule even after determining that an alternative would reduce adverse effects on competition, although such a rule certainly would be subject to judicial review. Under Section 9(c) (2), however, the Commission is required to make two findings regarding a proposed rule before it can issue a final rule. If it does not make these findings regarding a proposed standard or ban, it cannot promulgate that standard or ban as a final rule.

First, the rule and its effective date must be found to be "reasonably necessary" to eliminate or reduce the risk of injury associated with the project. The final rule must also affirmatively state the risk of injury which it is designed to reduce. Second, the promulgation of such rule must be determined to be in the "public interest."

As an additional condition precedent to promulgating a rule declaring a product to be a banned hazardous product, the Commission must find that "no feasible consumer product safety standard * * * would adequately protect the public from the unreasonable risk of injury associated with such product."

Effective Date

Any rule that formulates a consumer product safety standard must specify the date on which the rule is to take effect. The effective date will ordinarily be at least 30 days after the date of promulgation, and cannot be more than 180 days after promulgation. The Commission may, if it finds it to be in the public's interest, either set an earlier effective date or extend the 180-day period.

No rule embodying a consumer product safety standard may be given retroactive application, however. A rule explicating a safety standard can apply *only* to products manufactured *after* the rule's effective date. Products manufactured before the standard's effective date need not conform to the requirements of the standard.

Stockpiling

Since retroactive application of safety standards is precluded, a manufacturer could attempt to avoid the standard by producing at an increased rate before the standard's effective date, thus escaping the provisions of the standard for those products. Section 9(d) (2) empowers the Commission to exercise its rulemaking authority in order to prohibit such "stockpiling." The act defines "stockpiling" as manufacturing or importing a product at a "significantly greater" rate between the rule's date of promulgation and effective date than was the rate of manufacture during a defined base period before the date of promulgation. There is no restriction on any "stockpiling" between the time the Commission's first notice is published and the date the final rule is promulgated.

The ban on retroactive application applies only to safety standards and does not apply to rules banning hazardous products. Although the Act is silent as to the application of a rule declaring a product to be a banned hazardous product, it specifies only that a rule embodying a consumer product safety standard may not be given retroactive effect. The House committee report on the bill makes clear that "rules declaring a product to be a banned hazardous product may apply to products of new manufacture or to products already manufactured and distributed." Similar language also appears in the conference report on the bill.

Amendment by the Commission of a product safety rule is permitted by Section 9(e). Such amendment must be published in the Federal Register and must take effect within 180 days, unless the Commission extends the period for good cause. If the amendment involves a material change in a safety standard, the Commission must in effect treat it as a new rule and observe the full procedures requisite for the adoption of a new rule—including inviting interested persons to develop an amended standard.

Revocation of a rule is permitted only after a finding by the Commission that the rule is not "reasonably necessary" to eliminate or reduce an unreasonable risk of injury. Before the commission can make such a finding, it must publish in the Federal Register its proposal to revoke, and must then allow interested persons the opportunity to submit both oral and written evidence, under the same procedures applicable to adopting a rule.

E. JUDICIAL REVIEW

The Consumer Product Safety Act contains specific provisions for judicial review of any product safety rule promulgated by the Commission.

An integral factor, of course, in any judicial review provision, is, "Who is entitled to sue under the Act?" Can anyone challenge a proposed standard, or is it limited to those who actually participated in the decision at the Commission level?

Section 11 establishes two concepts of standing, both broadly based. First, any person "adversely affected" by a rule can maintain suit to challenge that rule. Under past judicial consideration of such language, a person need not have sustained direct economic injury in order to be adversely affected. The threat of potential economic injury is generally sufficient. Thus, a manufacturer who feels that a product safety rule will result in direct economic loss to him—through increased costs, loss of business or the like—will be able to challenge the rule, even though the loss may not have yet been sustained.

The second concept of standing established by the Act deals exclusively with consumer or consumer organizations. Under Section 11, "any" consumer or consumer organization has standing to review the rule. Thus, no economic injury need even be alleged if a person is challenging a rule in his status as a consumer.

Since judicial review is explicitly provided by Section 11, a petitioner seeking to review a rule need not meet the requisites ordinarily necessary to sue in federal court—diversity of citizenship of parties, for example, or a $10,000 interest at stake. Instead, a petitioner need only file suit within 60 days of the Commission's promulgation of the contested rule. Suit may be filed either in the U. S. Court of Appeals for the District of Columbia Circuit or in the court of appeals for the circuit in which the petitioner resides or has his principal place of business.

Record of Proceedings

Once suit is maintained, the Commission must then file with the court a record of the proceedings which formed the basis for the rule's promulgation. The record must include the rule itself; any notice or proposal published pursuant to Sections 7, 8, or 9; the transcript of any oral testimony concerning the proposed rule; any written evidence that was submitted to the Commission; and any other information which the Commission considers relevant to the promulgation of the rule.

Section 11(b) offers the person seeking review an opportunity to present evidence to the court that was not presented to the Commission during the rulemaking process. The petitioner must demonstrate that such additional evidence would be material in review of the case, and also must satisfactorily explain to the court why such evidence was not presented during the rulemaking process. Thus, a manufacturer affected by a rule who discovers new data to support his position after the Commission has already acted still has a forum in which to present such data. Such data, could, of course, perhaps alternatively serve to support a petition to modify or revoke a rule. If the court accepts such new evidence, the Commission can be given an opportunity to modify its findings or make new findings on the basis of the additional evidence.

Substantial Evidence

Court review of the rule and the basis for the rule is under the terms of "substantial evidence taken as a whole." This is a broader type of review than is generally used by courts in reviewing agency rulemaking. Under normal standards of review accorded informal rulemaking, a court will overturn the agency's decision only if it was clearly arbitrary or capricious. The "substantial evidence" test is generally used to review formal agency actions taken pursuant to a full trial-type hearing. The court looks to all the evidence presented in the case, and determines whether a substantial portion of that evidence supports the agency's actions.

Review under the "substantial evidence" test, since it is broader and offers the court more leeway, provides more opportunities for judicial intervention. An agency operating under the substantial evidence review rule will ordinarily be more cautious and more painstaking in preserving a record that can be affirmed by the court.

Final review of a product safety rule can be taken to the Supreme Court, if that Court votes to review the case upon petition for certiorari or if the appeals court certifies a question to the Court for review.

Section 11(e) makes clear that the procedures established by this section for review are not exclusive. Even after the 60-day period for review under this section has passed, a petitioner can avail himself of any other legal remedies, such as provided in the Administrative Procedure Act.

Section 11 contains no provision regarding the award by the court of damages or attorney's fees. The Senate version of the Act contained a provision permitting the court to award damages and attorney's fees to any manufacturer of a product declared to be a banned hazardous product if the court determined that the rule banning the product represented an abuse of the commission's discretion. That language was deleted from the final enactment, however.

F. CERTIFICATION OF COMPLIANCE

Section 14 of the Act requires manufacturers, importers, and private labelers of consumer products subject to product safety standards to issue certificates indicating compliance with the standards. The certificates are to be based on actual tests of the product (or a reasonable testing program), and are to show the name of the manufacturer, importer, or private labeler, and the date and place of manufacturee.

Although the certificate is required to accompany the product or be otherwise furnished to any distributor or retailer to whom it is delivered, the conference report makes it clear that it is not intended to require a certificate on each individual item. Where appropriate, the certificate may apply to an entire production run, batch, or group of products, which will be supplied, together with a bill of lading, at the time the first products are actually delivered to the distributor or retailer. It may even be possible, in some cases, to certify an entire model year, although in other cases, only a single day's production may be covered.

Where original shipments are divided and delivered to more than one retailer, the conference report stated, it will be sufficient to deliver a copy of the certificate to any party within the distribution chain to whom the product is delivered.

The Commission is given authority by Section 14(b) of the Act to promulgate rules prescribing reasonable testing programs upon which certification must be based. The conference committee has stated its intention that the Commission adopt rules that establish testing criteria or methods and the results to be achieved, rather than requiring manufacturers to observe specified production techniques or manufacturing practices.

Where there is more than one manufacturer of a consumer product—as, for example, in the case of an electronic product where different plants produce or assemble various components—Section 14(a) (2) authorizes the Commission to prescribe who shall make the certification. The same procedure would be followed where there is more than one private labeler of a particular product.

The provision authorizing the Commission to specify the form and content of product labels, according to the conference report, will permit use of codes in circumstances where the date of manufacture or other labeling information might create special economic hardships, or where the certifier is a private labeler and not the actual producer. If codes are permitted, however, they must be easily decipherable by consumers and persons within the distribution chain, once they are supplied with a key to the code. It is anticipated that manufacturers and private labelers who use coded information will have to assume added responsibilities to assure adequate notice in the event of a product recall.

CHAPTER VI
ENFORCEMENT

The enforcement authority provided by the Consumer Product Safety Act is broad and varied, ranging from notification to condemnation, including civil and criminal penalties, and providing for private as well as public agency enforcement. Included in this panoply of legislative authority are unusual enforcement provisions providing a violator with the opportunity for choosing among appropriate remedies, and establishing a private right to bring an action seeking to enforce Commission rules and orders.

A. REPAIR, REPLACEMENT, REFUND

A potentially significant remedy contained in this Act is the power the Commission is given to order a manufacturer, distributor, or retailer to repair, replace, or refund the cost of hazardous products. In order for the Commission to undertake this action, it must first determine both that the product presents a substantial product hazard and that ordering such action is in the public interest. "Substantial product hazard" is defined in the Act as a failure to comply with an applicable consumer product safety rule, which causes a risk of death, personal injury, or serious or frequent illness, or a product defect which, because of its severity or pattern of distribution, causes a similar risk.

Before making this determination the Commission must give interested parties an opportunity for an adjudicatory hearing under the provisions of the Administrative Procedure Act, including notice of the time, place, and subject of the hearing, an opportunity to present facts and arguments in support of their position by written or oral testimony, cross-examination of witnesses, and an impartial presiding officer. Where there is a class of participants sharing an identity of interest, the Commission may limit participation to a single representative designated by the class.

Notification

Once the Commission determines that it is in the public interest to take action against a substantial hazard and that notification to the public is necessary to avoid injuries, it may order the manufacturer or any distributor or retailer of the product to provide public notice of the hazard, mail notices to each commercial entity handling the product, or mail notices to each known purchaser. The Commission has the authority to specify the form and content of any such notice.

In addition to, or in lieu of, such notification, the Commission may order remedial action by giving the respondent the choice of bringing the product into conformity with the applicable rule or repairing the defect, replacing the product with one that meets the applicable standard, or refunding the purchase price, less a reasonable allowance for use if the consumer has possessed the product for one year or more.

The Commission may also require the person to whom the order is directed to submit its plan for corrective action. In cases where the order is directed to more than one person, the Commission is to specify which person has the power to decide what remedial action will be taken. The House Committee Report noted that it is expected that the Commission, in making this determination, will consider where the ultimate legal responsibility for the hazard lies. The Commission's authority to issue multiple orders will enable it to attack a hazardous product all along its line of distribution, from manufacturer or importer to distributor to retailer.

If the remedy of refund is chosen, the Commission is given wide authority to determine parties, terms, and procedures for the refund, including whether only first purchasers are covered and whether a sales slip or other proof of purchase is necessary. There is no specific requirement in the Act that consumers must tender products in order to obtain a refund.

Consumers taking advantage of any remedy provided by the Commission may not be charged—indeed, must be reimbursed—for any reasonable and foreseeable expenses incurred in availing themselves of the remedy. The Commission can also order any manufacturer, distributor, or retailer to reimburse any other person in the distribution chain for his expenses in carrying out any remedy. While commonly those at fault will be expected to bear the loss, the House Committee report noted, each instance will be treated individually and the Commission can take into account which party is best able to bear the loss.

B. CIVIL PENALTIES

Any person who knowingly commits any prohibited act is subject to a civil penalty not to exceed $2,000 for each violation. The Commission may impose multiple penalties, not to exceed $500,000, for any related series of violations. In addition to penalties for violations of product safety rules, each refusal to permit access to or copying of records, to furnish reports or information, or to permit entry or inspection under Section 19(a)(3) is considered a separate violation. Commission of any other act prohibited by Section 19(a) is considered a separate transaction for each product involved.

Any person not a manufacturer, distributor, or private labeler who knowingly violates Section 19 is not subject to multiple penalties unless he had actual knowledge or notice from the Commission that this action would constitute violation of the Act. It should be noted that for the purposes of Section 20 of the Act, dealing with civil penalties, "knowingly" is defined as actual knowledge or knowledge presumed to be possessed by a reasonable man acting in the circumstances, including knowledge obtainable upon the exercise of due care to ascertain the truth of representations.

The Commission is also given authority to compromise civil penalties, considering the size of the business involved and the gravity of the violation.

C. CRIMINAL PENALTIES

Any person who knowingly and willfully commits any of the acts prohibited by Section 19 after having received notice of noncompliance from the Commission is liable for a fine of not more than $50,000 or imprisonment for not more than one year, or both. Any individual director, officer, or agent of a corporation who knowingly or willfully authorizes, orders, or performs any prohibited act with knowledge that notice of noncompliance has been received by the corporation is subject to the same penalties, without regard to any that may be imposed upon the corporation.

D. INJUNCTIONS

United States district courts are given authority to issue injunctions preventing any person from committing any prohibited act or distributing in commerce any product that does not comply with a consumer product safety rule. Either the Commission, with the concurrence of the Attorney General, or the Attorney General on his own may seek such action in any judicial district where any act, omission, or transaction constituting the violation occurred, or where the defendant is found or transacts business. Under this section, process may be served on a defendant in any other district where he resides or may be found.

E. SEIZURES

Any consumer product that fails to conform to an applicable consumer product safety rule when introduced into commerce, while in commerce, or when held for sale after shipment in commerce is liable to be seized after proceedings in the United States district court in the district where the product is found. Proceedings for seizure are to conform "as nearly as possible" to proceedings *in rem* in admiralty. When proceedings involving substantially similar products are pending in two or more judicial districts, they are to be consolidated for trial by application of any party and order of any court in which an action is pending.

F. DAMAGE SUITS

Section 23(a) of the Act authorizes personal injury suits in the federal courts for "any knowing (including willful) violation" of any Commission rule or order, subject to the $10,000 jurisdictional requirement of Section 1331 of the Judicial Code. The bill reported by the House Commerce Committee would have authorized actions under this section without regard to the amount in controversy (see Appendix G, p. 238), but the limitation was inserted during debate on the floor of the House in order to avoid overcrowding of the federal courts with insubstantial cases (see Appendix H, p. 281). Also deleted from the committee-approved bill was Section 23(b), which contained a variety of affirmative defenses for defendants who acted with due care and in good faith.

There is a specific provision that the remedies here provided are in addition to, and not in lieu of, any other remedies provided by common law or under Federal or state statutory law—that is, the traditional products liability suits. Whether the new provision for suits in the federal courts will have any major impact on the customary personal injury litigation will depend on many factors that will have to be considered by injured consumers and their attorneys. For one thing, it may be easier in some cases to prove noncompliance with a mandatory federal standard than to prove the existence of a product defect. On the other hand, Section 23 authorizes actions only for a "knowing" violation of a Commission rule or order, while the "strict liability" doctrine applicable in most jurisdictions does not even require a showing of negligence. Also to be considered is the specific provision in Section 23 authorizing the court to award costs, including attorneys' fees, if considered appropriate by the court, as against the typical products liability suit where the attorney is compensated on a contingency basis out of the award.

It should be noted that this section does not define "knowing (including willful)" and does not refer to the definition of "knowingly" contained in Section 20, dealing with civil penalties (see Section B, supra). The phrase "knowing (including willful)" was not included in the House bill as reported by the committee, but was added on the House floor during debate (see Appendix H, p. 281)

The committee stated in its report that it "anticipates" that federal court actions under this section will in general apply state law as to the extent of recoverable damages and the parties other than the injured person who may recover damages. It noted, also, that the committee intended that any person who recovers damages by reason of injury, illness, or death would also be able to recover for any property damage resulting from the defendant's noncompliance.

G. PRIVATE ENFORCEMENT OF RULES

Private actions for injunctive relief to enforce Commission rules or orders are also authorized by the Act (Section 24), with provision for costs and attorneys' fees to the "prevailing party." At least 30 days before any such action is instituted to enforce a product safety rule or a remedial order calling for repair, replacement, or refund, the prospective plaintiff is required to provide notice by registered mail to the Consumer Product Safety Commission, the Attorney General, and the person against whom the action is directed. No such private action may be instituted, however, if the same alleged violation is the subject of a pending civil or criminal action by the United States under this Act. This restriction on private injunctive actions, of course, has no relevance to any private damage suits that may be appropriate.

The private injunctive action is not limited to "affected" or "aggrieved" persons or to those injured by the alleged noncompliance, but is available to "any interested person," without definition.

H. EFFECT ON PRIVATE REMEDIES

The limited impact of this new product safety legislation on the traditional forms of products liability litigation is spelled out in Section 25 of the Act.

Compliance with product safety standards or other rules or orders promulgated by the Commission, Section 25(a) provides, "shall not relieve any person from liability at common law or under State statutory law to any other person." It is to be expected, however, that at least one of the parties in personal injury suits will have an additional fact to be presented to the court and the jury—i.e., the fact of compliance or noncompliance with the mandatory federal standard.

On the other hand, subsection (b) states that the Commission's failure to take any action with respect to the safety of a consumer product "shall not be admissible in evidence in litigation at common law or under State statutory law relating to such product."

Probably the most significant change wrought by the Act in products liability cases—affecting the preparation and presentation of the case, rather than procedural or substantive issues—is Section 25(c), which states that the Commission's accident or investigative reports "shall be made available to the public," although without identifying the injured person or his doctor, except with their consent. The availability of such reports is subject only to the provisions of Section 6(a)(2) and 6(b) of the Act, dealing with trade secrets and procedures to protect individual manufacturers, and is not restricted by the provisions of Section 6(a)(1), relating to the Freedom of Information Act. In addition, the Commission is required to make available all reports on research projects, demonstration projects, and other related activities.

Deleted by the Conference Committee from the final enactment was an additional provision of the House bill that would have required the Commission to make available, subject only to the confidentiality provisions of Section 6(a)(1), "accident and investigation reports * * * for use in any civil, criminal, or other judicial proceeding arising out of the accident," plus the testimony of Commission officers or employees as to the facts developed in the investigation (see Appendix J, p. 338).

CHAPTER VII
IMMINENT HAZARDS

In addition to the authority given to the Consumer Product Safety Commission to promulgate product safety rules administratively, Section 12 of the Act gives it the power to seek immediate judicial relief in emergency situations affecting the public's safety, without requiring formal administrative rulemaking or adjudicatory action.

Whenever the Commission finds that a hazardous consumer product is presenting, or is likely to present, an imminent and unreasonable risk of death, illness, or severe personal injury, it may file an action in the federal district courts seeking one or more of a variety of remedial orders. The Commission, through its own attorneys, may file one or both of the following types of suits: (1) an action *in rem* against the offending product, looking to its seizure; (2) an *in personam* action against the manufacturer, importer, distributor, or retailer of the product, in order to get injunctive relief and/or an order requiring notification, recall, repair, or replacement of the product.

Suit may be instituted whether or not there is a consumer product safety rule applicable to the product, and whether or not there is pending any standard-setting or other administrative or judicial proceeding under the Act. However, if there is no product safety rule covering the particular product hazard, Section 12(c) provides that, "where appropriate," the Commission shall initiate proceedings for such a rule, either concurrently with the filing of the suit or as soon as practicable thereafter.

Unlike other provisions in the Act dealing with Commission-instituted suits, which permit the Commission to be represented by its own attorneys only with the concurrence of the Attorney General, whose Justice Department attorneys would ordinarily handle Commission cases as they do suits by almost all other federal agencies, Section 12 dealing with imminent hazards states specifically, that "notwithstanding any other provision of law, in any action under this section, the Commission may direct attorneys employed by it to appear and represent it."

In Rem Actions

An *in rem* action against the offending merchandise can be filed in any district in which the products may be found. The proceeding would be a libel for the seizure or condemnation of the product, comparable to proceedings *in rem* in admiralty law, "as nearly as possible." In admiralty, an action against the *res*—usually a vessel—is ordinarily a private action instituted by a person holding a maritime lien; clearly, in a public action brought by the Consumer Product Safety Commission, no such requirement would be applicable. However, as in admiralty, while the *res*, not its owner, is the party defendant, persons having an interest in the product may be deemed parties to the suit, with full opportunities to defend against the Commission's claim.

Also as in admiralty, it is expected that a personal judgment against the owner cannot be entered on a libel *in rem.* While in admiralty law, there is sometimes an apparent exception to this rule when the owner has posted a bond to obtain the release of the *res* during the pendency of the proceeding (the bond usually being twice the value of the seized property), there is no indication in the statute or its legislative history that similar flexibility is contemplated in suits under the Consumer Product Safety Act. Although release under bond will apparently be subject to the discretion of the court, it can be expected that the Commission will urge that products it has deemed to be imminently hazardous should be kept off the market completely until a final determination on the merits is made. In this, the procedure would be comparable to that involving imported consumer products deemed to be hazardous, where no provision is made for entry under bond (see Chapter IX, *infra*).

In Personam Actions

Commission suits against the manufacturer, importer, distributor, or retailer of a product deemed imminently hazardous may be brought in any district where the defendant is found, is an inhabitant, or transacts business. Process may be served on a defendant in any other district in which he may be found, and subpenas may run in any district. Provision is made for convenience of the parties to be considered in instances where the action may be brought in more than one judicial district. Private labelers are not considered as manufacturers for purposes of this section, as they are for other purposes of the Act. They are therefore not subject to be sued under Section 12 as private labelers, although they would presumably be covered as either distributors or retailers.

In the event of multidistrict litigation involving identical consumer products, Section 12(e)(2) provides that the suits shall be consolidated for trial by order of any court in which one or more of the suits is pending, upon application by any party in interest and with notice to all parties.

In any action against the commercial establishments subject to Section 12, the federal court is granted authority to provide such temporary or permanent relief as may be necessary to protect the public from the stated risk, including mandatory orders requiring notification to the public or to known purchasers, the recall, repair, or replacement of the product, or refunds to purchasers.

Before commencing any action under Section 12, the Commission is told that it may consult the Product Safety Advisory Council about the institution of the suit and may request Council recommendations as to the appropriate relief. The Council may hold hearings or offer the opportunity for written comments in preparing its recommendations, but the opportunities will clearly be limited, since Section 12(d)(2) requires any Council recommendations to be submitted to the Commission within one week of the Commission's request.

CHAPTER VIII
INSPECTION AND RECORDKEEPING

Section 16 of the Act gives the Consumer Product Safety Commission broad authority to:

1. Conduct on-site inspections of all industrial and commercial premises on which consumer products may be found, including conveyances used to transport the products;
2. Issue regulations prescribing the form and nature of records to be kept and reports to be made by manufacturers, importers, private labelers, and distributors (but *not* retailers unless they are also manufacturers, distributors or private labelers); and
3. Inspect books, records, and papers of manufacturers, importers, private labelers, and distributors to determine whether they are operating in compliance with the Act and the rules issued under it.

The inspection and recordkeeping provisions of the Act are those that were contained in the House-approved bill (Appendix I), differing in several significant respects from the Senate-approved legislation (Appendix F), and the legislative history of this section is certain to be a much-debated issue in future litigation.

A. INSPECTION

Officers or employees of the Commission are authorized to enter any factory, warehouse, or other commercial establishment in which consumer products are manufactured or held and inspect any area "which may relate to the safety of such products." The same authority is granted with respect to conveyances being used to transport such products in commerce, presumably including common carriers, contract carriers, and freight forwarders, despite the fact that such firms are, by definition (Section 3(b) of the Act), not to be considered as manufacturers, distributors, or retailers for the purposes of the Act.

The inspecting officer must present appropriate credentials and a written notice from the Commission, and the inspection must be conducted at reasonable times, in a reasonable manner, and with reasonable promptness. According to the House committee report, the Commission has authority to conduct periodic or random inspections, in addition to inspections for cause (see Appendix G, p. 234).

"In the early stages of this program, however," the report continues, "it is expected that the Commission in marshalling its resources will place primary emphasis on inspections to test for compliance with applicable standards and concentrate on instances where it has reason to believe that the methods, tests, or procedures related to the manufacture and storage of a product may not be adequate or reliable."

Unlike the Senate version of the product safety legislation, Section 16 contains no reference to the taking of samples by Commission inspectors, for which the Senate would have required appropriate receipts. Whether the Act's broad grant of inspection authority to the Commission includes such power will be a matter for Commission and, ultimately, judicial determination. (The Commission's authority to *purchase* consumer products for testing purposes, at the seller's cost, is spelled out in Section 27(f), and its power to require the submission of performance and technical data in Section 27(e).)

In some respects, the Senate version of the product safety legislation would have restricted the Commission's authority. For example, the Senate bill limited the inspection authority to the premises of companies handling only consumer products that are subject to a product safety rule; the conference report uses the phrase "whether or not required to conform to a consumer public [sic] safety standard" (see Appendix J, p. 333). As enacted, this section applies to all consumer products, whether or not a standard or rule has been promulgated.

On the other hand, the Senate bill contained a specific provision authorizing U.S. district courts to issue any warrants needed by the Commission in aid of an inspection or investigation. As enacted, the law contains no such provision. However, among the prohibited acts listed in Section 19 is a failure to permit entry or inspection, and the Commission is clearly authorized by Section 22 of the Act to seek injunctive relief to restrain any violation of Section 19.

It is much too early to determine whether the Consumer Product Safety Commission, in administering the Act, will adhere to the conclusion reached in June 1970 by the National Commission on Product Safety, that "inspections of plants to check the safety of products at their source is a more efficient method of protecting the public than ferreting out noncomplying units on the market and then seizing them."

B. RECORDKEEPING

One of the greatest concerns of industry spokesmen who testified on the various product safety bills was the possibility of "onerous" and expensive recordkeeping requirements, particularly those related to the identification of every purchaser of a consumer product in the event notification, replacement, repair, or refund should be ordered. There was little concern with major items, such as automobiles and television sets, where records are usually kept anyway, but the problems involved in maintaining complete lists of all purchasers of such low-priced volume items as aerosol sprays, toys, household cleaners, children's football helmets, matches, and hundreds of other products were cited by many witnesses, particularly those at the retail level.

There was much discussion during the House and Senate hearings of a minimum dollar limit for such requirements, such as the $50 cut-off provision in the Radiation Control Act, but the large number of low-priced items that could present safety problems to consumers was cited by several committee members in opposition to any such limitation.

The bill approved by the Senate would have extended the recordkeeping authority of the Commission to "every person who manufactures, assembles, distributes, or sells in commerce, or imports," thus including retailers of consumer products. The objective was to promulgate "reasonable" procedures for securing and maintaining the names and addresses of the first public purchasers of consumer products subject to a product safety rule, with the Commission to consider the severity of the potential injuries, the likelihood of noncompliance, and the burden imposed on the recording companies.

The conference committee, however, rejected the Senate requirements and adopted the House provisions, which authorize the Commission to require all manufacturers (including importers), distributors, and private labelers to "maintain such records, make such reports, and provide such information" as may be necessary to implement the Act or determine compliance with its provisions. As in the case of Commission inspections, the recordkeeping requirements are applicable whether or not the particular consumer product is subject to a product safety rule. Records, books, and papers must be made available upon request to officers or employees designated by the Commission.

Retailers Excluded

The House committee report noted that retailers were excluded from the recordkeeping provision "in the belief that mandatory customer recordkeeping requirements could prove unduly burdensome for a large number of small retailers and could materially add to the costs of consumer products. Manufacturers, of course, are free to develop such arrangements with their retailers as they may believe are necessary to facilitate the efficient and economic recall and remedy of defective and nonconforming consumer products. Such arrangements will remain a matter of private agreement."

Examples of such arrangements, cited often during subcommittee hearings, included warranty registration cards or self-addressed identification cards that could be mailed by the consumers to the manufacturer, private labeler, or importer of the product.

It should be noted that the notification provisions of Section 15, specifying the notice that is to be given whenever the Commission determines that a product presents a substantial hazard, apply to retailers as well as to manufacturers and distributors. In such instances, the Commission is empowered to order the manufacturer or any distributor or retailer to provide notification through a published notice, a mailed notice to any commercial enterprise handling the product, or a mailed notice to "every person to whom the person required to give notice knows such product was delivered or sold."

The Commission also is given authority, under Section 29(a)(2), to commission any qualified officer or employee of any state or local government to conduct inspections or investigations.

CHAPTER IX
IMPORTED PRODUCTS

All United States imports of consumer products are subject to the provisions of the Consumer Product Safety Act and to the rules and regulations issued thereunder. As a result, U. S. importers and their overseas suppliers, as well as the U. S. Customs Bureau that oversees all importations, will be forced to adopt substantial changes in their traditional methods of doing business.

With respect to imports of all consumer products covered by the Act, the Consumer Product Safety Commission is:

1. Required to ban completely the entry of unsafe consumer products, without any provision for entry under bond while the product is being inspected for possible noncompliance;
2. Authorized to condition the importation of any such products on the foreign manufacturer's willingness to permit Commission-designated inspectors to make on-site investigations of the manufacturing or warehousing premises;
3. Authorized to condition the importation of the products on the foreign manufacturer's willingness to establish and maintain such records as the Commission may require;
4. Empowered to require of the U. S. importer compliance with all the inspection and recordkeeping regulations applicable to U. S. manufacturers of consumer products, as well as rules on new products;
5. Empowered to apply any of its many enforcement procedures to U. S. importers in the event of noncompliance; and
6. Authorized to ban any "stockpiling" of imported consumer products—that is, any substantial increase in the volume of imports—during the period between the promulgation of a product safety rule and its effective date.

No Entry under Bond

Section 17(a) provides that any consumer product "offered for importation" into the customs territory of the United States "shall be refused admission" if it fails to comply with an applicable safety standard, is not accompanied by proper certification, is imminently hazardous, or has a hazardous product defect. Provision is made in Section 17(b) for customs to turn over a reasonable number of samples for inspection by the Commission.

There is no provision in the Act allowing the merchandise to be taken out of the custody of the Customs Bureau during the period of inspection, even by the posting of a bond as specified in Section 449 of the Tariff Act (19 U.S.C. 1499). The Senate bill contained authorization for entry of the products under bond (see Appendix F, Section 317), with provisions for redelivery of the merchandise if the inspection showed noncompliance or, upon a failure to redeliver, forfeiture of the bond. In the conference committee, the Senate provisions were deleted and the outright ban of the House bill was incorporated into final enactment.

The owner or consignee of the imported consumer product (who would ordinarily be the U. S. importer, but could in some circumstances be the customs broker) is entitled to a full adjudicatory hearing before the Commission on the safety status of his merchandise. Section 17(b) states that the importer may have a full hearing under Section 5 of the Administrative Procedure Act (5 U.S.C. 554), dealing with administrative adjudications and providing for testimony under oath, the issuance of subpoenas, cross-examination, a decision made on the record and other accoutrements of formal agency hearings. (It should be noted that Section 5 of the APA exempts from its procedural requirements "proceedings in which decisions rest solely on inspections [or] tests.") The only exception to the requirement for an agency hearing relates to imported products that are, or have been, the subject of judicial proceedings under Section 12 of the Act for seizure and condemnation as "imminently hazardous consumer products" (see Chapter VII).

If the Commission determines that the imported product is not entitled to entry into the commerce of the United States, the merchandise must be exported or destroyed, unless the importer can persuade the Commission that the product can be so modified as to permit its admission. In that case, under regulations to be jointly prepared by the Commission and the Treasury Department, the importer may post a bond, remove the merchandise from customs custody, and attempt to make the necessary modifications, subject to the supervision of an official of either the Commission or the Customs Bureau. If the attempted modification is not successful, or is not proceeding to the satisfaction of the Commission, the customs officials will be directed to demand redelivery of the merchandise, which will then be exported or destroyed. All expenses connected with storage, cartage, labor, and destruction of the merchandise will be to the importer's account, and, if unpaid, will constitute a lien against any of his future importations.

Inspection and Recordkeeping

The authority to impose inspection and record-keeping requirements on foreign manufacturers is covered by Section 17(g), which provides that the Commission may adopt regulations that condition the importation of any merchandise on the manufacturer's compliance with such requirements. If the Commission informs the Customs Bureau that a foreign manufacturer has not complied with such requirements, his products shipped to the United States are to be barred from entry into the country. In comments on the bill originally before the Senate, the U. S. State Department pointed out that "many countries almost certainly would dispute the right under international law of the Consumer Product Safety Commission to inspect records and facilities of manufacturers located outside the jurisdiction of the United States. Some countries may refuse to allow their nationals to comply even voluntarily with these requirements." They suggested that the provisions for inspection of the imports after they reach U. S. ports, plus the provisions for certification procedures, including third-party inspection and certification, should be sufficient to guarantee the safety of imported products. Even more significant, according to the State Department, is the fact that "provisions of our law imposing criminal sanctions for conduct occurring in another country would produce even stronger resentment and reactions than regulatory provisions." In a later memo to the Senate Commerce Committee, the Department, asserting its strong support for the goal of protecting consumers against risks of injury from hazardous products, stated that "the satisfactory achievement of this goal * * * may require international coordination of information on safety hazards and negotiation of international arrangements to assure that established safety standards are met."

The comments of the Treasury Department took no issue with the provision for overseas inspection and recordkeeping, perhaps because that Department's customs officials have long been involved in similar overseas investigations under the Anti-Dumping Act of 1921. While "dumping" investigations relate to pricing information rather than manufacturing processes or product performance, the Treasury Department has found that most foreign companies, however reluctantly, have agreed to provide answers to detailed questionnaires and even to open their books and vouchers to on-site investigators when faced with the alternative of being denied access to the U. S. market. In the case of a "dumping" investigation, the Department, faced with overseas recalcitrance, can impose "dumping duties" that would make the importation uneconomic. Under the Consumer Product Safety Act, the Commission has the authority to bar the importation without further ado.

The U. S. importer will be subject to the same inspection and recordkeeping requirements applicable to U. S. manufacturers of consumer products, whether or not the particular products handled by the importer are subject to a Commission product safety standard or other rule. (For details of the inspection and recordkeeping powers of the Commission, see Chapter VIII *supra.*)

Problems for Customs

The problems created for the Customs Bureau by the requirements of the new statute relate to both physical and procedural matters. The physical problem is the matter of storage facilities for an undetermined quantity of consumer product shipments that may be subject to inspections, tests, or other examinations to determine compliance with the product safety rules. In almost every instance under other legislation, the importer is permitted to enter his merchandise into the country even before it is appraised or classified under the Tariff Act or before it is examined for compliance with applicable statutes or regulations. The entry is made under bond, determined by the Customs Bureau to be sufficient to assure compliance with the financial or other requirements. When the merchandise is required to be kept in customs custody for more than a few days, it must be sent to a General Order Warehouse until the papers can be cleared through customs. In most major ports, such as New York, Los Angeles, and New Orleans, the Bureau anticipates that storage space in such warehouses should present few problems, unless the quantity of consumer product importations in any time period becomes large and their clearance is substantially delayed. In many smaller port areas, however, such warehousing is not available, or not available in sufficient degree to handle any quantity of stored products. How such importations are to be handled will depend on joint arrangements to be worked out by the Commission and the Bureau.

Similarly, joint regulations will be required to govern the procedures involved in the selection and forwarding of samples to the Commission, the release of imported merchandise for necessary modification, the destruction or exportation of unsafe products, and the other joint steps required in the enforcement of the Act's requirement.

Date of Manufacture

An additional problem presented to the Customs Bureau has no ready solution under present procedures, but it is likely that the burden will be passed on to the importer or his customs broker. Any product safety standard adopted by the Consumer Product Safety Commission may not be made applicable to a product manufactured before the effective date of the standard (Section 9(d)(1) of the Act). Customs invoices and other papers accompanying imported shipments, however, while they provide information as to date of exportation, price information, and other pertinent data, contain no information as to the date on which the products in the shipment were manufactured. Such information may, indeed, not be in the possession of the foreign exporter, who often is a person other than the manufacturer. How, then, is the customs official to determine whether a product safety standard issued by the Commission is "applicable" to the merchandise being offered for entry into the United States?

Customs officials may avoid the problem by making a determination that the imported merchandise contains products on which the Commission has issued safety standards, and place the burden on the importer or his broker to prove that they were manufactured before the effective date of the standard. If any such procedure is actually adopted, it is not yet clear what type of proof the Customs Bureau will require before allowing the merchandise to enter the United States.

There may still be some question, also, as to the applicability of the effective date provision to imported products. Various versions of the product safety legislation considered by Congress appeared to require compliance on the part of imported products with any product safety rule issued at the time of the importation, and several witnesses at committee hearings urged such a requirement. Authority to impose such a ban was, in fact, included in the Senate bill (Appendix F). The language finally adopted in the Act is that an imported consumer product is to be barred if it "fails to comply with an applicable consumer product safety rule." Query: What is the meaning of the word "applicable"—does it refer merely to any product that is described in the text of the rule, or does it incorporate the effective date provisions of Section(9)(d)(1)?

Stockpiling

The anti-stockpiling provision of the Act also will pose special problems for U. S. importers, who ordinarily order their merchandise in large quantities many weeks or months before the importation is actually made. Section 9(d)(2) of the Act does not impose an outright ban on stockpiling, as the Senate version of the legislation did. Instead, it authorizes the Commission to adopt regulations spelling out the standards of any anti-stockpiling rule. How the Commission exercises its discretion—whether applying to the date of importation rather than the date of purchase, whether having due regard to seasonal merchandise, etc.—will have a significant impact on the volume and nature of future importations.

Since the Act refers to merchandise "offered for importation," rather than merchandise "imported"—statutory language to which the Treasury Department objected, in view of its uncertain meaning—it is possible that arrangements can be made for prior inspection and clearance of product samples, in advance of the actual importation, in order to speed up the importing process for both the importers and the Customs Bureau. Any such program, which would require substantial changes in the operations of many importers, would have to be worked out jointly by the Customs Bureau and the Consumer Product Safety Commission.

The conference committee's adoption of the Senate's broad definition of "State" in Section 3(a)(10) of the Act extends the law's regulatory powers to certain territories in which importations are not subject to Customs Bureau control. Presumably, in those areas, the import controls will be administered by the appropriate territorial offices.

Although the new Act itself contains no reference to the establishment of international safety standards and procedures, the legislative history of the statute is replete with such references and suggestions, starting with the Final Report of the National Commission on Product Safety. This may be a matter for at least preliminary discussion during the trade negotiations scheduled for 1973 under the auspices of the General Agreement on Tariffs and Trade.

CHAPTER X
FEDERAL-STATE RELATIONS

The program established by the Consumer Product Safety Act to rid the market of unsafe consumer products is a nationwide program, deliberately designed to avoid—and end—the problem of differing product safety standards in different state and local communities. Indeed, the proliferation of such state and local safety regulations was one of the prime factors behind industry's general support—sometimes lukewarm, often enthusiastic—of a federal consumer safety program. Industry's natural reluctance to subject itself to strict federal regulation was overcome in most instances by a realization of the much greater burdens imposed on both production and marketing operations by the existence of varying standards in major markets across the country.

With a few specific exceptions, therefore, the Consumer Product Safety Act provides for federal preemption of problems involving the safety of consumer products. However, the new law also makes provision for a maximum of cooperation between federal and state agencies and officials concerned with product safety.

It has been generally recognized that, aside from the problem of diverse standards applicable to similar products, state and local agencies cannot be expected to cope effectively with imports, out-of-state purchases, out-of-state enforcement, and similar problems affecting consumer products that move in interstate commerce. On the other hand, as the National Commission on Product Safety noted, they may be uniquely well equipped to regulate the installation and use of consumer products, such as electric, gas, or plumbing appliances.

Moreover, the new statute's definition of "commerce" offers some opportunities for state and local regulation of consumer products that move only within a single state. The conference committee rejected the Senate's definition, which would have included commerce "within" as well as between the states, and adopted the House definition, which appears to include the full reach of the Federal Government's constitutional authority—including not only all consumer products that move in interstate or foreign commerce, but also all products that "affect" such commerce. Presumably, there are some consumer products that are produced and sold locally and have no effect on interstate commerce, but their number is certain to be small and their impact on the consumer safety program minimal.

A. EFFECT ON STATE STANDARDS

State statutes and local ordinances dealing with product safety will not be affected by enactment of the federal Consumer Product Safety Act, unless and until the Commission issues a product safety rule. Once the federal rule becomes effective, states and their political subdivisions will be barred from enforcing their own standards, or establishing new standards, unless their standards are identical with those issued by the federal Commission.

The federal preemption relates to particular hazards associated with consumer products, not to the products themselves. If, for example, the Commission should adopt standards designed to prevent short-circuits in powered hand saws, the state and local governments could still enforce, or establish, their own standards for blade guards on such saws, since each standard is aimed at a different hazard. But once the Commission promulgates a safety rule dealing with a particular hazard, the state and local governments are barred from prescribing any different requirements as to the performance, composition, contents, design, finish, construction, packaging, or labeling of such products that are designed to deal with the same hazard.

The House Commerce Committee, whose version of these provisions prevailed in the final legislation, explained that it was intended that the state or local government maintain its own enforcement mechanisms over its own product safety rules, and be able to establish its own criminal and civil penalties for violation of those rules. By permitting dual enforcement of identical rules, however, the committee said it was not intended that the provisions would be used as a means of subjecting violators to double penalties. In instances where violators have already been adequately penalized under state law, it is expected that federal, civil and criminal penalties would not be sought by the Commission or would not be imposed in full measure.

In addition, in instances where state action follows the imposition of federal penalties, it is expected that the Commission would take this into consideration in determining whether to compromise any civil penalty already imposed.

There are only two exceptions to these broad preemptive provisions of the new Act:

1. State and local governments, like the Federal Government, may establish a higher standard of performance than the otherwise applicable Commission standard on consumer products they purchase for their own use.

2. The Consumer Product Safety Commission is authorized to exempt any state or local government from the preemption provisions of the Act, if the proposed standard is higher than the applicable Commission standard, is "required by compelling local conditions," and does not unduly burden interstate commerce. On application by a state or local government under Section 26(c) of the Act, the Commission is to provide notice and opportunity for oral presentation of views on the proposal, after which it may issue an exemption order, under such conditions as it may choose to impose.

B. COOPERATION WITH STATES

A program to promote federal-state cooperation in carrying out the provisions of the new law is to be established by the Commission. In implementing that program, the Commission may accept and pay for help from state or local authorities engaged in activities relating to health, safety, or consumer protection. The assistance may involve such activities as injury data collection, investigation, and educational programs. The Commission also may accept and pay for other assistance in the administration and enforcement of the Act which the states and localities may be "able and willing to provide."

The Act provides that the Commission may authorize any qualified state or local officer or employee to conduct examinations, investigations, and inspections.

In determining whether the state and local programs are "appropriate," the Commission is directed to give favorable consideration to programs establishing separate state and local agencies to consolidate functions relating to product safety and other consumer protection activities.

The extent to which the new Commission will utilize the services of state and local officials to carry out its own delegated functions—an authority that has been provided in other statutes, such as the Occupational Safety and Health Act, and the degree of cooperation with state and local enforcement officers will depend entirely on the discretion of the members of the Commission.

CHAPTER XI
OTHER PROVISIONS

A. TRANSFERS OF FUNCTIONS

A major goal of the National Commission on Product Safety was to consolidate virtually all consumer safety regulatory activities within a single independent agency concerned only with problems of product safety. This goal has been largely achieved through enactment of the Consumer Product Safety Act of 1972. With only a few exceptions—food, drugs, cosmetics, motor vehicles, aircraft, boats, tobacco, firearms, and economic poisons—the Consumer Product Safety Commission will not only exercise authority over the broad range of hitherto unregulated consumer products, but will also assume operating responsibility under existing product safety legislation.

Transferred to the new Commission—with the transfers to take effect on or about March 26, 1973—are all the regulatory functions under:

1. The Hazardous Substances Act, including its amendments designated as the Caustic Poisons Act and the Child Protection and Toy Safety Act—which was administered by the Department of Health, Education and Welfare;
2. The Poison Prevention Packaging Act—previously administered by HEW except for pesticide packaging, which is the responsibility of the Environmental Protection Agency;
3. The Flammable Fabrics Act—which had been administered jointly by HEW, the Department of Commerce, and the Federal Trade Commission; and
4. The Refrigerator Safety Act—which was under the Department of Commerce. (The reference in Section 30(c) of the Act to the transfer of functions of the Secretary of Commerce and the Federal Trade Commission under the Act of August 2, 1956, is apparently an oversight, since the FTC had no operating authority relating to the safety of refrigerators.)

These transfers involve not only the regulatory powers under the various statutes, but also the personnel, property, records, obligations, and commitments, with only one exception. Section 30(e)(1)(A) provides that this transfer provision shall not affect the research activities of the Commerce Department's National Bureau of Standards on fire and flammability.

The transfer does not abrogate regulations already issued or other actions taken under these laws. To the contrary, the Act provides that all orders, determinations, rules, regulations, permits, contracts, certificates, licenses, and privileges of these various departments and agencies shall remain in effect unless and until they are amended or abrogated through normal administrative procedures by the Consumer Product Safety Commission.

The transfer section of the Act includes what is essentially a pro forma, but necessary, provision that any suits brought under transferred laws or rules involving their former overseers will not be affected, except that they will be taken over by the Commission. Thus, a suit brought by or naming HEW, for example, will not have to be started all over again just to accommodate the jurisdictional change.

In transferring the Hazardous Substances Act, the Poison Prevention Packaging Act, and the Flammable Fabrics Act—but not the Refrigerator Safety Act—the new Act clearly limits the Commission's authority to that prescribed under those laws; the product safety law does not in any way alter the regulatory or enforcement authority of the pre-existing statutes.

As the Conference Report states (Appendix J, p. 318): "A product hazard which could be prevented or reduced to a sufficient extent by action taken under the Federal Hazardous Substances Act, the Poison Prevention Packaging Act, or the Flammable Fabrics Act could be regulated by the Commission only in accordance with the provisions of those Acts."

The members of the conference committee deliberately omitted the Refrigerator Safety Act from this limitation, leaving the new Commission with much broader regulatory authority over refrigerators under the provisions of the new law.

Pre-Existing Legislation

The Hazardous Substances Act, as amended by the Caustic Poisons Act and the Child Protection and Toy Safety Act, is designed to protect the public from any substance or mixture used in a toy or household product that is deemed to be hazardous by reason of being toxic, corrosive, an irritant, a strong sensitizer, flammable or combustible, or a product that "generates pressure through decomposition, heat, or other means, if such substance or mixture of substances may cause substantial personal injury or substantial illness during or as a proximate result of any customary or reasonably foreseeable handling or use, including reasonably foreseeable ingestion by children." Under this Act, the new Commission takes over HEW's responsibility, which includes authority to issue regulations (1) naming any substance as hazardous if it meets the above criteria, (2) requiring labeling of any radioactive substance, (3) covering toys that present an electrical, mechanical, or thermal hazard. The Act also says that additional labeling requirements may be ordered for a product if the standard format outlined in the Act is insufficient to protect the public. Designated hazardous substances cannot be packaged in containers formerly used for food or in packages that resemble food containers.

Products can be banned if cautionary labeling is insufficient to protect the public, but the Act authorizes exemptions for hazardous substances that are included in a product because of the product's "functional purpose," so long as directions and warnings for safe use are given—for example, chemical sets and fireworks. Other exemptions are authorized for substances that as a practical matter cannot be made to comply with labeling requirements, and those which do not present a danger sufficient to warrant cautionary labeling or for which adequate safeguards for protecting consumers are provided by some other federal law.

In the case of a substance presenting an "imminent hazard" to the health and safety of the public, an order may be issued immediately banning the item from sale in interstate commerce, even before completion of prescribed administrative proceedings to declare the product "banned." But in the case of hazardous substances or toys, the normal banning regulations must follow hard upon the emergency order. Banned or misbranded hazardous substances introduced into interstate commerce may be subject to seizure under court order, but the court may authorize the regulatory body to assure that the product is brought into compliance as an alternative to destruction.

The Poison Prevention Packaging Act of 1970 is designed to set standards for packaging of household substances that are easily accessible to children and would be harmful to them if handled or ingested. Types of products used around the household that could be subject to special child protection packaging rules include: hazardous substances, pesticides, foods, drugs, or cosmetics. The Commerce Secretary, before the transfer, had authority to set packaging requirements for all substances except pesticides, which were regulated by the Environmental Protection Agency. The Act also provides that products may be packaged in one size that is not child-proofed, to accommodate the elderly or handicapped who would find them difficult to open otherwise.

New Commission's Authority

Standards and regulations issued by the departments and agencies enforcing these various statutes will remain in effect and are to be enforced by the Consumer Product Safety Commission, unless and until they are changed by Commission regulation, court action, or operation of law.

Under the Hazardous Substances Act, for example, this would include regulations covering ball point ink cartridges using toxic ink, cigarette lighters using butane fuel, and charcoal briquettes; under the Poison Prevention Packaging Act, the existing standards on liquid furniture polishes containing petroleum distillates, aspirin, liquid preparations containing wintergreen oil, household liquid products containing methanol, household substances containing sodium and/or potassium hydroxide, and household products containing turpentine; under the Flammable Fabrics Act, the standards covering children's sleepwear up to size 6X, carpets and rugs, and mattresses; and under the Refrigerator Safety Act, the rule governing inside latches.

On various proposals that were pending at the time the Consumer Product Safety Act was passed, however, the new Commission has complete authority to make its own determination, provided the decisions have not been made by the transferee agencies prior to the effective date of the transfer. Pending proposals under the Hazardous Substances Act, for example, include one for pacifiers that can present a mechanical hazard to children, another for federal preemption of state and local labeling requirements for household products, and a third (subsequently withdrawn, but being reconsidered) to regulate the repurchase provisions of the Act.

With regard to administrative procedures, the new Commission is bound by existing regulations. For example, the two-hearing procedure adopted by the Department of Commerce under the Flammable Fabrics Act—calling for one proposal, hearing, and determination on the *need* for a flammability standard, and another on the *nature* of the standard—will be binding on the new Commission, unless and until it takes formal action to change its rules of practice. If, as the National Commission on Product Safety believed, the Flammable Fabrics Act does not require the two separate hearings and determinations, the Consumer Product Safety Commission would be empowered to change the administrative procedure and consolidate the two issues into one notice, hearing, and decision.

Except for the Refrigerator Safety Act, the new Commission is limited to operating under the language of the pre-existing statutes, to the extent that those statutes provide a sufficient basis for the elimination or reduction of a particular risk of injury. If the risk can be reduced "to a sufficient extent" under the old law, the Commission may not utilize any of its authority under the new product safety law, even if the exercise of that authority might produce a more satisfactory result. However, it is possible for a single class of products to be regulated both under the old statutes and under the new, if the preexisting statute provides adequate protection against one hazard, but not against another.

Since the personnel of the departments and agencies having authority under the earlier laws will undoubtedly form the nucleus of the new Commission's staff, and in view of the time lag between the appointment of the new Commission and the transfer of these functions, it is expected that the turnover of authority will be accomplished with a minimum of disruption and confusion. What happens thereafter is largely within the discretion of the members of the Consumer Product Safety Commission.

B. NEW PRODUCTS

For new consumer products not yet on the market, the only specific authority given to the Consumer Product Safety Commission is the promulgation of regulations requiring the manufacturer to furnish notice and a description of the product *before* its distribution in commerce. The rule may also be applied to importers.

Of course, new products as well as those on the market are covered by other applicable provisions of the Act, including the authority to promulgate product safety rules, ban hazardous products, seek a court order to seize imminently hazardous products, and also the power under Section 27(e) to require a manufacturer to provide product performance and technical data related to performance and safety "as may be required to carry out the purposes of this Act."

Section 13 defines a new product as one incorporating a design, material, or form of energy exchange that (1) has not previously been used substantially in consumer products, and (2) as to which there exists a lack of information adequate to determine its safety for use by consumers.

The House Commerce Committee explained that the provisions are designed to give the Commission an opportunity to keep abreast of new products entering the marketplace, so that it can head off imminently hazardous products in the courts or promptly institute a proceeding to ban the product or develop appropriate safety standards. However, the committee emphasized in its report (see Appendix G, p. 230) that it did not intend the Commission's rulemaking powers to be used to require pre-market clearance of new consumer products, as in the case of certain drugs. Therefore, the Commission would not have authority to require a manufacturer to postpone distribution until the Commission can run tests on the product or make an analysis of its potential for harm.

The Senate bill would have authorized the new agency to require by regulation that a consumer product not subject to a consumer product safety standard be subjected to a detailed safety analysis. The provision, dropped from the final version by the House-Senate conferees, would have allowed the detailed safety analysis to be conducted by the manufacturer, an independent testing laboratory, or any other person designated by the agency.

C. CARRIERS

As specified in Section 3(b) of the Act, common carriers, contract carriers, and freight forwarders are not to be considered manufacturers, distributors, or retailers of a consumer product solely by reason of receiving or transporting products in the ordinary course of business. This provision excludes the carriers and forwarders from most of the provisions of the Act.

The House Commerce Committee, which drafted the provision, explained that, unless specifically excluded, carriers and forwarders "would be swept up" in the broad definitions of the terms "manufacturer," "distributor," and "retailers."

In Section 16 of the Act, however, the Commission is authorized to enter and inspect conveyances being used to hold or transport consumer products in connection with distribution in commerce, in addition to the authority to enter and inspect factories and warehouses. Carriers are therefore subject to the provisions of Section 19(a)(3), which states that it is unlawful for any person to fail or refuse to permit entry or inspection, and such failure or refusal would be subject to the penalties set out in Section 20. In addition, carriers and forwarders would presumably be subject to the injunctive provisions of Section 22(a), which gives the U.S. district courts jurisdiction to restrain any violation of Section 19 or to restrain any person from distributing a product in commerce which does not comply with a consumer product safety rule.

In the case of an imminently hazardous consumer product, Section 12 provides the Commission with authority to file a court action against the product, as well as against any manufacturer, distributor, or retailer of the product. Thus, an imminently hazardous consumer product could be seized from a carrier or forwarder, even though the Commission could not proceed against him individually. The recordkeeping requirements of Section 16(b) cannot be made applicable to a carrier, but are limited to manufacturers, importers, private labelers, and distributors.

D. AUTHORIZATIONS

For the fiscal year ending June 30, 1973, the Act authorizes the appropriation of $55 million, increasing to $59 million for fiscal 1974, and to $64 million for fiscal 1975, as provided in Section 32(a).

An exception to this is provided in subsection 32(b), which authorizes "such sums as may be necessary" for the planning and construction of research, development, and testing facilities. No appropriation for these facilities in excess of $100,000 may be made without prior approval of the House and Senate Commerce Committees. In order to gain such approval, the Commission must submit to Congress a prospectus of the proposed facility, including a brief description, the location and estimated maximum cost, a statement of those groups which will use the facility, together with a report on the contribution to be made by each toward the cost, and a statement of justification of the need for the facility.

The estimated maximum cost of the facility may be increased by an amount up to 10 percent of the increase in general construction costs, as determined by the Commission.

These provisions for authorization are identical to those included in the bill originally passed by the House, but are substantially different from the Senate-approved language (see Appendix F, p. 198) The Senate measure would have authorized $250 million for fiscal 1973, $300 million for fiscal 1974, and $350 million for fiscal 1975. Provision for these sums was approved during the debate on the Senate floor in an amendment proposed by Senator Norris Cotton (R-NH).

There was considerable debate over federal spending in the last few months of the 92nd Congress, and the House-Senate conferees on the product safety bill decided in favor of the substantially lower figures in the House measure.

It is interesting to note that the National Commission on Product Safety included in its proposed Consumer Product Safety Act of 1970 authorization of $5 million for fiscal 1971, $7.5 million for fiscal 1972, and $10 million for fiscal 1973.

E. EFFECTIVE DATES

The Consumer Product Safety Act, with the exception of three provisions, took effect on December 26, 1972, the sixtieth day after the October 27 date of enactment.

The provisions for establishment of the Consumer Product Safety Commission (Section 4) and for authorization of funds (Section 32) took effect on October 27, the day President Nixon signed the bill into law.

Provisions for the transfer of activities (Section 30) under the Federal Hazardous Substances Act, the Poison Prevention Packaging Act, the Flammable Fabrics Act, and the Refrigerator Safety Act take effect either on March 26, 1973—150 days after enactment—or the date on which at least three members of the Commission first take office, whichever is later.

These effective dates were approved by the House and adopted by the House-Senate conferees, although the Senate-passed bill included different provisions. The Senate had approved a general effective date of 90 days after the Administrator of the agency first took office or on such earlier date as the President might designate. Officers were to be appointed at any time after date of enactment.

In the Senate bill, provisions for amendment to the Food, Drug, and Cosmetic Act regarding labeling of cosmetics were to take effect one year after enactment, while provisions for amending the Federal Hazardous Substances Act and repealing the Federal Caustic Poison Act were to take effect in 180 days.

APPENDICES

Appendix page

Public Law 92-573
92nd Congress, S. 3419
October 27, 1972

An Act

To protect consumers against unreasonable risk of injury from hazardous products, and for other purposes.

Be it enacted by the Senate and House of Representatives of the United States of America in Congress assembled,

SHORT TITLE; TABLE OF CONTENTS

SECTION 1. This Act may be cited as the "Consumer Product Safety Act".

TABLE OF CONTENTS

FINDINGS AND PURPOSES

SEC. 2. (a) The Congress finds that—

(1) an unacceptable number of consumer products which present unreasonable risks of injury are distributed in commerce;

(2) complexities of consumer products and the diverse nature and abilities of consumers using them frequently result in an inability of users to anticipate risks and to safeguard themselves adequately;

(3) the public should be protected against unreasonable risks of injury associated with consumer products;

(4) control by State and local governments of unreasonable risks of injury associated with consumer products is inadequate and may be burdensome to manufacturers;

(5) existing Federal authority to protect consumers from exposure to consumer products presenting unreasonable risks of injury is inadequate; and

(6) regulation of consumer products the distribution or use of which affects interstate or foreign commerce is necessary to carry out this Act.

(b) The purposes of this Act are—

(1) to protect the public against unreasonable risks of injury associated with consumer products;

(2) to assist consumers in evaluating the comparative safety of consumer products;

(3) to develop uniform safety standards for consumer products and to minimize conflicting State and local regulations; and

(4) to promote research and investigation into the causes and prevention of product-related deaths, illnesses, and injuries.

DEFINITIONS

SEC. 3. (a) For purposes of this Act:

(1) The term "consumer product" means any article, or component part thereof, produced or distributed (i) for sale to a consumer for use in or around a permanent or temporary household or residence, a school, in recreation, or otherwise, or (ii) for the personal use, consumption or enjoyment of a consumer in or around a permanent or temporary household or residence, a school, in recreation, or otherwise; but such term does not include—

(A) any article which is not customarily produced or distributed for sale to, or use or consumption by, or enjoyment of, a consumer,

(B) tobacco and tobacco products,

(C) motor vehicles or motor vehicle equipment (as defined by sections 102 (3) and (4) of the National Traffic and Motor Vehicle Safety Act of 1966),

(D) economic poisons (as defined by the Federal Insecticide, Fungicide, and Rodenticide Act),

(E) any article which, if sold by the manufacturer, producer, or importer, would be subject to the tax imposed by section 4181 of the Internal Revenue Code of 1954 (determined without regard to any exemptions from such tax provided by section 4182 or 4221, or any other provision of such Code), or any component of any such article,

(F) aircraft, aircraft engines, propellers, or appliances (as defined in section 101 of the Federal Aviation Act of 1958),

(G) boats which could be subjected to safety regulation under the Federal Boat Safety Act of 1971 (46 U.S.C. 1451 et seq.); vessels, and appurtenances to vessels (other than such boats), which could be subjected to safety regulation under title 52 of the Revised Statutes or other marine safety statutes administered by the department in which the Coast Guard is operating; and equipment (including associated equipment, as defined in section 3(8) of the Federal Boat Safety Act of 1971) to the extent that a risk of injury associated with the use of such equipment on boats or vessels could be eliminated or reduced by actions taken under any statute referred to in this subparagraph,

(H) drugs, devices, or cosmetics (as such terms are defined in sections 201 (g), (h), and (i) of the Federal Food, Drug, and Cosmetic Act), or

(I) food. The term "food", as used in this subparagraph means all "food", as defined in section 201(f) of the Federal Food, Drug, and Cosmetic Act, including poultry and poultry products (as defined in sections 4 (e) and (f) of the Poultry Products Inspection Act), meat, meat food products (as defined in section 1(j) of the Federal Meat Inspection Act), and eggs and egg products (as defined in section 4 of the Egg Products Inspection Act).

See sections 30(d) and 31 of this Act, for limitations on Commission's authority to regulate certain consumer products.

(2) The term "consumer product safety rule" means a consumer products safety standard described in section 7(a), or a rule under this Act declaring a consumer product a banned hazardous product.

(3) The term "risk of injury" means a risk of death, personal injury, or serious or frequent illness.

(4) The term "manufacturer" means any person who manufactures or imports a consumer product.

(5) The term "distributor" means a person to whom a consumer product is delivered or sold for purposes of distribution in commerce, except that such term does not include a manufacturer or retailer of such product.

(6) The term "retailer" means a person to whom a consumer product is delivered or sold for purposes of sale or distribution by such person to a consumer.

(7)(A) The term "private labeler" means an owner of a brand or trademark on the label of a consumer product which bears a private label.

(B) A consumer product bears a private label if (i) the product (or its container) is labeled with the brand or trademark of a person other than a manufacturer of the product, (ii) the person with whose brand or trademark the product (or container) is labeled has authorized or caused the product to be so labeled, and

(iii) the brand or trademark of a manufacturer of such product does not appear on such label.

(8) The term "manufactured" means to manufacture, produce, or assemble.

(9) The term "Commission" means the Consumer Product Safety Commission, established by section 4.

(10) The term "State" means a State, the District of Columbia, the Commonwealth of Puerto Rico, the Virgin Islands, Guam, Wake Island, Midway Island, Kingman Reef, Johnston Island, the Canal Zone, American Samoa, or the Trust Territory of the Pacific Islands.

(11) The terms "to distribute in commerce" and "distribution in commerce" mean to sell in commerce, to introduce or deliver for introduction into commerce, or to hold for sale or distribution after introduction into commerce.

(12) The term "commerce" means trade, traffic, commerce, or transportation—

(A) between a place in a State and any place outside thereof, or

(B) which affects trade, traffic, commerce, or transportation described in subparagraph (A).

(13) The terms "import" and "importation" include reimporting a consumer product manufactured or processed, in whole or in part, in the United States.

(14) The term "United States", when used in the geographic sense, means all of the States (as defined in paragraph (10)).

(b) A common carrier, contract carrier, or freight forwarder shall not, for purposes of this Act, be deemed to be a manufacturer, distributor, or retailer of a consumer product solely by reason of receiving or transporting a consumer product in the ordinary course of its business as such a carrier or forwarder.

CONSUMER PRODUCT SAFETY COMMISSION

SEC. 4. (a) An independent regulatory commission is hereby established, to be known as the Consumer Product Safety Commission, consisting of five Commissioners who shall be appointed by the President, by and with the advice and consent of the Senate, one of whom shall be designated by the President as Chairman. The Chairman, when so designated, shall act as Chairman until the expiration of his term of office as Commissioner. Any member of the Commission may be removed by the President for neglect of duty or malfeasance in office but for no other cause.

(b)(1) Except as provided in paragraph (2), (A) the Commissioners first appointed under this section shall be appointed for terms ending three, four, five, six, and seven years, respectively, after the date of the enactment of this Act, the term of each to be designated by the President at the time of nomination; and (B) each of their successors shall be appointed for a term of seven years from the date of the expiration of the term for which his predecessor was appointed.

(2) Any Commissioner appointed to fill a vacancy occurring prior to the expiration of the term for which his predecessor was appointed shall be appointed only for the remainder of such term. A Commissioner may continue to serve after the expiration of his term until

his successor has taken office, except that he may not so continue to serve more than one year after the date on which his term would otherwise expire under this subsection.

(c) Not more than three of the Commissioners shall be affiliated with the same political party. No individual (1) in the employ of, or holding any official relation to, any person engaged in selling or manufacturing consumer products, or (2) owning stock or bonds of substantial value in a person so engaged, or (3) who is in any other manner pecuniarily interested in such a person, or in a substantial supplier of such a person, shall hold the office of Commissioner. A Commissioner may not engage in any other business, vocation, or employment.

(d) No vacancy in the Commission shall impair the right of the remaining Commissioners to exercise all the powers of the Commission, but three members of the Commission shall constitute a quorum for the transaction of business. The Commission shall have an official seal of which judicial notice shall be taken. The Commission shall annually elect a Vice Chairman to act in the absence or disability of the Chairman or in case of a vacancy in the office of the Chairman.

(e) The Commission shall maintain a principal office and such field offices as it deems necessary and may meet and exercise any of its powers at any other place.

(f)(1) The Chairman of the Commission shall be the principal executive officer of the Commission, and he shall exercise all of the executive and administrative functions of the Commission, including functions of the Commission with respect to (A) the appointment and supervision of personnel employed under the Commission (other than personnel employed regularly and full time in the immediate offices of commissioners other than the Chairman), (B) the distribution of business among personnel appointed and supervised by the Chairman and among administrative units of the Commission, and (C) the use and expenditure of funds.

(2) In carrying out any of his functions under the provisions of this subsection the Chairman shall be governed by general policies of the Commission and by such regulatory decisions, findings, and determinations as the Commission may by law be authorized to make.

(g)(1) The Chairman, subject to the approval of the Commission, shall appoint an Executive Director, a General Counsel, a Director of Engineering Sciences, a Director of Epidemiology, and a Director of Information. No individual so appointed may receive pay in excess of the annual rate of basic pay in effect for grade GS–18 of the General Schedule.

(2) The Chairman, subject to subsection (f)(2), may employ such other officers and employees (including attorneys) as are necessary in the execution of the Commission's functions. No full-time officer or employee of the Commission who was at any time during the 12 months preceding the termination of his employment with the Commission compensated at a rate in excess of the annual rate of basic pay in effect for grade GS–14 of the General Schedule, shall accept employment or compensation from any manufacturer subject to this Act, for a period of 12 months after terminating employment with the Commission.

(h)(1) Section 5314 of title 5, United States Code, is amended by adding at the end thereof the following new paragraph:

"(59) Chairman, Consumer Product Safety Commission."

(2) Section 5315 of such title is amended by adding at the end thereof the following new paragraph:

"(97) Members, Consumer Product Safety Commission (4)."

PRODUCT SAFETY INFORMATION AND RESEARCH

SEC. 5. (a) The Commission shall—

(1) maintain an Injury Information Clearinghouse to collect, investigate, analyze, and disseminate injury data, and information, relating to the causes and prevention of death, injury, and illness associated with consumer products; and

(2) conduct such continuing studies and investigations of deaths, injuries, diseases, other health impairments, and economic losses resulting from accidents involving consumer products as it deems necessary.

(b) The Commission may—

(1) conduct research, studies, and investigations on the safety of consumer products and on improving the safety of such products;

(2) test consumer products and develop product safety test methods and testing devices; and

(3) offer training in product safety investigation and test methods, and assist public and private organizations, administratively and technically, in the development of safety standards and test methods.

(c) In carrying out its functions under this section, the Commission may make grants or enter into contracts for the conduct of such functions with any person (including a governmental entity).

(d) Whenever the Federal contribution for any information, research, or development activity authorized by this Act is more than minimal, the Commission shall include in any contract, grant, or other arrangement for such activity, provisions effective to insure that the rights to all information, uses, processes, patents, and other developments resulting from that activity will be made available to the public without charge on a nonexclusive basis. Nothing in this subsection shall be construed to deprive any person of any right which he may have had, prior to entering into any arrangement referred to in this subsection, to any patent, patent application, or invention.

PUBLIC DISCLOSURE OF INFORMATION

SEC. 6. (a)(1) Nothing contained in this Act shall be deemed to require the release of any information described by subsection (b) of section 552, title 5, United States Code, or which is otherwise protected by law from disclosure to the public.

(2) All information reported to or otherwise obtained by the Commission or its representative under this Act which information contains or relates to a trade secret or other matter referred to in section 1905 of title 18, United States Code, shall be considered confidential and shall not be disclosed, except that such information may be disclosed to other officers or employees concerned with carrying out this Act or when relevant in any proceeding under this Act. Nothing in this Act shall authorize the withholding of information by the Commission or any officer or employee under its control from the duly authorized committees of the Congress.

(b)(1) Except as provided by paragraph (2) of this subsection, not less than 30 days prior to its public disclosure of any information obtained under this Act, or to be disclosed to the public in connection therewith (unless the Commission finds out that the public health and safety requires a lesser period of notice), the Commission shall, to the extent practicable, notify, and provide a summary of the information to, each manufacturer or private labeler of any consumer product to which such information pertains, if the manner in which such consumer product is to be designated or described in such information will permit the public to ascertain readily the identity of such manufacturer or private labeler, and shall provide such manufacturer or private labeler with a reasonable opportunity to submit comments to the Commission in regard to such information. The Commission shall take reasonable steps to assure, prior to its public disclosure thereof, that information from which the identity of such manufacturer or private labeler may be readily ascertained is accurate, and that such disclosure is fair in the circumstances and reasonably related to effectuating the purposes of this Act. If the Commission finds that, in the administration of this Act, it has made public disclosure of inaccurate or misleading information which reflects adversely upon the safety of any consumer product, or the practices of any manufacturer, private labeler, distributor, or retailer of consumer products, it shall, in a manner similar to that in which such disclosure was made, publish a retraction of such inaccurate or misleading information.

(2) Paragraph (1) (except for the last sentence thereof) shall not apply to the public disclosure of (A) information about any consumer product with respect to which product the Commission has filed an action under section 12 (relating to imminently hazardous products), or which the Commission has reasonable cause to believe is in violation of section 19 (relating to prohibited acts), or (B) information in the course of or concerning any administrative or judicial proceeding under this Act.

(c) The Commission shall communicate to each manufacturer of a consumer product, insofar as may be practicable, information as to any significant risk of injury associated with such product.

CONSUMER PRODUCT SAFETY STANDARDS

SEC. 7. (a) The Commission may by rule, in accordance with this section and section 9, promulgate consumer product safety standards. A consumer product safety standard shall consist of one or more of any of the following types of requirements:

(1) Requirements as to performance, composition, contents, design, construction, finish, or packaging of a consumer product.

(2) Requirements that a consumer product be marked with or accompanied by clear and adequate warnings or instructions, or requirements respecting the form of warnings or instructions.

Any requirement of such a standard shall be reasonably necessary to prevent or reduce an unreasonable risk of injury associated with such product. The requirements of such a standard (other than requirements relating to labeling, warnings, or instructions) shall, whenever feasible, be expressed in terms of performance requirements.

(b) A proceeding for the development of a consumer product safety standard under this Act shall be commenced by the publication in the Federal Register of a notice which shall—

(1) identify the product and the nature of the risk of injury associated with the product;

(2) state the Commission's determination that a consumer product safety standard is necessary to eliminate or reduce the risk of injury;

(3) include information with respect to any existing standard known to the Commission which may be relevant to the proceeding; and

(4) include an invitation for any person, including any State or Federal agency (other than the Commission), within 30 days after the date of publication of the notice (A) to submit to the Commission an existing standard as the proposed consumer product safety standard or (B) to offer to develop the proposed consumer product safety standard.

An invitation under paragraph (4)(B) shall specify a period of time, during which the standard is to be developed, which shall be a period ending 150 days after the publication of the notice, unless the Commission for good cause finds (and includes such finding in the notice) that a different period is appropriate.

(c) If the Commission determines that (1) there exists a standard which has been issued or adopted by any Federal agency or by any other qualified agency, organization, or institution, and (2) such standard if promulgated under this Act, would eliminate or reduce the unreasonable risk of injury associated with the product, then it may, in lieu of accepting an offer pursuant to subsection (d) of this section, publish such standard as a proposed consumer product safety rule.

(d)(1) Except as provided by subsection (c), the Commission shall accept one, and may accept more than one, offer to develop a proposed consumer product safety standard pursuant to the invitation prescribed by subsection (b)(4)(B), if it determines that the offeror is technically competent, is likely to develop an appropriate standard within the period specified in the invitation under subsection (b), and will comply with regulations of the Commission under paragraph (3) of this subsection. The Commission shall publish in the Federal Register the name and address of each person whose offer it accepts, and a summary of the terms of such offer as accepted.

(2) If an offer is accepted under this subsection, the Commission may agree to contribute to the offeror's cost in developing a proposed consumer product safety standard, in any case in which the Commission determines that such contribution is likely to result in a more satisfactory standard than would be developed without such contribution, and that the offeror is financially responsible. Regulations of the Commission shall set forth the items of cost in which it may participate, and shall exclude any contribution to the acquisition of land or buildings.

(3) The Commission shall prescribe regulations governing the development of proposed consumer product safety standards by persons whose offers are accepted under paragraph (1). Such regulations shall include requirements—

(A) that standards recommended for promulgation be suitable for promulgation under this Act, be supported by test data or such other documents or materials as the Commission may reasonably require to be developed, and (where appropriate) contain suitable test methods for measurement of compliance with such standards;

(B) for notice and opportunity by interested persons (including representatives of consumers and consumer organizations) to participate in the development of such standards;

(C) for the maintenance of records, which shall be available to the public, to disclose the course of the development of standards recommended for promulgation, the comments and other information submitted by any person in connection with such development (including dissenting views and comments and information with respect to the need for such recommended standards), and such other matters as may be relevant to the evaluation of such recommended standards; and

(D) that the Commission and the Comptroller General of the United States, or any of their duly authorized representatives, have access for the purpose of audit and examination to any books, documents, papers, and records relevant to the development of such recommended standards or to the expenditure of any contribution of the Commission for the development of such standards.

(e)(1) If the Commission has published a notice of proceeding as provided by subsection (b) of this section and has not, within 30 days after the date of publication of such notice, accepted an offer to develop a proposed consumer product safety standard, the Commission may develop a proposed consumer product safety rule and publish such proposed rule.

(2) If the Commission accepts an offer to develop a proposed consumer product safety standard, the Commission may not, during the development period (specified in paragraph (3)) for such standard—

(A) publish a proposed rule applicable to the same risk of injury associated with such product, or

(B) develop proposals for such standard or contract with third parties for such development, unless the Commission determines that no offeror whose offer was accepted is making satisfactory progress in the development of such standard.

In any case in which the sole offeror whose offer is accepted under subsection (d)(1) of this section is the manufacturer, distributor, or retailer of a consumer product proposed to be regulated by the consumer product safety standard, the Commission may independently proceed to develop proposals for such standard during the development period.

(3) For purposes of paragraph (2), the development period for any standard is a period (A) beginning on the date on which the Commission first accepts an offer under subsection (d)(1) for the development of a proposed standard, and (B) ending on the earlier of—

(i) the end of the period specified in the notice of proceeding (except that the period specified in the notice may be extended if good cause is shown and the reasons for such extension are published in the Federal Register), or

(ii) the date on which it determines (in accordance with such procedures as it may by rule prescribe) that no offeror whose offer was accepted is able and willing to continue satisfactorily the development of the proposed standard which was the subject of the offer, or

(iii) the date on which an offeror whose offer was accepted submits such a recommended standard to the Commission.

(f) Not more than 210 days after its publication of a notice of proceeding pursuant to subsection (b) (which time may be extended by the Commission by a notice published in the Federal Register stating good cause therefor), the Commission shall publish in the Federal Register a notice withdrawing such notice of proceeding or publish a proposed rule which either proposes a product safety standard applicable to any consumer product subject to such notice, or proposes to declare any such subject product a banned hazardous consumer product.

BANNED HAZARDOUS PRODUCTS

SEC. 8. Whenever the Commission finds that—

(1) a consumer product is being, or will be, distributed in commerce and such consumer product presents an unreasonable risk of injury; and

(2) no feasible consumer product safety standard under this Act would adequately protect the public from the unreasonable risk of injury associated with such product,

the Commission may propose and, in accordance with section 9, promulgate a rule declaring such product a banned hazardous product.

ADMINISTRATIVE PROCEDURE APPLICABLE TO PROMULGATION OF CONSUMER PRODUCT SAFETY RULES

SEC. 9. (a)(1) Within 60 days after the publication under section 7 (c), (e)(1), or (f) or section 8 of a proposed consumer product safety rule respecting a risk of injury associated with a consumer product, the Commission shall—

(A) promulgate a consumer product safety rule respecting the risk of injury associated with such product if it makes the findings required under subsection (c), or

(B) withdraw by rule the applicable notice of proceeding if it determines that such rule is not (i) reasonably necessary to eliminate or reduce an unreasonable risk of injury associated with the product, or (ii) in the public interest;

except that the Commission may extend such 60-day period for good cause shown (if it publishes its reasons therefor in the Federal Register).

(2) Consumer product safety rules which have been proposed under section 7 (c), (e)(1), or (f) or section 8 shall be promulgated pursuant to section 553 of title 5, United States Code, except that the Commission shall give interested persons an opportunity for the oral presentation of data, views, or arguments, in addition to an opportunity to make written submissions. A transcript shall be kept of any oral presentation.

(b) A consumer product safety rule shall express in the rule itself the risk of injury which the standard is designed to eliminate or reduce. In promulgating such a rule the Commission shall consider relevant available product data including the results of research, development, testing, and investigation activities conducted generally and pursuant to this Act.

(c) (1) Prior to promulgating a consumer product safety rule, the Commission shall consider, and shall make appropriate findings for inclusion in such rule with respect to—

(A) the degree and nature of the risk of injury the rule is designed to eliminate or reduce;

(B) the approximate number of consumer products, or types or classes thereof, subject to such rule;

(C) the need of the public for the consumer products subject to such rule, and the probable effect of such rule upon the utility, cost, or availability of such products to meet such need; and

(D) any means of achieving the objective of the order while minimizing adverse effects on competition or disruption or dislocation of manufacturing and other commercial practices consistent with the public health and safety.

(2) The Commission shall not promulgate a consumer product safety rule unless it finds (and includes such finding in the rule)—

(A) that the rule (including its effective date) is reasonably necessary to eliminate or reduce an unreasonable risk of injury associated with such product;

(B) that the promulgation of the rule is in the public interest; and

(C) in the case of a rule declaring the product a banned hazardous product, that no feasible consumer product safety standard under this Act would adequately protect the public from the unreasonable risk of injury associated with such product.

(d) (1) Each consumer product safety rule shall specify the date such rule is to take effect not exceeding 180 days from the date promulgated, unless the Commission finds, for good cause shown, that a later effective date is in the public interest and publishes its reasons for such finding. The effective date of a consumer product safety standard under this Act shall be set at a date at least 30 days after the date of promulgation unless the Commission for good cause shown determines that an earlier effective date is in the public interest. In no case may the effective date be set at a date which is earlier than the date of promulgation. A consumer product safety standard shall be applicable only to consumer products manufactured after the effective date.

(2) The Commission may by rule prohibit a manufacturer of a consumer product from stockpiling any product to which a consumer product safety rule applies, so as to prevent such manufacturer from circumventing the purpose of such consumer product safety rule. For purposes of this paragraph, the term "stockpiling" means manufacturing or importing a product between the date of promulgation of such consumer product safety rule and its effective date at a rate which is significantly greater (as determined under the rule under this paragraph) than the rate at which such product was produced or imported during a base period (prescribed in the rule under this paragraph) ending before the date of promulgation of the consumer product safety rule.

(e) The Commission may by rule amend or revoke any consumer product safety rule. Such amendment or revocation shall specify the date on which it is to take effect which shall not exceed 180 days from the date the amendment or revocation is published unless the Commission finds for good cause shown that a later effective date is in the public interest and publishes its reasons for such finding. Where an amendment involves a material change in a consumer product safety rule, sections 7 and 8, and subsections (a) through (d) of this section shall apply. In order to revoke a consumer product safety rule, the Commission shall publish a proposal to revoke such rule in the Federal Register, and allow oral and written presentations in accordance with subsection (a)(2) of this section. It may revoke such rule only if it determines that the rule is not reasonably necessary to eliminate or reduce an unreasonable risk of injury associated with the product. Section 11 shall apply to any amendment of a consumer product safety rule which involves a material change and to any revocation of a consumer product safety rule, in the same manner and to the same extent as such section applies to the Commission's action in promulgating such a rule.

COMMISSION RESPONSIBILITY—PETITION FOR CONSUMER PRODUCT SAFETY RULE

SEC. 10. (a) Any interested person, including a consumer or consumer organization, may petition the Commission to commence a proceeding for the issuance, amendment, or revocation of a consumer product safety rule.

(b) Such petition shall be filed in the principal office of the Commission and shall set forth (1) facts which it is claimed establish that a consumer product safety rule or an amendment or revocation thereof is necessary, and (2) a brief description of the substance of the consumer product safety rule or amendment thereof which it is claimed should be issued by the Commission.

(c) The Commission may hold a public hearing or may conduct such investigation or proceeding as it deems appropriate in order to determine whether or not such petition should be granted.

(d) Within 120 days after filing of a petition described in subsection (b), the Commission shall either grant or deny the petition. If the Commission grants such petition, it shall promptly commence an appropriate proceeding under section 7 or 8. If the Commission denies such petition it shall publish in the Federal Register its reasons for such denial.

(e)(1) If the Commission denies a petition made under this section (or if it fails to grant or deny such petition within the 120-day period) the petitioner may commence a civil action in a United States district court to compel the Commission to initiate a proceeding to take the action requested. Any such action shall be filed within 60 days after the Commission's denial of the petition, or (if the Commission fails to grant or deny the petition within 120 days after filing the petition) within 60 days after the expiration of the 120-day period.

(2) If the petitioner can demonstrate to the satisfaction of the court, by a preponderance of evidence in a de novo proceeding before such court, that the consumer product presents an unreasonable risk of injury, and that the failure of the Commission to initiate a rulemaking proceeding under section 7 or 8 unreasonably exposes the petitioner or other consumers to a risk of injury presented by the consumer product, the court shall order the Commission to initiate the action requested by the petitioner.

(3) In any action under this subsection, the district court shall have no authority to compel the Commission to take any action other than the initiation of a rule-making proceeding in accordance with section 7 or 8.

(f) The remedies under this section shall be in addition to, and not in lieu of, other remedies provided by law.

(g) Subsection (e) of this section shall apply only with respect to petitions filed more than 3 years after the date of enactment of this Act.

JUDICIAL REVIEW OF CONSUMER PRODUCT SAFETY RULES

SEC. 11. (a) Not later than 60 days after a consumer product safety rule is promulgated by the Commission, any person adversely affected by such rule, or any consumer or consumer organization, may file a petition with the United States court of appeals for the District of Columbia or for the circuit in which such person, consumer, or organization resides or has his principal place of business for judicial review of such rule. Copies of the petition shall be forthwith transmitted by the clerk of the court to the Commission or other officer designated by it for that purpose and to the Attorney General. The Commission shall transmit to the Attorney General, who shall file in the court, the record of the proceedings on which the Commission based its rule, as provided in section 2112 of title 28 of the United States Code. For purposes of this section, the term "record" means such consumer product safety rule; any notice or proposal published pursuant to section 7, 8, or 9; the transcript required by section 9(a)(2) of any oral presentation; any written submission of interested parties; and any other information which the Commission considers relevant to such rule.

(b) If the petitioner applies to the court for leave to adduce additional data, views, or arguments and shows to the satisfaction of the court that such additional data, views, or arguments are material and that there were reasonable grounds for the petitioner's failure to adduce such data, views, or arguments in the proceeding before the Commission, the court may order the Commission to provide additional opportunity for the oral presentation of data, views, or arguments and for written submissions. The Commission may modify its findings, or make new findings by reason of the additional data, views, or arguments so taken and shall file such modified or new findings, and its recommendation, if any, for the modification or setting aside of its original rule, with the return of such additional data, views, or arguments.

(c) Upon the filing of the petition under subsection (a) of this section the court shall have jurisdiction to review the consumer product safety rule in accordance with chapter 7 of title 5, United States Code, and to grant appropriate relief, including interim relief, as provided in such chapter. The consumer product safety rule shall not be affirmed unless the Commission's findings under section 9(c) are supported by substantial evidence on the record taken as a whole.

(d) The judgment of the court affirming or setting aside, in whole or in part, any consumer product safety rule shall be final, subject to review by the Supreme Court of the United States upon certiorari or certification, as provided in section 1254 of title 28 of the United States Code.

(e) The remedies provided for in this section shall be in addition to and not in lieu of any other remedies provided by law.

IMMINENT HAZARDS

SEC. 12. (a) The Commission may file in a United States district court an action (1) against an imminently hazardous consumer product for seizure of such product under subsection (b)(2), or (2) against any person who is a manufacturer, distributor, or retailer of such product, or (3) against both. Such an action may be filed notwithstanding the existence of a consumer product safety rule applicable to such product, or the pendency of any administrative or judicial proceedings under any other provision of this Act. As used in this section, and hereinafter in this Act, the term "imminently hazardous consumer product" means a consumer product which presents imminent and unreasonable risk of death, serious illness, or severe personal injury.

(b)(1) The district court in which such action is filed shall have jurisdiction to declare such product an imminently hazardous consumer product, and (in the case of an action under subsection (a)(2)) to grant (as ancillary to such declaration or in lieu thereof) such temporary or permanent relief as may be necessary to protect the public from such risk. Such relief may include a mandatory order requiring the notification of such risk to purchasers of such product known to the defendant, public notice, the recall, the repair or the replacement of, or refund for, such product.

(2) In the case of an action under subsection (a)(1), the consumer product may be proceeded against by process of libel for the seizure and condemnation of such product in any United States district court within the jurisdiction of which such consumer product is found. Proceedings and cases instituted under the authority of the preceding sentence shall conform as nearly as possible to proceedings in rem in admiralty.

(c) Where appropriate, concurrently with the filing of such action or as soon thereafter as may be practicable, the Commission shall initiate a proceeding to promulgate a consumer product safety rule applicable to the consumer product with respect to which such action is filed.

(d)(1) Prior to commencing an action under subsection (a), the Commission may consult the Product Safety Advisory Council (established under section 28) with respect to its determination to commence such action, and request the Council's recommendations as to the type of temporary or permanent relief which may be necessary to protect the public.

(2) The Council shall submit its recommendations to the Commission within one week of such request.

(3) Subject to paragraph (2), the Council may conduct such hearing or offer such opportunity for the presentation of views as it may consider necessary or appropriate.

(e)(1) An action under subsection (a)(2) of this section may be brought in the United States district court for the District of Columbia or in any judicial district in which any of the defendants is found, is an inhabitant or transacts business; and process in such an action may be served on a defendant in any other district in which such defendant resides or may be found. Subpenas requiring attendance of witnesses in such an action may run into any other district. In determining the judicial district in which an action may be brought under this section in instances in which such action may be brought in more than one judicial district, the Commission shall take into account the convenience of the parties.

(2) Whenever proceedings under this section involving substantially similar consumer products are pending in courts in two or more judicial districts, they shall be consolidated for trial by order of any such court upon application reasonably made by any party in interest, upon notice to all other parties in interest.

(f) Notwithstanding any other provision of law, in any action under this section, the Commission may direct attorneys employed by it to appear and represent it.

NEW PRODUCTS

Sec. 13. (a) The Commission may, by rule, prescribe procedures for the purpose of insuring that the manufacturer of any new consumer product furnish notice and a description of such product to the Commission before its distribution in commerce.

(b) For purposes of this section, the term "new consumer product" means a consumer product which incorporates a design, material, or form of energy exchange which (1) has not previously been used substantially in consumer products and (2) as to which there exists a lack of information adequate to determine the safety of such product in use by consumers.

PRODUCT CERTIFICATION AND LABELING

Sec. 14. (a) (1) Every manufacturer of a product which is subject to a consumer product safety standard under this Act and which is distributed in commerce (and the private labeler of such product if it bears a private label) shall issue a certificate which shall certify that such product conforms to all applicable consumer product safety standards, and shall specify any standard which is applicable. Such certificate shall accompany the product or shall otherwise be furnished to any distributor or retailer to whom the product is delivered. Any certificate under this subsection shall be based on a test of each product or upon a reasonable testing program; shall state the name of the manufacturer or private labeler issuing the certificate; and shall include the date and place of manufacture.

(2) In the case of a consumer product for which there is more than one manufacturer or more than one private labeler, the Commission may by rule designate one or more of such manufacturers or one or more of such private labelers (as the case may be) as the persons who shall issue the certificate required by paragraph (1) of this subsection, and may exempt all other manufacturers of such product or all other private labelers of the product (as the case may be) from the requirement under paragraph (1) to issue a certificate with respect to such product.

(b) The Commission may by rule prescribe reasonable testing programs for consumer products which are are subject to consumer product safety standards under this Act and for which a certificate is required under subsection (a). Any test or testing program on the basis of which a certificate is issued under subsection (a) may, at the option of the person required to certify the product, be conducted by an independent third party qualified to perform such tests or testing programs.

(c) The Commission may by rule require the use and prescribe the form and content of labels which contain the following information (or that portion of it specified in the rule)—

(1) The date and place of manufacture of any consumer product.

(2) A suitable identification of the manufacturer of the consumer product, unless the product bears a private label in which case it shall identify the private labeler and shall also contain a code mark which will permit the seller of such product to identify the manufacturer thereof to the purchaser upon his request.

(3) In the case of a consumer product subject to a consumer product safety rule, a certification that the product meets all applicable consumer product safety standards and a specification of the standards which are applicable.

Such labels, where practicable, may be required by the Commission to be permanently marked on or affixed to any such consumer product. The Commission may, in appropriate cases, permit information required under paragraphs (1) and (2) of this subsection to be coded.

NOTIFICATION AND REPAIR, REPLACEMENT, OR REFUND

SEC. 15. (a) For purposes of this section, the term "substantial product hazard" means—

(1) a failure to comply with an applicable consumer product safety rule which creates a substantial risk of injury to the public, or

(2) a product defect which (because of the pattern of defect, the number of defective products distributed in commerce, the severity of the risk, or otherwise) creates a substantial risk of injury to the public.

(b) Every manufacturer of a consumer product distributed in commerce, and every distributor and retailer of such product, who obtains information which reasonably supports the conclusion that such product—

(1) fails to comply with an applicable consumer product safety rule; or

(2) contains a defect which could create a substantial product hazard described in subsection (a)(2),

shall immediately inform the Commission of such failure to comply or of such defect, unless such manufacturer, distributor, or retailer has actual knowledge that the Commission has been adequately informed of such defect or failure to comply.

(c) If the Commission determines (after affording interested persons, including consumers and consumer organizations, an opportunity for a hearing in accordance with subsection (f) of this section) that a product distributed in commerce presents a substantial product hazard and that notification is required in order to adequately protect the public from such substantial product hazard, the Commission may order the manufacturer or any distributor or retailer of the product to take any one or more of the following actions:

(1) To give public notice of the defect or failure to comply.

(2) To mail notice to each person who is a manufacturer, distributor, or retailer of such product.

(3) To mail notice to every person to whom the person required to give notice knows such product was delivered or sold.

Any such order shall specify the form and content of any notice required to be given under such order.

(d) If the Commission determines (after affording interested parties, including consumers and consumer organizations, an opportunity for a hearing in accordance with subsection (f)) that a product distributed in commerce presents a substantial product hazard and that action under this subsection is in the public interest, it may order the manufacturer or any distributor or retailer of such product to take whichever of the following actions the person to whom the order is directed elects:

(1) To bring such product into conformity with the requirements of the applicable consumer product safety rule or to repair the defect in such product.

(2) To replace such product with a like or equivalent product which complies with the applicable consumer product safety rule or which does not contain the defect.

(3) To refund the purchase price of such product (less a reasonable allowance for use, if such product has been in the possession of a consumer for one year or more (A) at the time of public notice under subsection (c), or (B) at the time the consumer receives actual notice of the defect or noncompliance, whichever first occurs).

An order under this subsection may also require the person to whom it applies to submit a plan, satisfactory to the Commission, for taking action under whichever of the preceding paragraphs of this subsection under which such person has elected to act. The Commission shall specify in the order the persons to whom refunds must be made if the person to whom the order is directed elects to take the action described in paragraph (3). If an order under this subsection is directed to more than one person, the Commission shall specify which person has the election under this subsection.

(e) (1) No charge shall be made to any person (other than a manufacturer, distributor, or retailer) who avails himself of any remedy provided under an order issued under subsection (d), and the person subject to the order shall reimburse each person (other than a manufacturer, distributor, or retailer) who is entitled to such a remedy for any reasonable and foreseeable expenses incurred by such person in availing himself of such remedy.

(2) An order issued under subsection (c) or (d) with respect to a product may require any person who is a manufacturer, distributor, or retailer of the product to reimburse any other person who is a manufacturer, distributor, or retailer of such product for such other person's expenses in connection with carrying out the order, if the Commission determines such reimbursement to be in the public interest.

(f) An order under subsection (c) or (d) may be issued only after an opportunity for a hearing in accordance with section 554 of title 5, United States Code, except that, if the Commission determines that any person who wishes to participate in such hearing is a part of a class of participants who share an identity of interest, the Commission may limit such person's participation in such hearing to participation through a single representative designated by such class (or by the Commission if such class fails to designate such a representative).

INSPECTION AND RECORDKEEPING

SEC. 16. (a) For purposes of implementing this Act, or rules or orders prescribed under this Act, officers or employees duly designated by the Commission, upon presenting appropriate credentials and a written notice from the Commission to the owner, operator, or agent in charge, are authorized—

(1) to enter, at reasonable times, (A) any factory, warehouse, or establishment in which consumer products are manufactured or held, in connection with distribution in commerce, or (B) any conveyance being used to transport consumer products in connection with distribution in commerce; and

(2) to inspect, at reasonable times and in a reasonable manner such conveyance or those areas of such factory, warehouse, or establishment where such products are manufactured, held, or transported and which may relate to the safety of such products. Each such inspection shall be commenced and completed with reasonable promptness.

(b) Every person who is a manufacturer, private labeler, or distributor of a consumer product shall establish and maintain such records, make such reports, and provide such information as the Commission may, by rule, reasonably require for the purposes of implementing this Act, or to determine compliance with rules or orders prescribed under this Act. Upon request of an officer or employee duly designated by the Commission, every such manufacturer, private labeler, or distributor shall permit the inspection of appropriate books, records, and papers relevant to determining whether such manufacturer, private labeler, or distributor has acted or is acting in compliance with this Act and rules under this Act.

IMPORTED PRODUCTS

SEC. 17. (a) Any consumer product offered for importation into the customs territory of the United States (as defined in general headnote 2 to the Tariff Schedules of the United States) shall be refused admission into such customs territory if such product—

(1) fails to comply with an applicable consumer product safety rule;

(2) is not accompanied by a certificate required by section 14, or is not labeled in accordance with regulations under section 14 (c);

(3) is or has been determined to be an imminently hazardous consumer product in a proceeding brought under section 12;

(4) has a product defect which constitutes a substantial product hazard (within the meaning of section 15(a)(2)); or

(5) is a product which was manufactured by a person who the Commission has informed the Secretary of the Treasury is in violation of subsection (g).

(b) The Secretary of the Treasury shall obtain without charge and deliver to the Commission, upon the latter's request, a reasonable number of samples of consumer products being offered for import. Except for those owners or consignees who are or have been afforded an opportunity for a hearing in a proceeding under section 12 with respect to an imminently hazardous product, the owner or consignee of the product shall be afforded an opportunity by the Commission for a hearing in accordance with section 554 of title 5 of the United States Code with respect to the importation of such products into the customs territory of the United States. If it appears from examination of such samples or otherwise that a product must be refused admission under the terms of subsection (a), such product shall be refused admission, unless subsection (c) of this section applies and is complied with.

(c) If it appears to the Commission that any consumer product which may be refused admission pursuant to subsection (a) of this section can be so modified that it need not (under the terms of paragraphs (1) through (4) of subsection (a)) be refused admission, the Commission may defer final determination as to the admission of such product and, in accordance with such regulations as the Commission and the Secretary of the Treasury shall jointly agree to, permit such product to be delivered from customs custody under bond for the purpose of permitting the owner or consignee an opportunity to so modify such product.

(d) All actions taken by an owner or consignee to modify such product under subsection (c) shall be subject to the supervision of an officer or employee of the Commission and of the Department of the Treasury. If it appears to the Commission that the product cannot be so modified or that the owner or consignee is not proceeding satisfactorily to modify such product, it shall be refused admission into the customs territory of the United States, and the Commission may direct the Secretary to demand redelivery of the product into customs custody, and to seize the product in accordance with section 22(b) if it is not so redelivered.

(e) Products refused admission into the customs territory of the United States under this section must be exported, except that upon application, the Secretary of the Treasury may permit the destruction of the product in lieu of exportation. If the owner or consignee does not export the product within a reasonable time, the Department of the Treasury may destroy the product.

(f) All expenses (including travel, per diem or subsistence, and salaries of officers or employees of the United States) in connection with the destruction provided for in this section (the amount of such expenses to be determined in accordance with regulations of the Secretary of the Treasury) and all expenses in connection with the storage, cartage, or labor with respect to any consumer product refused admission under this section, shall be paid by the owner or consignee and, in default of such payment, shall constitute a lien against any future importations made by such owner or consignee.

(g) The Commission may, by rule, condition the importation of a consumer product on the manufacturer's compliance with the inspection and recordkeeping requirements of this Act and the Commission's rules with respect to such requirements.

EXPORTS

SEC. 18. This Act shall not apply to any consumer product if (1) it can be shown that such product is manufactured, sold, or held for sale for export from the United States (or that such product was imported for export), unless such consumer product is in fact distributed in commerce for use in the United States, and (2) such consumer product when distributed in commerce, or any container in which it is enclosed when so distributed, bears a stamp or label stating that such consumer product is intended for export; except that this Act shall apply to any consumer product manufactured for sale, offered for sale, or sold for shipment to any installation of the United States located outside of the United States.

PROHIBITED ACTS

SEC. 19. (a) It shall be unlawful for any person to—

(1) manufacture for sale, offer for sale, distribute in commerce, or import into the United States any consumer product which is not in conformity with an applicable consumer product safety standard under this Act;

(2) manufacture for sale, offer for sale, distribute in commerce, or import into the United States any consumer product which has been declared a banned hazardous product by a rule under this Act;

(3) fail or refuse to permit access to or copying of records, or fail or refuse to make reports or provide information, or fail or refuse to permit entry or inspection, as required under this Act or rule thereunder;

(4) fail to furnish information required by section 15(b);

(5) fail to comply with an order issued under section 15 (c) or (d) (relating to notification, and to repair, replacement, and refund);

(6) fail to furnish a certificate required by section 14 or issue a false certificate if such person in the exercise of due care has reason to know that such certificate is false or misleading in any material respect; or to fail to comply with any rule under section 14(c) (relating to labeling); or

(7) fail to comply with any rule under section 9(d)(2) (relating to stockpiling).

(b) Paragraphs (1) and (2) of subsection (a) of this section shall not apply to any person (1) who holds a certificate issued in accordance with section 14(a) to the effect that such consumer product conforms to all applicable consumer product safety rules, unless such person knows that such consumer product does not conform, or (2) who relies in good faith on the representation of the manufacturer or a distributor of such product that the product is not subject to an applicable product safety rule.

CIVIL PENALTIES

SEC. 20. (a)(1) Any person who knowingly violates section 19 of this Act shall be subject to a civil penalty not to exceed $2,000 for each such violation. Subject to paragraph (2), a violation of section 19(a) (1), (2), (4), (5), (6), or (7) shall constitute a separate offense with respect to each consumer product involved, except that the maximum civil penalty shall not exceed $500,000 for any related series of violations. A violation of section 19(a)(3) shall constitute a separate violation with respect to each failure or refusal to allow or perform an act required thereby; and, if such violation is a continuing one, each day of such violation shall constitute a separate offense, except that the maximum civil penalty shall not exceed $500,000 for any related series of violations.

(2) The second sentence of paragraph (1) of this subsection shall not apply to violations of paragraph (1) or (2) of section 19(a)—

(A) if the person who violated such paragraphs is not the manufacturer or private labeler or a distributor of the products involved, and

(B) if such person did not have either (i) actual knowledge that his distribution or sale of the product violated such paragraphs or (ii) notice from the Commission that such distribution or sale would be a violation of such paragraphs.

(b) Any civil penalty under this section may be compromised by the Commission. In determining the amount of such penalty or whether it should be remitted or mitigated and in what amount, the appropriateness of such penalty to the size of the business of the person charged and the gravity of the violation shall be considered. The amount of such penalty when finally determined, or the amount agreed on compromise, may be deducted from any sums owing by the United States to the person charged.

(c) As used in the first sentence of subsection (a)(1) of this section, the term "knowingly" means (1) the having of actual knowledge, or (2) the presumed having of knowledge deemed to be possessed by a reasonable man who acts in the circumstances, including knowledge obtainable upon the exercise of due care to ascertain the truth of representations.

CRIMINAL PENALTIES

Sec. 21. (a) Any person who knowingly and willfully violates section 19 of this Act after having received notice of noncompliance from the Commission shall be fined not more than $50,000 or be imprisoned not more than one year, or both.

(b) Any individual director, officer, or agent of a corporation who knowingly and willfully authorizes, orders, or performs any of the acts or practices constituting in whole or in part a violation of section 19, and who has knowledge of notice of noncompliance received by the corporation from the Commission, shall be subject to penalties under this section without regard to any penalties to which that corporation may be subject under subsection (a).

INJUNCTIVE ENFORCEMENT AND SEIZURE

Sec. 22. (a) The United States district courts shall have jurisdiction to restrain any violation of section 19, or to restrain any person from distributing in commerce a product which does not comply with a consumer product safety rule, or both. Such actions may be brought by the Commission (with the concurrence of the Attorney General) or by the Attorney General in any United States district court for a district wherein any act, omission, or transaction constituting the violation occurred, or in such court for the district wherein the defendant is found or transacts business. In any action under this section process may be served on a defendant in any other district in which the defendant resides or may be found.

(b) Any consumer product which fails to conform to an applicable consumer product safety rule when introduced into or while in commerce or while held for sale after shipment in commerce shall be liable to be proceeded against on libel of information and condemned in any United States district court within the jurisdiction of which such consumer product is found. Proceedings in cases instituted under the authority of this subsection shall conform as nearly as possible to proceedings in rem in admiralty. Whenever such proceedings involving substantially similar consumer products are pending in courts of two or more judicial districts they shall be consolidated for trial by order of any such court upon application reasonably made by any party in interest upon notice to all other parties in interest.

SUITS FOR DAMAGES BY PERSONS INJURED

SEC. 23. (a) Any person who shall sustain injury by reason of any knowing (including willful) violation of a consumer product safety rule, or any other rule or order issued by the Commission may sue any person who knowingly (including willfully) violated any such rule or order in any district court of the United States in the district in which the defendant resides or is found or has an agent, subject to the provisions of section 1331 of title 28, United States Code as to the amount in controversy, and shall recover damages sustained, and the cost of suit, including a reasonable attorney's fee, if considered appropriate in the discretion of the court.

(b) The remedies provided for in this section shall be in addition to and not in lieu of any other remedies provided by common law or under Federal or State law.

PRIVATE ENFORCEMENT OF PRODUCT SAFETY RULES AND OF SECTION 15 ORDERS

SEC. 24. Any interested person may bring an action in any United States district court for the district in which the defendant is found or transacts business to enforce a consumer product safety rule or an order under section 15, and to obtain appropriate injunctive relief. Not less than thirty days prior to the commencement of such action, such interested person shall give notice by registered mail to the Commission, to the Attorney General, and to the person against whom such action is directed. Such notice shall state the nature of the alleged violation of any such standard or order, the relief to be requested, and the court in which the action will be brought. No separate suit shall be brought under this section if at the time the suit is brought the same alleged violation is the subject of a pending civil or criminal action by the United States under this Act. In any action under this section, such interested person may elect, by a demand for such relief in his complaint, to recover reasonable attorney's fees, in which case the court shall award the costs of suit, including a reasonable attorney's fee, to the prevailing party.

EFFECT ON PRIVATE REMEDIES

SEC. 25. (a) Compliance with consumer product safety rules or other rules or orders under this Act shall not relieve any person from liability at common law or under State statutory law to any other person.

(b) The failure of the Commission to take any action or commence a proceeding with respect to the safety of a consumer product shall not be admissible in evidence in litigation at common law or under State statutory law relating to such consumer product.

(c) Subject to sections 6(a)(2) and 6(b) but notwithstanding section 6(a)(1), (1) any accident or investigation report made under this Act by an officer or employee of the Commission shall be made available to the public in a manner which will not identify any injured person or any person treating him, without the consent of the person so identified, and (2) all reports on research projects, demonstration projects, and other related activities shall be public information.

EFFECT ON STATE STANDARDS

SEC. 26. (a) Whenever a consumer product safety standard under this Act is in effect and applies to a risk of injury associated with a consumer product, no State or political subdivision of a State shall have any authority either to establish or to continue in effect any provision of a safety standard or regulation which prescribes any requirements as to the performance, composition, contents, design, finish, construction, packaging, or labeling of such product which are designed to deal with the same risk of injury associated with such consumer product, unless such requirements are identical to the requirements of the Federal standard.

(b) Nothing in this section shall be construed to prevent the Federal Government or the government of any State or political subdivision thereof from establishing a safety requirement applicable to a consumer product for its own use if such requirement imposes a higher standard of performance than that required to comply with the otherwise applicable Federal standard.

(c) Upon application of a State or political subdivision thereof, the Commission may by rule, after notice and opportunity for oral presentation of views, exempt from the provisions of subsection (a) (under such conditions as it may impose) a proposed safety standard or regulation described in such application, where the proposed standard or regulation (1) imposes a higher level of performance than the Federal standard, (2) is required by compelling local conditions, and (3) does not unduly burden interstate commerce.

ADDITIONAL FUNCTIONS OF COMMISSION

SEC. 27. (a) The Commission may, by one or more of its members or by such agents or agency as it may designate, conduct any hearing or other inquiry necessary or appropriate to its functions anywhere in the United States. A Commissioner who participates in such a hearing or other inquiry shall not be disqualified solely by reason of such participation from subsequently participating in a decision of the Commission in the same matter. The Commission shall publish notice of any proposed hearing in the Federal Register and shall afford a reasonable opportunity for interested persons to present relevant testimony and data.

(b) The Commission shall also have the power—

(1) to require, by special or general orders, any person to submit in writing such reports and answers to questions as the Commission may prescribe; and such submission shall be made within

such reasonable period and under oath or otherwise as the Commission may determine;

(2) to administer oaths;

(3) to require by subpena the attendance and testimony of witnesses and the production of all documentary evidence relating to the execution of its duties;

(4) in any proceeding or investigation to order testimony to be taken by deposition before any person who is designated by the Commission and has the power to administer oaths and, in such instances, to compel testimony and the production of evidence in the same manner as authorized under paragraph (3) of this subsection;

(5) to pay witnesses the same fees and mileage as are paid in like circumstances in the courts of the United States;

(6) to accept gifts and voluntary and uncompensated services, notwithstanding the provisions of section 3679 of the Revised Statutes (31 U.S.C. 665(b));

(7) to initiate, prosecute, defend, or appeal any court action in the name of the Commission for the purpose of enforcing the laws subject to its jurisdiction, through its own legal representative with the concurrence of the Attorney General or through the Attorney General; and

(8) to delegate any of its functions or powers, other than the power to issue subpenas under paragraph (3), to any officer or employee of the Commission.

(c) Any United States district court within the jurisdiction of which any inquiry is carried on, may, upon petition by the Commission with the concurrence of the Attorney General or by the Attorney General, in case of refusal to obey a subpena or order of the Commission issued under subsection (b) of this section, issue an order requiring compliance therewith; and any failure to obey the order of the court may be punished by the court as a contempt thereof.

(d) No person shall be subject to civil liability to any person (other than the Commission or the United States) for disclosing information at the request of the Commission.

(e) The Commission may by rule require any manufacturer of consumer products to provide to the Commission such performance and technical data related to performance and safety as may be required to carry out the purposes of this Act, and to give such notification of such performance and technical data at the time of original purchase to prospective purchasers and to the first purchaser of such product for purposes other than resale, as it determines necessary to carry out the purposes of this Act.

(f) For purposes of carrying out this Act, the Commission may purchase any consumer product and it may require any manufacturer, distributor, or retailer of a consumer product to sell the product to the Commission at manufacturer's, distributor's, or retailer's cost.

(g) The Commission is authorized to enter into contracts with governmental entities, private organizations, or individuals for the conduct of activities authorized by this Act.

(h) The Commission may plan, construct, and operate a facility or facilities suitable for research, development, and testing of consumer products in order to carry out this Act.

(i)(1) Each recipient of assistance under this Act pursuant to grants or contracts entered into under other than competitive bidding procedures shall keep such records as the Commission by rule shall prescribe, including records which fully disclose the amount and disposition by such recipient of the proceeds of such assistance, the total cost of the project undertaken in connection with which such assistance is given or used, and the amount of that portion of the cost of the project or undertaking supplied by other sources, and such other records as will facilitate an effective audit.

(2) The Commission and the Comptroller General of the United States, or their duly authorized representatives, shall have access for the purpose of audit and examination to any books, documents, papers, and records of the recipients that are pertinent to the grants or contracts entered into under this Act under other than competitive bidding procedures.

(j) The Commission shall prepare and submit to the President and the Congress on or before October 1 of each year a comprehensive report on the administration of this Act for the preceding fiscal year. Such report shall include—

(1) a thorough appraisal, including statistical analyses, estimates, and long-term projections, of the incidence of injury and effects to the population resulting from consumer products, with a breakdown, insofar as practicable, among the various sources of such injury;

(2) a list of consumer product safety rules prescribed or in effect during such year;

(3) an evaluation of the degree of observance of consumer product safety rules, including a list of enforcement actions, court decisions, and compromises of alleged violations, by location and company name;

(4) a summary of outstanding problems confronting the administration of this Act in order of priority;

(5) an analysis and evaluation of public and private consumer product safety research activities;

(6) a list, with a brief statement of the issues, of completed or pending judicial actions under this Act;

(7) the extent to which technical information was disseminated to the scientific and commercial communities and consumer information was made available to the public;

(8) the extent of cooperation between Commission officials and representatives of industry and other interested parties in the implementation of this Act, including a log or summary of meetings held between Commission officials and representatives of industry and other interested parties;

(9) an appraisal of significant actions of State and local governments relating to the responsibilities of the Commission; and

(10) such recommendations for additional legislation as the Commission deems necessary to carry out the purposes of this Act.

(k) (1) Whenever the Commission submits any budget estimate or request to the President or the Office of Management and Budget, it shall concurrently transmit a copy of that estimate or request to the Congress.

(2) Whenever the Commission submits any legislative recommendations, or testimony, or comments on legislation to the President or the

Office of Management and Budget, it shall concurrently transmit a copy thereof to the Congress. No officer or agency of the United States shall have any authority to require the Commission to submit its legislative recommendations, or testimony, or comments on legislation, to any officer or agency of the United States for approval, comments, or review, prior to the submission of such recommendations, testimony, or comments to the Congress.

PRODUCT SAFETY ADVISORY COUNCIL

Sec. 28. (a) The Commission shall establish a Product Safety Advisory Council which it may consult before prescribing a consumer product safety rule or taking other action under this Act. The Council shall be appointed by the Commission and shall be composed of fifteen members, each of whom shall be qualified by training and experience in one or more of the fields applicable to the safety of products within the jurisdiction of the Commission. The Council shall be constituted as follows:

(1) five members shall be selected from governmental agencies including Federal, State, and local governments;

(2) five members shall be selected from consumer product industries including at least one representative of small business; and

(3) five members shall be selected from among consumer organizations, community organizations, and recognized consumer leaders.

(b) The Council shall meet at the call of the Commission, but not less often than four times during each calendar year.

(c) The Council may propose consumer product safety rules to the Commission for its consideration and may function through subcommittees of its members. All proceedings of the Council shall be public, and a record of each proceeding shall be available for public inspection.

(d) Members of the Council who are not officers or employees of the United States shall, while attending meetings or conferences of the Council or while otherwise engaged in the business of the Council, be entitled to receive compensation at a rate fixed by the Commission, not exceeding the daily equivalent of the annual rate of basic pay in effect for grade GS–18 of the General Schedule, including traveltime, and while away from their homes or regular places of business they may be allowed travel expenses, including per diem in lieu of subsistence, as authorized by section 5703 of title 5, United States Code. Payments under this subsection shall not render members of the Council officers or employees of the United States for any purpose.

COOPERATION WITH STATES AND WITH OTHER FEDERAL AGENCIES

Sec. 29. (a) The Commission shall establish a program to promote Federal-State cooperation for the purposes of carrying out this Act. In implementing such program the Commission may—

(1) accept from any State or local authorities engaged in activities relating to health, safety, or consumer protection assistance in such functions as injury data collection, investigation, and educational programs, as well as other assistance in the administration and enforcement of this Act which such States or

localities may be able and willing to provide and, if so agreed, may pay in advance or otherwise for the reasonable cost of such assistance, and

(2) commission any qualified officer or employee of any State or local agency as an officer of the Commission for the purpose of conducting examinations, investigations, and inspections.

(b) In determining whether such proposed State and local programs are appropriate in implementing the purposes of this Act, the Commission shall give favorable consideration to programs which establish separate State and local agencies to consolidate functions relating to product safety and other consumer protection activities.

(c) The Commission may obtain from any Federal department or agency such statistics, data, program reports, and other materials as it may deem necessary to carry out its functions under this Act. Each such department or agency may cooperate with the Commission and, to the extent permitted by law, furnish such materials to it. The Commission and the heads of other departments and agencies engaged in administering programs related to product safety shall, to the maximum extent practicable, cooperate and consult in order to insure fully coordinated efforts.

(d) The Commission shall, to the maximum extent practicable, utilize the resources and facilities of the National Bureau of Standards, on a reimbursable basis, to perform research and analyses related to risks of injury associated with consumer products (including fire and flammability risks), to develop test methods, to conduct studies and investigations, and to provide technical advice and assistance in connection with the functions of the Commission.

TRANSFERS OF FUNCTIONS

SEC. 30. (a) The functions of the Secretary of Health, Education, and Welfare under the Federal Hazardous Substances Act (15 U.S.C. 1261 et seq.) and the Poison Prevention Packaging Act of 1970 are transferred to the Commission. The functions of the Administrator of the Environmental Protection Agency and of the Secretary of Health, Education, and Welfare under the Acts amended by subsections (b) through (f) of section 7 of the Poison Prevention Packaging Act of 1970, to the extent such functions relate to the administration and enforcement of the Poison Prevention Packaging Act of 1970, are transferred to the Commission.

(b) The functions of the Secretary of Health, Education, and Welfare, the Secretary of Commerce, and the Federal Trade Commission under the Flammable Fabrics Act (15 U.S.C. 1191 et seq.) are transferred to the Commission. The functions of the Federal Trade Commission under the Federal Trade Commission Act, to the extent such functions relate to the administration and enforcement of the Flammable Fabrics Act, are transferred to the Commission.

(c) The functions of the Secretary of Commerce and the Federal Trade Commission under the Act of August 2, 1956 (15 U.S.C. 1211) are transferred to the Commission.

(d) A risk of injury which is associated with consumer products and which could be eliminated or reduced to a sufficient extent by action taken under the Federal Hazardous Substances Act, the Poison Prevention Packaging Act of 1970, or the Flammable Fabrics Act may be regulated by the Commission only in accordance with the provisions of those Acts.

(e) (1) (A) All personnel, property, records, obligations, and commitments, which are used primarily with respect to any function transferred under the provisions of subsections (a), (b) and (c) of this section shall be transferred to the Commission, except those associated with fire and flammability research in the National Bureau of Standards. The transfer of personnel pursuant to this paragraph shall be without reduction in classification or compensation for one year after such transfer, except that the Chairman of the Commission shall have full authority to assign personnel during such one-year period in order to efficiently carry out functions transferred to the Commission under this section.

(B) Any commissioned officer of the Public Health Service who upon the day before the effective date of this section, is serving as such officer primarily in the performance of functions transferred by this Act to the Commission, may, if such officer so elects, acquire competitive status and be transferred to a competitive position in the Commission subject to subparagraph (A) of this paragraph, under the terms prescribed in paragraphs (3) through (8) (A) of section 15(b) of the Clean Air Amendments of 1970 (84 Stat. 1676; 42 U.S.C. 215 nt).

(2) All orders, determinations, rules, regulations, permits, contracts, certificates, licenses, and privileges (A) which have been issued, made, granted, or allowed to become effective in the exercise of functions which are transferred under this section by any department or agency, any functions of which are transferred by this section, and (B) which are in effect at the time this section takes effect, shall continue in effect according to their terms until modified, terminated, superseded, set aside, or repealed by the Commission, by any court of competent jurisdiction, or by operation of law.

(3) The provisions of this section shall not affect any proceedings pending at the time this section takes effect before any department or agency, functions of which are transferred by this section; except that such proceedings, to the extent that they relate to functions so transferred, shall be continued before the Commission. Orders shall be issued in such proceedings, appeals shall be taken therefrom, and payments shall be made pursuant to such orders, as if this section had not been enacted; and orders issued in any such proceedings shall continue in effect until modified, terminated, superseded, or repealed by the Commission, by a court of competent jurisdiction, or by operation of law.

(4) The provisions of this section shall not affect suits commenced prior to the date this section takes effect and in all such suits proceedings shall be had, appeals taken, and judgments rendered, in the same manner and effect as if this section had not been enacted; except that if before the date on which this section takes effect, any department or agency (or officer thereof in his official capacity) is a party to a suit involving functions transferred to the Commission, then such suit shall be continued by the Commission. No cause of action, and no suit, action, or other proceeding, by or against any department or agency (or officer thereof in his official capacity) functions of which are transferred by this section, shall abate by reason of the enactment of this section. Causes of actions, suits, actions, or other proceedings may be

asserted by or against the United States or the Commission as may be appropriate and, in any litigation pending when this section takes effect, the court may at any time, on its own motion or that of any party, enter an order which will give effect to the provisions of this paragraph.

(f) For purposes of this section, (1) the term "function" includes power and duty, and (2) the transfer of a function, under any provision of law, of an agency or the head of a department shall also be a transfer of all functions under such law which are exercised by any office or officer of such agency or department.

LIMITATION ON JURISDICTION

SEC. 31. The Commission shall have no authority under this Act to regulate any risk of injury associated with a consumer product if such risk could be eliminated or reduced to a sufficient extent by actions taken under the Occupational Safety and Health Act of 1970; the Atomic Energy Act of 1954; or the Clean Air Act. The Commission shall have no authority under this Act to regulate any risk of injury associated with electronic product radiation emitted from an electronic product (as such terms are defined by sections 355 (1) and (2) of the Public Health Service Act) if such risk of injury may be subjected to regulation under subpart 3 of part F of title III of the Public Health Service Act.

AUTHORIZATION OF APPROPRIATIONS

SEC. 32. (a) There are hereby authorized to be appropriated for the purpose of carrying out the provisions of this Act (other than the provisions of section 27(h) which authorize the planning and construction of research, development, and testing facilities), and for the purpose of carrying out the functions, powers, and duties transferred to the Commission under section 30, not to exceed—

(1) $55,000,000 for the fiscal year ending June 30, 1973;

(2) $59,000,000 for the fiscal year ending June 30, 1974; and

(3) $64,000,000 for the fiscal year ending June 30, 1975.

(b)(1) There are authorized to be appropriated such sums as may be necessary for the planning and construction of research, development and testing facilities described in section 27(h); except that no appropriation shall be made for any such planning or construction involving an expenditure in excess of $100,000 if such planning or construction has not been approved by resolutions adopted in substantially the same form by the Committee on Interstate and Foreign Commerce of the House of Representatives, and by the Committee on Commerce of the Senate. For the purpose of securing consideration of such approval the Commission shall transmit to Congress a prospectus of the proposed facility including (but not limited to)—

(A) a brief description of the facility to be planned or constructed;

(B) the location of the facility, and an estimate of the maximum cost of the facility;

(C) a statement of those agencies, private and public, which will use such facility, together with the contribution to be made by each such agency toward the cost of such facility; and

(D) a statement of justification of the need for such facility.

(2) The estimated maximum cost of any facility approved under this subsection as set forth in the prospectus may be increased by the amount equal to the percentage increase, if any, as determined by the Commission, in construction costs, from the date of the transmittal of such prospectus to Congress, but in no event shall the increase authorized by this paragraph exceed 10 per centum of such estimated maximum cost.

SEPARABILITY

SEC. 33. If any provision of this Act, or the application of such provision to any person or circumstance, shall be held invalid, the remainder of this Act, or the application of such provisions to persons or circumstances other than those as to which it is held invalid, shall not be affected thereby.

EFFECTIVE DATE

SEC. 34. This Act shall take effect on the sixtieth day following the date of its enactment, except—

(1) sections 4 and 32 shall take effect on the date of enactment of this Act, and

(2) section 30 shall take effect on the later of (A) 150 days after the date of enactment of this Act, or (B) the date on which at least three members of the Commission first take office.

Approved October 27, 1972

APPENDIX B

CONSUMER PRODUCT SAFETY BILL PROPOSED BY NATIONAL COMMISSION ON PRODUCT SAFETY

(June 1970)

Table of Contents

A BILL

To protect consumers against unreasonable risk of injury from hazardous products and for other purposes.

Be it enacted by the Senate and House of Representatives of the United States of America in Congress assembled: That this act may be cited as the "Consumer Product Safety Act of 1970."

Findings and Purposes

Section 2(a).–The Congress hereby finds:

(1) The public has a right to be protected against risk of death or injury from hazardous consumer products when such hazards can reasonably be eliminated or minimized;

(2) Unacceptable numbers of hazardous consumer products now affect interstate commerce;

(3) The increasing number and complexity of consumer products make it essential to act promptly to avoid unnecessary death and injury in the future;

(4) Complexities of modern consumer products and the diverse nature and abilities of consumers using them frequently result in an inability of users to anticipate hazards and to safeguard themselves adequately;

(5) Voluntary efforts by industry to develop means of preventing the sale of unsafe products, while sometimes contributing to consumer safety, often have not been adequate to protect consumers;

(6) Preservation of free competition precludes enforcement of voluntary product safety standards by private groups;

(7) The production and sale of consumer products generally affects interstate commerce, making control of unreasonable hazards by state and local governments inadequate and often burdensome to manufacturers.

(*b*) The purposes of this Act are:

(1) To protect the public against unreasonable product hazards to their health and safety;

(2) To assist consumers in evaluating the comparative safety of consumer products;

(3) To aid manufacturers of consumer products by encouraging industry to develop uniform safety standards for consumer products and by minimizing conflicting state and local regulations;

(4) To promote research and investigation into the causes and prevention of product-related deaths and injuries.

Consumer Product Safety Commission

Section 3(a).–A Commission is hereby created and established, to be known as the Consumer Product Safety Commission (hereinafter referred to as the "Commission"), consisting of five Commissioners who shall be appointed by the President, by and with the advice and consent of the Senate, one of whom shall be designated by the President as Chairman. The Chairman shall be the principal executive officer of the Commission and, when so designated, shall act as Chairman until the expiration of his term of office. Any member of the Commission may be removed by the President for neglect of duty or malfeasance in office but for no other cause.

(*b*) The Commissioners first appointed under this section shall continue in office for terms of 1, 2, 3, 4, and 5 years, respectively, from the date of the enactment of this Act, the term of each to be designated by the President at the time of nomination. Their successors shall be appointed each for a term of 5 years from the date of the expiration of the term for which his predecessor was appointed and until his successor is appointed and has qualified, except that he shall not so continue to serve beyond the expiration of the next session of Congress subsequent to the expiration of said fixed term of office and except that any person appointed to fill a vacancy occurring prior to the expiration of the term for which his predecessor was appointed shall be appointed only for the unexpired term.

(*c*) Not more than three of the Commissioners shall be appointed from the same political party. No person in the employ of, or holding any official relation to, any person, firm, association, or corporation engaged in selling or manufacturing consumer products or owning stock or bonds of substantial value in such a firm, association, or corporation or who is in any other manner pecuniarily interested in such a firm, association, or corporation, or a substantial supplier thereof, shall enter upon the duties of or hold the office of Commissioner. Commissioners shall not engage in any other business, vocation, or employment.

(*d*) No vacancy in the Commission shall impair the right of the remaining Commissioners to exercise all the powers of the Commission. Three members of the Commission shall constitute a quorum for the transaction of business. The Commission shall have an official seal of which judicial notice shall be taken. The Commission shall annually elect a Vice Chairman to act in the absence or in case of the disability of the Chairman or in case of a vacancy in the office of the Chairman.

(*e*) The Commission shall maintain a principal office and such field offices as it deems necessary and may meet and exercise any or all of its powers at any other place. The Commission may, by one or more of its members or by such agents or agency as it may designate, prosecute any inquiry necessary to its function anywhere in the United States. A Commissioner who participates in such an inquiry shall not be disqualified from subsequently participating in a decision of the Commission in the same matter.

(*f*) The Commission shall prepare and submit to the President for transmittal to the Congress on or before October 1 of each year a comprehensive report on the administration of this Act for the preceding fiscal year. Such report shall include:

(1) A thorough appraisal, including statistical analyses, estimates, and long-term projections, of the incidence of injury and effects to the population resulting from consumer products, with a breakdown, insofar as practicable, among the various sources of such injury;

(2) A list of consumer product safety standards in effect in such year, with identification of standards newly added during such year;

(3) An evaluation of the degree of observance of consumer product safety standards, including a list of enforcement actions, court decisions, and compromises of alleged violations, by location and company name;

(4) A summary of outstanding problems confronting the administration of this Act in order of priority;

(5) An analysis and evaluation of consumer product safety research activities completed and in progress as a result of government and/or private sponsorship and technological progress achieved during such year;

(6) A list, with a brief statement of the issues, of completed or pending judicial actions under this Act;

(7) The extent to which technical information was disseminated to the scientific and commercial communities and consumer information was made available to the public;

(8) The extent of cooperation between Commission officials and representatives of industry and other interested parties in the implementation of this Act, including a log or summary of meetings held between Commission officials and representatives of industry and other interested parties; and

(9) An appraisal of significant actions of state and local governments relating to the responsibilities of the Commission.

(*g*) The report required by subsection (*f*) shall contain such recommendations for additional legislation as the Commission deems necessary to promote cooperation among the several states in the improvement of consumer product safety and to strengthen national consumer safety efforts.

(*h*) The Commission shall appoint an Executive Director, a General Counsel, a Director of Engineering Sciences, a Director of Epidemiology, a Director of Information, and such other officers and employees as are necessary in the execution of its functions. Commission employees, other than those specifically enumerated in the preceding sentence, shall be subject to the provisions of Title 5, United States Code, governing appointments in the competitive service.

Consumer Safety Advocate

Section 4.—There shall be an independent safety advocate to the Commission, appointed by the President, with the advice and consent of the Senate, for a term of 7 years. The independent safety advocate shall be known as the Consumer Safety Advocate, shall represent the interests of consumers before the Commission, and shall have the following additional authority and responsibility:

(*a*) To receive and act upon complaints from the public, Congress, or the Executive agencies regarding actions or inactions by the Commission;

(*b*) To evaluate, where appropriate, proposed or existing standards, proposed orders and regulations, hazards and potential hazards, and to hire and contract for such personnel which will enable such evaluation;

(*c*) To obtain information from the Commission concerning any proposed, pending, or completed standard, regulation or other proceeding;

(*d*) To appear before the Commission, at his discretion, in any proceeding as a party, or witness;

(*e*) To recommend modification of any proposed regulation, order or standard;

(*f*) To request the development of a regulation or standard by the Commission;

(*g*) To request commencement of other proceedings by the Commission;

(*h*) To appeal to any appropriate court of the United States any order, regulation, or standard issued by the Commission;

(*i*) To issue public statements with respect to any matter within his responsibilities under subsections (*a*) through (*h*).

Injury Information Clearinghouse

Section 5(*a*).—The Commission shall establish and operate an Injury Information Clearinghouse to collect, investigate, analyze, and disseminate information relating to the causes and prevention of product-related injuries to consumers. The Commission may, under the provisions of Section 31 utilize the facilities and personnel of state and local governments to collect, investigate, analyze, and disseminate such data.

(*b*) The Commission, in cooperation with appropriate federal agencies, shall conduct additional continuing studies and investigations of deaths, injuries, diseases, other health impairments, and economic losses resulting from accidents involving consumer products as it deems necessary.

(*c*) Independently or, in cooperation with appropriate public and private agencies, the Commission is authorized to:

(1) Conduct research and investigation into the safety of consumer products;

(2) Conduct studies on improvement of consumer products;

(3) Test consumer products and develop product safety test methods and testing devices;

(4) Offer training in product safety investigation and test methods; and

(5) Assist public and private organizations, administratively and technically, in the development of safety standards and test methods.

(*d*) The Commission is authorized to carry out the functions described in this section by making grants or entering into contracts for the conduct of such functions with governmental entities, private organizations or individuals.

(*e*) The Commission shall employ personnel of scientific and technical competence adequate to implement the provisions of this Act.

(*f*) Whenever the federal contribution for any information, research, or development activity authorized by this Act is more than minimal, the Commission shall include in any contract, grant, or other arrangement for such research or development activity, or in rules or regulations applicable to such information function, provisions effective to insure that all information, uses, processes, patents, and other developments resulting from that activity will be made freely and fully available to the general public. Nothing herein shall be construed to deprive the owner of any background patent of any right which he may have thereunder.

(*g*) The Commission is authorized to plan, design, construct and operate a facility or facilities suitable for research, development and testing of consumer products pursuant to the purposes of this Act.

Commission Priorities

Section 6.–The Commission shall annually evaluate information obtained by it for the purpose of establishing an order of priorities for its informational, educational, and regulatory activities. After such evaluation the Commission shall publish in the *Federal Register* a list of the categories of consumer products which it believes warrant primary attention, with the reasons therefor. The Commission may from time to time add to, delete from, or modify such list of priorities. The failure to include any category of products in such list of priorities shall not preclude Commission action with respect thereto.

Consumer Product Safety Standards

Section 7.–The Commission shall have authority to promulgate consumer product safety standards or other regulations for consumer product safety including:

(*a*) Any requirement as to performance, composition, contents, design, construction, finish, packaging, or otherwise relating to any consumer product or any component part thereof, as is reasonably necessary to prevent or reduce risk of death or personal injury.

(*b*) Any requirement that any consumer product or any component part thereof be marked with or accompanied by clear and adequate warnings or instructions, or form of warnings or instructions, as is reasonably necessary to prevent or reduce risk of death or personal injury.

Consumer Product Safety Standards–Proceedings by Commission

Section 8(a).–Whenever the Commission finds that a consumer product safety standard or other regulation authorized by Section 7 is necessary to prevent or reduce risk of death or personal injury to the public from an identified product hazard, the Commission shall commence a proceeding for the development of such a standard or regulation.

(*b*) A proceeding for the development of such a standard or regulation shall be commenced by the publication of a notice in the *Federal Register*.

The notice shall state:

(1) The nature of an identified product hazard found by the Commission;

(2) That the Commission has determined a consumer product safety standard or regulation is necessary to prevent or reduce unreasonable risk of death or personal injury to the public from such hazard; and

(3) That any person or organization which is competent and willing to develop a proposed standard or regulation to prevent or reduce such hazard is invited to advise the Commission within 30 days of the date of such notice.

(*c*) If, within such period, a person or organization offers to develop such a proposed standard or regulation and the Commission determines that such person or organization:

(1) Is technically competent to undertake such a project; and

(2) If an organization operates pursuant to fair procedures, including: (i) reasonable notice to and adequate participation by all interested parties including consumers, (ii) due process to all participants, (iii) maintenance of adequate records of deliberations which are available to the public, (iv) a requirement that all dissenting views on proposed standards be recorded and furnished to the Commission, and (v) such other procedures as the Commission deems necessary,

–the Commission shall suspend its proceeding for the development of a consumer product safety standard for not more than 180 days and authorize such person or organization to develop a proposed standard or regulation. The Commission, for good cause shown, may extend such suspension for such additional period as it finds in the public interest and shall publish its reasons for such determination. During such suspension the Commission may authorize its staff to develop proposals for a standard or regulation, or contract with third parties for such development.

(*d*) If, within such period, a proposed consumer product safety standard or regulation is developed by such person or organization, the Commission shall resume its proceeding and shall take such proposed standard or regulation into consideration, along with the views of its staff, prior to publishing a proposed consumer product safety standard or regulation in the *Federal Register.* A consumer product safety standard or regulation shall thereafter be published within 60 days of submission of such proposed standard unless the Commission, for good cause shown, finds an extension of such period is in the public interest and publishes its reasons for such determination. Such standard or regulation shall include a finding that the Commission determines it is reasonably necessary to prevent or reduce unreasonable risk of death or personal injury to the public from the hazard described.

(*e*) If no person or organization offers and is authorized by the Commission to develop such a proposed consumer product safety standard or regulation, the Commission shall publish a consumer product safety standard or regulation within 180 days of the publication of the notice commencing the proceeding unless the Commission, for good cause shown, finds an extension of such period is in the public interest and publishes its reasons for such determination. Such standard or regulation shall include a finding that the Commission determines it is reasonably necessary to prevent or reduce unreasonable risk of death or personal injury to the public from the hazard described.

(*f*) Each consumer product safety standard or regulation shall specify the date such standard or regulation is to take effect not exceeding 90 days from the date issued, unless the Commission finds, for good cause shown, that a later effective date is in the public interest and publishes its reasons for such finding.

(*g*) The Commission may by order amend or revoke any consumer product safety standard or regulation established under this section. Such order shall specify the date on which such amendment or revocation is to take effect which shall not exceed 90 days from the date the order is issued unless the Commission finds for good cause shown that a later effective date is in the public interest and publishes its reasons for such finding. Where an amendment involves a material change in a standard or regulation subsections (*a*) - (*e*) of this section shall apply.

(*h*) In issuing a consumer product safety standard pursuant to this section, (1) the Commission shall not issue any standard unless there is an expression in the standard itself of the hazard which the standard is designed to prevent or reduce; (2) shall whenever possible promulgate performance standards; and (3) shall consider relevant available product data including the results of research, development, testing, and investigation activities conducted generally and pursuant to this Act.

(*i*) Section 553 of Title 5, United States Code, shall apply to all proceedings for the purpose of establishing, amending, or revoking a consumer product safety standard or other regulation pursuant to this Act.

Consumer Product Safety Standards–Imminent Hazards

Section 9.–Whenever the Commission makes the findings specified in Section 8(*a*) and, in addition, at any time finds (1) that such identified product hazard presents an imminent risk to public health or safety and (2) the consumer product in question is already being distributed, or is about to be distributed in interstate commerce, the Commission may issue an interim consumer product safety standard or regulation and make such standard or regulation effective immediately or within such time as the Commission deems necessary in the public interest. The Commission shall specify such findings in a *Federal Register* notice promulgating such interim standard or regulation, and such findings shall be subject to judicial review pursuant to Section 28. In any such review proceeding an interim standard or regulation of the Commission shall be sustained unless the party asserting its invalidity establishes by clear and convincing proof that it is arbitrary. In the event the Commission issues an interim consumer product safety standard or other regulation, it shall commence and complete a proceeding under Section 8 with reasonable promptness.

Consumer Product Safety Standards–Petition by Interested Party

Section 10(a).–Any consumer or other interested party may petition the Commission to commence a proceeding for the issuance, amendment, or revocation of a consumer product safety standard or other regulation.

(*b*) Such petition shall be filed in the principal office of the Commission and shall set forth:

(1) Facts which it is claimed establish the existence of an identified product hazard;

(2) Facts which it is claimed establish that a consumer product safety standard or other regulation or an amendment or revocation thereof is necessary; and

(3) The terms of any such consumer product safety standard or other regulation or amendment thereof which it is claimed should be issued by the Commission.

(*c*) The Commission may, in its discretion, hold a public hearing or may conduct such investigation or proceeding as it deems appropriate in order to determine whether or not such petition should be granted.

(*d*) If the Commission grants such petition, it shall promptly commence an appropriate proceeding for the issuance of a consumer product safety standard, or other regulation or, pursuant to Section 14, declare such product a banned hazardous product or take such other action as it deems appropriate. If the Commission denies such petition it shall publish its reasons for such denial.

New Products

Section 11(*a*).–The Commission shall have authority to promulgate standards and procedures for the purpose of insuring that new consumer products are adequately designed and tested to minimize unreasonable risk of death or personal injury to the public.

(*b*) For purposes of this section, a "new consumer product" is a consumer product which incorporates a design, material, or form of energy exchange which (1) has not previously been used substantially in consumer products and (2) as to which there exists a lack of information adequate to determine the safety of such product in use by consumers.

Suits by Commission

Section 12(*a*).–Whenever the Commission shall have reason to believe that a make, model, or type of consumer product incorporating an identified product hazard is being marketed or is about to be marketed, it is authorized to commence an action for temporary and permanent injunctive relief with respect to such consumer product in an appropriate federal district court.

(*b*) Such a proceeding by the Commission shall be commenced by the filing of a complaint setting forth the facts which establish that the marketing of such consumer product presents or may present an unreasonable risk of death or personal injury to the public and the nature of injunctive relief which the Commission believes is necessary with respect thereto.

(*c*) The district courts of the United States shall have jurisdiction over such actions commenced by the Commission.

(*d*) The Commission may commence such actions in any district court in the United States in a district where any act, omission, or transaction constituting the alleged violation occurred, or is threatened, or in such court for the district wherein the defendant is found or transacts business. In such cases, process may be served in any other district in which the defendant is an inhabitant or wherever the defendant may be found.

Injunctive Relief

Section 13(a).–If the court determines that the risk is unreasonable and the Commission is entitled to relief pursuant to Section 12 hereof, it may (i) enter an appropriate order enjoining the marketing of such consumer product, and (ii) enter an appropriate order directing the defendant or defendants to establish such procedures with respect to such consumer product as are necessary to avoid unreasonable risk of death or personal injury to the public in the future.

(*b*) Those procedures which may be the subject of an affirmative order of the court pursuant to this section may include:

(i) collection and retention of information on the identity of purchasers and claims of injury or hazards;

(ii) collection and retention of information on product performance and servicing, to the extent it relates to safety;

(iii) procedures for adequate product design and performance;

(iv) procedures for adequate conduct of testing and inspection;

(v) inclusion of necessary warnings and instructions with consumer products; and

(vi) procedures for adequate quality control.

Banned Hazardous Products

Section 14(a).–Whenever the Commission finds:

(1) That a consumer product incorporating an identified product hazard is being marketed, or is about to be marketed, and such consumer product presents an unreasonable risk of death or personal injury to the public; and

(2) Notwithstanding any cautionary labeling, regulation, or safety standard as is or may be required under this Act, the degree or nature of the hazard involved in the use of the consumer product is such that protection of the public health and safety can be adequately served only by keeping such product out of the channels of interstate commerce

—the Commission may, by regulation pursuant to Section 553 of Title 5, United States Code, declare such product a banned hazardous product.

(*b*) If, before or during a proceeding pursuant to subparagraph (a) of this section, the Commission finds that because of an identified product hazard, distribution of a consumer product affecting interstate commerce presents an imminent hazard to the public health, and by order published in the *Federal Register* it gives notice of such finding, such consumer product shall be deemed to be a banned hazardous product for the purposes of this Act until the proceeding has been completed. If not yet initiated when such an order is published, such a proceeding shall be commenced and completed with reasonable promptness.

(*c*) Orders pursuant to this section shall be subject to judicial review pursuant to Section 28. In any such review proceeding an order pursuant to subsection (*b*) shall be sustained unless the party asserting its invalidity establishes by clear and convincing proof that the order is arbitrary.

Product Safety Advisory Council

Section 15(*a*).—The Commission shall establish a Product Safety Advisory Council which it may consult before prescribing a consumer product safety standard or other regulation. The Council shall be appointed by the Commission and shall be composed of fifteen members, each of whom shall be qualified by training and experience in one or more of the fields applicable to the safety of products within the jurisdiction of the Commission. The Council shall be constituted as follows:

(1) Five members shall be selected from governmental agencies including federal, state, and local governments;

(2) Five members shall be selected from consumer product industries including at least one representative of small business;

(3) Five members shall be selected from among consumer organizations, community organizations, and recognized consumer leaders.

(*b*) The Council may propose product safety standards or other regulations to the Commission for its consideration and may function through subcommittees of its members. All proceedings of the Council shall be public, and a record of each proceeding shall be available for public inspection.

(*c*) Members of the Council who are not officers or employees of the United States and members of any ad hoc advisory committees created pursuant to subsection (*d*) shall, while attending meetings or conferences of the Council or while otherwise engaged in the business of the Council, be entitled to receive compensation at a rate fixed by the Commission, not exceeding $100 per diem, including travel time and while away from their homes or regular places of business they may be allowed travel expenses, including per diem in lieu of subsistence, as authorized by Section 5703 of Title 5, United States Code. Payments under this subsection shall not render members of the Council officers or employees of the United States for any purpose.

(*d*) The Commission is authorized to establish, in addition to the aforesaid Product Safety Advisory Council, such ad hoc advisory committees as it deems necessary to advise it with respect to any safety standard or other regulation considered by it under this Act. Where practicable, such ad hoc committees shall be composed of representatives of differing interests in the same proportions specified in subsection (*a*) hereof. Such ad hoc committees shall terminate upon termination of the proceeding with respect to such standard or regulation. All proceedings shall be public, and a record of each proceeding shall be available for public inspection.

Notification of Defects; Repair or Replacement of Hazardous Products

Section 16(*a*).–Every manufacturer of consumer products who discovers or acquires information tending to show that:

(1) A consumer product produced, assembled or imported by him contains a defect which creates a substantial risk of personal injury to the public; or

(2) A consumer product produced, assembled or imported by him on or after the effective date of an applicable standard or regulation prescribed pursuant to Sections 8, 9, or 14 fails to comply with such standard or regulation,

–shall immediately notify the Commission of such defect or failure to comply if such product has left the place of manufacture and shall, except as authorized by paragraph (*c*), with reasonable promptness furnish notification of such defect or failure to comply to the persons specified in subsection (*d*) of this section.

(*b*) The Commission is authorized to promulgate regulations defining "defect which creates a substantial risk of personal injury to the public" pursuant to this section.

(*c*) If, in the opinion of such manufacturer the defect or failure to comply (i) is not such as to create a substantial risk of personal injury, or (ii) a special limited form of notice is appropriate, or (iii) the Commission and not the manufacturer should furnish and pay for the notification specified, he may, at the time of giving notice to the Commission of such defect or failure to comply, apply to the Commission for a partial or complete exemption from the requirement of notice specified in subsection (*d*). If such application states grounds for such exemption, the Commission may afford such manufacturer an opportunity to present his views in support of the application, the burden of proof being on the manufacturer. Where the Commission determines it is in the public interest it may publish notice of such application in the *Federal Register* and afford interested parties, including consumers, an opportunity to comment thereon. If, after such presentation, the Commission for good cause shown finds (1) that such defect or failure to comply is not such as to create a substantial risk of injury and (2) that exemption would be in the public interest, it may exempt such manufacturer from the requirement of notice to the persons specified in subsection (*d*) of this section or from the requirements of repair, refund, or replacement imposed by subsection (*h*) of this section, provided, that it shall publish its reasons for such findings in the *Federal Register*. If, after such presentation the Commission, for good cause shown, finds that a special limited form of notice is appropriate or that it is in the public interest that the Commission furnish the notification specified, it may grant such partial or complete exemption from subsection (*d*) and shall publish its reasons for such finding in the *Federal Register*.

(*d*) The notification, other than to the Commission, required by subparagraph (*a*) of this section shall be accomplished:

(1) by certified mail to the first purchaser of such product for purposes other than resale and to any subsequent transferee of such product where known to the manufacturer, and

(2) by certified mail or other more expeditious means to the dealers or distributors of such manufacturer to whom such product was delivered.

(*e*) The notification required by subparagraph (*a*) of this section shall contain a clear description of such defect or failure to comply, an evaluation of the hazard reasonably related thereto, and a statement of the measures to be taken to correct such defect. In the case of a notification to a person referred to in subsection (*d*)(1) of this section, the notification shall also advise the person of his rights under subsection (*h*) of this section.

(*f*) Every manufacturer of consumer products shall furnish to the Commission a true copy of all notices, bulletins, and other communications to dealers or distributors of such manufacturer or to purchasers, or subsequent transferees, of consumer products of such manufacturer regarding any such defect in such product or any failure to comply with a standard, regulation, or order applicable to such product. The Commission shall disclose to the public so much of the information contained in such notices or other information in its possession as it deems will assist in carrying out the purposes of this Act, but it shall not disclose any information which contains or relates to a trade secret unless it determines that it is necessary to carry out the purposes of this Act.

(*g*) If through testing, inspection, investigation, research or examination of reports carried out pursuant to this Act the Commission determines that any consumer product:

(1) fails to comply with an applicable standard or regulation prescribed pursuant to Section 8, 9 or 14; or

(2) contains a defect which creates a substantial risk of personal injury to the public,

and if the Commission determines that notification or other remedies provided under this section are appropriate, it shall notify the manufacturer of the product of such defect or failure to comply. The notice shall contain the findings of the Commission and shall include a synopsis of the information upon which the findings are based. Unless the Commission determines that delay will unreasonably harm the public health and safety, it shall afford such manufacturer an opportunity to present his views to establish that there is no failure of compliance or that the alleged defect does not exist or does not create a substantial risk of personal injury. Where the Commission determines it is in the public interest, it may publish notice of such proceeding in the *Federal Register* and afford interested parties, including consumers, an opportunity to comment thereon. If after such presentation by the manufacturer the Commission determines that such product does not comply with an applicable standard or regulation, or that it contains a defect which creates a substantial risk of personal injury, the Commission may direct the manufacturer to furnish the notification specified in subsection (*e*) of this section to the persons specified in subparagraph (*d*) of this section. The Commission may in its discretion use the sanctions provided by Sections 25, 26, or 27 of this Act with or without utilizing the procedures specified in this section.

(*h*) If any consumer product is found under subparagraph (*a*) or (*g*) to fail to comply with an applicable standard or regulation or to have a defect which creates a substantial risk of personal injury, and the notification specified in subsection (*e*) is required to be furnished on account of such failure or defect, the manufacturer of such product shall,

(1) without charge, bring such product into conformity with such standard or regulation, or remedy such defect and provide reimbursement for any expenses, including transportation expenses incurred in connection with having such product brought into conformity or having such defect remedied, or

(2) replace such product with a like or equivalent product which complies with each applicable standard, regulation or order under this Act and which has no defect relating to the safety of its use, or

(3) refund the purchase price of such product upon tender of the product by the owner.

The manufacturer shall take the action required by this subsection in such manner and with respect to such persons as the Commission shall by order prescribe.

Product Certification and Labeling

Section 17(a).–Every manufacturer of a product subject to a consumer product safety standard or regulation issued under Sections 8 or 9 shall furnish to the distributor or dealer at the time of delivery of such product a certification that such product conforms to all applicable safety standards and shall specify such standards. Such certification shall be based on a test of such specific product set forth in such standard or regulation or upon a reasonable testing program and shall state the name of the manufacturer and date and place of manufacture.

(*b*) The Commission may by rule or regulation prescribe reasonable tests or testing programs for consumer products pursuant to this section.

(*c*) The Commission may by rule or regulation require the use and prescribe the form and content of labels which, where practicable, may be required by the Commission to be permanently affixed to any consumer product and which shall furnish to the extent practicable the information specified in this section.

(*d*) The Commission may order that any product subject to a consumer product safety standard or regulation pursuant to Section 8 shall be subject to a reasonable testing program operated by an independent third-party qualified to perform such program and that an appropriate mark so certifying appear on the product. Where a product is subject to such an order, the certification under subparagraph (*a*) of this section shall so state and shall state the name of the party operating such testing program. The Commission may, by regulation, prescribe procedures for such programs and requirements with respect to reporting of compliance with applicable regulations and standards by independent third-parties conducting such certification programs.

(*e*) The Commission may, with the advice of the Secretary of Commerce, designate parties who are qualified to operate such independent third-party certification programs.

Inspection and Record Keeping

Section 18(*a*).–The Commission is authorized to conduct such inspection and investigation as may be necessary to implement this Act and regulations and standards prescribed pursuant hereto. It shall furnish the Attorney General and, when appropriate, the Secretary of the Treasury, any information obtained indicating noncompliance (except noncompliance with Sec. 19(*b*) of this Act) for appropriate enforcement action.

(*b*) For purposes of implementation of orders, regulations, or standards promulgated under this Act, officers or employees duly designated by the Commission, upon presenting appropriate credentials and a written notice from the Commission to the owner, operator, or agent in charge, are authorized:

(1) To enter, at reasonable times, any factory, warehouse, or establishment in which consumer products or component parts thereof are manufactured, assembled, or held for introduction into interstate commerce or are held for sale after such introduction; and

(2) To inspect, at reasonable times and in a reasonable manner those areas of such factory, warehouse or establishment where such products are produced or stored and which may relate to the safety of such products. Each such inspection shall be commenced and completed with reasonable promptness.

(*c*) Every manufacturer of consumer products or component parts thereof shall establish and maintain such records, make such reports, and provide such information as the Commission may reasonably by regulation require. Establishment and maintenance of records of purchasers of products, product design, testing, quality control, defects and claims for five (5) years, shall not be deemed unreasonable. Upon request of an officer or employee duly designated by the Commission, every such manufacturer shall permit the inspection of appropriate books, records, and papers relevant to determining whether such manufacturer has acted or is acting in compliance with this Act and regulations and standards prescribed pursuant hereto.

(*d*) The Commission or its representatives shall not disclose any information reported to, or otherwise obtained by it pursuant to this section which contains or relates to a trade secret unless it determines that it is necessary to carry out the purposes of this Act. Such information may be disclosed to other officers or employees of the United States concerned with carrying out this Act or, when relevant in any administrative or judicial proceeding under this Act. Nothing in this section shall authorize the withholding of information by the Commission or by any officer or employee under his control from the duly authorized Committees of Congress.

Additional Powers of Commission

Section 19(*a*).—The Commission, or any two members thereof as authorized by the Commission, may conduct hearings anywhere in the United States or otherwise secure data and expressions of opinion pertinent to the safety of consumer products. The Commission shall publish notice of any proposed hearing in the *Federal Register* and shall afford a reasonable opportunity for interested persons to present relevant testimony and data.

(*b*) The Commission shall also have the power:

(1) To require, by special or general orders, corporations, business firms, and individuals to submit in writing such reports and answers to questions as the Commission may prescribe; such submission shall be made within such reasonable period and under oath or otherwise as the Commission may determine;

(2) To administer oaths;

(3) To require by subpoena the attendance and testimony of witnesses and the production of all documentary evidence relating to the execution of its duties;

(4) In the case of disobedience to a subpoena or order issued under this subsection, to invoke the aid of any district court of the United States in requiring compliance with such subpoena or order;

(5) In any proceeding or investigation to order testimony to be taken by deposition before any person who is designated by the Commission and has the power to administer oaths and, in such instances, to compel testimony and the production of evidence in the same manner as authorized under paragraphs (3) and (4) of this subsection; and

(6) To pay witnesses the same fees and mileage as are paid in like circumstances in the courts of the United States.

(*c*) Any district court in the United States within the jurisdiction of which any inquiry is carried on may, upon petition by counsel for the Commission, in case of refusal to obey a subpoena or order of the Commission issued under subsection (*b*) of this section, issue an order requiring compliance therewith; and any failure to obey the order of the court may be punished by the court as a contempt thereof.

(*d*) When the Commission finds that publication of any information obtained by it is in the public interest and would not give an unfair competitive advantage to any person, it is authorized to publish such information in the form and manner deemed best adapted for public use, except that data and information which relates to a trade secret, shall be held confidential and shall not be disclosed, unless the Commission determines that it is necessary to carry out the purposes of this Act.

(*e*) Every manufacturer of consumer products or component parts thereof shall provide to the Commission such performance and technical data related to performance and safety as may be required to carry out the purposes of the Act. The Commission is authorized to require the manufacturer to give such notification of such performance and technical data at the time of original purchase to prospective purchasers and to the first purchaser of such product, for purposes other than resale, as it determines necessary to carry out the purposes of this Act.

(*f*) The Commission is authorized to obtain without charge from any manufacturer of consumer products written authorization to distributors and retailers to obtain a reasonable number of such products for purposes of determining compliance of such products with the provisions of this Act.

(*g*) The Commission is authorized to enter into contracts with governmental entities, private organizations or individuals for the conduct of activities authorized by this Act.

(*h*) The Commission is authorized to establish such policies, criteria, and procedures and to prescribe such rules and regulations as it deems necessary to administration of this Act and its functions hereunder. Unless otherwise specified the provisions of Title 5, United States Code, Section 553 shall apply to such proceeding.

Cooperation With Federal Agencies

Section 20.–The Commission is authorized to obtain from any federal department or agency such statistics, data, program reports, and other materials as it may deem necessary to carry out its functions under this Act. Each such department or agency is authorized to cooperate with the Commission and, to the extent permitted by law, to furnish such materials to it The Commission and the heads of other departments and agencies engaged in administering programs related to product safety shall, to the maximum extent practicable, cooperate and consult in order to insure fully coordinated efforts.

Imported Products

Section 21(*a*).–Any consumer product offered for importation into the United States which fails to comply with an applicable standard or regulation prescribed under this Act, which is not accompanied by a certification in the form prescribed by Section 17, or which contains a defect which creates an unreasonable risk of personal injury to the public shall be refused admission to the United States.

(*b*) The Secretary of the Treasury shall obtain without charge and deliver to the Commission, upon the latter's request, a reasonable number of samples of consumer products being offered for import. The owner or consignee of such product may have a hearing before the Commission with respect to admission of such imports into the United States. If it appears from examination of such samples or otherwise that a product fails to comply with the provisions of this Act, unless subsection (*c*) of this section applies and is complied with,

(1) such product shall be refused admission, and

(2) the Secretary of the Treasury shall cause destruction of such product unless it is exported, under regulations prescribed by the Secretary of the Treasury, within 90 days after notice to the importer or consignee.

(*c*) If it appears to the Commission that any consumer product refused admission pursuant to subsection (*a*) of this section can be brought into compliance with applicable regulations, standards, or orders, final determination as to the admission of such product may be deferred, and the Commission may permit the applicant to perform such operations to bring such product into conformity. The Commission may by regulation prescribe the means of compliance with this subsection, including execution of a sufficient bond for payment of damages and expenses incurred with respect to the imported product.

(*d*) It shall be the duty of every manufacturer offering a consumer product for importation to the United States to designate in writing an agent upon whom service of all administrative and judicial process may be made and to file such designation with the Commission. Such designation shall be public and may from time to time be changed by like writing similarly filed. Service of all administrative and judicial processes, notices, orders, decisions, and requirements may be made upon said manufacturer by service upon such designated agent with like effect as if made personally upon said manufacturer. In default of such designation, the Commission or any court of the United States may effect service of process upon such manufacturer by posting such process, notice, order, requirement, or decision in the office of the Executive Director of the Commission.

(*e*) No consumer product shall be imported into the United States unless the manufacturer of such product complies with the inspection and record keeping requirements of this Act and the Commission's regulations with respect thereto.

Exported Products

Section 22.–Regulations, orders, and standards issued by the Commission under this Act shall apply to consumer products intended for export unless the manufacturer of any consumer product subject thereto obtains and files with the Commission a certification by the responsible official of the country to which export is intended stating that the safety provisions of such regulations, orders, or standards are waived.

Antitrust Laws

Section 23.–Nothing contained in this Act shall be deemed to exempt from the antitrust laws of the United States any conduct that would otherwise be unlawful under such laws.

Prohibited Acts

Section 24(a).–It shall be unlawful for any person to:

(1) Manufacture for sale, sell, offer for sale, assemble, introduce or deliver for introduction in interstate commerce, or import into the United States any consumer product which is not in conformity with an applicable regulation or standard prescribed pursuant to this Act, if such product was manufactured after the effective date of such regulation or standard;

(2) Manufacture for sale, sell, offer for sale, assemble, introduce or deliver for introduction in interstate commerce, or import into the United States any consumer product which has been declared a banned hazardous product by the Commission;

(3) Fail or refuse to permit access to or copying of records, or fail or refuse to make reports or provide information, or fail or refuse to permit entry or inspection, as required under this Act;

(4) Fail to furnish a notification of any defect as required by Section 16, unless exempted from the requirements of that section by order of the Commission;

(5) Fail to comply with the requirements of Section 16(*h*) with respect to repair, replacement, or refund of certain consumer products;

(6) Fail to furnish a certificate required by Section 17 or issue a false certificate if such person in the exercise of due care has reason to know that such certificate is false or misleading in any material respect.

(*b*) Paragraphs (1) and (2) of Section (*a*) shall not apply to any person who, prior to the first purchase of such consumer product, holds a certificate issued by the manufacturer or importer of such consumer products to the effect that such consumer product conforms to all applicable federal regulations and safety standards, unless such person knows that such consumer product does not conform.

Civil Penalties

Section 25(*a*).–Any person who violates Section 24 of this Act shall be subject to a civil penalty not to exceed $2,000 for each such violation. A violation of Section 24(*a*)(1), (2), (4), (5) and (6) shall constitute a separate violation with respect to each consumer product involved, except that the maximum civil penalty shall not exceed $500,000 for any related series of violations. A violation of Section 24(*a*)(3) shall constitute a separate violation with respect to each failure or refusal to allow or perform an act required thereby. If such violation is a continuing one, each day of such violation shall constitute a separate offense, except that the maximum civil penalty shall not exceed $500,000 for any related series of violations.

(*b*) Any such civil penalty may be compromised by the Commission. In determining the amount of such penalty or whether it should be remitted or mitigated and in what amount, the appropriateness of such penalty to the size of the business of the person charged and the gravity of the violation shall be considered. The amount of such penalty when finally determined, or the amount agreed on compromise, may be deducted from any sums owing by the United States to the person charged.

Criminal Penalties

Section 26.–Any person who knowingly or willfully violates Section 24 of this Act shall be guilty of a misdemeanor and upon conviction thereof shall be fined not more than $50,000 or be imprisoned not more than 180 days or both, in the discretion of the court, provided that nothing herein shall limit other provisions of this Act.

Whenever any corporation knowingly or willfully violates Section 24 of this Act, any individual director, officer, or agent of such corporation who knowingly or willfully authorized, ordered, or performed any of the acts or practices constituting in whole or in part such violation shall be subject to such penalties, in addition to the corporation.

Enforcement

Section 27(a).–The district · courts of the United States shall have jurisdiction to enforce the provisions of Section 24 of this Act. Such actions may be brought in any district court of the United States for a district wherein any act, omission or transaction constituting the violation occurred, or in such court for the district wherein the defendant is found or transacts business. In such cases process may be served in any other district in which the defendant is an inhabitant or wherever the defendant may be found.

(*b*) The district courts of the United States shall have jurisdiction, for cause shown, to restrain violations of Section 24, except when such products are disposed of by returning them to the distributor or manufacturer from whom they were obtained.

(*c*) Any consumer product that fails to conform to an applicable consumer product safety standard or regulation or which has been declared a banned hazardous product pursuant to Section 14 of this Act, when introduced into or while in interstate commerce or while held for sale after shipment in interstate commerce shall be liable to be proceeded against on libel of information and condemned in any district court of the United States within the jurisdiction of which such consumer product is found. Proceedings in cases instituted under the authority of this section shall conform as nearly as possible to proceedings in rem in admirality. Whenever such proceedings involving identical consumer products are pending in two or more jurisdictions they shall be consolidated for trial by order of any such court upon application seasonably made by any party in interest upon notice to all other parties in interest.

Judicial Review

Section 28(a).–In a case of actual controversy over the validity of any Commission order

(1) Issuing, amending, or revoking a consumer product safety standard or regulation pursuant to Section 8 or 9, or

(2) Declaring a product to be a banned hazardous product under Section 14, or

(3) Granting or denying an exemption under Section 16, or

(4) Issuing, amending, or revoking any other final regulation or order under this Act,

any person who will be adversely affected by such regulation or order, including any consumer or group of consumers, may at any time prior to the 60th day after such order is issued file a petition with the United States Court of Appeals for the circuit wherein such person resides or has his principal place of business for judicial review of such order. A copy of the petition shall be forthwith transmitted by the clerk of the court to the Commission. The Commission thereupon shall file in the court the record of the proceedings upon which it based its order, as provided in Section 2112 of Title 23 of the United States Code.

(*b*) If the petitioner applies to the court for leave to adduce additional evidence and shows to the satisfaction of the court that such additional evidence is material and that there were reasonable grounds for the failure to adduce such evidence in the proceeding before the Commission. the court may order such additional evidence (and evidence in rebuttal thereof) to be taken before the Commission, or to be adduced upon a hearing, in such manner and upon such terms and conditions as to the court may seem proper. The Commission may modify its findings as to the facts, or make new findings by reason of the additional evidence so taken and shall file such modified or new findings, and its recommendation, if any, for the modification or setting aside of its original order, with the return of such additional evidence.

(*c*) Upon the filing of the petition referred to in subsection (*a*) of this section, the court shall have the jurisdiction to review the order in accordance with Sections 701-706 of Title 5 of the United States Code and to grant appropriate relief as provided in such sections.

(*d*) The judgment of the court affirming or setting aside, in whole or in part, any such order of the Commission shall be final, subject to review by the Supreme Court of the United States upon certiorari or certification as provided in Section 1254 of Title 28 of the United States Code.

(*e*) The remedies provided for in this section shall be in addition to and not in substitution for any other remedies provided by law.

(*f*) A certified copy of the transcript of the record and proceedings under this section shall be furnished by the Commission to any interested party at his request, upon payment of the costs thereof, and shall be admissible in any civil, criminal, exclusion of imports or other proceeding arising under or in respect of this title, irrespective of whether proceedings with respect to the order have previously been initiated or become final under subsection (*a*). The Commission may by regulation provide for furnishing such transcripts without charge to interested persons unable to pay costs therefor, where in the public interest.

Private Remedies

Section 29(a).—Compliance with consumer product safety standards, regulations, or orders under this Act shall not relieve any person from liability at common law or under state law to any other person.

(*b*) Evidence that an entire finished product complies with regulations or standards issued by the Commission shall be inadmissible in any private litigation except an action to recover treble damages pursuant to Section 30.

(*c*) The failure of the Commission to take any action or commence a proceeding with respect to the safety of a consumer product shall not be admissible in evidence in litigation at common law or under state law relating to such consumer product.

(*d*) Accident and investigation reports made under this Act by any officer, employee, or agent of the Commission shall be available for use in any civil, criminal or other judicial proceeding arising out of such accident. Any such officer, employee, or agent may be required to testify in such proceedings as to the facts developed in such investigations. Any such report shall be made available to the public in a manner which need not identify injured persons. All reports on research projects, demonstration projects, and other related activities shall be public information.

Suits for Treble Damages by Persons Injured

Section 30.—Any person who shall be injured by reason of any knowing or willful violation of a consumer product safety standard, regulation, or order issued by the Commission may sue therefor in any district court of the United States in the district in which the defendant resides or is found or has an agent, without respect to the amount in controversy, and shall recover threefold the damages sustained, and the cost of suit, including a reasonable attorney's fee.

Federal-State Cooperation

Section 31(a).–The Commission shall promote federal-state cooperation for the purpose of reducing or eliminating unreasonable risk of injury to the public from identified product hazards. In implementing such program the Commission may:

(i) Accept from any state or local authorities engaged in activities relating to health, safety, or consumer protection assistance in such functions as injury data collection, investigation, and educational programs, as well as other assistance in the administration and enforcement of this Act which it may request and which such states or localities may be able and willing to provide and, if so agreed, may pay in advance or otherwise for the reasonable cost of such assistance, and

(ii) Commission any qualified officer or employee of any state or local agency as an officer of the Commission for the purpose of conducting examinations, investigations, and inspections.

(*b*) In determining whether such proposed state and local programs are appropriate in implementing the purposes of this Act the Commission shall give favorable consideration to programs which establish separate state and local agencies to consolidate functions relating to product safety and other consumer protection activities.

Effect on State Standards

Section 32(a).–Whenever a consumer product safety standard or regulation established under this Act is in effect, no state or political subdivision of a state shall have any authority either to establish or to continue in effect any safety standard or regulation applicable to the same aspect of performance of such consumer product which is not identical to the federal standard.

(*b*) Nothing in this section shall be construed to prevent the Federal government or the government of any state or political subdivision thereof from establishing a safety requirement applicable to a consumer product for its own use if such requirement imposes a higher standard of performance than that required to comply with the otherwise applicable federal standard.

(*c*) The Commission may, upon application of a state or political subdivision thereof, exempt such application from the provisions of subsection (*a*) where a proposed standard or regulation (1) imposes a higher level of performance than the federal standard, (2) is required by compelling local conditions, and (3) does not unduly burden interstate commerce.

Definitions

Section 33(*a*).–"Commission" means the Consumer Product Safety Commission.

(*b*) "Consumer product" means any product, or component part, which affects interstate commerce and is customarily produced or distributed for sale (i) to a consumer for use in or around a household or residence, or (ii) for the personal use, consumption, or enjoyment of a consumer. Such term does not include hazards associated with such products to the extent such hazards are subject to duly promulgated regulations under the National Traffic and Motor Vehicle Safety Act of 1966 (15 U.S.C. 1381 et seq.), the Flammable Fabrics Act (15 U.S.C. 1191 et seq.), the Food, Drug and Cosmetic Act (21 U.S.C. 301 et seq.), the Federal Cigarette Labeling and Advertising Act (15 U.S.C. 1331 et seq.), the Federal Insecticide, Fungicide, and Rodenticide Act (7 U.S.C. 135 et seq.) and the Radiation Control for Health and Safety Act (42 U.S.C. 262 et seq.).

(*c*) "Identified product hazard" means a hazard associated with a consumer product which presents or may present an unreasonable risk of death or personal injury to the public and which the Commission describes in a regulation, standard, order, or complaint issued pursuant to this Act. The Commission may, in determining whether a hazard is an "identified product hazard," consider, among other factors frequency or potential frequency of injury, severity or potential severity of injury., number of products in use, potential for hazard reduction, awareness of hazard by consumers, increase of hazard with age of product, and hazard to nonusers, if it deems such factors applicable to its determination.

(*d*) "Consumer product safety standard" means a minimum safety standard relating to a consumer product, promulgated by the Commission pursuant to Sections 8 or 9 of this Act for the purpose of preventing or reducing risk of death or personal injury from an identified product hazard. A consumer product safety standard establishes the minimum acceptable safety level for a consumer product. Compliance with a consumer product safety standard may or may not be evidence of adequate care to avoid death or personal injury caused by a specific consumer product.

(*e*) "Manufacturer" means any person that manufactures or assembles consumer products or imports or distributes consumer products manufactured or assembled elsewhere.

(*f*) "Person" means an individual, partnership, corporation, association, or any other form of business enterprise.

(*g*) "State" includes a state of the United States, the District of Columbia, the Commonwealth of Puerto Rico, the Virgin Islands, and Guam.

(*h*) "Interstate commerce" means commerce between any place in a state and any place in another state, or between places in the same state through another state.

(*i*) "Importation" includes reimportation of consumer products manufactured or processed, in whole or in part, in the United States.

(*j*) Use of the singular includes the plural wherever appropriate.

Interpretation and Separability

Section 34.–The provisions of this Act shall be held to be in addition to and not in substitution for or limitation of the provisions of any other law. If any provision of this Act or the application thereof to any person or circumstances is held invalid, the remainder of the Act and the application of such provision to any other person or circumstances shall not be affected thereby.

Authorization of Appropriations

Section 35.–There are hereby authorized to be appropriated for the purpose of carrying out the provisions of this Act the following sums:

$5,000,000 for the fiscal year ending June 30, 1971;

$7,500,000 for the fiscal year ending June 30, 1972; and

$10,000,000 for the fiscal year ending June 30, 1973.

The foregoing sums do not apply to facilities to be constructed pursuant to Section 5 (*g*) of this Act.

Effective Date

Section 36.–This Act shall take effect on the 60th day following the date of its enactment.

APPENDIX C

REPORT OF SENATE COMMERCE COMMITTEE

92D CONGRESS *2d Session*	SENATE	REPORT No. 92–749

CONSUMER SAFETY ACT OF 1972

APRIL 13 (legislative day, APRIL 12), 1972.—Ordered to be printed

Filed, under authority of the order of the Senate of MARCH 24, 1972

Mr. MAGNUSON, from the Committee on Commerce, submitted the following

REPORT

together with

MINORITY AND ADDITIONAL VIEWS

The Committee on Commerce, to which was referred the bill (S. 3419) to protect consumers against unreasonable risk of injury from hazardous products, and for other purposes, having considered the same, reports favorably thereon without amendment and recommends that the bill do pass. An original bill (S. 3419) is reported in lieu of S. 983 and S. 1797 which were considered by the Committee.

SUMMARY AND PURPOSE

It is the purpose of S. 3419 (1) to create a new, independent agency within the Federal structure which has undiluted responsibility for preventing consumers from being exposed to unsafe foods, drugs, and other consumer products; and (2) to consolidate within the new Agency various consumer product safety activities now being handled by a number of different government entities. In order to accomplish this two-fold purpose, the proposed bill creates an independent Consumer Safety Agency, transfers to that Agency the present food, drug, and product safety activities of the Secretary of Health, Education, and Welfare, the Secretary of Commerce, and the Federal Trade Commission and repeals various consumer safety laws directed at particular products or specific hazards and replaces them with a single, comprehensive consumer product safety law capable of reaching any consumer product in the marketplace presenting an unreasonable risk of injury.[1]

Background

That the consumer has a right to purchase consumer products in the marketplace which do not present an unreasonable risk of injury or death is not disputed. Nor is the government's role in protecting that right disputed. For more than half a century Federal, State, and local governments have been involved in setting safety standards for certain consumer products. The government's historic concern for the safety of foods and drugs testifies to the traditional nature of the consumer's right to safety and the government's longstanding protection of it.

In recent years the Federal Government has become more involved in the protection of the consumer's right to safety for several reasons. In the first place, the technological revolution has brought to the American consumer a variety of new products employing new energy sources with potential for injury which is both greater and less easily comprehended. Secondly, the number of consumer products has increased dramatically, thereby increasing the consumer's exposure to risk of injury from consumer products. In addition, continuing product development has demonstrated that previously acceptable risk levels may no longer be reasonable in light of available safety technology.[2]

The increase in government involvement in consumer product safety is also the result of a growing concern over the quality, as opposed to the mere quantity, of consumer products available in the marketplace. There is a final reason for an increased government involvement in the protection of the consumer's right to safety. Neither self-interest nor competition has impelled manufacturers to produce products that are safe. The reasons have been well stated by Philip Elman, former Commissioner of the Federal Trade Commission:

> The answer, very simply, is that competition and voluntary actions of businessmen do not always suffice to safeguard the public

---

[1] In addition to the food and drug safety program transfers, other food and drug regulatory programs presently administered by the Food and Drug Administration are transferred from the Food and Drug Administration to the new Consumer Safety Agency. In other words, its regulatory functions will not be confined to matters of safety only. Under authority of the Food, Drug and Cosmetic Act, agency officials would not only examine the safety but also the efficacy of foods and drugs. The new Consumer Safety Agency would also be responsible for administering food, drug and cosmetic aspects of the Fair Packaging and Labeling Act, the Import Tea Act, the Filled Milk Act, and the Import Milk Act.

[2] In its Final Report the National Commission on Product Safety estimated that 20 million Americans are injured each year as a result of incidents connected with household consumer products:

"Of the total, 110,000 are permanently disabled and 30,000 are killed. A significant number could have been spared if more attention had been paid to hazard reduction. The annual cost to the Nation of product-related injuries may exceed $5.5 billion.

"The exposure to consumers to unreasonable consumer product hazards is excessive by any standard of measurement. (See Final Report at page 1.)"

It is important to note that these figures do not include injuries resulting from automobile accidents.

In hearings before the Senate Commerce Committee, Arnold B. Elkind, Chairman of the National Commission on Product Safety estimated that approximately 20 percent of the injuries associated with the use of consumer products could be prevented. He stated: "This translates into 6,000 lives, 22,000 permanent cripples, 4,000,000 injuries, and $1.1 billion in treasure that could be saved each year by an effective system for making products safe to use." (Senate hearings at page 142.)

Although estimates of injury prevention resulting solely from the setting of product safety standards are estimated at only five percent. (See Senate hearings at page 515).

> interest. Competition does not inevitably take the form of a rivalry to produce the safest product. Indeed, the competitive struggle may sometimes lead to a "shaving" of the costs of manufacture involving some sacrifice of safety. Nor does competition always reward, in the form of greater volume and higher profits, the manufacturer who trys to sell "safety" as a feature of his product. (Heffron report at 3.)

During the so-called Consumer Decade of the 60's the Federal Government's increasing concern over the consumer's right to safety was demonstrated through the consideration and enactment of a number of different categorical product safety laws. Beginning with the landmark National Traffic and Motor Vehicles Safety Act of 1966, Congress considered and passed the Child Protection Amendments of 1966, the Flammable Fabrics Act Amendments of 1967, the Gas Pipeline Safety Act of 1968, the Radiation Control for Health and Safety Act of 1968, the Child Protection and Toy Safety Act of 1969, and the Poison Prevention Packaging Act of 1970. Each of these legislative endeavors was directed toward a particular product category that had received some public notoriety prior to legislative treatment. Each authorized an existing agency of government to set appropriate standards of safety for the particular product. For the most part, the concept of "unreasonable risks" was to guide the standard-setter in fulfilling his statutory safety responsibility, but the standard-setter was to establish standards that were technically and economically feasible.

As early as 1967 those legislators responsible for the creation of the categorical consumer safety laws recognized that a continued piecemeal approach to consumer product safety might not adequately protect the right of the American consumer to safety in the products he purchased. Therefore, those legislators proposed the creation of a National Commission on Product Safety to survey consumer product safety problems in general and to make recommendations concerning the government's proper role in securing the consumer's right to safety.

As a study commission, the National Commission on Product Safety was notably successful. It publicized the need for increased government involvement in the setting of product safety standards by conducting informational hearings on a variety of subjects in every section of the country. As a result of its hearings on toy safety, the stopgap Child Protection and Toy Safety Act of 1969 was recommended to Congress, considered, and enacted into law.

The final report of the National Commission on Product Safety recommended that the government chart a new course in its effort to provide consumers safe products. Rather than continuing to pass piecemeal legislation, the Commission recommended creation of an independent Product Safety Agency to establish standards of reasonable risks for all consumer products.

Despite the legislative efforts mentioned above, the Commission concluded:

> Consumers assume that the Federal Government exercises broad regulatory authority in the interest of their safety. And yet the short answer * * * is that Federal authority to curb hazards in consumer products is virtually nonexistent.
>
> Federal product safety legislation consists of a series of isolated acts treating specific hazards and narrow product categories. No

> government agency possesses general authority to ban products which harbor unreasonable risks or to require that consumer products conform to the minimum safety standards.
>
> Such limited Federal authority as does exist is scattered among many agencies. Jurisdiction over a single category of products may be shared by as many as four different departments of agencies. Moreover, where it exists, Federal product safety regulation is burdened by unnecessary procedural obstacles, circumscribed investigative powers, inadequate and ill-fitting sanctions, bureaucratic lassitude, timid administration, bargain-basement budgets, distorted priorities, and misdirected technical resources. (Final report at 2.)

The Commission recommended that "the Congress of the United States enact an omnibus Consumer Product Safety Act committing the authority and resources of the Federal Government to the elimination of unreasonable product hazards" and "that an independent Consumer Product Safety Commission be established as a Federal agency concerned exclusively with the safety of consumer products."

The National Commission on Product Safety strongly recommended that any new product safety authority be independent. Discussing existing product safety programs, the Commission stated:

> The reasons for their weaknesses include lack of adequate funding and staffing because of competition with other deserving programs within an Agency; lack of vigor in enforcing the law caused by an absence of authority and independence of some Federal administrators; and a low priority assigned to programs of low visibility.
>
> Of course, not all Federal safety programs which are part of larger agencies exhibit these symptoms. The broad based Federal Trade Commission displayed admirable vigor in proceeding against health hazards of cigarettes . . .
>
> Notwithstanding these efforts, when a Federal agency must take up substantial and controversial issues of consumer safety and economics, we believe it needs independent status. (Final report at 5.)

While the National Commission on Product Safety was conducting its investigation, the Senate Commerce Committee was holding legislative oversight hearings to evaluate the success of the various safety acts upon which it had favorably reported. For example, the Committee held extensive oversight hearings on the National Traffic and Motor Vehicle Safety Act and Flammable Fabrics Act.

Building upon the final report of the National Commission of Product Safety and the investigations of the Committee, Chairman Magnuson, together with Senator Moss and others, introduced first in June 1970, S. 4054 and then in February 1971, S. 983 a bill to create an independent Product Safety Commission. This bill was identical to the legislation recommended by the National Commission. In response to this legislative initiative, the Administration offered an alternative proposal (S. 1797) which would have extended the product safety authority of the Federal Government for most consumer products but would have retained that authority within the existing Food and Drug Administration of the Department of Health, Education, and Welfare.

In July 1970, the Committee held 10 days of hearings on these two proposals to expand the government's role in consumer product safety. In general, industry witnesses supported the Administration's bill because of its greater reliance on voluntary standards as a basis for Federal mandatory safety standards. Consumer organizations, in general, supported the bill creating an independent commission. At the outset of the hearings the President wrote to Chairman Magnuson about his plans for reshaping the Food and Drug Administration into a Consumer Safety Agency within the present Department of Health, Education, and Welfare. (See letter from President Nixon to Chairman Magnuson in Appendix to Minority Views.)

After studying the hearings, the reports of the National Commission on Product Safety, the Committee's own oversight hearings, and other studies of Federal product safety efforts, Chairman Magnuson presented to the Committee for its consideration a revised bill incorporating many of the features of both the Administration's proposal and the National Commission's proposal for a comprehensive product safety statutory authority. Building upon the concept of "independence" advocated by the National Commission on Product Safety and the Administration's own proposal to create a consumer safety agency within the Department of Health, Education, and Welfare, the new bill provided for the creation of an independent Consumer Safety Agency similar in design and concept to the Environmental Protection Agency. After careful executive consideration by the Committee, a bill following the basic design suggested by Chairman Magnuson was ordered to be reported from the Committee by a vote of 17 to 1. The bill was designed to meet the following needs.

NEEDS

(1) *Resource Commitment*

Without the proper resource commitment no Federal consumer safety effort can succeed. The Agency must request the money and personnel it needs to carry out its assigned missions; the Office of Management and Budget must assign sufficient priority to the government's safety mission; and the Congress must appropriate the necessary funds whether or not the executive branch has requested such funds. In the Heffron Report of the National Commission on Product Safety the following observation was made:

> While Congress has committed vast paper power to agency discretion, it has failed to provide agency resources commensurate with the regulatory problems presented. Only one full time employee within the Food and Drug Administration's Bureau of Compliance has been responsible for enforcing the banning or labeling of thousands of potentially hazardous products regulated under the Hazardous Substances Act * * *
>
> The agencies have also contributed to their own ineffectiveness. For years, the Food and Drug Administration failed to make open and public demands for adequate appropriations to implement the hazardous substances legislation * * * (at 1 and 2)

There is a certain irony in the above observation. Nowhere is mentioned the omnipresent role of the Office of Management and Budget in resource allocation decisions. In most product safety programs the Congress has matched or exceeded the budget requests of the Administration. Nevertheless, resource commitment to consumer product safety has been wholly inadequate in the past, and no amount of government reorganization or increased statutory power will produce greater consumer protection unless there is a commensurate increase in money and competent, committed personnel.

(2) *Detection of Products Causing Injury or Death*

In order to take effective action against products in the marketplace which are injuring consumers, the Federal Government must establish a sophisticated injury detection system which indicates which products are involved in how many accidents and what kind of injuries they are producing. This data base is absolutely essential if the Federal Government is to order its priorities and move in the first instance to eliminate those products which have presented or are presenting the most unreasonable risk of injury or death.

The Federal Government should not, however, depend upon the "after-the-fact" detection of products involved in accidents. It must not, for example, wait for the burning of thousands of small children before it moves to establish flammability standards for children's sleepwear. The government must develop a capability for identifying hazardous elements, conditions and potential accidents; the significance of their potential effect; and recommendations for safety requirements to eliminate or control the hazards *before* these hazards expose consumers to injury. The Federal Government must cooperate with the manufacturers of consumer products to insure that, in the design stage, hazards are properly identified and minimized. By having the authority to require a safety analysis study of marketed products, the Federal Government would be better able to meet the need for prior detection of products presenting unreasonable risk of injury or death.

(3) *Determination of which products are presenting unreasonable risk of injury or death*

Many products in the marketplace present risk of injury or death. The need is to differentiate between those products whose risks of injury or death are reasonable or those products whose risks are unreasonable. A determination of unreasonable risk must be predicated upon the following factors: 1) the degree of the anticipated injury; 2) the frequency of such injury; 3) the effect upon the performance or availability of a product when the degree of the anticipated injury or the frequency of such industry is reduced; and 4) an evaluation of the utility of the product, in absolute terms and in varying modes of risk. For example, it is possible to anticipate that a knife will cause injury; that to reduce its injury causing potential by blunting it would interfere with its purpose, namely cutting; and that knives are essential for a number of purposes. An overall evaluation of the knife, then, might lead one to conclude that it does not present an unreasonable risk of injury. However, such a general conclusion does not preclude a determination that a particular knife designed for a particular purpose presents an unreasonable risk of injury. Suppose the existence of a child's silverware set which has a knife with a very acute point and a razor sharp blade. Such a knife might present an unreasonable risk of injury or death. In any event, there is a need for the Federal Government to consider all factors relative to a determination of which products are presenting an unreasonable risk of injury or death and then to take appropriate action.

(4) *Elimination of products presenting unreasonable risk of injury or death*

There is a need for the government to have information regarding the safety characteristics of particular consumer products. A safety analysis can serve as an important preventive tool in the elimination of unsafe consumer products. By requiring the manufacturer of a particular class of consumer products to consider the safety implications of those products, the government can advance to a considerable degree the cause of safety by encouraging the voluntary removal of hazards associated with a given product.

There is also a need to create a responsive, not procedurally burdensome, standard-setting authority which mandates minimum safety performance standards for a consumer product or class of consumer products. Such standard setting authority must draw upon the scientific community for its expertise in the design of a standard which sets the appropriate performance level, which is based upon test methods which are reproducible, and which covers all relevant aspects of the safety performance of the particular product. It is absolutely essential that the standard-setting process be completed within a reasonable period of time and that undue delay be resisted.

In addition to the need for authority to set minimum safety performance standards, there is a need for authority to ban products from sale when the setting of minimum safety performance standard is not practicable. The Federal Government should also have authority to take emergency action to remove immediately from the marketplace products likely to cause injury or death during the period when performance standards or orders to ban are being considered.

The need to eliminate products presenting unreasonable risks cannot be satisfied without bestowing authority upon the Federal government to recall those products which are manufactured in violation of any applicable consumer product safety standards or orders to ban or which contain manufacturing defects which render a normally safe product unsafe. The Federal Government also needs the authority to utilize the electronic and other media to warn consumers of defective or noncomplying products and to require the repurchase of those products which are defective or noncomplying.

Recall, however, is expensive, time consuming, and only partially effective. Therefore, the Federal Government needs a vigorous compliance program to insure that products meet applicable safety standards and thereby do not present unreasonable risk of injury. Such compliance programs should include inspection of manufacturing facilities, compliance testing of finished products, and monitoring of quality control procedures. In those situations where existing quality control procedures have been shown deficient, then the Federal Government should have authority to prescribe proper quality control procedures.

Finally, in order to insure the elimination of products presenting unreasonable risks of injury or death, there is need to apply strong sanction to those manufacturers who produce products not in compliance with applicable product safety standards or who fail to comply with other requirements of the product safety program. There is a need to provide for criminal sanctions for willfull violations and for strong civil penalties for other than willfull violations. In this way, the Federal Government will be able to exercise both the carrot and the stick to insure that American consumers are protected against the marketing of unsafe products.

(5) *The responsiveness of the government to its product safety mission*

There is an urgent need to make the Federal Government responsive to its mission to protect consumers against unsafe products. *Independence* is a crucial element in fulfilling such a need. An independent agency with publicly accountable decision makers is able to make determinations as to which products present unreasonable risk of injury or death unfettered by political dictates, self-interested industry pressure, or blind consumer zeal.

Independence alone, however, does not automatically assure responsiveness to the legislative mission. As mentioned above, the Agency must be adequately funded and staffed. It must also make visible decisions based upon input from all constituencies. In other words, both consumer and industry points of view must be made publicly known to the decision maker, and the public accountability for the decision must be placed upon the person actually making it. A prerequisite to meaningful participation in Agency activities by both consumer and industry groups is availability of information. It is therefore important that the Agency make accessible to interested persons reports, documents, communications, studies and all other materials (other than competitively harmful information) which would enable them to monitor and participate in all proceedings in an informed manner.

There is a final need to insure the responsiveness of the government to its product safety mission. In addition to the judicial review of Agency action, there is a need to subject Agency inaction to judicial review through the mandamus process. Unfortunately, the false distinctions created by the thaumaturgical words "ministerial" and "discretionary" presently impose limitations on mandamus in needed areas. For example, the determination of which products present unreasonable risk of injury or death is "discretionary" and therefore not subject to mandamus. But this is the very area of decisionmaking which should be reviewable if the Federal Government is to be responsive to its mission of protecting consumers against unreasonable risk of injury or death. Therefore, it is necessary to limitedly expand the mandamus action so that it can reach into certain carefully defined discretionary areas.

Brief Description

Title I of S. 3419 establishes an independent Consumer Safety Agency with responsibility for the safety and efficacy of food, drugs, and consumer products. The new Agency would be headed by an Administrator appointed for a term of five years. The Administrator would be the coordinator of the Agency and handle all enforcement. Food, drug, or consumer product safety standards would be set by separate Commissioners appointed by the President to serve at his pleasure. There would be a Commissioner of Foods and Nutrition, a Commissioner of Drugs, and a Commissioner of Product Safety. The appointment of the Administrator and each of the Commissioners would have to be confirmed by the Senate.

Several innovative provisions designed to remedy shortcomings in existing government agencies are set forth in Title I. For example, the bill creates an Office of Consumer Information and Representation headed by a Director appointed by the Administrator for a term concurrent with that of the Administrator. The Director of the Office of Consumer Information and Representation is required to establish a Consumer Safety Information Center capable of responding to consumers' requests for safety information. The Director would also conduct consumer education programs designed to minimize injury resulting from the use of consumer products. He would also be responsible for insuring public access to information concerning pending or completed actions of the Consumer Safety Agency. To insure that the consumer point of view is properly presented to the decision makers in the Agency, the Director is empowered to retain counsel to present the consumer point of view in Agency proceedings. It is anticipated that such attorney would be retained from the Consumer Protection Agency if and when it were established.

Another innovative provision in S. 3419 permits individuals to bring a mandamus action against the Agency upon a showing that persons in the Agency, by their acts or omissions, have exposed individuals to foods, drugs, devices, or consumer products presenting unreasonable risks of injury or death. The Federal district court would have jurisdiction to entertain such an action and order performance or cessation of performance, as appropriate, if it finds that any person or persons in the Agency have by any act or omission exposed individuals to foods, drugs, devices, or consumer products presenting unreasonable risks of injury or death.

In addition to this "mandamus-like" action for insuring Agency responsibility, the bill provides that no former Agency employee may assist any other person in any transaction involving the Agency if he at any time personally participated in such transaction during his Agency employment. It also prohibits a person from participating in any transaction involving the Agency which was under his responsibility but in which he was not directly involved for a period of 18 months following such transaction. Unlike existing conflict of interest statutes (see, e.g., 18 U.S.C. 207), the prohibitions in the conflict of interest section of S. 3419 are civil, not criminal.

Title I of S. 3419 also provides for the creation of a Joint Scientific Committee chaired by a Director of Science to be appointed by the Administrator. The purpose of the committee is to advise the Administrator and the Commissioners on technical matters and make recommendations for the soliciting of outside expert scientific opinion. Title I also requires the Administrator to file detailed annual reports with the Congress and contains a section designed to assure broad public access to information.

Title II

Title II of S. 3419 transfers the functions of the Secretary of Health, Education, and Welfare administered through the Food and Drug Administration to the Administrator of the Consumer Safety Agency. In addition to transfers of function, all personnel, property, records, obligations, commitments, and so forth, including HEW overhead, which are used primarily by, or allocated to, the Food and Drug Administration are also transferred to the new Agency. In transferring personnel, Civil Service status is preserved, but the Administrator is permitted to make new assignments of responsibility as he deems appropriate.

Title II also requires the Administrator to delegate certain aspects of the authority transferred to him to each of the respective Commissioners. For example, the food responsibilities under the Food, Drug and Cosmetic Act would be transferred to the Commissioner of Foods and Nutrition. The Administrator, however, would retain all enforcement authority.

Finally, Title II would repeal the Federal Hazardous Substances Act, Flammable Fabrics Act, the cosmetic chapter of the Food, Drug and Cosmetic Act, the Radiation Control for Health and Safety Act, the Poison Prevention Packaging Act, and the Refrigerator Safety Act. Existing orders or regulations promulgated under authority of these acts would be retained and administered by the Commissioner of Product Safety until such time as they were amended or superseded by authority granted under Title III. In other words, there would be no hiatus between ongoing consumer protection programs and new consumer protection programs when creating the new Agency.

Title III

Title III of S. 3419 sets forth the comprehensive consumer product authority conferred upon the Consumer Safety Agency. Basically, the Commissioner is given authority to set product safety standards for all consumer products presenting unreasonable risk of injury or death. The Commissioner would be empowered to proceed as follows:

(1) On the basis of injury information provided by the Injury Information Clearinghouse, his own accident investigation work, or risk-based analysis (including engineering data) the Commissioner would determine that there was a need for a product safety standard and initiate a proceeding to promulgate such a standard.

(2) The next step would be the development of a proposed product safety standard, and such development could be facilitated by the use of an existing voluntary standard or by contracting with interested parties to develop a proposed standard.

(3) A proposed standard would be offered and comments would be received.

(4) A final standard would be promulgated.

The product safety standard would draw the line between reasonable and unreasonable risk of injury presented by consumer products or classes of consumer products. Products whose risks could not be made reasonable by the setting of a product safety standard could be banned by the Commissioner. In addition, the Commissioner would be empowered to request the court to take emergency action to remove a product presenting an unreasonable risk of injury pending the completion of proceedings authorized by the bill.

The bill also authorizes the Commissioner to request manufacturers to make safety analysis reports on their products to insure that hazards associated with such products are minimized. The Commissioner would establish by regulation the criteria that would have to be followed in preparing any safety analysis report.

The technical resources of the private sector could also be used to assist the Commissioner in setting appropriate product safety standards. Such resources should be utilized to the maximum extent possible, under scrutiny of the Agency, to solve product safety problems efficiently and effectively.

Compliance with product safety standards would be facilitated by provisions in the bill which authorize the Commissioner to inspect manufacturing operations, conduct compliance tests, and, when necessary, prescribe quality control procedures which would insure that consumer products subject to product safety standards complied with any applicable standards following their manufacture.

The Commissioner of Product Safety would also be authorized, following a formal hearing, to order the recall of consumer products presenting unreasonable risk of injury or death when they failed to comply with any applicable standard or when they contained a manufacturing defect. To facilitate such recall, the Commissioner would be empowered to require the use of the electronic and other media when necessary to protect the public health and safety to communicate to consumers the fact that certain consumer products were being recalled.

To further insure compliance with requirements established under authority of Title III, S. 3419 prescribes a variety of sanctions. For example, any manufacturer who willfully produces a consumer product with the knowledge that it does not comply with any applicable product safety standard may be criminally prosecuted. Any manufacturer who knowingly produces a product not in compliance with the product safety standard may be subject to civil fine. The Administrator is also given authority to seek injunctive relief to prevent violations of the Act.

Private sanctions are also provided for in S. 3419. A consumer may seek an injunction in Federal court to prevent the manufacture of a product not in compliance with applicable product safety standards. In addition, a consumer whose injuries exceed $10,000 as a result of a knowing violation of a product safety standard would be able to sue the manufacturer in Federal court to recover damages resulting from injuries sustained by such non-conforming consumer product.

The preemption section of S. 3419 provides that Federal consumer product safety standards would preempt any inconsistent State standards. The preemption section, however, permits a State to petition the Consumer Safety Agency for the right to set a higher standard of care upon a showing that such higher standard is necessary to protect the public health and safety of the citizens of that State.

A final provision in the new bill treats the following problem. In the past when product safety standards have been promulgated to take effect in six months or a year, some manufacturers have drastically increased their production of products which do not meet the soon-to-be-required product safety standard. These "stockpiled" products have then been distributed after the effective date of the standard. A provision in the bill would prevent this stockpiling by prohibiting any drastic increase in the quantity of products manufactured between the date of setting a new standard and its effective date.

In sum, S. 3419 recognizes that the issue of consumer safety encompasses not only hazardous household products but also food, drugs and devices. Therefore, government action designed to insure the production of safe foods, drugs and other consumer products is centralized in one independent Agency which is to be innovatively structured and responsively operated. Finally, a comprehensive consumer product safety legislative authority is created to replace the present piecemeal legislation which inadequately and inconsistently attempts to protect the consumer's right to safety.

Section-by-Section Analysis

TITLE I

Definitions (Section 101)

"Consumer product" is a term central to the operation of the comprehensive product safety authority set forth in Title III of the bill. The term prescribes the scope of the Product Safety Commissioner's authority to move against products in the marketplace. Because the product safety authority is designed to be comprehensive in its scope, the definition of "consumer product" by necessity is comprehensive. Rather than attempt to catalogue those items included within the concept of "consumer product," paragraph (1) of section 101 catalogues those products which are not "consumer products."

By definition a "consumer product" is a product produced or distributed for sale to an individual for his personal use, consumption, or enjoyment in or around a household or residence (including a residential farm), a school, in recreation, or otherwise. To qualify as a "consumer product," therefore, the product must be one capable of production or distribution for sale to an individual but it is not necessary that the product actually be sold. For example, new razor blades distributed free of charge as a promotion would be considered "consumer products" under the terms of S. 3419, or a product offered "free" but requiring other consideration would be a consumer product. The definition does not include products produced solely by an individual for his own personal use, consumption or enjoyment.

The "personal use, consumption, or enjoyment" focus in the definition is intended to differentiate the "consumer" product from the "industrial" product. Where there is overlap, the definition would pick up the "industrial" product personally used. However, such product might be excluded if it were subject to safety regulation under the Occupational Safety and Health Act of 1970. To the extent that action is taken against a "consumer product" which is used "in or around a household or residence" and also in a factory, the risk evaluation for that product would be made in terms of its use in or around a residence and not its use in the factory.

There is one category of products which the bill expressly excludes from the definition of "consumer product". That product is tobacco. Because the safety regulation of tobacco is the subject of separate legislation before the Committee and because hearings are being held on that legislation, the Committee has decided not to include tobacco under the general safety law.

Other products excluded from the definition of "consumer product" include products "subject to regulation" under the National Traffic and Motor Vehicle Safety Act of 1966, aircraft or other aeronautical products "subject to safety regulations" by the Federal Aviation Administration, foods, drugs, or devices subject to safety regulation under the Food, Drug and Cosmetic Act, products "subject to safety regulations" under the Federal Insecticide, Fungicide, and Rodenticide Act, the Occupational Safety and Health Act of 1970, the Gas Pipeline Safety Act, the Atomic Energy Act of 1954, and vessels, or appertenances and equipment subject to various laws administered by the Department in which the Coast Guard is operating, including the Federal Boat Safety Act of 1971. It should be noted that cosmetics are to be treated as "consumer products" (See Section 204 (a) *infra*).

The language "subject to safety regulation" indicates that products capable of being regulated under one of the enumerated acts but not actually "subject to safety regulation" can be reached by the Product Safety Commissioner when in response to a written inquiry to the appropriate agency it is ascertained that such products are not "subject to safety regulation." For example, the Secretary of Transportation may not have promulgated safety standards for mini-bikes which might be considered "motor vehicles" under the National Traffic and Motor Vehicle Safety Act. If the Commissioner on Product Safety found these bikes were presenting unreasonable risk of injury or death, he could promulgate a safety standard on them if he ascertained from the Secretary of Transportation that mini-bikes were not "subject to regulation."

Because many inquiries concerning mobile home safety have been directed to the Committee, it would seem appropriate to express the Committee's intent with respect to mobile home safety. It is the Committee's intent with respect to mobile home safety. It is the Committee's intent to include mobile homes under the definition of "consumer product."

Much confusion has been generated by the words in the definition of "consumer product" which seem to single out electronic products for particular consideration. That is not the purpose of defining consumer products to include electronic products. The purpose for the specific reference to "electronic product" is to insure that even though the Radiation Control for Health and Safety Act is repealed there is the same authority in title III to take action against such products. Therefore, the definition of "electronic product" and "electronic product radiation" are incorporated verbatim from the Radiation Control for Health and Safety Act and referenced in the definition of "consumer product." The Committee does not intend non-consumer electronic products to be subject to regulation for other than radiation hazard.

Paragraph (2) of section 101 defines "commerce" to mean commerce among, between, or within the several States. This term is relevant in determining the jurisdictional reach of the comprehensive product safety authority set forth in title III of the Act. For example, under section 315 it is unlawful for any person to manufacture for sale or lease, "in commerce," any consumer product which does not comply with an applicable consumer product safety standard. Products manufactured for sale or lease only in one State are covered under this bill because of the affect that such products have on interstate commerce.

"Consumer product safety standard" means a minimum standard promulgated under authority of the bill which is designed to prevent a product from presenting an unreasonable risk of injury or death. This definition read in conjunction with section 319(c), establishes Federal Government action as "minimum" action which is not necessarily the optimum level of safety and therefore not conclusive evidence of "due care" in product liability litigation.

As mentioned above, the definition of "electronic product" is incorporated verbatim from the Radiation Control for Health and Safety Act (42 USC 262 et seq.). Together with the definition of "electronic product radiation," the term provides that products presently included within the ambit of the Radiation Control for Health and Safety Act are covered under title III of this bill.

Paragraph (6) of section 101 defines "injury" to mean "*accidental* harm (including illness) produced by biologic, chemical, thermal, mechanical, electrical, or radiological agents . . ." This definition would include all harm suffered by humans except that which is intentionally inflicted.

The definition of "State" has been expanded to include all of those territories, possessions, and commonwealths in which the United States has a direct responsibility for protecting the well-being of the inhabitants. This definition should be read in conjunction with the definition of "commerce" in paragraph (2) of section 101.

The definition of "unreasonable risk of injury presented by a consumer product" in paragraph (8) of section 101 highlights those factors which are relevant when drawing the line between risks which are reasonable and those which are unreasonable. The definition sets forth a balancing test which emphasizes the primacy of health safety factors. Two particular measures of public health and safety are to be considered: 1) the degree of *anticipated* injury, and 2) the frequency of such injury. In those situations where either the degree of anticipated injury or the frequency of such injury can be reduced without affecting the "performance" or "availability" of that class of consumer product, then almost any risk capable of producing injury becomes unwarranted. When "performance" or "availability" are affected, then a balancing of competing interests must be undertaken.

The word "performance" focuses attention on the functional impediments which safety standards or actions may impose. For example, a safety standard covering the sharpness of a knife may impinge upon its performance. The word "availability" focuses attention on those matters related to additional costs of safety, the impact of that cost on the frequency of purchase, and the impact upon the consumer if reduction in risk would adversely affect the consumer's decision to purchase. For example, in determining whether clacker balls present an unreasonable risk of injury or death, the Commissioner would exercise his judgment as to the likely impediments to performance which a product safety standard would impose. He might determine that there would be no impediment to performance. He would then determine whether there might be additional costs associated with the manufacture of clacker balls in order to reduce the risk. Suppose he determines there would be added costs. The added costs might affect the number of clacker balls sold but their overall usefulness, he might determine, would not justify the existence of additional risks to children simply to avoid any detrimental impact upon availability. Having gone through this analysis, he might decide to set a rather stringent performance standard on clacker balls. On the other hand, a product such as a knife, which in absolute terms might contain the same hazards as the original clacker balls, might not contain "unreasonable" risks because of the utility of the product, the awareness of the consumer to the risks involved in using the knife, and the type of person who is likely to be exposed to the risk. Thus, the definition of "consumer product presenting unreasonable risk of injury or death" is intended to guide the Commissioner of Product Safety in his attempt to define the line between the reasonable and unreasonable risk of injury or death. Whenever specific data or other information are available they must be reflected in his decision, but lack of such data or information would not preclude him from acting on the basis of reasonable judgment.

The definition of "use" in paragraph (9) of Section 101, read in conjunction with the Commissioner's authority to promulgate standards for consumer products, defines the ambit of risk that the Product Safety Commissioner is to consider in determining which products present unreasonable risk of injury and in formulating appropriate action to eliminate those products. (See section 302.) The definition of "use" includes exposure to and any normal use. In addition, it includes reasonably foreseeable misuse. The ambit of risk, then, extends beyond exposure and normal use to those risks presented by consumer products being misused if such misuse is "reasonably foreseeable." For example, a child's doll in normal use is cuddled and loved. But it is reasonably foreseeable that such a product can be misused—that a child may tug at the hair ribbon of the doll, thereby exposing a dangerous, sharp pin. In such a case, the Commissioner may determine there is an unreasonable risk of injury associated with the use (including reasonably foreseeable misuse) of the doll which has a hair ribbon attached with a long, sharp pin.

In paragraph (10) of Section 101 the term "risk-based analysis" is defined. This is the first time that the definition has been included in product safety legislation. In effect, it introduces a new approach to product safety regulation—an approach which identifies hazardous elements, conditions and potential accidents, determines the significance of their potential effect, and provides, through the exercise of reasonable judgment, an analytical basis for design and procedural safety requirements to eliminate or control hazards *prior to the time* that these hazards produce actual injury or death. Although a new concept in the area of consumer product safety regulation, this type of analysis has been used in manufacturing endeavors to insure the safety of products when first introduced. For example, the aerospace industry has incorporated this kind of analysis in their manufacturing processes to insure the production of safe space equipment in the first instance.

Establishment of the Agency (Section 102)

Section 102 of the bill creates an independent Consumer Safety Agency and establishes within that Agency a Commission of Foods and Nutrition, a Commission of Drugs, and a Commission of Product Safety, each to be headed by a separate Commissioner.

Administrator (Section 103)

The new Consumer Safety Agency is to be headed by an Administrator appointed, with the advice and consent of the Senate, for a term of five years. The Administrator may be reappointed only once in succession.

The Administrator is empowered to coordinate [3] the activities of the separate Commissions, select personnel for the Agency, direct and supervise the personnel so selected, employ experts and consultants, constitute advisory committees, utilize the services, personnel and facilities of other Federal agencies, enter into and perform contracts, leases, cooperative agreements and other transactions as may be necessary, accept gifts, or voluntary and uncompensated services, designate representatives to serve or assist on such Committees, conduct public hearings, and undertake such other activities as are necessary to carry out his duties. Furthermore, the Administrator is empowered to obtain by subpena, where necessary, such information as he is authorized by the terms of the bill to acquire. His power to obtain by subpena the information is expressly provided; his authority to seek court enforcement of such a subpena is granted by implication.

The Administrator is also authorized to construct research and test facilities if: he first utilizes the personnel, facilities and other technical support available in other Federal agencies, and he obtains special authorization and appropriation from the Congress to plan, design, and construct these facilities. This qualified construction authority is designed to prevent duplication of facilities and save tax dollars.

Finally, the Administrator is empowered to delegate any of his powers (with the exception of his subpena powers) to the Commissioners or other officers or employees of the Agency. It should be noted that the Commissioners are granted independent subpena authority in section 106(d)(2). (See also section 301(b)).

Duties of the Administrator (Section 104)

Section 104 sets forth the Administrator's duty to coordinate the activities of the three Commissions. The Administrator is also under a duty to "attempt, in good faith, to secure levels of funding for the Agency" that will permit it to carry out it's safety mission on behalf of the public. This section also establishes his duty to create an Office of Consumer Information Representation, a National Injury Information Clearinghouse, and a Joint Scientific Committee. In addition, the Administrator must appoint a General Counsel who would serve as the legal representative of the Administrator and coordinate the efforts of the legal representatives of each Commission and publish notice of any proposed public hearing in the Federal Register. Finally, section 104 clarifies the Administrator's exclusive enforcement authority.

---

[3] The coordination function of the Administrator is not precisely defined in the bill. In section 107(5) the Administrator is given authority to coordinate, in essence by "veto" power, the field operations of the various Commissioners. Under section 114 the Administrator would coordinate the requests for the other agencies of government to assist the Consumer Safety Agency. Finally, the Administrator is given all of the functions that the Secretary of Health, Education, and Welfare now administers through the Food and Drug Administration and the functions now administered by the Division of Biologics Standards in the National Institutes of Health. (See Sec. 201). The authority to assign personnel from the transferred agencies is also given to the Administrator.

Section 202(a) of the bill requires the Administrator to delegate the "standard setting functions" transferred to him to the various Commissioners. "Standard setting" includes all regulatory functions and does not have the narrow legislative meaning of "standard" contained in the Food, Drug and Cosmetic Act. The Administrator, however, would retain the regulatory functions relating to color additives. Under subsection (c) of section 202, the Administrator is required to present to Congress a detailed plan of delegation in which he could further resolve the way in which his "coordination" function would be accomplished. In effect, the delegation plan would enable the Administrator to spell out the responsibilities retained by the Administrator and those delegated by him to the Commissioners. In effect, then, subsection (c) of section 202 authorizes the Administrator to modify, to some extent the delegation requirements set forth in subsection (a) of section 202.

Obligations of Agency Contractors (*Section 105*)

Section 105 sets forth the requirement that Agency contractors to maintain appropriate records. The Administrator and the Comptroller General of the United States are given access to such records.

Commissioners (*Section 106*)

This section requires the President to appoint a Commissioner to head each of the three Commissions. These Commissioners would serve as standard-setters in their respective product areas. The Commissioners would be appointed by the President, with the advice and consent of the Senate. It should be noted that the President now appoints the Commissioner of the Food and Drug Administration without the advise and consent of the Senate.

Commissioners are not appointed for a fixed term; they are to serve at the pleasure of the President. In the event of a vacancy, the Administrator shall appoint an acting Commissioner to serve until the President appoints another Commissioner.

Each Commissioner is empowered to undertake such activities as are necessary to carry out his particular duties, including those delegated to him by the Administrator. He is also empowered to conduct public hearings anywhere in the United States and compel the attendance of witnesses by subpena at those hearings.

Duties of the Commissioners (*Section 107*)

Each Commissioner is under a duty to eliminate products presenting unreasonable risk of injury in accordance with procedures set forth in laws which he is given authority to administer. The duty to eliminate products presenting unreasonable risk of injury is not absolute. The Commissioner is required only to "attempt, in good faith," to eliminate such products. (See also section 111 *infra.*) Each Commissioner is also required to establish a capability within his Commission to engage in "risk-based analysis". This analytical capability is extremely important if the Consumer Safety Agency is to have a proper accident *prevention* focus.

In addition, each Commissioner is required to establish an interdisciplinary epidemiological capability to build upon the injury reporting system of the National Injury Information Clearinghouse. This capability would enable the Commissioner to properly evaluate the sequence of events which leads to consumer injuries and allow him to formulate proper plans to break the causal chain. In the auto safety area interdisciplinary crash investigation teams have been very helpful in facilitating an understanding of accident causation and in formulating improved motor vehicle standards.

The Commissioner is also required to establish a scientific capability within the Commission to assist in hazard detection, test method development and quality control improvement. And the Commissioner is under a duty to establish field operations as authorized by the Administrator, to facilitate detection of conditions which might lead to injury or death, to monitor compliance with required levels of safety performance, to report violations, and to assist the Administrator in any enforcement action.

Finally, each Commissioner would have to appoint a counsel to assist him as his legal representative in carrying out his duties. Each

Commissioner would also be required to publish notices of any proposed public hearing in the Federal Register and to afford a reasonable opportunity for interested persons, including consumers, to present relevant testimony and data.

Office of Consumer Information and Representation (*Section 108*)

Section 108 requires the Administrator to appoint a Director of the Office of Consumer Information and Representation. The Director, in effect, would have a fixed term of office equal to the duration of the term of the Administrator, although he may be removed by the Administrator for good cause shown. It is the purpose of this section to insure public participation in, and public understanding of, Agency decision-making.

The Director of the Office of Consumer Information and Representation is required to establish a Consumer Safety Information Center capable of responding to written inquiries from consumers (including Congressional referrals) concerning consumer safety. The Director is also to conduct consumer information programs based upon data supplied by the Commissioners. These programs are to inform the public about specific hazards and the steps which consumers should take to minimize the risks associated with those hazards. It is the intent of the Committee that "such consumer education programs shall not be relied upon by any Commissioner as a substitute for action designed to minimize any hazard unless the Director publishes in the Federal Register a finding that such reliance would sufficiently reduce the risk of such product so that its use would not present an unreasonable risk of injury or death."

In fulfillment of his information duty, the Director is to insure public access to information concerning pending or completed actions of the Administrator or Commissioners related to consumer safety. His duty, however, does not transcend the prohibitions in the bill against unqualified disclosure of trade secrets. (See section 113 *infra.*) To facilitate public access to information, the bill requires the Director to establish within his office a "public information room" equipped with a self-help copying machine from which the public can make copies at the cost of production of the copy. However, the bill is silent as to who is to pay for the cost of the search of the documents to be reproduced if such documents cannot reasonably be retained in the public information room.

In order to insure that the decisionmakers within the Agency hear "all sides" before they make a judicious decision, section 108 empowers the Director to appoint a consumer counsel to represent the consumer interests in any rule making proceedings undertaken by any Commissioner or the Administrator. The Director is to make such appointment from attorneys engaged privately in the practice of law or employed by the United States or any State thereof "unless he determines that the consumer interest will be adequately represented * * * without such appointment." In the event that a consumer advocacy agency is created, it is the intent of the Committee that the Director rely upon an advocate furnished by that Agency for representation of the consumer interests. The Director is also empowered to appoint other experts but the Administrator has the ability to veto in writing these appointments. The words "objects in principle" are designed to indicate that the Administrator's veto is not to be directed at the particular expert to be retained but rather to the concept of retaining experts in the particular proceeding.

The bill requires that "any person appointed * * * shall be chosen for his ability to represent the consumer interests fairly, effectively, and without conflict of interest." In other words, the representative must consult with consumers or consumer organizations in order to develop a consumer position in any rule-making proceeding. Nothing contained in this section of the bill, however, would prevent any other person with requisite standing from participating in the proceedings on behalf of the consumer interests.

Compensation for individuals appointed pursuant to the authority contained in this section would be provided in accordance with section 103(c)(4) of this bill.

National Injury Information Clearinghouse (Section 109)

Section 109 of S. 3419 directs the Administrator to appoint a Director of the National Injury Information Clearinghouse. Utilizing sophisticated computer technology, the Director of the National Injury Information Clearinghouse would establish injury reporting centers throughout the United States to monitor accident occurrences that produce injury, identify the agents which cause the injury, and describe the way in which the agents came into contact accidentally with the victim. In addition, the injury surveillance system would evaluate the severity of the injury.

As a result of the National Commission on Product Safety's initial injury reporting efforts, the Food and Drug Administration is presently monitoring product related injuries utilizing computer terminals located in selected hospitals throughout the United States. This National Electronic Injury Surveillance System (NEISS) should serve as a useful model for an expanded National Injury Information Clearinghouse.

In order to augment injury data, the Director of the Clearinghouse is empowered to require manufacturers, importers, processors, distributors, retailers or distributors of foods, drugs or other products to submit information concerning injuries resulting from the use of their products. The only qualification upon this power is the following: the information cannot be used to compromise any pending litigation. This would not prevent, however, the Administrator from requiring information concerning pending litigation. Experience in the auto safety field shows that an examination of such pending litigation could turn up safety problems which a general injury surveillance program might miss.

The Director of the Injury Information Clearinghouse is not permitted to disclose information obtained by him which concerns or relates to a trade secret unless such information is requested by other Federal agencies and departments or Committee's of Congress or unless it is relevant in any judicial proceeding under a court order formulated to preserve the confidentially of such information. The Director is also free to disclose information concerning or relating to a trade secret if relevant in any proceeding under the bill or if necessary to protect the public health and safety. In the latter situation, notice and opportunity to comment in writing or to discuss in closed session the public release of trade secrets is given to the manufacturer of the product to which the information appertains.

In no event is the Director permitted to disclose the names or other means of identification of injured persons without the express written consent of such persons. And nothing in section 109 requires the release of information not required to be released under the terms of the Freedom of Information Act (5 U.S.C. 552(b)). (For a more detailed discussion of the disclosure of information provisions in section 109, see the discussion accompanying section 113 *infra.*)

Joint Scientific Committee (Section 110)

Section 110 requires each Commissioner to designate five persons within his Commission involved in the scientific detection of hazards or the establishment of standards to serve on a joint Scientific Committee chaired by a Director of Science to be appointed by the Administrator. The purpose of this Committee is to insure the coordination of scientific endeavors in each of the Commissions and to serve as a technical advisor to the Administrator and the Commissioners on scientific matters. The Committee, under the terms of section 110, is required to meet at least once a month.

Agency Responsibility (Section 111)

This section permits an individual or class of individuals to bring suit against the Agency for "mandamus-like" relief upon a showing that a person or persons in the Agency, by their acts or omissions, have exposed the individual or individuals to foods, drugs, devices, or consumer products presenting unreasonable risks of injury or death. The court is empowered to order the performance or cessation of performance, as appropriate, in order to eliminate any food, drug, device, or consumer product presenting an unreasonable risk of injury or death *if the court finds that any person or persons in the Agency by any act or omission or by any series of acts or omissions, have exposed the individuals to such unsafe products.*

Section 111 provides that the Attorney General shall defend the Agency against any action brought under the section. In order to guard against the prosecution of frivolous suits, section 111 authorizes the court, where appropriate, to apportion the costs of litigation to either the plaintiff or the Agency.

In effect, section 111 of the bill extends the availability of the mandamus action beyond the areas of "ministerial" or "mandatory" functions. The reasons for the extension is to allow the action or inaction of the Agency to be reviewed by the court and thereby provide further assurance that the public health and safety would be protected.

This limited extension of the mandamus action is not intended to alter the basic American system of jurisprudence. Traditionally courts have not, through writs of mandamus, required officials of the Executive Branch to perform or not to perform functions which were discretionary. The historical line between "ministerial" and "discretionary" insured the preservation of three independent, co-equal branches of government. Any intervention of the court into discretionary areas of the Executive Branch would have done violence to the separation of powers principle.

The "mandamus-like" action prescribed in section 111 does not impair the separation of powers principle. The functions to be performed by the employees of the Consumer Safety Agency cannot be categorized as Executive Branch functions. The functions are multifaceted, incorporating activities resembling legislative, executive and judicial functions. Therefore, intervention by the Judicial Branch in a regulatory function which is quasi-legislative, quasi-executive and quasi-judicial does no more violence to the principal of separations of powers than the very existence of a regulatory agency itself.[4]

There is another reason that judicial intervention as prescribed in section 111 does no violence to basic principles of American jurisprudence. The Judicial Branch has traditionally been called upon to determine which products in the marketplace present unreasonable risks of injury, first under traditional tort doctrines and now under principles resembling strict liability. It would seem appropriate for the court to be authorized to order government officials to remove products presenting unreasonable risks of injury, since it has been traditional for the court, after an injury has occurred, to make determinations of unreasonable risk before assessing damages against manufacturers of those products.

In addition to authorizing concerned citizens to bring mandamus-like actions, section 111 prohibits certain post-agency employment activities and goes beyond the criminal prohibitions in section 207 of Title 18 of the United States Code. Unlike section 207, subsection (c) of section 111 establishes civil, not criminal, prohibitions against certain post-employment practices of employees of the Consumer Safety Agency constituting a conflict of interest. Agency employees are forever prohibited from participating, whether or not for compensation, in any transaction involving the Agency in which he at any time personally and not collaterally, casually, or incidentally partcipated during his Agency employment. If the transaction involving the Agency was under the official responsibility of an Agency employee, then he is prohibited from participating himself, or assisting any other person, in that transaction for a period of 18 months following the time the person terminates his employment with the Agency.

Annual Reports (*Section 112*)

Section 112 of S. 3419 requires the Administrator of the Agency to file a detailed annual report within 120 days following the convening of each regular session of the Congress. Such report is to be prepared and submitted to Congress and the President without review of the Office of Management and Budget. The report is to contain the detailed summary of the activities of the Agency and its recommendation for legislative action. Among the details to be included are the following: budget information containing the budget requests of the President, the Administrator, and each of the Commissioners, the appropriation of the Congress, and the distribution of appropriated funds for the

---

[4] The Administration's product safety bill (S. 1797) recognized that intervention by the Judicial Branch in the regulatory function was appropriate. In section 12 of S. 1797 the Administration relied upon the court to determine whether or not a consumer product was imminently hazardous. Section 12 specifically authorized the court to grant such temporary or permanent equitable relief as may be necessary to protect the public from such risks, including a mandatory order requiring the notification of the original purchasers, public notice, the recall, the repair, the replacement, or the seizure of such product. This provision has been incorporated in S. 3419. In section 16 of S. 1797 the Administration authorized interested persons to bring actions in district court to enforce product safety standards or enforce any order "and to obtain appropriate injunctive relief." This section has also been incorporated in S. 3419. Both of these provisions permit the intervention of the Judicial Branch in "discretionary" activities of the Consumer Safety Agency.

fiscal year of the report and for the preceding three fiscal years; an account of the activities of the National Injury Information Clearinghouse, the Office of Consumer Information and Representation, and the Joint Scientific Committee detailing the number and type of personnel employed and the monies expended by each; a detailed summary of the activities of each Commission prepared by its Commissioner which presents information as to its injury detection efforts, standard-setting efforts, certification programs, scientific activities, and its field operations; a detailed summary of the enforcement activities of the Agency including violations reported to the Administrator by each Commissioner, a summary of the disposition of non-technical violations including but not limited to voluntary agreements, seizures, recalls, civil fines, and criminal prosecutions; and legislative recommendations of each Commissioner, the Administrator, and the Director of the Office of Consumer Information and Representation. The purpose of this annual report is to provide Congress on a yearly basis a detailed document which will facilitate the Congressional oversight of the independent Consumer Safety Agency mandated by the Legislative Reorganization Act of 1970.

Public Access to Information (Section 113)

Section 113 of the bill establishes as a general principle that "copies of any communications, documents, or reports, or other information received or sent by the Administrator or the Commissioner shall be made available to the public, upon identifiable request, and at reasonable costs . . ." Subsection (c) of section 113 mandates that any communication from a person to the Administrator, the Commissioners, or any other employee of the Agency concerning a matter presently under consideration in a rulemaking or adjudicatory proceeding in the Agency should be made part of the public file of that proceeding unless it is a communication entitled to protection as outlined below.

Whereas subsection (a) of section 113 establishes as a general principle complete access of the public to information there is no *legal requirement* to make information available if it is not required to be made available under the Freedom of Information Act (5 U.S.C. 552 (b)). Subsection (a) must be read in conjunction with paragraph (2) of subsection (b) which states: "Nothing contained in this section shall be deemed to require the release of any information described by subsection (b) of section 552, Title 5, United States Code, or which is otherwise protected by law from disclosure to the public." Although nothing in the Section "shall be deemed to require" release of any information, section 113 *authorizes* the Administrator, the Commissioner, or any officer or employee of the Agency to make public any communications, documents, reports, or other information which are not trade secrets.

Trade secrets may not be disclosed by the Administrator, Commissioner or employees of the Agency except under certain specified situations. The purpose for this qualification is to protect the business community from competitive harm. Black's Law Dictionary defines "trade secret" to mean: "a plan or process, tool, mechanism, or compound known only to its owner and those of his employees to whom it is necessary to confide it . . .; a secret formula or process not patented, but known only to certain individuals using it in compounding some article of trade having a commercial value. . . ." To give added protection to possessors of trade secrets, public disclosure of trade secrets could not be made without notice to the manufacturer and an opportunity for comment in writing or for personal discussion in closed session during a period of 15 days following the notice. Of course, the 15 day period could be waived if the resultant delay would be detrimental to the public health and safety.

There is a final qualification to the general principle of complete public access to information. Section 113 prevents disclosure of the names or other means of identification of injured persons without their expressed written consent.

Cooperation of Federal Agencies (Section 114)

Section 114 establishes cooperation between the Consumer Safety Agency and other agencies and departments. For example, the Commissioner of Drugs may wish to consult with the Institutes of Health or obtain information from medical facilities administered by the Armed Forces. This section would permit the Commissioner to ask for their cooperation and assistance. There is also a general authorization that each Federal Agency "furnish to the Consumer Safety Agency such information, data, estimates, and statistics, and to allow the Agency access to all information in its possession, as the Administrator may reasonably determine to be necessary for the performance of the functions" of the Consumer Safety Agency.

Separability (Section 115)

Section 115 sets forth the separability principle: if any provision in the bill, or the application of such provision to any person or circumstance, is held invalid, the remainder of the bill is not to be affected.

Authorization of Appropriations (Section 116)

Section 116 grants a three year authorization of appropriations with a step up in authorization for each fiscal year. Authorization for the fiscal year beginning July 1, 1972, is not to exceed $180,000,000, for the fiscal year beginning July 1, 1973, $200,000,000, and for the fiscal year beginning July 1, 1974, $225,000,000. Congress would have to renew the authorization for succeeding fiscal years. To complement paragraph (12) of subsection (c) of section 103, section 116 also provides that "no part of the funds so authorized to be appropriated shall be used to plan, design, or construct any research and test facilities unless specifically authorized by the Congress by law."

Executive Level Schedules (Section 117)

Section 117 establishes Executive Schedule pay levels for the Administrator and the Commissioners.

Effective Dates; Initial Appointment of Officers (Section 118)

This section states that the bill will take effect 90 days after the Administrator first takes office, or on such prior date as the President prescribes. The President is authorized to appoint the Administrator and Commissioners, and they, in turn, to appoint their officers, at any time after the date of enactment. Section 118 provides that such officers are to be compensated from the date they first take office at the rates provided for in this bill, and that the compensation and related expenses are to be paid from funds available from the functions transferred to the Agency under Title II of the bill.

TITLE II—TRANSFERS OF FUNCTION

Section 201 (a) transfers all functions of the Secretary of Health, Education, and Welfare administered through the Food and Drug Administration to the Administrator of the Consumer Safety Agency. Subsection (b) transfers all functions of the Secretary of Health, Education, and Welfare administered by the Division of Biological Standards to the Administrator.

All personnel, property, records, obligations, commitments, and unexpended balances of appropriations, and so forth which are used primarily by the Food and Drug Administration or the Bureau of Biological Standards would be transferred to the Administrator under authority of subsection (c) of section 201. That subsection states that the transfer of personnel is to be without reduction in classification or compensation for one year. Although the Administrator must reassign personnel from the Food and Drug Administration or the Bureau of Biological Standards to jobs in the new Agency, he is given the freedom to utilize their services in whatever position he deems most appropriate. The Administrator is also to consult with the Civil Service Commission and assist the Commission in preparing competitive examinations for new Civil Service positions in the Consumer Safety Agency.

Section 202 of the bill requires the Administrator to delegate all standard setting—i.e. regulation setting—functions transferred to him to the appropriate Commissioner. The Administrator would retain all enforcement powers. For example, the Commissioner of Foods and Nutrition would assume the standard-setting responsibilities under the food section of the Food, Drug and Cosmetic Act, the Fair Packaging and Labeling Act, the Import Milk Act, the Filled Milk Act, and the Imported Tea Act. The Commissioner of Drugs would assume responsibility for the drug chapter of the Food, Drug and Cosmetic Act and the Division of Biologics Standards. The Commissioner on Product Safety would assume the standard-setting responsibilities for products other than foods and drugs. For example, the safety of devices is to be regulated under authority of the Food, Drug and Cosmetic Act by the Commissioner on Product Safety.

To assure flexibility of organization, final plans for the delegations discussed above are to be submitted to Congress 90 days after the bill is enacted and are to become effective within 90 days of such a submission if not disapproved by the Congress.

Section 203 of the bill assures that all laws relating to any office, agency, bureau, or function transferred under authority of the bill would remain in full force and effect. In addition, orders, rules, regulations, permits, or other privileges made, issued, or granted by any transferred office, agency, or bureau which were in effect at the time of transfer would continue in effect to the same extent as if such transfer had not occurred until modified, superseded or repealed. Section 203 also preserves any suit, action or other proceeding commenced by any office, agency or bureau prior to transfer.

Section 204 of S. 3419 repeals the cosmetic chapter (Chapter VI) of the Food, Drug and Cosmetic Act and classifies cosmetics as "consumer products". (See Section 101(1) discussed *supra.*) Several other statutes would be repealed and regulation under them would be replaced by the comprehensive consumer product safety authority set forth in Title III of S. 3419. The statutes that would be repealed are as follows:

1. The Federal Hazardous Act, as amended (15 USC 1261 et seq.);
2. The Flammable Fabrics Act, as amended (15 USC 1191 et seq.);
3. The Radiation Control for Health and Safety Act (42 USC 262 et seq.);
4. The Poison Prevention Packaging Act of 1970 (15 USC 1471–76); and
5. The Act of August 2, 1956, (15 USC 1211) pertaining to refrigerator doors.

Subsection (b) of Section 204 preserves any orders, rules, regulations, permits or other privileges made, issued, or granted, or in the process of being made, issued, or granted by authority of the laws which are repealed under Section 204(a). The Commissioner on Product Safety is given authority to administer, and the Administrator to enforce, any such orders, rules, regulations, as if the legislation enumerated above had not been repealed. Such orders, rules, regulations would stay in effect until modified, amended, or repealed under authority granted to the Commissioner of Product Safety in title III of the bill.

For example, regulations requiring pertinent labeling on cosmetics which were in the process of being issued under authority of chapter VI of the Food, Drug and Cosmetic Act would not be negated by the passage of this bill. The Commissioner on Product Safety could continue to pursue such labeling for cosmetics under authority of the Food, Drug and Cosmetic Act. Any such requirements would be administered and enforced as if chapter VI of the Food, Drug and Cosmetic Act had not been repealed. In other words, the repeal of the acts enumerated in Section 204 of S. 3419 is a "qualified" repeal. The Administrator would be empowered to enforce any provisions in accordance with the enforcement authority in the laws enumerated above by virtue of the language in subsection (b) of Section 204 which states that orders, rules, regulations and so forth "shall continue in effect and be administered by the Commissioner and enforced by the Administrator to the same extent as if the laws under which they had been made, issued, or granted, or are being made, issued, or granted, or are being made, issued, or granted, had not been repealed and superseded . . ."

TITLE III—CONSUMER PRODUCT SAFETY

Collection and Disclosure of Information on Consumer Product Risks (Section 301)

This section mandates that the Commissioner of Product Safety collect, evaluate, and disseminate, on a continuing basis information on the types, frequency, severity, and causes of injury associated with the use of consumer products. The activities of the Commissioner would be undertaken in conjunction with the National Injury Information Clearinghouse. By collecting and disclosing information on consumer product risks the Commissioner would be able to prevent many injuries, have a data base for facilitating the design of relevant standards, and evaluate the efficacy of existing standards.

The Commissioner of Product Safety is also required under section 301 to conduct and make available, through publications and other appropriate means, the results of research and studies relating to the nature and extent of the risks associated with consumer products. To fulfill this and related requirements, the Commissioner would maintain a capability for risk-based analysis and make his own recommendations for reducing product risks.

Under subsection (b) of Section 301 the Commissioner is authorized to obtain, by subpena if necessary, information in the form of books, records, or other writings pertinent to the frequency or causes of death, or the types, frequency, severity, or causes of illnesses or injury associated with exposure to the use of consumer products, including litigation records.

The Commissioner is under the same prohibition against information disclosure discussed in section 113 above. He may disclose everything but trade secrets, and he may disclose trade secrets in certain situations. He is not required by law to disclose any information not required to be disclosed under the Freedom of Information Act.

When the Commissioner discovers information about unreasonable or significant risks associated with products he has surveyed, he is required to communicate his findings to the manufacturers of such products. And if his investigations disclose that exposure to an aspect of the household environment other than a consumer product presents an unreasonable risk of personal injury or death and that a recognized building, electrical, or other code covers that aspect of the household environment, he may recommend to the appropriate code-making authority, and to those authorities responsible for enforcing the code, those code changes which he thinks will reduce the perceived risk to a reasonable level. Any recommendations so made would be advisory only.

Authority To Promulgate Standards for Consumer Products (Section 302)

Section 302 authorizes the Commissioner, whenever he finds that there is a need for eliminating unreasonable risk of injury or death, associated with a particular consumer product, to promulgate for such product, or type of class or such product a consumer product safety standard or amend any standard previously established. Section 302 makes explicit the Committee's intent that a product safety standard should be, insofar as practicable, compatible with any Federal environmental standards established for consumer products. The following discussion of subsequent sections describes the way in which consumer product safety standards would be established under the provisions of Title III of S. 3419.

Initiation of Proceeding To Promulgate a Consumer Product Safety Standard (Section 303)

Section 303 (a) requires the Commissioner to publish a "notice of proceeding" which would invite public comment on the need to control any risk or risks presented by a consumer product or type or class of consumer products which the Commissioner identifies in the notice. Paragraph (3) of section 303 (a) requires the Commissioner to include in the notice of proceeding a summary description of the information upon which the Commissioner has found a need to initiate the proceeding, and the manner (consistent with the information disclosure provisions of Title III) in which interested persons may examine such information. Although it is the purpose of the bill and the Commissioner's prime responsibility to eliminate known injuries, this requirement is not intended to place a burden upon the Commissioner of producing proof of actual injuries in order to justify the notice of proceeding. The information upon which the Commissioner bases his need could consist of injury information collected by the National Injury Information Clearinghouse, his own investigations and judgments, risk-based analysis, or other engineering data.

The notice of proceeding would include an invitation for any person, including any Federal agency, within 30 days after the date of publication of the notice to submit information challenging the need to control the identified risks, to submit to the Commissioner an existing standard which might be used to control any identified risk, or to offer to develop a proposed consumer product safety standard in accordance with regulations prescribing procedures for such development developed pursuant to subsection (a) of section 303.

Subsection (b) of section 303 authorizes "any consumer or other interested party" to petition the Commissioner to commence a proceeding for the issuance, amendment, or revocation of consumer product safety standard or other appropriate action. This section provides an important mechanism for public initiation of, and participation in, the protection of the public health and safety. A petition submitted under authority of subsection (b) must set forth with particularity the reasons for such petition, and the Commissioner must publish such petition in the Federal Register and allow opportunity for comment. If the Commissioner denies a petition he must publish his reasons for the denial.

Section 303 (c) requires the Commissioner to receive and evaluate any information disputing the need to control a risk or risks presented by a consumer product designated in the notice of proceeding. His determination as to whether or not there is a need is not reviewable.

If the Commissioner determines that there exists a need, he then proceeds toward the publishing of a proposed consumer product safety standard. The Commissioner is given 180 days from the notice of proceeding to publish a proposed consumer product safety standard. In extraordinary situations, the Commissioner could extend the 180 days if he publishes in the Federal Register the reasons for such extension. (See Section 306 (a) (1).)

There are several avenues open to the Commissioner as he proceeds toward the publication of a proposed consumer product safety standard. If he finds an existing standard which he has referenced in his notice of proceeding and if he is satisfied that the standard will alleviate the risks intended to be controlled, then he may immediately publish such standard as a proposed consumer product safety standard. If these pre-conditions have not been satisfied, the Commissioner may accept one or more offers to develop a proposed consumer product safety standard. The Committee believes that the utilization of the technical knowhow and facilities of independent testing laboratories, trade associations, and certain manufacturers could aid the Commissioner in developing a sufficient and fair standard. Consumer organizations could also contribute significantly to the development of an appropriate standard.

Subsection (e) of section 303 prohibits any acceptance of any offer if the offeror is not technically competent and is not likely to develop an appropriate standard within 150 days (or such longer period of time not to exceed 360 days from the date of the notice of proceeding). The offeror must also have the capacity to comply with regulations governing development of consumer product safety standards prescribed pursuant to section 305 of the bill.

The Commissioner is authorized to contribute to the offeror's cost in developing a proposed consumer product safety standard if he determines that such contribution is likely to result in a more satisfactory standard. Consumer organizations would be likely recipients of such financial aid. If the Commissioner accepts an offer to develop a proposed consumer product safety standard, he must publish the name and address of the offeror or offerors he selects in the Federal Register and provide a summary of the terms of each accepted offer.

Development of Standard by Commissioner (*Section 304*)

In order to have the capability of making technical judgments concerning different proposals for consumer product safety standards and to insure that the public is protected from unsafe consumer products, the Commissioner is required to proceed to develop a proposed consumer product safety standard whether or not he has accepted offers to develop a proposed standard. Such development would be particularly appropriate, where, for example, the risks were significant, the corrective technology uncertain, or conflicting commercial interests were likely to interfere with private sector development. Of course, if the Commissioner determines that his own development would not be of benefit to the public, he need not develop an in-house consumer product safety standard. Needless, duplicative efforts should not be undertaken. If he does proceed with in-house development, he should make sure that his technical staff, when evaluating other proposals, does not express preferences for their own approaches for reasons of "pride of authorship" alone.

Regulations Governing Development of Standards (*Section 305*)

The development of proposed standards is to be guided by regulations promulgated in accordance with section 305 of the bill. This section requires the Commissioner to prescribe regulations in accordance with section 553 of Title 5 United States Code. The language "which regulation shall not be considered rules of agency organization, procedure, or practice for purposes of section 553 of Title 5" is included to insure that there will be opportunity for comment by interested parties when these regulations are established. The regulations are to include requirements: that standards recommended for promulgation be supported by test data or other such documents or materials; be suitable for promulgation as a proposed product safety standard; and contain test methods that appropriately measure compliance with the established standard. The regulations must also provide that there be opportunities for interested persons to participate in the development of standard; that records be maintained so as to disclose the course of the development, the comments and other information submitted by any person in connection with the development and such other matters as may be relevant to the evaluation of the recommended standard; and that the appropriate government officials be given access for the purpose of auditing and examination of any books, documents, papers, and records relevant to the expenditure and any contribution which the Commissioner might make in aid of the development of a standard. The Committee intends by these requirements to make the private sector development of standards open and fair.

Promulgation of Standards (Section 306)

One hundred and eighty days following publication of a notice of proceeding, the Commissioner is required to publish in the Federal Register either a notice withdrawing the notice of proceeding, a proposal to promulgate a consumer product safety standard, or a proposal to declare a consumer product a banned hazardous product. If the Commissioner chooses to publish a proposal to promulgate a consumer product safety standard, such proposal shall contain only one proposed standard formulated by the Commissioner after evaluating any standard developed for him by any offerors or by his own personnel. The Commissioner is given authority to combine the features of the various developed proposals in formulating his own proposal.

A proposal to promulgate a consumer product safety standard or to declare a product a banned hazardous substance, under the terms of section 306 of the bill, must set forth a proposed standard or the reasons for the declaration to ban, the manner in which interested persons may examine data and other information upon which such proposed standard or declaration is based, and the period within which all interested persons should present their comments on such standard or declaration, and the need therefore, orally or in writing.

The Commissioner is authorized to conduct a hearing in such manner as he deems appropriate for the purpose of resolving any issue of material fact raised by any person presenting comments on the proposed standard or declaration to ban. Any hearing which the Commissioner holds should afford all interested persons, including consumers, opportunity to comment on the proposed standard. It must also be expeditious because under section 306(d) the Commissioner must publish an order to promulgate a consumer product safety standard or an order to declare a ban hazardous consumer product within 60 days after publication of a proposal to promulgate a standard or to declare a consumer product a banned hazardous consumer product.

In the 60 days between the issuance of the proposal and the final order, the Commissioner is also required to consider and make appropriate findings where available (for inclusion in the final order), concerning the significance of data, and comments submitted in the course of the proceeding leading to the development of the order; the types, frequency, severity, and causes of injury that have been attributed to those aspects of the consumer product being regulated under the order; the approximate number of consumer products, or types or classes thereof, subject to the order; the need of the public for the consumer product subject to the order, the probable effect of such order upon the utility, cost, or availability of such products; and any means of achieving the objective of the order which minimizes adverse effects on competition or disruption or dislocation of manufacturing and commercial practices "consistent with the public health and safety."

Any order published by the Commissioner must include a determination that the findings enumerated above establish the need for the standard or declaration produced by the order.

The final order must also set forth reasons for the Commissioner's action (including reasons materially different than those set forth in the proposal). If the Commissioner takes no action, he must explain his failure to promulgate any standard. Of course, the effective date of the standard must be included in the order. The effective date must not be later than six months after publication of the order unless the Commissioner publishes his reasons for making exception to this six month rule. (See section 312 regulating the stockpiling of consumer products between the time of promulgation of a final order and the effective date of the consumer product safety standard.)

Subsection (e) of section 306 requires the Commissioner to promulgate product safety standards which pertain to the safety performance characteristics of consumer products. The Committee has expressed its preference for performance standards in order to assure that product innovation is not stifled by government action. However, the bill permits safety standards to apply to the composition, design, construction, or finish of a consumer product if a performance standard for that aspect of the product is not feasible.

Performance standards would include standards relating to the safe packaging of products—e.g. packaging making it difficult for small children to open or packaging deceiving children into thinking the contents were foods or other harmless substances. Safety performance characteristics include safe packaging characteristics in order to prevent someone from arguing that a safe packaging standard is not a performance standard.

A consumer product safety standard relating to performance would be required to set forth the "test procedures (including instrumentation) capable of producing reproducible results" to measure such performance characteristics. Without proper test procedures covering all relevant safety performance characteristics and producing reproducible results, it would be very difficult for industry to comply with applicable standards *and for the Administrator to enforce such standards.*

Paragraph (2) of subsection (e) of section 306 authorizes the Commissioner either in a product safety performance standard or a separate standard to require consumer products to be "marked, tagged, or accompanied by clear and adequate warnings or instructions." This would include symbols as well as words. For example, the Commissioner might promulgate a product safety standard requiring manufacturers of aerosals to place a warning or a symbol on the aerosal can to indicate its explosive potential. Or, when setting a performance standard, the Commissioner might require that products manufactured after the effective date of the standard bear a label explaining that the product complies with the new required safety standard. This would permit the consumer to differentiate between those products manufactured before the effective date and those manufactured after the effective date, thereby enabling the consumer to purchase the safer product if he wishes. A product safety standard requiring marking, tagging or labeling (including symbols) could prescribe placement and type size and could require the identification of the manufacturer to be printed, endorsed or otherwise permanently affixed.

In the past the Federal Government has relied upon labeling as a substitute for setting performance standards for consumer products. The explicit authority in S. 3419 to "mark, tag, or require clear and adequate warnings or instructions" should not be interpreted as authority to perpetuate previous government regulatory propencities to "label" where that action does not effectively protect the public health and safety. Labeling can be a useful tool for informing the consumer of risks associated with the use of consumer products, particularly when used as an adjunct to consumer product safety performance standards. But labeling alone cannot protect the young, the illiterate, or the inattentive from injury. And too many warnings, labels or symbols can reduce the overall effectiveness of any one such warning label or symbol. Only performance standards which eliminate the risks are able, in most situations, to protect adequately the public health and safety.

In addition to the authority to promulgate performance or other consumer product safety standards, or to promulgate labeling standards, the Commissioner of Product Safety would be authorized to promulgate consumer product safety standards which require consumer products to be "subject to safety precautions related to physical distribution, as may be reasonably necessary for the protection of the public health or safety." For example, in normal distribution channels a product may not present an unreasonable risk of injury or death to such children because of the parents awareness of the danger and their ability to remove the product from the child's reach. But a manufacturer may decide to distribute free samples of a consumer product door-to-door. Small children may gain access to such consumer products and thereby be exposed to unreasonable risk of injury. It is this type of activity which the Commissioner could reach through a consumer product safety standard related to the physical distribution of the consumer product. Other examples might include requirements that retailers make sure that required labels or warnings are properly affixed to a consumer product at the time of sale. This provision would not allow the Commissioner to reach advertising.

Subsection (f) of section 306 sets forth the Commissioner's authority to declare a consumer product a "banned hazardous consumer product." Before banning a consumer product the Commissioner must find (and include such finding in the order to ban) that no feasible consumer product safety standard would adequately protect the public from unreasonable risk of injury or death presented by the product. Subsection (f) prohibits the Commissioner from declaring a firearm or ammunition a banned hazardous consumer product. But nothing in S. 3419 prohibits the Commissioner from setting a consumer product safety standard for firearms or ammunition. In light of the recent publicity about "Saturday night specials" and the dangers they present to their users (as well as those they might be used upon), it is possible that the Commissioner of Product Safety would direct his attention to eliminating such unsafe consumer products. But it is not the Committee's intent that the Commissioner on Product Safety intervene in the gun control controversy.

If a consumer product is declared a banned hazardous consumer product, then it is subject to the repurchase provisions set forth in paragraph (2) of subsection (f) of section 306. Any product sold after the date on which the notice to ban is published is required to be repurchased. The Administrator is authorized to set out regulations clarifying and facilitating this repurchase. If the Commissioner believes it is necessary to require the repurchase of banned hazardous consumer products sold prior to the date on which the proposal to ban was issued, he would have to proceed under authority of section 311 and request a Federal district court to order such repurchase.

The repurchase provisions are to work as follows: the consumer would return the product to retailer; the retailer would refund the purchase price paid for the consumer product by the person "less a reasonable allowance for use if the product had been in the possession of the consumer for one year or more"; the retailer would resell it to the distributor and be reimbursed for the amount paid to the consumer and any "reasonable and necessary expenses" incurred in returning it to the distributor; the distributor would, in turn, be reimbursed by the manufacturer to the extent of the refund as well as the "reasonable and necessary expenses" incurred in returning the product to the manufacturer if the manufacturer so requires. It should be noted the manufacturer, under the repurchase provisions in the bill, is required to absorb any price mark ups in the distribution chain. Nothing in the bill, however, would prevent agreements between the manufacturer and distributor and retailer that would limit the price to be paid for the repurchase to the amount refunded to the consumer less the mark up of the retailer or distributor. (But see section 309 (d).)

Safety Analysis Study (Section 307)

Section 307 of S. 3419 authorizes, the Commissioner where appropriate, by regulation, to require a consumer product, or type or class of consumer products, to be subjected to a detailed safety analysis. The Commissioner would not be permitted to require a manufacturer to conduct such safety analysis if the product is already subject to a consumer product safety standard.

The purpose of the safety analysis study is to illuminate and thereby eliminate risks associated with the use of consumer products short of promulgating a consumer product safety standard. In any proceeding to establish a consumer product safety standard for products that have been subjected to safety analysis study requirements, the fact that such products have been subjected to safety analysis study would be considered in determining the need for a consumer product safety standard on such product.

The Commissioner is authorized to demand of the manufacturer a copy of any required safety analysis report. Failure to provide such safety analysis report meeting the criteria set forth in the regulations requiring the report would constitute an unlawful act under section 315 of S. 3419.

The ability of the Commissioner to require a manufacturer to subject his product to a detailed safety analysis should better enable the Commissioner to take action to reduce the risk of injury associated with the use of a wide variety of consumer products. The Committee does not intend, however, that the Commissioner propose a blanket requirement that every consumer product in the marketplace be subjected to a detailed safety analysis. The Commissioner should only require safety analysis of those products he determines are presenting or may present significant risks of injury, but which at that time should not be subject to a notice of proceeding to develop a proposed consumer product safety standard.

It is the intent of the Committee that the Commissioner on Product Safety when requiring detailed safety analysis of particular consumer products, or types or classes of consumer products, will provide technical assistance to the small businessman in order to insure that any safety analysis requirement does not unduly prejudice the competitive position of the small businessman.

Revocation or Amendment of Standard (*Section 308*)

Section 308 authorizes the Commissioner to amend or revoke a consumer product safety standard. Such revocation and amendment authority would extend to safety standards which the Commissioner on Product Safety inherits from consumer product safety programs transferred to the new Consumer Safety Agency.

Revocation would be accomplished by publishing the proposed revocation in the Federal Register, offering interested persons an opportunity to examine data and other information relevant to the Commissioner's determination to revoke the standard, and then issuing an order (also published in the Federal Register) revoking the standard and indicating the reasons for, and the effective date of, the revocation.

Subsection (b) of section 308 describes two approaches for amending consumer product safety standards. If the amendment is a material amendment, it is to be treated as if it were a new product safety standard. In other words, the beginning point for the proceeding would be the "notice of proceeding" required under section 303 (a). If the amendment is other than a material amendment, the Commissioner is authorized to promulgate the amendment as a proposal to promulgate a consumer product safety standard. Within 60 days he would then promulgate the final amendment. During those 60 days he would be authorized to conduct a hearing for the purpose of resolving any issue of material fact raised by any person when presenting comments on the proposal to amend an existing consumer product safety standard.

Compliance (*Section 309*)

Although primary responsibility for compliance remains with the manufacturer or importer, section 309 authorizes the Commissioner to take steps to assure compliance. In the first place, he is authorized to conduct compliance testing of production products. These products are to be furnished without cost to the Commissioner by any person who manufactures or imports a consumer product. The bill requires that such products be "drawn from regular production runs." Any products furnished to the Commissioner are to be returned to the manufacturer upon completion of the complance testing unless such product did not comply with an applicable standard. In subsequent sale or lease of a tested product, the manufacturer would be obligated to disclose that the product had been subjected to compliance testing and to indicate the extent of damage, if any, prior to repair.

Under S. 3419 compliance is also facilitated through the provision which authorizes the Product Safety Commissioner to establish procedures to be followed by those persons in the distribution chain and consumers themselves in securing and maintaining the names and addresses of first purchasers of certain consumer products. In determining whether or not to require the maintenance of the names and addresses of the first purchasers, the Commissioner is required to consider the severity of the injury that could result if the consumer product was manufactured not in compliance with an applicable standard, the likelihood that a particular type or class of consumer product would be manufactured not in compliance, and the burden imposed upon the manufacturer or importer, and ultimately the consumer, in requiring the maintenance of the names. Although the names of first purchasers would not be required to be maintained for all consumer products subject to consumer product safety standards, the recall of non-complying consumer products is made very difficult without the names of the first purchasers. (See section 313(b)(1) where the Commissioner is given authority to require the manufacturer to notify "each consumer of such product known to such manufacturer" notification of a defect or failure to comply.)

Subsection (d) of section 309 requires the manufacturer or importer, and in turn the distributor, to furnish a certification to the distributor or dealer at the time of delivery that the consumer product conforms to any and all applicable consumer product safety standards. Such certification could create a warranty between a manufacturer and distributor or the distributor and the dealer in order to protect such person from the losses sustained as a result of the failure of the consumer product to comply with any applicable consumer product safety standards as set forth in such certification.

A final weapon in the arsenal of compliance is subsection (a) of section 309 which authorizes the Commissioner whenever he "has good cause to believe that a particular manufacturer is producing a consumer product with a significant incidence of non-compliance with a particular consumer product safety standard" to require the manufacturer to submit a description of the relevant quality control procedures followed and to undertake to revise such quality control procedures "to the extent necessary" to assure compliance, including pre-market testing. Any revision of the quality control procedures of a particular manufacturer would not be accomplished without a formal hearing pursuant to section 554 Title 5, United States Code. Subsection (a) authorizes the Commissioner, after receiving indications that a particular manufacturer has significant difficulty producing products conforming to applicable consumer product safety standards, to prescribe quality control procedures that would insure future compliance. This provision would permit the Commissioner and the Administrator a flexible enforcement response. Rather than levying fines to the point of putting a particular manufacturer out of business because he produces products not in compliance with applicable standards, the Commissioner and Administrator would have a second line of defense, namely the prescription of quality-control procedures to assure future compliance with applicable standards. These quality-control procedures, however, would be used in conjunction with, rather than in lieu of, the enforcement proceedings set forth in section 316.

Judicial Review (Section 310)

Section 310 sets forth the procedure for judicial review of final orders or regulations promulgated pursuant to sections 305 (regulations governing the development of standards), 306(d) (order to set safety standard or ban), 307 (safety analysis study), 308 (revocation or amendment of standard) or 309 (compliance). Any interested person, including consumers, affected by a final order would be permitted to file a petition for judicial review in the United States Court of Appeals for the District of Columbia or any circuit in which such person resides or has his principal place of business. Upon notice of such petition, the Administrator would file in the court the record of the proceedings on which the Commissioner based his order. Subsection (b) authorizes the court to stay the effective date of any order during the review process if in the public interest. The subsection also assures "substantial evidence" review of the entire record of an order or regulation. This imposes a greater standard of review than would normally be accorded rules or regulations promulgated in accordance with section 553 of Title 5 of the United States Code. Any determinations, regulations, or orders not subject to the judicial review process of section 310 would be reviewable in accordance with chapter 7 of Title 5 of the United States Code. (See, e.g., sections 303 and 313.)

Emergency Action (Section 311)

Section 311 allows the Administrator or the Attorney General to file an action seeking a Federal court to restrain any person in the distribution chain who is marketing a consumer product which is "imminently hazardous". An "imminently hazardous consumer product" is defined as a "consumer product presenting an unreasonable risk of injury or death which requires action to protect adequately the public health and safety prior to the completion of administrative proceedings held pursuant to this Act." For example, a toy may possess an electrical hazard which could cause injury to children during the period for promulgation a product safety standard. In that situation, the Administrator could ask the court to take action to remove the dangerous toy from the marketplace pending completion of the standard-setting process. Or, a product that has been declared a banned hazardous substance may be so dangerous as to require its total recall instead of a recall limited to those products sold after the publication of the proposal to ban.

Any district court entertaining an emergency action would be authorized to declare the product an "imminently hazardous consumer product" and grant such temporary or permanent equitable relief as may be necessary to protect the public from such risks. The relief could include a mandatory order "requiring a notification of the first purchasers of such product of such risk, public notice, the recall, the repurchase, the repair, the replacement, or the seizure of such product."

In those situations where the emergency action is taken prior to any other formal action, the Commissioner is required to immediately initiate a proceeding for the development of a consumer product safety standard or for the banning of the hazardous consumer product. But subsection (c) should not be interpreted as limiting emergency action only to those cases involving products not yet subject to an order to ban or to promulgate a consumer product safety standard.

Stockpiling (*Section 312*)

This section requires the Commissioner to take action to prevent the stockpiling of consumer products not in compliance with a newly promulgated consumer product safety standard between the time of promulgation and the effective date of such standard. This section prohibits any manufacturer or importer, in an effort to stockpile a non-complying consumer product, from producing or importing such product in quantities significantly greater than quantities he had produced for a base period established by the Commissioner. The Commissioner is required to establish this base period prior to the promulgation of the final order establishing a consumer product safety standard.

Notification of Failure to Comply; Repair or Replacement of a Non-Complying Consumer Product (*Section 313*)

Subsection (a) of section 313 imposes a statutory duty upon every manufacturer, importer, distributor, or dealer who discovers that a consumer product has a defect which relates to the safety of use of the product or is not in compliance with an applicable consumer product safety standard to immediately notify the Commissioner of such defect or failure to comply "if such products has left the place of manufacture." The notification required must contain a clear description of the defect or failure to comply; an evaluation of the hazard reasonably related to the defect or failure or to comply; and a statement of the measures to be taken to effect repair to such defect or failure to comply. Any breach of the above statutory duty would constitute a prohibited act under section 315(2). (Note that the use of "consumer" is synonymous with the previous use of the term "individual".)

Subsection (b) authorizes the Administrator of the Consumer Safety Agency, by order after opportunity for hearing pursuant to the provisions of section 554 of Title 5, United States Code, to require public notice whenever a consumer product fails to comply with an applicable order or has a manufacturing defect which causes it to present an unreasonable risk of injury or death. It should be noted that the duty to notify in subsection (a) runs to all defects, but the Administrator's authority to require public notice relates only to "manufacturing defects". If a design defect were to present an unreasonable risk of injury or death, the Commissioner could proceed under authority of section 311 to remove immediately the product from the marketplace or could resort to the standard-setting procedures contained in the bill.

In addition to the authority to require public notice, including notice through the electronic media when necessary to protect the public health and safety, the Administrator could by order require anyone in the distribution chain to mail to each consumer of such product a notification of a failure to comply or a manufacturing defect containing such information as the Administrator may prescribe, upon the Administrator's determination that such notification is required to protect adequately the public health or safety. In any such notice, the manufacturer should not be permitted to disclaim the existence of the defect or the failure to comply.

Finally, the Administrator could order the manufacturer or the appropriate person in the distribution chain to bring the product into conformity with the requirements of any order—i.e. repair—without charge to the consumer. The Administrator may also order either the replacement of the product with a like or equivalent consumer product or the refund of the purchase price of such product upon its tender, whichever option is elected by the manufacturer, importer, distributor, or dealer whose product fails to comply with an applicable standard or contains a defect. If an election is made to refund the purchase price, the price could be less a reasonable allowance if the product has been in the possession of the consumer for more than one year at the time of tender. The words "without charge to the consumer" indicate that during the repair, replacement, or refund process the consumer should not be required to make expenditures in connection with the repair, replacement, or refund. For example, cost of transportation in order to accomplish repair, replacement, or refund would be borne by the manufacturer, importer, distributor or dealer.

Inspection and Record Keeping (*Section 314*)

Section 314 authorizes any officers or employees duly designated by the Commissioner, upon presenting appropriate credentials and a written notice to the owner, operator, or agent in charge to enter at reasonable times those places in which consumer products are manufactured, assembled, or held for introduction into, or sale in, commerce or those vehicles in which consumer products are transported. (A similar provision is found in the Radiation Control for Health and Safety Act (42 U.S.C. 262 et seq.)). In addition, such employees or officers would be authorized to enter at reasonable times and in a reasonable manner those areas in which consumer products are produced, stored, or transported, and examine all pertinent equipment, materials, containers, and labeling in those areas. It would be appropriate for the Commissioner to request from any manufacturer a list of all such places.

Section 314 requires that a separate written notice be given for each inspection, but does not require that one be given for each entry made during the period of inspection set forth in the written notice. For example, a written notice to the owner could state that between date *X* and date *Y* employees of the Consumer Safety Agency would be making inspections of the factory. At any reasonable time during the stated period, employees of the Agency could enter the premises to make their inspections. The inspections must be completed with reasonable promptness. If an officer or employee making an inspection obtains any sample in the course of the inspection, he is required, prior to leaving the premises, to give the owner, operator, or agent in charge, a receipt for the sample.

Subsection (b) of section 314 authorizes the Commissioner to establish by regulation requirements for record keeping related to the safety of consumer products. This provision was expressly limited to safety related records by the Committee in order to avoid any undue hardship on small business. These records would be available to any officer or employee designated by the Commissioner upon request.

Subsection (c) states that the district courts of the United States "shall have jurisdiction to issue any warrant in aid of an inspection or investigation under this section, if such warrant is required by the constitution or laws of the United States, upon a finding that such inspection or investigation is for the purpose of enforcing this Act."

Prohibited Acts (Section 315)

Section 315 makes it unlawful for any person engaged in the business of making consumer products available to consumers, either directly or indirectly, to manufacture, sell, or lease a consumer product not in compliance with any applicable consumer product safety standard. Section 315 also prohibits the manufacture, importation, and sale, or lease of any consumer product which has been declared a banned or imminently hazardous consumer product.

It would also be unlawful to fail to comply with any notification requirement or repair, replacement or refund requirement under section 313 or to fail or refuse to comply with any requirement established under the compliance section (section 309), the stockpiling section (section 312) or the inspection and record keeping section (section 314). Any alteration, modification, destruction, or removal of any portion of a consumer product, or the labeling thereon, is unlawful if it renders the product a banned or imminently hazardous consumer product or makes a previously complying consumer product a non-complying product.

It is also unlawful for a person to refuse to provide information concerning injuries as required in section 109(c) (1) (B) or to provide any required safety analysis (section 307).

Enforcement (Section 316)

The Attorney General and the Administrator of the Consumer Safety Agency are granted broad enforcement powers under section 316 to enable them to prevent or deter the commission of unlawful acts. In the first place, the Attorney General or Administrator may institute a civil action against whoever knowingly commits any act prohibited by section 315. In such action the corporation (or other business entity) "and any individual director, officer, or agent of such corporation" who knowingly caused the corporation (or other business entity) to commit the act would be subject to a civil penalty of not more than $10,000 for each such act. "Each such act" might mean the production of each product in violation of an applicable product safety standard or might only include the single decision which lead to the marketing of a number of products not in compliance with an applicable product safety standard. The term "knowingly" includes actual knowledge, presumed knowledge based upon the knowledge deemed to be possessed by a reasonable man in like circumstances, including knowledge obtainable upon the exercise of due care to ascertain the truth of representations and knowledge that the probable consequences of actions in disregard of reasonable safeguards.

Whoever willfully commits an act prohibited by section 315 "shall be guilty of a misdemeanor and, upon conviction, fined not more than $10,000 for each such act or imprisoned not more than one year, or both. The Administrator of the Consumer Safety Agency or the Attorney General is empowered to prosecute such criminal cases under authority of subsection (a) of section 316.

Subsection (b) of section 316 authorizes both the Administrator and the Attorney General to ask the district courts of the United

States to enjoin the commission of acts prohibited by the bill and to compel the taking of any action required under the bill.

Subsection (c) of section 316 permits the Administrator to seize any consumer product not in compliance with an applicable consumer product safety standard either because of its manufacturer or alteration, or because a consumer product has been declared a banned or imminently hazardous consumer product. Condemnation, following complaint for forfeiture by the Administrator, would be made in any district court in the United States within whose district the consumer product is found.

Subsection (d) of section 316 authorizes private citizens to bring suits to compel the enforcement of a consumer product safety standard or an order to ban a product or declare it an imminently hazardous product, and to obtain appropriate injunctive relief. (See also section 111.) Prior to commencing such suit, the person must give notice by registered mail to the Commissioner, to the Administrator, and to the person against whom such action is directed. The notice must state the nature of the alleged violation, the relief to be requested, and the court in which the action will be brought. No private suit may be brought if the same alleged violation is the subject of a pending action by the United States under authority of this title.

In order to finance the cost of private litigation, subsection (d) provides that the person may elect, by demand for such relief in his complaint, to recover a reasonable attorney's fees. If such demand is made, the court is required to award reasonable attorney's fee to the prevailing party.

Paragraph (2) of subsection (d) authorizes any person who sustains injury by reason of knowing (including willful) violation of a consumer product safety standard, regulation, or order issued by the Commissioner to bring suit in any district court of the United States in the district in which the defendant resides or is found or has an agent, subject to the provisions of section 1331 of Title 28 of the United States Code. In such suit the person is permitted to recover the damages sustained, the cost of suit, including a reasonable attorney's fee if considered appropriate in the discretion of the court. By making the suit subject to the jurisdictional requirements of section 1331 of Title 28, the section prohibits the use of the Federal courts unless a person sustains damage of $10,000 or more. If that jurisdictional requirement is met, than a class action suit in accordance with Rule 23 of the Federal Rules of Civil Procedure might be possible.

Subsection (e) of section 316 states "the remedies provided for in this section shall be in addition to and not in substitution for any other remedies provided by law." This subsection insures that common law remedies, or other statutory remedies, are not displaced by section 316.

Imports (*Section 317*)

Section 317 establishes the procedure for handling imported consumer products so as to assure their compliance with applicable orders and regulations of the Consumer Safety Agency. For example, subsection (c) authorizes the Secretary of the Treasury to obtain without charge and deliver to the Commissioner upon his request a reasonable number of samples of consumer products being offered for import. If it appears from the examination or testing of such samples that a product fails to comply with any applicable requirements, the product would be refused admission and the Secretary would cause destruction of the product unless it was exported (under regulations prescribed by the Secretary of the Treasury) within 90 days after the notice to the importer or consignee.

It is the Committee's intent to assure that the regulation for safety of imports is equal to the regulation for safety of domestically-produced products. Section 317 is designed to insure this equality of treatment. In addition, the Committee expects that the compliance authority set out in section 309 will be equally applicable to imported products. This means, where necessary, that foreign inspections are to be made and quality-control procedures are to be prescribed where necessary and appropriate.

Exports (*Section 318*)

Section 318 exempts from title III any consumer product manufactured, sold, or held for sale for export from the United States (or to any consumer product imported for export) *if* such consumer product, and any container in which it is enclosed, bears a stamp or label stating that the consumer product is intended for export and *if* it is, in fact, exported from the United States. However, consumer products manufactured for sale, offered for sale, or sold for shipment to any installation in the United States located outside the United States must comply with the provisions of title III of S. 3419. Products manufactured for domestic consumption which the manufacturer decides to export may be exported after notice to the Commissioner.

Effect on State Law (*Section 319*)

Section 319 prohibits any State or political subdivision thereof from establishing or continuing in effect any consumer product safety standard that is not identical to a consumer product safety standard established pursuant to title III. This "qualified" preemption would not take effect until such time as the Commissioner on Product Safety promulgated a consumer product safety standard for a particular consumer product.

Section 319 would not prohibit a State or political subdivision thereof from establishing or continuing in effect any health or safety requirement applicable to a consumer product *for its own use* as long as the requirement imposed a higher standard of health or safety than that required by the Federal consumer product safety standard.

Subsection (b) of section 319 authorizes the Administrator, upon application of a State or political subdivision thereof, to exempt a State or political subdivision from the "qualified" preemption if it promulgates a consumer product safety standard which: imposes a level of health or safety higher than the Federal standard; is required by compelling local conditions; does not unduly burden commerce; and is adopted by such State or political subdivision pursuant to procedures and requirements comparable to those in title III.

Subsection (c) of section 319 states that compliance with any consumer product safety standard issued under Title III does not exempt any person from liability under common law. This subsection reaffirms the fact that product safety standards promulgated in accordance with this bill are "minimum" standards. Therefore, in product liability litigation compliance with applicable Federal safety standards would not automatically create a defense for the manufacturer.

Utilization of Other Federal Agencies (Section 320)

Subsection (a) of section 320 directs the Administrator and the Commissioner of Product Safety to utilize, to the maximum extent practicable, the personnel facilities and other technical support available in other Federal agencies. (See also section 301 (c) (12).) Subsection (b) requires that technical research support for fire safety projects undertaken by the Administrator or the Commissioner be provided by the National Bureau of Standards on a reimbursable basis. In other words, any in-house research that the Administrator or Commissioner would engage in is to be done by the National Bureau of Standards and not by their own research personnel.

COSTS

The Committee estimates that costs for implementation of S. 3419 would be as follows:

First year	$180, 000, 000
Second year	200, 000, 000
Third year	225, 000, 000
Fourth year	250, 000, 000
Fifth year	250, 000, 000

* * *

MINORITY VIEWS OF MR. COTTON

S. 3419, the Consumer Safety Act of 1972, is an omnibus bill comprising three titles. Its objective is to protect consumers against unreasonable risk of injury from hazardous products.

Title I sets forth definitions applicable to the Act (S. 3419) and establishes a new independent Consumer Safety Agency.

Title II transfers various functions under existing law to the new independent Consumer Safety Agency and repeals the following six categorical consumer safety statutes:

(1) The Federal Hazardous Substances Act, as amended (15 U.S.C. 1261 et seq.);

(2) The Flammable Fabrics Act, as amended (15 U.S.C. 1191 et seq.);

(3) Chapter VI of the Food, Drug, and Cosmetics Act (21 U.S.C. 361–363) concerning adulterated cosmetics;

(4) The Radiation Control for Health and Safety Act (42 U.S.C. 263b–263n);

(5) The Poison Prevention Packaging Act of 1970 (15 U.S.C. 1471–76); and

(6) The Act of August 2, 1956 (15 U.S.C. 1211) concerning household refrigerator safety devices.

Title III sets forth the substantive provisions concerning consumer product safety—i.e., authority to set consumer product safety standards, enforcement procedures and sanctions. Except for vesting this authority in the new independent Consumer Safety Agency rather than the Department of Health, Education, and Welfare, its provisions are substantially the same as those set forth in a draft bill submitted by the Secretary of Health, Education, and Welfare to the President of the Senate by letter dated April 20, 1971, which was introduced by Senator Magnuson and myself (by request) on May 6, 1971, as S. 1797. Its objective was "to reduce or eliminate unreasonable risk of death, or of serious or frequent illness or injury, associated with exposure to or use of such products, *by establishing in the Department of Health, Education, and Welfare a product safety program under which the Secretary* would collect and disseminate information on consumer product hazards, and promulgate mandatory standards for consumer products *insofar as the need for such standards is supported by injury and other data.*" [1] (Emphasis supplied)

Another bill considered by the Committee on Commerce along with S. 1797 was S. 983, introduced by Senator Magnuson and Senator Moss on February 25, 1971.[2] S. 983 was a legislative recommendation of the National Commission on Product Safety contained in its final report transmitted to the President and to the Congress on June 30, 1970.

The National Commission on Product Safety was established pursuant to S.J. Res. 33 which was approved on November 30, 1967, as P.L. 90–146. The Commission's principal duty was to "conduct a comprehensive study and investigation of the scope and adequacy of measures now employed to protect consumers against unreasonable risk of injuries which may be caused by hazardous household products." [3] The term "household products" was defined to mean "products customarily produced or distributed for sale through retail sales agencies or instrumentalities for use by a consumer or any member of his family in or around the household." It was further provided, however, that "Such term does *not* include *products which are subject to regulations prescribed* under the National Traffic and Motor Vehicle Safety Act of 1966 (15 U.S.C. 1381 et seq.), the Flammable Fabrics Act (15 U.S.C. 1191 et seq.), the Federal Food, Drug, and Cosmetic Act (21 U.S.C. 301 et seq.), the Federal Hazardous Substances Labeling Act (15 U.S.C. 1261 et seq.), the Federal Cigarette Labeling and Advertising Act (15 U.S.C. 1331 et seq.), the Federal Firearms Act (15 U.S.C. 901 et seq.), the National Firearms Act (26 U.S.C. 5801 et seq.), and the Federal Insecticide, Fungicide, and Rodenticide Act (7 U.S.C. 135 et seq.)." [4] (Emphasis supplied.)

I joined with the Chairman of our Committee on Commerce, Senator Magnuson, in co-sponsoring S.J. Res. 33 which served to establish the National Commission on Product Safety. When the Senate considered that legislation almost five years ago, I stated in part the following:

> I believe that the Committee felt that to plunge into legislation and undertake the task in the Committee, to deal fairly and justly, with careful analysis, with all the multitudinous appliances on the market being manufactured, sold, and utilized in and about the home, would be a hasty and perhaps unfair method of pursuing this task.
>
> Therefore, it was our opinion that a Commission to make a careful study and analysis and recommend how far we should go, in enacting laws for the protection of the consumer and his family, would be a wiser and better approach. That is the rea-

---

1 Congressional Record, May 6, 1971, S. 6329.
2 *See also* S. 4054, 91st Congress, 2d Session.
3 Public Law No. 90–146, section 2(a).
4 *Ibid.*, section 6.

son for my enthusiastic support of this resolution creating this Commission.[5]

If in 1967 I had known what I now know about how far the final product, S. 3419, would go, then my earlier support would have been something less than enthusiastic. S. 3419 goes well beyond the bounds established for the Commission pursuant to P.L. 90–146 and the recommendation set forth in its final report. As a matter of fact, during that same earlier consideration of S.J. Res. 33 I also stated that "great oaks from little acorns grow, and whenever we scratch the surface of a subject of legislation, immediately during the hearings that result, and the study of legislation, there is brought to light many other steps that should be taken."[6] Little did I realize that the seed we planted would blossom into a patch of poison oak which will have legitimate business breaking out in a rash from the fear of potential regulatory harassment and scratching for years to come if the Committee bill is enacted!

My opposition to S. 3419 was not without considerable soul-searching and deep personal regret. I sincerely felt that the work of the National Commission on Product Safety was a worthwhile effort and that it produced what was in large measure a commendable work product. As a matter of fact, when S. 3419 was ordered reported by our Committee on Commerce it was my intention to limit my views solely to registering opposition to Titles I and II establishing and transferring certain functions to a new independent Consumer Safety Agency. I then felt and I feel now that such a new independent Agency, in addition to the Consumer *Protection* Agency proposed in legislation now pending before the Senate Committee on Government Operations (i.e., H.R. 10835 and S. 1177) would be redundant, regressive, and a waste of the taxpayers money.[7] However, after examining the Committee report on S. 3419, I am compelled to raise further objections as a result of the legislative interpretations placed by that report upon certain key provisions of the bill.

My three principal objections to S. 3419, upon which I shall elaborate further may be summarized as follows:

(A) There is no demonstrated need for the establishment of a new independent Consumer *Safety* Agency, especially in light of pending legislation (H.R. 10835) which would establish a new independent Consumer *Protection* Agency, and which is, unlike that proposed in S. 3419, supported by the Administration;

(B) The apparent unknown impact of including "an electronic product" in the definition of "Consumer product" coupled with the repeal of the Radiation Control for Health and Safety Act (42 U.S.C. 263b–263n);[8] and

(C) The erroneous and mischievous legislative interpretation given in the Committee report to the terms "subject to regulation" and "subject to safety regulation" found in section 101(1) of S. 3419 which could lead to dual and duplicative regulation in the following product areas:

---

[5] Congressional Record, June 6, 1967, S7740.

[6] *Ibid.*

[7] *See also* similar bill, S. 4459. 91st Congress, 2d Session, which passed the Senate on December 1, 1970 on a vote of 74–4 and which I supported.

[8] *See* S. 3419, section 101(1) and section 204(a)(4).

(1) "products subject to regulation under the National Traffic and Motor Vehicle Safety Act of 1966 (15 U.S.C. 1381 et seq.);

(2) "aircraft or other aeronautical products subject to safety regulations by the Federal Aviation Administration;

(3) "foods, drugs or devices subject to safety regulations under the Food, Drug, and Cosmetic Act (21 U.S.C. 301 et seq.), as amended by section 204(a) of this Act;

(4) "products subject to safety regulations under the Federal Insecticide, Fungicide, and Rodenticide Act (7 U.S.C. 135 et seq.);

(5) "products subject to regulation under the Occupational Safety and Health Act of 1970 (29 U.S.C. 651 et seq.);

(6) "products subject to safety regulations under the Gas Pipeline Safety Act (49 U.S.C. 1671 et seq.); [and]

(7) "products subject to safety regulations under the Atomic Energy Act of 1954 (42 U.S.C. 2011 et seq.)".

A. Consumer Safety Agency

The establishment of a new independent Consumer Safety Agency is objectionable for several reasons.

1. CONTRARY TO RECOMMENDATIONS OF THE PRESIDENT AND MEMBERS OF CONGRESS

First, the establishment of such an independent Agency is contrary to recommendations on reorganization submitted by the President to this Congress, *as well as, ironically enough, legislative proposals advanced by several of the proponents of the new Consumer Safety Agency.*

On March 25, 1971, the President submitted to the Congress his Message on Government Reorganization in which he proposed four new departments.[9] One of the four proposed new departments would be the Department of Human Resources which would include the applicable functions of the Department of Health, Education, and Welfare and several of which, pursuant to S. 3419, are now being proposed to be transferred to the new independent Consumer Agency. As the President noted in his message:

> The problem with government is not, by and large, the people in government.
>
> * * * * * * *
>
> Good people cannot do good things with bad mechanisms. But bad mechanisms can frustrate even the noblest aims.[10]

Again on March 29, 1972, the President submitted to the Congress another message on his proposed reorganization of the Executive Branch. In that message the President noted in part the following:

> The plethora of diverse and fragmented Federal activities * * * is a glaring case in point.[11]

[9] H. Doc. 92–75.
[10] *Ibid.*
[11] Congressional Record, March 29, 1972, S5164.

In my opinion the new independent Consumer Safety Agency proposed in S. 3419 is just such a "bad mechanism" and a further fragmenting of Federal activities referred to in the two messages from the President on the reorganization of the Executive Branch.

Additionally, there have been legislative proposals on reorganization of the Executive Branch recently advanced by members of the Senate, on which I find myself somewhat in sympathetic accord. For example, on March 29, 1972, the very day of the President's second message on his reorganization proposals and but eight days following the action of the Committee on Commerce in ordering reported S. 3419, the distinguished senior Senator from Connecticut (Mr. Ribicoff), himself a former Secretary of HEW, introduced, along with more than 20 co-sponsors, the bill, S. 3432. I think it is particularly significant that *four of the several co-sponsors of S. 3432 are members of the Committee on Commerce who support the independent Consumer Safety Agency proposed to be established pursuant to S. 3419.*[12] S. 3432, however, proposes to establish a separate Department of Health. Moreover, of the several existing statutes proposed to be transferred to this new Department of Health, three would be repealed entirely; one, in part; and four, transferred to the new independent Consumer Safety Agency proposed in S. 3419.

Complementing S. 3432, the Senator from Minnesota (Mr. Humphrey) introduced on April 7, 1972, the bill, S. 3464, which would establish a Department of Education. (See Congressional Record of that date, at page S561.)

Another proposed approach is the bill, S. 3312, introduced on March 8, 1972. This bill proposes to establish a Commission to study and appraise the organization and operation of the Executive Branch of the Federal Government. On the occasion of the introduction of S. 3312 its author noted in part the following:

> It is time that we once again step back and see what we have created. We know that our great bureaucracies do not function properly at all times. We know that they waste tax dollars through duplication of activities and mismanagement of physical resources and personnel. *We cannot afford to limp along with piecemeal reorganizations by the Congress or the Executive.*[13] (Emphasis supplied)

The point to be made, I believe, is a highly significant one. S. 3419 prejudges in part the legislative proposals both of the President and the several members of the Senate noted above. One cannot have it both ways—further study or a positive legislative proposal—and still adjudge that a new independent Consumer Safety Agency is the more viable mechanism.

Someone once observed that reorganizing "[s]hould be undergone about as often as major surgery." [14] And, we should make no mistake that S. 3419 does represent major, if not radical, surgery upon the Government organizational structure. But, perhaps this allure for

---

[12] Senators Magnuson, Hartke, Pastore, and Hart; *See* Congressional Record, March 29, 1972, at page S5050.

[13] *See* Congressional Record, March 8, 1972, at page S. 3612 *re* S. 3312 introduced by Senator Pearson.

[14] Townsend, Robert, *Up the Organization* (Alfred A. Knopf, New York, 1970), p. 162.

reorganizing, like that proposed by the proponents of an independent Consumer Safety Agency, was best expressed by the Roman author, G. Petronius Arbiter who made the following observation:

> I was to learn later in life that we tend to meet any new situation by reorganizing; and a wonderful method it can be for creating the illusion of progress while producing confusion, inefficiency, and demoralization.[15]

2. AN INDEPENDENT AGENCY IS NOT A PANACEA

Proponents of the independent Agency including the National Commission on Product Safety are prone to represent it as some sort of a panacea. It is argued that such an independent Agency would have greater public visibility than an organization structured within an existing Executive Department; that it would be better able to resist pressures that often cause regulators to identify their interests with those of the industries they regulate; and that it would be able to secure a higher level of funding than would an organization situated within a Cabinet-level department. Such arguments have a particular appeal to Congressional frustrations over the ever-growing size of the Executive bureaucracy, but there is to my knowledge no empirical evidence to support this view.

On the contrary, Secretary of HEW Elliot Richardson rebutted such arguments by noting the following:

> I doubt that these observations hold true over the long run. As examples, actions of the Federal Trade Commission or Interstate Commerce Commission have never seemed to me to be more "visible" than an action of the Food and Drug Administration, even though they are independent agencies. Nor do I think that independent regulatory agencies have historically shown a greater resistance than other agencies to the pressures that often cause agencies to identify their interests with those of the industries they regulate.[16]

Moreover, on the issue of increased funding the following table comparing the budget authority for the Food and Drug Administration with the *independent* Federal Trade Commission does little to support the view of the proponents of the proposed new independent Consumer Safety Agency:

Fiscal year	Amount	Increase (percent)
Food and Drug Administration:		
1971	$87,503,000	
1972	110,745,000	[1] 26
1973 (proposed)	182,869,000	[2] 65
Federal Trade Commission:		
1971	22,470,000	
1972	25,092,000	[1] 12
1973 (proposed)	27,073,000	[2] 8

[1] Fiscal year 1972 percentage increase over base fiscal year 1971.
[2] Fiscal year 1973 (proposed) percentage increase over base fiscal year 1972.

[15] *Ibid.* (From Petronius Arbiter (circa. A.D. 60))

[16] U.S. Congress, House. Committee on Interstate and Foreign Commerce. Hearings on *Consumer Product Safety Act.* (Part 3) 92d Congress, 1st and 2d Sessions (Serial No. 92–61), p. 973. *See also* Kohlmeier, Jr., Louis, M., *The Regulators* (Harper & Row, New York, 1969), Part Two, Chapter 6.

Perhaps the distinguished Chairman of the Committee on Government Operations of the House of Representatives (Mr. Holifield) best expressed the rebuttal to those who would argue that the independency of an agency results in increased funding during the 1966 debate on the Department of Transportation Act in the following manner:

> Will they obtain a dynamic, viable * * * program by withdrawing themselves from the mainstream of * * * attention, and getting off to one side and playing solitaire in the back room, or if they allow themselves to be put into this Department * * * —and that is where the chips are—they might be able to sit in and get a few more chips from that game.[17]

Reports from agencies and departments of the Executive Branch including the Office of Management and Budget, are uniformly opposed to the establishment of an independent Consumer Safety Agency. And, this position in opposition to the proliferation of independent agencies is hardly unique to this Administration.

For example, the Honorable Charles L. Schultze, Director, Bureau of the Budget, under the Administration of President Lyndon B. Johnson, noted in part the following with respect to a legislative proposal to create an independent Federal Maritime Administration:

> Consolidation, not fragmentation, is the direction we should follow.
>
> * * * * * * *
>
> Many groups in our community seek to have independent agencies established within the executive branch which can act as advocates for their particular interests. This is an understandable desire * * *.
>
> With the growing complexity of our Federal Government and the increasing demands on the time of both the President and the Congress, a relatively small independent agency . . . can easily get lost in the shuffle. It has little chance to bring decisive weight to bear on Government-wide policy issues. It is at a disadvantage in competing with major departments and large agencies for scarce resources. A Cabinet Secretary, on the other hand, has ready access to the President. In discussions of any policy affecting his Department he necessarily plays a major role—even though the particular policy is Government-wide in nature. This is much less likely to be the case with a small independent agency.
>
> The small independent agency, moreover, cannot hope to bring to bear the special resources—in terms of research capacity, systems design, attraction of top flight personnel, computer capability, and other services—that a large department can muster.[18]

Perhaps the issue was phrased even more succinctly by another cabinet officer under the Administration of President Johnson when the

---

[17] Congressional Record, August 24, 1966, p. 20380.

[18] U.S. Congress, House. Committee on Merchant Marine and Fisheries. Hearings on *Independent Federal Maritime Administration.* 90th Congress, 1st Session (Serial No. 90–9, pp. 124–125.

first Secretary of Transportation, Allen S. Boyd, made the following observation:

> A separate chapter in the Government Organization Manual is not going to be any magic elixir * * *[19]

3. CONFLICT WITH CONSUMER *PROTECTION* AGENCY

There presently is pending before the Senate Committee on Government Operations the bill, S. 1177, and the House-passed bill which is supported by the Administration, H.R. 10835. Each proposes, *inter alia*, to establish a new independent Consumer *Protection* Agency. Those legislative measures still are under consideration by the Senate Committee on Government Operations.

Most significantly, H.R. 10835, as passed by the House of Representatives and referred to the Senate Committee on Government Operations, contains a section 208 entitled "Consumer Safety". This section makes it mandatory upon the proposed new independent Consumer Protection Agency to "conduct studies and investigations of the scope and adequacy of measures employed to protect consumers against unreasonable risk of injury which may be caused by hazardous household products, * * *" This provision enters into the very study area of the National Commission on Product Safety conducted pursuant to P.L. 90–146 and more importantly, stands in direct conflict with the provisions of S. 3419.

Accordingly, until such time as the issues raised by such legislative measures pending before the Senate Committee on Government Operations are resolved, action by the Senate on S. 3419 proposing to establish yet *another* new independent agency pertaining to consumer matters is definitely premature, inconsistent, and a shameful waste of the taxpayers' money.

4. THE ANALOGY OF THE ENVIRONMENTAL PROTECTION AGENCY DOES NOT SUPPORT THE ESTABLISHMENT OF AN INDEPENDENT CONSUMER SAFETY AGENCY

The establishment of the independent Environmental Protection Agency (EPA) pursuant to Reorganization Plan No. 3 of 1970 does *not* justify the creation of an independent Consumer Safety Agency as argued by the proponents for the latter.

In the first place, prior to the establishment of EPA, the programs and authorities now contained within that Agency were distributed among several Federal departments and agencies. On the other hand, the authorities proposed to be transferred into the new independent Consumer Safety Agency are essentially those which now reside within the single Department of Health, Education, and Welfare.

The Food and Drug Administration, many of the function of which are proposed by S. 3419 to be transferred to the Consumer Safety Agency are essentially regulatory in nature and are dependent upon an existing regional and field office system integrated within the network of regional offices of the Department of Health, Education, and Welfare. No such single system existed for the components which were transferred into EPA.

[19] *Ibid.*, p. 414.

Similarly, there is an Operational Planning System within the Department of HEW which the Secretary uses to insure inter-agency cooperation, program performance, etc. The Food and Drug Administration is tied in closely with this system. There was no analogous system for the various components transferred into EPA.

The Food and Drug Administration's regulatory responsibilities also require a significant amount of legal and judicial activity. These services are available through the Office of the General Counsel of HEW whereas the components transferred into EPA had no such single source for this type of assistance.

Finally, a very definite relationship exists between the Food and Drug Administration and the health components of the Department of HEW. No such single unit of supporting services existed for the component transferred into EPA. In summary, to "bootstrap" a new independent Consumer Safety Agency using the analogy of the independent Environmental Protection Agency is both specious and grossly misleading.

5. THE ESTABLISHMENT OF AN INDEPENDENT CONSUMER SAFETY AGENCY COULD PROVE TO BE REGRESSIVE RATHER THAN PROGRESSIVE

On March 16, 1972, Secretary of HEW Richardson issued a press release on the bill, S. 3419, strongly opposing the establishment of an independent Consumer Safety Agency.[20] In that press release Secretary Richardson charged that "[t]he bill for a separate agency is regressive. It will deal the cause of consumer safety a crushing set back." This position recognizes the close mission relationship between the Food and Drug Administration's medical devices and radiological health programs and the product safety functions because of common technology and emphasis upon safe products through engineering design. Certainly the establishment of any new agency or department constitutes a major reorganization with a new administrative superstructure consisting of budget, personnel, procurement and computer services amongst others. Such a resulting time delay cannot but help slow down the increasing momentum the Food and Drug Administration and the Department of HEW have been building in the field of consumer safety.

Moreover, as was pointed out by Secretary Richardson, the establishment of the independent Consumer Safety Agency would destroy vital relationships between the Food and Drug Administration's food, drug, cosmetic and product safety regulatory processes and the other health responsibilities of the Department of HEW.

In Secretary Richardson's own words,

> I think * * * that if the Food and Drug Administration is going to have any problems of digestion of new responsibilities, the problems would be multiplied severalfold by the effort to create a new agency duplicating administrative authorities and having to seek scientific capabilities and resources that are already within the Food and Drug Administration.

---

[20] *See* Appendix A for full text of Secretary of HEW Richardson's press release.

> * * * the opportunity to move forward effectively and quickly in the enforcement of the kinds of legislation being considered * * * is much greater if we build upon the experience and capabilities of the Food and Drug Administration, than if we start all over again through the creation of a comparatively small, isolated outside body.[21]

Again on March 9, 1972, Secretary Richardson appeared before the Subcommittee on Labor, Health, Education, and Welfare and Related Agencies of the Senate Appropriations Committee and at that time I questioned him concerning the advisability of removing such functions from the Department of HEW and placing them within the proposed new independent Consumer Safety Agency. The colloquy at that time was as follows:

> Senator COTTON. We have a bill sponsored by the Chairman of the Subcommittee and the Chairman of the Full Committee which would move them out of the Department.
>
> What's your feeling about that?
>
> Secretary RICHARDSON. We oppose that, as I've had occasion to testify before the Chairman in his capacity as Chairman of the Commerce Committee, for the reason primarily that we think the Food and Drug Administration and our consumer safety role in general is strengthened by replacement [sic] of the Food and Drug Administration within a department having health responsibilities generally. And it can draw on the resources of, for example, the Communicable Disease Center in Atlanta and the research of the National Institutes of Health in Bethesda. The case for separation is basically that the regulatory agencies can benefit from independence, but we think that the record is highly ambiguous on that score, that indeed, it can be argued quite effectively that regulatory agencies in isolation have tended to come under the control of the regulated industry.
>
> So the case should then turn on whether or not the Food and Drug is able effectively to draw on the other resources of the Department.

6. A VIABLE ALTERNATIVE DOES EXIST TO THE PROPOSED NEW INDEPENDENT CONSUMER SAFETY AGENCY

On July 19, 1971 the Honorable Elliot L. Richardson, Secretary of the Department of Health, Education, and Welfare, appeared before the Senate Committee on Commerce. At the very beginning of his testimony, he read into the record a letter of the same date from the President to the Chairman of the Committee which noted in part the following:

> Today, Secretary Richardson will announce with my approval, that upon enactment of this bill [i.e., S. 1797], he will create within DHEW a new Consumer Safety Administration. This unit will build upon the activities, personnel, and

[21] U.S. Congress, House. Committee on Interstate and Foreign Commerce Hearings on *Consumer Product Safety Act* (Part 3) 92d Congress, 1st and 2d Sessions (Serial No. 92–61), p. 1045.

> facilities of the Food and Drug Administration, which has a long and distinguished history in the field of consumer safety, primarily in the vital regulation of the foods we eat and the drugs we use.[22]

Secretary Richardson went on to note the following:

> Upon its enactment, therefore, I propose to build, as the President's letter has just informed the Committee, upon the FDA framework by establishing a new Consumer Safety Administration to be composed of three major offices:
>
> The Office of Product Safety Regulation;
> The Office of Drug Regulation; and
> The Office of Food Regulation.[23]

Certainly, such an organizational structure within the Department of Health, Education, and Welfare would give "consumer safety" the required visibility and provide it equal status to its major components. The proposed Offices would be supported by information collection, field surveillance, and research capabilities, foundations for which already exist within the Department. Furthermore, a national center for consumer safety statistics would be established to collect, analyze and disseminate information on injuries and their causes, as they are associated with foods, drugs, and consumer products.

B. EFFECT UPON ELECTRONICS AND REPEAL OF THE RADIATION CONTROL FOR HEALTH AND SAFETY ACT

Section 101(1) of S. 3419 provides the definition for "Consumer product" which includes "an electronic product as defined in paragraph (3)" [sic.]. Paragraphs (3) [sic.] and (4) [sic.] provide the definitions for "Electronic product" and "Electronic product radiation", respectively, which are taken directly from the Radiation Control for Health and Safety Act of 1968 (42 U.S.C. 263b–263n).

Section 204(a) of S. 3419 in paragraph (4) repeals the Radiation Control for Health and Safety Act and provides that such is "superseded by the authority granted in title III of this Act * * *" (i.e., that Title dealing with consumer product safety and which vests such authority in a Commissioner of Product Safety.)

The purpose of the Radiation Control for Health and Safety Act was to so amend the Public Health Service Act as to provide for the protection of the public health from *radiation emission* from electronic products. What S. 3419 has done by virtue of including "electronic product" within the definition of "Consumer product", and at the same time repealing the Act and superseding it by authority in Title III, is to subject such electronic products not only to regulation concerning radiation emissions but to an entire panoply of regulation which might evolve from the establishment of a consumer product safety standard not necessarily limited solely to radiation emissions. Thus, the electronic industry could be subject to a series of regulations for which no hearing record whatsoever has been developed in justification for such an extension.

---

[22] Op. cit. infra note 23 at p. 95; see Appendix B for full text of letter from President Nixon to Chairman Magnuson.

[23] U.S. Congress, Senate. Committee on Commerce. Hearings on *Consumer Product Safety Act of 1971.* (Part 1) 92d Congress, 1st Session (Serial No. 92–27) p. 101.

For example, the inclusion of such product within the definition of "Consumer product" and the repeal of the Radiation Control for Health and Safety Act would eliminate the product exemptions now permitted with respect to certain electronic products which are intended for use by, and of a type used solely by, departments or agencies of the United States and for which certain procurement specifications have been prescribed, as well as the further exemption for the purpose of research, investigations, studies, demonstrations, or training or for reasons of national security. This one example alone is cause for concern and I would hope that the Committees to which S. 3419 has been referred for consideration will closely examine this aspect, taking whatever remedial action may be necessary.

C. Legislative Interpretation of "Subject to Safety Regulation"

Section 101(1) of S. 3419 defines "Consumer product" and then quite properly excludes certain products subject to regulation under enumerated existing statutes. Unfortunately, the Committee report contains the following concerning this provision:

> The language "subject to safety regulation" indicates that products capable of being regulated under one of the enumerated acts but not *actually* "subject to safety regulation" can be reached by the Product Safety Commissioner when in response to a written inquiry to the appropriate agency it is ascertained that such products are not "subject to safety regulation." (Emphasis supplied)

Such a legislative interpretation is not only erroneous but is fraught with mischief since what it clearly means is that where the Commissioner of Product Safety has found that a particular consumer product, although coming within the purview of one of the enumerated statutes is not *in fact regulated*, then he, the Commissioner of Product Safety, would be able after notice to the administering agency to promulgate a safety standard. It would make the Consumer Safety Agency a "super agency", which could enter into all such areas not *actually* regulated! If so, then this would seem to prejudge the effectiveness of the Consumer *Protection* Agency proposed in legislation now pending before the Senate Committee on Government Operations and which, in its "watchdog" advocacy functions on behalf of the consumer, is designed to see that such consumer products are regulated where there is a demonstrated need.

In other words, if carried to its logical conclusion, the Ford Motor Company and the General Motors Corporation may be subject to regulation not only by the Department of Transportation under the National Traffic and Motor Vehicle Safety Act of 1966, but by the Commissioner of Product Safety. Similarly, manufacturers of aircraft or other aeronautical products such as the Boeing Company and Beech Aircraft Corporation, might be subject to safety regulations issued by both the Federal Aviation Administration and the Commissioner of Product Safety. This same could hold true for the regulatory area of the Atomic Energy Commission. This could very well lead to an untenable situation.

This legislative interpretation is all the more suspect when comparing it with the language to be found in section 6 of P.L. 90–146 establishing the National Commission on Product Safety. That section provides the definition for the term "household products" and in the second sentence provides in part the following:

> Such term does *not* include products which are *subject to regulations* prescribed * * * (Emphasis supplied)

under eight enumerated acts, one of which was the National Traffic and Motor Vehicle Safety Act of 1966. More importantly, when on June 24, 1970, the National Commission on Product Safety presented its final report to the Committee on Commerce, the following exchange occurred between the Senator from Utah (Mr. Moss) and the Chairman of the National Product Safety Commission (Mr. Elkind):

> Senator Moss. The proposed legislation for the creation of a Consumer Product Safety Commission exempts from the Commission's authority automobiles, flammable fabrics, cigarettes, foods, drugs, cosmetics, pesticides, and radiation hazards, because these products have already been covered by other legislation.
>
> Why didn't the Commission evaluate these programs and make recommendations with respect to which programs would remain independent of the Consumer Product Safety Commission and which should be brought into the Commission?
>
> Mr. Elkind. Well, we didn't want to extend our work into an area that *we didn't think had been assigned to us.*
>
> * * * * * * *
>
> We felt it would be presumtious on our part to express opinions in this area. * * * [24] (Emphasis supplied)

Thus, not only does S. 3419 repeal the several categorical safety statutes enumerated in section 204(a) which have provided the cornerstone for consumer safety, but through a legislative interpretation which even the National Commission on Product Safety did not accord similar language, it now seeks to reach into areas which already *may* be regulated under existing statutes. This, too, is an area which warrants most careful consideration by the two Senate Committees to which the bill, S. 3419 has been referred.

Conclusion

In conclusion, my opposition to S. 3419, the Consumer Safety Act of 1972, is not motivated by any desire to reduce the safety of consumer products. On the contrary, my opposition to this bill centers upon a genuine concern over the following:

(1) The efficacy of establishing a new independent Consumer Safety Agency;

(2) The unknown but apparent impact upon the electronic industries of including within the definition of consumer product, electronic products, coupled with the repeal of the Radiation Control for Health and Safety Act; and

[24] U.S. Congress, Senate, Committee on Commerce. Hearings on *National Commission On Product Safety*. 91st Congress, 2d Session, (Serial No. 91–82), p. 16.

(3) The erroneous and mischievous interpretation given in the Committee report to the terms "subject to regulation" and "subject to safety regulation".

I sincerely fear that the proponents of this new independent Consumer Safety Agency have been blinded by the "gold glitter" of what can be accomplished through the establishment of yet another independent agency. As pointed out in *The Regulators by* Louis M. Kohlmeier, Jr.:

> Perhaps the only sure conclusion to be drawn is that government, as presently constituted, has made more promises than it can keep.[25]

I fear that the organizational structure proposed in S. 3419 could very well prove to be yet another such promise which the Federal government will not be able to keep.

Accordingly, while in general support for the need for new and improved authority with respect to consumer product safety, I must in all honesty register both my disappointment and my opposition to S. 3419 for the foregoing reasons.

Norris Cotton.

Appendix A

HEW NEWS—MARCH 16, 1972

HEW Secretary Elliot L. Richardson charged today that a bill before Congress to establish a separate consumer safety agency would sell the American consumer a phony bill of goods by moving away from, rather than toward, greater product safety for the consumer.

"The bill for a separate agency is regressive. It will deal the cause of consumer safety a crushing setback," the Secretary said.

"It would abandon the field to exploiters of the consumer by destroying existing mechanisms for regulation. It would create a serious vacuum—one lasting as long as three years—into which the exploiters could move while the new agency is being set into motion. It would have an adverse impact on the public health and the public purse," he said.

"This Administration has submitted its own strong product safety legislation to the Congress along with a letter from the President committing HEW to establishing within the Department a new consumer safety administration which would have an upgraded Food and Drug Administration as its core.

"Yet, to my complete disbelief, the Senate Commerce Committee seems to have chosen to counter this strong proposal by adding to it a disruptive reorganization which threatens to harm the health concerns of consumers," Secretary Richardson said.

Instead of helping consumers, the Secretary said, the regressive bill now before the Senate Commerce Committee moves counter to this with its load of fatal flaws:

—It would slow down the increasing momentum the FDA and HEW have been building in consumer safety.

—It would destroy vital relationships between the FDA's food, drug, cosmetic, and product safety regulatory processes and the other health responsibilities of HEW.

—It would require duplication of health accident and injury data collection which is now centralized in HEW.

—It would inevitably follow the path of other so-called independent regulatory agencies which have not fared as well in budget terms as those within Departments of the Executive Branch.

—It runs counter to the recommendations of numerous bipartisan national commissions studying Federal executive organization in recent years, all of which

[25] Kohlmeier, Jr., Louis M., *The Regulators* (Harper & Row, New York, 1969), p. 15.

have recommended consolidation, not further fragmentation, of Federal agencies and departments.

Secretary Richardson focused his attack on the bill for a separate agency on the premise that it would divorce consumer protection from public health.

"Public health is a prime responsibility of HEW and this will not change," he said. "FDA, as part of the Public Health Service, now draws on the total health resources of HEW. A separate agency would find such wide ranging support impossible to acquire.

"HEW is seeking a 70 percent increase in the FDA budget for the coming fiscal year—the largest increase for this agency in its history. For the first time, the FDA will have the people and the money it needs to do its job," the Secretary said.

APPENDIX B

THE WHITE HOUSE,
Washington, D.C., July 19, 1971.

Hon. WARREN G. MAGNUSON,
U.S. Senate,
Washington, D.C.

DEAR MR. CHAIRMAN: In my Consumer Message of February 24, I proposed comprehensive product safety legislation authorizing the Department of Health, Education, and Welfare to regulate hazardous consumer products. Subsequently S. 1797, a bill incorporating this proposal, was introduced on behalf of the Administration and referred to your Committee.

As part of the preparation of this bill, I asked Secretary Richardson to undertake a careful study of the organizational structure within the Department of Health, Education, and Welfare that would most effectively implement the consumer product safety authority proposed in S. 1797.

Today, Secretary Richardson will announce, with my approval, that upon enactment of this bill, he will create within the Department of Health, Education, and Welfare a new Consumer Safety Administration. This unit will build upon the activities, personnel and facilities of the Food and Drug Administration which has a long and distinguished history in the field of consumer safety, primarily in the vital regulation of the foods we eat and the drugs we use.

The Consumer Safety Administration will continue the work of the Food and Drug Administration. At the same time, the new unit will be structured so that the regulation of hazardous consumer products authorized in S. 1797 will have the facilities, the personnel, and the organizational prominence that will ensure an effective, efficient and responsive product safety program. Finally, where possible, common facilities such as laboratories and field offices will be utilized to gain the maximum possible cost effectiveness.

S. 1797 is a strong bill which will fully satisfy the public need for adequate protection against hazardous consumer products, and Secretary Richardson has acted to ensure that his Department is fully capable of implementing this needed authority. I urge your Committee to report S. 1797 favorably to the Senate.

Sincerely,

RICHARD NIXON.

ADDITIONAL VIEWS OF SENATOR STEVENS

I oppose the establishment of an independent Consumer Safety Agency because I feel the recent proliferation of independent agencies has compounded the problems of administration of Federal laws. I support the consumer protection and safety concepts, but believe that they should not be divorced from the responsibilities already imposed upon the Department of Health, Education, and Welfare by other laws.

TED STEVENS.

APPENDIX D

REPORT OF SENATE LABOR COMMITTEE

92D CONGRESS *2d Session*	SENATE	REPORT No. 92–835

FOOD, DRUG, AND CONSUMER PRODUCT SAFETY ACT OF 1972

JUNE 5, 1972.—Ordered to be printed

Mr. KENNEDY, from the Committee on Labor and Public Welfare, submitted the following

REPORT

together with

SUPPLEMENTAL VIEWS

[To accompany S. 3419]

The Committee on Labor and Public Welfare, to which was referred the bill (S. 3419), to having considered the same, reports favorably thereon with amendments and recommends that the bill as amended do pass.

PURPOSE

The purpose of this bill is to establish an independent agency in the Executive branch to regulate foods, drugs, and consumer products. It would combine into a single agency (1) the authority of the Food and Drug Administration over food, drugs, and consumer products; (2) the authority of the Division of Biologics Standards over human biological drugs; (3) the authority of the Center for Disease Control over clinical laboratory licensing; (4) the authority of the Department of Commerce and the FTC over flammable fabrics and refrigerator doors; and (5) the authority of the Agriculture Department over food inspection and animal biological drugs. The result will be one agency with comprehensive jurisdiction and authority to regulate all food, drugs, and common household products.

Since many of the primary components of the new agency come from the Food and Drug Administration, the Committee on Labor and Public Welfare expects that it shall retain its present jurisdiction respecting regulatory authority exercised by the new agency. The Committee also expects that it shall share the responsibility for holding confirmatory hearings on the administrator of such agency with the Senate Commerce Committee.

HEARINGS

The Subcommittee on Health held two days of hearings on May 2 and 3, 1972. On the first day of hearings Elliot Richardson, Secretary of Department of Health, Education, and Welfare, voiced the Administration's opposition to removing the Food and Drug Administration from HEW. James Goddard, M.D., former Commissioner of the Food and Drug Administration, strongly supported transferring the FDA to an independent agency and expanding its responsibilities. Dr. Goddard also emphasized the importance of the provisions to establish a National Injury Information Clearing House and to require the new Agency to file an annual report to Congress without the review of the Office of Management and Budget.

The subcommittee heard testimony on the final day of hearings from consumer and public health witnesses. James R. Kimmey, M.D., Executive Director, American Public Health Association, strongly supported expansion of the responsibilities of the FDA to promote and protect public health but favored retention of the FDA within a department concerned with health affairs. James Turner, author of the "Chemical Feast," a critical book about the FDA, favored transferring the FDA to a new independent regulatory agency where regulation would be a top priority. Martha Robinson, Information Director, Consumer Federation of America, affirmed support for the transfer of the FDA citing the need for an independent agency.

Among those who filed statements to the committee were the Pharmaceutical Manufacturer's Association, the Proprietary Association, the Grocery Manufacturer's Association, and the American Medical Association.

In addition to the hearings of the Subcommittee on Health, the Subcommittee on Executive Reorganization, and Government Research of the Government Operations Committee held 4 days of hearings on S. 3419. The latter hearings included 15 witnesses who provided sharply contrasting views on the bill, and the Committee on Labor and Public Welfare took into consideration this testimony in formulating its recommendations.

Arnold Elkind, former chairman of the National Commission on Product Safety, and Judy Jackson, of the Public Interest Research Group, favored transferring the FDA to the new agency. J. Edward Day, representing the Consumers Electronics Group of the Electronic Industries Association, and C. Joseph Stetler, President of the Pharmaceutical Manufacturers Association, opposed the transfer of the FDA and the expanding of its responsibilities. Gregory Ahart, Director of the Manpower and Welfare Division of the General Accounting Office, told the Subcommittee that organizational placement was not as important as "public and political concern for the importance of the mission."

Dr. Leonard Hayflick, a professor at the Stanford University School of Medicine and Dr. Peter Isacson, Project Director of the Vaccine Evaluation Unit, at the State University of New York in Buffalo, presented a critical evaluation of the work of the Division of Biologics Standards in the National Institutes of Health and urged support of the provision transferring the regulatory activities of DBS to FDA.

Rodney Leonard, former Administrator of the Consumer and Marketing Service of the Department of Agriculture told the Subcommittee that the food inspection programs of USDA should be transferred to the new agency. This view was supported in a statement to the Subcommittee by John Schnittker, former under-Secretary of Agriculture. Gregory Ahart, of GAO, pointed out the conflict of interest between USDA's consumer protection functions and its responsibility to promote the marketing of agricultural products.

Agency Independence

The final report of the National Commission on Product Safety in 1970, and the Commerce Committee report on the bill, make a strong and persuasive case for an independent agency. Nevertheless, the Committee considered this issue de novo. We reach the same conclusion.

The Committee began from the well-accepted proposition that new independent agencies should be created only on evidence of compelling need. We should guard against unnecessary fragmentation of the Federal structure. However, in this instance, the weight of the evidence argues for an independent agency.

The primary components of the new agency would come from the Food and Drug Administration, currently in the Department of Health, Education, and Welfare. Since its creation in 1906, FDA has functioned under several larger agencies and undergone many reorganizations. In none of these organizational structures and in none of these departments has the FDA been able to achieve optimum results. Repeated GAO reports and the work of Congressman Fountain's Subcommittee and others have brought many of these failures to light.

FDA's shortcomings have not been a matter of partisan politics; the same kinds of problems have plagued the FDA in Democratic as well as Republican administrations. Under all administrations, the agency has failed either to provide full protection to consumers against unsafe products or to articulate clear regulatory policies to industry.

The most important reason for this failure has been the agency's lack of clear-cut responsibility for accomplishing its mission. Authority for the regulation of food, drugs, and consumer products is widely fragmented within the federal government: the FDA sets standards for the leval of dangerous drug residues in meat and poultry, but testing and inspection is done by the Department of Agriculture; the FDA has responsibility to investigate the safety of flammable fabrics, but regulatory authority is vested with the Federal Trade Commission, the Department of Commerce and the Department of the Treasury. The same division of authority is present in other areas.

FDA has never had independent authority to regulate those matters within its jurisdiction. As presently structured within the Department of HEW, the Commissioner of the Food and Drug Administration must report to the Assistant Secretary for Health and Scientific Affairs, who must report to the Under Secretary of the Department of Health, Education, and Welfare, who must report to the Office of the Secretary of Health, Education, and Welfare, who must report to the Office of Management and Budget, to the Domestic Council, and finally, once all those channels have been exhausted, to the President. At any step along that route, a regulatory decision by the Commissioner could be reversed. Because of this structure, the Agency has not been able to make clear-cut regulatory decisions or even to make clear to consumers and to industry what its basic policies are.

In addition, despite the fact that many agencies have regulatory authority over food, drugs, and consumer products, in none is regulation the principal mission of the agency. In the Agriculture Department, for example, programs for the inspection of meat, poultry, and egg processing are under the direction of the same Assistant Secretary responsible for promoting the marketing of these very products. The basic orientation of the Department is to promote agricultural interests, not to make regulatory decisions which food producers might resist.

Similarly, in the Department of Health, Education, and Welfare, basic health programs are directed toward health research and health delivery systems. Even if all of FDA is considered health-related, 98% of the health resources of the Department and 88% of the manpower in fiscal year 1972 was devoted to health research and delivery. Health regulatory functions of FDA are only a small part of HEW's total health responsibility and cannot receive the attention they deserve.

Futhermore, in addition to health regulation, FDA plays an important role in economic regulation. It is concerned not only with adulteration of food and drugs which may be harmful to health, but with misbranding and deceptive labeling. With respect to adulteration of food, there are problems that are important but which do not, strictly speaking, involve dangers to health. For example, the FDA has published guidelines governing the amount of filth and foreign matter that may be permitted on food. In hearings before the Subcommittee on Executive Reorganization and Government Research, the Secretary stated that the presence of such foreign matter as rodent hairs in chocolate bars raised no health problem. Implicit in his statement was the assumption that since no health problem was raised, there was no pressing need for effective regulation to improve the purity of food. Yet there is clearly an interest in regulation to assure the purity of food, even when impurities are merely displeasing and do not pose a clear danger to health.

It is unlikely, however, that interests in economic and non-health regulation will ever be given appropriate consideration in a department in which health responsibilities focus on research and delivery. Nor is it likely that the entire program of regulation of food, drugs, and consumer products can ever be given the attention resources, support and services it deserves in as enormous and multifaceted a department as HEW. This problem is built in to the very structure of the Department, and is as prevalent in Democratic as in Republican administrations. It will continue to exist so long as the secretary is called upon to choose between competing needs. In short, to be an effective policeman of the marketplace, the agency must be free from the restraints of competing policies, priorities and objectives.

Examples are numerous. In the regulation of cyclamates, confusion over whose policy would prevail led the industry to build up vast inventories of products ultimately and unexpectedly banned from the market. This would not have happened if clear-cut authority to determine policy had been placed in one responsible official. Another example is the confusion concerning the use of detergents containing phosphates. Neither consumers, environmentalists, nor industry can tell for sure what the Government's regulatory policy is.

Finally, once a policy is enunciated, the FDA lacks the authority to enforce these decisions. The FDA must turn to the Department of Justice which because of other priorities may inadvertently frustrate or delay implementation of the FDA policy.

The committee also believes that the problem of food, drug, and consumer product regulation satisfies both of the basic criteria for the creation of an independent agency set out by the President in his message proposing the Environmental Protection Agency. The first, was that responsibility is divided among several agencies, but is not the primary function of any of them, and the other functions affect the agencies' views of the regulatory issues. The committee record shows that this situation exists in food, drug, and consumer product regulation.

The President stated a second criterion justifying the creation of an independent agency: a situation must exist in which the centralizing of authority in one agency would better enable that agency to make decisions about the activities of other agencies. The President stated that such decision-making functions were better lodged in an independent agency than in an existing cabinet department. He reasoned that a Cabinet agency, with multifarious non-regulatory responsibilities, might be regarded by other agencies as a representative of competing interests and constituencies and a promoter of its own programs at the expense of those of other agencies. He felt that it would be unwise in such a situation to transfer regulatory responsibilities to such a Cabinet agency.

It is entirely possible that promotion of HEW's health research and health delivery programs might appear to be in conflict with the promotion, marketing, and manufacturing of certain products. This problem could arise, for example, from the transfer of all authority over the use of the hormone diethylstilbesterol (DES), used to promote growth in cattle. The hormone has been shown to cause cancer in some animals, and residues of it in human food are prohibited. At present, authority is divided between HEW and the Department of Agriculture; largely because of this division, the government's policies have been inadequate and neither consumers nor industry have been satisfied with the result. Consolidation of authority would be desirable. But if all authority were transferred to HEW, heavily influenced by the need to promote its health delivery and research programs, the concerns of the Department of Agriculture might be ignored. Similarly, if all authority were transferred to the Department of Agriculture, health interests in HEW would feel uneasy.

A similar situation exists in the area of flammable fabrics, where the division of authority among the FDA, the FTC, the Department of Commerce and the Department of the Treasury has produced great confusion and no effective regulation. Consolidation is necessary, but authority would be lodged in an independent, wholly regulatory agency, without promotional programs designed to serve particular constituencies.

The Committee also strongly believes it essential to keep product safety regulation together with food and drug regulation. Enforcement and field operations in the three areas are already shared. To establish product safety regulation in a separate agency would cause needless duplication of staff, facilities, training, and other resources.

These transfers are based on precedent and widely accepted principles of government organization. The transfer of the poultry inspection program will simply reestablish it in the organization from which it was taken 15 years ago. The animal drug program properly belongs with the corresponding human drug programs in FDA. The Egg Inspection Act begins operation July 1, and hence involves no transfer of existing authority. The only transfers affecting programs historically associated with the Agriculture Department are meat and food inspection. The Committee believes that for both improved consumer protection and more efficient organization these programs should be transferred with the others.

The creation of a new agency will not sever the relationship between FDA and HEW. The Committee anticipates that there will be strong ties between the Department of HEW and the new Agency, just as there are presently strong ties between FDA and its sister agencies such as, FTC, EPA and USDA. Removing FDA from the Department of HEW is simply an organizational move to increase responsiveness and accountability, and need have no adverse impact on its relations with the health components of that Department in the future. In fact, these relationships may be substantially improved once the new Agency is established and is in a position to operate with the new strength and mandate given it in this legislation.

Committee Amendments

As reported by the Committee on Commerce, S. 3419 contained the short title of the "Consumer Safety Act of 1972." However, the bill extends considerably beyond issues of safety, and covers such matters as misbranding of food, drugs, cosmetics, and medical devices. The additional authorities transferred to the new Agency also encompass provisions that protect the health and pocketbook of the consumer, as well as his safety. As amended, S. 3419 covers food, drugs, and a wide variety of other consumer products. Accordingly, the short title of the bill has been changed to "The Food, Drug, and Consumer Product Act of 1972." The title change will also help reduce confusion with another bill before the Committee, S. 1177, the Consumer Protection Organization Act.

Title I

For the same reasons that the short title of the bill has been changed, the name of the new independent regulatory Agency created by the bill has been changed to "The Food, Drug, and Consumer Product Agency." This title more adequately describes the precise regulatory function of the new Agency. Further, it draws upon the name of its predecessor Agency, the Food and Drug Administration, which has been well-known since it was first adopted in 1931, and thus has 41 years of recognition by the public.

Findings and Declaration of Policy (Section 101)

As reported by the Committee on Commerce, S. 3419 contained no findings or declaration of policy. This Committee believes that findings will strengthen the legislation by explicitly setting out the basis on which it has been developed and enacted, thereby aiding in its subsequent interpretation and application.

The findings state the Congressional conclusion that the present fragmentation of regulation of food, drugs, and other consumer products throughout a number of federal departments and agencies has resulted in inconsistent policies and incomplete regulations, to the detriment of the consuming public. Effective food, drug and consumer product regulation requires creation of a new agency with independence to exert the leadership and vigorous enforcement necessary for consumer protection. Past experience shows that, unless the agency has the power to issue regulations, direct the course of all litigation, and make legislative and budgetary recommendations, without approval or clearance by outside agencies, its effectiveness will be substantially impaired.

In addition to consolidating present regulatory efforts relating to food, drugs, and consumer products within one agency, new legislative authority is also necessary to cover the safety hazards posed by household products for which present law establishes no safety regulation. The new legislation is intended to prevent needless injury to many Americans. In order to regulate these products most effectively, it is necessary to utilize the full reach of the commerce power under the Constitution, and to regulate intrastate commerce where it affects interstate commerce in these products.

Definitions (Section 102)

The definition of "consumer product" has been revised to delete the requirement that the distribution of the product must be "for sale," since any distribution of a hazardous product should properly be within the purview of the definition. The definition of "electronic" product has been deleted as well as the definitions for "electronic product" and "electronic product radiation," as unnecessary, since they are properly covered by the definition of "consumer product."

The definition of "consumer product" has been broadened to include "a component" of the product, so that the Agency could regulate just a part of a product, if only such regulation is warranted.

The Committee on Commerce provided that certain products "subject to safety regulation" under other listed statutes were excluded from the definition of a consumer product, and hence from regulation under Title III of this Act. The Committee has added a definition of "subject to safety regulation," in order to clarify the intended meaning. Under this definition, the enumerated products would not be considered "consumer products" if they were authorized to be regulated under the other statutes so as to eliminate any unreasonable risk of injury or death. Thus, the primary jurisdiction of other agencies has been recognized. The Administrator will determine whether a product is authorized to be regulated by another agency through communication and consultation with appropriate agency officials.

To be certain that products exempt from regulation by the Agency under the definition of a consumer product do not fail to be regulated for safety, the Committee has added a new power for the Administrator under section 104(c)(17). This grants him the right to petition the agency with primary jurisdiction to develop an appropriate safety regulation, and to participate in that proceeding. If the other agency requests, the Administrator may actually develop and enforce the new safety regulation himself.

Tobacco and tobacco products were completely exempted from the definition of consumer product by the Committee on Commerce. This Committee has also totally exempted food and drugs as defined in the Federal Food, Drug, and Cosmetic Act, since these products are completely regulated under present law with respect to safety. The definitions of "food" and "drug" under the Federal Food, Drug, and Cosmetic Act include all forms of food and drugs, including products presently regulated under more specific statutory provisions (such as the Federal Meat Inspection Act and the provisions in Section 351 of the Public Health Service Act relating to human biologics), thus this exclusion from Title III covers all food and drugs of any type.

The exclusion does not, however, cover cosmetics and medical devices regulated under the Federal Food, Drug, and Cosmetic Act. These two categories of products are presently regulated by incomplete and inadequate statutory provision of that Act. Under S. 3419 as reported by the Committee on Commerce, only cosmetics would have been included within the definition of a consumer product. There is no substantial reason for the exclusion of medical devices. This Committee believes that such products should also be included within the definition of consumer product.

This means that cosmetics and devices will be subject to the present provisions of the Federal Food, Drug, and Cosmetic Act, and to the new provisions of Title III of this bill. Since these two statutes are complementary, and in no way inconsistent, this will afford significant new consumer protection.

There is other pending legislation which would impose new regulatory requirements on cosmetics and devices. It is premature at this time to determine whether, and to what extent, those additional requirements may be appropriate, in addition to the present law contained in the Federal Food, Drug, and Cosmetic Act (which will remain applicable to cosmetics and devices after enactment of this bill) and the new supplemental requirements added by Title III and Title IV of this bill. It should be noted, in particular, that Title III contains no premarketing clearance provisions. Legislation presently pending with respect to devices would impose premarketing clearance for some devices, particularly those which are used in life-threatening situations. Enactment of this legislation is in no way intended to indicate that such additional legislation should not promptly be considered by the Congress. Titles III, and IV of this bill will, however, provide additional needed authority pending consideration of that additional legislation.

The definition of "injury" in S. 3419, as reported by the Committee on Commerce, appeared to focus on consumer products to the exclusion of food and drugs. Food and drugs are not taken unintentionally or accidentally, and the adverse reactions sometimes experienced from approved drugs are not "accidental" as that term is commonly understood. Accordingly, the requirement that an injury be "accidental" has been deleted. Similarly, adverse reactions have been added as one example of injury. Finally, a general all-inclusive reference to other natural or manmade agents has been added, to make it clear that all forms of food, drugs, and consumer products are intended to be encompassed.

Changes have been made in the definition of "risk-based analysis" to make clear that such analysis will provide standards for the Agency in fulfilling its responsibilities to minimize hazards and promote the public health and safety.

Establishment of Agency (Section 103)

In keeping with the change in name for the new Agency, to the Food, Drug, and Consumer Product Agency, this section has been amended to show that its mission includes protecting consumers against adulteration, misbranding, and illegal distribution of food, drugs, cosmetics, and medical devices, as well as against injury resulting from the use of consumer products.

Administrator (Sec. 104)

As reported by the Committee on Commerce, S. 3419 provided that the Administrator would "coordinate" the activities of the Commissions of Foods and Nutrition, and Drugs and Consumer Products. The word "coordinate" left unclear whether the Administrator could direct the activities of the commissions when necessary to resolve conflicts between the Commissions or provide consistent policy development. In order to provide the Administrator with this authority explicitly, the word "direct" was adeed to paragraph (1) of the Administrator's powers so that he is now specifically empowered to "direct and coordinate the activities of the Commissions of Food and Nutrition, Drugs and Consumer Products."

Section 202(a) of the bill makes it clear that each of the Commissioners will have delegated to him substantial final authority in his particular area of expertise. For example, the Commissioner of Product Safety will have authority to set product safety standards for most consumer products. Section 202(a), however, authorizes the Administrator to confer additional authority upon the Commissioners or to rescind expressly any delegation in the interest of sound administration and in order to protect the public health and safety.

This Committee struck the phrase which provided that advisory committees may be composed of persons appointed "with-out regard to any conflict of interest statutes." Adherence to conflict of interest statutes will in no way preclude utilization of the best qualified citizens and officials available, including those with industry connections, and waiver of the conflict of interest provisions would raise a dangerous precedent.

This Committee has also made it clear that the Administrator may promulgate such regulations as may be necessary to carry out his functions, and to enforce the statutes subject to his jurisdiction as efficiently and effectively as possible. Rulemaking will, of course, be subject to the provisions of the Administrative Procedure Act.

The subpoena authority contained in two separate paragraphs of S. 3419 was imprecise and did not provide for court enforcement. Consistent with the intent of the Commerce committee this Committee has therefore provided full subpoena power, access to documentary evidence, and authority to require general or special orders. This will make the authority of the Administrator to issue subpoenas equal to that contained in sections 6 and 9 of the Federal Trade Commission Act. The new authority will cover products presently regulated by the Food and Drug Administration as well as all of the other products over which jurisdiction is granted to the new Agency. The FDA does not now possess subpoena authority. In testimony before the Executive Reorganization Subcommittee, Secretary Richardson agreed that the FDA should be granted such power. This amendment remedies an important gap in the enforcement authority of the new Agency.

This Committee has also added five other new paragraphs providing additional authority for the Administrator.

Paragraph 13 permits the Administrator to prepare and submit, directly to the President without review by the Office of Management and Budget for review and transmittal to Congress, an annual budget estimate. It also requires that all appropriated funds be obligated and expended by the Agency, without the possibility that they may be reduced by the Office of Management and Budget. This language is modeled on section 407(b)(9) of the Public Health Service Act, as added by the recently-enacted National Cancer Act of 1971, P.L. 92–218. It will ensure that the Congress receives the undiluted judgment of the Administrator concerning his budget needs and that no funds appropriated for the Agency will be withheld.

Paragraphs 14 and 15 authorize the Administrator to prescribe personnel policies and to submit legislative recommendations and testimony to Congress without the usual prior approval or clearance from the Office of Management and Budget or the President. If the Agency is to be effective, the Administrator must be capable of informing Congress, directly and without outside interference, exactly what he and his Agency believe to be the facts about the matters before it. The inevitable compromise softening of approach and delays achieved through a review process, which often includes several departments and agencies, is inconsistent with the type of strong new Agency envisioned by this bill. Similarly, it is important that the Administrator establish his own personnel policies in a manner suited to the regulatory mission of the new Agency, rather than the judgment of some official outside the Agency.

Paragraph 16 authorizes the Administrator to initiate and litigate all court action in the name of the Agency. He will be represented in court by his own representative, the General Counsel of the Agency, or through the United States Attorneys, representing the Attorney General. The Secretary of Health, Education, and Welfare, in his testimony before the Executive Reorganization Subcommittee, endorsed this authority for FDA in principle. Secretary Richardson pointed out, and this Committee agrees, that in most instances legal action would continue to be filed through the United States Attorneys, as the Food and Drug Administration has done in the past. It may be unnecessary for the new Agency to establish its own network of local attorneys to handle routine matters. In the past, the Food and Drug Administration has prepared all pleadings for the United States

Attorneys, has sent its own attorneys who are experts in the field to assist in the litigation of the case, and has prepared all appellate briefs. The Committee intends this to continue, but the authority granted here will safeguard the independence of the new Agency.

It is important that the litigation of the Agency, which is critical to enforcement of the laws it administers, be directed and controlled by the Administrator. No one else has the responsibility for enforcement of those laws, and no one else should be in the position to frustrate their enforcement. The decision whether to file a criminal information, and the decision whether to include or to dismiss individual defendants, must be made by the Administrator. The Administrator must also be in the position to file, within hours, seizure or injunction actions, in order to prevent continued violation of the law. Similarly, the decision as to what legal arguments are to be made and how to make them most effectively for orderly development of the law through trial and appellate litigation is best handled by the Administrator who is responsible solely for enforcing the food, drug and product safety laws.

Paragraph 17 provides that where a product is subject to safety regulation under certain other laws, the Administrator may petition the appropriate Federal department or agency to establish and enforce necessary safety regulations for such product. The Administrator may establish and enforce such regulations upon request of other agencies and may participate in proceedings of other agencies to establish safety regulations.

Duties of the Administrator (Section 105)

This Committee agrees in general with the Administrator's duties established in S. 3419 as reported by the Committee on Commerce. Technical changes have been made to reflect our decision that the Administrator should direct as well as coordinate the Commissions, that the Agency has a broader mission than just safety regulation, and that injury encompasses illness and adverse reactions as well as accidental occurrences. Section 108(6) of the Commerce Committee bill provided that each Commissioner would appoint a counsel to carry out his legal work. The Committee consolidated these separate legal staffs and have provided that the Administrator shall appoint an Assistant General Counsel, within the office of the General Counsel, for each Commission, in addition to a General Counsel for the Agency. The General Counsel may, of course, appoint additional Assistant General Counsels as necessary to perform the legal duties of the Agency.

Obligations of Agency Contractors (Section 106)

This Committee has no significant change to suggest in this section.

Commissioners (Section 107)

S. 3419, as reported by the Committee on Commerce, provided that the President shall appoint the three Commissioners with the advice and consent of the Senate. This Committee has concluded that the Administrator, if he is to be ultimately responsible for the work of the Agency, must have the authority to appoint individuals in whom he has confidence to the position of Commissioner. If the Commissioners are not appointed by the Administrator, conflicts could arise which might disrupt the work of the Agency. Accordingly, to insure the independence and effectiveness of the Agency, the Committee has provided for appointment of the Commissioners by the Administrator.

Duties of the Commissioners (Section 108)

This Committee agrees, in general, with the duties of the Commissioners as set out by the Committee on Commerce in S. 3419. Technical changes have been made to reflect modifications already described above.

The bill has been amended to provide that as authorized by the Administrator, the Commissioners shall utilize where practicable, and establish where necessary, field operations. The majority of the field staff will consist of personnel transferred from the Food and Drug Administration. These personnel are largely separate and identifiable within the Department of Health, Education, and Welfare and there should be no difficulty in separating and transferring them to the new Agency.

Office of Consumer Information (Section 109)

The Committee has substantially modified this section. Conforming amendments and technical changes have been made in subsections (a), (b) and (c). With respect to the public information room, it is specifically provided that all funds collected for copying, or for search for and production of documents, shall be paid directly to the Agency and obligated and expended to finance the Consumer Information Program, after start up costs have been met. The Freedom of Information Act does not provide that funds paid for copying should remain available to the agency involved. As a result, the information program is a drain on an agency's resources. This new provision corrects that deficiency. The Agency will be able to hire personnel and finance a program out of the funds collected for copying.

Subsection (c) has also been amended to provide that the charge for search and copying shall be the minimum practicable amount, not exceeding actual cost. The bill also directs the Agency to take all reasonable measures to reduce or waive charges which would be financially burdensome to any person. These provisions are intended to carry out the basic policy of this bill to encourgae consumer participation in the procedures and processes of the agency. This can only be achieved if ordinary citizens are provided access to all essential agency information free or at a reasonable cost. It is intended to apply to small numbers of documents that can reasonably be obtained without significant burden to the agency, and not to permit fishing expeditions or requests for large numbers of documents that could impede the regulatory work of the agency.

The Committee deleted the Subsection (d) which provided for the appointment of private attorneys to represent consumers in proceedings before the Agency. We took this action to avoid potential conflict with the proposed Consumer Protection Agency bill, S. 1177. This legislation is pending before the Government Operations Committee and is expected to be reported soon. It contemplates that the

CPA will represent the consumer interest in proceedings before other government agencies. While several witnesses testified before the Executive Reorganization Subcommittee that they could foresee no duplication or overlap between the two agencies, since the CPA will have no regulatory authority, the Committee believed it to be the wiser course to take this action now.

The Committee added a new Subsection (d) establishing a Consumer Information Library. There is no single location in government where the vast amount of literature on foods, drugs and consumer products is available to the general public. This provision will cover that deficiency.

National Injury Information Clearinghouse (Section 110)

This section has been slightly modified to reflect the changes discussed earlier. They make it clear that the clearinghouse will monitor all illness, adverse reaction, and accidents associated with food, drugs, and consumer products, in order to assist the Commissioners and the Administrator to carry out their functions. This monitoring will include such diverse matters as surveillance of the nation's nutritional level, monitoring of foodborne illness, epidemiological surveys of adverse reactions, reporting systems designed to identify both serious and relatively inconsequential accidental injuries, and other similar matters.

It is not intended that these monitoring systems be operated conjointly. Surveillance of food-borne illness may well require a different capability and methodology from surveillance of accident injuries. The bill simply requires that a Clearinghouse must be established, through which such information is available, both to the Agency and to the public.

In this connection, the Committee intends that an expansive interpretation be given to the provision that injury "associated with" products should be monitored. It is often not possible to determine whether a causal relation exists between a product and an injury. This Committee believes it important that all injuries even associated with a product be monitored, in order adequately to survey the field and to begin to prevent future injury.

The confidentiality provisions of this section are largely a restatement of existing law. However, another ground for disclosure has been added where public health and safety are involved. Section 110(c) also provides that the identification of persons who treat injured persons shall not be disclosed. This is important because any system of injury surveillance will necessarily depend upon the cooperation of large numbers of physicians and other treatment professionals. Unless the confidentiality of their reports is assured, protecting their anonymity to avoid unwarranted litigation, there is a danger that this information would not be made available.

Joint Scientific Committee (Section 111)

This Committee has modified the provisions of S. 3419 to provide that the Administrator shall appoint one representative of each Commission to the Committee and that it shall be chaired by an Associate Administrator for Science.

AGENCY RESPONSIBILITY (SECTION 112)

S. 3419, as reported by the Committee on Commerce, authorized a civil mandamus action by individuals against the Agency where its act or omission has exposed a person to an unreasonable risk of injury or death from a food, drug or consumer product. This Committee fully agrees with the concept underlying this provision, but has revised it to streamline its functioning and to make it more efficient. The basic policy behind this provision is that the Agency should be responsive and accountable to the public.

The section now provides that an individual, by himself or as a representative of a class, who believes he has been exposed by an act or omission of the Agency to a food, drug, or consumer product presenting an unreasonable risk of injury or death shall first petition the Agency to take specific action sufficient to eliminate the alleged unreasonable risk. This permits a petition by an individual or class complaining that a product such as a new drug presents an unreasonable risk, and does not permit a person to submit a petition with respect to an Agency act or omission removing a product from the market or failing to allow it on the market.

After submission of the petition, and a 30-day period during which interested parties will be permitted to comment, the Agency must issue a decision either refusing to take action or taking action which it determines sufficient to eliminate any unreasonable risk. This decision is to be made within 120 days following the filing of the petition. The parties may, of course, stipulate to a longer period of time.

If the petitioner disagrees with the Agency decision, he may commence a civil action in a United States Court of Appeals against the Agency. Any such action must be filed within 60 days after the decision of the Agency. (If such an action is not filed within that time period, the petitioner may seek judicial review of the Agency decision pursuant to the applicable provisions of the Administrative Procedure Act.)

The Court of Appeals may remand the matter to the Agency for the gathering of additional evidence upon a request by the petitioner for good cause shown. The Court may place any conditions it wishes upon such a remand for additional evidence. Such new evidence might then require the Agency to reconsider its decision.

The United States Court of Appeals is charged with determining whether a preponderance of the evidence in the record on which the Agency made its decision (which is limited to the petition, all information submitted by the petitioner, and all information identified in the Agency's decision as part of the record) shows that the Agency has exposed the petitioner to a food, drug, or consumer product presenting an unreasonable risk of injury or death. In making this determination, the Court must consider whether the risk is unreasonable in light of all the relevant circumstances shown in the record. The burden of proof is on the petitioner to show that a preponderance of record evidence establishes the unreasonableness of the risk associated with the product, and that an act or omission of the Agency has exposed him to such risk.

If the petitioner prevails, the remedy available to the Court is to remand the matter to the Agency for appropriate action. The Agency will then have an opportunity to consider what alternatives are available to eliminate the unreasonable risk determined by the Court to exist, and to choose among those alternatives one that will be sufficient. Should the petitioner again dispute the Agency decision, the same type of civil action could again be undertaken. The Court has no power to award money damages against the Agency or any individual.

The Committee recognizes that this provision establishes a new standard of review applicable only in these cases. In our view, this departure from the Administrative Procedure Act is justified by the nature of the right involved. In these cases an individual, or a group, is seeking protection from some food, drug or consumer product which may expose them to an unreasonable risk of injury or death.

Agency action affecting interests in life and health should be subject to the most searching judicial examination. In our view, the importance of these interests justifies a departure from the normal standard of review. In such cases, substantial evidence in the record should not be sufficient to sustain the agency action.

The petitioner must prove the unreasonable risk by a preponderance of the evidence, the usual standard in civil cases. The Committee contemplates that most agency actions will withstand the scrutiny. Since this right of action gives the plaintiff no economic incentive—only costs may be recovered in the discretion of the court—it is unlikely that a large number of suits will disturb the orderly processes of Agency decision. Yet the possibility of suit will serve as a constant spur to action safeguarding the public.

The Committee struck the conflict of interest provision in section 111(c) as reported by the Commerce Committee which was applicable only to this Agency. It is not appropriate or efficient public administration to authorize special conflict of interest laws for a single agency. The policy on such matters of general importance should be uniform. This is not proper legislation for revising our conflict of interest laws.

Annual Reports (Section 113)

This section remains basically unchanged from S. 3419, as reported by the Committee on Commerce, except for a few conforming amendments. The annual report, like the budget, will be submitted directly to the President and Congress. It will contain the budget requests of the Administrator and the budget recommendations of each Commissioner. It will also contain a summary of regulatory efforts and of all violations, not just non-technical violations.

Public Access to Information (Section 114)

This Committee concurs with the provisions of S. 3419 with respect to public access to information The Committee has made only a few technical changes to conform it to the provisions in section 110 already mentioned above.

Cooperation of Federal Agencies (Section 115)

The Committee added a new Subsection authorizing the Administrator to utilize the resources and facilities of the National Bureau of Standards in the development of food, drug, and consumer product standards. The Bureau has traditionally focused upon economic matters. We believe its priorities should be changed to emphasize questions of public health and safety.

Authorization of Appropriations (Section 117)

The Commerce Committee authorized $180 million, $200 million, and $225 million for the Agency for fiscal 1973, 1974, and 1975 respectively.

This Committee believes that there should be authorized to be appropriated simply such sums as may be necessary to carry out the provisions of the bill. We believe a specific level of authorization would be unwise at this time. The Food and Drug Administration presently does not operate under any specific authorization for appropriation. The budget request for FDA alone this year is $187 million. It is unlikely that the substantial budgetary increase sought for the coming fiscal year would be possible if such an authorization existed.

Substantial new authorities are transferred to the new Agency under this bill, and new administrative powers are also granted. Accordingly, it is not feasible to anticipate the budgetary levels which will be necessary to carry out these responsibilities at this time.

Executive Schedule Levels (Section 118)

This Committee concurs in the conclusion of the Committee on Commerce that the Administrator should be at level III, of the executive pay scale and the Commissioners at level IV. This Committee also believes that the General Counsel should be at level IV.

It should be noted that the Chairman of the Federal Trade Commission and the heads of other similar agencies and commissions are at level III of the Executive Schedule. Since the responsibilities and duties of the Administrator of the new Agency are intended to be at least commensurate with the responsibilities and duties of those other officials, it is appropriate that he be placed at level III also. Similarly, the members of other commissions and their general counsels are at level IV.

The Committee believes that the appointment of the commissioners and general counsel by the administrator has ample precedence. In the General Services Administration the Deputy Administrator is appointed by the Administrator, and in the National Aeronautics and Space Administration the associate administrators are appointed by the administrator.

Effective Date (Section 119)

No change is recommended in this section.

Title II—Transfers of Functions

Section 201(a) transfers all functions of the Secretary of Health, Education, and Welfare presently administered through the Food and Drug Administration to the Administrator of the new Agency. The list of those functions, as set out in 21 CFR 2.120 and 36 Federal Register 12803, (July 7, 1971) and as otherwise transferred to or performed by the Food and Drug Administration. is as follows:

Federal Food, Drug, and Cosmetic Act (21 U.S.C. 301 et seq.)
Filled Milk Act (21 U.S.C. 61 et seq.)

Federal Import Milk Act (21 U.S.C. 141 et seq.)
Tea Importation Act (21 U.S.C. 41 et seq.)
Federal Caustic Poison Act (44 Stat. 1406)
Federal Hazardous Substances Act (15 U.S.C. 1261 et seq.)
Fair Packaging and Labeling Act (15 U.S.C. 1451 et seq.)
Flammable Fabrics Act (15 U.S.C. 1201(a))
Radiation Control for Health and Safety Act (42 U.S.C. 263b et seq.)
Various Provisions of the Comprehensive Drug Abuse Prevention and Control Act of 1970 (84 Stat. 1236)
Functions pertaining to sections 301, 308, 311, 314, 315, and 361 of the Public Health Service Act (42 U.S.C. 241, 242f, 243, 246, 247, and 264) which relate to pesticides, product safety, interstate travel sanitation, (except interstate transportation of etiologic agents under 42 CFR 72.25), milk and food service sanitation, shellfish sanitation, and poison control.
Egg Products Inspection Act (21 U.S.C. 1031 et seq.)
Poison Prevention Packaging Act of 1970 (15 U.S.C. 1471 et seq.)
Section 409(b) of the Federal Meat Inspection Act (21 U.S.C. 679 (b)).
Section 24(b) of the Poultry Products Inspection Act (21 U.S.C. 467f(b))

For some of these statutory provisions (eg, the Fair Packaging and Labeling Act, the Flammable Fabrics Act, the Comprehensive Drug Abuse Prevention and Control Act, the Public Health Service Act, and the Egg Products Inspection Act) the Food and Drug Administration presently exercises joint jurisdiction with other federal departments or agencies. For some of these statutes (eg, the Meat and Poultry Acts) the Food and Drug Administration apparently presently exercises its functions without formal delegation of authority from the Secretary.

Section 201(b) transfers to the Administrator of the new Agency all functions of the Secretary of Health, Education, and Welfare under the Clinical Laboratories Improvement Act of 1967 (42 U.S.C. 263a) and sections 351 and 352 of the Public Health Service Act (42 U.S.C. 262 and 263). The Clinical Laboratories Improvement Act contains authority to regulate laboratories operating in interstate commerce which examine human specimens to provide information for the diagnosis, prevention, or treatment of disease or the assessment of health. This function, which is the only regulatory function undertaken by the Center for Disease Control within the Department of Health, Education, and Welfare, is very closely related to the Food and Drug Administration's regulation of drugs and devices. The Act authorizes standards to be established to assure consistent performance by such laboratories, and thus includes as an integral function standards for the equipment, reagents, diagnostic products, drugs, and other products utilized in the laboratory. Since the passage of the Act in 1967, the CDC has instituted only one court action to enforce it. Accordingly, we conclude that sound regulatory policy dictates that this regulatory function should be combined with the Food and Drug Administration's regulatory authority. This will provide for the strongest and most effective regulation.

Sections 351 and 352 of the Public Health Service Act provides for the licensing of manufacturing establishments for human biologics, and for the biologic products themselves. This function has, until now, been administered by the Division of Biologics Standards of the National Institutes of Health. It is the only regulatory function undertaken by NIH. We concur with the Committee on Commerce that it is properly combined with the other human drug regulatory functions performed by the Food and Drug Administration. The Secretary of Health, Education, and Welfare indicated to the Committee that he favors the transfer of these functions to the Food and Drug Administration, and has recently announced this transfer.

Section 201(c) makes five additional transfers not recommended by the Commerce Committee. It transfers to the Administrator all functions now performed by the Secretary of Agriculture under five statutes:

> The virus, serum, toxin, and analogous products provisions applicable to domestic animals of the Act of Congress approved March 4, 1913 (21 U.S.C. 151 et seq.)
>
> Poultry Products Inspection Act (21 U.S.C. 451 et seq.)
>
> Federal Meat Inspection Act (21 U.S.C. 601 et seq.)
>
> Egg Products Inspection Act (21 U.S.C. 1031 et seq.)
>
> Food Inspection and Grading performed pursuant to 7 U.S.C. 1622(h).

Two of these statutes, the Meat and Poultry Acts, were amended in 1967 and 1968 to modernize them and to bring them in conformity with the Federal Food, Drug, and Cosmetic Act. The Egg Products Inspection Act which is to be jointly administered by the Department of Agriculture and the Food and Drug Administration when it becomes effective on July 1, 1972. Until 1957, the Food and Drug Administration had jurisdiction over poultry and this transfer represents a return to prior practice. The animal virus, serum, and toxin law is the counterpart for animals to the provisions of the Public Health Service Act relating to human biologics.

Virtually every study which has considered the Administration of food inspection programs during the past few years has concluded that the regulatory functions of the Department of Agriculture over meat and poultry should be consolidated with the Food and Drug Administration's regulatory functions with respect to all other food. The Hoover Commission first suggested this approach. The White House Conference on Food, Nutrition and Health in 1969, pointed to conflicting regulatory policies between the two agencies and recommended establishment of a committee to determine "whether a single federal regulatory agency for foods should be established" that would include both agencies. This same report also criticized the policy of continuous inspection after post-mortem inspection of fresh meat and poultry, and called for modern methods of inspection to insure the wholesomeness of the entire nation's food supply. Shortly thereafter, in June, 1970, the Government Accounting Office issued a report criticizing the overlapping of Federal inspection activities between the Department of Agriculture, the Food and Drug Administration, and other governmental agencies. All of this criticism was recognized in the report of the President's advisory council on executive organization recommending a Department of Human Resources in which the Department of Agriculture and the Food and Drug Administration food regulatory authorities would be combined. Thus, there is broad agreement that this step should be taken.

This Committee considered whether combining these activities should be undertaken at this time or should be delayed to a more comprehensive reorganization. In view of the fact that a new and independent regulatory agency is being created, the Committee could find no persuasive reason not to make these transfers now. The consumer benefits that can result, in the form of more balanced and effective inspections throughout the country, and greater efficiency through elimination of duplicative efforts, are too important to ignore. The food regulatory functions of the Department of Agriculture, which cover just a portion of the nation's food supply, involve resources in funds, manpower, organization, and scientific capability which are greater than those available to the Food and Drug Administration for regulation of all other food, drugs, and consumer products. Yet three GAO reports[1] on meat and poultry inspection programs in the past 2½ years have shown that USDA is not adequately protecting public health. Consolidating these programs with those of FDA should result in a more effective national food inspection effort.

Section 201(d) transfers the functions of the Secretary of Commerce and the Federal Trade Commission under the Flammable Fabrics Act (15 U.S.C. 1191 et seq.) and the functions of the Secretary of Commerce with respect to safety standards for refrigerator doors under the Act of August 2, 1956 (15 U.S.C. 1211 et seq.), to the Administrator of the new Agency. The Flammable Fabrics Act is a strong and useful regulatory statute, whose implementation has been virtually nullified because it is split among three federal agencies (the Department of Commerce, the Federal Trade Commission, and the Food and Drug Administration). Combining these functions in one strong regulatory agency is necessary if the law is to be effectively implemented. The Refrigerator Door Act, is so much a part of the product safety aspects of Title III of this bill that its inclusion in the new Agency is obvious.

S. 3419, as reported by the Committee on Commerce, would have repealed the Federal Hazardous Substances Act, the Flammable Fabrics Act, the cosmetic provisions of the Federal Food, Drug, and Cosmetic Act, the Radiation Control for Health and Safety Act, the Poison Prevention Packaging Act of 1970, and the Refrigerator Door Act. This Committee concluded, after studying the matter, that it was unwise to repeal any of these statutes until experience is gained in the administration of Title III of the new bill for two important reasons. First, some of the provisions that would have been repealed, such as the misbranding provisions for cosmetics, could not be reestablished under Title III of this bill. And second, some of the very explicit statutes, such as the Refrigerator Door Act and the Poison Prevention Packaging Act, embody important policy declarations and mandates from the Congress, which should not be diluted by more general statutory language. Furthermore, it may well be preferable in some cases, as with the self-executing enforcement provisions under the Federal Hazardous Substances Act, to utilize the existing statutory authority for many years to come, rather than engage in duplicative regulation-making activity under the new bill. In short, this Com-

[1] Enforcement of Sanitary, Facility and Moisture Requirements at Federally Inspected Poultry Plants B-163450—September 10, 1969. Weak Enforcement of Federal Sanitation Standards at Meat Plants by the Consumer and Marketing Service B-163450—June 24, 1970. Consumer and Marketing Service's Enforcement of Federal Sanitation Standards at Poultry Plants Continues to be Weak B-163450—November 16, 1971.

mittee is convinced that the statutory framework found in prior legislation has continuing utility and should not lightly be discarded. Accordingly, rather than repeal these statutes, they are continued in full force and effect and are transferred to the new Agency. As a result, the Agency will be able to proceed either under Title III of this bill, or the substantive provisions of those laws, whichever is considered more advantageous.

It may be that, after the new Agency has substantial experience in impleminting Title III of this bill, repeal of part or all of the provisions of some or all of these existing statutes should be considered. The new Agency has full authority to make such recommendations to the Congress, and those recommendations will undoubtedly be given serious consideration. For the present, however, it would be unwise to repeal existing laws without first being certain that the provisions designed to replace them will serve at least as well or better.

Section 201(e) transfers all personnel, property, records, funds, and other resources related to the functions that are transferred under the bill. This is intended to transfer not just those resources that are immediately involved with the transferred functions, but also an allocable share of overhead, such as general administrative resources, libraries, equipment, legal and other staff resources, and so forth. It is intended that these functions be left, after transfer, with the same ability to perform their regulatory mission as they had before the transfer.

Section 202 provides that, insofar as practicable and consistent with sound administration of the laws subject to his jurisdiction, the Administrator shall delegate all or part of the regulatory functions transferred to him to the three Commissioners. The bill defines those statutory provisions which appear to be within the province of each of the three Commissioners. In some cases, such as the Federal Food, Drug, and Cosmetic Act, each of the Commissioners will administer a portion of the statute.

As reported by the Committee on Commerce, S. 3419 would have required that the standard setting functions of certain statutes designated in the bill be totally delegated to the respective Commissioners. In keeping with this Committee's conclusion that the Administrator must be responsible for the overall functioning of the Agency, this standard-setting delegation provision has been modified to state that such delegation shall be done, in whole or in part, in so far as is practicable and consistent with sound administration. The Committee intends by this change to make more flexible the process whereby the standard setting function is delegated to a particular Commissioner. There is no intent, however, by this language to deny the Commissioner final authority to set appropriate standards in any situation. The Committee expects the Administrator to make appropriate delegations of standard setting and any other appropriate authority and to rescind such delegations if and when they interfere with the overall objectives of the Agency.

Under Section 203, all of the provisions of the statutes which are transferred for implementation to the new Agency, would remain in full force and effect. Insofar as the authority of the Agency to act was granted under a statute, or transferred for implementation to the new Agency, the full force and effect of such statute and all regulations promulgated thereunder shall be applicable.

TITLE IV—AMENDMENTS TO THE FEDERAL FOOD, DRUG, AND COSMETIC ACT

Title IV adds to the present cosmetic provisions of the Federal Food, Drug, and Cosmetic Act three new substantive labeling provisions. These provisions in effect bring the cosmetic requirements of the Act more closely into conformity with the labeling requirements for food, drugs, and devices.

The first provision [Sec. 401(a)] requires each cosmetic to be labeled with the common or usual name of the cosmetic (e.g., "lipstick" or "deodorant"), and with the common or usual name of each ingredient. Color and fragrance ingredients may be declared generally by "color" and "fragrance," without specifying each color and fragrance ingredient. This is the same type of requirement as presently applies to food under section 403 of the Act, where each food ingredient must be declared except that color and flavor may be declared as such. Where appropriate, the Secretary may of course use his general rulemaking authority to establish an official name for any ingredient or product.

The provision permits exemptions to be established where there is a showing that ingredient disclosure would be impracticable or deceptive. This would permit exemptions for small packages or perhaps for declaration of ingredients by category when the specific ingredient used in changed frequently.

The Committee intends that flexibility be permitted in the type of label that will be regarded as satisfying this provision. Where decorator containers are used, for example, tear-off labels or tags may be permitted.

The provision retains a reference to the "Secreatary," even though enforcement of the Act is transferred to the Administrator, to retain consistency throughout the Act since all other references are also to the Secretary.

The second provision [Sec. 410(b)] requires warnings in all labeling for any cosmetic which would be dangerous under any reasonably forseeable conditions of use or misuse. The Committee intends that such warnings shall, like warnings required for drugs under a comparable provision in section 502 of the Act, contain directions for proper use of the product to avoid a hazard, or directions for steps to be taken if a problem does occur (e.g., if shampoos gets in your eyes, wash it out immediately with clear water). It is the purpose of the Committee, in amending the Federal Food, Drug and Cosemtic Act in this manner to insure the availability of whatever information is appropriate to warn consumers about potential hazards, to guide them about proper use, and to provide first-aid instructions in the event of an accident with the product.

The third provision [Sec. 401(c)] deletes the present exemption for soap from the cosmetic requirements of the Act. The Act is presently applicable to soap to which any cosmetic ingredient is added (e.g., cold cream or a detergent ingredient), to all shampoos, and to soap for which any drug claim is made. The narrow exemption for plain soap is obsolete and should be deleted.

In addition to the safeguards imposed by these amendments with respect to cosmetics, the Committee recognizes that cosmetics are covered by the definition of "consumer product" contained in Sec. 102 of the bill and are therefore subject to the provisions of Title III.

The Committee intends that the Administrator shall take such additional action under Title III as may be necessary to protect consumers against the marketing of cosmetics that pose an unreasonable risk.

Conclusion

The Committee has made many amendments to the bill, yet its basic framework remains intact. We believe our amendments strengthen and improve the bill. We have expanded the mandate of the agency, broadened its powers and increased the authority of the Administrator to manage the business of the Agency efficiently. These changes will help assure that the bill's promise of better consumer protection in foods, drugs and consumer products becomes a reality.

Cost Estimates Pursuant to Sec. 252 of the Legislative Reorganization Act of 1970

Since Title III of S. 3419 is not within the jurisdiction of this Committee the Committee has made no estimate of the costs of implementing that title. The Committee believes that implementation of the other titles of this bill will involve no significant additional costs since they involve primarily transfers of functions now being performed by other agencies.

Tabulation of Votes Cast in Committee

Pursuant to section 133(b) of the Legislative Reorganization Act of 1946, as amended, the following is a tabulation of votes in committee:

The vote to report favorably the bill S. 3419.

Mr. Williams
Mr. Randolph
Mr. Pell
Mr. Kennedy
Mr. Nelson
Mr. Mondale
Mr. Eagleton
Mr. Cranston
Mr. Hughes
Mr. Stevenson
Mr. Javits
Mr. Dominick
Mr. Schweiker
Mr. Packwood
Mr. Beall
Mr. Stafford

Changes in Existing Law

In compliance with subsection (4) of Rule XXIX of the Standing Rules of the Senate, changes in existing law made by the bill as reported are shown as follows (existing law proposed to be omitted is enclosed in black brackets, new matter is printed in italic, existing law which no change is proposed is shown in roman):

SUBCHAPTER II OF CHAPTER 53 OF TITLE V, UNITED STATES CODE

§ 5314. Positions at level III

Level IV of the Executive Schedule applies to the following positions, for which the annual rate of basic pay is $29,500:

(58) Administrator, Food, Drug, and Consumer Product Agency.

§ 5315. Positions at level IV

Level IV of the Executive Schedule applies to the following positions, for which the annual rate of basic pay is $28,750:

(95) Commissioners, Food, Drug, and Consumer Product Agency.

(96) General Counsel, Food, Drug, and Consumer Product Agency.

FEDERAL FOOD, DRUGS, AND COSMETIC ACT, AS AMENDED

CHAPTER II—DEFINITIONS

SEC. 201 [321]. For the purposes of this Act—

* * * * * * *

(i) The term "cosmetic" means (1) articles intended to be rubbed, poured, sprinkled, or sprayed on, introduced into, or otherwise applied to the human body or any part thereof for cleansing, beautifying, promoting attractiveness, or altering the appearance, and (2) articles intended for use as a component of any such [articles; except that such term shall not include soap.] *article.*

* * * * * * *

CHAPTER VI—COSMETICS

ADULTERATED COSMETICS

SEC. 601 [361]. A cosmetic shall be deemed to be adulterated—

(a) If it bears or contains any poisonous or deleterious substance which may render it injurious to users under the conditions of use prescribed in the labeling thereof, or, under such conditions of use as are customary or usual: *Provided,* That this provision shall not apply to coal-tar hair dye, the label of which bears the following legend conspicuously displayed thereon: "Caution—This product contains ingredients which may cause skin irritation on certain individuals and a preliminary test according to accompanying directions should first be made. This product must not be used for dyeing the eyelashes or eyebrows; to do so may cause blindness.", and the labeling of which bears adequate directions for such preliminary testing. For the purposes of this paragraph and (1) of this subsection, the Secretary shall promulgate regulations exempting such drug or class of drugs from such requirements. The provisions of subsection (c) of section 507 of this Act (other than the first sentence thereof) shall apply under this paragraph.

(4) The Secretary shall promulgate regulations exempting from any requirement of this subsection—

(A) drugs which are to be stored, processed, labeled, or repacked at establishments other than those where manufactured, on condition that such drugs comply with all such requirements upon removal from such establishments; and

(B) drugs which conform to applicable standards of identity, strength, quality, and purity prescribed pursuant to this subsection and are intended for use in manufacturing other drugs.

(5) On petition of any interested person for the issuance, amendment, or repeal of any regulation contemplated by this subsection, the procedure shall be in accordance with subsection (f) of section 507 of this Act.

(6) Where any drug is subject to this subsection and not exempted therefrom by regulations, the compliance of such drug with sections 501(b) and 502(g) shall be determined by the application of the standards of strength, quality, and purity applicable under paragraph (1) of this subsection, the tests and methods of assay applicable under provisions of regulations referred to in paragraph (2)(A) of this subsection, and the requirements of packaging and labeling on the basis of which the application with respect to such drug filed under subsection (b) of this section was approved.

MISBRANDED COSMETICS

SEC. 602 [362]. A cosmetic shall be deemed to be misbranded—

(a) If its labeling is false or misleading in any particular.

(b) If in package form unless it bears a label containing (1) the name and place of business of the manufacturer, packer, or distributor; and (2) an accurate statement of the quantity of the contents in terms of weight, measure, or numerical count: *Provided*, That under clause (2) of this paragraph reasonable variations shall be permitted, and exemptions as to small packages shall be established, by regulations prescribed by the Secretary.

(c) If any word, statement, or other information required by or under authority of this act to appear on the label or labeling is not prominently placed thereon with such conspicuousness (as compared with other words, statements, designs, or devices in the labeling) and in such terms as to render it likely to be read and understood by the ordinary individual under customary conditions of purchase and use

(d) If its container is so made, formed, or filled as to be misleading.

(e) If it is a color additive, unless its packaging and labeling are in conformity with such packaging and labeling requirements, applicable to such color additive, as may be contained in regulations issued under section 706. This paragraph shall not apply to packages of color additives which, with respect to their use for cosmetics, are marketed and intended for use only in or on hair dyes (as defined in the last sentence of section 601(a)).

(f) If its packaging or labeling is in violation of an applicable regulation issued pursuant to section 3 or 4 of the Poison Prevention Packaging Act of 1970.

(g) If in package form unless its lable bears (1) the common or usual name of the cosemtic, if any there be, and (2) in case it is fabricated from two or more ingredients, the common or usual name of each such ingredient; except that fragrance and color may be designated as fragrance and color without naming each ingredient: Provided, that to the extent that compliance with the requirements of clause (2) is impracticable, or results in deception or unfair competition, exemptions may be established by regulations promulgated by the Secretary.

(h) Unless its labeling bears adequate warnings against use where it may be dangerous to health.

REGULATIONS MAKING EXEMPTIONS

SEC. 603 [363]. The Secretary shall promulgate regulations exempting from any labeling requirement of this act cosmetics which are, in accordance with the practice of the trade, to be processed, labeled, or repacked in substantial quantities at establishments other than those where originally processed or packed, on condition that such cosmetics are not adulterated or misbranded under the provisions of this act upon removal from such processing, labeling, or repacking establishment.

SUPPLEMENTAL VIEWS OF MR. DOMINICK

Senator Cotton's minority views pointed out several deficiencies in S. 3419, as reported by the Commerce Committee. While the changes recommended by this Committee would appear to remedy some of those deficiencies (for that reason I voted to report the bill favorably), the most serious one remains: Titles I and II of the bill would create an unnecessary independent agency.

I agree that additional household product regulatory authority is needed in order to protect consumers adequately. But a persuasive case has not been made that such authority would be more effectively utilized by a new independent agency than by a strengthened and reorganized Food and Drug Administration within the Department of Health, Education and Welfare, as the Administration has proposed. Independent agencies have no more visibility or accountability to the public than agencies within Cabinet-level Departments; have less access to the President; and are probably more vulnerable to political pressure.

Moreover, it is difficult to see how consumers will benefit from disruption of the close relationships between the regulatory functions of the Food and Drug Administration and the consumer-related functions of other agencies within the Department of Health, Education and Welfare. Of equally questionable merit is the proposed transfer to the new agency of the Agriculture Department's Meat, Poultry, and Egg Products Inspection functions.

While a new independent "Consumer Safety Agency" would certainly make it easier to demonstrate to a constituent that Congress has done something, it would not be easy to demonstrate to that same constituent specifically how he would be more effectively served. In short, I am inclined to agree with Secretary Richardson's testimony that the new independent agency would amount to "reorganization for its own sake", and would sell the consumer "a phony bill of goods".

PETER H. DOMINICK.

APPENDIX E

EXCERPTS FROM DEBATE ON FLOOR OF SENATE

(from the Congressional Record for June 21, 1972, starting at page S 9875)

Deleted from this Appendix are various procedural references, as well as extensive debates over Senate proposals that did not appear in the final enactment, including provisions to abolish the Food and Drug Administration, to include within the new agency regulatory authority over food, drugs, and cosmetics, to transfer the meat, poultry, and egg inspection functions of the U.S. Department of Agriculture, to amend the Federal Hazardous Substances Act, and others.

THE FOOD, DRUG, AND CONSUMER PRODUCT SAFETY ACT OF 1972

* * *

Mr. MAGNUSON. Mr. President, this bill would usher in a new era in product safety—an era in which Government, industry, and the consumer would work together to assure the safety and efficacy of our foods, drugs, and other products.

The bill grants the Federal Government the authority to move decisively against any unsafe product in the marketplace. It also grants the consumer the right to cause such Government movement when the Government fails to act. Piecemeal product safety programs are broadened and combined in a single Food, Drug, and Consumer Product Agency which is given undiluted responsibility for insuring the safety and efficacy of, products in the marketplace. The bill is designed to bring about the rapid detection and the rapid elimination of those products determined to present unreasonable risk of injury or death. To enable the Agency to do these things the bill provides for functional independence, incentives for proper resource commitment, and increased public accountability.

The bill would transfer to this new, independent agency, first, the authority of the Food and Drug Administration over foods, drugs, and other consumer products; second, the authority of the Division of Biologics Standards over human biological drugs; third, the authority of the Center for Disease Control over clinical laboratory licensing; fourth, and the authority of the Department of Commerce, and the Federal Trade Commission over flammable fabrics and such things as refrigerator doors.

This legislation has been in the works a long time. In 1967 those of us responsible for the creation of categorical consumer safety laws recognized that the continued piecemeal approach to consumer product safety might not adequately protect the right of the American consumer to safety in the products he purchases. Therefore, we proposed the creation of a National Commission on Product Safety to survey consumer product safety problems and to make recommendations concerning the Government's proper role in securing the consumer's right to safety.

The final report of the National Commission on Product Safety—and they worked a long time—which recommended the creation of an independent Product Safety Commission gave great impetus to S. 3419.

I am pleased to report to my Senate colleagues that S. 3419 was reported favorably as an original bill by the Senate Commerce Committee by a vote of 17 to 1. Because the bill is broad in its scope and treats important safety matters which are within the jurisdiction of other committees, the Government Operations Committee and the Labor and Public Welfare Committee have also carefully examined the bill as originally reported to the Senate Commerce Committee. The Executive Reorganization Subcommittee of the Government Operations Committee and the Labor and Public Welfare

Committee, in consultation with representatives of the Commerce Committee, have formulated certain improving and strengthening amendments to the Commerce Committee bill. The Labor and Public Welfare Committee has reported S. 3419, as amended, to the floor without a dissenting vote.

Mr. President, I would at this time like to yield the floor to my distinguished colleagues who have all worked diligently to forge improvements in S. 3419. They will be able to describe these improvements to the Members of the Senate.

Mr. President, the Senator from Utah did yeoman work on this bill, as did the Senator from Connecticut in his committee.

Does the Senator from Utah wish to make an opening statement?

Mr. MOSS. I thank the Senator for yielding.

Mr. President, I will take 2 or 3 minutes to indicate that this is a bill on which all members of the committee worked very diligently. We held long sessions on the matter. I think it is a landmark bill, because it now brings together, as the chairman has mentioned, bits of piecemeal legislation that we have passed during many years dealing with various consumer items. As this has gone on, the jungle has sort of grown like "Topsy."

This is an attempt, first of all, to expand the principle of safety in the marketplace to all products, not just certain selected ones, and to bring together the administration of the safety features of the marketing process under one independent agency that is not deterred or deflected in any way by other functions than making appropriate assessments of the safety in products that come before it, and to take appropriate measures to be sure that those who market the products and distribute them abide by the laws and the regulations to protect the consumers. This, of course, will become apparent as we discuss the structure of the agency.

I commend the chairman, the ranking Republican member of the committee, and all other members of the Commerce Committee and the other committees for the great diligence displayed in preparing this measure. The staff also has done yeoman work on it.

I probably will speak later with respect to amendments that are offered, but that is all I want to say by way of an opening statement.

I again thank the chairman for yielding to me.

Mr. PEARSON. Mr. President, the Senate today considers landmark legislation to promote the manufacture of safer consumer products for use in and around the home. The Food, Drug and Consumer Product Safety Act of 1972 is the result of more than a decade of effort to perfect the "consumer's right to safety" through responsible Federal laws and regulations.

The Committee on Commerce has attempted over the years to eliminate the most obvious hazards to the physical safety of the American people. The committee has approved—and the Congress has passed—the Child Protection Amendments of 1966, the Flammable Fabrics Act of 1967, the Gas Pipeline Safet Act of 1968, the Radiation Control for Health and Safety Act of 1968, the Child Protection and Toy Safety Act of 1969, and the Poison Prevention Packaging Act of 1970.

This piecemeal approach to product safety has reduced the incidence of unreasonable risk to the unsuspecting consumer of hazardous products, but has been wholly inadequate in responding to the broad spectrum of risks which confronts all of us in our daily lives.

An estimate by the National Center for Health Statistics indicates that each year, in and around the home, about 30,000 persons are killed, 110,000 permanantly disabled, 585,000 hospitalized, and more than 20 million injured seriously enough to require medical treatment or be absent from work a day or more. One estimate has put the annual dollar cost to the economy at more than $5 billion. Other surveys provide additional information, but none indicates that the accident toll is of less magnitude.

The legislation before the Senate today creates an independent agency with responsibility for the safety and efficacy of food, drugs, and consumer products. This reorganization of the Federal bureaucracy is needed to insure vigorous implementation of the mandate for consumer safety.

The new agency will be responsible to the consuming public and to the Congress. Its work will be visible, its leaders will be in the public spotlight. The budget of the new agency will not be buried in the budget of a larger department of the executive branch. The commitment to product safety will not be deemphasized or diminished by competing considerations, or competing requests for limited funds. The ultimate responsibility for consumer safety will not be fragmented among the various agencies of the Government—the responsibility will be vested in a single entity.

I do not believe the reorganization contemplated in S. 3419 will produce a bigger Federal bureaucracy—only a more effective one.

Mr. President, the Committees on Commerce and Labor and Public Welfare have considered this legislation in some detail; and 33 Senators have voted in committee to report the bill favorably. This degree of unanimity could not have been achieved without the strong commitment of Mrs. Knauer, Secretary Richardson, and President Nixon to effective product safety legislation. The administration is to be commended for recommending S. 1797, a bill containing language upon which the committees have drawn heavily.

The administration and the committees are of a single mind on the critical policy determination: That the Federal Government must have authority to identify hazardous products, promulgate standards of safety, and ban those products which create an unreasonable risk to the consumer. This consensus will permit this Congress to adopt meaningful legislation in the public interest. This consensus will promote full funding and adequate staffing for the agency charged with the heavy responsibilities enumerated in the bill.

Mr. President, I am moved to pay tribute to the distinguished chairman of the Commitee on Commerce (Mr. MAGNUSON). His leadership has been instrumental in developing a bill which enjoys such broad-based bipartisan support. This act will be a testament to Chairman MAGNUSON's legislative skills and commitment to consumer protection. I am honored to have the opportunity to serve as cosponsor of S. 3419, and join the chairman in urging its adoption by the Senate.

Mr. MAGNUSON. Mr. President, I yield to the Senator from Connecticut such time as he may require.

Mr. RIBICOFF. Mr. President, I commend the distinguished chairman of the Committee on Commerce for another great achievement in behalf of the consumers of America. Due to the work of the distinguished Senator from Washington over the past 6 years, the consumers of this country have been provided increasingly more effective protection in the marketplaces of America.

Mr. President, I support the bill as amended by the Committee on Labor and Public Welfare. It has now been approved by two committees and the Subcommittee on Executive Reorganization of the Government Operations Committee. It deserves the approval of the Senate.

This bill was favorably reported from the Commerce Committee on March 24. Titles I and II were then jointly referred to the Government Operations and Labor and Public Welfare Committees. My Subcommittee on Executive Reorganization held 4 days of hearings on the legislation in April and May. We heard testimony from consumer spokesmen, industry groups, and the administration. Some thought that the new Food, Drug, and Consumer Product Agency should become a part of the Department of Health, Education, and Welfare. Others thought it should be an independent agency or a part of some other organization. But there was broad agreement that, for effective operation, the new agency should have a large measure of legal and functional independence.

After considering all the issues, we concurred in the judgment of the Commerce Committee that an independent agency should be established. This is the best way to assure that the programs entrusted to the agency will be carried out in the manner Congress intended. Plainly and simply, if the agency remained part of HEW, the regulatory decisions of the Administrator could be overruled by political appointees in the Department. Nor could Congress obtain the unaltered views of the Administrator on important matters such as the agency budget and legislation affecting its work. Though there is a strong policy against the establishment of new independent agencies, in these circumstances it is justified.

The amendments added by the Labor and Public Welfare Committee improve the organization and operation of the new agency. Overall, they will make the agency more efficient by giving the Administrator greater authority and flexibility in managing the agency.

I ask unanimous consent that a chart comparing the major provisions of titles I and II of S. 3419 as reported by the Commerce and Labor and Public Welfare Committees be printed at this point in the RECORD.

There being no objection, the chart was ordered to be printed in the RECORD, as follows:

S. 3419	REVISED BILL
1. Titled Consumer Safety Act of 1972.	1. Title changed to Food, Drug and Consumer Product Safety Act of 1972.

2. No provision.	2. Consumer products subject to safety regulation under other laws are defined as "authorized to be regulated for the purpose of eliminating unreasonable risk of injury or death." Such products may be regulated by the Consumer Product Agency after a petition to the agency with jurisdiction over the product, asking to regulate it, and a request by that agency to the Consumer Product Agency to regulate it.
3. Administrator authorized only to "coordinate" activities of the three Commissioners.	3. Administrator authorized to "direct and coordinate" the Commissioners.
4. Mandatory delegation of standard setting to Commissioners by Administrator.	4. Discretionary delegation of regulatory authority "insofar as practicable and consistent with sound administration."
5. Subpena authority limited to witnesses at hearings and "information."	5. Subpena broadened to cover access to records and general or special reports by producers.
6. No provision.	6. Direct submission of budget to President, for review and transmittal to Congress, and direct receipt of all funds from OMB.
7. No provision.	7. Authority to prescribe personnel policies "without prior approval of clearance," subject to civil service laws .
8. Law enforcement through Justice Department.	8. Law enforcement by Agency plus authority to "direct the course of all agency litigation."
9. Separate legal staffs for Administrator and three Commissioners.	9. One legal staff for Agency.
10. Commissioners appointed by President, no fixed term.	10. Commissioners appointed by Administrator.
11. Authorized appointment of private attorneys to represent consumers in agency proceedings.	11. No provision.
12. Mandamus action against agency where its act or omission has exposed a person to unreasonable risk of injury or death. DeNova trial in District Court.	12. Petition to agency for action to eliminate the unreasonable risk. Review in Court of Appeals on agreed record. Court will remand to Agency if petition shows by preponderance of evidence that agency action was not sufficient to eliminate risk.
13. Authorizes \$180, \$200 and \$225 million for next three fiscal years.	13. Authorizes such sums as may be necessary.
14. No provision.	14. Transfers USDA authority under Meat, Poultry, Egg and other Agricultural Product Inspection Acts to Administrator, plus authority over animal drugs.
15. Repealed Hazardous Substances Act, Flammable Fabrics Act, Radiation Control for Health and Safety Act, Poison Prevention Packaging Act, Refrigerator Door Safety Act and Chapter VI of the Food, Drug and Cosmetic Act.	15. Transfers authority under these laws to the new Agency.

Mr. RIBICOFF. These amendments were unanimously approved by the Subcommittee on Executive Reorganization on May 18. However, action on them could not be completed by the Government Operations Committee due to lack of a quorum at three scheduled meetings.

The most significant of these amendments is the transfer of the food inspection and animal drug programs from the Department of Agriculture. In my view these transfers are fully justified. Three GAO reports on the meat and poultry inspection programs in the past 2½ years have demonstrated that the Agriculture Department is not adequately protecting the public health. There is wide agreement that these programs should be combined with the food inspection programs in FDA. The 1969 White House Conference on Food and Nutrition, the GAO in June 1970 and the administration in 1971 all recommended this move. Mr. Rodney Leonard, former head of the Consumer and Marketing Service, which operated these programs until an internal reorganization in April, strongly urged the transfer, as did John Schnittker, former Under Secretary of Agriculture.

At recent hearings, FDA Commissioner Edwards recognized the overlap in food inspection programs between USDA and FDA, commented that the transfer of the USDA activities would increase FDA inspection capability and said the transfer was primarily a matter of timing. In my view the time is now.

The bill also transfers the Division of Biologics Standards to the new agency. The regulatory failures of DBS are well documented in a recent GAO report, which I requested. The GAO found that DBS had allowed at least 32 ineffective vaccines to remain on the market. Several of them had serious side effects. GAO also revealed that between 1966 and 1968, DBS allowed millions of doses of diluted influenza vaccine to be marketed. Combining DBS with FDA in the new agency will provide more effective vaccine regulation.

Mr. President, this bill shows that Congress is responding to the growing public demand for better consumer protection. Consumers will no longer accept the morals of the marketplace. They expect their Government to act as guardian of the market to assure that the goods they purchase are safe, effective, and meet the claims made for them.

American consumers no longer want just a larger pie. They want to know the quality of the ingredients and their nutritional value. There is a rising tide of concern over the quality of all our goods and services.

Too often Government and industry have defaulted on their promises of consumer protection. While no law can be any better than the people administering it, and the amount of resources committed to it, this bill provides a strong new framework for assuring the safety of hundreds of products. It will help assure that our promises to consumer protection become a reality.

Mr. President, I urge the adoption of the amendment and approval of the bill.

Mr. MAGNUSON. I say to the Senator from Connecticut that I tried to make clear and to explain the work he has been doing on this type of legislation for many years.

I thoroughly agree with him that here we are trying to bring together many things that we thought of piecemeal. I authored the Flammable Fabrics Act in 1953, and there has been a series of subsequent safety legislation resulting in different modes of administration. Some were badly administered, and some were not administered at all. Now we are putting them together for the purpose of efficient adminstration.

What the Senator and I are saying to the American people is that we are putting it together so that the consumer will get a better deal.

Mr. RIBICOFF. Mr. President, it has been a special privilege for me to work with the distinguished chairman of the Committee on Commerce.

Since we started our hearings on automobile safety many years ago, the Government Operations Committee has cooperated with the Commerce Committee on consumer protection legislation. During this entire period, the cooperative efforts between our committees have been of the highest quality.

I also want to commend the respective staffs of our committees, who worked closely to improve this bill and other legislation. I do not recall any proposal that went to our two committees for consideration on which we could not reach a meeting of the minds, and by our joint efforts improve the legislation finally presented to the Senate.

I again commend the distinguished chairman for his outstanding contribution and cooperation in the cause of consumer protection.

Mr. MAGNUSON. I thank the Senator

Mr. President, I believe the Senator from New Hampshire wishes to speak at this time.

Mr. COTTON. I yield myself, on my share of the time, such time as necessary for a brief opening statement.

Mr. President, S. 3419—the Food, Drug, and Consumer Product Safety Act of 1972—is a far-reaching omnibus bill. It is a legislative measure which has a most praiseworthy objective of protecting consumers against unreasonable risk of injury from hazardous products.

It is a bill which has been considered by our Committee on Commerce and subsequently, by the Committee on Government Operations and the Committee on Labor and Public Welfare. Although the Subcommittee on Executive Reorganization and Government Research of the Committee on Government Operations did hold hearings on this bill and did consider it, it was not possible for that committee to complete its deliberations within the time limitation specified in the referral. However, the Committee on Labor and Public Welfare was able to complete its consideration and was able to report on this measure.

Mr. President, when the bill, S. 3419, was considered by our Committee on Commerce I was in general support for the need for new and improved authority with respect to consumer product safety. As a matter of fact, I joined with the distinguished chairman of our Committee on Commerce, (Mr. MAGNUSON), in cosponsoring Senate Joint Resolution 33 of the 90th Congress which established the National Commission on Product

Safety, the report of which provided the genesis for the legislation now under consideration, S. 3419.

Unfortunately, Mr. President, I felt compelled to vote in the Committee on Commerce against reporting this bill owing to the following three principal objections as set forth in my minority views in that committee's report—No. 92-749 at page 139:

(A) There is no demonstrated need for the establishment of a new independent Consumer *Safety* Agency, especially in light of the pending legislation (H.R. 10835) which would establish a new independent Consumer *Protection* Agency, and which is, unlike that proposed in S. 3419, supported by the Administration;

(B) The apparent unknown impact of including "an electronic product" in the definition of "Consumer product" coupled with the repeal of the Radiation Control for Health and Safety Act (42 U.S.C. 263b-263n); and

(C) The erroneous and mischievous legislative interpretation given in the Committee report to the terms "subject to regulation" and "subject to safety regulation" found in section 101(1) of S. 3419 which could lead to dual and duplicative regulation in [several] product areas. . . .

Mr. President, the Committee on Labor and Public Welfare is in my opinion, to be complimented for meeting at least in part two of my three principal objections. It has met my second objection concerning the inclusion of "an electronic product" in the definition of "consumer product" by appropriately striking language from the definition provision of section 102 appearing on pages 3 and 5, as well as the repealing provisions of section 204 affecting several existing categorical consumer safety statutes. This, Mr. President, constitutes a definite improvement in this legislative measure.

The Committee on Labor and Public Welfare also met in part my third objection concerning the erroneous and mischievous legislative interpretation given in the Commerce Committee report to the terms "subject to regulation" and "subject to safety regulations" as found in section 101(1) of the bill. If the legislative interpretation placed upon these terms by the Committee on Commerce in its report had been left standing then we would have been confronted with the following situation as pointed out in my minority views:

Where the Commissioner of Product Safety has found that a particular consumer product, although coming within the purview of one of the enumerated statutes is not *in fact regulated,* then he, the Commissioner of Product Safety, would be able after notice to the administering agency to promulgate a safety standard. It would make the Consumer Safety Agency a "super agency", which could enter into all such areas not *actually* regulated! If so, then this would seem to prejudge the effectiveness of the Consumer *Protection* Agency proposed in legislation now pending before the Senate Committee on Government Operations and which, in its "watchdog" advocacy functions on behalf of the consumer, is designed to see that such consumer products are regulated where there is a demonstrated need.

In other words, if carried to its logical conclusion, the Ford Motor Company and the General Motors Corporation may be subject to regulation not only by the Department of Transportation under the National Traffic and Motor Vehicle Safety Act of 1966, but by the Commissioner of Product Safety. Similarly, manufacturers of aircraft or other aeronautical products such as the Boeing Company and Beech Aircraft Corporation, might be subject to safety regulations issued by both the Federal Aviation Administration and the Commissioner of Product Safety. This same could hold true for the regulatory area of the Atomic Energy Commission. This could very well lead to an untenable situation.

Mr. President, the Committee on Labor and Public Welfare quite appropriately, I believe, has added a definition of "Subject to safety regulation" in subsection 101(d) appearing on pages 5 and 6 which represent a definite improvement. As noted in the report of the Committee on Labor and Public Welfare accompanying S. 3419—No. 92-835:

The Committee has added a definition of "Subject to safety regulation", in order to clarify the intended meaning. Under this definition, the enumerated products would not be considered "consumer products" if they were authorized to be regulated under the other statutes so as to eliminate any unreasonable risk of injury or death. Thus, the primary jurisdiction of other agencies has been recognized.

Mr. President, there remains my first objection concerning the efficacy of establishing a new independent Consumer Safety Agency. I still am convinced that there has been no demonstrated need shown for the establishment of a new independent Consumer Safety Agency, particularly cognizant as I am that within the not-too-distant future the Senate Committee on Government Operations will be calling upon this body to support yet another independent agency, the Consumer Protection Agency. A proliferation of independent agencies makes neither good sense nor good government. As a matter of fact, Mr. President, as pointed out in my minority views on S. 3419 the establishment of an independent Consumer Safety Agency is—

Contrary to recommendations on reorganization submitted by the President to this

Congress, as well as, ironically enough, legislative proposals advanced by several of the proponents of the new Consumer Safety Agency.

I went on in my views to point out that there now is pending a conflicting legislative proposal, S. 3432, introduced by the distinguished Senator from Connecticut (Mr. RIBICOFF), himself a former Secretary of Health, Education, and Welfare, along with more than 20 cosponsors, four of whom are members of the Commerce Committee supporting the present proposal for an independent Consumer Safety Agency. Two more members of the Committee on Commerce have been added as cosponsors to this bill, S. 3432, since its introduction—the distinguished Senator from Nevada (Mr. CANNON) and the distinguished Senator from South Carolina (Mr. HOLLINGS).

I simply feel, Mr. President, that we in the Congress would be making a very grave mistake, indeed, if we continue what seems to be a growing trend to splinter off into separate independent agencies all those interests which seem to have an emotional appeal for such independence, especially at a time when we are confronted with a Government structure which constantly is being lamented as unmanageable. Agency independence certainly is no panacea. And, as a distinguished Cabinet officer under the administration of former President Johnson once observed:

> A separate chapter in the Government Organization Manual is not going to be any magic elixer. . . .

Accordingly, Mr. President, at an appropriate time during the consideration of S. 3419 I plan to offer an amendment placing these product safety functions more appropriately at this time within the Department of Health, Education, and Welfare.

Mr. President, the only other amendment which I presently contemplate offering deals with an amendment made by the Committee on Labor and Public Welfare with which I do not agree. The amendment concerns the authorization of appropriations for the purpose of carrying out the provisions of S. 3419 and which appears in section 117 on pages 32 and 33. As reported by our Committee on Commerce, this provision carried a specific dollar amount ceiling for the next 3 fiscal years which the Committee on Labor and Public Welfare deleted substituting an "open-ended" appropriation authorization of "such sums as may be necessary."

Mr. President, this provision of the bill deleted by the Committee on Labor and Public Welfare was an amendment which I offered in the Commerce Committee and which was adopted. As a member of the Committee on Appropriations, I feel very strongly about this particular issue. There is a need, if not an obligation, upon legislative committees to furnish the Committee on Appropriations some guidance in the funding requirements of legislation which they handle. It also is necessary for purposes of future budgetary control. Accordingly it is my intention to offer an amendment prior to the conclusion of debate on S. 3419 which will restore a specified monetary ceiling on appropriation authorizations for purposes of carrying out the provisions of this legislative measure. Since any such figures will be dependent upon amendments which may be adopted by the Senate, it will be necessary for me to await the final action on whatever substantive amendments may be made to the bill before offering in this particular amendment.

Mr. President, I wish to extend my compliments to the distinguished chairman of the Committee on Labor and Public Welfare (Mr. WILLIAMS), and the senior Republican Senator of that committee (Mr. JAVITS), for the commendable drafting improvements made by that committee in amending S. 3419 and I would join in urging that these amendments be adopted en bloc at such time as they are offered.

Mr. President, this product safety measure could be a good bill. However, as the ranking minority member on the Commerce Committee I did find it necessary to file dissenting views on certain important points. Thus, our distinguished chairman's (Mr. MAGNUSON) comment that the vote was 17 to 1 in committee was correct.

Now, in conclusion, Mr. President, I should note that "consumer" has become a sacred word and any dissent from any particular proposal that can be interpreted into being "anticonsumer" is a sacrilege. Nevertheless, I did feel compelled to do so in this instance on some very basic issues.

Mr. MAGNUSON. Mr. President, will the Senator from New Hampshire yield?

Mr. COTTON. I yield.

Mr. MAGNUSON. I want to say for the record that if there is any implication the Senator from New Hampshire has not been for the basic purposes of this bill or the goals of the bill, I deny it right here on the floor. We have all worked hard to perfect the bill. We could not agree on every amendment. That is what it is all about. But the Senator from New Hampshire has worked as hard on this bill with the members of the committee as any other member to achieve what we are trying to do in the total bill.

Mr. COTTON. I thank my chairman, the distinguished Senator from Washington (Mr. MAGNUSON). He is always fair. He is always considerate.

Let me say there has been no ill feeling engendered at any time during consideration of this legislation, because it is a bill with a worthy objective.

As I have always done in the past, I want to commend the distinguished chairman of the committee (Mr. MAGNUSON). I think, it can be honestly said—without disparaging the earnest efforts of many of our colleagues—that in the position he occupies the distinguished Senator from Washington probably has done more to advance the cause of the consumers of this Nation than almost any other man who has ever sat in the Senate.

Mr. President, as I have said, the purpose of this is a praiseworthy one. I have no doubt that it will pass.

I might add that I know of no intention on the part of any of our committee, to interfere, whatsoever, with functions which now repose in the Department of Agriculture. I understand that at an appropriate point an amendment will be offered to make this clear.

Mr. President, let me again say that there is no disagreement about the need for legislation in this area. The principal disagreement has to do with this matter of setting up a new and different agency of Government which confuses the picture more than clarifies it in the opinion of this Senator.

Mr. President, I again commend the chairman of our Committee on Commerce (Mr. MAGNUSON) and the other members who worked hard and diligently on this meritorious legislation. I also commend the Committee on Government Operations and the Committee on Labor and Public Welfare for their constructive work on the bill.

If this bill comes out with some amendments which this Senator feels are vitally necessary, I am confident that it will meet with the approval of the other body. I am also quite confident that it will meet with executive approval.

If this can be done, then the distinguished Senator from Washington (Mr. MAGNUSON), the chairman of the Committee on Commerce, and the chairman of the other two committees and the members of these committees will be able to pride themselves on the fact that they will have written on the statute books one of the most constructive measures of this session of Congress.

Mr. MAGNUSON. Mr. President, I yield to the distinguished Senator from Illinois.

The PRESIDING OFFICER. The Senator from Illinois is recognized.

Mr. PERCY. I thank my distinguished friend, the Senator from Washington. Mr. President, S. 3419, as amended by the Subcommittee on Executive Reorganization of the Government Operations Committee and by the Committee on Labor and Public Welfare, creates a new, independent agency within the Federal structure with undiluted responsibility for preventing consumers from being exposed to unsafe foods, drugs, devices, and other consumer products commonly found around the home. The measure would also consolidate within the new agency various consumer product safety activities now being handled by a number of Government entities by transferring to an independent Consumer Safety Agency the present food, drug, cosmetic, vaccine, and product safety activities of HEW and other product safety functions of the Commerce Department and the FTC.

S. 3419 would retain various existing consumer safety laws directed at particular products or specific hazards and complement them with a single omnibus product safety law capable of reaching any consumer product in the marketplace presenting an unreasonable risk of injury.

Although much of the discussion of S. 3419 concentrated primarily on organizational issues, I want to reaffirm the underlying reasons why the Congress is and should be addressing itself to a regulatory plan of this nature.

The American consumer has a right to safe products for use in his home. The safety of a product begins in its design, before it reaches the market, before it causes illness, injury, blindness, disfigurement, or death.

Today we are faced with a number of unreasonable hazards in and around the home. In determining their unreasonableness, we can ill-afford to sit by and await an epidemic of tragedies to verify that a hazard exists. Instead, it is the proper role of the Federal Government to stimulate American industry to reduce product risks by an omnibus legislative approach which will permit the Government, where necessary, to promulgate and enforce minimal standards of reasonableness in product design and manufacture.

Currently, however, the folly of Federal regulation of consumer products is all too plain. Legislation in this area consists of a hodgepodge of unrelated statutes dealing with specific hazards in very narrow product categories. There is no general Federal authority to seize or ban consumer products which exhibit unreasonable risks nor to require such products to conform to minimum safety standards.

And to the extent any Federal authority does exist, jurisdiction is commonly scattered among agencies or shared by as many as four different agencies. As the National Commission on Product Safety concluded:

> Federal product safety regulation is burdened by unnecessary procedural obstacles, circumscribed investigative powers, inadequate and ill-fitting sanctions, bureaucratic lassitude, timid administration, bargain-basement budgets, distorted priorities, and misdirected technical resources.

All this in the face of 20 million Americans injured in the home each year in accidents involving consumer products, 110,000 of whom are permanently disabled and 30,000 killed.

Through the passage of S. 3419, we hope to move away from the facade of Federal regulation in the area of consumer products. To date, and largely due to the fault of Congress itself, such regulation consists of piecemeal pablum which provides little more than a morsel of protection for the American consumer.

The Senate Commerce Committee has identified the problem. The question before us in the Senate today is how best to house the related functions of food, drug, and consumer product safety regulation. One thing is certain. If we accept a straw house for protection, we will have to rebuild it year after year. And if we accept a scare-crow to oversee the terrain, we will have to prop it up so often that it will hardly be worth the effort.

The Commerce Committee proposes an alternative to the house of straw and the man of straw by offering an independent Consumer Safety Agency headed by an administrator with a full panoply of powers.

Clearly, an "independent regulatory agency" is not some kind of magical formulation which will eliminate for all time lacklustre performance in the name of public protection. The history of such agencies as the Interstate Commerce Commission, the Federal Power Commission, and the Federal Maritime Commission, among others, attests all too sadly to that fact.

But after considering the alternate plans which were before us in the Executive Reorganization Subcommittee, I became convinced that, notwithstanding how we have treated this subject in the past, we cannot afford now to give less than the highest priority attention at the Federal level. Otherwise, I am afraid that our priorities are woefully askew.

The arrangement of a new and independent regulatory agency avoids mere box-shuffling, title changes, and pay raises which give the illusion of substance but in fact amounts to straw piled upon straw.

Significant changes reflected in consideration of the bill by the Executive Reorganization Subcommittee of the Government Operations Committee unanimously agreed upon, are as follows:

(1) The new agency is renamed "Food, Drug, and Consumer Product Agency" instead of "Consumer Safety Agency." This is to avoid confusion with the proposed Consumer Protection Agency, as well as to indicate that more than safety alone is involved (for example, nutritional labelling of foods, ingredient labelling of cosmetics, etc.).

(2) Section 101, containing findings and declaration of policy is added. The original bill had no comparable section.

(3) The definition of consumer product in Section 102 is clarified, primarily through the insertion of subsection (d), which defines the phrase "subject of safety regulation." This was one of the major points which Senator Cotton had appropriately raised in his minority views in the report accompanying S. 3419.

(4) The powers of the Administrator vis-a-vis the Commissioners under him are strengthened, in that practically all authority is vested in the Administrator who shall *direct and coordinate* the activities of the Commissions of Food, Drugs, and Consumer Products (see Section 104(c)(1)). The Administrator is, however, empowered to delegate any of his functions and duties under the Act to the Commissioners under him by virtue of Section 104(c)(20). See also Section 202(a).

(5) General subpoena power is granted not only to the Commission on Product Safety but also to the Commission on Food and the Commission on Drugs, by virtue of Section 104(c)(7). Omission in the original bill of enforcement authority by the courts is now corrected.

(6) The Agency is to submit directly to the President and transmit to the Congress its annual budget estimates, which is a departure from the typical OMB approval procedure (see Section 104(c)(14)).

(7) The Agency is to submit its legislative recommendations and testimony to the Congress without prior approval or clearance, as by OMB (see Section 104(c)(15)).

(8) The Agency would handle its own cases in court, without prior approval or recourse to the Justice Department (see Section 104(c)(17)).

(9) The Agency could petition other safety regulatory agencies (for example, FAA, Agriculture, AEC) to establish and enforce new safety regulations, to participate in the development of such regulations by that other agency, or, upon request of the other agency, to assist in establishing or enforcing such regulations (see Section 104(c)(18)).

(10) Elimination of an organizational defect, raised in the hearings, of four General Counsels, one reporting to each Commissioner (Section 105(f)). Now there is provision for a single General Counsel and an Assistant General Counsel for each Commission, reporting to the General Counsel and not to the individual Commissioners.

(11) Elimination of possible duplicative function involving the proposed Consumer Protection Agency. The Section 109 "Office of Consumer Information and Representation" is changed to simply an "Office of Consumer Information," and all consumer representation functions are eliminated.

(12) Instead of repealing the former product safety legislation now in effect as old Section 204(a) would have done, the new draft leaves that legislation in effect in order that there be no gap in coverage while new regulations, promulgated under the authority in Title III, are being developed over the next few years.

From my own experience of more than a quarter century in business, I think it is important to emphasize that the forces of competition, free enterprise, and profit motive are neither inherently conducive to nor inconsistent with consumer safety. But with the backing of Government, properly organized to do the job, these forces can be focused to reduce unreasonable product risks.

An investment of this kind in the safety of consumer products—from rotary lawnmowers, to power tools, to plate glass panels, to unvented floor furnaces, to children's toys, and the rest—can be expected to produce an exceptional rate of return on the capital required. Such investment will also result in a more productive economy, an expanded market for consumer goods that can be relied upon, and, most important of all, a safer home environment for ourselves and our children.

Mr. President, in closing I wish to commend very much, indeed, the Committee on Commerce, both the majority side and the minority side, for the outstanding job that has been done on this bill. There was no quarrel at all as to the objectives and purposes as we in the Government Operations Committee reviewed the bill. We addressed ourselves to how best to set this new function, organizationally.

My colleague, the Senator from New Hampshire, has a difference of opinion on this matter but it is not on the objectives we are trying to achieve.

I feel that this action today will culminate years and years of devotion to this subject by the distinguished Senator from Washington (Mr. MAGNUSON) and the ranking minority member from New Hampshire (Mr. COTTON) who had upupermost in their minds the fact that there is presumed to be a great deal more protection to the consumer in the consumer's mind than there is. Much of what we do is shallow, and we are now trying to beef up and give the support to this activity which it deserves.

The National Commission on Safety has done an excellent job and the members of that Commission should be commended for proposing comprehensive legislation of this nature. I particularly commend one member, Mr. Stuart Statler, whom we took on our staff as Chief Counsel to the minority of the Subcommittee on Executive Reorganization, and who has been the guiding spirit not only behind this legislation but also the drug abuse legislation and other matters of deep interest and concern, including the Consumer Protection Agency legislation that we will be dealing with very soon in the Senate.

But it is the outstanding work of members of this body and the staff that has made possible what I consider to be a landmark piece of legislation.

Mr. President, I ask unanimous consent that the committee amendments be agreed to en bloc and that the bill as thus amended be treated as original text for the purpose of further amendment.

* * *

Mr. PASTORE. Mr. President, I do not rise at this time to make any parliamentary observation on amendments proposed. Rather, I direct myself to the very complimentary statement the sound observation on this bill made by our distinguished colleague from Illinois (Mr. PERCY). I associate myself with everything he said. One significant element in my opinion, that lends tremendous credence to the statement by the Senator from Illinois is the fact that he was a distinguished businessman in his own right at the time he came to the Senate.

There has been some apprehension on the part of business as to whether or not we have gone too far in this product safety legislation. I think the end result will be that insofar as the legitimate businessman in this country is concerned, in time he is going to welcome this legislation. This legislation is for the benefit not only of the consumer but also for the benefit of the legitimate businessman who wants to produce a product that guarantees the safety of the people of this country who use it. I want to make that clear because I do not think that business is going to be harassed by any agency of government. This is true whether we go to HEW or an independent agency—and I think the independent agency is the best way to do this. But in either case I do not think any agency is going to harass business. This is a growing economy. What we want are more jobs created. We want them created by creating products that will be safe and salable in the open market.

I commend the Senator from Illinois.

Mr. PERCY. Mr. President, I thank the Senator from Rhode Island. I think the comment he has made is especially worthy of response because many of us have been subjected to tremendous pressures from the business community on this legislation and companion legislation to create an independent consumer advocacy agency. I warn all Senators ahead of time they will be subjected to similar pressures with respect to the Consumer Protection Agency legislation.

I have now appeared before the U.S. Chamber of Commerce and the National Conference of Better Business Bureaus. I have received close to four thousand letters from businessmen, many of whom I feel did not bother to read the bill.

They took the word of some executive director, perhaps fighting for his $35,000 job, and they responded by contacting me on things that most were just simply not properly informed about.

I feel that when I can specify the cost to American society and consumers—at least $5.5 billion a year in costs that we suffer, not to mention human hardship, as a result of products that never should have been put on the market by a company—when we have free license to market and distribute hazardous consumer products, it is time to do something.

I saw a rotary cutter at a hardware store that I would not even want around my house. It would be like putting a handgun on the open shelf for somebody to pick up. When we permit that to happen, the need is not simply to talk, but to do something about it.

Mr. PASTORE. Mr. President, talking about these rotary mowers, a very close friend of mine had a frightening experience, mowing his own lawn—it may have been through his own carelessness a mechanical fault, or it may have been for some other reason—accidentally he had three fingers of his hand severed. Should corporations be allowed to build these instruments with such disregard to product safety that younger people, as well as older people, cannot use them without practically taking their lives in their hands?

That is what the legislation is aimed at. Some have the idea that we are out to harass business. Of course we are not doing that. This country cannot survive without business. This Government cannot operate without taxes derived from business. Our wages cannot be paid without a prospering business. So we are not trying to put business out of business. What we are trying to do is to protect the consumer and at the same time to protect sound business.

Mr. PERCY. The greatest enemies of business are businessmen who do not adhere to reasonable laws. It is the 5 percent who put the taint on the 95 percent. We are not trying to get at the 95 percent. It is the 5 percent, or the 3 percent, or the 2 percent that will be especially affected by the provisions of this act and that must be regulated and controlled and kept to a reasonable level of responsibility with respect to consumer products.

Mr. MAGNUSON. Of course, this will stimulate more research by business itself, to be sure they are going to do the right thing.

Mr. PERCY. Absolutely.

Mr. MAGNUSON. Because when they see this law, they will not want to be hauled in and told they are not doing the right thing. I would say it is true of 98 percent of them. This is what we need. We have the technology to do many of these things. I have a friend who is a great technician, a research man in the electrical industry. He said to me, "There must be a better way to make an electric light plug than the way we are making it." It is things like this which will stimulate industry.

Mr. PERCY. Mr. President, if I may at this point, I would like to point out the social cost of injuries, including actual millions of dollars unrealized as income taxes as a result of preventable deaths and injuries: $446 million in public expenditures representing 1.7 percent of the current expenditures for health care. Injuries caused 2.1 percent of hospital admissions, filling 18,782 beds for acute care, a number equal to the annual construction of such beds at a capital expenditure of $600 million.

The loss to society is tremendous.

I once again commend our distinguished chairman for articulating so well how all of us agree on the purposes of this bill. I think virtually all of responsible business supports this purpose in legislation. I worry and wonder about those who say this is not a proper function of government after these and like figures are cited.

Mr. JAVITS. Mr. President, I support S. 3419 as reported by the Labor and Public Welfare Committee with amendments and have joined this bill in this form as a cosponsor. I believe the recommended changes improve the bill and more effectively serve consumer interests.

The Labor and Public Welfare Committee and the Executive Reorganization Subcommittee of the Government Operations Committee, on both of which I am the ranking member, had the responsibility for reviewing titles I and II. These titles were the executive reorganization provisions of S. 3419, "The Consumer Safety Act of 1972," as reported by the Commerce Committee. Since the bill extends considerably beyond issues of safety, and covers such matters as misbranding of food, drugs, cosmetics, and medical devices, and encompasses provisions that protect the health and pocketbook of the consumer, as well as his safety, the title of the bill has been changed to "The Food, Drug, and Consumer Product Act of 1972."

Title I of the bill would establish an independent agency in the executive branch with the responsibility to promote the public health and safety by protecting consumers against injury resulting from the use of foods, drugs, devices, and consumer products—as defined in the bill. Title II would transfer to the new agency all functions of the Secretary of Health, Education, and Welfare which are presently administered through the Food and Drug Administration or through the Division of Biologics Standards of the National Institutes of Health, and the authority of the center for disease control over clinical laboratory licensing. It would also transfer consumer safety laws directed at certain classes of products or hazards such as the authority of the Department of Commerce and the FTC over flammable fabrics and refrigerator doors; and the authority of the Agriculture Department over food inspection and animal biological drugs.

A new title IV adds to the present cosmetic provisions of the Federal Food, Drug, and Cosmetic Act three new substantive labeling provisions which, in effect, bring the cosmetic requirements of the Act more closely into conformity with the labeling requirements for food, drugs, and devices.

As reported by the Committee on Commerce, the bill established a new independent agency. However, the Labor and Public Welfare Committee, of which I am ranking minority member, began from the well-accepted proposition that new independent agencies should be created only on evidence of compelling need and we should guard against unnecessary fragmentation of the Federal structure. I join with my other colleagues who have so eloquently put the case for some new Federal structure to better protect the consumer from hazards associated with food, drugs and consumer products. In this instance, the weight of the evidence as presented in both of my committees argued for an independent agency.

The administration was concerned that the creation of a new agency would sever the relationship between FDA and HEW, and sought to retain these functions within HEW. Their proposal to structure a consolidated regulatory effort within HEW did not, I believe, offer sufficient safeguards to insure the fullest protection in the consumer's interest.

Essential ingredients that I believed would be required for the administration of a structure in HEW and which the administration could not support are:

First, a measure of authority to initiate and litigate all court action in the name of such structure as may be necessary to carry out its functions, and to enforce the statutes subject to its jurisdiction as efficiently and effectively as possible.

Second, a measure of authority to submit its budget request and legislative recommendations directly to Congress.

Third, the authority to prescribe its own personnel policies.

The Agency established by this bill clearly has the aforementioned authorities—and certain additional authorities—which permit it to perform in the public interest, and I anticipate that there will be strong ties between the Department of Health, Education, and Welfare and the new Agency. Removing FDA from the Department of HEW is simply an organizational move to increase responsiveness and accountability, and need have no adverse impact on its relations with the health components of that Department in the future. In fact, these relationships may be substantially improved once the new Agency is established and is in a position to operate with the new strength and mandate given it in this legislation.

Mr. JAVITS. Mr. President, as the ranking minority member of the Committee on Labor and Public Welfare, which revised this bill after the Committee on Commerce completed its work, I feel it my duty not only to state my support for the bill but also to ask unanimous consent to have printed in the RECORD at this point a table of the revisions made in the bill by the Committee on Labor and Public Welfare and concurred in by a large number of members of the Committee on Government Operations, which never had a chance formally to act on these changes but concurred in those of the Committee on Labor and Public Welfare.

There being no objection, the material was ordered to be printed in the RECORD, as follows:

REVISIONS

S. 3419	REVISED BILL
1. Titled Consumer Safety Act of 1972.	1. Title changed to Food, Drug and Consumer Product Safety Act of 1972.
2. Definition of "Consumer Product" authorized to be regulated under Title III. Exemption of certain products "subject to safety regulation" under certain other laws was confusing; could have been interpreted to authorize this Agency to regulate in those exempted areas (e.g. FAA, Motor Vehicles, Occupational Safety and Health, etc.).	2. "Consumer products subject to safety regulation under other laws" are defined as "authorized to be regulated for the purpose of eliminating unreasonable risk of injury or death." Such products may be regulated by the Food, Drug and Consumer Product Agency after it petitions the agency with jurisdiction over the product, asking to regulate it, and such agency requests the Food, Drug and Consumer Product Agency to regulate it. Sec. 102(a), p. 3. Sec. 104(c)(17), p. 13.
3. Administrator authorized only to "coordinate" activities of the Commissioners (Food, Drug and Consumer Products).	3. Administrator authorized to "direct" and coordinate" the Commissioners. Ultimate responsibility rests with the Administrator. Sec. 105(a), p. 14.
4. Mandatory delegation of standard setting to Commissioners by Administrator.	4. Delegation of regulatory authority "insofar as practicable and consistent with sound administration." Sec. 202, p. 37.
5. Subpoena authority limited to witnesses at hearings and for "information."	5. Subpoena broadened to cover access to records and general or special reports by producers (based on FTC). Sec. 104(c) (6), p. 10.
6. No provision.	6. Direct submission of budget to President, and direct receipt of all funds from OMB. Sec. 104(c) (13), p. 12.
7. No specific provision.	7. Authority to prescribe personnel policies "without prior approval or clearance" Sec. 104(c) (16), p. 12.
8. Law enforcement through Justice Department.	8. Law enforcement by Agency authorized plus authority to "direct" the course of all agency litigation." Sec. 104(c) (16), p. 12.
9. Separate legal staffs for Administrator and 3 Commissioners.	9. One legal staff for Agency. Sec. 105(f), p. 14.
10. Commissioners appointed by President, no fixed term of office.	10. Commissioners appointed by Administrator. Sec. 107(a), p. 16.
11. Authorized appointment of private attorneys to represent consumers in agency proceedings.	11. No provision. Consumer Protection Agency (advocacy), as embodied in S. 1177 now pending, will perform this function. "Representation" struck from Sec. 109, p. 18.
12. Mandamus action against agency where its act or omission has exposed a person to unreasonable risk of injury or death.	12. Rewritten to require suit against the Agency only after petitioning Agency for corrective action. Petitioner would have to show by preponderence of the evidence that act or omission has exposed a person to unreasonable risk of injury or death. Sec. 112, p. 25.
13. Authorizes $180-$200-and $225 million for next three fiscal years.	13. Authorizes such sums as may be necessary. (Subsequently modified by Senator Cotton's amendment to authorize $250-300-and 350 million for next three fiscal years). Sec. 117, p. 32.
14. No provision.	14. Transfers USDA authority under Meat, Poultry, Egg and other Agricultural Product Inspection Acts to Administrator. (Subsequently deleted by amendment offered by Senator Moss.) Sec. 201(c), p. 35.

REVISIONS

S. 3419	REVISED BILL
15. No provision	15. Transfers authorities of Division of Biologics Standards. (DBS works on vaccines, *inter alia*; is in NIH). Sec. 201(b), p. 34.
16. Repealed several consumer safety laws.	16. *Transfers* authority under these laws to the new Agency. Old Sec. 204, p. 40 struck; now in Sec. 202(a), p. 37.
17. No provision.	17. Adds certain labeling requirements for cosmetics by amending the Food, Drug and Cosmetic Act to bring cosmetics more closely into conformity with the labeling requirements for food drugs and devices. Title IV, p. 80.

Mr. JAVITS. The need for this new agency is clear. We were unable to work out any arrangement putting the essentials of this agency in HEW that would have best served the consumer with all the changes made by the Labor and Public Welfare Committee. This bill now deserves the support of the Senate.

* * *

Mr. MAGNUSON. Mr. President, I congratulate the members of the Government Operations Committee and the Labor and Public Welfare Committee for their efforts in improving S. 3419. I was, of course, pleased that both committees concurred in the judgment of the Senate Commerce Committee that an independent agency was essential in order to insure the safety and efficacy of foods, drugs, and other consumer products.

The changes in the agency responsibility section of the bill—section 112—bring clarity of meaning and administrative efficiency to the section. I still believe that this section is one of the most important in the bill. The section grants citizens in this country the right to overturn bureaucratic inertia in a court of law by showing, through a preponderance of the evidence, that the bureaucracy has failed in its mission to protect consumers from unsafe foods, drugs or other consumer products.

The Government Operations Committee and the Labor and Public Welfare Committee have also improved the definition of "consumer product." These committees have eliminated ambiguity with respect to the treatment of "electronic products" and clarified the words "subject to such regulation." These are both areas which appropriately concerned my distinguished colleague, Senator COTTON, in his minority views on S. 3419.

I also agree with the decision of these committees to retain the present authority over cosmetics and medical devices while simultaneously applying the new authority in title III to these products. I am also pleased with the transfer of the Center for Disease Control to the new Food, Drug, and Consumer Product Agency. Secretary Richardson in his statement before the Senate Commerce Committee mentioned that CDC was an important resource upon which the Food and Drug Administration drew. By having CDC and FDA under one roof, their exchange of resources should be significantly facilitated.

* * *

So Mr. COTTON's amendment was rejected.

* * *

Mr. HUMPHREY. Mr. President, I rise in support of S. 3419, the Food, Drug, and Consumer Product Safety Act of 1972.

I believe the enactment of this legislation is dictated by the clear need of the American consumer for adequate protection in obtaining safe foods, drugs, and cosmetics, and in avoiding accident hazards in the use of fabrics, toys, certain electronic products, toxic substances, and other articles, and in the prevention of deceptive packaging and inadequate labeling.

The heavy responsibilities laid upon existing Federal regulatory agencies in these areas cannot be met with full effectiveness without the establishment of an independent agency in the executive branch, directly responsible to the President and Congress and openly accountable to the public. The operations of the Food and Drug Administration, which will provide many of the primary components of this new agency can only be strengthened under this reorganization. This is an essential step that must be taken beyond the increase of FDA appropriations and the expansion of staff.

I do not regard the establishment of an independent Food, Drug, and Consumer Product Agency as an unnecessary fragmentation of the Federal structure. To the contrary, there is a compelling need for this consolidation of diverse and uncoordinated regulatory, research, and inspection functions in the Federal Government, if full protection is to be provided to consumers, and if a priority level of authority and responsibility is to be established to articulate clear regulatory policies to industry.

Further deliberation must be given to the need for providing in this legislation for the transfer of Department of Agriculture food inspection programs. But it is essential that the functions of the new Agency be organized as provided for under the three subordinate Commissions of Food and Nutrition, Drugs, and Consumer Products. A direct line of authority must also be provided to the Agency Administrator, appointed by the President, by and with the advice and consent of the Senate, for an initial term of 5 years with a one-time reappointment—a provision designed to achieve a reasonable Agency independence from immediate political pressures, but at the same time to assure the Agency's responsiveness to immediate public concerns. And this line of authority is further emphasized by the provision in this bill directing the Administrator to submit an annual Agency budget directly to the President for review and submittal to Congress, and prohibiting the Office of Management and Budget from impounding any funds appropriated to the Agency by Congress.

I applaud the initiatives taken in this bill to establish an Office of Consumer Information, a Consumer Information Library, and a National Injury Information Clearinghouse, as well as a Joint Scientific Committee to assume the coordination of functions within the Agency. An unacceptable number of hazardous consumer products now affect interstate commerce, and their increasing numbers and complexity make it imperative that the Federal Government act promptly to eliminate hazards resulting in death or injury.

I also strongly believe the Agency must adopt a position of openness toward and accessibility by the Amreican consumer public. It is for this reason that I fully support provisions in this legislation to assure public access to information received or sent by the Administrator or any Commissioner, subject only to specified and fair limitations on information relating to trade secrets as covered under Federal law. Further provision is made for a consumer to commence a civil action against the Agency, if it refuses to take action in response to a petition, or if its action is regarded by the petitioner as insufficient to eliminate an alleged unreasonable risk of injury or death. And specific guidelines are provided in this bill to assure that the promulgation of consumer product standards is expedited and that hazardous products are removed from the market, if necessary by emergency action initiated before the appropriate U.S. district court by the Agency Administrator or the Attorney General. Finally, I fully support the provisions in this bill giving the Agency Administrator the necessary powers to take all action necessary to enforce food, drug, and consumer product safety laws.

The time has come to end needless injury and death resulting from the inadequate regulation of consumer products under present Federal law. I urge the Senate to address this national issue forthrightly by passing the Food, Drug, and Consumer Product Safety Act.

Mr. KENNEDY. Mr. President, it gives me great pleasure to support S. 3419, the Food, Drug, and Consumer Product Safety Act of 1972, as amended and reported by the Committee on Labor and Public Welfare.

S. 3419 is far-reaching and comprehensive legislation to protect consumers in the vital areas of food, drugs, and consumer products. It provides a clear mandate to insure the safety and efficacy of drugs, the wholesomeness of foods, and the safety of consumer products to prevent unnecessary injury and harm to the consumer. S. 3419 is a giant step forward to implement and achieve a strong Federal commitment in an area of critical concern to all Americans. The Committee on Commerce and its distinguished chairman, Senator MAGNUSON, are to be highly commended, for once again reporting outstanding legislation for Senate consideration.

I strongly support S. 3419 as amended by the Committee on Labor and Public Welfare and believe the committee amendments merit strong support and consideration. S. 3419 would establish an independent agency in the executive branch to regulate foods, drugs, and consumer products. It would combine into a single agency; first, the authority of the Food and Drug Administration over food, drugs, and consumer products; second, the authority of the Division of Biologics Standards Over Human Biological Drugs; third, the authority of the Center for Disease Control over Clinical Laboratory Licensing; fourth, the authority of the Department of Commerce and the FTC over flammable fabrics and refrigerator doors; and fifth, the authority of the Agriculture Department over food inspection and animal biological drugs. The result will be one agency with comprehensive jurisdiction and authority to regulate all food, drugs, and common household products.

FDA's shortcomings have not been a matter of partisan politics; the same kinds of problems have plagued the FDA in Democratic as well as Republican administrations. Under all administrations, the Agency has failed either to provide full protection to consumers against unsafe products or to articulate clear regulatory policies to industry.

The most important reason for this failure has been the agency's lack of clear-cut responsibility for accomplishing its mission. Authority for the regulation of food, drugs, and consumer products is widely fragmented within the Federal Government: The FDA sets standards for the level of dangerous drug residues in meat and poultry, but testing and inspection is done by the Department of Agriculture; the FDA has responsibility to investigate the safety of flammable fabrics, but regulatory is vested with the Federal Trade Commission, the Department of Commerce, and the Department of the Treasury. The same division of authority is present in other areas.

FDA has never had independent authority to regulate those matters within its jurisdiction. As presently structured within the Department of Health, Education, and Welfare, the Commissioner of the Food and Drug Administration must report to the Assistant Secretary for Health and Scientific Affairs, who must report to the Under Secretary of the Department of Health, Education, and Welfare, who must report to the Office of the Secretary of Health, Education, and Welfare, who must report to the Office of Management and Budget, to the Domestic Council, and finally, once all those channels have been exhausted, to the President. At any step along that route, a regulatory decision by the Commissioner could be reversed. Because of this structure, the agency has not been able to make clear-cut regulatory decisions or even to make clear to consumers and to industry what its basic policies are.

In the Department of Health, Education, and Welfare, basic health programs are directed toward health research and health delivery systems. Even if all of FDA is considered health-related, 98 percent of the health resources of the Department and 88 percent of the manpower in fiscal year 1972 was devoted to health research and delivery. Health regulatory functions of FDA are only a small part of HEW's total health responsibility and cannot receive the attention they deserve.

Furthermore, in addition to health regulation, FDA plays an important role in economic regulation. It is concerned not only with adulteration of food and drugs which may be harmful to health, but with misbranding and deceptive labeling. With respect to adulteration of food, there are problems that are important but which do not, strictly speaking, involve dangers to health. For example, the FDA has published guidelines governing the amount of filth and foreign matter that may be permitted on food. In hearings before the Subcommittee on Executive Reorganization and Government Research, the Secretary stated that the presence of such foreign matter as rodent hairs in chocolate bars raised no health problem. Implicit in his statement was the assumption that since no health problem was raised, there was no pressing need for effective regulation to improve the purity of food. Yet, there is clearly an interest in regulation to assure the purity of food, even when impurities are merely displeasing and do not pose a clear danger to health.

It is unlikely, however, that interests in economic and non-health regulation will ever be given appropriate consideration in a department in which health responsibilities focus on research and delivery. Nor is it likely that the entire program of regulation of food, drugs, and consumer products can ever be given the attention resources, support, and services it deserves in as enormous and multifaceted a department as HEW. This problem is built into the very structure of the Department, and is as prevalent in Democratic as in Republican administrations.

It will continue to exist so long as the Secretary is called upon to choose between competing needs. In short, to be an effective policeman of the marketplace, the agency must be free from the restraints of competing policies, priorities, and objectives.

Examples are numerous. In the regulation of cyclamates, confusion over whose policy would prevail led the industry to build up vast inventories of products ultimately and unexpectedly banned from the market. This would not have happened if clear-cut authority to determine policy had been placed in one responsible official. Another example is the confusion concerning the use of detergents containing phosphates. Neither consumers, environmentalists, nor industry can tell for sure what the Government's regulatory policy is.

Finally, once a policy is enunciated, the FDA lacks the authority to enforce these decisions. The FDA must turn to the Department of Justice which because of other priorities may inadvertently frustrate or delay implementation of the FDA policy.

Mr. President, the problem of food, drug, and consumer product regulation also satisfies both of the basic criteria for the creation of an independent agency set out by the President in his message proposing the Environmental Protection Agency. The first, was that responsibility is divided among several agencies, but is not the primary function of any of them, and the other functions affect the agencies' views of the regulatory issues. The committee record shows that this situation exists in food, drug, and consumer product regulation.

The President stated a second criterion justifying the creation of an independent agency; a situation must exist in which the centralizing of authority in one agency would better enable that agency to make decisions about the activities of other agencies. The President stated that such decisionmaking functions were better lodged in an independent agency than in an existing Cabinet department. He reasoned that a Cabinet agency, with multifarious nonregulatory responsibilities, might be regarded by other agencies as a representative of competing interests and constituencies and a promoter of its own programs at the expense of those of other agencies. He felt that it would be unwise in such a situation to transfer regulatory responsibilities to such a Cabinet agency.

It is entirely possible that promotion of HEW's health research and health delivery programs might appear to be in conflict with the promotion, marketing, and manufacturing of certain products. This problem could arise, for example, from the transfer of all authority over the use of the hormone diethylstilbesterol—DES—used to promote growth in cattle. The hormone has been shown to cause cancer in some animals, and residues of it in human food are prohibited. At present, authority is divided between HEW and the Department of Agriculture; largely because of this division, the Government's policies have been inadequate and neither consumers nor industry have been satisfied with the result. Consolidation of authority would be desirable. But if all authority were transferred to HEW, heavily influenced by the need to promote its health delivery and research programs, the concerns of the Department of Agriculture might be ignored. Similarly, if all authority were transferred to the Department of Agriculture, health interests in HEW would feel uneasy.

A similar situation exists in the area of flammable fabrics, where the division of authority among the FDA, the FTC, the Department of Commerce and the Department of the Treasury, has produced great confusion and no effective regulation. Consolidation is necessary, but authority would be lodged in an independent, wholly regulatory agency, without promotional programs designed to serve particular constituencies.

It is essential to keep product safety regulation together with food and drug regulation, enforcement and field operations in the three areas are already shared. To establish product safety regulation in a separate agency would cause needless duplication of staff, facilities, training, and other resources.

The creation of a new agency will not sever the relationship between FDA and HEW. There should be strong ties between the Department of HEW and the new agency, just as there are presently strong ties between FDA and its sister agencies such as, FTC, EPA, and USDA. Removing FDA from the Department of HEW is simply an organizational move to increase responsiveness and accountability, and need have no adverse impact on its relations with the health components of that department in the future. In fact, these relationships may be substantially improved once the new agency is established and it is in a position to operate with the new strength and mandate given it in this legislation.

Mr. President, as amended, S. 3419 covers food, drugs, and a wide variety of other consumer products. Accordingly, the short title of the bill has been changed to "the Food, Drug, and Consumer Product Act of 1972," and the name of the new independent regulatory agency created by the bill has been changed to "the Food, Drug, and Consumer Product Agency." This title more adequately describes the precise regulatory function of the new agency. Further, it draws upon the name of its predecessor agency, the Food and Drug Administration, which has been well-known since it was first adopted in 1931, and thus has 41 years of recognition by the public.

Since many of the primary components of the new agency come from the Food and Drug Administration, the Committee on Labor and Public Welfare expects that it shall retain its present jurisdiction respecting regulatory authority exercised by the new agency. The committee also expects that it shall share the responsibility for holding confirmatory hearings on the administrator of such agency with the Senate Commerce Committee.

In keeping with the change in name for the new agency, section 103, establishment of agency, has been amended to show that its mission includes protecting consumers against adulteration, misbranding, and illegal distribution of food, drugs, cosmetics, and medical devices, as well as against injury resulting from the use of consumer products.

The Labor and Public Welfare Committee has amended section 104 to provide the Administrator of the agency full subpena power, access to documentary guidance, and authority to require general or special orders. This will make the authority of the Administrator to issue subpenas equal to that contained in sections 6 and 9 of the Federal Trade Commission Act. The new authority will cover products presently regulated by the Food and Drug Administration as well as all of the other products over which jurisdiction is granted to the new agency. The FDA does not now possess subpena authority. In testimony before the Executive Reorganization Subcommittee, Secretary Richardson agreed that the FDA should be granted such power. This amendment remedies an important gap in the enforcement authority of the new agency.

The committee has also added five other new paragraphs providing additional authority for the Administrator.

Paragraph 13 permits the Administrator to prepare and submit, directly to the President without review by the Office of Management and Budget for review and transmittal to Congress, an annual budget estimate. It also requires that all appropriated funds be obligated and expended by the Agency, without the possibility that they may be reduced by the Office of Management and Budget. This language is modeled on section 407(b) (9) of the Pubic Heath Service Act, as added by the recently enacted National Cancer Act of 1971, Public Law 92–218. It will insure that the Congress receives the undiluted judgment of the Administrator concerning his budget needs and that no funds appropriated for the Agency will be withheld.

Paragraphs 14 and 15 authorize the Administrator to prescribe personnel policies and to submit legislative recommendations and testimony to Congress without the usual prior approval or clearance from the Office of Management and Budget or the President. If the Agency is to be effective, the Administrator must be capable of informing Congress, directly and without outside interference, exactly what he and his Agency believe to be the facts about the matters before it. The inevitable compromise softening of approach and delays achieved through a review process, which often includes several departments and agencies, is inconsistent with the type of strong new Agency envisioned by this bill. Similarly, it is important that the Administrator establish his own personnel policies in a manner suited to the regulatory mission of the new Agency, rather than the judgment of some official outside the Agency.

Paragraph 16 authorizes the Administrator to initiated and litigate all court action in the name of the Agency. He will be represented in court by his own representative, the general counsel of the Agency, or through the U.S. attorneys, representing the Attorney General. The Secretary of Health, Education, and Welfare, in his testimony before the Executive Reorganization Subcommittee, endorsed this authority for FDA in principle. It may be unnecessary for the new Agency to establish its own network of local attorneys to handle routine matters. In the past, the Food and Drug Administration has prepared all pleadings for the U.S. attorneys, has sent its own attorneys who are experts in the field to assist in the litigation of the case, and has prepared all appellate briefs. The committee intends this to continue, but the authority granted here will safeguard the independence of the new Agency.

It is important that the litigation of the Agency, which is critical to enforcement of the laws it administers, be directed and controlled by the Administrator. No one else has the responsibility for enforcement of those laws, and no one else should be in the position to frustrate their enforcement. The decision whether to file a criminal information, and the decision whether to include or to dismiss individual defendants, must be made by the Administrator. The Administrator must also be in the position to file, within hours, seizure or injunction actions, in order to prevent continued violation of the law. Similarly, the decision as to what legal arguments are to be made and how to make them most effectively for orderly development of the law through trial and appellate litigation is best handled by the Administrator who is repsonsible solely for enforcing the food, drug, and product safety laws.

Paragraph 17 provides that where a product is subject to safety regulation under certain other laws, the Administrator may petition the appropriate Federal department or agency to establish and enforce necessary safety regulations for such product. The Administrator may establish and enforce such regulations upon request of other agencies and may participate in proceedings of other agencies to establish safety regulations.

The committee has also substantially modified section 109, Office of Consumer Information. Conforming amendments and technical changes have been made in subsections (a), (b), and (c). With respect to the public information room, it is specifically provided that all funds collected for copying, or for search for and production of documents, shall be paid directly to the Agency and obligated and expended to finance the consumer information program, after start up costs have been met. The Freedom of Information Act does not provide that funds paid for copying should remain available to the agency involved. As a result, the information program is a drain on an agency's resources. This new provision corrects that deficiency. The Agency will be able to hire personnel and finance a program out of the funds collected for copying.

Subsection (c) has also been amended to provide that the charge for search and copying shall be the minimum practicable amount, not exceeding actual cost. The bill also directs the Agency to take all reasonable measures to reduce or waive charges which would be financially burdensome to any person. These provisions are intended to carry out the basic policy of this bill to encourage consumer participation in the procedures and processes of the Agency. This can only be achieved if ordinary citizens are provided access to all essential Agency information free or at a reasonable cost. It is intended to apply to small numbers of documents that can reasonably be obtained without significant burden to the Agency, and not to permit fishing expeditions or requests for large numbers of documents that could impede the regulatory work of the Agency.

The committee deleted the subsection (d) which provided for the appointment of private attorneys to represent consumers in proceedings before the Agency to avoid potential conflict with the proposed Consumer Protection Agency bill, S. 1177, and added new subsection (d) establishing a Consumer Information Library. There is no single location in government where the vast amount of literature on foods, drugs, and consumer products is available to the general public. This provision will cover that deficiency.

The National Injury Information Clearinghouse established under section 110 is a most important and innovative provision. A system of monitoring should be invaluable to assist the Commissioners and the Adminstration to carry out their functions. A confidentiality provision is included for the names or identification of either the injured parties or the person treating them. Either party may waive such privilege concerning his or her own name.

S. 3419, as reported by the Committee on Commerce, authorized in section 112, agency responsibility, a civil mandamus action by individuals against the agency where its act or omission has exposed a person to an unreasonable risk of injury or death from a food, drug, or consumer product. The Committee on Labor and Public Welfare fully agrees with the concept underlying this provision, but has revised it to streamline its functioning and to make it more efficient. The basic policy behind this provision is that the Agency should be responsive and accountable to the public.

The section now provides that an individual, by himself or as a representative of a class, who believes he has been exposed by an act or omission of the Agency to a food, drug, or consumer product presenting an unreasonable risk of injury or death shall first petition the Agency to take specific action sufficient to eliminate the alleged unreasonable risk. This permits a petition by an individual or class complaining that a product such as a new drug presents an unreasonable risk, and does not permit a person to submit a petition with respect to an agency act or omission removing a product from the market or failing to allow it on the market.

After submission of the petition, and a 30-day period during which interested parties will be permitted to comment, the Agency must issue a decision either refusing to take action or taking action which it determines sufficient to eliminate any unreasonable risk. This decision is to be made within 120 days following the filing of the petition. The parties may, of course, stipulate to a longer period of time.

If the petitioner disagrees with the Agency decision, he may commence a civil action in a U.S. court of appeals against the Agency. Any such action must be filed within 60 days after the decision of the Agency—if such an action is not filed within that time period, the petitioner may seek judicial review of the Agency decision pursuant to the applicable provisions of the Administrative Procedure Act.

The court of appeals may remand the matter to the Agency for the gathering of additional evidence upon a request by the petitioner for good cause shown. The court may place any conditions it wishes upon such a remand for additional evidence. Such new evidence might then require the Agency to reconsider its decision.

The U.S. Court of Appeals is charged with determining whether a preponderance of the evidence in the record on which the Agency made its decision—which is limited to the petition, all information submitted by the petitioner, and all information identified in the Agency's decision as part of the record—shows that the Agency has exposed the petitioner to a food, drug, or consumer product presenting an unreasonable risk of injury or death. In making this determination, the court must consider whether the risk is unreasonable in light of all the relevant circumstances shown in the record. The burden of proof is on the petitioner to show that a preponderance of record evidence establishes the unreasonableness of the risk associated with the product, and that an act or omission of the Agency has exposed him to such risk.

If the petitioner prevails, the remedy available to the court is to remand the matter to the Agency for appropriate action. The Agency will then have an opportunity to consider what alternatives are available to eliminate the unreasonable risk determined by the court to exist, and to choose among those alternatives one that will be sufficient. Should the petitioner again dispute the Agency decision, the same type of civil action could again be undertaken. The court has no power to award money damages against the Agency or any individual.

This provision establishes a new standard of review applicable only in these cases, but this departure from the administrative procedure act is justified by the nature of the right involved. In these cases an individual, or a group, is seeking protection from some food, drug, or consumer product which may expose them to an unreasonable risk of injury or death.

Agency action affecting interests in life and health should be subject to the most searching judicial examination. The importance of these interests justifies a departure from the normal standard of review. In such cases, substantial evidence in the record should not be sufficient to sustain the Agency action. Since this right of action gives the plaintiff no economic incentive—only costs may be recovered in the discretion of the court—it is unlikely that a large number of suits will disturb the orderly processes of agency decision. Yet the possibility of suit will serve as a constant spur to action safeguarding the public, but this does not preclude an independent tort action against an individual by the injured party.

Mr. President, the committee also accepted an amendment proposed by Senator EAGLETON which adds to the present cosmetic provisions of the Federal Food, Drug, and Cosmetic Act three new substantive labeling provisions. These provisions in effect bring the cosmetic requirements of the act more closely into conformity with the labeling requirements for food, drugs, and devices.

The first provision requires each cosmetic to be labeled with the common or usual name of the cosmetic, and with the common or usual name of each ingredient. The provision permits exemptions to be established where there is a showing that ingredient disclosure would be impracticable or deceptive.

The second provision requires warnings in all labeling for any cosmetic which would be dangerous under any reasonably foreseeable conditions of use or misuse.

The third provision deletes the present exemption for soap from the cosmetic requirements of the act.

The committee strongly supports these provisions which shall insure greater safety for consumers in regard to cosmetics.

The committee believes cooperation among the Federal agencies is most important and has provided in section 115 for the administrator to utilize the resources and facilities of the National Bureau of Standards. The Bureau can be of invaluable assistance in the area of public health and safety. The committee does not intend for the administrator to delegate to the Bureau the setting and enforcement of standards.

Mr. President, the present fragmentation of regulation of food, drugs, and other consumer products throughout a number of Federal departments and agencies has resulted in inconsistent policies and incomplete regulations, to the detriment of the consuming public. Effective food, drug and consumer product regulation requires creation of a new agency with independence to exert the leadership and vigorous enforcement necessary for consumer protection. Past experience shows that, unless the agency has the power to issue regulations, direct the course of all litigation, and make legislative and budgetary recommendations, without approval or clearance by outside agencies, its effectiveness will be substantially impaired.

The Committee on Labor and Public Welfare has made many amendments to the bill, yet its basic framework remains intact. The amendments strengthen and improve the bill by expanding the mandate of the agency, broadening its powers and increasing the authority of the administrator to manage the business of the agency efficiently. These changes will help assure that the bill's promise of better consumer protection in foods, drugs and consumer products becomes a reality.

I commend the Senate Commerce Committee and its distinguished chairman, Senator Magnuson, for originally reporting out S. 3419, and I strongly urge that S. 3419, as amended by the Committee on Labor and Public Welfare do pass.

As chairman of the Health Subcommittee of the Committee on Labor and Public Welfare, I want to express my deep appreciation to the distinguished Senator from Wisconsin, GAYLORD NELSON, who was kind enough to chair the Health Subcommittee hearings on S. 3419. I also wish to thank the Subcommittee on Executive Reorganization, and Government Research of the Government Operations Committee and its distinguished chairman, Senator RIBICOFF, for the cooperation and support in respect to S. 3419.

Mr. EAGLETON. Mr. President, I rise in support of S. 3419, and particularly title IV which requires ingredient labeling of all cosmetics, and where applicable, cautionary labeling.

Federal law now requires that a cosmetic be labeled without false or misleading representations, with information about the manufacturer, packer or distributor of the product, and the quantity of its contents. The law also provides that a cosmetic be packaged in a safe and non-deceptive container, and that it be produced in a sanitary plant. That is all the law presently requires.

The inadequacy of these existing provisions under the Federal Food, Drug, and Cosmetic Act, is clearly demonstrated by the 60,000 persons injured annually by cosmetics, as reported by the National Commission on Product Safety. The Food and Drug Administration cannot require pretesting for safety of cosmetics before they are marketed. They cannot even demand that the manufacturers list the ingredients. The FDA can act to ban harmful products, but only after some damage has been done.

My amendment, which the committee adopted with no dissenting votes, would be the first step toward giving the consumer protection from potential harm. It is directed to protecting the consumer with a known allergic reaction to a particular ingredient. The provision requires each cosmetic to be labeled with the common or usual name of the cosmetic, and with the common or usual name of each ingredient. Color, fragrance, and flavor ingredients may be declared generally by "color", "fragrance", or "flavor", without specifying each color, fragrance, and flavor ingredient. This is the same type of requirement as presently applies to food under section 403 of the same act.

Despite the contention of the cosmetic industry that half the population is allergic to one or another ingredient and that manufacturers cannot possibly guard against all sensitivities, many consumers could protect themselves if they knew what a cosmetic contained before they bought it—simply by reading the label.

The cosmetic manufacturers have in the past protested vigorously that the listing of ingredients would give away jealously guarded trade secrets. We are not asking that they list formulations on the label, or that they give specific quantities of each ingredient; we are only asking that they list each ingredient of the product so that the consumer can protect him or herself by minimizing use of those containing suspected substances. Cases of cosmetic injury range from mild discomfort to temporary damage to serious disfigurement and permanent injury. Consumers have suffered underarm and skin irritations from deodorants and lotions, vision damage from shampoo, scalp burns and loss of hair from hair dye, eye infection from contaminated mascara, and systemic reactions from creams and powders.

Yet in most cases, all of this could be prevented. Upon reading the ingredient labeling, the consumer could know which products contain ingredients to which she is sensitive, and thus, which products not to use.

The second provision requires warnings in all labeling from any cosmetic which would be dangerous under any reasonably forseeable conditions of use or misuse. This cautionary label would also contain directions for proper use of the product to avoid a hazard, or direction for steps to be taken if a problem does occur.

The provisions before you now would be a major breakthrough for cosmetic safety. I urge that the Senate retain these provisions in the bill as reported from the Committee on Labor and Public Welfare.

Mr. TALMADGE. Mr. President, I send to the desk an amendment and ask that it be stated.

The PRESIDING OFFICER. The amendment will be stated.

The assistant legislative clerk read the amendment, as follows:

On page 64, after line 25, insert the following:

(d) (1) Any manufacturer of a product declared a banned hazardous consumer product under this Act, who seeks judicial review under this section, may be awarded at the discretion of the court, damages, interest, and the cost of suit, including reasonable attorney fees, for actual damages suffered by him due to any order of the Commissioner declaring a product to be a banned hazardous substance determined by the court to constitute an abuse of the discretion granted to the Commissioner under this Act.

(2) The Secretary of the Treasury is authorized and directed to pay, out of any money in the Treasury not otherwise appropriated the amount of damages, interest, and costs awarded by the court under paragraph (1).

Mr. TALMADGE. I yield myself as much time as I may require.

Mr. President, this is a very simple amendment. I have discussed it with the distinguished floor manager of the bill and his staff, and it is my information that they are agreeable to it.

The amendment I have offered will correct what I believe to be a fundamental inequity which exists in this act.

The situation which I am trying to correct can best be illustrated by the following example. Suppose we have a shoe manufacturer in Georgia. He has a relatively small operation. Let us assume that under the provisions of this bill, the Consumer Protection Agency orders that his shoes be banned because they cause injury to the feet of children.

Under the provisions of this act, he can take an appeal to the Federal courts. He can urge the courts to stay the effective date of this order until the appeal is settled, but there is no guarantee that the court will find that it is in the public interest to do so. I do not think it is unreasonable to assume that this appeal would take from 1 to 2 years. In the meantime, he will have no other choice than to close down his business and dismiss his employees. Even if he wins the court fight, what is he left with—a business which has been shut down, a life which has been wrecked, and an admission from the Government that they were wrong, and they are sorry that his business was closed down.

That is not enough, Mr. President. He is an American citizen, too, and the Government owes him more than that. In my amendment, I propose the following solution. If a Federal court finds that a product which was banned should not, in fact, have been banned, the court shall then make an inquiry into the question of whether or not the decision to ban the product constituted an abuse of discretion. If such an abuse is found, then a special master would be appointed to assess the manufacturer's actual damages and refund them to him from the public treasury, along with the payment of the legal rate of interest on this sum computed since the order to ban was issued.

This is only simple justice, Mr. President. Why should the American manufacturer be required to indemnify himself against abuses of discretion on the part of Government officials? The power to ban is an extensive one. If a manufacturer has only one product, the power to ban amounts to a life and death power over his entire enterprise. If we are going to assume this kind of power as a government, then we must take the responsibility which goes with it.

Some will say that this will have a "chilling effect" on the administrator. To them I say that when you are dealing with a power this broad, it should be exercised with maximum caution. If a manufacturer is victimized by an abuse of discretion on the part of the Government, then he deserves to be made as whole as possible.

Quite frankly, Mr. President, I think that he should be reimbursed even for those decisions to ban which are found to be good-faith errors of judgment on the part of the administrator. It is still an error. If it is not an error which was made by the manufacturer, why should he be called on to pay for it with his entire business?

But I am not asking for that, Mr. President, though I think it would be the fair thing to do. All I am asking the Senate to do is to say to the American manufacturer, "If a Government official abuses his discretion and takes action which causes you severe financial damage, then we will do what we can to make you whole again." I am not talking about punitive damages, Mr. President, only actual damages.

I would ask any Senator who is prepared to vote against this amendment to stop and think for a moment how he would try to explain to that shoe manufacturer in Georgia why his shoe plant was closed down because of a governmental abuse of discretion, and there is no recourse for him.

This is a new and viscous kind of eminent domain, Mr. President. I am totally opposed to it, and I hope the floor manager will accept this amendment.

Mr. MAGNUSON. Mr. President, I have conferred with the Senator from Georgia and the ranking minority member of the committee, and I think it is an amendment we can take and talk to the House. I think, as the Senator points out, it is only fair to the people to be made whole if something happens to them, if an administrator abuses his authority or his power. I think it is common justice.

Mr. TALMADGE. Mr. President, I thank the distinguished floor manager of the bill and I agree with him.

* * *

The amendment was agreed to.

Mr. TALMADGE. Mr. President, I send another amendment to the desk and ask that it be stated.

The PRESIDING OFFICER. The amendment will be stated.

The legislative clerk read the amendment, as follows:

On page 56, line 24, insert "except as provided in subsection (g)," after "(ii)".

On page 57, line 18, insert "except as provided in subsection (g)," after "(ii)".

On page 58, between lines 13 and 14, insert the following:

Notice by Manufacturer or Distributor

(g) If any maufacturer of a product which has been declared a banned hazardous consumer product under this Act furnishes notice by registered mail to a distributor or retail dealer of that product, his liability to reimburse that distributor or retail dealer under subsection (f)(2)(A)(ii) of this section with respect to the refunded purchase price of any such product sold by that distributor or retail dealer after the day on which he receives notice shall be limited to the price paid for the product by that distributor or retail dealer. If any distributor of such a product furnishes notice by registered mail to a retail dealer of that product, his liability to reimburse that retail dealer under subsection (f)(2)(B)(ii) of this section with respect to the refunded purchase price of any such product sold by that retail dealer after the day on which he receives notice shall be limited to the price paid for the product by that retail dealer.

Mr. TALMADGE. Mr. President, this is a simple amendment. I have discussed it with the distinguished floor manager of the bill and my understanding is that he is agreeable to accepting it.

Mr. President, the purpose of my amendment is to correct a defect which exists in the section of the bill dealing with repurchasing requirements.

Under the bill as it is currently written, when a manufacturer's product is banned, he is obligated to repurchase it from the distributors, retailers and general public. An aggrieved consumer can also resell the product to the retailer from whom he purchased it, in which case, the retailer resells it, in turn, to the manufacturer. The manufacturer is required to refund, to the retailer, the retail price paid for the product, and not the wholesale price.

The purpose of my amendment is to which he can protect himself. In the event that his product is banned, he can notify his distributors and retailers by registered mail of the fact that the product has been banned. They can then resell them to the manufacturer for the price they paid for them. But if they continue to sell these products after receiving the notice from the manufacturer, in the event that the manufacturer is required to repurchase such items from the retailer and distributor, he only has to pay them the wholesale price, and is not responsible for their mark-up as he would be in the case of goods sold before notice is received.

Mr. President, if this amendment is not accepted, we will have created a situation where a retailer could continue to sell products after learning that they are banned, knowing that even if they were returned by the consumer, he could resell them to the manufacturer at the retail price rather than the wholesale price. I think that this is a perfectly reasonable protection to extend to the manufacturer.

I urge the Senate to adopt this amendment.

Mr. MAGNUSON. Mr. President, the pending amendment pursues the same objectives as the Senator's first amendment. It does simple justice and I am in favor of it.

Mr. TALMADGE. I thank the distinguished floor manager of the bill and I agree with him.

* * *

The amendment was agreed to.

* * *

Mr. PERCY. Mr. President, I call up my amendment No. 1259 and ask that it be stated.

The PRESIDING OFFICER. The amendment will be stated.

The legislative clerk read the amendment as follows:

On page 58, line 23, delete the sentence beginning with the word "Such" down through line 25 and substitute in lieu thereof the following: "Such safety analysis shall be conducted in conformity with criteria set forth in such regulations promulgated by the Commissioner and may be conducted by the manufacturer, an independent testing laboratory, or any other person who the Commissioner may designate."

On page 62, line 11, delete the words "The Commissioner shall conduct compliance testing" and substitute in lieu thereof the following: "The Commissioner shall conduct or contract pursuant to section 104(c)(8) for compliance testing".

On page 63, line 1, insert the words "or cause to be returned," after the word "return"

On page 63, beginning on line 8, delete the sentence beginning with the word "Any" down through line 14 and substitute in lieu thereof the following:

"(d) CERTIFICATION.—Any manufacturer, importer, or distributor of a consumer product subject to a consumer product safety standard shall furnish to the distributor or dealer at the time of delivery of such consumer product certification

"(a) by said manufacturer, or importer, or distributor; or

"(b) by an independent testing laboratory qualified to perform such tests or testing program,

that each such consumer product conforms to all applicable consumer product safety standards. Any certification under this subsection shall be based upon test procedures in conformance with subsection 306(e)(1) or, where no procedures are prescribed, upon a reasonable testing program approved by the Commissioner.".

On page 78, line 9, delete the word "Act" and substitute in lieu thereof the word "title".

Mr. PERCY. Mr. President, as my general remarks on this bill indicate, I take great pleasure, as a cosponsor of S. 3419, in knowing that after so many years the American consumer will be afforded the protection he deserves in connection with the ordinary products used in and around the home.

My purpose at this time is to introduce an amendment on behalf of myself and the distinguished floor manager from the State of Washington (Mr. MAGNUSON), who, as chairman of the Committe on Commerce, has steadfastly and forcefully fought for this legislation for almost a decade. The fact that the Senate is taking up this bill today is a tribute to the persistence of Senator MAGNUSON.

This amendment consists of several parts, all directed to the single reality that private testing laboratories are and should be an important facet in any ongoing consumer safety program in this country.

The amendment is meant to make clear that the omission of any reference to private testing laboratories was unintended and that, upon the commencement of a Federal standards program as authorized by this bill, such laboratories will continue to perform a vital service to the manufacturing community of this Nation. Accordingly, in amending S. 3419, Senator MAGNUSON and I have provided that—in connection with any safety analysis study as provided for in section 307 and in connection with compliance testing as provided for in section 309 (c)—qualified independent testing laboratories be authorized to conduct such studies and tests as are prescribed, approved, or otherwise necessary to insure the safety of consumer products which may present an unreasonable risk of injury or death.

Typically today, with respect to many potential hazards—electrical, thermal, mechanical, toxic, or whatever—a manufacturer will ask an independent laboratory, such as Underwriters' Laboratories, to test his product to make sure that it complies with recognized consumer safety standards, most of which, to date, have been voluntarily promulgated by one or another industry. The amendment we offer at this time simply recognizes this state of affairs and asures that the legislation before us in now way impairs that procedure. Indeed, a firm like Underwriters', which has proven time and again to be eminently qualified to perform such tests, will I suspect in the future be more and more in demand as the Federal Government promulgates product standards in connection with particular hazards.

I am particularly interested in the increased sensitivity of a private, not-for-profit firm like Underwriters' Laboratories toward the safety problems that beset the American consumer today. I note that in its final report issued in June 1970, the National Commission on Product Safety referred to Underwriters' Laboratories as a "principal force in preventing electrical and fire hazards in the home," and went on to make the following observations:

Until recently, a product bearing a UL mark might have been tested with regard to only one hazard. An electric toy might be tested for shock hazards but not for sharp or protruding surfaces. UL announced in February 1970 that it would hereafter restrict its Listing Service for household products to those which have been evaluated with respect to "all significant hazards."

With its acknowledged technical competence and inspection force, UL has been an important factor in self-regulation by private industry. Its standards are particularly important to consumers, since UL listings are frequently relied upon by county and municipal electrical inspectors in discharging their duties under the National Electrical Code.

Considering the technical and economic realities, UL has been relatively independent of the manufacturers who finance its work. None of its 124 "members"—elected by the board of trustees to 4-year terms—has a financial connection with manufacturers of products which UL might test. Nonetheless, its president says it must "successfully walk the tightrope of responsibility" between setting standards too high to be acceptable to manufacturers and permitting an unacceptable number of injuries. The problem of drafting an acceptable standard is also locked into the capacity of the manufacturer to produce and the willingness of the consumer to pay. UL says:

"Getting safe equipment into the hands of the public is not always achieved by simply publishing a standard whose requirements provide for a high level of safety. Standards could and sometimes do provide such high levels of safety that no one manufactures to them, hence, they are self-defeating."

Underwriters' Laboratories, Inc., is an independent, not-for-profit corporation founded in 1894, chartered by the State of Illinois in 1901, and incorporated under the laws of Delaware in 1936. Its certificate of incorporation provides that it shall have no capital stock; it shall be for service and not for profit.

The certificate further provides that members and trustees shall be associated with one of the following categories: insurance industry, consumer interest, governmental body or agency, education, public safety body or agency, safety expert, standardization expert, public utility, or officer of the corporation. No more than one-third of the board of trustees may be from any one of the above categories.

Its objectives, as stated in the certificate of incorporation are:

By scientific investigation, study, experiments, and tests, to determine the relation of various materials, devices, products, equipment, constructions, methods, and systems to hazards appurtenant thereto or to the use thereof, affecting life and property and to ascertain, define and publish standards, classifications and specifications for materials, devices, products, equipment, constructions, methods, and systems affecting such hazards, and other information tending to reduce and prevent loss of life and property from such hazards.

Underwriters' is supported solely by charges made to clients and subscribers for its services. These charges are generally on a time and material basis and are not affected by the nature of the report rendered, whether favorable or unfavorable.

Operations are primarily in two phases: New work engineering and factory followup services. The new work engineering is conducted by six engineering departments: burglary protection and signaling; casualty and chemical hazards; electrical; fire protection; heating, air-conditioning and refrigeration; and marine.

The engineering departments, by test and examination of submitted products, ascertain their conformity or nonconformity with established requirements. The factory followup service is for the purpose of auditing the procedures of the manufacturer that provide for conformance with the established requirements.

Testing laboratories are located in Chicago, Ill.; Northbrook, Ill.; Melville, N.Y.; Santa Clara, Calif.; and Tampa, Fla. Inspection services at factories are conducted on a worldwide basis.

The factory followup services encompass all the procedures by which Underwriters' audits those mechanisms manufacturers employ to assure compliance with the laboratories' requirements.

Factory inspection visits in 1971 increased to 209,673, an increase of 2.8 percent over the previous year.

The number of labels issued in 1971 to identify listed products increased 25.8 percent, to a total of 1,685,589,950—the largest single annual increase in the number of labels issued in the laboratories' history. This reflects a wider use of UL's method of identifying products that meet nationally-recognized safety requirements.

While there is no record of the units of production to which the listing mark was applied during the past year, it is estimated that in the electrical appliance industry alone, over 100,000,000 units were identified by manufacturers as having met the laboratories' requirements.

The number of full-time domestic inspection centers increased by 15 during the year, while 25 part-time centers were closed or consolidated into the full-time centers, resulting in 190 domestic inspection centers in operation at year's end.

New domestic inspection centers were opened during the year in the following cities:

Casper, Wyo., Chicago, Ill. (North Shore), Chicago, Ill. (South Shore), Cody, Wyo., Electra, Tex., Huskerville, Nebr., International Falls, Minn., Laurens, S.C., Lower Brule, S. Dak., Lumberton, N.C., Mobile, Ala., and Pawtucket, R.I.

Supplementing the factory inspection program, the market survey program, inaugurated in mid-1970, continued throughout 1971 with 3,483 shopping visits in 81 different cities. This activity frequently included unannounced visits to trade shows where new developments are exhibited to prospective buyers for the first time.

I have gone into this detail, Mr. President, to point up that with respect to Underwriters' Laboratories and several other qualified testing laboratories throughout the country, the major new legislative impetus of S. 3419 in the consumer product safety area will not disrupt what is now a most beneficial and worthwhile service to the manufacturing community and to the consumer. With the approval of this amendment to S. 3419, the compliance and certification role of such laboratories will be preserved in a manner consistent with the original intention of this measure.

* * *

The amendment was agreed to.

AMENDMENTS NOS. 1260 AND 1261, AS MODIFIED

Mr. GURNEY. Mr. President, I send to the desk two amendments and ask for their immediate consideration.

* * *

The legislative clerk read as follows:

On page 65, beginning with line 2, strike out through line 17 and insert in lieu thereof the following:

"SEC. 311. (a) Whenever the Administrator has reason to believe that a consumer product presents an unreasonable risk of injury or death, necessitating immediate action to protect adequately the public health and safety prior to the completion of administrative proceedings held pursuant to this Act, he or the Attorney General may bring suit in a district court of the United States having venue thereof to enjoin any person from engaging in the manufacture for sale, sale, offering for sale, or otherwise offering for public consumption, in commerce, or the importation into the United States of such an imminently hazardous consumer product. Upon a proper showing, and after notice to the defendant, a preliminary injunction may be granted without bond under the same conditions and principles as injunctive relief against conduct or threatened conduct that will cause loss or damage is granted by courts of equity. Notwithstanding the existence of a consumer product safety standard applicable to such product, such an action may be filed or the pendency of proceedings initiated pursuant to section 303 of this Act.".

On page 65, line 21, strike out the words "or permanent".

On page 65, line 23, insert before the period "prior to completion of administrative proceedings held pursuant to this Act".

On page 2, line 13, strike out the word "enforce" and insert in lieu thereof the words "assure the enforcement of".

On page 2, line 15, strike out the first comma and the words "prosecute court actions".

On page 3, line 23, strike out "(17)" and insert in lieu thereof "(16)".

On page 12, beginning with line 22, strike out through line 2 on page 13.

On page 13, line 3, strike out "(17)" and insert in lieu thereof "(16)".

On page 13, line 12, strike out the word "enforce" and insert in lieu thereof "assure the enforcement of".

On page 13, line 16, strike out "(18)" and insert in lieu thereof "(17)".

On page 13, line 20, strike out "(19)" and insert in lieu thereof "(18)".

On page 29, line 12, strike out the words "of the Agency" and insert in lieu thereof the words "of this Act".

On page 72, beginning with the words "or the Agency" on line 15, strike out through the comma in line 16.

On page 73, beginning with the word "upon" in line 4, strike out through the word "the" the first time it appears in line 5, and insert in lieu thereof the following: "The".

On page 73, beginning with the word "on" in line 16, strike out through the comma in line 17.

* * *

Mr. GURNEY. Mr. President, these two amendments to S. 3419, the Food, Drug, and Consumer Product Safety Act of 1972, would bring this legislation into line with previous congressional enactments on similar issues and longstanding Government policy.

Briefly, the net effect of these two amendments would be to eliminate any duplication in enforcement procedure while, at the same time, making it possible for the new Food, Drug and Consumer Product Agency—FDCPA—to act quickly in an emergency situation involving an imminent health or safety danger to the consumer.

The first amendment, entitled the emergency protection amendment, permits the Administrator of the FDCPA to apply to the courts for an injunction whenever a product appears to constitute a real and imminent threat to the buying public. Furthermore, during the preliminary injunction period, the products in question will be kept off the market, giving FDCPA time to take proper administrative action without any risk to purchasers. This represents an effective compromise between the need for speedy remedial action and the desirability of having the enforcement function separate from that of the investigative.

Obviously, the American public deserves protection from products that might present an immediate threat to consumer health and/or safety. That is not the question here. What is at stake is whether we are going to compromise the separation of powers—so essential to due process—in order to provide this protection. In my opinion, this amendment helps balance the rights of consumers and producers and, at the same time, provides a highly acceptable alternative which avoids the necessity of compromising a right so basic as due process.

The second amendment, known as the efficient administration amendment, consists of a series of changes that would remove from the FDCPA any enforcement powers, other than those provided for in this emergency protection amendment, now vested in the Department of Justice. Instead of having a single agency interpret and enforce the law on consumer protection cases, the Department of Justice would prosecute the cases and the courts would decide them. This method of operating is both cheaper and more efficient. This approach is fairer to all concerned. Just as the interests of consumers must be protected, so too must the overall public interest in a workable economy.

Now, with this bill, the question is not the desirability of consumer product safety, but whether the enforcement power of FDCPA should be different from that of other agencies. The Justice Department and the courts should enforce consumer protection decisions as they do in the case of other agencies rather than the Food, Drug and Consumer Protection Agency.

Fifty years ago, when Americans went to buy something they went to the corner grocery or the local dry goods store. There were no supermarkets, no radio, no television, no mass advertising campaigns, no huge shopping centers and far fewer goods than there are today. If somebody bought something, he could generally see what he was getting and if he was not satisfied, he could go back and get a refund or replacement without too much difficulty. A merchant just couldn't afford to alienate too many customers or he would soon be out of business.

But now, the technological revolution, bringing with it all the conveniences of modern day to day living, has changed all that. Products have proliferated as transportation has improved and the demand for additional goods and services has increased. But, wonderful as such progress has been, it has not come without a pricetag; in the changeover to the mass consumerism of the 1970's, something important has been lost—the personal relationship between producer and consumer that helped promote a mutally beneficial exchange of quality goods for a fair price. What we are seeing now, in this concern for consumer protection, is the search for a satisfactory substitute. And we are all interested in that. This measure does that.

However, this search, like the progress that has spawned it, is not new. The first Pure Food and Drugs Act was passed in 1906, the first meat inspection act a year later, and the Federal Trade Commission has been in business since 1914. What is new about this proposal and some others like it that will probably be before us soon is that it contradicts the constitutionally rooted and time-tested principle of separation of legislative, executive and judicial functions.

The American consumer must be provided with an adequate means of protection against dangerous or harmful products—and my amendment in the way interferes with that. But I see no reason for duplicating enforcement functions, adding to the bureaucratic tangle, or casting aside the best means of assuring fair treatment for all parties concerned. By giving the FDCPA administrator the right to seek a preliminary injunction, during which time the product in question would not be available for purchase, the consumers are well protected. If the injunction has merit, the courts will so rule; if not, efficiency and fairness will still have been served.

There is another aspect to this issue, one to which I have briefly alluded, and that is this business of adding to the bureaucratic tangle. If we begin with giving separate enforcement functions to this Agency, where will we stop? In the months ahead, we will be considering the formation of numerous new Federal agencies, in connection with the reorganization of the executive branch.

Another consumer product bill will come before us shortly. Shall we give each Federal agency a complete set of huge legal offices throughout the country, all of them suing and being sued by each other and the public? The inefficient bureaucratic tangle which would result can well be imagined.

No one questions the need for attention to product safety. The figures given in the final report of the National Commission on Product Safety are reason enough for concern; each year 30,000 deaths, 20 million injuries and $5.5 billion worth of expense result from incidents connected with consumer products. This is a high price to pay—unnecessarily high—but certainly with a reasonable legislative approach and with the realization, by producers and consumers alike, that greater care must be exercised in the production and utilization of goods, these figures can be reduced.

In conclusion, I believe that the amendments I have offered provide the reasonable, balanced legislative approach that is necessary to bring about greater safety for all without discriminating against either producers or consumers. I, therefore, urge adoption of these amendments.

Mr. COOPER. Mr. President, will the Senator yield?

Mr. GURNEY. I am pleased to yield to the Senator from Kentucky.

Mr. COOPER. Mr. President, I have read the Senator's amendment and have also read section 311(a) that it seeks to amend. What is the distinction between the language of the amendment and section 311(a), not merely the language of the amendment, but its effect?

Section 311(a) and the amendment seem to be similar.

Mr. GURNEY. The distinction is this. My amendment to the bill limits the legal procedures available to the new agency to obtaining a preliminary injunction. If the Administrator thinks a product coming on the market is unsafe and hazardous he can go to court with his lawyers and get an injunction.

In the bill section 311(a) is much broader. It allows him to go to the full extent, as stated in the bill, insofar as enforcing penalties under it with his own legal staff.

For example, he could bring several actions and penalties under the bill. He could apply for permanent injunction or apply to stop the manufacture of hazardous products with his own legal staff.

Under the time-honored system we have in the Government of the United States under the Constitution, we have all kinds of agencies that have powers much like this but they cannot go into court with their own attorneys and do these things.

They go to the Department of Justice and say that there has been a violation of procedures under the act. They say, "This person is violating the procedures of the act and, Mr. Attorney General, please bring action against him." That is the way we do things. They do things in most departments and agencies of Government. But this bill would place all those legal duties and prerogatives in the new agency, and this is what I seek to prevent.

Mr. COOPER. I thank the Senator. I note that section 311(a) provides as follows: "The Administrator or the Attorney General may file, in a district court of the United States having venue thereof, an action."

The amendment also gives authority to both the Administrator and the Attorney General to institute a civil action. The Senator has stated that under his amendment only preliminary injunctive relief could be granted.

Aside from the question of such a limitation, it appears fairer that the court consider the case as a whole, with whatever determinations are necessary.

I am trying to find the distinction. Under the bills' section 311(c) either the Administrator or the Attorney General may file an action and secure injunctive relief. What is the difference?

Mr. GURNEY. Perhaps I was not able to explain to the distinguished Senator from Kentucky the difference between my section and that section 311 which is in the bill now. In my amendment the Administrator would be permitted to file for preliminary injunction, but not a permanent injunction. During the time the preliminary injunction was in effect the Administrator would go through his administrative proceedings and procedures set out in other parts of the bill to determine with his own hearings, which are rather extensive in most cases, if a product is hazardous or unsafe, rather than to burden the court with that. My amendment would seek to avoid getting the court tied up in those things the Administrator should do.

Mr. COTTON. Mr. President, will the Senator yield?

Mr. GURNEY. I yield.

Mr. COTTON. Mr. President, as I read the language on page 72 of the bill, the new agency is authorized through its own attorneys not only to seek injunctions and civil penalties, but also criminal penalties.

Mr. GURNEY. It does exactly that, and the legal staff of the administrator would have all those powers shown on page 27.

Mr. COTTON. And it would carry a penalty of imprisonment?

Mr. GURNEY. That is correct.

Mr. COTTON. I wish to ask one more question. The Senator from Florida is aware of the fact that a bill is about to be reported by the Committee on Government Operations, according to the Senator from Illinois who is on that committee. The subcommittee already has acted favorably on it. So we will surely have on the heels of this bill another bill called the "Consumer Protection Agency" bill, which creates yet another independent agency.

As I understand the bill presently, and probably as it will be reported to the committee, the agency will have an advocacy role. It is not a prosecuting agency. But if I know the temper of the Senate, as I have observed it today, and knowing of the power of the magic word of "consumer," before it passes the Senate there will be a second agency with powers to prosecute. Does the Senator feel this makes it doubly necessary to take this provision out of the bill? My amendment would have taken it out of the bill.

Mr. GURNEY. The Senator from New Hampshire has made the precise point I was making just a moment ago: That if we go ahead with this one now, then we are going ahead with other independent agencies and doing the same thing. As the Senator pointed out, perhaps there will be an amendment on the floor to give the Consumer Protection Agency, when it comes before us, the broad legal powers that are in this bill. It seems to me that we are tampering with the structure of the Government we have. The Department of Justice was set up in the beginning under the Constitution to be the legal enforcement part of the U.S. Government. When a department or an agency has a legal problem and has enforcement which it wishes to be carried out, it goes to the Department of Justice under the law of the land and has it done. This completely departs from that procedure and changes the structure of the Government and sets up in this agency a great big new law firm so they can hire a lot of lawyers and after the investigation is done by the administrative section, then the lawyers can swing into action and file a lot of lawsuits. I do not think that is a good precedent. I have not heard any complaints about the Department of Justice so far as to the way they carry out the legal obligations of Government with respect to any other department or agency. I think we should continue to do it that way.

Mr. COOPER. Mr. President, will the Senator yield for another question?

Mr. GURNEY. I yield to the distinguished Senator from Kentucky.

Mr. COOPER. The Senator has made a good argument about the separation of the authority to prosecute criminal actions from the investigative authority. It is a proper argument accepted by statute and reason.

But again, I do not see where the Senator's amendment separates such authority. It deals with civil action.

Mr. GURNEY. That is only for the preliminary injunction. As far as all other actions are concerned that now can be done by the agencies. As was pointed out in the colloquy between the Senator from New Hampshire and me, under the amendment the agency would not be able to do these things, but only the Department of Justice in behalf of the agency.

Mr. COOPER. Are you referring to the language on page 2? Would that be an effect of the Senator's second amendment? Would that be the consequence of the second amendment?

Mr. GURNEY. The Senator is correct. That would be the consequence of my second amendment.

Mr. COOPER. If the Senator's amendment were adopted, would authority for criminal action be retained by the Department of Justice?

Mr. GURNEY. The Senator is correct.

Mr. COOPER. The Senator is attempting to separate criminal action from the investigating and civil action.

Mr. GURNEY. That is exactly right, although at the same time I have preserved the needed, and I think it is needed, power in the administrator for a preliminary injunction. If he believes a product is hazardous to the safety of people he has the right to go into court, with his own people and get a preliminary injunction. I think it is important to preserve that right, and I have done that under the amendment, but all the other legal enforcement procedures that are in the bill are lodged in the Department of Justice.

Mr. PERCY. Mr. President, will the Senator yield for a point of clarification?

Mr. GURNEY. I yield.

Mr. PERCY. The distinguished Senator from Florida is a valued member of the Government Operations Committee, and I think he will certify that in the Consumer Protection Agency bill we will totally delete any regulatory responsibility and jurisdiction over consumer safety. That agency has an advocacy function only. In the bill we are considering right now, the committee specifically deleted the subsection which provided for appointment of private attorneys to represent people before the Food, Drug, and Consumer Product Agency. As explained in the report, the committee took this action to avoid potential conflict with the Consumer Protection Agency bill's provisions. Thus, we did take into account the obvious need, to avoid possible duplication and overlap, and we took preventive action in that area.

I hope that answers satisfactorily the comments of the Senator from New Hampshire.

Mr. COTTON. Mr. President, will the Senator yield?

Mr. GURNEY. I yield.

Mr. COTTON. I thank the Senator from Illinois, and I certainly take that as a complete answer as far as the committee is concerned. As far as the Senate is concerned, I would not want to guarantee anything.

I requested from the Department of Justice an analysis of this prosecution power of this bill and received a memorandum on this point. The appendix to the memorandum cites the following from section 519 of title 28, United States Code:

Except as otherwise authorized by law, the Attorney General shall supervise all litigation to which the United States, an agency, or officer thereof is a party, and shall direct all United States attorneys, assistant United States attorneys, and special attorneys appointed under section 543 of this title in the discharge of their respective duties.

I repeat the words "Except as otherwise authorized by law." Clearly the word "otherwise" authorizes separate enforcement by the new agency proposed in S. 3419.

* * *

Mr. GURNEY. I thank the Senator from New Hampshire, and amplifying what he just said, I inquired of the Department of Justice how much law enforcing of this kind it did for the Federal Government. The Senator from New Hampshire may be interested to learn that all of the criminal proceedings done under any of the agencies or departments are done by the Department of Justice now. This is a completely new departure here. This is criminal procedure, where this agency may bring criminal prosecution. So far as the civil end is concerned, the amount of business done by the Department of Justice for the rest of the government in proceedings like this amounts to about 95 percent. There are a few special cases here and there where agencies have been given legal power of their own, but these are rare exceptions. About 95 percent of the legal business of the United States is done by the Department of Justice. For the life of me, I do not see why we should give this new agency all kinds of broad new legal power.

Mr. COTTON. Mr. President, will the Senator yield?

Mr. GURNEY. I yield.

Mr. COTTON. The memorandum I have just introduced confirms what the Senator said. It recites in great detail the precedents.

Let me make it clear that the memorandum does not comment on this particular bill. I did not ask for that kind of comment. I asked for a memorandum of the law on this subject from the Department of Justice and it clearly indicates that this bill constitutes, in the criminal enforcement angle of it, a real departure from precedent.

Mr. GURNEY. I thank the Senator. That is my understanding. May I inquire of the Chair how much time I have remaining?

The PRESIDING OFFICER. The Senator from Florida has 5 minutes.

Mr. GURNEY. In summary, then, let me say that here we are singling out for special treatment this bureau. We are duplicating in this field of law enforcement. We are providing added expense. It is a deviation from the structure of Government, as we know it now under the Constitution, so far as the duties of the Justice Department are concerned, and I think it would set an exceedingly bad precedent.

I would hope the Senate would adopt my amendment which, I again say, in no way weakens this bill in any fashion so far as the protection of consumers is concerned.

* * *

Mr. MAGNUSON. Mr. President, I listened with great interest to the colloquy. Of course this is a departure. That is exactly what we want to do with this bill. We want to give authority to this agency to act quickly. We did it with the Federal Trade Commission. It was a pretty substantial departure when we did it for the Federal Trade Commission, so it could go in and get some action. Under this proposal the agency could go to the Attorney General. It is an alternate method. But if we require the agency to go through the Attorney General, it may be a long, long time before anything happens, and when we are dealing with dangerous substances, we have to have some place where we can get quick action and allow these people to go into court, as we do with the Federal Trade Commission, where there might be some reason to hold something up.

In another part of the amendment, the amendment denies any court the right to order a recall of dangerous products on the market. This is not the intent of the bill, and it is not the intent of the committee. We were unanimous on this. Of course it is a departure. That is exactly what we want it to be, so we can get some action in this particular field.

They may use the Attorney General for 90 percent of their cases, but sometime they will want to go into court, just as the Federal Trade Commission and other agencies do. That is the purpose of it.

Mr. GURNEY. Mr. President, will the Senator yield?

Mr. MAGNUSON. They may have to go into court quickly to take some dangerous product off the market. That is the exact purpose of the bill. I know the Senator from Florida objects to that, but I do not want to suggest that we are saying this is not a departure in this field. It is, and that is what we want it to be. Otherwise we will never get anything done.

Mr. GURNEY. Mr. President, will the Senator yield on that point?

Mr. MAGNUSON. Well, all right, I yield, but I am going to yield back the remainder of my time.

Mr. GURNEY. I would like to point out to the distinguished manager of the bill that my amendment takes care of exactly what the Senator wants so far as quick action is concerned, because it still retains within the agency and its administrator the power to go into court at once if it wants to get a preliminary injunction against a hazardous product.

Mr. MAGNUSON. I understand that.

Mr. GURNEY. So it does exactly what the Senator wants it to do. The only thing it does not do is permit the administrator to get a permanent injunction or to do the other things that can later be done by the Justice Department, which have absolutely nothing whatever to do with immediate urgency of doing something then.

So my amendment in no way militates against what the Senator wants.

Mr. MAGNUSON. I think the Senator's amendment does. It stops quick action. If they went in for a preliminary injunction, they could hang around for days, and we are dealing with hazardous substances. They have got to go to court; the court has to order this, no matter what we do. But they have a right to go in and get quick action. That is the purpose of this.

Mr. GURNEY. That is exactly my point.

Mr. MAGNUSON. If they have some big cases that can hang around, the court would probably say, "Mr. Attorney General, nobody has a privilege of immediate hearing on routine matters in this court, not even the Attorney General's Office." We want them to be able to move fast, and this is exactly what we did in the Federal Trade Commission.

Mr. COTTON. Mr. President, will the Senator yield?

Mr. MAGNUSON. I yield.

Mr. COTTON. I find myself halfway between my two friends here. It was my understanding that the amendment of the Senator from Florida permitted only preliminary injunctions. I thought he was striking out of this bill all power for the attorneys in this new agency to handle criminal prosecutions.

Mr. MAGNUSON. The agency cannot do that.

Mr. COTTON. Yes, it can, under this——

Mr. MAGNUSON. The agency has got to go to court.

Mr. COTTON. The agency goes to court for the injunction, certainly.

Mr. MAGNUSON. Or for the imposition of any fines or anything like that.

Mr. COTTON. But the agency can directly invoke criminal penalties, which is really——

Mr. MAGNUSON. If the court agrees with them.

Mr. COTTON. Well, criminal prosecution, to my mind, should be left for the Department of Justice. As to the temporary and permanent injunctions, I would like to see this amendment permit the use of injunctions to stop dangerous products. But, when it comes to going to Federal court to send a businessman to a Federal penitentiary, I do not think that should be in the hands of attorneys hired by the proposed new agency.

Mr. MAGNUSON. Well, that may be true. I hope they would be of the same caliber as the attorneys hired in the Attorney General's office. They would be Government attorneys in this particular field, like the fine attorneys we have down at the Federal Trade Commission.

This does not allow an order to get a product recalled, does it?

Mr. GURNEY. What was the question?

Mr. MAGNUSON. We cannot get an unsafe product off the market, under the Senator's amendment.

Mr. GURNEY. Sure we can.

The PRESIDING OFFICER. Who yields time?

Mr. GURNEY. Mr. President, if I may answer——

Mr. MAGNUSON. I have no more to say about it. I have studied the two amendments—not the second one, but the first one. The danger of it is that you cannot get swift action; and as to the fact that it is a departure, of course it is a departure. That is what we intended to have, a departure.

Mr. COOPER. Mr. President, will the Senator yield?

Mr. MAGNUSON. We voted this for the Federal Trade Commission, the same thing. But in dealing with dangerous products, if they are to get a product off the market that involves fraud or things like that, we have said they can go into court. This deals with dangerous products, and it may be a serious matter. I suppose they will use the Attorney General for many, many of their cases, where they have a lot of appeals and the case does not require immediate attention.

Mr. COOPER. Will the Senator yield?

Mr. MAGNUSON. I have no more to add to it. I yield to the Senator from Kentucky.

Mr. COOPER. Mr. President, I do not want to turn attention away from the question raised by the Senator from Florida, but I want to ask about section 316(a), which is related to it.

Mr. MAGNUSON. Oh, excuse me. Let me add to the RECORD a more complete statement about the amendment of the Senator from Florida.

Mr. President, quite a bit has been said today with respect to the merits of an independent consumer product safety function within the Federal Government. Achieving the goal of an independent agency, however, involves more than the creation of a new regulatory body. The new agency must also be equipped with procedures and safeguards which will be out of the reach of any particular corporate or political pressure.

One provision of S. 3419 designed to insure both independence and the expeditious handling of the enforcement function of the agency would be eliminated by the amendment proposed by my colleague from the State of Florida (Mr. GURNEY). Section 104(c)(1) of the bill now authorizes the administrator of the agency to initiate, prosecute, defend, or appeal any court action in the name of the agency to enforce any laws subject to his jurisdiction, through his own legal representatives or through the Attorney General. The proposed Gurney amendment would allow the agency to perform this similar function only through the Attorney General.

An effective compliance and enforcement mechanism is absolutely essential. It does little good to equip an agency with the authority and personnel to locate defective or nonconforming products and then not equip it with the ability to take action against manufacturers or processors of those products. This amendment would not only wipe out the ability of the agency to go to court to seize products, obtain injunctions or enforce regulations, but also destroy the agency's ability to criminally prosecute offenders.

Adoption of the Gurney amendment would add another layer of review to any agency court proceeding and result in delayed proceedings. The need for quick action is obvious: If an adulterated food is located in a warehouse, then it is crucial that the agency be able to obtain a seizure order before that food is introduced in interstate commerce. Requiring the agency to utilize Justice Department lawyers oftentimes results in delay. In fact, almost one-tenth of all seizure orders obtained by FDA since 1968 have been meaningless because Justice Department delay resulted in the defective foods or drugs being introduced in interstate commerce and beyond the reach of seizure.

But the need for quick action is not the only argument in opposition to the amendment offered by my colleague from Florida (Mr. GURNEY). In a recent letter to Congressman PAUL ROGERS, William W. Goodrich who was FDA's chief counsel for well over two decades, endorsed the concept of direct agency action and outlined several other convincing arguments in support of his views. Among other things, Goodrich noted that the area of Food and Drug law and technology is exceedingly complex. Needless to say, this description is also applicable to product safety law. It requires an advocate for the Government's position who is equipped with the necessary expertise to match wits with the highly paid and qualified representatives of the defendants. Obviously, a Justice Department lawyer cannot be expected to possess this degree of specialization and in fact, FDA attorneys themselves are the only ones within Government who possess this knowledge.

Accordingly, to put the Government on an equal par with those who are being prosecuted, it is often necessary for the Justice Department to allow FDA lawyers to argue the cases themselves, under the supervision of the U.S. attorneys. This is particularly true in situations where agency action is required on short notice such as a temporary injunction.

The waste in resources and manpower due to this duplication of effort is obvious. But of even more concern to me is the question of what possible function the Justice Department attorney can play in a Food and Drug case? I am afraid that the answer to this question is that the presence of such lawyers from Justice presents a unique opportunity for making political decisions about the prosecution proceeding. It enables political manipulation or influence of Agency enforcement actions by administration representatives—the very influence that this legislation was designed to prevent. As currently structured, Justice can refuse to file or even dismiss a case without FDA approval. It can even drop parties or accept settlements without the presence of the FDA legal staff.

Those who endorse the Gurney amendment argue that since 1870, the Justice Department has been the sole representative of the United States in the court rooms throughout the land and should remain in that position. In 1870 however, we were not involved in the highly technical litigation to which a Food, Drug, and Consumer Product Agency is forced to address itself. At present, FDA prepares all of its own cases for court including brief writing, evidence gathering and arranging for witnesses; since it is most intimately involved in the case, it should also argue it.

Moreover, the Congress holds FDA and its Commissioner responsible for the efficient administration of laws under its jurisdiction. Yet, the Department of Justice is charged with the role of deciding when and whom to prosecute and how to settle cases once they have been initiated. To be perfectly frank, the record of the Justice Department in the last few years has not only been outrageous, but also the most effective argument against this amendment that I can muster.

Let's look at the record:

Thus far in 1972, the Food and Drug Administration submitted to the Department of Justice a total of 32 cases for criminal prosecution for violation of the Food and Drug Act. Justice declined outwardly to prosecute four of the cases. In addition, a total of 10 cases were not filed by the U.S. Attorney in the District where the action was to be commenced. This is in spite of the fact that the case was completely prepared by the FDA attorneys and all that was necessitated was walking the papers over to the courthouse. Hence, over 40 percent of the cases for criminal prosecution that FDA requested to be filed were blocked by Justice.

It must be remembered in considering this statistic that FDA inspectors discover almost 5,000 potential criminal prosecutions per year and it is only through a screening process from the inspector to a Food and Drug Officer; to a bureau within the administration; and finally through the General Counsel's office that a case finally goes to Justice. Only about 60 cases per year are recommended for criminal prosecution; the point of this being that FDA itself is quite selective in the cases it chooses to prosecute. In view of the fact that the most recent critical GAO report recommended an increased number of criminal prosecutions by FDA, Justice seems to be substantially mitigating the effectiveness of FDA enforcement activities.

But statistics alone do not tell the story. Let me cite for you some of the cases that the Department of Justice refused to prosecute or file in the last 6 months.

Case No. 1: FDA action 57724 against Delchamps, Inc. The offenses complained of occurred in late 1970 and early 1971 and involved quantities of popcorn, kidney beans, flour, blackeye peas and sugar held in the defendants' warehouse which were contaminated by rodents. To be specific the foods were contaminated with rodent hairs, rodent urine, excreta pellets, and were being held under insanitary conditions. To be even more explicit, the FDA inspector was able to photograph mice scampering about in the warehouse, a mouse carcass found on a case of frosting mix, mice tracks in spilled flour, baby mice nesting in packaging materials, excreta pellets, and rodent gnawed food packaging. Those who are not convinced by my description are free to come forward and view the photographs of the rodent infestation of the Delchamps warehouse. In this instance, FDA had done its job but the Department of Justice refused to prosecute.

Case No. 2: United States against Wendt Laboratories, Inc. The case was filed by the U.S. attorney but later dismissed by Justice. The defendant was accused by the FDA of processing, packaging, and labeling an injectable for animals which was unsafe since no approval of an application for use of the drug was ever issued by FDA. Further, the methods used for manufacture and facilities and controls for processing, packing and holding did not conform with current good manufacturing principles. This is of particular concern in view of the fact that there are indications that harmful tissue residues resulting from use of the drug may be ingested by humans. It should also be added that this case was dismissed by the Justice Department without even first consulting the FDA.

Case No. 3: FDC No. 57320 involving the Rala Singh Farms. Rala Singh was cited by FDA for shipping in interstate commerce, lettuce which exceeded the HEW tolerance levels for pesticides. Although a seizure was effected, the Justice Department refused to file the criminal charges despite FDA advice to the contrary.

There are other cases. One where the U.S. attorney failed to move against a company and it was later discovered that the father of the wife of the attorney owned the company. In two districts: the Eastern District of Missouri and the Northern District of Texas, the U.S. attorney refused to file any FDA cases submitted to them. I could cite more cases, but the point has been made. The current situation is intolerable. It is hard enough to get the Food and Drug Administration to act at all. But when they finally do act and their inspectors do discover situations such as the ones outlined above, they should not have their hands tied. To insure that this recent Justice Department record is never again duplicated, I emphasize the importance of defeating the amendment and adopting the proposal of S. 3419.

Frankly, I am somewhat confused as to where the administration stands on this issue. On the one hand, in hearings before the Rogers subcommittee in the House, Steve Kurzman, Assistant Secretary of Health, Education, and Welfare for legislation stated unequivocally, that authorizing the FDA Administrator to prosecute his own cases would be duplicative and disruptive. On the other hand, the Secretary of Health, Education, and Welfare, Mr. Richardson stated before Senator PERCY at Government Operations Committee hearings, and I quote:

> I think it would be useful for the Commissioner to have the authority (to bring his own cases). I am not sure he would want to exercise it in every case, nor does the legislation propose so.

The provision in S. 3419 fulfills the authority that Secretary Richardson has endorsed: granting the Product Safety Agency the authority to bring its own cases or allow Justice to handle them itself.

For these reasons, Mr. President, I respectfully urge the Members of this body to defeat the amendment proposed by my colleague from Florida.

Mr. COOPER. Mr. President, will the Senator from Washington yield so that I may ask a couple of questions?

As I have said, I do not want to turn the interest of the Senate away from the question raised by the Senator from Florida, but reference was made to section 316(a), and it does have pertinence to this question, because the administrator would be able to take both civil and criminal action under section 316(a).

More and more we are legislating the imposition of civil penalties. Section 316(a) provides a civil penalty of not more than $10,000 for each such act which shall accrue to the United States and may be recovered in a civil action.

This may seem a specious question, but does not mean a $10,000 civil penalty can be imposed by the administrator, and then that the burden of proof against its imposition would be upon the defendant?

Mr. MAGNUSON. No; the administrator has to go to court and say to a judge——

Mr. COOPER. This is what I want to know.

Mr. MAGNUSON. "We think this man should be subject to a penalty because," and the judge will say, "Tell me the becauses," and then, after a hearing, he may waive a penalty, or he may not. The Administrator cannot fine anyone, send anyone to jail, or either, unless he goes to court and the judge says, "This is a good case; I will grant it."

Mr. COOPER. That is what I wanted to find out about and have interpreted. We have passed a number of acts in the last 3 years giving authority to agencies to impose civil penalties, with only a subsequent hearing. It is a proceeding without due process.

Mr. MAGNUSON. Yes.

Mr. COOPER. I want to know if there is due process in section 316 A1.

Mr. MAGNUSON. Well, the Administrator cannot place a fine on anyone. He has got to go to court and make the suggestion to the judge, and tell the judge why.

Mr. COOPER. He has to prove it?

Mr. MAGNUSON. Of course he does.

Mr. COOPER. He has the burden of proof?

Mr. MAGNUSON. I do not think a Federal judge would grant it willy-nilly. Of course, they might, but he would have to prove it.

Mr. COOPER. I am not just bringing up a frivolous question. The section goes to due process and justice?

Mr. MAGNUSON. I might say most Federal judges I know would not.

Mr. COOPER. We have passed several acts in the last 3 years which give to agencies a power to impose a civil penalty and only a subsequent hearing. As an example, the Coal Mine Safety Act. I am very familiar with it.

Mr. MAGNUSON. The Senator from New Hampshire and I will give the Senator another example. The Senator from Colorado was there also. The Occupational Safety and Health law.

Mr. COOPER. Yes; that is another one.

Mr. MAGNUSON. Yes; you could go out and fine a man. The investigator can fine him, not the Administrator but the investigator.

Mr. COOPER. And without the due process.

Mr. MAGNUSON. Yes. And the review board down here, or the Department of Labor, can fine the guy.

Mr. COOPER. There have been some cases in the past on this issue——

Mr. MAGNUSON. And the Senator is correct that in most safety measures we have gone much farther than this bill.

Mr. COOPER. I want to be sure we are not following the two acts to which we have alluded, in this bill, because it is a failure of due process.

Mr. MAGNUSON. Yes.

Mr. COOPER. The Supreme Court will probably finally rule on the two acts. There have been some cases in the past which have suggested that the imposition of a civil penalty of size, is in fact a criminal penalty, and would require a criminal trial; and I assume it is still true that in Federal courts a unanimous verdict by all the members of a jury would be required. But I wanted to raise the question.

Mr. MAGNUSON. The court must approve it, and the lawyer who comes in for the agency will have to do like I used to do when I used to be a U.S. attorney: We would recommend to the judge, "Put this fellow away and throw the key away," or "Let him go," or somewhere in between on a lot of them. But that is all these lawyers would do, is the same thing. The judge has to approve it.

Mr. COOPER. I am glad the Senator has made this very clear. I have been concerned about this imposition of civil penalties without a hearing, without due process, and I must say this: There are people in our country who express very liberal and correct views for justice, but who seem to have no feeling at all about due process in such cases as I have cited.

Mr. MAGNUSON. That is not contained in this bill, I assure the Senator of that.

Mr. COTTON. And, if the Senator will yield, I want to join the Senator from Washington in assuring the Senator from Kentucky that there is no such thing in this bill. The only thing in the bill I find objectionable—and it is no departure as far as the injunctive powers or civil penalties are concerned. I agree with my distinguished chairman that there is no departure.

The only departure I am talking about is the departure of starting the custom of having the attorneys retained by these departments pursuing criminal prosecutions in the Federal courts. I think that criminal prosecutions have been and should continue to be confined to the Department of Justice.

Mr. GURNEY. Mr. President, again I want to make clear to the Senate, because of the colloquy I had with the distinguished manager of the bill, that my amendment gives just as much power as the bill presently does to the Administrator to go into court and stop by injunction, right now, any hazardous product. It says:

> To enjoin any person from engaging in the manufacture for sale, sale, offering for sale, or otherwise offering for public consumption . . . an imminently hazardous consumer product.

If that does not take it off the market, I do not know what does.

After that preliminary injunction has been issued, the administration is going through the administrative process. Sometimes that takes a year or two. Some of the Federal Trade Commission actions, when the hearings are printed, occupy whole shelves. We do not want the Federal district court to do that. We want that to be done by the Administrator.

But so far as setting up a legal department within this new agency is concerned and giving it special treatment and allowing it to duplicate what the Justice Department is now doing at extra expense, a complete deviation from the enforcement procedures we now have, that is a mistake and a bad precedent. That is what my amendment would seek to stop, and it should stop.

One other comment, with respect to what the Senator from New Hampshire was talking about. Section 316(a) does give to the Administrator, the agency, or his lawyers acting on his behalf, the right to go into court and seek a conviction of somebody. It says that it would be guilty of a misdemeanor or, upon conviction, fined not more than $10,000 for each such act, or imprisoned not more than 1 year, or both.

If the Senate is going to permit an agency to do that and take that criminal procedure away from the Department of Justice, we are making a very bad mistake. I hope the Senate adopts my amendment, which puts the procedures in the proper perspective, as we always have done.

Mr. ALLOTT. Mr. President, will the Senator yield?

Mr. GURNEY. I yield.

Mr. ALLOTT. Mr. President, being present on the floor during this discussion, I cannot let the discussion take place without stating my own stand upon these very important issues.

The Senator from Kentucky and the Senator from Florida have stated a position which the Senator from Colorado believes in very firmly and very thoroughly.

The Senator from Washington, the manager of this bill, spoke of the Occupational Safety and Hazard Act. In my opinion, one of the greatest mistakes the Senate has made in the last few years was to permit that department to go in and exercise the right of fine upon the people who violate that act. If we want to do anything really great, one of the things we ought to do is to bring this back.

The purpose for the formation of the Department of Justice was to file and proceed with criminal procedures against people who violate Federal laws. Regardless of any power that has been put into the Federal Trade Commission—I was for writing their powers in the field of injunction—I still believe that any time we permit this to go on, we are making a great error.

The PRESIDING OFFICER. All time of the Senator from Florida has expired.

Mr. ALLOTT. Mr. President, will the Senator from Washington yield me 2 minutes?

Mr. MAGNUSON. I yield.

Mr. ALLOTT. The prosecuting powers of this Government should lie with the Attorney General and no one else. I do not believe, as the Senator from New Hampshire said, that we should permit the Government lawyers hired by an individual agency to pursue the right of prosecution of people for criminal acts. In that respect, I am particularly and wholly opposed to the law as it is proposed in section 316.

Mr. PERCY. Mr. President, will the Senator yield?

Mr. MAGNUSON. I yield 5 minutes to the Senator.

Mr. PERCY. Mr. President, I would submit as evidence that we need go no further than an article published this morning in the Washington Post, written by Mr. Morton Mintz, whom I consider one of the Nation's most knowledgeable and capable reporters in the field of consumer protection. This article very carefully documents a single case that occurred last year.

A Food and Drug Administration inspector, Lewis R. Sikes, began an inspection at a wholesale grocery warehouse in Alabama that stores beans, flour, peas, popcorn, sugar, and other foods. I read from the article:

> The inspection showed evidence of heavy rodent habitation . . . throughout the food storage area which is not only unsanitary and obnoxious, but a possible source of disease.
>
> Twenty-five live adult mice were seen and four nests were found containing a total of 19 live baby mice," Hutt continued. "One live mouse ran out of a bag of kidney beans while the lot was being examined.
>
> Twenty-five lots of human food were found to be defiled by rodents in varying degrees; and at least 15 of these lots were rodent-gnawed or were in rodent gnawed containers.
>
> Fifteen lots were found to have rodent excreta pellets or urine stains on the immediate product container or the shipping containers.

I read this simply because it is not an isolated case but because we have taken testimony time after time after time indicating that there are the conditions that frequently are found.

What do you do with an injunction? Do you issue an injunction to enjoin the mice from coming in, the rats from excreting on food, the rodents from depositing urine strains all over the kidney beans and flour and whatever else? How do you operate? What do you do under the law as it now exists or as this amendment would provide.

You go to the U.S. attorney—and they did. They did not go once or twice. They went several times. The FDA lawyer told the prosecutor of the conditions that were found, and his belief that a criminal action was clearly warranted. But the U.S. attorney wrote that he did not feel that action was appropriate at that particular time.

I wish the RECORD was capable of printing pictures. Certainly, as the former head of a camera company, I would like to see the RECORD in color. I now submit pictures of actual conditions that existed in that warehouse, which were subsmitted to the U.S. attorney. If these pictures do not cause anyone not to have a good appetite fro dinner this evening after they peruse them, I would like to know what would. But the U.S. attorney, after these facts were stated and these pictures presented, simply said:

> I continue to be of the same opinion, that prosecution is not appropriate.

What do you have to do to break the law in a food warehouse? This is not an isolated case. It has been documented many times over that these conditions exist. The hearings held before the Committee on Government Operations are filled with instances of this kind.

I maintain that we must do something more than we are now doing if we intend merely to fulfill our public responsibility.

* * *

Mr. COTTON. Mr. President, I send to the desk an amendment.

The PRESIDING OFFICER. The clerk will report the amendment.

The assistant legislative clerk read as follows:

Commencing on page 72, line 16, insert a period after "purpose" and strike out all thereafter through page 73, line 2.

Mr. COTTON. Mr. President, this amendment simply leaves everything in the bill. It leaves in the injunction authority. It leaves in the enforcement of civil penalties up to $10,000. It merely takes from the bill the authority for the attorneys of the new agency to prosecute criminally in the courts. That is all it does. It leaves everything else intact which, in my opinion, would give the new agency all the power it needs, including the situation outlined by the distinguished Senator from Illinois (Mr. PERCY). But it does not start the precedent of having the attorneys employed by the various agencies becoming criminal prosecutors in the Federal courts.

Mr. MAGNUSON. I want to ask one question. I oppose the amendment because that is exactly what the Senator from Florida is trying to do, to take away from the agencies and do it through the U.S. attorneys.

Mr. COTTON. It would do much more than that——

Mr. MAGNUSON. It would not take care of certain things, such as the matter the Senator from Illinois raised, because the U.S. attorneys would not act.

* * *

Mr. COTTON. Mr. President, may I have 1 minute to say to my friend from Washington (Mr. MAGNUSON), that the amendment of the Senator from Florida goes much further. It would strike out the civil penalties in the case of the rats the Senator from Illinois talked about. If my amendment is adopted they could still go ahead with their own attorneys regardless of the district attorneys and they could seek to impose the $10,000 penalty.

Mr. MAGNUSON. As to the civil penalties, I understand that, but it takes away from the agency to bring the action into the Federal court—routes it through the Attorney General—and that is what I would not like to see happen. I think many members of the committee and members of the other two committees feel the same way about it. I have a feeling about cases like that going through any Attorney General's office. They take too long. It is too much trouble. But we are talking about emergencies like this one example. There are many, many others, I can think of, where they find some fish in a warehouse, say, it is supposed to be fresh fish, but it might make thousands of people sick, and we have to act immediately and we cannot find a U.S. attorney, perhaps, that will say that they will do it. That is what the bill intended. We may have been wrong in our contention but I do not think we are.

I believe that the bill would not have any force or effect on hazardous substances if we routed this through the U.S. attorney's office. They can go there anyway. On a particular case, they may go out and want the U.S. attorney to handle it and they would, but we have to have some emergency measures. We are not going to get the people by just saying, "Mr. Judge, I hope you will fine them," when there are some criminal acts involved somewhere along the line. Toys are an example.

* * *

So Mr. GURNEY's amendments were rejected.

Mr. COTTON. Mr. President, I send an amendment to the desk.

* * *

The amendment, ordered to be printed in the RECORD, is as follows:

On page 72, line 6, strike "and Criminal".

On page 72, line 16, insert a period after "purpose"; strike the comma and all through "both." on line 20.

Mr. COTTON. Mr. President, this amendment simply would eliminate from the bill the authority for attorneys for the new agency to bring criminal prosecution. It takes out criminal fines and prison sentences, but would leave them free for temporary injunctions and permanent injunctions. That is all it would do.

* * *

Mr. MAGNUSON. Mr. President, the Senator from Washington opposes the amendment. The committee discussed part of this amendment and decided against it. I think it seriously weakens the bill.

* * *

Mr. COOPER. Mr. President, this is a complex bill.

Under the bill, as I understand, the Administrator would have vast powers, as the Senator from New Hampshire said, to proceed to secure the imposition of civil penalties up to $10,000 and wide emergency powers in securing preliminary and permanent injunctions, and to do all these things necessary to prevent distribution of these products on the market.

I think it is correct that in the case of criminal actions, jurisdiction has always been held by the Department of Justice, and I think it should remain there. We have been giving more and more power to the Administrators of agencies, and the very fact that their lawyers can go into court and prosecute, if they choose, and the suggestion of such powers provides too great authority—the power to investigate, to bring changes, to prosecute criminal action.

I have had some complaints about other acts, and agencies which have been given these powers. I have been told when civil penalties are imposed these agencies suggest, "Well, if you do not take this civil penalty we can impose a larger one or prosecute you." That is a veiled threat which is unjust. I hope that with the vast powers given the Administrator in this bill, we would leave jurisdiction of criminal action to the Department of Justice.

* * *

So Mr. COTTON's amendment was rejected.

* * *

Mr. BROCK. Mr. President, I call up an amendment which I have at the desk, and ask for its immediate consideration.

The PRESIDING OFFICER. The amendment will be stated.

The assistant legislative clerk read as follows:

On page 22, line 7; page 30, line 7; and page 43, line 17, strike the phrase:

"referred to" and substitute therefore the phrase "or other confidential business information; not related to a consumer product in such a way as to indicate the presence of an unreasonable risk of injury or death, described".

Mr. BROCK. Mr. President, I yield myself such time as I may consume.

My amendment is designed to give greater protection to confidential business information, the release of which would be to the competitive disadvantage and detriment of domestic corporations, particularly with respect to international competition. The amendment does not restrict the specific authority of the Agency to release confidential information to committee of Congress, to courts and Federal agencies, or to the public when necessary to protect health or safety as provided by the bill.

This amendment is necessary to make it clear that the Agency is not intended to be free to disclose, without any limitations, the kinds of confidential business information—including confidential processes, cost and pricing statistics, confidential statistical data, and other similar business information—the disclosure of which, absent statutory authority, would constitute a criminal act under section 1905 of title 18 of the United States Code.

The present language of section 301 (c)(1), referring only to "trade secrets" is not adequate to insure that this critical information will not be regularly disclosed in a manner by which it would be readily available to competitors, both domestic and foreign. As a matter of statutory construction, it is highly possible that a court would conclude that because section 301(c)(1) refers only to "trade secrets" in section 1905, it was not intended to protect the other confidential data referred to in section 1905.

Moreover, there is considerable precedent for a narrow reading of the term "trade secrets" which would exclude from its protection some formulas (*e.g., Drew Chemical Corp.* v. *Star Chemical Co.,* 258 F. Supp. 827, 836 (W.D. Mo. 1966); *cf. Venn.* v. *Goedert,* 319 F. 2d 812 (8th Cir. 1963)), cost and pricing information (*e.g., Cudahy Co.* v. *American Laboratories, Inc.,* 313 F. Supp. 1339 (D. Neb. 1970)), and other information protected by section 1905.

The amendment will insure confidential treatment of such information except as it is necessary for the Agency to disclose it in carrying out its functions under the bill.

The same question arose under the language in section 208(c) of S. 1177, the Consumer Protection Organization Act of 1972, when that bill was being considered by the Subcommittee on Executive Reorganization of the Senate Committee on Government Operations. I was pleased that that subcommittee amended section 208(c) to provide protection not only of "trade secrets" but also of "other confidential business information" described by section 1905 of title 18, United States Code. It would appear to me that this has been a drafting oversight which can and should be curbed by my proposed amendment..

I have discussed this amendment with the distinguished floor manager of the bill and with the Senator from New Hampshire. They have suggested amendments which I think would improve the effect of the amendment, and their suggestions have been incorporated.

The simple purpose of the amendment is to protect businessmen against the release of confidential information, statisti cal data, cost data, and related information which has no relevance to health and safety, and to prevent the agency from wantonly abusing American industry and creating a competitive disadvantage, particularly with international competition.

My amendment, very simply, prohibits the unwarranted disclosure of confidential business information.

I am prepared to yield back the remainder of my time, if the manager of the bill is.

Mr. MAGNUSON. I am prepared to yield my time back, too. The committee is willing to accept the amendment. We intended to discuss this matter in conference, anyway.

I yield back the remainder of my time.

The PRESIDING OFFICER. All remaining time having been yielded back, the question is on agreeing to the amendment of the Senator from Tennessee.

The amendment was agreed to.

* * *

Mr. NELSON. Mr. President, I send to the desk two amendments, and I ask unanimous consent that they be acted upon en bloc.

The amendments are as follows:

On page 50, delete lines 17 and 18, and substitute in lieu thereof the following:

"(3) that the offeror, where the Commissioner has accepted an offer or offers under section 303, provide opportunity for all interested persons including consumers to participate in the offeror's development of a proposed consumer safety standard in accordance with accepted standards of due process, including adequate notice to all participants and access to all relevant records and documents;"

On page 49, between lines 3 and 4, insert the following:

"(C) the offeror, including any person assisting the offeror in the development of the proposal, is not a manufacturer, distributor or retailer or the employee of a manufacturer, distributor or retailer of a consumer product proposed to be included in the consumer product safety standard to which the offer applies."

On page 48, line 22 delete the word "and"; on page 48, line 25 delete the period, add a semi-colon, and the word "and".

Mr. NELSON. Mr. President, these amendments are designed to insure that, whenever the Consumer Agency delegates to a nongovernment group the responsibilities for suggesting proposed consumer product safety standards, that group or any of its members does not have an economic stake in the manufacture or sale of the products involved.

The amendments also insure that such groups outside the Government follow fair procedures in their standard making so that all interested parties, including consumers, are afforded due process participation in the standard making.

These amendments apply only to the development of suggested standards, which are offered to the Agency for consideration. The Agency, in seeking to develop a standard, first promulgates a notice of need for a standard. Outside groups may offer to suggest such standards. In promulgating standards, the Agency must follow administrative procedures, and may include in its own proposed standards—as published in the Federal Register—whatever it chooses from the suggestions developed by outside expertise.

The proposals drawn up under these amendments do not give outside groups legal authority to set standards—only to propose standards for consideration by the Agency.

The provision in the bill, to allow suggested standard making outside of the Government agency, is designed to enable the Agency to take advantage of technical competence existing in the scientific and engineering communities, including independent testing laboratories, university connected experts, professional societies, and such consumer organizations as Consumers Union.

The amendments prevent a conflict of interest between companies setting standards for, and marketing, the same product, and insure that fair procedures are followed in the proposed standard making.

The most serious condemnation of the voluntary standards system which emerged from the studies of the Product Safety Commission and others—upon whose recommendations this entire bill is based—was the chronic tendency of the standards committees to be dominated by companies with an economic stake in the product. The result was that standards generally met the lowest common denominator in the marketplace.

Because consumers have had little or no voice in these voluntary standard-making procedures, the standards have been industry dominated.

I would like to quate from the Product Safety Commission report:

> We have studied this system (of voluntary safety standard-setting) and found it is valuable in marshalling technical competence but has certain inherent limitation. . . .
>
> In no standards procedure can it be said that consumers have a substantial voice. Rarely have they an effective veto. . . . The need for a consensus commonly waters down a proposed standard until it is little more than an affirmation of the status quo. . . .
>
> At the same time, voluntary safety programs, with due regard for the public interest, need and warrant Federal technical and financial assistance and oversight.

These amendments are offered to strengthen the voluntary standard-making procedure, if such suggested standards are offered to the Agency for consideration.

They require:

First. That anyone offering to suggest proposed standards not be a manufacturer, distributor, or retailer, or the employee of a manufacturer, distributor, or retailer, of a consumer product proposed to be included in the consumer product safety standard; and

Second. That anyone drawing up such suggested standards follow fair procedures, by providing an opportunity for all interested persons, including consumers, to participate in the standard-making procedure in accordance with accepted standards of due process, including adequate notice to all participants and access to all revelant records and documents.

Mr. President, these two amendments clarify at least what I think is the intent of the bill. The bill provides that the Administrator may contract with an outside organization for the purpose of developing proposed safety standards.

One amendment provides that the private contractor must guarantee the opportunity for all interested persons, including consumers, "to participate in the offeror's development of a proposed consumer safety standard in accordance with accepted standards of due process."

The other amendment provides that the independent contractor must be one who is not manufacturing or selling the product.

The objective of the proposals is to permit the Administrator to contract with such independent organizations as the Underwriters Laboratories, American Society for Testing Materials, American National Standards Institute, and so forth.

Mr. MAGNUSON. Mr. President, the Senator from Wisconsin and I have discussed this matter with the staffs, and we think it is a good amendment. It clarifies what we all probably wanted to do, anyway, but it nails it down.

I accept the amendment.

Mr. COTTON. Mr. President, I could not hear what the chairman said, and I am not familiar with these amendments. I heard the second amendment, and I can see no objection to it. I did not quite get the first amendment, but I have a feeling that it raised havoc with the "instant action" about which the chairman has been talking.

Mr. MAGNUSON. No; it does not do that.

Mr. COTTON. What is the first one?

Mr. NELSON. The first amendment provides that, when an outside agency, outside the Government, or a university has a contract to propose standards—they cannot establish them—they must afford the opportunity for all interested persons, including consumers, "to participate in the offeror's development of a proposed consumer safety standard in accordance with accepted standards of due process."

In other words, if a university or the American Society of Testing Materials is going to contract to propose some safety standards, the manufacturer and the consumers have the right to submit their arguments before the proposed standard is sent up to the Agency.

Mr. COTTON. Must all this take place before any product can be placed on the market?

Mr. NELSON. That takes place during the course of the independent agency, outside the government—whatever it is—proposing standards that go back to the Administrator, who then does with them what he wishes and follows the regular Administrative Procedure Act.

Mr. COTTON. Is this prior to or after the product is on the market?

Mr. NELSON. I am assuming that standards will be established for products that are already on the market under the act as well as prior to.

Mr. COTTON. But after that, nothing new can come on the market until the process has been gone through?

Mr. MAGNUSON. Not necessarily. It is just that they ask for a review and they get the independent agency—the agencies which businesses use now—so that everybody can participate. It may be a product on the market. There may be some change in it. Or it could be a new product, too.

Mr. NELSON. This only relates to the authority of the Administrator to establish minimum safety standards. He can do that himself within the Department and file in the Federal Register, or he can contract outside the agency.

They would develop a proposed standard and would come back to the administrator. They would modify it, reject it, accept it—whatever they please—and then file the Federal Register, according to the regular procedure.

Mr. EAGLETON. Mr. President, I send to the desk an amendment.

The PRESIDING OFFICER. The amendment will be stated.

The assistant legislative clerk read the amendment, as follows:

On page 3, line 22, before the word "but" insert the following: "and includes any mobile home;".

Mr. EAGLETON. Mr. President, I rise to offer a clarifying amendment to the Food, Drug and Consumer Product Safety Act. This amendment places mobile homes specifically within the definition of "consumer product" to eliminate any doubt as to the Commissioner of Product Safety's authority over them.

My amendment is consistent with the report of the Commerce Committee, which states:

It is the committee's intent to include mobile homes under the definition of "consumer product."

It is intended only to clarify that intent, as the language of S. 3419 as presently written may be subject to misinterpretation on this point.

Over 7 million Americans now live in mobile homes. Half the one one-family houses built in this country today are mobile homes and 95 percent of the houses sold for under $15,000 are mobile homes. In this day of high costs for real property and housing, mobile homes with a median price of $6,000 to $7,000 provide an affordable alternative for many—including a significant number of young married people and elderly people—who want homes of their own.

Unfortunately, there remains a crying need for stricter regulation of the mobile home industry. Each year, defects in mobile homes result in an inexcusably high toll in property damage, personal injury, and death. There are now far too many complaints of defective electrical wiring, inadequate mooring, insufficient exits and window construction that inhibits emergency escape.

The greatest threats to property and life for mobile homeowners are the likelihood of fire and damage by high winds. Because mobile homes are so susceptible to damage by fire and wind under current law, insurance rates for mobile homeowners have skyrocketed.

Mobile homes are now regulated neither as motor vehicles under the Motor Vehicles Safety Act nor as housing under local housing codes of most communities. They are subject only to minimal standards which the mobile home industry itself has promulgated. These standards were prepared under the aegis of the American National Standards Institute—ANSI—with the participation of the Mobile Homes Manufacturers Association as required guidelines for MHMA members.

While some States have incorporated some or all of the ANSI standards into their law, enforcement is generally poor. These standards thus form the basis of what is essentially a voluntary compliance program, with manufacturers self-certifying that their vehicles meet ANSI standards. Even where ANSI standards are met, mobile homeowners may not be adequately protected. The National Commission on Product Safety found serious deficiencies in these standards at the time of their report in 1970. It is my understanding that these standards have been upgraded to some extent since that report, but it is apparent that they should be subjected to a systematic review by the Federal Government and stricter standards promulgated where they are needed.

I believe that the hazards to property and life presented by defective mobile homes require the promulgation of stringent, uniform standards coupled with effective enforcement authority. The question now is not whether such standards are necessary, but how most effectively to accomplish this end. I share the view of the members of the Commerce Committee that the bill before us provides the most effective vehicle.

Mr. President, the essence of the amendment is to clarify the language of the statute itself by adding to it mobile homes so as to conform with the statement in the committee report that certain mobile homes are included under the aegis of the act.

I reserve the remainder of my time.

Mr. COTTON. Mr. President, will the Senator from Missouri yield?

Mr. EAGLETON. I yield.

Mr. COTTON. I gather that the Senator from Missouri had this brought to his attention because it was in the committee report?

Mr. EAGLETON. Yes, sir.

Mr. COTTON. Does the Sena [illegible] om Missouri consider a mobile home to be a hazardous substance, impure food, or an appliance?

Mr. EAGLETON. I believe it is a product manufactured under the act.

Mr. COTTON. Would the Senator include submarines and battleships in this bill then?

Mr. EAGLETON. No, no.

Mr. COTTON. They might be a little too big?

Mr. EAGLETON. That is correct.

Mr. COTTON. I merely want to say for myself, and I am not speaking for minority. But, I personally never knew that this was in the report.

The report was, naturally, prepared by the staff. It is getting now so that the tail is wagging the dog. The staff is running the committee most of the time.

I did not know it was in there. I think it is utterly absurd and utterly ridiculous.

I made a statement early this afternoon that whether my amendments, which I thought were important, were adopted or rejected, I thought this was a good bill. I would vote for it. This has changed my mind. I am not going to vote for any monstrosity that carries any such silly amendments as this one.

In saying that, I am not reflecting on the distinguished Senator from Missouri (Mr. EAGLETON), because it was in the committee report. Some of us were responsible for what goes into that committee report.

Mr. SPARKMAN. Mr. President, will the Senator from New Hampshire yield?

Mr. COTTON. I yield.

Mr. SPARKMAN. Mr. President, I strongly object to the amendment. First of all, housing comes under the jurisdiction of an entirely different committee. It has only been within the past couple of years that we have authorized the FHA to insure mobile homes. We have provided that the Secretary of Housing shall set standards, and I do not see why we have to go to any other committee bill or to any other piece of legislation with reference to mobile homes which are clearly within the jurisdiction of our committee. We might as well apply it to single-family dwellings or to apartment houses, or to anything else, if we are going to start here on mobile homes.

I strongly object to the amendment.

Mr. TOWER. Mr. President, will the Senator from New Hampshire yield?

Mr. COTTON. I yield.

Mr. TOWER. Mr. President, as the ranking minority member on the Committee on Banking, Housing and Urban Affairs, I should like to second what our distinguished chairman, the Senator from Alabama (Mr. SPARKMAN) has just said, that if we are going to extend it to mobile homes, why not extend it to modular housing which has just become a breakthrough in construction in order to bring it within the reach of low-income families.

Our distinguished colleague from Tennessee (Mr. BROCK) already has a bill before the committee. It should be left to this committee which has the appropriate jurisdiction and not be dealt with on the Senate floor now in the form of an amendment to the pending bill.

Mr. MOSS. Mr. President, in dealing with this matter of ridiculing the amendment affecting mobile homes, that we might as well take some other kind of home, and so forth, the fact is, this was considered by the committee. There is testimony on it. We did consider it at length. So, it seems to me to be a logical amendment and I should like to support it.

I understood the Senator from Texas to say that there had been some bill or an amendment offered recently in which they intended to take it up in the Committee on Banking, Housing, and Urban Affairs; but a mobile home, under these circumstances, is quite different from any other living quarters which people occupy. A mobile home is a movable, transferable vehicle. It is a manufactured product. The deficiencies were outlined by Mr. Karl Herrmann, the State fire marshal of the State of Washington, so that there is little question about the need for safety regulation of mobile homes.

The mobile home industry has experienced phenomenal growth in a short period of time. The concept of the mobile home has changed from that of portable, temporary living quarters for travelers and transient workers of limited means to that of semipermanent dwellings for a large portion of our population. The industry has not had the benefit of long years of experience in designing construction and voluntary standards have proved inadequate for insuring safety.

The inadequacy of the voluntary standard was documented in the final report of the National Commission on Product Safety. It noted that the standard does not provide exits opening out on either side at opposite ends, in the event of fire or upset. In addition, provisions for safety glazing were braking to prevent fishtailing are not included. Other deficiencies of the standard include permitting the use of gas-fired floor heaters which generate excessive grate surface temperatures and the lack of requirements that the heater be constructed to preclude blocking.

Similar deficiencies were outlined in testimony before the Commerce Committee during hearings on S. 3419 by Karl Hermann, State fire marshal of the State of Washington. He noted that private standards do not include combustibility provisions for all structural and finished materials, establish flame spread requirements that are too high, and do not include design requirements to provide for fire separation between sleeping areas and other portions of the mobile home.

In short, there is little question that there is a great need for Federal regulation of mobile homes. The Commission on Consumer Products is best qualified to perform this function, and for this reason I support adoption of the amendment proposed by the Senator from Missouri (Mr. EAGLETON).

Mr. EAGLETON. Mr. President, I thank the Senator from Utah for his comments and his support of my amendment.

Mr. COTTON. Mr. President, what I am about to say is no reflection on the Senator from Missouri because this was in the committee report, although God knows why, but it seems to me that this simply shows how far afield we are getting.

Here we are trying to pass a bill to protect the consumer, and this is the first time I ever knew that one could consume a mobile home. If we are going to have mobile homes in the bill, we might as well put in bowling alleys, or dance halls, or make this a whole new and extraordinary department of government to maintain control over our whole society.

I have never heard of a more ridiculous thing in my life.

When we write into a committee report a provision for mobile homes in a bill that seeks to protect the consumer against improper food, medicine, and electrical appliances, then I think we are making monkeys of ourselves. It is not conducive to the dignity of the Senate.

I did not intend to speak so strongly, but this turn of events took me by surprise.

Mr. SPARKMAN. Mr. President, if the Senator will yield, I refer the Senator to the bottom of page 12 of the committee report and invite his attention to the following:

> Other products excluded from the definition of "consumer product" include products "subject to regulation" under the National Traffic and Motor Vehicle Safety Act of 1966, aircraft or other aeronautical products "subject to safety regulations" by the Federal Aviation Administration, foods, drugs, or devices subject to safety regulation under the Food, Drug and Cosmetic Act, . . .

This is subject to regulation under the laws that we passed authorizing the FHA to grant insurance. We do require standards. They are required already. The Senator from Tennessee (Mr. BROCK) has introduced a bill that strengthens those requirements. There is a bill before our committee now and we will have hearings on it.

* * *

Mr. BROCK. Mr. President, I rise in opposition to the amendment and in support of the statement of the Senator from Alabama, the chairman of the Committee on Banking, Housing and Urban Affairs.

I think this amendment really goes to the wrong point. The point is that we have statutes today. We have existing regulations and controls which have been established. We also have my bill which seeks to provide uniformity and improvement of existing standards before the Committee on Banking, Housing and Urban Affairs. Moreover, the Senator from Alabama (Mr. SPARKMAN) has graciously afforded my legislation the opportunity for hearings.

The fact of the matter is that the Senator's amendment tries to equate a waffle iron with a home. The Senator from Utah said that there is something different about a mobile home. I was always taught all my life that if something looks like a duck, waddles like a duck, and sounds like a duck, it is a duck. A mobile home looks like a house, functions as a house, sleeps as a house, it is a house.

There are 7 million Americans who live in these mobile homes. They call them homes. There is no possible way we could put them under this Agency in this bill without diminishing the effectiveness of the control and the opportunity for greater safety to the consumers, because they would be swept in with a hodgepodge of things like toasters and everything else.

Each piece of equipment in a mobile home, such as toasters, refrigerators, and other components, is covered under the present proposal. However, to try to say that a mobile home is not a house and should be covered under the Consumer Product Act is ridiculous and certainly is not logical.

This is a serious problem. I agree with all of the Senator's objectives of achieving greater safety for the homeowners. However, in this instance this is the wrong way to go about it.

The Senator from Utah mentioned the witnesses who testified. Three witnesses testified about this bill before the committee. Two of those witnesses endorse my bill to create standards. Two of the witnesses who testified before the Senate Commerce Committee. The National Association of Independent Insurers endorsed my bill. As a body, the mobile home manufacturers have not. However, the people who insure those homes have. They say that it costs as much per family to insure a mobile home costing $6,000 as it does to insure a $40,000 conventional home.

There is something very wrong here. The Senator from Missouri does not solve the problem. He creates a problem and compounds a felony by putting one more item and 7 million families under the Product Safety Act.

We have duplicate standards between FHA, DOT, VA, FHLB, and this agency. And nobody will win. We know that.

It makes a great deal more sense to treat it as a home under the jurisdiction of the Committee on Banking, Housing and Urban Affairs. Let us write the bill. We will do it and then we will respond to the actual need.

Mr. President, the distinguished junior Senator and I both agree standards are imperative for mobile homes. But to seek to place mobile homes under the jurisdiction of this new agency would be to dilute the effectiveness of what we are both attempting to achieve. If this new agency is designed to give the assurances of safety to consumers "of products for his use, consumption, or enjoyment in or around a household or residence, a school, in recreation," then to give its Commissioner authority over already regulated items such as minibikes, boats, automobiles, or mobile homes can only result in a dilution of competence and effectiveness of the Agency. This is particularly true in the case of mobile homes. For if this amendment were to be adopted the Consumer Product Safety Agency would be thrust into an area which relates solely to housing. A mobile home is a dwelling. These domiciliary units have become a vital and critical component of America's future housing capability. They are practically the only form of housing available to the home buyer for less than $15,000. To attempt to place mobile homes within the definition of a consumer product as envisioned by this act is tantamount to denying the consumer the protection which undeniably should be his when he purchases his home.

If this amendment were adopted, mobile homes would be the only form of housing contained in this legislation although presently modular homes also are not presently regulated by local building codes in most parts of the country. To bury mobile homes in an agency with jurisdiction over items such as irons, televisions, and diet pills is absurd when you think that nearly 7 million people occupy mobile homes as their place of residence.

Mr. President, separate regulation and treatment of mobile homes in an agency with the expertise is required. There is a severe safety problem. But it cannot be solved by an agency without the expertise and resources. Since there is no one agency with established authority over mobile homes today, the ability of the Consumer Product Safety Agency would place these dwellings in dubious priority at a time when action is imperative.

We cannot ignore the fact that the mobile home is the fastest growing sector of American housing and provides 95 percent of all single family dwellings under $15,000. For this reason, I have emphasized in my legislation that the per unit cost of a regulation be considered before promulgation of final standards. There is no such provision in the bill presently under consideration. We must realize that the mobile home is the only mode of housing within reach of the average American. Young people and the elderly are the principal purchasers of mobile homes and we must consider the effects of regulations on their continued ability to own this type of home. Regulation of mobile homes under the Consumer Product Safety Act could push the cost of such a dwelling beyond the reach of these consumers and I believe factors of cost must be weighed.

Thus, regulation should be administered by HUD, not HEW or a new consumer agency. And the goal of such regulation should be to establish minimum uniform safety standards while at the same time promoting the use of the mobile home as a low-cost desirable form of housing.

Mr. President, the use of mobile homes have grown at an astounding rate. In

1967 the manufacturers of mobile homes produced 240,000 units. In less than 3 years in 1970 production was over 500,000. There can be little doubt that mobile homes are the wave of the future.

People are being killed everyday in mobile homes unnecessarily. To seek to relegate mobile homes to the status of toasters, waffle iron, diet pills and the like is to perpetrate the worst kind of injustice on the consumer. We are not talking about an item that is used once a year, once a month, or even once a day. We are talking about a home in use daily where many people, especially the elderly, spend literally thousands of hours. We cannot hope for adequate protection of the mobile homebuyer if we shove him to the side and tell him to wait behind the man with the broken toaster, waffle iron or whatever. These people need protection which is effective. They do not want their homes seized because of a failure to meet an administratively determined standard. This is not consumer protection. It is consumer be damned.

NEED FOR FURTHER EXAMINATION

Mr. President, during consideration of this bill the Senate Commerce Committee scheduled three witnesses on mobile homes. None were technical witnesses, but nevertheless their testimony was enlightening. During hearings on this Consumer Product Safety bill in the other body, now witnesses were heard on Mobile Home safety and it is my understanding that agreement has been reached to exclude mobile homes from their bill in favor of a hearing on specific legislation introduced by my former colleague, Lou Frey of Florida.

Mr. President, all this shows we need to examine this subject carefully before we act, so the result will have the desired effect. At present we have four Federal agencies with statutory authority over mobile home safety. We have 29 States with some sort of regulatory programs covering mobile homes.

Yet, after hearing from a grand total of three witnesses who state something is needed, we are being presented with an amendment which seeks to define a mobile home as a consumer product in the same category with a toaster.

What we need to do is gather representatives from the four Federal programs and the various States with existing safety legislation. Give them a hearing which will result in a reasonable, effective bill.

If we do not, if we pass this proposal we run the risk of establishing yet another unsynchronized federal program for mobile homes.

We risk diminishing the real priority status of mobile home safety.

We risk forcing prices on mobile homes to a level beyond the purchase power of average Americans.

We risk the establishment of standards which are ineffective and ill-conceived.

I urge my colleagues to reject this amendment. I urge them not to run these risks.

Mr. TAFT. Mr. President, I do not believe that mobile homes should be included under the purview of the Food, Drug, and Consumer Product Agency.

The need for establishing Federal safety standards for mobile homes cannot be overemphasized. Unlike conventional housing, mobile homes are not subject to local building ordinances. More than half of the States have adopted standards covering mobile home construction, but in most States that have such standards only those mobile homes manufactured and sold in the State are regulated. There is no control over mobile homes manufactured in a State without regulations. Even in States with adequate standards, the enforcement of such standards is often lackadaisical or hampered by a lack of funding and personnel.

In view of the fires and other tragedies involving mobile homes which have recently been reported, this situation is clearly unacceptable.

At the same time, however, it is clear that any standards for mobile homes should be promulgated with the full benefit of all the expertise available. Ninety-five percent of all homes sold for under $15,000 in America are mobile homes; 400,000 last year. For many Americans earning modest incomes, the only kind of new home which they can afford is a mobile home.

It would be a tragic blow to those low-income consumers if Federal mobile home standards were established which unnecessarily raised the price or complicated the financing of mobile homes.

For those reasons, I have agreed to cosponsor S. 3604, Senator BROCK's bill to establish a national safety standard for mobile homes. That bill calls for the establishment of these standards in consultation with a National Mobile Home Safety Advisory Council, consisting of representatives of the general public, the standards-setting research agencies and the mobile home industry. In promulgating any standard, HUD is directed to consider all relevant mobile home safety data, the advice of the States, the practicality of the standard and the possible financial burden which the standard may place on the manufacturers or dealers.

I feel strongly that this is a more fitting method for regulating mobile homes than allowing the Food, Drug, and Consumer Product Agency to establish the standards as it sees fit. Mobile homes are dwellings, and HUD has the technical expertise necessary to deal with complicated structural problems which may arise when evaluating a dwelling's safety. In addition, HUD is familiar with the financing arrangements which would be made for mobile homes but not for the other types of products which the Food, Drug, and Consumer Product Agency is to regulate.

I urge the Senate not to accept the Eagleton Amendment because of its impatience with the under-regulation of mobile homes. I look forward to hearings and subsequent action on S. 3604 in the near future. At that time, Congress will have an opportunity to determine in a more considered manner the way to regulate mobile homes which will be most beneficial to consumers.

Mr. EAGLETON. Mr. President, I yield myself 3 minutes.

The PRESIDING OFFICER. The Senator from Missouri is recognized for 3 minutes.

Mr. EAGLETON. Mr. President, mobile homes are now regulated neither as motor vehicles under the Motor vehicles Safety Act, nor as housing under local housing codes of most communities. Mobile homes are subject only to minimal standards which the Mobile Home Association itself has promulgated. These standards were prepared under the aegis of the American National Standards Institute with the participation of the Mobile Homes Manufacturers Association.

Thus, they are a product, a sizable product to be sure. However, they are a manufactured product. They are risky. They cause death and injury to human beings and they are yet unregulated.

It seems to me that the vehicle before the Senate is an appropriate vehicle by which to bring some semblance of regulation and control to this otherwise unrelated and uncontrolled industry.

* * *

So Mr. EAGLETON's amendment was rejected.

The PRESIDING OFFICER. The bill is open to further amendment.

Mr. MAGNUSON. Mr. President, while everyone is here I will ask for the yeas and nays on final passage.

The yeas and nays were ordered.

Mr. EAGLETON. Mr. President, I nervously rise to offer another amendment.

The PRESIDING OFFICER. The amendment will be stated.

The amendment was read as follows:

On page 67, lines 12 and 13, strike "manufacturing".

Mr. EAGLETON. Mr. President, I offer an amendment to section 313(b) of the Food, Drug, and Consumer Product Safety Act. This section, as currently drafted, provides the Product Safety Commissioner with strong remedial authority when he finds that a product is either substandard or has a manufacturing defect which presents an unreasonable risk of injury or death. Under this section, he may require manufacturers or others in the distribution chain to give public notice of such defects or to repair the defect without charge or refund the purchase price.

As reported by the Commerce Committee, this section applies only to "manufacturing defects," that is, defects which occur as a result of an oversight or error on the production line or during the inspection process or use of materials not up to design specifications. It does not apply where the defect is so-called design defect. Design defects are those which occur when a product is constructed according to a plan, without production error, but the plan itself results in a product which presents a risk to safety.

We need only look to our recent experience with safety-related defects in automobiles to see that any effective product safety program must provide adequate remedies for all safety-related defects, whether they are technically deemed "manufacturing" or "defect" related. Some of the most serious safety defects found in cars have related to design—including, for example, the recall of 7 million Chevrolets for faulty engine mounts and the recall of all Corvairs manufactured in the 1960's for faulty heaters which propelled noxious fumes into the car interior.

There are countless examples of dangerous designs in the kinds of products that would be covered by the Product Safety Act. For example, Consumer Reports recently rated some of the following products "unacceptable" for purchase:

A $40 washing machine which has neither 3-wire grounding cord nor double insulation to protect the user against the possibility of a shock hazard;

An $80 humidifier which has large openings in the motor housing at the back of the unit making it possible to touch electrical windings accidentally, causing shock;

A $9 portable electric drill with a trigger which locks too easily in the "on" position;

A $25 bench grinder with a ¼ inch gap between the work rest and the grinding wheels, posing the chance of jamming the work between the wheel and the housing; and

A $40 electric hair setter in which terminal pins on rollers go through holes in plate to make contact with conductors. Severe shock could result from attempting to retrieve a hairpin while the electricity is alive.

Moreover, the Commission on Product Safety Report refers to design defects in floor furnaces, high-rise bicycles, infant furniture, power tools, and other products likely to be found around the average household.

Consumers need protection against design defects even more than they need protection against manufacturing defects. A manufacturing defect may affect a day's run on the assembly line. But a design defect, unless caught and rectified, will affect an entire production run of a product—all the 1972 models, say, of a particular bicycle or toaster.

We must keep in mind that the legislation before us does not deal simply with esthetic complaints, but with safety-related defects—those which pose an unreasonable risk to health and safety. I think it is fair to say that anyone stuck with a product which poses a threat to him or his family does not care whether the danger results from the failure of someone on the line to use the proper bolt, or from the fact that the master plans called for an improper bolt in the first place.

I would also stress the fact that no other product safety legislation of which I am aware—including the statutes which now regulate automobile safety and the safety of products with a potential radiation hazard—make a distinction between manufacturing and design defects. These laws go to any safety defect when it presents a sufficient danger to justify action. Nor does the proposed legislation of the Commission on Product Safety, after which the pending legislation is modeled, make such a distinction.

The Commerce Committee report refers only briefly to this point, stating that—

If a design defect were to present an unreasonable risk of injury or death, the Commissioner could proceed under authority of section 311 to remove immediately the product from the marketplace or could resort to the standard-setting procedures contained in the bill.

It is clear to me, however, that more attention should be focused on this point. For the reasons I am about to set out, neither the standard setting procedure nor the emergency injunctive authority under section 311 provide an effective alternative for defectively designed products which are already on the market.

Turning first to the standard-setting alternative proposed by the committee, the most obvious drawback in relying on standards is delay. Realistically, we cannot expect that the Commissioner of Product Safety will turn to standard setting for a defectively designed product on the day he learns about the defect. There will be many competing demands. Moreover, even when he determines that standards should be set, promulgating of final standards can be expected to take at least 240 days—180 days for development, 60 days for Commissioner action—with an effective date at least 6 months later in most instances. During this period, defective products will be sold at the risk of injury to consumers.

Furthermore, even where standards are eventually promulgated, they have only prospective effect. Thus, those who have been buying defective products until the effective date of the standard are simply out of luck. The standards afford them no remedy whatever.

Nor does section 311 provide an effective remedy in the case of a defective product already on the market. This section provides for emergency power to seek injunctive relief through the courts for products deemed to be "imminently hazardous." These are products for which no safety standards can be fashioned which would adequately protect consumers. These products are by their very nature dangerous.

Moreover, the section presumes that some administrative proceeding is underway at the time of the court action—a presumption that would not be met in the case of a design defect just discovered by the Commissioner of Product Safety.

The importance of the notification and recall provisions of section 313(b) is that they provide a relatively quick, effective mode of action for the Commissioner when he knows that a product already in the hands of consumers is potentially dangerous. Neither the standard setting procedure nor the emergency injunctive remedy if defects relating to design are excluded from its scope.

Mr. MAGNUSON. Mr. President, I have just conferred with my colleague from New Hampshire. I think we can accept the amendment. It clarifies the difference between design and manufacture. Some of it I do not understand but there is a difference in the question of safety. The testimony was to that effect. We accept the amendment.

* * *

The amendments were agreed to en bloc.

The PRESIDING OFFICER. Are there further amendments? If there be no further amendments, the question is on the engrossment and third reading of the bill.

The bill was ordered to be engrossed for a third reading, and was read the third time.

Mr. MAGNUSON. Mr. President, I would like to clarify three matters which have been raised in discussions of the text of S. 3419. They are as follows:

First. Section 306(d) provides that the Commissioner may set a later effective date for a standard beyond the 6 month norm, but that the Commissioner must publish his reasons therefore. It is of course contemplated that, in accordance with the provisions of the Freedom of Information Act, all of the documents upon which the Commissioner has relied in making such determination will be made public.

Second. In regard to section 315(b) which authorizes the Commission to inspect records, in accordance with normal practice it is contemplated that the right to inspect includes the authority to make appropriate copies of such records.

Third. Section 305(4), providing for the maintenance of records of the development of proposed standards requires that "comments and other information submitted by any person in connection with such development" be disclosed. This provision contemplates that any dissenting views submitted to the person or persons developing a proposed standard will be made public in a timely manner.

RADIATION SAFETY

Mr. President, S. 3419 meets the recommendations of the National Product Safety Commission in the key area of electronic product radiation safety by transferring the administration of the Radiation Control for Health and Safety Act from the Food and Drug Administration to the new agency. Under the authority of this consumer protection legislation, over 34,000 products have been repaired at no cost to the purchaser. S. 3419 carefully preserves this effective consumer protection measure and, in the process, avoids duplication of effort. Today, there are over 116 Federal employees—of whom 70 are engineers and physicists—working on radiation hazards to the public from television receivers, microwave ovens, lasers, ultrasonic products, and X-ray equipment. However, as noted by the National Product Safety Commission—

> Legislation for a single hazard often fails to cover other serious hazards. . . . The Radiation Control for Health and Safety Act authorized inspection of television sets for radiation but not for fire hazards.

It is prudent, therefore, that these highly competent and trained persons be permitted to work on the solution of the full range of problems associated with electronic products—whether it be radiation, fire, or electrical shock. Furthermore, over 33,000 square feet of electronic laboratories now exist, and these should also be made available to the new agency. Otherwise, these facilities will have to be duplicated at a cost of over $3 million.

The progress that has been made under the Radiation Control for Health and Safety Act has been almost solely oriented toward product safety: Radiation safety standards for demonstration tubes used in high schools, television receivers, microwave ovens, and medical X-ray equipment. Each of these standards deals specifically with the engineering and physical principles of how the product is to perform. As noted in the June 12 issue of Product Safety Letter—

> Despite the Buck Rogers aura that surrounds lasers, a number of products could move quickly from the R&D stage to the marketplace. Their future depends on radiation limits that will be set by the government.

The new agency to be established by S. 3419 will need expertise in this area, because lasers not only present a potential radiation hazard, but also have potential problems in electrical shock.

It is the full intent of S. 3419 to draw together into one agency the existing Federal authority and expertise which is needed to provide the fullest possible protection to the consumer from hazardous products. We should not place an unneeded burden on a manufacturer to have to report to separate safety agencies on the same products and thus require the Congress to fund two groups when one could do it. Failure to place the administration of the Radiation Control for Health and Safety Act with the new agency proposed by S. 3419 would deny to the agency, and to the consumer, an immediate and demonstrated ability to respond to the complex engineering problems involved in product safety.

* * *

(S. 3419 was passed by a vote of 69-10)

APPENDIX F

TEXT OF BILL AS PASSED BY SENATE

(June 21, 1972)

S. 3419

An act to protect consumers against unreasonable risk of injury from hazardous products, and for other purposes

Be it enacted by the Senate and House of Representatives of the United States of America in Congress assembled, That this Act may be cited as the "Food, Drug, and Consumer Product Safety Act of 1972".

TITLE I—CREATION OF FOOD, DRUG, AND CONSUMER PRODUCT AGENCY

FINDINGS AND DECLARATION OF POLICY

SEC. 101. The Congress hereby finds and declares—

(1) that the regulation of foods, drugs, and consumer products is scattered widely throughout several Federal departments and agencies, and that inconsistent policies and incomplete regulation has resulted from this diffusion of regulatory efforts within the Federal Government;

(2) that effective consumer product regulation requires creation of a new independent agency with the power to take all action necessary to enforce food, drug, and consumer product safety laws, including the power to promulgate regulations, prosecute court actions, and make legislative and budgetary recommendations;

(3) that each year many Americans are needlessly injured in their homes because present Federal law inadequately regulates most consumer products;

(4) that in addition to consolidating present food, drug, and product safety regulation in a new independent regulatory agency, new statutory authority is needed to protect consumers against the hazards of many household products not covered by present Federal safety regulation;

(5) that because intrastate and interstate commerce in consumer products are closely intertwined and directly affect each other, Federal control over intrastate commerce in consumer products is essential to the effective control of the interstate commerce in such products;

(6) that unacceptable numbers of hazardous consumer products now affect interstate commerce, and their increasing number and complexity make it imperative that the Federal Government act promptly to eliminate unnecessary death and injury in the future; and

(7) that the American public has a right to be protected against risk of death or injury from hazardous consumer products when such hazards can reasonably be eliminated or minimized.

DEFINITIONS

SEC. 102. As used in this Act—

(a) "Consumer product" means a product, or a component thereof, produced for or distributed to an individual for his personal use, consumption, or enjoyment in or around a household or residence, a school, in recreation, or otherwise, but, except to the extent provided in section 104(c)(17), it does not include—

(1) tobacco and tobacco products;

(2) products subject to safety regulation under the National Traffic and Motor Vehicle Safety Act of 1966 (15 U.S.C. 1381 et seq.);

(3) aircraft or other aeronautical products subject to safety regulation by the Federal Aviation Administration;

(4) food or drugs as defined in the Federal Food, Drug, and Cosmetic Act (21 U.S.C. 201 et seq.);

(5) products subject to safety regulation under the Federal Insecticide, Fungicide, and Rodenticide Act (7 U.S.C. 135 et seq.);

(6) products subject to safety regulation under the Occupational Safety and Health Act of 1970 (29 U.S.C. 651 et seq.) insofar as such products are regulated for use in employment;

(7) products subject to safety regulation under the Gas Pipeline Safety Act (49 U.S.C. 1671 et seq.);

(8) products subject to safety regulation under authority of the Atomic Energy Act of 1954 (42 U.S.C. 2011 et seq.); and

(9) vessels, appurtenances, and equipment subject to safety regulation under title 52 of the Revised Statutes, as amended, the Federal Boat Safety Act of 1971 (46 U.S.C. 1451 et seq.), or other marine safety statutes administered by the Department in which the Coast Guard is operating.

(b) "Commerce" means commerce among, between, or within the several States.

(c) "Consumer product safety standard" means a minimum standard promulgated under this Act which prevents such product from presenting an unreasonable risk of injury or death.

(d) "Subject to safety regulation" means authorized to be regulated for the purpose of eliminating any unreasonable risk of injury or death, as determined by the Administrator through communication and consultation with appropriate department or agency officials.

(e) "Injury" means harm (including adverse reactions and illness) produced by biologic, chemical, thermal, mechanical, electrical, radiological, or other natural or man-made agents.

(f) "State" means a State of the United States, the District of Columbia, the Commonwealth of Puerto Rico, the Virgin Islands, American Samoa, Guam, Wake Island, Midway Island, Kingman Reef, Johnston Island, the Trust Territory of the Pacific Islands, or the Canal Zone.

(g) "Unreasonable risk of injury presented by a consumer product" means that degree of risk which the Commissioner determines is incompatible with the public health and safety either because the degree of anticipated injury or the frequency of such injury, or both, is unwarranted because—

(A) the degree of anticipated injury or the frequency of such injury can be reduced without affecting the performance or availability of the consumer product, or

(B) the degree of anticipated injury or the frequency of such injury cannot be reduced without affecting the performance or availability of the consumer product but the effect on such performance or availability is justified when measured against the degree of anticipated injury or the frequency of such injury.

(h) "Use" means: (A) exposure to, and (B) normal use or reasonably foreseeable misuse.

(i) "Risk-based analysis" means analysis which (A) identifies hazardous elements, conditions of use, and potential accidents, (B) determines the significance of their potential effect, and (C) provides the bases for limitations on use and design and procedural safety requirements to eliminate, control, or minimize hazards and to promote health and safety.

ESTABLISHMENT OF AGENCY

SEC. 103. There is hereby created an independent Food, Drug, and Consumer Product Agency (hereinafter referred to as the "Agency") whose function it is to promote the public health, safety, and welfare by protecting consumers against adulteration, misbranding, and illegal distribution of food, drugs, devises, and cosmetics, and against injury resulting from the use of consumer products. Within such Agency there shall be established a Commission of Food and Nutrition, a Commission of Drugs, a Commission of Veterinary Medicine, and a Commission of Consumer Products, each to be headed by a Commissioner as provided in section 107 of this Act.

ADMINISTRATOR

SEC. 104. (a) APPOINTMENT.—The President shall appoint, with the advice and consent of the Senate, an Administrator of the Agency.

(b) TERM OF OFFICE.—The Administrator shall serve for a term of five years. He may be reappointed to the position of Administrator only once in succession.

(c) POWERS.—In order to fulfill his duties under this title, the Administrator is empowered to—

(1) direct and coordinate the activities of the Commissions of Food and Nutrition, Drugs, Veterinary Medicine, and Consumer Products;

(2) direct and supervise all personnel of the agency;

(3) employ experts and consultants (including such experts as provided for in section 109 of this title) in accordance with section 3109 of title 5, United States Code, and compensate individuals so employed for each day (including traveltime) at rates not in excess of the maximum rate of pay for grade GS–18 as provided in section 5332 of title 5, United States Code, and, while such experts and consultants are so serving away from their homes or regular place of business, to pay such employees travel expenses and per diem in lieu of subsistence at rates authorized by section 5703 of title 5, United States Code, for persons in Government service employed intermittently;

(4) appoint advisory committees composed of such private citizens and officials of the Federal, State, and local governments as he deems desirable to advise him with respect to his functions under this Act, and to pay such members (other than those regularly employed by the Federal Government) while attending meetings of such committees, or otherwise serving at the request of the Administrator, compensation and travel expenses at the rate provided for in paragraph (3) of this subsection with respect to experts and consultants;

(5) promulgate such regulations as may be necessary to carry out the functions vested in him and for the efficient enforcement of the laws subject to the jurisdiction of the Agency;

(6) issue subpenas to require the attendance and testimony of witnesses and the production of documentary evidence relating to any matter within his statutory authority which is the subject of a public hearing, have access for the purpose of examining and copying any documentary evidence relating to any matter within his statutory authority, and require by general or special orders signed by him the submission of annual or special reports or answers in writing to specific questions containing such data and information relating to any matter within his statutory authority as will enable him to enforce the laws subject to his jurisdiction. The district courts of the United States shall have jurisdiction to enforce such subpenas or general or special orders or to require access to such documentary evidence upon application of the Attorney General or the Administrator. An action for such enforcement may be brought in any district court of the United States for the district wherein the person involved is found or transacts business;

(7) utilize, with their consent, the services, personnel, and facilities of other Federal agencies and of State and private agencies and instrumentalities with or without reimbursement therefor;

(8) enter into and perform such contracts, leases, cooperative agrements, or other transactions as may be necessary in the conduct of the work of the Agency and on such terms as the Administrator may deem appropriate,

with any agency or instrumentality of the United States, or with any State, territory, or possession, or any political subdivision thereof, or with any public or private person, firm, association, corporation, independent testing laboratory, or institution;

(9) accept gifts and voluntary and uncompensated services, notwithstanding the provisions of section 665(b) of title 31, United States Code;

(10) designate representatives to serve or assist on such committees as the Administrator may determine to be necessary to maintain effective liaison with Federal agencies and with State and local agencies and independent standard-setting bodies carrying out programs and activities related to the protection of consumers against injury resulting from the use of foods, drugs, and consumer products;

(11) construct such research or test facilities as may be necessary to carry out the purposes of this Act, (A) after fully utilizing the personnel, facilities, and other technical support available in other Federal agencies, (B) when authorized by the Congress to plan, design, and construct such facilities, and (C) subject to the appropriation of funds for this purpose by the Congress;

(12) conduct public hearings anywhere in the United States to consider the safety of foods, drugs, or consumer products;

(13) prepare and submit, directly to the President for review and transmittal to Congress, an annual budget estimate for the administration and enforcement of the laws subject to his jurisdiction, and receive from the President and Office of Management and Budget directly all funds appropriated by Congress for obligation and expenditure by the Agency;

(14) prescribe personnel policies for the Agency including selecting, appointing, fixing compensation of, hiring, firing, promoting, and transferring of employees without prior approval or clearance, subject to the civil service and classification laws;

(15) submit legislative recommendations and testimony to Congress without prior approval or clearance;

(16) initiate, prosecute, defend, or appeal any court action in the name of the Agency to enforce the laws subject to his jurisdiction, through his own legal representative or through the Attorney General, and direct the course of all litigation involving the Agency;

(17)(A) petition any Federal department or agency which has jurisdiction over products included within the definition of consumer product in section 102(a) but exempt under paragraphs (1)–(9) to establish and enforce appropriate safety regulations for any such product;

(B) participate in the establishment of such regulations; and

(C) upon request of such department or agency, establish and enforce such regulations in accordance with title III of this Act. Upon such request, such product shall be deemed to be a consumer product under section 102(a);

(18) undertake such other activities as are necessary to carry out his duties under this Act, including those enumerated in other sections of this Act; and

(19) delegate any of his functions and duties under this Act, including functions and duties transferred to him pursuant to title II, other than subpena powers, to the Commissioners or other officers or employees of the Agency.

DUTIES OF THE ADMINISTRATOR

SEC. 105. The Administrator shall—

(a) direct and coordinate the activities of the Commissions of Food and Nutrition, Drugs, Veterinary Medicine, and Product Safety;

(b) attempt to secure levels of funding for the Agency that will permit it to carry out its mission on behalf of the public;

(c) establish an Office of Consumer Information in accordance with the provisions of section 109 of this title;

(d) establish a National Injury Information Clearinghouse which shall systematically monitor and report injuries or deaths associated with foods, drugs, and consumer products and identify the agent or agents associated with such injuries or deaths;

(e) establish and supervise the activities of the Joint Scientific Committee;

(f) appoint a General Counsel for the Agency and an Assistant General Counsel for each Commission, to assist him as his legal representative in carrying out his duties under this Act;

(g) enforce the laws which he is required under title II of this Act to administer; and

(h) publish notice of any proposed public hearing in the Federal Register, and afford a reasonable opportunity for interested persons, including consumers, to present relevant testimony and data.

OBLIGATIONS OF AGENCY CONTRACTORS

SEC. 106. (a) MAINTENANCE OF RECORDS.—Each recipient of assistance under this Act pursuant to grants or contracts entered into under other than competitive bidding procedures shall keep such records as the Administrator shall prescribe, including records which fully disclose the amount and disposition by such recipient of the proceeds of such assistance, the total cost of the project undertaken in connection with which such assistance is given or used, and the amount of that portion of the cost of the project or undertaking supplied by other sources, and such other records as will facilitate an effective audit.

(b) ACCESS TO RECORDS.—The Administrator and the Comptroller General of the United States or their duly authorized representatives, shall have access for the purpose of audit and examination to any books, documents, papers, and records of the recipients that are pertinent to the grants or contracts entered into under section 104(c)(8) under other than competitive bidding procedures.

COMMISSIONERS

SEC. 107. (a) APPOINTMENT.—The Administrator shall appoint a Commissioner of Food and Nutrition, a Commissioner of Drugs, a Commissioner of Veterinary Medicine, and a Commissioner of Consumer Products.

(b) POWERS.—In order to fulfill his duties under this title, a Commissioner is empowered to—

(1) undertake such activities as are authorized and necessary to carry out his duties under this title, including those delegated to him by the Administrator and those enumerated in other sections; and

(2) conduct public hearings anywhere in the United States to consider the safety of foods, drugs, or consumer products.

DUTIES OF THE COMMISSIONERS

SEC. 108. Each Commissioner, in cooperation with the other Commissioners and as directed and coordinated by the Administrator, shall—

(1) attempt to eliminate products presenting unreasonable risk of injury;

(2) establish a capability within his Commission to engage in risk-based analysis;

(3) establish an interdisciplinary epidemiology capability and undertaken investigations in coordination with the National Injury Information Clearinghouse to facilitate regulation-making and to assist in risk-based analysis;

(4) establish a scientific capability within the Commission to assist in hazard detection, test method development, and quality control requirements;

(5) utilize where practicable, and establish where necessary, field operations as authorized by the Administrator to facilitate detection of conditions which might lead to injury or death, to monitor compliance with required levels of safety performance, to report violations, and to assist the Administrator in any enforcement action taken by him; and

(6) publish notice of any proposed public hearing in the Federal Register, and afford a reasonable opportunity for interested persons, including consumers, to present relevant testimony and data.

OFFICE OF CONSUMER INFORMATION

SEC. 109. (a) DIRECTOR.—The Administrator shall appoint a Director of the Office of Consumer Information.

(b) DUTIES OF DIRECTOR.—The Director shall—

(1) establish a Consumer Information Center which can respond to written inquires from consumers;

(2) conduct consumer education programs so as to inform the public about certain specified hazards and thereby reduce the risk of those hazards. Such consumer education programs shall not be relied upon by the Administrator or any Commissioner as a substitute for action designed to minimize any hazard unless the Director publishes in the Federal Register a finding that such reliance would sufficiently reduce the risk of such product so that its use would not present an unreasonable risk of injury or death; and

(3) insure public access to information concerning pending or completed actions of the Administrator in accordance with section 114 of this title.

(c) PUBLIC INFORMATION ROOM.—In addition to publishing information in the form and manner best adopted for widespread distribution, information available for public disclosure shall be made available in a "Public Information Room" within the Director's office, equipped with a self-help copying machine, from which the public can make copies at the cost of the production of the copy. The Agency shall charge the public the minimum practicable amount for the search for and production of documents, shall take all reasonable measures to reduce or waive, where appropriate, any charge to persons to whom such charge would be financially burdensome, and in no event shall charge any amount which exceeds the actual cost of such search and production. All funds collected for copying and for search for and production of documents shall be paid to the Administrator and shall be obligated and expended by him to finance the Agency's consumer information program.

(d) The Director shall establish a Consumer Information Library.

NATIONAL INJURY INFORMATION CLEARINGHOUSE

SEC. 110. (a) DIRECTOR.—The Administrator shall appoint a Director of the National Injury Information Clearinghouse.

(b) DUTIES OF DIRECTOR.—The Director shall establish a system of nationwide reporting centers to monitor injury associated with food, drugs, and consumer products, to identify any natural or man-made biologic, chemical, mechanical, electrical, thermal, radiological, or other agents that caused such injury, to describe the way in which such agents came into contact with the victim, and to ascertain the severity of the injury.

(c) POWERS OF DIRECTOR.—(1) The Director may—

(A) obtain injury data from other governmental and nongovernmental sources; and

(B) require manufacturers, importers, processors, distributors, retailers or assemblers of food, drugs, or consumer products, and their insurers, to submit information concerning injuries associated with such food, drugs, and consumer products that have come to their attention in accordance with regulations promulgated by the Administrator, which ensure that such persons providing such information are not compromised in any claim or pending litigation.

(d) LIMITATIONS.—(1) The Director shall not disclose information obtained by him under this section which concerns or relates to a trade secret or other confidential business information, not related to a consumer product in such a way as to indicate the presence of an unreasonable risk of injury or death, described in section 1905 of title 18, United States Code, except that such information may be disclosed—

(A) to other Federal Government departments, agencies, and officials for official use upon request;

(B) to committees of Congress having jurisdiction over the subject matter to which the information relates;

(C) in any judicial proceeding under a court order formulated to preserve the confidentiality of such information without impairing the proceeding;

(D) if relevant in any proceeding under this Act, in a manner designed to preserve confidentiality to the greatest practicable extent; and

(E) to the public in order to protect their health and safety after notice and opportunity for comment in writing or for discussion in closed session within fifteen days by the manufacturer of any product to which the information appertains (if the delay resulting from such notice and opportunity for comment would not be detrimental to the public health and safety).

In no event shall the names or other means of identification of injured persons or person treating them be made public without their express written consent.

(2) Nothing contained in this section shall be deemed to require the release of any information described by subsection (b) of section 522, title 5, United States Code, or which is otherwise protected by law from disclosure to the public.

JOINT SCIENTIFIC COMMITTEE

SEC. 111. (a) DESIGNATION.—After consultation with the Commissioners, the Administrator shall establish and appoint the members of a Joint Scientific Committee which shall be composed of at least one representative of each Commission and chaired by an Associate Administrator for Science appointed by the Administrator.

(b) MEETINGS.—Such Committee shall meet at least once a month.

(c) DUTIES.—

(1) The Associate Administrator and members of the Committee shall insure that there is an exchange of scientific information between the Commissions and shall report to the Administrator on the needs of the scientific personnel in each of the Commission.

(2) The Committee shall advise the Administrator or any of the Commissioners on technical matters and shall make recommendations for the soliciting of expert scientific opinion on particular issues.

AGENCY RESPONSIBILITY

SEC. 112. (a) PETITION OF THE AGENCY.—Any individual or class of individuals who alleges that he or they have been exposed by an act or omission of the Agency to a food, drug, or consumer product presenting an unreasonable risk of injury or death, shall first petition the Agency to take specific action sufficient to eliminate the alleged unreasonable risk of injury or death. After opportunity for interested parties to comment on the petition not to exceed thirty days, the Agency shall determine whether an unreasonable risk of injury or death exists as a result of an act or omission of the Agency and issue a decision either refusing to take any action or taking action designed to eliminate any unreasonable risk of injury or death. The Agency shall make such determination and issue such decision within a reasonable period of time, but in no event more than one hundred and twenty days following the presentation of the petition to the Agency.

(b) CIVIL ACTION AGAINST THE AGENCY.—If the Agency refuses to take any action in response to the petition or if the Agency action taken in response to the petition is regarded by the petitioner or petitioners as insufficient to eliminate the alleged unreasonable risk of injury or death, a petitioner or petitioners may commence a civil action in a United States court of appeals. Any such action shall be filed within sixty days after the decision of the Agency pursuant to subsection (a) to take or refuse to take any action. If a petitioner or petitioners apply to the court to adduce additional evidence and show to the satisfaction of the court that such additional evidence is material and that there were reasonable grounds for the failure of the petitioner or petitioners to adduce such evidence in the proceeding before the Agency the court may order such additional evidence (and evidence in rebuttal thereof) to be taken before the Agency in a hearing or in such other manner, and upon such terms and conditions, as to the court may seem proper.

(c) POWERS OF THE COURT.—(1) If the court finds, based upon a preponderance of the evidence which constitutes the record of the Agency, that the Agency, by an act or omission, has exposed such petitioner or petitioners to a food, drug, or consumer product presenting unreasonable risk of injury or death, the court shall remand the matter to the Agency for appropriate action. The "record of the Agency" means the information upon which the Agency based its decision, including the petition and any information submitted by the petitioner or petitioners and all other information identified in the decision of the Agency as part of the record, and any additional evidence adduced in accordance with procedures established in subsection (b) of this section.

(2) No action pursuant to any section may be filed for the purpose of requiring the Agency to permit the sale, distribution, use, or shipment in commerce of any food, drug, or consumer product, and no award of money damages may be made in any court action pursuant to this section.

(d) COSTS OF PETITION AND CIVIL ACTION.—Costs of the petition and civil action (including reasonable attorney's fees) may be apportioned to the parties as the interests of justice require.

ANNUAL REPORTS

SEC. 113. (a) TIME OF REPORT.—Within one hundred and twenty days following the convening of each regular session of each Congress, the Administrator shall prepare and submit directly to Congress and the President a report on the activities of the Agency and its recommendation for legislative action.

(b) CONTENTS.—Such reports shall contain the following—

(1) budget information containing the budget requests of the President and the Administrator, the budget recommendations of each of the Commissioners, the appropriation of the Congress, and the distribution of appropriated funds for the fiscal year following the year of the report, for the fiscal year of the report, and for the preceding three fiscal years;

(2) a detailed summary of the activities

of the Agency, including but not limited to an account of the activities of the National Injury Information Clearinghouse, the Office of Consumer Information, and the Joint Scientific Committee detailing the number and type of personnel employed and the moneys expended by each;

(3) a detailed summary of the activities of each Commission prepared by its Commissioner which presents information as to its epidemiology efforts, risk-based analysis activities, regulation-making efforts (including a brief description of final regulations promulgated), certification programs, scientific activities (including basic research and test methods development) undertaken by the Commission or by other Government agencies or private persons under contract with the Agency, and its field operations;

(4) a detailed summary of the enforcement activities of the Agency including violations reported to the Administrator by each Commissioner, a summary of the disposition of violations including but not limited to voluntary agreements, seizures, recalls, civil fines, and criminal prosecutions; and

(5) legislative recommendations of each Commissioner, the Administrator, and the Director of the Office of Consumer Information.

PUBLIC ACCESS TO INFORMATION

SEC. 114. (a) AVAILABILITY.—Copies of any communications, documents, reports, or other information received or sent by the Administrator or any Commissioner shall be made available to the public, upon identifiable request, and at reasonable cost, through the Office of Consumer Information unless such information may not be publicly released under the terms of subsection (b) of this section.

(b) (1) LIMITATIONS.—The Administrator, Commissioner, or any officer or employee of the Agency shall not disclose information obtained by him under this section which concerns or relates to a trade secret or other confidential business information, not related to a consumer product in such a way as to indicate the presence of an unreasonable risk of injury or death, described in section 1905 of title 18, United States Code, except that such information may be disclosed—

(A) to other Federal Government departments, agencies, and officials for official use upon request;

(B) to committees of Congress having jurisdiction over the subject matter to which the information relates;

(C) in any judicial proceeding under a court order formulated to preserve the confidentiality of such information without impairing the proceeding,

(D) if relevant in any proceeding under this Act, in a manner designed to preserve confidentiality to the greatest practicable extent; and

(E) to the public in order to protect their health and safety, after notice and opportunity for comment in writing or for discussion in closed session within fifteen days by the manufacturer of any product to which the information appertains (if the delay resulting from such notice and opportunity for comment would not be detrimental to the public health and safety).

In no event shall the names or other means of identification of injured persons or persons treating them be made public without their express written consent.

(2) Nothing contained in this section shall be deemed to require the release of any information described by subsection (b) of section 552, title 5, United States Code, or which is otherwise protected by law from disclosure to the public.

(c) PROCEEDING COMMUNICATIONS—Any communication from a person outside the Agency to the Administrator, the Commissioners, or any other employee of the Agency concerning a matter presently under consideration in a rulemaking or adjudicatory proceeding in the Agency shall be made a part of the public file of that proceeding unless it is a communication entitled to protection under subsection (b) of this section.

COOPERATION OF FEDERAL AGENCIES

SEC. 115. (a) The Administrator is authorized to utilize the resources and facilities of the National Bureau of Standards in the Department of Commerce, with or without reimbursement, for the purpose of developing food, drug, or consumer product safety standards, testing, enforcing compliance or for other purposes related to carrying out the authorities of the Administrator under the Act. The Administrator shall report to the Congress each year on his implementation of this section.

(b) Upon request by the Administrator, each Federal agency is authorized—

(1) to make its services, personnel, and facilities available with or without reimbursement to the greatest practicable extent within its capability to the Agency to assist it in the performance of its functions; and

(2) to furnish to the Agency such information, data, estimates, and statistics, and to allow the Agency access to all information in its possession, as the Administrator may reasonably determine to be necessary for the performance of the functions of the Agency as provided by this Act.

SEPARABILITY

SEC. 116. If any provision of this Act, or the application of such provision to any person or circumstance, shall be held invalid, the remainder of this Act, or the application of such provisions to persons or circumstances other than those as to which it is held invalid, shall not be affected thereby.

AUTHORIZATION OF APPROPRIATIONS

SEC. 117. There are authorized to be appropriated for the purpose of carrying out the provisions of this Act not to exceed $250,000,000 for the fiscal year beginning July 1, 1972, not to exceed $300,000,000 for the fiscal year beginning July 1, 1973, not to exceed $350,000,000 for the fiscal year beginning July 1, 1974, and for succeeding fiscal years only such sums as the Congress may specifically authorize by law. No part of the funds appropriated to carry out this Act may be used to plan, design, or construct any research or test facilities unless specifically authorized by the Congress by other law.

SEC. 118. (a) EXECUTIVE SCHEDULE LEVEL OF ADMINISTRATOR.—Section 5314 of title 5, United States Code, is amended by adding at the end thereof the following new paragraph:

"(59) Administrator, Food, Drug, and Consumer Product Agency."

(b) EXECUTIVE SCHEDULE LEVEL OF COMMISSIONERS.—Section 5315 of title 5, United States Code, is amended by adding at the end thereof the following new paragraphs:

"(96) Commissioners, Food, Drug, and Consumer Product Agency.

"(97) General Counsel, Food, Drug, and Consumer Product Agency."

(c) ADDITIONAL POSITIONS.—Section 5108(c) of title 5, United States Code, is amended by:

(1) striking out the word "and" at the end of paragraph (9);

(2) striking out the period at the end of paragraph (10) and inserting in lieu thereof a semicolon and the word "and"; and

(3) by adding immediately at the end of such subsection the following new paragraph:

"(11) The Administrator of the Food, Drug, and Consumer Product Agency, without regard to this chapter (except section 5114), may place twenty-five positions in the Food, Drug, and Consumer Product Agency in GS-16, 17, and 18 for the purposes of carrying out his responsibilities under the Food, Drug, and Consumer Product Safety Act of 1972.".

EFFECTIVE DATE; INITIAL APPOINTMENT OF OFFICERS

SEC. 119. (a) This Act shall take effect ninety days after the Administrator first takes office, or on such prior date after enactment of this Act as the President shall prescribe and publish in the Federal Register.

(b) Any officers provided for in this Act may (notwithstanding subsection (a)) be appointed in the manner provided for in this Act at any time after the date of enactment of this Act. Such officers shall be compensated from the date they first take office at the rates provided for in this Act. Such compensation and related expenses of their offices shall be paid from funds available for the functions to be transferred to the Agency pursuant to this Act.

TITLE II—TRANSFERS OF FUNCTION

SEC. 201. (a) All functions of the Secretary of Health, Education, and Welfare administered through the Food and Drug Administration are transferred to the Administrator of the Food, Drug, and Consumer Product Agency.

(b) All functions of the Secretary of Health, Education, and Welfare under the Clinical Laboratories Improvement Act of 1967 (42 U.S.C. 263(a)) and under sections 351 and 352 of the Public Health Service Act (42 U.S.C. 262, 263) are transferred to the Administrator of the Food, Drug, and Consumer Product Agency.

(c) All functions of the Secretary of Commerce and the Federal Trade Commission under the Flammable Fabrics Act (15 U.S.C. 1191 et seq.) and under the Act of August 2, 1956 (15 U.S.C. 1211) are transferred to the Administrator of the Food, Drug, and Consumer Product Agency.

(d)(1) All personnel, property, records, obligations, commitments, and unexpended balances of appropriations, allocations, and other funds, which are used primarily with respect to any office, agency, bureau, or function transferred under the provisions of this section are transferred to the Administrator of the Food, Drug, and Consumer Product Agency. The transfer of personnel pursuant to this subsection shall be without reduction in classification or compensation for one year after such transfer, and this provision shall not be construed to impair the authority of the Administrator to assign personnel during this period to carry out the functions of the Agency most effectively.

(e) The Civil Service Commission shall establish criteria, in consultation with the Administrator, when preparing competitive examinations for positions in the Agency.

(2) Any commissioned officer of the Public Health Service who, upon the day before the effective date of this Act, is serving as such officer primarily in the performance of functions transferred by this Act to the Agency or the Administrator may, if such officer so elects, acquire competitive status and be transferred to a competitive position in the Agency subject to paragraph (1) of this subsection, under the terms prescribed in section 15(b)(3)-(8)(A) of the Clean Air Amendments of 1970 (84 Stat. 1676; 42 U.S.C. 215 nt).

SEC. 202. (a) The Administrator shall, insofar as practicable and consistent with sound administration of the laws subject to his jurisdiction, delegate all or part of the authority transferred to him to—

(1) the Commissioner of Food and Nutrition with respect to functions relating to human food, including but not limited to functions under the Federal Food, Drug, and Cosmetic Act (21 U.S.C. 301 et seq.), the Fair Packaging and Labeling Act (15 U.S.C. 1451 et seq.), the Federal Import Milk Act (21 U.S.C. 141 et seq.), the Filled Milk Act (21 U.S.C. 61 et seq.), the Tea Importation Act (21 U.S.C. 41 et seq.), the Federal Caustic Poison Act (44 Stat. 1406), and the provisions relating to pesticides, interstate travel sanitation, milk and food service sanitation, and shellfish sanitation under the Public Health Service Act (42 U.S.C. 241, 243, 246, and 264);

(2) the Commissioner of Drugs with respect to functions relating to human drugs, including but not limited to functions under the Federal Food, Drug, and Cosmetic Act (21 U.S.C. 301 et seq.), the Fair Packaging and Labeling Act (21 U.S.C. 1451 et seq.), the Federal Caustic Poison Act (44 Stat. 1406), sections 351 and 352 of the Public Health Service Act (42 U.S.C. 262, 263), the Clinical Laboratories Improvement Act of 1967 (42 U.S.C. 263a), the Comprehensive Drug Abuse Prevention and Control Act of 1970 (84 Stat 1236);

(3) the Commission of Veterinary Medicine with respect to functions relating to food and drugs for use in animals other than man, including but not limited to functions under the Federal Food, Drug, and Cosmetic

Act (21 U.S.C. 301 et seq.), the Fair Packaging and Labeling Act (21 U.S.C. 1451 et seq.), the Federal Caustic Poison Act (44 Stat. 1406), and the Comprehensive Drug Abuse Prevention and Control Act of 1970 (84 Stat. 1236); and

(4) the Commissioner of Consumer Products with respect to functions relating to other consumer products over which the Administrator has jurisdiction, including but not limited to functions under title III of this Act, the Federal Food, Drug, and Cosmetic Act (21 U.S.C. 301 et seq.), the Fair Packaging and Labeling Act (21 U.S.C. 1451 et seq.), the Federal Hazardous Substances Act (15 U.S.C. 1261 et seq.), the Poison Prevention Packaging Act (15 U.S.C. 1471 et seq), the Radiation Control for Health and Safety Act (42 U.S.C. 263b et seq.), the Federal Caustic Poison Act (44 Stat. 1406), the Flammable Fabrics Act (15 U.S.C. 1191 et seq.), the Act of August 2, 1956 (15 U.S.C. 1211), and the provisions relating to product safety under the Public Health Service Act (42 U.S.C. 241, 244, 246, and 264).

(b) The Administrator shall annually present to Congress as part of his annual report under section 113 a detailed statement of delegation.

SEC. 203. All laws relating to any office, agency, bureau, or function transfered under this Act shall, insofar as such laws are applicable, remain in full force and effect. And orders, rules, regulations, permits, or other privileges made, issued, or granted by any office, agency, or bureau or in connection with any function transferred by this Act, and in effect at the time of the transfer, shall continue in effect to the same extent as if such transfer had not occurred until modified, superseded, or repealed. No suit, action, or other proceeding lawfully commenced by or against any office, agency, or bureau or any officer of the United States acting in his official capacity shall abate by reason of any transfer made pursuant to this Act, but the court, on motion or supplemental petition filed at any time within twelve months after such transfer takes effect, showing a necessity for a survival of such suit, action, or other proceedings to obtain a settlement of the questions involved, may allow the same to be maintained by or against the appropriate office, agency, bureau, or officer of the United States.

TITLE III—CONSUMER PRODUCT SAFETY

COLLECTION AND DISCLOSURE OF INFORMATION ON CONSUMER PRODUCT RISKS

SEC. 301. (a) The Commissioner of Product Safety (hereinafter referred to as the "Commissioner") shall collect, evaluate, and disseminate, on a continuing basis in conjunction with the National Injury Information Clearinghouse, information on the types, frequency, severity, and causes of injury associated with the use of consumer products, and on means to test, measure, or evaluate the risks of such injury. In carrying out his functions under this section the Commissioner in addition to or in aid of the foregoing—

(1) shall collect data or perform research or studies to facilitate the establishment of consumer product safety standards and to evaluate their efficacy in reducing risks associated with consumer products;

(2) shall use interdisciplinary epidemiological teams where appropriate to ascertain the details and causation of injury resulting from the use of a consumer product;

(3) shall plan, conduct, coordinate, or provide technical assistance to research activities, development of methods, training of personnel, or operations, designed to minimize the risks associated with consumer products, or designed to develop means to test, measure, or evaluate such risks;

(4) shall secure information on the risks associated with consumer products from other Federal or State departments and agencies with related interests, professional organizations, industry, or labor associations, and other public or private agencies, organizations, or institutions;

(5) shall make available, through publications and by other appropriate means, the results of, and other information concerning, research and studies relating to the nature and extent of the risks associated with consumer products, and may include recommendations for the reduction of such risks, or information on the means of testing consumer products for risks; and

(6) shall obtain (by negotiation or otherwise) consumer products for research and testing purposes, and sell or otherwise dispose of such products.

(b) The Commissioner is authorized to obtain from any person by subpena, issued pursuant to regulation, information in the form of books, records, or other writings in his possession pertinent to the frequency or causes of death, or the types, frequency, severity, or causes of illness or injury associated with exposure to or use of consumer products. The district courts of the United States shall have jurisdiction to enforce such subpenas upon application of the Attorney General or the Administrator. An action for such enforcement may be brought in any district court of the United States for the district wherein such person is found or transacts business.

(c)(1) The Commissioner shall not disclose information obtained by him under this section which concerns or relates to a trade secret or other confidential business information, not related to a consumer product in such a way as to indicate the presence of an unreasonable risk of injury or death, described in section 1905 of title 18, United States Code, except that such information may be disclosed—

(A) to other Federal Government departments, agencies, and officials for official use upon request;

(B) to committees of Congress having jurisdiction over the subject matter to which the information relates;

(C) in any judicial proceeding under a court order formulated to preserve the confidentiality of such information without impairing the proceeding;

(D) if relevant in any proceeding under this Act; and

(E) to the public in order to protect their health and safety, after notice and opportunity for comment in writing or for discussion in closed session not to within 15 days by the manufacturer of any product to which the information appertains (if the delay resulting from such notice and opportunity for comment would not be detrimental to the public health and safety).

In no event shall the names or other means of identification of injured persons be made public without their express written consent.

(2) Nothing contained in this section shall be deemed to require the release of any information described by subsection (b) of section 552, title 5, United States Code, or which is otherwise protected by law from disclosure to the public.

(d) The Commissioner shall communicate to each manufacturer of a consumer product, insofar as may be practicable, information as to any unreasonable or significant risk to health or safety associated with such product.

(e) Whenever the Commissioner finds, on the basis of information available to him, that exposure to an aspect of the household environment other than a consumer product presents an unreasonable risk of personal injury or death and that a recognized building, electrical, or other code covers that aspect of the household environment, he may recommend to the appropriate code-making authority, and to those authorities responsible for enforcing the code having jurisdiction over that aspect, the code changes he considers warranted to reduce the risk to a reasonable level.

AUTHORITY TO PROMULGATE STANDARDS FOR CONSUMER PRODUCTS

SEC. 302. Whenever the Commissioner finds a need for action to eliminate unreasonable risk of injury or death associated with the use of a consumer product, or any type or class of such products, he may by regulation, in accordance with the requirements of this Act, promulgate for such product, or type or class of such products, a consumer product safety standard or amend any standard previously established. Such standard or amendment to a standard, insofar as practicable, shall be compatible with any environmental standards established for any consumer product by the Federal Government.

INITIATION OF PROCEEDING TO PROMULGATE A CONSUMER PRODUCT SAFETY STANDARD

Notice of Proceeding

SEC. 303. (a) A proceeding to promulgate a consumer product safety standard shall be initiated by the Commissioner by publication in the Federal Register of a notice of proceeding. Such notice shall invite public comment with respect to the initiation of such proceeding and shall include—

(1) a description or other appropriate designation of the consumer product or type or class of such products with respect to which the proceeding is initiated;

(2) the risk or risks intended to be controlled;

(3) a summary description of the information upon which the Commissioner has found a need to initiate the proceeding, and the manner, consistent with subsection (c) of section 301, in which interested persons may examine such information;

(4) information with respect to any existing standard known to the Commissioner which may be relevant to the proceeding; and

(5) an invitation for any person, including any Federal agency, within thirty days after the date of publication of the notice—

(A) to submit information challenging the need to control any risk or risks presented by the consumer product, or type or class of such products, with respect to which the proceeding is initiated;

(B) to submit to the Commissioner an existing standard as such proposed consumer product safety standard; or

(C) to offer to develop such proposed consumer product safety standard in accordance with regulations of the Commissioner prescribing procedures for such development.

Petititon by Interested Party

(b) Any consumer or other interested party may petition the Commissioner to commence a proceeding for the issuance, amendment, or revocation of a consumer product safety standard or other action. Such petition shall set forth with particularity the reasons for such petition. The Commissioner shall publish petitions in the Federal Register and allow opportunity for comment. If the Commissioner denies such petition he shall publish his reasons for such denial.

Decision To Proceed

(c) If the Commissioner determines, after receiving and evaluating any information to the contrary, that there exists a need to control a risk or risks presented by the designated consumer product, or type or class of such products with respect to which the proceeding to promulgate a consumer product safety standard was initiated, then he shall proceed toward the publishing of a proposed consumer product safety standard.

Use of Existing Standard

(d) If the Commissioner—

(1) finds that there exists a standard which has been published by any Federal agency or other qualified agency, organization, or institution;

(2) has made reference to such standard (unless it is a standard submitted pursuant to section 303(a)(5)(B)) in his notice pursuant to subsection (a)(4); and

(3) determines that such standard may be acceptable to him as a consumer product safety standard, then he may, in lieu of accepting an offer pursuant to this section, publish such standard as a proposed consumer product safety standard pursuant to section 306.

Acceptance of Offers To Develop Proposed Consumer Product Safety Standards

(e)(1) Except as provided by subsection (b), the Commissioner may accept one, or more than one, offer to develop a proposed consumer product safety standard pursuant to the invitation prescribed by subsection (a)(5)(C), upon his determination that—

(A) the offeror is technically competent and is likely to develop an appropriate standard within one hundred and fifty days of the notice of proceeding or such longer period of time not to exceed three hundred and sixty days from the date of such notice;

(B) the offeror has the capacity to comply with regulations of the Commissioner prescribed pursuant to section 305; and

(C) the offeror, including any person assisting the offeror in the development of the proposal, is not a manufacturer, distributor or retailer or the employee of a manufacturer, distributor or retailer of a consumer product proposed to be included in the consumer product safety standard to which the offer applies.

The Commissioner shall publish in the Federal Register the name and address of each person whose offer he accepts, and a summary of the terms of such offer as accepted.

(2) Upon an offeror's application therefor prior to the acceptance of his offer under this subsection, the Commissioner may agree to contribute to the offeror's cost in developing a proposed consumer product safety standard, if the Commissioner determines that such contribution is likely to result in a more satisfactory standard than would be developed without such contribution, and that the offeror is financially responsible. Regulations of the Commissioner shall set forth the items of cost in which he may participate, and shall exclude any contribution to the acquisition of land or buildings.

DEVELOPMENT OF A PROPOSED CONSUMER PRODUCT SAFETY STANDARD BY THE COMMISSIONER

SEC. 304. If the Commissioner has published a notice of proceeding as provided by section 303(a), and he has not accepted an existing standard pursuant to section 303(d) then the Commissioner shall proceed to develop a proposed consumer product safety standard whether or not he has accepted offers to develop a proposed standard if he has determined that his own development will be of benefit to the public.

REGULATIONS GOVERNING DEVELOPMENT OF STANDARDS

SEC. 305. The Commissioner shall prescribe regulations governing the development of proposed consumer product safety standards under sections 303 and 304 of this Act, which regulations shall not be considered rules of agency organization, procedure, or practice for purposes of section 553 of title 5, United States Code. Such regulations shall include requirements—

(1) that standards recommended for promulgation be supported by test data or such other documents or materials as the Commissioner may reasonably require to be developed, and be suitable for promulgation pursuant to section 306;

(2) that standards recommended for promulgation contain such test methods as may be appropriate for measurement of compliance with such standards;

(3) that the offeror, where the Commissioner has accepted an offer or offers under section 303, provide opportunity for all interested persons including consumers to participate in the offeror's development of a proposed consumer safety standard in accordance with accepted standards of due process, including adequate notice to all participants and access to all relevant records and documents;

(4) for the maintenance of such records as the Commissioner prescribes in such regulations to disclose the course of the development of standards recommended for promulgation, the comments and other information submitted by any person in connection with such development, including comments and information with respect to the need for such recommended standards, and such other matters as may be relevant to the evaluation of such recommended standards; and

(5) that the Commissioner, the Administrator, and the Comptroller General of the United States, or any of their duly authorized representatives, have access for the purpose of audit and examination to any books, documents, papers, and records, relevant to the expenditure of any contribution of the Commissioner, pursuant to section 303(e), to the development of such recommended standards.

PROMULGATION OF CONSUMER PRODUCT SAFETY STANDARDS; DECLARATION OF BANNED HAZARDOUS CONSUMER PRODUCT

Proposal To Promulgate Consumer Product Safety Standard or To Declare a Banned Hazardous Consumer Product

SEC. 306. (a)(1) Not more than one hundred and eighty days after his publication of a notice of proceeding pursuant to subsection (a) of section 303 (which time may be extended by the Commissioner by a notice published in the Federal Register stating good cause therefor), the Commissioner shall publish in the Federal Register either a notice withdrawing such prior notice or a proposal to promulgate a consumer product safety standard applicable to any consumer product subject to such notice, or a proposal to declare any such subject product a banned hazardous consumer product. A proposal to promulgate a consumer product safety standard and a proposal to declare a product a banned hazardous consumer product may be published in the alternative with respect to any consumer product subject to such notice.

(2) A proposal to promulgate a consumer product safety standard shall contain only one such proposed standard formulated by the Commissioner on the basis of the proposed standard developed by an offeror under section 303(e) of this title or by the Commissioner, or both.

(3) A proposal to promulgate a consumer product safety standard, or to declare a product a banned hazardous consumer product, shall set forth such proposed standard, or the reason for such declaration, the manner in which interested persons may examine data and other information upon which such proposed standard or declaration, or need therefor, is based (consistent with subsection (c) of section 301), and the period within which all interested persons may present their comments on such standard or

declaration, or the need therefor, orally or in writing.

Disputes of Fact

(b) The Commissioner may conduct a hearing in accordance with such conditions or limitations as he may make applicable thereto, for the purpose of resolving any issue of material fact raised by any person when presenting comments in accordance with paragraph (3) of subsection (a) of this section.

Findings

(c)(1) Prior to his issuance of an order to promulgate a consumer product safety standard pursuant to subsection (d) or to declare a product a banned hazardous consumer product pursuant to subsection (f), the Commissioner shall consider, and shall make appropriate findings for inclusion in such order with respect to—

(A) data and comments submitted in the course of any proceeding under section 303 relevant to such order;

(B) the types, frequency, severity, and causes of injury that may be attributed to those aspects of the consumer products subject to such order;

(C) the approximate number of consumer products, or types or classes thereof, subject to such order;

(D) the need of the public for the consumer products subject to such order; and the probable effect of such order upon the utility, cost, or availability of such products to meet such need; and

(E) any means of achieving the objective of the order while minimizing adverse effects on competition or disruption or dislocation of manufacturing and other commercial practices consistent with the public health and safety.

(2) The Commissioner shall include in any order promulgating a consumer product safety standard or banning a hazardous consumer product, a determination that his findings pursuant to paragraph (1), upon which such order shall be based, show that such standard or declaration is reasonably necessary to carry out the purposes for which such standard or declaration is authorized.

Order To Promulgate Consumer Product Safety Standard or To Declare a Banned Hazardous Consumer Product

(d) Within sixty days after the publication of a proposal to promulgate a consumer product safety standard, or to declare a consumer product a banned hazardous consumer product, the Commissioner shall, by order published in the Federal Register, act upon such proposed standard or declaration, or withdraw the applicable notice of proceeding. The order shall set forth the consumer product safety standard or declaration, if any, the reasons for the Commissioner's action (including reasons for the promulgation of a consumer product safety standard materially different than that set forth in the proposal or for his failure to promulgate any standard), and the date or dates upon which such standard or declaration, or portions thereof, shall become effective. If such effective date is later than six months after publication of an order setting forth a consumer product safety standard, the Commissioner shall publish his reasons therefor.

Characteristics of Consumer Product Safety Standards

(e)(1) Consumer product safety standards shall, where feasible, pertain to the safety performance characteristics (including safe packaging characteristics) of a consumer product, or type or class of such products, and shall to the extent practicable set forth test procedures (including instrumentation) capable of producing reproducible results to measure such performance characteristics, except that any such standard may apply to the composition, design, construction, or finish of a consumer product (or any component thereof), or type or class of such products, if the Commissioner determines that it is not feasible to protect the public health or safety by development of a consumer product safety standard pertaining to safety performance characteristics or any other consumer product safety standard authorized by this subsection.

(2) A consumer product safety standard may require that a consumer product (or any component thereof), or type or class of such products, (1) be marked, tagged, or accompanied by clear and adequate warnings or instructions, or (2) be subject to safety precautions related to physical distribution, as may be reasonably necessary for the protection of the public health or safety.

Ban of Product

(f)(1) The Commissioner may declare a consumer product to be a "banned hazardous consumer product", in accordance with the procedures of this section, only upon his finding, to be included in the Commissioner's order pursuant to subsection (d), that no feasible consumer product safety standard will adequately protect the public from unreasonable risk of injury or death presented by such product. A firearm or ammunition may not be declared a banned hazardous consumer product.

(2) Any banned hazardous consumer product sold after the date on which notice was published of the proposal to declare such product a banned hazardous consumer product shall, in accordance with regulations promulgated by the Administrator, be repurchased as follows:

(A) The manufacturer of any such consumer product shall repurchase it from the person to whom he sold it, and shall—

(i) refund that person the purchase price paid for such consumer product, upon tender of the product, less a reasonable allowance for use if such product has been in the possession of the consumer for one year or more at the time of such tender,

(ii) except as provided in subsection (g), if that person has repurchased such consumer product pursuant to subparagraph (B) or (C), reimburse him for any amounts paid in accordance with that paragraph for the return of such consumer product, and

(iii) if the manufacturer requires the return of such consumer product in connection with his repurchase of it in accordance with this subparagraph, reimburse that person for any reasonable and necessary expenses incurred in returning it to the manufacturer.

(B) The distributor of any such consumer product shall repurchase it from the person to whom he sold it, and shall—

(i) refund that person the purchase price paid for such consumer product, upon tender of the product, less a reasonable allowance for ues if such product has been in the possession of the consumer for one year or more at the time of such tender.

(ii) except as provided in subsection g, if that person has repurchased such consumer product pursuant to subparagraph (C), reimburse him for any amounts paid in accordance with the subparagraph for the return of such consumer product in connection with its repurchase, and

(iii) if the distributor requires the return of such consumer product in connection with his repurchase of it in accordance with this subparagraph, reimburse that person for any reasonable and necessary expenses incurred in returning it to the distributor.

(C) In the case of any such consumer product sold at retail by a dealer, if the person who purchased it from the dealer or a subsequent owner returns it to him, the dealer shall refund that person the purchase price upon tender of such product, less a reasonable allowance for use if such product has been in the possession of the consumer for one year or more at the time of such tender and reimburse him for any reasonable and necessary transportation charges incurred in its return.

Notice by Manufacturer or Distributor

(g) If any manufacturer of a product which has been declared a banned hazardous consumer product under this Act furnishes notice by registered mail to a distributor or retail dealer of that product, his liability to reimburse that distributor or retail dealer under subsection (f) (2) (A) (ii) of this section with respect to the refunded purchase price of any such product sold by that distributor or retail dealer after the day on which he receives notice shall be limited to the price paid for the product by that distributor or retail dealer. If any distributor of such a product furnishes notice by registered mail to a retail dealer of that product, his liability to reimburse that retail dealer under subsection (f) (2) (B) (ii) of this section with respect to the refunded purchase price of any such product sold by that retail dealer after the day on which he receives notice shall be limited to the price paid for the product by that retail dealer.

SAFETY ANALYSIS STUDY

SEC. 307. In order to insure that a manufacturer gives adequate consideration to the safety aspects of a consumer product, so as to prevent an unreasonable risk of injury or death from such consumer product, the Commissioner, where applicable, may require by regulation that a consumer product (or component thereof), or type or class of consumer products, be subjected to a detailed safety analysis, if such consumer product is not subject to a consumer product safety standard under this Act. Such safety analysis shall be conducted in conformity with criteria set forth in such regulations promulgated by the Commissioner and may be conducted by the manufacturer, an independent testing laboratory, or any other person who the Commissioner may designate. If such consumer product is later subject to a proceeding under section 303 of this Act, then the Commissioner may take into consideration such safety analysis when considering the need for a consumer product safety standard on such consumer product. The Commissioner may demand of the manufacturer a copy of any required safety analysis report.

REVOCATION OR AMENDMENT OF STANDARD

SEC. 308. (a) The Commissioner may revoke, in whole or in part, any consumer product safety standard, upon the ground that there no longer exists a need therefor or that such standard is no longer in the public interest. Such revocation shall be published as a proposal in the Federal Register and shall set forth such standard or portion thereof to be revoked, a summary of the reasons for his determination that there may no longer be a need therefor or that such standard (or any part thereof) may no longer be in the public interest, the manner (consistent with subsection (c) of section 301) in which interested persons may examine data and other information relevant to the Commissioner's determination, and the period within which all interested persons may present their views, orally or in writing, with respect to such revocation. As soon as practicable thereafter, the Commissioner shall by order act upon such proposal and shall publish such order in the Federal Register. The order shall include the reasons for the Commissioner's action, and the date or dates upon which such revocation shall become effective.

(b) The requirements of sections 303, 304, 305, and 306 of this title for the promulgation of a consumer product safety standard shall apply to the promulgation of a material amendment of a consumer product safety standard. The Commissioner may promulgate an amendment of a consumer product safety standard, other than a material amendment, without regard to section 303, 304, or 305, but shall comply with the procedures set forth in subsections (a) and (b) of section 306, and shall set forth, in his order promulgating such amendment, such findings as he may deem appropriate in explanation thereof. As used in this subsection, the term "material amendment" means an amendment that would substantially increase any performance standard applicable to a consumer product, or substantially after the composition, design, finish, or packaging of such product.

COMPLIANCE

SEC. 309. (a) QUALITY CONTROL PROCEDURES.—Whenever the Commissioner has good cause to believe that a particular manufacturer is producing a consumer product with a significant incidence of noncompliance with a particular consumer product safety standard—

(1) he may require such manufacturer to submit to the Commissioner a description

of the relevant quality control procedures followed in the manufacture of such product; and

(2) if the Commissioner thereafter determines that such noncompliance is attributable to the inadequacy of the manufacturer's control procedures, he may, after notice and opportunity for hearing pursuant to section 554 of title 5, United States Code, order the manufacturer to revise such quality control procedures to the extent necessary to remedy such inadequacy.

(b) NAMES OF FIRST PURCHASERS.—(1) The Commissioner may establish, by order at any time, procedures to be followed by manufacturers or importers, including procedures to be followed by distributors, dealers and consumers to assist manufacturers or importers in securing and maintaining the names and addresses of the first purchasers (other than dealers or distributors) of consumer products for which consumer product safety standards have been promulgated. Such procedures shall be reasonable for the particular type or class of consumer products for which they are prescribed.

(2) In determining whether to require the maintenance of the names and addresses of the first purchasers, the Commissioner shall consider—

(A) the severity of the injury that could result if a consumer product were not manufactured in compliance with an applicable consumer product safety standard;

(B) the likelihood that a particular type or class of consumer products would be manufactured not in compliance with an applicable consumer product safety standard; and

(C) the burden imposed upon the manufacturer or importer by requiring the maintenance of the names and addresses of the first purchasers (including the cost to consumers of such maintenance).

(c) COMPLIANCE TESTING.—(1) The Commissioner shall conduct or contract pursuant to section 104(c)(8) for compliance testing of consumer products subject to consumer product safety standards in order to insure that such products are in compliance with applicable consumer product safety standards pursuant to regulations promulgated in accordance with section 553 of title 5, United States Code.

(2)(A) Any person who manufactures or imports a consumer product for which a consumer product safety standard is in effect shall furnish a reasonable number of such products without cost to the Commissioner upon request. Consumer products furnished to the Commissioner under this subsection shall be drawn from regular production runs of such product.

(B) Upon the completion of any compliance testing, the Commissioner shall return or cause to be returned the consumer product in compliance with any applicable consumer product safety standard to the manufacturer or importer from whom he obtained it, and such manufacturer or importer, in any subsequent sale or lease of such product, shall disclose that it has been subjected to compliance testing and shall indicate the extent of damage, if any, prior to repair.

(d) CERTIFICATION.—Any manufacturer, importer, or distributor of a consumer product subject to a consumer product safety standard shall furnish to the distributor or dealer at the time of delivery of such consumer product certification

(a) by said manufacturer, or importer, or distributor; or

(b) by an independent testing laboratory qualified to perform such tests or testing program,

that each such consumer product conforms to all applicable consumer product safety standards. Any certification under this subsection shall be based upon test procedures in conformance with subsection 306(e)(1) or, where no procedures are prescribed, upon a reasonable testing program approved by the Commissioner.

JUDICIAL REVIEW

SEC. 310. (a) Any interested person affected by a final order or regulation of the Commissioner promulgated pursuant to sections 305, 306(d), 307, 308, or 309 may, at any time after such order is published by the Commissioner, file a petition with the United States Court of Appeals for the District of Columbia, or any circuit in which such person resides or has his principal place of business for a judicial review of such order. Copies of the petition shall be forthwith transmitted by the clerk of the court to the Commissioner or other officer designated by him for that purpose and to the Administrator. The Commissioner shall transmit to the Administrator, who shall file in the court, the record of the proceedings on which the Commissioner based his order, as provided in section 2112 of title 28, United States Code. Such record shall include such order of the Commissioner and, if issued, held, or obtained in connection therewith, the notice of proceeding published pursuant to subsetcion (a) of section 303; any notice or proposal published pursuant to sections 350, 306(a), 307, 308, or 309; the transcript or summary of any proceedings and the findings arising therefrom; and any other information, including comments of interested persons, required to be considered by the Commissioner in the promulgation of such order.

(b) Upon the filing of the petition under subsection (a) of this section the court shall have jurisdiction to review the order of the Commissioner in accordance wtih chapter 7 of title 5, United States Code, and to grant appropriate relief, including interim relief, as provided in such chapter. The order of the Commissioner shall be affirmed if supported by substantial evidence on the record taken as a whole.

(c) The judgment of the court affirming or setting aside, in whole or in part, any order of the Comimssioner shall be final, subject to review by the Supreme Court of the United States upon certiorari or certification, as provided in section 1254 of title 28, United States Code.

(d)(1) Any manufacturer of a product declared a banned hazardous consumer product under this Act, who seeks judicial review under this section, may be awarded at the discretion of the court, damages, interest, and the cost of suit, including reasonable attorney fees, for actual damages suffered by him due to any order of the Commissioner declaring a product to be a banned hazardous substance determined by the court to constitute an abuse of the discretion granted to the Commissioner under this Act.

(2) The Secretary of the Treasury is authorized and directed to pay, out of any money in the Treasury not otherwise appropriated the amount of damages, interest, and costs awarded by the court under paragraph (1).

EMERGENCY ACTION

SEC. 311. (a) The Administrator or the Attorney General may file, in a district court of the United States having venue thereof, an action against a consumer product to have such product described an imminently hazardous consumer product, or against any person who manufactures for sale, sells, or offers for sale, in commerce, or imports into the United States, such product. Such an action may be filed, notwithstanding the existence of a consumer product safety standard applicable to such product, or the pendency of proceedings initiated pursuant to section 303. As used in this section, and hereinafter in this Act, the term "imminently hazardous consumer product" means a consumer product presenting an unreasonable risk of injury or death which requires action to protect adequately the public health and safety prior to the completion of administrative proceedings held pursuant to this Act.

(b) The district court in which such action is filed shall have jurisdiction to declare such product an imminently hazardous consumer product, and to grant (as ancillary to such declaration or in lieu thereof) such temporary or permanent equitable relief as may be necessary to protect the public from such risk. Such relief may include a mandatory order requiring the notification of the first purchasers of such product of such risk, public notice, the recall, the repurchase, the repair, the replacement, or the seizure of such product.

(c) Concurrently with the declaration of an imminent hazard, the Commissioner shall initiate a proceeding, pursuant to section 303, to promulgate a consumer product safety standard applicable, to the consumer product with respect to which such declaration is made, or, if the initiation of such proceeding is not feasible, shall initiate a proceeding, pursuant to section 306, to declare such product a banned haazrdous consumer product.

STOCKPILING

SEC. 312. Between the time a final order establishing a consumer product safety standard is issued and the time such order becomes effective, no manufacturer or importer, in an effort to stockpile that consumer product, shall produce or import such product in quantities significantly greater than quantities he had produced for a base period establihed by the Commissioner prior to the promulgation of a final order establishing a consumer product safety standard.

NOTIFICATION OF FAILURE TO COMPLY; REPAIR OR REPLACEMENT OF NONCOMPLYING CONSUMER PRODUCT

SEC. 313. (a) Every manufacturer, importer, or distributor of, or dealer in, a consumer product who discovers that such product has a defect which relates to the safety of use of such product or that such product fails to comply with an applicable consumer safety standard shall immediately notify the Commissioner of such defect or failure to comply if such product has left the place of manufacture. The notification required by this subsection shall contain (1) a clear description of such defect or failure to comply with an applicable consumer product safety standard, (2) an evaluation of the hazard reasonable related to such defect or failure to comply, and (3) a statement of the measures to be taken to effect repair to such defect or failure to comply.

(b) If any consumer product fails to comply with any applicable order issued pursuant to this title and thereby presents an unreasonable risk of injury or death or has a defect which causes it to present an unreasonable risk of injury or death, the manufacturer, importer, or distributor of, or dealer in, such product may be required by the Administrator (by order after opportunity for hearing pursuant to the provisions of section 554 of title 5, United States Code) to give public notice (including notice through electronic media when necessary to protect the public health and safety) and—

(1) to mail to each consumer of such product known to such manufacturer, importer, distributor, or dealer, and, in the case of a manufacturer or importer, to each distributor or dealer to whom he delivered such product, a notification of such failure containing such information as the Administrator may prescribe, upon the Administrator's determination that such notification is required in order adequately to protect the public health or safety,

(2) to bring such product into conformity with the requirements of such order without charge to the consumer, or

(3) to either replace such product with a like or equivalent consumer product which complies with such order without charge to the consumer or to refund the purchase price of such product upon its tender, whichever option is elected by the manufacturer, importer, distributor, or dealer whose product fails to comply. If an election is made to refund the purchase price, the price shall be less a reasonable allowance for use, if such product has been in the possession of the consumer for more than one year at the time of tender.

The manufacturer, importer, distributor, or dealer against whom an order is issued under this subsection shall reimburse each consumer of the product which is the subject of such order for any reasonable and foreseeable expenses (including transportation expenses) incurred by such consumer in availing himself of the remedies provided by such order.

INSPECTION AND RECORDKEEPING

SEC. 314. (a) For purposes of carrying out regulations, standards, or orders promulgated under this Act, officers or employees duly designated by the Commissioner, upon presenting appropriate credentials and a written notice to the owner, operator, or agent in charge, are authorized—

(1) to enter, at reasonable times, any factory, warehouse, or establishment in which consumer products are manufactured, assembled, or held for introduction into commerce or are held for sale after such introduction; or to enter any vehicle being used to transport consumer products in interstate commerce; and

(2) to inspect, at reasonable times and in a reasonable manner, those areas of such factory, warehouse, establishment, or vehicle where or in which such products are produced, stored, or transported, and all pertinent equipment, materials, containers, and labeling therein.

A separate written notice shall be given for each inspection, but a notice shall not be required for each entry made during the period of inspection set forth in such notice. Each such inspection shall be completed with reasonable promptness. If the officer or employee who makes such inspection obtains any sample in the course thereof, he shall, prior to leaving the premises, give to the owner, operator, or agent in charge, a receipt therefor describing such sample.

(b) Every person who manufactures, assembles, distributes, or sells in commerce, or imports, a consumer product required to conform to a consumer product safety standard shall establish and maintain such records, and make such reports, and provide such information as the Commissioner may by regulation reasonably require with respect to the safety of such product. Upon request of an officer or employee duly designated by the Comimssioner every such person shall permit the inspection of such records and other books, records, and papers relevant to determining whether such person is in compliance with this Act and regulations, standards, and orders prescribed thereunder.

(c) The district courts of the United States shall have jurisdiction to issue any warrant in aid of an inspection or investigation under this section, if such warrant is required by the Constitution or laws of the United States, upon a finding that such inspection or investigation is for the purpose of enforcing this Act.

PROHIBITED ACTS

SEC. 315. It shall be unlawful for any person engaged in the business of making consumer products available to consumers, either directly or indirectly, to—

(1) (A) manufacture for sale or lease, in commerce, any consumer product which does not comply with a consumer product safety standard; (B) sell or lease, or offer for sale or lease, in commerce, and consumer product which does not comply with a consumer product safety standard (i) if such product was manufactured or assembled in the United States after the effective date of such standard, or (ii) if such product was imported into the United States in violation of clause (C); (C) import into the United States any consumer product which does not comply with a consumer product safety standard; or (D) manufacture for sale or lease, sell or lease, or offer for sale or lease, in commerce, or import into the United States, any consumer product which has been declared a banned or imminently hazardous consumer product;

(2) fail or refuse to comply with any order of the Commissioner pursuant to section 313;

(3) fail or refuse to comply with any requirement of sections 309, 312, and 314;

(4) alter, modify, destroy, or remove any portion of, or do any other act with respect to, a consumer product or labeling thereon or attached thereto, if such act is done while such product is being held or transported for sale, and results in the consumer product or its labeling failing to conform to a consumer product safety standard, or renders the product a banned or immanently hazardous consumer product;

(5) fail to provide to the Director of the National Injury Information Clearinghouse the information concerning injuries as required in section 109(c)(1)(B); or

(6) fail to provide, pursuant to section 307, any required safety analysis.

ENFORCEMENT

Civil and Criminal Penalties

SEC. 316. (a) Whoever knowingly commits any act prohibited by section 315, or, in case of commission of any such act by a corporation, the corporation and any individual director, officer, or agent of such corporation who knowingly caused in whole or in part the corporation to commit such act, shall be subject to a civil penalty of not more than $10,000 for each such act which shall accrue to the United States and may be recovered in a civil action brought by the United States or the Agency in its own name by any of its attorneys designated by the Administrator for such purpose, and, if such act was willfully committed, shall be guilty of a misdemeanor and, upon conviction, fined not more than $10,000 for each such act or imprisoned not more than one year or both. As used in this subsection, the term "knowingly" means (1) the having of actual knowledge, or (2) the presumed having of knowledge deemed to be possessed by a reasonable man who acts in the circumstances, including (A) knowledge obtainable upon the exercise of due care to ascertain the truth of representations, and (B) knowledge of the probable consequences of action taken in disregard of reasonable safeguards.

Injunctions

(b) Upon application by the Administrator or the Attorney General, the district courts of the United States shall have jurisdiction to enjoin the commission of acts prohibited by section 315, and to compel the taking of any action required by this Act.

Seizure

(c) Any consumer product which is not manufactured in compliance with an applicable consumer product safety standard, or which is not in compliance with such a standard as the result of an action made unlawful by clause (4) of section 315, or which is declared a banned or imminently hazardous consumer product, shall be liable to be proceeded against while in commerce or at any time thereafter, on complaint for forfeiture by the Administrator, and condemned in any district court of the United States within whose district the consumer product is found.

Private Suits

(d) (1) Any person who may be exposed to unreasonable risk of injury or death presented by a consumer product may bring an action in any district court for the district in which the defendant is found or transacts business to enforce a consumer product safety standard, or to enforce any order under subsection (f) of section 306, or under section 311, and to obtain appropriate injunctive relief. Not less than thirty days prior to the commencement of such action, such interested person shall give notice by registered mail to the Commissioner, to the Administrator, and to the person against whom such action is directed. Such notice shall state the nature of the alleged violation of any such standard or order, the relief to be requested, and the court in which the action will be brought. No separate suit shall be brought under this subsection if the same alleged violation is the subject of a pending action by the United States under this title. In any action under this section, such interested person may elect, by a demand for such relief in his complaint, to recover reasonable attorney's fees, in which case the court shall award reasonable attorney's fees to the prevailing party.

(2) Any person who shall sustain injury by reason of any knowing (including willful) violation of a consumer product safety standard, regulation, or order issued by the Commissioner may sue therefor in any district court of the United States in the district in which the defendant resides or is found or has an agent, subject to the provisions of section 1331 of title 28, United States Code, and shall recover damages sustained, and the cost of suit, including a reasonable attorney's fee, if considered appropriate in the discretion of the court.

(e) The remedies provided for in this section shall be in addition to and not in substitution for any other remedies provided by law.

IMPORTS

SEC. 317. (a) Any consumer product imported into the United States to which a consumer product safety standard applies (except insofar as the Commissioner may otherwise provide with respect to a consumer product accompanied by a certification of compliance with such standard in a form prescribed by the Commissioner) or which is declared a banned or imminently hazardous consumer product, shall not be delivered from Customs custody except as provided in section 499 of the Tariff Act of 1930. In the event an imported consumer product is delivered from Customs custody under bond, as provided in section 499 of the Tariff Act of 1930, and is declared a banned or imminently hazardous consumer product or fails to conform with a consumer product safety standard in effect on the date of entry of such merchandise, the Administrator shall so inform the Secretary of the Treasury, and unless it appears to the Administrator that the product can be brought into compliance with all applicable requirements under this title shall request the Secretary of the Treasury to demand redelivery. Upon a failure to redeliver, the Secretary of the Treasury shall assert a claim for liquidated damages for breach of a condition of the bond arising out of such failure to conform or redeliver in accordance with regulations prescribed by the Secretary of the Treasury or his delegate. When asserting a claim for liquidated damages against an importer for failure to redeliver such nonconforming goods, the liquidated damages shall not be less than 10 per centum of the value of the nonconforming merchandise if, within five years prior thereto, the importer has previously been assessed liquidated damages for failure to redeliver nonconforming goods in response to a demand from the Secretary of the Treasury as set forth above.

(b) If it appears to the Administrator that the consumer product can be brought into compliance with all applicable requirements under this title, final determination as to admission of such consumer product may be deferred and, upon filing of timely written application by the owner or consignee and the execution by him of a bond as provided in the preceding provisions of this section, the Administrator may, in accordance with regulations, authorize the applicant to perform such action specified in such authorization (including destruction or export of rejected consumer products or portions thereof, as may be specified in such authorization). All such action pursuant to such authorization shall, in accordance with regulations, be under the supervision of an officer or employee of the Agency or of the Department of the Treasury.

(c) The Secretary of the Treasury shall obtain without charge and deliver to the Commissioner, upon his request, a reasonable number of samples of consumer products being offered for import. The owner or consignee of any such product may have a hearing before the Administrator with respect to admission of such imports into the United States. If, except as provided by subsection (b), it appears from examination or testing of such samples or otherwise that a product fails to comply with the requirements of this Act, such product shall be refused admission, and the Secretary of the Treasury shall cause destruction of such product unless it is exported, under regulations prescribed by the Secretary of the Treasury, within ninety days after notice to the importer or consignee.

(d) All expenses (including travel, per diem or subsistence, and salaries of officers or employees of the United States) in connection with the destruction provided for in this section, the amount of such expenses to be determined in accordance with regulations of the Secretary of the Treasury, and all expenses in connection with the storage, cartage, or labor with respect to any consumer product refused admission under this section, shall be paid by the owner or consignee and, in default of such payment, shall constitute a lien against any future importations made by such owner or consignee.

EXPORTS

SEC. 318. This title shall not apply to any consumer product manufactured, sold, or held for sale for export from the United States (or to any consumer product imported for export), if such consumer product, and any container in which it is enclosed, bears a stamp or label stating that such consumer product is intended for export and such consumer product is in fact exported from the United States; except that this title shall apply to any consumer product manufactured for sale, offered for sale, or sold for shipment to any installation of the United States located outside of the United States.

EFFECT ON STATE LAW

SEC. 319. (a) No State or political subdivision thereof shall establish or continue in effect, with respect to any consumer product, any standard or similar regulation prescribing requirements applicable to any aspect of health or safety of such consumer product, if such aspect is required to conform to a consumer product safety standard under this title unless that standard or similar regulation is identical to a consumer product safety standard established pursuant to this title. Nothing in this section shall be construed to prevent any State or political subdivision thereof from establishing or continuing a health or safety requirement applicable to a consumer product for its own use, if such requirement imposes a higher standard of health or safety than that required to comply with the applicable consumer product safety standard under this title.

(b) The Administrator may, upon application of a State or political subdivision thereof, exempt such State or political subdivision from the limitation of subsection (a) if a consumer product safety standard proposed by such application (1) imposes a higher level of health or safety than the Federal consumer product safety standard with respect to consumer products to be manufactured, sold, held for sale, or used in such State or political subdivision thereof, (2) is required by compelling local conditions, (3) does not unduly burden commerce, and (4) is adopted by such State or political subdivision pursuant to procedures and requirements which in the judgment of the Administrator are substantially comparable to those prescribed for consumer product safety standards under this title.

(d) Compliance with any consumer product safety standard issued under this title does not exempt any person from any liability under common law.

UTILIZATION OF OTHER FEDERAL AGENCIES

SEC. 320. (a) In carrying out their duties under this Act, the Administrator and the Commissioner shall, to the maximum practical extent, utilize the personnel, facilities, and other technical support available in other Federal agencies.

(b) Technical research support for fire safety projects undertaken by the Administrator or the Commissioner shall be provided by the National Bureau of Standards on a reimbursable basis.

TITLE IV—FEDERAL FOOD, DRUG, AND COSMETIC ACT AMENDMENTS

SEC. 401. (a) The Federal Food, Drug, and Cosmetic Act (21 U.S.C. 301 et seq.) is amended as follows:

(1) Section 602 of such Act is amended by adding at the end thereof the following new subsection:

"(g) If in package form unless its label, or labeling affixed to or within the package, bears conspicuously and in such terms as to render it likely to be read and understood by the ordinary individual under customary conditions of purchase, (1) the common or usual name of the cosmetic, if any there be, and (2) in case it is fabricated from two or more ingredients, the common or usual name of each such ingredient; except that fragrance, color, and flavor may be designated as fragrance, color, and flavor without naming each ingredient: *Provided,* That to the extent that compliance with the requirements of clause (2) is impracticable, or results in deception or unfair competition, exemptions may be established by regulations promulgated by the Secretary."

(2) Section 602 of such Act is amended by adding at the end thereof the following new subsection:

"(h) Unless its labeling bears adequate warnings against use where it may be dangerous to health."

(3) Section 201(i) of such Act is amended by striking "articles; except that such terms shall not include soap.", and inserting in lieu thereof "articles.".

(b) The amendments made by paragraphs (1) and (2) of subsection (a) shall take effect one year after the date of enactment of this Act.

TITLE V—FEDERAL HAZARDOUS SUBSTANCES ACT AMENDMENTS

SEC. 500. This title may be cited as the "Hazardous Substances Registration Act of 1972".

SEC. 501. Section 2(p) of the Federal Hazardous Substances Act (15 U.S.C. 1261 (p)) is amended by adding at the end thereof the following new paragraph:

"The term 'misbranded hazardous substance' also includes any hazardous substance required to be registered under section 16 of this Act if such substance fails to bear prominently and conspicuously on the label, in accordance with regulations issued by the Secretary, a registration number issued by the Secretary for the substance pursuant to section 16."

SEC. 502. The Federal Hazardous Substances Act is further amended by redesignating sections 16, 17, and 18 as sections 17, 18, and 19, respectively, and adding after section 15 the following new section 16:

"REGISTRATION OF CERTAIN SUBSTANCES

"SEC. 16. (a) Before beginning commercial distribution of any substance intended, or packaged in a form suitable, for use in or around the household or by children that may be 'toxic' or 'corrosive' a manufacturer or distributor shall conduct all screening tests prescribed by the Secretary or, where applicable, the Administrator of the Environmental Protection Agency, by regulation to determine whether the substance is toxic or corrosive. A copy of the results of such screening tests shall be maintained by the manufacturer or distributor for two years after the last shipment of the substance, and shall be available upon request by the Secretary.

"(b) The manufacturer or distributor of a substance which falls within any such screening level for a toxic or corrosive substance shall register such substance with the Secretary in accordance with regulations promulgated by the Secretary. The registration shall include the formulation of the product, a brief summary of the results of all screening tests, and the proper antidote or treatment for the substance.

"(c) If the Secretary determines that the substance is a hazardous substance, he shall issue a registration number for the substance, which number shall appear on the label of the substance prominently and conspicuously in accordance with regulations promulgated by the Secretary. Such a registration number shall be the same as any registration number for such substance that is required to appear on the label under any other provision of Federal law. Such registration number for any drug shall be the same as that assigned pursuant to the National Drug Code.

"(d) The Secretary shall establish a central office through which information contained in the registrations submitted under this section (except for trade secret information referred to in section 1905 of title 18, United States Code) shall be immediately available to any physician, hospital, clinic, poison control center, or other person requesting such information to provide treatment to any person injured, or who may be injured, as a result of the ingestion of, contact with, or exposure to any such substance. The Secretary shall notify physicians, hospitals, clinics, poison control centers and other persons who may have use for such information, of the availability of such information and the methods by which it may be obtained at any time.

"(e) The Secretary may exempt from any requirement of this section any substance for which he determines such requirement is unnecessary to protect the public health."

"SEC. 503. Subsection 2(f)(2) of the Federal Hazardous Substances Act (15 U.S.C. 1261(f)(2)) is amended by deleting "nor to foods, drugs, and cosmetics subject to the Federal Food, Drug, and Cosmetic Act, nor to substances intended for use as fuels when stored in containers and used in the heating, cooling or refrigeration system of a house,".

SEC. 504. (a) Section 19(a) of the Federal Hazardous Substances Act, as redesignated by section 502 of this Act (15 U.S.C. 1277(a)) is amended by striking out "except as specified in section 19" and replacing the comma after "Congress" with a period.

(b) Section 19 of such Act is hereby repealed.

SEC. 505. Section 4 of the Federal Hazardous Substances Act (15 U.S.C. 1263) is amended by adding at the end thereof the following new subsection:

"(i) The failure to conduct screening testing, maintain a copy of the results of such testing, or to provide the results of such screening testing, or to register, or to label a hazardous substance with a registration number, as required by section 16."

SEC. 506. Subsection 11(b) of the Federal Hazardous Substances Act (15 U.S.C. 1270 (b)) is amended by deleting "and" immediately before "(3)" in the first sentence, changing the period to a semicolon, and adding the following: "and (4) to inspect and copy the results of screening tests as required pursuant to section 16."

SEC. 507. The Federal Caustic Poison Act (44 Stat. 1406) is hereby repealed.

SEC. 508. Title V shall become effective one hundred and eighty days after the date of enactment of this Act except that the Secretary may postpone the applicability in the case of persons who were engaged on the date of enactment of this Act in the manufacture, compounding, or processing of a substance subject to these amendments if he determines such action is necessary to afford sufficient time for the proper and orderly testing and registration of such substances.

APPENDIX G

REPORT OF HOUSE COMMERCE COMMITTEE

This report accompanied H.R. 15003, which was subsequently approved by the House as S. 3419, and became the basis for the law that was ultimately enacted.

92D CONGRESS *2d Session*	HOUSE OF REPRESENTATIVES	REPORT No. 92–1153

CONSUMER PRODUCT SAFETY ACT

JUNE 20, 1972.—Committed to the Committee of the Whole House and ordered to be printed

Mr. STAGGERS, from the Committee on Interstate and Foreign Commerce, submitted the following

REPORT

together with

MINORITY VIEWS

[To accompany H.R. 15003]

The Committee on Interstate and Foreign Commerce, to whom was referred the bill (H.R. 15003) to protect consumers against unreasonable product hazards, having considered the same, report favorably thereon with an amendment and recommend that the bill as amended do pass.

* * *

PURPOSE AND SUMMARY OF THIS LEGISLATION

This legislation proposes that the Federal Government assume a major role in protecting the consumers from unreasonable risks of death, injury, or serious or frequent illness associated with the use or exposure to consumer products. To carry out that objective, this bill would create a new, independent regulatory commission with comprehensive authority to take action across the full range of consumer products to reduce or prevent product-related injuries. The powers and procedural requirements contained in this legislation, for the most part, draw and improve upon concepts and practices which the Congress has previously employed in other safety laws.

In its barest terms this bill would vest in the independent regulatory commission, which it establishes, authority to:

(1) collect and disseminate information on consumer product related injuries;

(2) establish mandatory safety standards where necessary to prevent or reduce unreasonable product hazards, or—where such standards are not feasible—to ban the product from the marketplace;

(3) obtain equitable relief in the courts to protect the public from products which pose imminent hazards to health and safety; and

(4) administratively order the notification and remedy of products which fail to comply with Commission safety rules or which contain safety related defects.

The bill would also provide a system of product certification and permit the Commission to compel inclusion of certain safety-related information in product labels. The Commission would be given broad inspection and record keeping powers. Enforcement of the bill may be obtained through court injunctive process or through imposition of criminal and civil penalties. Also, private suits for damages are allowed to be brought in Federal courts and consumer suits are permitted to compel compliance with safety rules and certain Commission orders.

Basis for Legislation

It is considered self-evident that the public is entitled to purchase products without subjecting themselves to unreasonable risk of injury or death. At the present time, however, consumers are not able to confidently rely on the safety of products which are distributed for their use or enjoyment.

The National Center for Health Statistics estimates that each year 20 million Americans are injured in and around the home. Of this total, 110,000 injuries result in permanent disability and 30,000 in death. One estimate has placed the annual dollar cost to the economy of product-related injuries at over $5 billion. Moreover, home accidents reap a death toll among children under the age of 15 which is higher than that of cancer and heart disease combined. Yet, despite the public's widely held assumption that the Federal government exercises broad authority in the interest of their safety, existing federal authority to curb hazards in a majority of consumer products is virtually non-existent.

Within the last six years, the Congress has exhibited an increasing concern with the safety of the products which consumers encounter in their daily lives. This concern has been manifested in the passing of a series of acts designed to deal with specific hazards and categories of products for which a substantial regulatory need had been established. These acts include the National Traffic and Motor Vehicle Safety Act of 1966, the Gas Pipeline Safety Act of 1968, the Flammable Fabrics Act Amendments of 1967, the Radiation Control for Health and Safety Act of 1968, the Child Prevention and Toy Safety Act of 1969, and the Poison Prevention Packaging Act of 1970.

While each of these acts is meritorious in its own right and deserving of enactment, this legislative program has resulted in a patchwork pattern of laws which, in combiantion, extend to only a small portion of the multitude of products produced for consumers. Moreover, the technological revolution and ever-increasing public demand for consumer products has produced over the last several years thousands of new products whose applications are not easily understood by consumers and whose use may pose great potential for harm.

Recognizing this problem, Congress created in 1967 the National Commission on Product Safety with a mandate to "conduct a comprehensive study and investigation of the scope and adequacy of measures now employed to protect consumers against unreasonable risks of injuries which may be caused by household products." The work of the Commission extended over a period of two years. Much of the Commission's investigative effort was concentrated in a series of widely publicized informational hearings which were held at different locations throughout the country. In the course of these proceedings, the Commission was presented with evidence from over 225 witnesses whose testimony contributed to a hearing record in excess of 7,000 pages. The Commission's final report was transmitted to both the President and the Congress in July 1970.

In general terms, the Commission confirmed both the absence of and the need for a strong, vigorous Federal presence to protect the public from hazardous consumer products. The Commission's findings set out in sharp terms the shortcomings of past Federal safety efforts.

> Federal products safety legislation consists of a series of isolated acts treating specific hazards in narrow product categories. No Government agency possesses general authority to ban products which harbor unreasonable risks or to require that consumer products conform to minimum safety standards.
>
> Such limited Federal authority as does exist is scattered among many agencies. Jurisdiction over a single category of products may be shared by as many as four different departments or agencies. Moreover, where it exists, Federal product safety regulation is burdened by unnecessary procedural obstacles, circumscribed investigative powers, inadequate and ill-fitting sanctions, bureaucratic lassitude, timid administration, bargain-basement budgets, distorted priorities, and misdirected technical resources.

In addition, the Commission found State and local laws to be a "hodgepodge of tragedy-inspired responses to challenges which cannot be met by restricted geographical entities."

Perhaps even more significant, however, are the Commission's findings that self-interest and competitive forces are not of themselves sufficient to influence manufacturers to produce safe products. Attempts at self-regulation through industry trade associtaions and standards groups was found "patently inadequate." Here, the Commission's findings bear repeating in some detail:

> "Competitive forces may require management to subordinate safety factors to cost consideration, styling, and other marketing imperatives.
>
> "There is a dearth of factors motivating producers toward safety. Only a few of the largest manufacturers have coherent, articulated safety engineering programs. Manufacturers' efforts

to obtain data on injuries and on the costs and benefits of design changes that will reduce unreasonable hazards can be charitable described as sketchy and sporadic.

"The consensus principle, which is at the heart of all voluntary standards making, is not effective for elevating safety standards. It permits the least responsible segment of an industry to retard progress in reducing hazards.

"The protection afforded by various seals of approval is no better than the technical competence, product-testing protocols, and independence of the certifier. When an industry association awards the seal, or when it is awarded in return for paid advertising, the seal may convey a deceptive implication of third-party independence. Consumers appear to attribute to such endorsements a significance beyond their specific meaning."

There is today no central facility for the systematic collection and evaluation of injury data. And, for this reason, it is impossible to measure the true magnitude of product-related injuries or to determine with confidence what portion of the annual toll of 30,000 deaths or 20 million injuries which are estimated to occur around the American home are actually caused by unsafe products.

Innumerable individual reports, nevertheless, persuaded the Commission—and have persuaded your Committee—that a significant number of deaths and injuries are directly attributable in whole or in part to unsafe consumer products. The Commission's report catalogs a large number of products which it found, on an ad hoc basis, to present unreasonable hazards to consumers. These included various makes, models, or types of: architectural glass, color television sets, fireworks, floor furnaces, glass bottles, high-rise bicycles, hot water vaporizers, household chemicals, infant furniture, ladders, power tools, protective headgear, rotary lawnmowers, toys, unvented gas heaters, and wringer washing machines. In a section of its report entitled "Unfinished Business", the Commission went on to list an additional sixteen products which it believed warranted further safety investigation. By any standard of measurement, the Commission concluded "the exposure of consumers to unreasonable consumer product hazards is excessive."

Rather than propose individual legislation designed to deal with the product hazards which it had identified, however, the Commission decided that the Federal Government should abandon its traditional case by case approach to product safety and consolidate in a single agency authority sufficient to regulate the full spectrum of products which are sold to or used by consumers. To this end, the Commission submitted with its final report legislative proposals to create a new independent regulatory commission with comprehensive powers to minimize or eliminate unreasonably hazardous products.

Committee Consideration

In the first session of this Congress, the Chairman of the committee's Subcommittee on Commerce and Finance, John E. Moss of California, introduced a bill which substantially embodied the Product Safety Commission's legislative recommendations. Also, drawing upon the Commission's report, the President transmitted legislation to the Congress which proposed the establishment of omnibus product safety authority in the Federal government.

These two proposals formed the focus of 13 days of hearings before the Subcommittee on Commerce and Finance which extended over a four-month period. After 8 meetings in executive session, the Subcommittee unanimously reported a clean bill which represented an accommodation between the legislative recommendations of the National Commission on Product Safety and those of the Administration. This bill, HR 15003, with certain amendments, was ordered favorably reported on voice vote by the full committee after 2 days in executive session.

Structure

All witnesses who testified on this legislation—including virtually every segment of the manufacturing industry—supported the proposition that the Federal government should assume a major role in assuring the safety of consumer products. Disagreement among witnesses primarily centered on the organizational structure for regulating product hazards and the procedures to be employed in the exercise of governmental authority. Indeed, the most fundamental difference between the recommendations of the National Commission on Product Safety and those submitted by the Administration relate to the form of the governmental agency which is to assume responsibility for protecting the public from hazardous products.

The Commission had recommended that a new independent federal agency be established; the Administration had asked that this authority be given to HEW. It was the Administration's plan to build on the activities, personnel and existing facilities of the Food & Drug Administration and to reorganize FDA for the purpose of assuming the additional responsibilities contained in this legislation.

Your committee has decided on the approach recommended by the National Commission on Product Safety, and, therefore, proposes to vest comprehensive authority to protect the public from hazardous products in an independent regulatory agency. This decision reflects the committee's belief that an independent agency can better carry out the legislative and judicial functions contained in this bill with the cold neutrality that the public has a right to expect of regulatory agencies formed for its protection. Independent status, and bi-partisan commissioners with staggered and fixed terms, will tend to provide greater insulation from political and economic pressures than is possible or likely in a cabinet-level department. The Commission's decisions under this legislation will necessarily involve a careful meld of safety and economic considerations. This delicate balance, the committee believes, should be struck in a setting as far removed as possible from partisan influence. Also, the creation of a new independent agency, it is thought, will assure that the regulatory program contained in this bill will be highly visible to get off to a firm and vigorous start.

The committee's decision to delegate product safety responsibility to a new independent commission also stems, in part, from a reluctance to assign substantial additional responsibilities to FDA in the face of a series of studies in recent years which have been sharply critical of the agency's abilities to carry out effectively the responsibilities already assigned to it under existing law. Principal among these studies are internal analyses: beginning with the so-called

Kinslow report in July 1969 (which offered an analysis of FDA's consumer protection objectives and programs); followed by a departmental review of FDA conducted by then Deputy Under Secretary Frederic V. Malek completed in December 1969; and ending with the Ritts Committee review of FDA's "total scientific effort" which was completed in May 1971.[1] Each of these studies identified structural shortcomings in FDA, citing inadequacies in internal procedures and organization. Following each study, the prescription has been for more money and manpower and for reorganization.

There is today evidence that FDA is beginning to take strong, positive steps to strengthen its regulatory capability. Moreover, the Department of HEW has recently taken long overdue action to increase the agency's budget.

There is no assurance, however, that the regulatory program for product safety envisioned in this legislation would be free from organizational and funding difficulties if the Congress were to assign this authority to FDA, as suggested. On the contrary, it has been the committee's experience that when regulatory programs are placed in Executive Departments which have broad and diverse responsibilities, the regulatory effort has typically suffered from a lack of adequate funding and staffing. This has often been the result of the regulatory program s inability to compete effectively with other deserving programs within the Department or to gain public attention and support. In this regard, it would be difficult to find another Department of the Executive branch whose responsibilities are more broad than HEW's, or where the internal competition for the Secretary's attention and for funds is more intense.

PROCEDURES GOVERNING THE EXERCISE OF FEDERAL REGULATORY AUTHORITY

In addition to the need to establish comprehensive and effective regulation over the safety of unreasonably hazardous consumer products, there is a need to insure that the procedures relating to consumer products are fair to both industry and consumers. The Committee heard extensive testimony from manufacturers and trade associations documenting some of the potential difficulties that might be faced in complying with the regulations of a product safety agency. This testimony convinces the Committee that it is essential to establish both an effective and fair product safety program, impacting to the minimum extent practicable on the manufacturing process. In addition, an effective consumer safety program must insure an adequate opportunity for participation and judicial review by consumers and regulated industries.

---

[1] Copies of these studies were submitted in the committee's hearings on this legislation. The "Kinslow Report" entitled "Report from the Study Group on Food and Drug Administration Consumer Protection Objectives and Programs" appears in the published hearings at p. 1025; the "Malek Report" which is entitled "Analysis and Recommendations: The Food and Drug Administration Organizational Review. . . . December 10, 1969" appears at p. 982; and the Ritts Committee report which is entitled "Report to the Commissioner of Food and Drugs from the FDA Ad Hoc Science Advisory Committee, May 1971" appears at p. 986. These studies were repeatedly relied on by consumer groups participating in the subcommittee's hearings as evidence that FDA should not be assigned additional responsibilities for product safety. These critics also called the committee's attention to a recent report completed by GAO in April of this year which found a "serious problem of insanitary conditions" in food-manufacturing plants. In addition to placing fault on the manufacturers, it blamed inadequate resources of the FDA and the agency's "lack of timely and aggressive enforcement action" as contributing to the problem.

With these goals in mind the Committee has fashioned legislation which for the first time affords industry and consumer groups an opportunity to directly participate in the development of safety standards. In addition, the Consumer Product Safety Commission created under this bill may, where appropriate, agree to contribute to the cost of development of such standards.

Product safety standards or proposed banning rules must be issued pursuant to the procedures of the Administrative Procedure Act. In addition, the bill incorporates added requirements for an oral presentation of arguments and the keeping of a transcript in such proceedings. Review by the courts, where sought, would be on the basis of "substantial evidence" in support of the agency's action, rather than on the usual rule, which sustains the agency's rule-making action if it is neither arbitrary nor capricious.

While the Committee has determined that it is essential to include authority to recall substantially hazardous products and products which do not meet safety standards from the marketplace, it has provided for an informal hearing prior to public notification, and a formal hearing prior to repair, replacement or refund under these provisions. Whether to utilize either of the remedies of repair, replacement or refunds would be at the election of the manufacturer.

Through these procedures the Committee has sought to develop legislation which will afford effective protection to consumers and fairness to the industries of the nation.

Explanation of Reported Bill by Section

Finding and Purposes

Section 2(a) contains congressional findings respecting the subject matter of the bill. These include a finding that—in order to effectively regulate products distributed in interstate commerce—it is necessary to regulate hazards associated with products the distribution or use of which affects interstate commerce. The committee's decision to extend the reach of this bill to hazards associated with products the distribution or use of which "affects" commerce has two bases:

First, that effective enforcement of consumer product safety standards would be impracticable if the standards applied only to products in interstate commerce; and second, that the very substantial economic effects of accidents involving consumer products are by themselves sufficient to justify Federal intervention without regard to whether the particular product crosses State lines.

Subsection (b) of section 2 states the purposes of the bill, which are to protect the public against unreasonable hazards associated with consumer products, to assist consumers in evaluating product safety, to develop uniform consumer product safety standards, and to promote product safety research.

Definitions

Section 3 defines 13 terms which are to have particular application under this bill. Several of these are definitions commonly found in Federal statutes; others are unique to this bill and require special mention.

The definition of the term "consumer product" delimits the jurisdictional reach of this bill. Because it is intended to vest omnibus product safety authority in a single Federal agency, the definition is broadly stated to include any article which is produced or distributed for sale to or for the use, consumption or enjoyment of a consumer in or around a household or residence, a school, in recreation, or otherwise. Special attention should be paid to the use of the phrase: "produced or distributed for sale to * * * or for the use of * * * a consumer." It is not necessary that a product be actually sold to a consumer, but only that it be produced or distributed for his use. Thus products which are manufactured for lease and products distributed without charge (for promotional purposes or otherwise) are included within the definition and would be subject to regulation under this bill. Also, products which are primarily or exclusively sold to industrial or institutional buyers would be included within the definition of consumer product so long as they were produced or distributed for *use* of consumers.

It is not intended that true "industrial products" be included within the ambit of the Product Safety Commission's authority. Thus, your committee has specifically excluded products which are not *customarily* produced or distributed for sale to or use of consumers. The occasional use of industrial products by consumers would not be sufficient to bring the product under the Commission's jurisdiction. The term "customarily" should not be interpreted as intending strict adherence to a quantum test, however. Your committee is aware that some products which were initially produced or sold solely for industrial application have often become broadly used by consumers. If the manufacturer or distributor of an industrial product fosters or facilitates its sale to or use by consumers, the product may lose its claim for exclusion if a significant number of consumers are thereby exposed to hazards associated with the product.

The committe has also excluded from the definition of consumer product certain product categories which are either regulated under other safety laws or which the Committee has yet to determine should be subjected to safety regulation of the type envisioned in this bill. In this grouping are: tobacco and tobacco products, motor vehicles and motor vehicle equipment, economic poisons, firearms and ammunition, medical devices and cosmetics. So that there may be no uncertainty as to the committee's intent with respect to the exclusion of food from this bill, the term is separately defined to make clear that poultry, meats, and eggs, and poultry, meat, and egg products are meant to be excluded. The specific listing of these foods and the failure to list others should not be interpreted as an intention to exclude some foods or food products while including others. The committee intends to exclude from application of this bill all foods within the broad meaning given to that term in section 201 of the Food, Drug and Cosmetic Act.

There has been some confusion over the intended application of this bill to mobile homes and the increasingly important problem of mobile home safety. It is the committee's understanding that the definition of the term "consumer product" would include any component, equipment, or appliance sold with or used in or around a mobile home. It is not thought that the term is so broadly stated as to bring the basic structure of the mobile home within the reach of this legislation. It is the committee's intent that the Consumer Product Safety Commission to be created under this legislation would have full authority, however, to regulate all appliances and appurtenances of the household environment of the mobile home.

In several sections of this bill, private labelers are required to assume the same duties and responsibilities as manufacturers. This follows the committee's belief that, if a person holds himself out as manufacturing a product and as standing behind the product's quality or performance, it is reasonable to ask him to assume certain responsibilities for that product.

For the purposes of this bill, a "private labeler" is defined to mean an owner of a brand or trademark which is placed on a consumer product in lieu of that of the manufacturer's. A product is not considered to bear a private label, however, if the manufacturer's brand or trademark also appears on the label.

The term "consumer product safety rule" is defined to include both a rule which establishes a safety standard, and a rule which declares a consumer product a banned hazardous product.

The term "hazard" is defined to mean a risk of death, injury, or serious or frequent illness. The phrase "unreasonable hazard" is used throughout the bill as a short-form reference to unreasonable risk of death, personal injury, or serious or frequent illness.

The term "manufacturer" is defined to include any person who manufactures, assembles or imports a consumer product. As a result, those engaged in the assembly of a consumer product are subjected to the same regulatory control as producers of the product. Also, to assure parity of regulation, importers are made subject to the same responsibilities as domestic manufacturers.

Subsection (b) of section 3 provides that common carriers, contract carriers, or freight forwarders shall not be deemed manufacturers, distributors, or retailers under this bill if the sole reason they would be considered as such arises out of their receiving or transporting a consumer product in the ordinary course of their business as carriers or forwarders. Unless excluded, carriers and forwarders would be swept up in the broad definitions of the terms "manufacturer," "distributor," and "retailers."

Consumer Product Safety Commission

Section 4 of this bill establishes an independent regulatory commission to carry out the assigned duties and responsibilities to protect consumers from unreasonably hazardous products. This section implements the National Commission on Product Safety's recommendation to create a strong independent product safety authority. In using the term independent, the committee intends that the agency be independent of the executive department and to be removed as far as possible from the influence of partisan politics or political control.

Section 4 creates the Consumer Product Safety Commission in the image of other regulatory commissions which have been created by the Congress to regulate the essential industries of rail and air transportation, oil and gas production, communications, and the securities markets. As such, the Consumer Product Safety Commission is made subject to traditional requirements relating to the appointment and organization of independent regulatory agencies. For example, to promote evenhanded regulation, the Commission is to consist of 5 members selected on a bipartisan basis to serve for seven-year terms. In the interest of efficiency and good organization, however, staffing authority is concentrated in the office of the Chairman—subject only to the general guidance of the Commission.

The committee has incorporated several provisions which depart from and improve upon traditional agency practice. Because the Commission's Chairman is designated as the principal executive officer and assigned special powers to control the operation of the agency, the committee does not believe that the Chairman should serve at the pleasure of the President. As Mr. Justice Sutherland once noted in a case involving the attempted removal of a member of the Federal Trade Commission "[i]t is quite evident that one who holds his office only during the pleasure of another cannot be depended upon to maintain an attitude of independence against the latter's will." Accordingly, section 4(a) qualifies the presidential appointment powers by requiring that the Chairman, when designated as such by the President, shall continue to serve as Chairman until the expiration of his term of office as a member of the Commission. Thus, if the President designates a member of the Commission to serve as Chairman at the time of his appointment to the Commission, that person shall continue in office as Chairman for his full seven-year term on the Commission. The President would not be empowered to designate some other Commissioner to serve as Chairman within this period. Also, if the seven-year term of office runs into another administration, the incumbent President would not be able to remove the Chairman and replace him with his own designee.

In order to properly isolate members of the Commission from removal from office at the whim of the executive, section 4(a) states that members of the Commission may be removed for neglect of duty or malfeasance in office, but for no other cause. By delineating the bases for removal, your committee intends to restrict the Preisdent's power to remove from office to these grounds alone.

Subsection 4(c) states that no person may hold office as a member of the Commission if he is a member of, or holds any official relation to, any person engaged in selling or manufacturing consumer products. Commissioners are also disqualified if they own stocks or bonds in substantial valuation in a person engaged in selling or manufacturing consumer products or if they are in any way pecuniarily interested in such person or in a substantial supplier of such person. The committee recognizes that these restrictions are severe. It is intended by them to create a standard for members of the Commission which will assure that they are their own masters and are known to be such.

These requirements, of course, are in addition to conflict of interest codes contained in the criminal provisions of title 18 (see 18 U.S.C. 207). Also, to assure that Commissioners and principal agency employees carry out their responsibilities vigorously and without compromise, this section makes it unlawful for any member of the Commission or individual employee who receives compensation at a rate in excess of GS–14 to accept employment or compensation from any manufacturer subject to this act for a period of one year after terminating employment with the Commission. This restriction is intended to assure that persons will not seek employment with the agency or use their Federal office as a means of subsequently gaining employment in the regulated industry or as a means of acquiring members of industry as future clients.

Product Safety Information and Research

Section 5 directs the Commission to maintain an injury information clearing house to collect, investigate, analyze, and disseminate information relating to the causes and prevention of death, injury, and illness associated with consumer products. The Commission is also directed to conduct such accident investigations and studies as it considers necessary to this function.

The committee expects that, in the exercise of its responsibilities under this section, the Commission will develop the means to monitor accident occurrences throughout the United States, to determine whether they are product related and to measure the severity of the injury caused. Information which discloses that a product may be hazardous must be promptly transmitted to the manufacturer. In this regard it is expected that responsible manufacturers, once notified of the dangers attendant to their products, will act to correct the problem without requiring governmental action.

It is recognized, of course, that the powers given the Commission to collect and analyze injury data far exceed the abilities of any single manufacturer or industry association to acquire information concerning the accident experience associated with their products. Private industry however, should not rely totally on the Government to discover product hazards. Each manufacturer has today and should continue to have the responsibility to assure through testing and other independent means that his products are free from defect or hazard and are properly designed for the use for which they are intended or applied.

Section 5(b) authorizes the Commission to conduct research, studies, and investigations on the safety of consumer products; to test products and to develop safety testing methods and testing devices; and to offer training in product safety investigation; and to assist others in the development of safety standards and test procedures. This authority is designed to give the Commission the means of identifying hazards before consumers are exposed to them. The application of modern technology makes possible sophisticated analysis of product design and testing for product degradation so that potential accidents may be foreseen and avoided. And such analyses may well provide a proper basis for regulatory action without awaiting an accumulation of accident statistics of the maimed and injured.

The Commission is given broad authority to make grants and enter into contracts to conduct any of these functions. Where the contribution of technical assistance or financial aid is more than minimal, such contracts, grants or other arrangements must provide that the rights to all information, processes, patents, and other developments resulting from any research and development activities must be available to the public without charge on a nonexclusive basis. Nothing in this section is intended to deprive the contracted party or grant recipient from any patent, patent application, or invention which he may have had prior to entering within the arrangement with the Commission. Subject to this qualification, it is intended that all information developed under these grants would be freely and fully available to the public.

Public Disclosure of Information

If the Commission is to act responsibly and with adequate basis, it must have complete and full access to information relevant to its statutory responsibilities. Accordingly, the committee has built into this bill broad information-gathering powers. It recognizes that in so doing it has recommended giving the Commission the means of gaining access to a great deal of information which would not otherwise be available to the public or to Government. Much of this relates to trade secrets or other sensitive cost and competitive information. Accordingly, the committee has written into section 6 of the bill detailed requirements and limitations relating to the Commission's authority to disclose information which it acquires in the conduct of its responsibilities under this act.

Subsection (a) makes clear that nothing in this act shall be deemed to compel the Commission to disclose information which would not otherwise be available to the public under the Freedom of Information Act (5 U.S.C. 552(b)). There is one exception to this requirement. The Freedom of Information Act would not require a Federal agency to permit public access to investigatory files compiled for law enforcement purposes. Section 25(c) of this bill qualifies the Commission's authority to deny access to investigatory files by making accident investigations specifically available to the public so long as they do not identify injured parties or attending physicians (unless a release is obtained from such persons).

Subsection (a)(2) contains an absolute prohibition against the Commission's disclosure of trade secrets and other information referred to in section 1905 of title 18—except to other officers or employees concerned with carrying out responsibilities under this act or when relevant in any proceeding under this act. The committee intends that the term "trade secrets" shall be given the same judicial construction as that term has acquired under 18 U.S.C. 1905. Accordingly, for the purposes of section 6 of this act, a trade secret means "an unpatented, secret, commercially valuable plan, appliance, formula, or process, which is used for the making, preparing, compounding, treating, or processing of articles or materials which are trade commodities."[1]

Before disseminating any information which identifies the manufacturer or private labeler of a product, the Commission is directed to give the manufacturer or private labeler 30 days in which to comment on the proposed disclosure of information. This procedure is intended to permit the manufacturer or private labeler an opportunity to come forward with explanatory data or other relevant information for the Commission's consideration. There is no intention that the Commission be required to include a manufacturer's or private labeler's explanation in the materials which it determines to disseminate at the end of the 30-day period. This was suggested to the committee and rejected

The committee recognizes that the Commission has a responsibiilty to assure that the information which it disseminates is truthful and accurate. Where it is discovered that the disclosure of information has been inaccurate or misleading and reflects adversely on the safety of

---

[1] See *Consumers Union of United States* v. *Veterans Administration*, 301 F. Supp. 796 (1969), citing with approval *United States ex rel. Norwegian Nitrogen Products Co.* v. *United States Tariff Comm.*, 6 F. 2d 491, 495 (1925).

a consumer product or the practices of any manufacturer, distributor, or retailer of the product, the Commission is directed to publish a retraction in a manner similar to that in which the original disclosure was made. It is intended that a retraction receive at least the same notoriety as the original disclosure. Accordingly, if the Commission had publicly released information to the news media which was inaccurate or misleading, the retraction must also be released to the news media and not simply placed in the Federal Register. By requiring that the Commission publish its retraction in a manner similar to that in which the original disclosure was made, the committee does not intend to limit the Commission to these means. There may be circumstances where equity requires fuller disclosure of the Commission's mistakes in order to repair the damage to any manufacturer, distributor, or retailer of the product which may have resulted from publication of the inaccurate information.

The Commission is not required to give prior notification to manufacturers of any information which may be disclosed with respect to a product for which an action has been brought under section 12 (relating to imminently hazardous products) or a product which the Commission has reasonable cause to believe is in violation of section 19. The Commission also need not notify manufacturers and await the tolling of the 30-day period prior to the disclosure of information in the course of or concerning an administrative or judicial proceeding under the act.

Consumer Product Safety Standards

Section 7 authorizes the Commission to promulgate mandatory consumer product safety standards where it finds that such standards are reasonably necessary to prevent or reduce an unreasonable hazard to the public associated with a consumer product. These standards may prescribe requirements relating to the performance, composition, content, design, construction, finish, or packaging of a product or prescribe requirements relating to the labeling of a product. Safety standards may contain any combination of these requirements which the Commission determines is necessary to prevent or reduce the hazard to the public.

Section 7(a) contains the statutory admonition that, wherever feasible, a standard must be expressed in terms of performance requirements. Your committee has expresed a strong preference for performance standards in the recognition that such standards permit industry to make the fullest use of its technological resources in meeting safety requirements. Mandatory standards which prescribe performance requirements can often be expected to foster rather than stifle competition. Your committee expects that the Commission will exercise its authority to establish standards relating to a product's composition, content, design, construction, finish, or packaging only in circumstances where it is persuaded that it would not be feasible to establish performance criteria.

It should be noted that the Commission's authority to promulgate standards under this bill is limited to instances where the hazard associated with a consumer product presents an unreasonable risk of death, injury, or serious or frequent illness. Your committee has not included a definition of "unreasonable hazards" within this bill. Protection against unreasonable risks is central to many Federal and State safety statutes and the courts have had broad experience in interpreting the term's meaning and application. It is generally expected that the determination of unreasonable hazard will involve the Commission in balancing the probability that risk will result in harm and the gravity of such harm against the effect on the product's utility, cost, and availability to the consumer. An unreasonable hazard is clearly one which can be prevented or reduced without affecting the product's utility, cost, or availability; or one which the effect on the product's utility, cost or availability is outweighed by the need to protect the public from the hazard associated with the product. There should be no implication, however, that in arriving at its determination the Commission would be required to conduct and complete a cost-benefit analysis prior to promulgating standards under this act. Of course, no standard would be expected to impose added costs or inconvenience to the consumer unless there is reasonable assurance that the frequency or severity of injuries or illnesses will be reduced.

Procedures for the Development of a Consumer Product Safety Standard

Section 7 contains detailed procedures for the development of consumer product safety standards. Briefly stated, your committee has attempted to outline a process which makes maximum use of the expertise available in the private sector and permits maximum participation by industry and consumer interests in the standard-setting process, while at the same time reserving to the Commission that measure of discretion and authority necessary to permit it to efficiently and effectively carry out its responsibilities.

Initiation of the Standard-Making Process

A proceeding to develop a consumer product safety standard is initiated by publication of notice in the *Federal Register* which: (1) identifies the product and the nature of the hazard associated with it; (2) states the Commission's determination that a consumer product safety standard is necessary to prevent or reduce the hazard; (3) includes information respecting any existing standard which may be relevant; and (4) invites interested persons to come forward within 30 days with an existing standard suitable to be proposed as a consumer product safety standard under this act or to offer to develop a proposed consumer product safety standard to deal with the product hazard.

The notice is required to state a development period within which the Commission must receive final recommendations from any person whose offer to develop a standard is accepted. The Commission is to allow 150 days for the development of a recommended standard unless, for good cause, it finds a longer or shorter period is appropriate.

Subsection (c) would permit the Commission, in lieu of accepting an offer for the development of a standard to publish an existing standard which it finds would adequately prevent or reduce the hazard associated with the product if promulgated as a Federal consumer product safety standard under this act. There are, of course, many thousands of existing standards which have been issued by a multitude of public and private organizations and agencies. Many of these relate to consumer product safety. In some cases an existing voluntary standard may be entirely adequate to prevent or reduce an unreasonable hazard associated with a product, but is ineffective in protecting the public because it is not widely accepted by industry or because the promulgating agency or organization lacks authority to require adherence to its terms.

Except in circumstances where the Commission determines that an existing standard would satisfactorily prevent or reduce the hazard, the Commission is required to accept an offer for the development of a standard made by an offeror which it determines is technically competent; is likely to develop an appropriate standard within the required period; and is willing and able to comply with certain regulations relating to procedures for the development of the standard. The requirement of technical competence contemplates that an offeror may be called upon to demonstrate his expertise and capability to carry out the undertaking to develop the proposed standard. It is not intended to require that an offeror have past standards-writing experience or particular knowledge of the product for which the standard is to be developed. It is anticipated that universities and research laboratories could be found technically competent even though they may have had no experience relating to the product to be regulated.

Subsection (d) makes it mandatory that the Commission accept an offer to develop a proposed standard in order to assure that, in the first instance, private standard-making organizations or technical committees as well as consumer groups and other public and private agencies will have an opportunity to prepare a proposed solution to the problem. If the Commission accepts an offer for the development of a standard, it may agree to contribute to the offeror's cost. It is expected that the Commission will exercise its authority under this section to provide assistance to consumer organizations or groups which are less likely to be able to bear the costs of standards development than are industrial trade organizations. Also, in instances where an offer from a technical committee or standard-writing organization is accepted, it is contemplated that the Commission would have authority under this section to limit its contribution to such of the offeror's costs as are attributable to assuring adequate participation by public representatives in the development process.

Subsection (d)(3) directs the Commission to adopt regulations to assure that offerors whose offers are accepted proceed fairly and openly in the development of the standard. To a large measure, these regulations parallel requirements which the Administrative Procedure Act (5 U.S.C. 551 et seq.) prescribes for Federal agencies. Accordingly, the regulations require the offeror to provide notice and opportunity for interested persons to participate in the development process; to keep public records showing the course of the standard's development and any information submitted to the offeror which relates to the development of the standard or other matter relevant to the evolution of the standard. Such regulations must also provide that the standards recommended for promulgation be suitable; be supported by test data or such other documentation as the Commission may reasonably require; and, in appropriate cases, that they contain suitable test methods for determining compliance with the standard. Each offeror must permit the Commission and the Comptroller General access to any books or records which are relevant to the development of the standard or to the expenditure of any contribution made by the Commission to the standard's development.

Commission Development of a Proposed Standard

Section 7(e) imposes restrictions on the ability of the Commission to proceed independently to develop a proposed standard once it has accepted an offer for its development. The committee has imposed these limitations in order to avoid duplication and to help assure that a proposed standard submitted by an offeror will be given serious consideration and will not be readily discarded by the Commission in favor of its own solutions to the problem.

Under subsection (e)(2), if the Commission accepts an offer to develop a standard, it may not, during the development period, develop proposals for such standard itself or contract with third parties for the development of such a standard. The Commission is also prohibited from publishing a proposed rule applicable to the same hazard associated with the product during this period. Subsection (e)(2) should not be interpreted, however, as preventing the Commission or its staff—while awaiting the submission of recommended standards—from developing or acquiring the technical capability necessary to properly evaluate the standards recommended to it.

If the Commission determines that no offeror is making satisfactory progress, it may proceed to develop its own proposals or contract with third parties for that purpose. It is hoped that this action will prompt an offeror to move more diligently to develop a recommended standard within the period allowed for its development. If, however, the Commission determines that no offeror is able or willing to continue satisfactorily to develop the standard, the Commission may end the development period and immediately publish a proposed product safety rule applicable to the product hazard with which the standard was to have dealt. This proposed rule may take the form either of a proposed standard or rule declaring the product a banned hazardous product.

Publication of Proposed Rule

Section 7(f) mandates that the Commission act within 210 days after publication of the original notice initiating a proceeding for the development of a standard to (1) withdraw the notice of proceeding, or (2) publish a proposed rule which either proposes a consumer product safety standard applicable to the product or proposes to declare the product a banned hazardous product. The Commission may extend the 210 day period for good cause shown.

Banned Hazardous Products

Section 8 grants authority to the Commission to administratively ban hazardous consumer products if it finds that the product presents an unreasonable hazard and that no feasible consumer safety standard would adequately protect the public from the hazard. Section 9(c)(2) requires that these findings must be affirmatively made and incorporated in any adopted rule which declares a product to be a banned hazardous consumer product. The Commission need not attempt to first develop a proposed standard to deal with the hazard under section 7, but may proceed directly to ban a hazardous product. Interested persons may obtain judicial review under section 11 of a banning rule and may thereby require the Commission to support with substantial evidence its finding that no feasible standard would adequately protect the public.

Administrative Procedures Applicable to Promulgation of Consumer Product Safety Rules

Section 9 requires the Commission to act to either adopt a final rule or withdraw the proposed rule within 60 days of publication of any proposed consumer product safety rule under this act. If the Commission determines to withdraw the proposed rule, it must find that withdrawal is in the public interest, or that the proposed rule is not reasonably necessary to prevent or reduce the hazard associated with the product. The 60-day period may be extended by the Commission for good cause shown.

Consumer product safety rules under this bill are to be promulgated pursuant to section 553 of title 5 of the United States Code. The committee has modified the informal rulemaking procedures of the Administrative Procedure Act by requiring that the Commission give interested persons an opportunity for the oral presentation of views, data, or arguments in addition to providing an opportunity for the submission of written comments. Also, a transcript must be kept of this proceeding to assure that the views of participating parties will be preserved and available to a reviewing court under section 11.

In traditional agency rulemaking, it is discretionary with the agency whether to provide an oral hearing under section 553 of title 5. Your committee has decided to remove that discretion and make mandatory that interested persons be afforded an opportunity to orally present arguments to the Commission. In so doing, the Committee sought to reach an accommodation between the informal requirements of section 553 and the formal trial type procedures of sections 556 and 557 of title 5. The informal procedures were not thought to provide the desired opportunity for interested parties to participate in the Commission's rulemaking proceeding; the formal, on the other hand, were thought to unduly involve the Commission in adjudicatory procedures inappropriate to the essentially legislative nature of the rulemaking procedure. The committee has accordingly crafted an administrative procedure to be employed in this bill which it believes will maximize opportunities to participate in the rulemaking proceeding without unduly entangling the Commission in trial type procedures.

Consumer product safety rules are required to express the nature of the hazard the rule is designed to prevent or reduce and state the rule's effective date. Rules are required to take effect not more than 180 days from the date issued unless the Commission finds for good cause that a later effective date is in the public interest. Consumer product safety standards may be made applicable only to consumer products which are manufactured after the date a standard is promulgated. Thus the Commission could not establish a retroactive effective date for any consumer product safety rule which embodies a product safety standard. Rules declaring a product to be a banned hazardous consumer product, however, may apply to products of new manufacture or to products already distributed in commerce.

In determining whether to promulgate a final consumer product safety rule the Commission is directed to consider all relevant data available to it including the results of research, development, testing, and investigation activities. The Commission is instructed to make appropriate findings to be included in any final rule with respect to

(1) the nature and degree of the hazard, (2) the approximate number of consumer products or types or classes of consumer products which are to be made subject to the rule, (3) the public need for the consumer products which are to be subject to the rule and (4) the probable effect of the rule upon the utility, cost, or availability of such product.

As a condition precedent to issuing a consumer product safety rule, the Commission must make findings that (1) the rule (including the effective date) is reasonably necessary to prevent or reduce an unreasonable hazard to the public and (2) the promulgation of the rule is in the public interest. In instances where the rule declares a product to be a banned hazardous product, the Commission must make an affirmative finding that no feasible consumer product safety standard would adequately protect the public.

Amendment and Revocation of Consumer Product Safety Rules

Under section 9(e) the Commission is permitted to adopt rules amending or revoking any consumer product safety rule which it has promulgated. An amendment or revocation must take effect within 180 days unless the Commission extends the period for good cause. If the amendment involves a material change in a consumer product safety rule, the Commission must observe the full procedures required for the promulgation of rules contained in sections 7, 8, and 9. For example, where the Commission proposes to make a material amendment in a rule which embodies a consumer product safety standard, it must publish notice under section 7 and invite interested persons to offer to develop an amended standard. In instances where the Commission proposes to revoke a rule, it must provide an opportunity for the oral presentation of views, data, and arguments and for written submissions in accordance with the provisions of section 9(a)(2). A rule may only be revoked if the Commission determines that the rule is no longer reasonably necessary to prevent or reduce the hazard.

Persons adversely affected or any consumer or consumer organization may obtain judicial review under section 11 of any rule which materially amends or revokes an existing consumer product safety rule.

Petition by Interested Parties for Consumer Product Safety Rules

Section 10 establishes a mechanism for interested persons to petition the Commission to commence a proceeding to issue, amend, or revoke a consumer product safety rule. The right to petition agency action is, of course, fundamental and already a part of the Administrative Procedure Act (5 U.S.C. 553(e)). This section would add to that privilege by requiring the Commission to explain its reasons if it determines to deny the petition. As a result, interested persons are given a means of requiring the Commission to explain the basis for inaction with respect to a particular product or class of consumer products.

Judicial Review of Consumer Product Safety Rules

Section 11 provides a procedure under which any person adversely affected by a consumer product safety rule or any consumer or consumer organization may obtain judicial review of the rule upon application to a U.S. court of appeals within 60 days following promulgation of the rule. The reviewing court, upon application of the petitioner, may order the Commission to adduce additional data, views, or arguments. Commission rules are to be overturned unless each of the findings which the Commission is required to make under section 9(c) is shown to be supported by "substantial evidence" on the record taken as a whole. Thus, although the Commission's rule-making proceeding is permitted to follow the informal procedures of section 553 of title 5 of the U.S. Code (subject to the further requirement that the Commission afford an opportunity for the oral presentation of views, data, and arguments) its determinations are subjected to the stricter standard of review that is normally reserved for formal agency proceedings under sections 556 and 557 of title 5.

Judicial review under this section is in addition to, not in lieu of, other legal rights or remedies. Accordingly, this section should not be interpreted as abridging in any way a person's right to collaterally attack a product safety rule to the extent otherwise provided by law in civil or criminal proceedings brought after the expiration of the 60-day period. Nor should the failure to subject other Commission rules or orders to review under this section be read as derogating from customary rights of judicial review of such rules and orders which are made available under applicable provisions of the Administrative Procedure Act (5 U.S.C. 701–06).

Imminent Hazards

Section 12 gives the Commission emergency authority to deal with hazardous products which present an imminent and unreasonable risk of death, serious illness, or severe personal injury. In such circumstances the Commission may file an action in U.S. district court to seize and condemn the offending product and may bring an action against any manufacturer, distributor, or retailer of the product for such equitable remedy as may be necessary to adequately protect the public from the hazard.

The district court is granted authority to issue mandatory orders requiring notification to purchasers known to the defendant, to require public notice, recall, repair, replacement, or repurchase of such product. The Commission may request and the court may order any combination of these remedies.

In determining whether to initiate an action and what type of equitable relief to request, the Commission may consult with the Product Safety Advisory Council which is established under section 28 of this bill. The Council is authorized to conduct such hearings or offer such opportunity for the presentation of views as it may consider necessary or appropriate. In light of the emergency nature of the proceeding, however, the Council is required to submit its recommendations to the Commission within one week. It is to be emphasized that the Commission has complete discretion whether to consult the Council and its failure to seek advice shall not in any way affect the validity of a proceeding under this section.

In appropriate cases, the Commission is required to initiate a proceeding to promulgate a consumer product safety rule applicable to the product concurrently with the filing of an action with the court under this section or as soon thereafter as may be practical. If the hazard is of a type which would not reasonably be corrected by a safety standard or by banning the product, the Commission would not be required to initiate such a proceeding.

New Products

Section 13 gives the Commission rulemaking authority to establish procedures requiring manufacturers of new consumer products to furnish notice and a description of the product to the Commission before its distribution in commerce. The term "new consumer product" is defined to mean any consumer product which incorporates a design, material, or form of energy exchange which (1) has not previously been used substantially in consumer products *and* (2) as to which there exists a lack of information adequate to determine the safety of the product.

This section is designed to provide the Commission with a means of keeping abreast of new products entering the market place so that it can head off imminently hazardous products in the courts or promptly institute a proceeding to ban or develop standards for products which it determines are unreasonably hazardous. It is not intended that the Commission's rulemaking powers under this section be used to require premarket clearance of new consumer products. Thus, the Commission would not have authority under this section to require a manufacturer to postpone distribution of a new product until the Commission has had an opportunity to run tests on the product or make an analysis of its potential for harm.

Product Certification and Labeling

Section 14 provides that manufacturers (including importers) and private labelers of products subject to safety standards shall issue certificates which certify that their products conform to all applicable consumer product safety rules. Your committee has determined to require private labelers who distribute a product as if it were their own, to assume the same responsibilities with respect to certification that this section would impose upon a manufacturer of the product.

Certificates are to be issued on the basis of actual tests conducted of each product or upon a reasonable testing program, and shall state the name of the manufacturer or private labeler issuing a certificate and include the date and place of manufacture. The certificate must accompany the product or be otherwise furnished to any distributor or retailer to whom the product is delivered. Your committee does not intend to require that the certificate accompany delivery of each item. Where it is reasonable and appropriate to certify an entire production run, or batch or group of products based upon a reasonable testing program, the certificate may apply to the entire production run, batch, or group of products and may be furnished to the distributor or retailer together with a bill of lading (or otherwise) at the time the first product from the production run, batch, or group is delivered to the distributor or retailer. For some products it may be possible to certify an entire model year; for others, testing results would be valid for only a single day's production.

The committee understands that an original shipment is frequently divided in the course of its distribution and portions of the shipment will end up in the possession of more than one retailer. In these circumstances, manufacturers, importers, or private labelers would not be expected to issue original certificates to each distributor or retailer. It would satisfy the requirements of this section to deliver a copy of the certification to any party within the distribution chain to whom the product is delivered.

Under subsection (b), the Commission is given rulemaking authority to prescribe reasonable testing programs upon which certification must be based. In this connection it is the committee's intention that the Commission would adopt rules which establish testing criteria or methods for testing products and the results to be achieved therefrom. Your committee does not intend that this rulemaking authority be used by the Commission to require manufacturers to observe specified production techniques or manufacturing practices in the manufacture or assembly of products.

Section 14(b)(2) gives the Commission authority to prescribe rules applicable to certification where there is more than one manufacturer of a consumer product. This was thought necessary because, in an attempt to reach the fullest range of persons engaged in the production of a consumer product, the bill defines the process of manufacture to include the assembly or production of a product or any of its component parts. In the case of certain electrical products, therefore, it would be common for several "manufacturers" to have participated in the production of the product. In such a case it is expected that the Commission could designate one or more such manufacturers as the manufacturer required to issue a certificate under paragraph (1) of this subsection and could provide that other manufacturers of the product would be relieved of the requirement of issuing a certificate or seeing to it that a certificate accompanied delivery of the product or component. The Commission would have the same authority in cases in which there is more than one private labeler of a product.

Subsection (c) of this section permits the Commission to prescribe rules which may require any consumer product to be labeled with the date and place of manufacture and contain suitable identification of the manufacturer or private labeler. The Commission is given authority to specify the form and content of such labels and, where practicable, to require that they be permanently marked on or affixed to the consumer product. Where products are subject to applicable product safety standards under this act, the Commission also may require that labels certify that the product conforms to all standards and specify those standards which are applicable to the product.

The committee recognizes that there may be circumstances where open dating of particular types or classes of consumer products may create special economic hardships, or cause a restruction of marketing techniques which may unduly affect the cost and availability of the product. In appropriate cases, therefore, it is expected that the Commission would permit manufacturers and private labelers to express in code the date of manufacture and other labeling information. Information which may be required by the Commission under this section is intended among other things to facilitate product identification in connection with a notification and recall under section 16 or pursuant to court order under section 12. Accordingly, if the Commission permits the required information to be expressed in code it should make certain that consumers and persons within the distribution chain, once supplied with the key to the code, will have no difficulty in decifering its meaning. In this regard, manufacturers and private labelers who use coded information may be required to assume added responsibilities to assure that adequate notice is given in the event recall of their product proves necessary.

Notification and Repair, Replacement, or Refund

Section 15 would require that every manufacturer of a consumer product which is distributed in commerce and every distributor or retailer of the product notify the Commission on obtaining information which reasonably supports the conclusion that the product (1) fails to comply with an applicable consumer product safety rule, or (2) contains a defect that could create a substantial product hazard. A manufacturer, distributor, or retailer is relieved from this obligation if he has actual knowledge that the Commission has been adequately informed of the defect or failure to comply.

If the Commission, based upon information which it receives from manufacturers, distributors, or retailers or on any other information which it may independently acquire, determines that a product presents a substantial hazard and that notification is required in order to adequately protect the public, it may order the manufacturer or distributor or retailer of the product to give public notice of the defect or failure to comply and require that notice be mailed to known customers and persons within the distribution chain. The Commission may specify the form and content of any notice required.

It is contemplated that a Commission order requiring public notice may, in appropriate cases, include a requirement that the manufacturer, distributor, or retailer purchase broadcasting time or buy advertising space in magazines or newspapers. While broadcasters and other media may wish to make time and space available without charge, there is no compulsion that they do so. Nor is it intended that broadcasters or news media be required to sell time or space in order to facilitate public notice under this section. A manufacturer, retailer, or distributor who is ordered to purchase broadcasting time, but is unable to do so, would be deemed to have complied with the Commission's order so long as he exercised good faith in attempting to carry out the Commission's directive.

It should be noted that manufacturers, distributors, and retailers may only be required to mail notice to customers who are known to them. This is intended to mean customers of whom they have actual knowledge. Thus, the Commission would not have authority to require a manufacturer to comb the files of its retailers to learn the names of customers who have purchased the product.

In order to compel notification under this section, the Commission must afford interested persons an opportunity to orally present their views in addition to affording them the opportunity to make written presentations. Like the administrative procedures contained in section 9, this marks a departure from traditional informal rulemaking authority.

Section 15(a) defines the term "substantial product hazard" to mean a defect which because of the pattern of defect, the number of defective products distributed in commerce and the severity of the risk or otherwise, can be determined to pose a substantial hazard to the public. This definition looks to the extent of the public exposure to the hazard. A few defective products will not normally provide a proper basis for compelling notification under this section.

Section 15(d) permits the Commission to order a manufacturer, distributor, or retailer to take remedial action with respect to the product if the Commission finds both that the product presents a substantial hazard and that it is in the public interest to order such action. The Commission must afford interested persons an opportunity for a hearing in accordance with section 554 *et seq.* of title 5 of the United States Code before it may order remedy of the product defect or failure to comply. Thus, before being compelled to take remedial action, manufacturers, distributors, and retailers may avail themselves of the procedural safeguards available under the formal adjudicatory procedures of the Administrative Procedure Act.

If the Commission orders that remedial action be taken, the person to whom the order is directed may elect whether to (1) bring the product into conformity with the applicable rule or to repair the defect in such product; (2) replace such product, or (3) refund the purchase price of such product—less a reasonable allowance for use in certain cases. When the Commission orders more than one person to take action, it may specify which of those persons shall be entitled to elect the remedies listed above. It is expected that in the exercise of this authority the Commission give consideration to where the ultimate legal responsibility for the defect or failure to comply may lie. The authority to issue multiple orders under this section is designed to allow the Commission to order retailers of a product to take action to remedy the product defect or failure to comply, while permitting the manufacturer to determine whether remedy shall take the form of repair, replacement, or refund.

A manufacturer, retailer, or distributor ordered to take remedial action under this section may be required to submit a plan satisfactory to the Commission which sets forth the action he intends to take in compliance with the Commission order. This is intended to give the Commission authority to supervise the remedy of the hazard associated with the product so as to disallow intended repairs which do not in fact prevent or sufficiently reduce it.

The Commission is also authorized to specify which persons are to receive refunds where that remedy is elected. This would permit the Commission to control not only who will be entitled to refund but also what proof of claim must be made in order for a person to recover the purchase price. Accordingly, the Commission is intended to have authority to specify whether present owners or only first purchasers are entitled to refund and whether the product must be tendered or whether the sales slip or some other proof of purchase or ownership must be made. The Committee has decided against an absolute requirement that consumers must tender products in order to be entitled to the refund in favor of this more flexible approach. The Committee was concerned that, in some instances, to require the tender of the product might unduly expose consumers and persons within the distribution chain to the hazards associated with the product. Also, the offending product may no longer be in a form which would allow its tender.

Consumers who avail themselves of the remedy provided by Commission order shall not be charged and must be reimbursed for any reasonable and foreseeable expenses incurred in availing himself of the remedy. The Commission is given authority to require any manufacturer, distributor, or retailer to reimburse any other person in the distribution chain for his expenses in carrying out the Commission's order. While it is expected that the Commission in the exercise of this authority will most commonly order those at fault to reimburse others for their expenses, it is contemplated that the Commission would have the authority to place this obligation on the person most able to bear the cost where equitable and other considerations appear to warrant such action in the public interest. In this area, general rules are neither appropriate or feasible. The Commission would be expected to exercise this power on an ad hoc basis taking into account the individual circumstances of each case.

Inspection and Recordkeeping

In pursuance of the act's purpose of protecting the public health and safety, section 16 grants the Commission broad authority to conduct on-site inspections of any factory, warehouse, or establishment in which consumer products are manufactured or held in connection with their distribution in commerce, or to enter and inspect any conveyance being used to transport consumer products. Such inspections may extend to any portion of any premises or facility which may relate to the safety of such products.

Inspections under this section may be conducted of any factory, warehouse, establishment, or conveyance in which consumer products are manufactured or held whether or not those consumer products are subject to an applicable product safety rule. The Commission is intended to have authority under this section to conduct periodic or random inspections in addition to inspections for cause. In the early stages of this program, however, it is expected that the Commission in marshalling its resources will place primary emphasis on inspections to test for compliance with applicable standards and concentrate on instances where it has reason to believe that the methods, tests, or procedures related to the manufacture and storage of a product may not be adequate or reliable.

Inspections are required to be conducted at reasonable times, in a reasonable manner, and are to be completed with reasonable promptness. By so conditioning the time, scope, and length of inspections, the committee has sought to allay manufacturers' fears that the inspection process may be used as a harassing technique or otherwise abused.

Section 16(b) gives the Commission authority to require manufacturers, private labelers, or distributors of consumer products to establish and maintain such records, make such reports, and provide such information as the Commission may reasonably require for purposes of implementing this act or to determine compliance with applicable rules or orders. It should be noted that this authority does not extend to retailers who are not also manufacturers, private labelers, or distributors (as defined in section 3 of the bill). Such persons have been excluded by the committee in the belief that mandatory customer recordkeeping requirements could prove unduly burdensome for a large number of small retailers and could materially add to the costs of consumer products. Manufacturers, of course, are free to develop such arrangements with their retailers as they may believe are necessary to facilitate the efficient and economic recall and remedy of defective and nonconforming consumer products. Such arrangements will remain a matter of private agreement.

Records required to be established and maintained by the Commission must be made available for inspection upon request of a duly designated officer or employee of the Commission. In exercising its recordkeeping authority under this section, the committee expects that the Commission will take due consideration of the cost of establishing and maintaining the records and benefits to be achieved.

Imported Products

Section 17(a) requires that any consumer product offered for importation be refused admission into the United States customs territory if the product (1) fails to comply with an applicable consumer product safety rule; (2) does not meet the certification or labeling requirements of section 14; (3) is, or has been, determined to be an imminently hazardous consumer product under section 12; (4) has a product defect which constitutes a substantial product hazard (within the meaning of section 15(a)(2)); or (5) manufactured by a person who the Commission has informed the Secretary of the Treasury is in violation of subsection (g).

Subsection (b) directs the Secretary of the Treasury to obtain without charge and deliver to the Commission, upon the latter's request, a reasonable number of samples of consumer products being offered for import. If it appears from examination of these samples or otherwise that a product cannot be admitted under the terms of subsection (a), such product must be refused admission unless modified under subsection (c).

Owners and consignees are entitled to an adjudicatory type hearing with respect to importation of their products (unless an opportunity for such a hearing has already been afforded under section 12).

Subsections (c) and (d) permit the owner or consignee to modify any product so that it may be admitted under the terms of subsection (a). The modification would be subject to requirements respecting bonds and would be under the supervision of the Commission and the Treasury Department.

Subsection (e) requires that products refused admission under this section be exported or destroyed.

Subsection (f) requires that the owner or consignee pay expenses in connection with the destruction of, and storage, cartage, or labor with respect to any consumer product refused admission under this section. If the expenses are not paid, they will be a lien against any future importations made by such owner or consignee.

Subsection (g) authorizes the Commission by rule to condition the importation of a consumer product on the manufacturer's compliance with certain inspection and record-keeping requirements.

Exports

Section 18 excludes exported products from the provisions of this act. This provision has been drawn to exclude only products which are exported or those which can be shown to have been manufactured, sold or held for sale for export and which are marked with a stamp or label stating that the product is intended for export. If a consumer product is, in fact, distributed in commerce for the use in the United States, it will be subject to the act.

The committee wishes to point out that any person claiming exemption under this section for any product found within the United States has the burden of proving that the product was manufactured, sold, or held for sale for export. Also, it should be noted that in cases where such product has been distributed in commerce, in order to qualify for an exemption, the product (or its container) must bear a stamp or label stating that the product is intended for export.

Any person engaged in the distribution or sale of products which are not labeled "for export" must proceed on the premise that the product is subject to the act and must comply with applicable standards or rules and, in appropriate circumstances, be accompanied by a certificate.

Prohibited acts

Section 19 lists prohibited acts under this bill for which civil and criminal penalties may be imposed or injunctive action brought.

Paragraphs 1 and 2 of subsection (a) make it unlawful for any person to manufacture for sale, offer for sale, distribute in commerce, or import any consumer product which does not conform to an applicable consumer product safety standard or which has been declared a banned hazardous product by rule authorized by section 8. This language is intended to insure that the act may apply to each stage of the process followed in the manufacture and distribution of consumer products.

Several persons have expressed the fear that the broad sweep of this language, would hold in violation of the Act, a manufacturer whose product failed to comply with applicable standards as it came off the assembly line, even though the non-conformity was corrected prior to the products distribution in commerce. This would not be the intention of the committee. In interpreting the term "manufacture for sale" the Commission and the courts should look to whether the manufacturer evidenced an intention to distribute the product. Where the manufacturer could show his intention to correct a non-conforming product or where he has, in fact, made the required correction, this paragraph should not be read as permitting the manufacturer to be held in violation on the technical basis that the product as initially produced or assembled did not comply with applicable standards or rules.

Paragraph 3 makes it unlawful for any person to fail or refuse to comply with inspection and record-keeping requirements or to furnish reports or other information required under this act or by Commission rule.

Paragraphs 4 and 5 make it unlawful to fail to give notice to the Commission as required by section 15(b) or to fail to comply with a Commission order under section 15 to give notice to or to repair, replace, or refund the purchase price of products which present substantial hazards.

Paragraph 6 would make it unlawful to fail to furnish a certificate required by section 14 or to issue a false certificate where such person, in the exercise of due care, would have reason to know is false or misleading in any material respect. It is also made a prohibited act to fail to comply with Commission rules issued under section 14(c) relating to the labeling of consumer products.

It would not be a prohibited act under this section for a distributor or retailer to distribute, sell, or offer for sale any product which does not conform to applicable standards or which has been declared a banned hazardous product if the retailer or distributor (1) holds a certificate certifying that the product conforms to all applicable consumer product safety rules (unless he knows that such consumer product does not so conform) or (2) relies in good faith on the representation of the manufacturer or distributor that the product is not subject to an applicable product safety rule. The representation that the product is not subject to an applicable product safety rule may be either expressed or implied. In some cases a retailer or distributor may properly assume that a product is not subject to safety rules. However, where the distributor or retailer relies on implied representations, he must be prepared to demonstrate his good faith in not pursuing further inquiry to determine whether a product was, in fact, subject to an applicable product safety rule.

Civil Penalties

Section 20 makes any person who knowingly commits a prohibited act under section 19 subject to a civil penalty of not more than $2,000 for each violation. The Commission may impose multiple penalties for any related series of violations not to exceed $500,000. In this respect a separate violation is committed with respect to each failure or refusal to perform a required act under section 19(a)(3). With respect to violations of paragraphs (1), (2), (4), (5), and (6) of section 19(a) it shall be considered a separate violation for each product involved.

A person who is not also a manufacturer, distributor, or private labeler (e.g. certain retailers) who knowingly violate section 19 may not be subjected to "multiple penalties" under this section unless he had actual knowledge that his sale or distribution of the product would violate the act or unless he received notice from the Commission that such action would constitute a violation of the act.

The Commission is given authority to compromise penalties which are imposed under this section.

It is to be noted that civil penalties may be imposed only for violations which are knowingly committed. In this regard the committee has defined the term "knowingly" to mean (1) actual knowledge, or (2) knowledge presumed to be possessed by a reasonable man acting in the circumstances including knowledge obtainable upon the exercise of due care to ascertain the truth of representation.

Criminal Penalties

Under section 21, any person who knowingly and wilfully violates section 19 of the act after receiving notice of noncompliance from the Commission may be fined not more than $50,000 or imprisoned for not more than one year or both.

Where individual directors of corporations or their officers or agents knowingly and wilfully authorized, ordered, or performed acts which constituted a violation of the act with knowledge that the Commission had notified the corporation of its noncompliance, both the corporation and the individual director, officer, or agent may be subject to criminal penalties under this section.

Injunctive Enforcement and Seizure

Section 22(a) provides that the U.S. district courts shall have jurisdiction to restrain violations of section 19 or to restrain any person from distributing in commerce any product which does not comply with a consumer product safety rule. This section contains its own venue requirements and would permit process to be served on a defendant in any district in which he is resident or may be found.

Under subsection (b), any consumer product which fails to conform to an applicable safety rule or which is not promptly returned to customs custody upon the order of the Secretary of the Treasury, may be proceeded against in an action in U.S. district court, seized, and condemned. Proceedings under this section shall conform as nearly as possible to proceedings in rem in admiralty. To avoid a multiplicity of actions, this section provides that proceedings initiated against identical consumer products in two or more judicial destricts, may be consolidated by order of the court upon motion of any party in interest.

Suits for Damages by Persons Injured

Section 23 provides a private remedy for damages to persons injured by reason of noncompliance with certain provisions of the bill. If an individual dies or sustains personal injury or illness by reason of the failure of a consumer product to comply with an applicable consumer product safety rule under the bill, then he (or his survivors or legal representative) may sue any manufacturer, distributor, or retailer of the noncomplying product, and may recover any damages sustained as a result of such failure to comply. Likewise if a person dies or sustains personal injury or illness by reason of a failure to comply with an order under section 15(c) or section 15(d) (relating to notification respecting, and repair, etc., of products presenting substantial product hazards), then he (or his survivors or legal representative) may sue any person who failed to comply with such order under section 15, and may recover any damages sustained as a result of such failure to comply.

The committee anticipates, in cases in which it is established that death, personal injury, or illness occurred by reason of noncompliance with the consumer product safety rule or section 15 order, that the courts will in general apply State law as to questions of which types of damages may be recovered and which parties in addition to the injured person can recover damages. The committee intends that any person who recovers damages by reason of personal injury, illness, or death, would also be able to recover for any property damage occurring by reason of the noncompliance giving rise to the injury, illness, or death.

Actions under this section may be brought without regard to the amount in controversy. In any action under this section, whenever a plaintiff prevails the court may award the plaintiff the costs of the suit, including a reasonable attorney's fee.

Section 27(b) contains affirmative defenses to actions under subsection (a). In the case of an action brought for noncompliance with an applicable consumer product safety rule, no liability will be imposed upon any manufacturer, distributor, or retailer who establishes (1) that he did not have reason to know in the exercise of due care that the product did not comply with the consumer product safety rule, and (2) in the case of a manufacturer or a private labeler of such noncomplying product, that the product was designed so as to comply with all applicable consumer product safety rules and that due care was used in the manufacture of the product so as to assure that the product complied with such rule. In the case of an action for noncompliance with a section 15 order, no liability will be imposed upon any manufacturer, distributor, or retailer who establishes that he took all steps as may be reasonable in the exercise of due care to comply with the order.

Subsection (c) makes it clear that remedies provided for in section 27 are in addition to and not in lieu of any other remedies provided by common law or under Federal or State statutory law.

Private Enforcement of Product Safety Rules and of Section 15 Orders

Section 24 permits any interested person to bring an action in the United States district court to enforce a consumer product safety rule or an order under section 15, and to obtain appropriate injunctive relief. Thirty days prior notice to the Commission, the Attorney General, and the defendant is required. A separate suit under this section is prohibited if at the time the suit is brought the same alleged violation is the subject of a pending civil or criminal action by the United States under the bill. In an action under this section, the plaintiff may elect at the time he files his complaint to recover reasonable attorney's fees. If he makes such an election, the court must award reasonable attorney's fees to the prevailing party. In determining which party is the "prevailing party" in multi-issue or multiparty litigation, the trial court should award attorney's fees in a manner which it determines will carry out the purpose of this section.

Effect on Private Remedies

Sections 25(a) and 25(b) provide that compliance with consumer product safety rules or other rules or orders under the bill will not relieve any person from liability at common law or under State statutory law to any other person; and that the Commission's failure to take any action or commence a proceeding with respect to the safety of a consumer product shall not be admissible in evidence in litigation at common law or under State statutory law relating to such consumer product.

Section 25(c)(1) provides accident and investigation reports by any officer, employee, or agent of the Commission will be available for use in any judicial proceeding arising out of such accident, and that any such officer, employee, or agent may be required to testify in such proceedings as to the facts developed in such investigations. The availability of such reports and testimony is subject to the bill's restrictions on disclosure of trade secrets but not otherwise subject to the restrictions of section 6.

Section 25(c)(2) requires that any such accident or investigation report be made available to the public in a manner which will not identify any injured person or any person treating him, without the consent of the person so identified, and that all reports on research projects demonstration projects, and other related activities shall be public information. The availability of reports under this provision is subject to all of the restrictions of section 6 except those of section 6(a)(1) (providing that matter exempted from the disclosure requirements of the Freedom of Information Act need not be disclosed under the bill).

Effect on State Standards

Section 26 provides that at such time as the Commission prescribes a product safety standard under this act and such standard takes effect, no State or political subdivision shall have authority to establish or continue in effect any safety standard or regulation which prescribes any requirement as to the performance, composition, contents, design, construction, finish, packaging, or labeling of such product which is devised to protect the public from the same hazard associated with the product (unless such requirements are identical to the Federal standard). It is intended that Federal authority—once exercised—occupy the field and broadly preempt State authority to regulate the same product hazards. Accordingly, the Federal preemption is intended to extend not only to State authority to set standards on labeling requirements but also to prevent States from acting to ban products which conform to applicable Federal safety standards where the purpose of the ban is to protect the public from the same product hazard.

This section would, however, permit States to establish or to continue standards which are identical to the Federal standard. Also, under certain conditions, States may be permitted by the Commission to impose standards which call for a higher level of performance. In both instances it is intended that the State or political subdivision will maintain its own enforcement mechanisms and be able to establish its own criminal and civil penalties for violation of the standard. By permitting dual enforcement, it is not intended that this section will be used as a means of subjecting violators to double penalties. In instances where violators have already been adequately penalized under State law, it is expected that Federal civil and criminal penalties will not be sought by the Commission or will not be imposed in their full measure. Moreover, in instances where State action follows the imposition of Federal penalties, it is expected that the Commission will take this into consideration in determining whether to compromise any civil penalty already imposed under section 21.

Additional Functions of Commission

Section 27(a) authorizes the Commission, its members, or its designated agent or agency, to conduct any hearing or other inquiry necessary or appropriate to its functions anywhere in the United States. Commissioners who participate in such a hearing or inquiry are not disqualified solely by reason of such participation from subsequently participating in Commission decisions in the same matter. The Commission is directed to give notice of any hearing, and an opportunity to participate therein.

Subsection (b) of section 27 authorizes the Commission to require any person to submit reports and answers to questions; to administer oaths; to require by subpena the attendance and testimony of witnesses and the production of documentary evidence; to take depositions; and to pay witnesses' fees. United States district courts are authorized under subsection (c) to enforce the Commission's subpenas.

Section 27(d) permits the Commission to require, for purposes of carrying out the legislation, that manufacturers provide to the Commission with performance and technical data related to performance and safety, and that they give notification of such performance and technical data at the time of original purchase to certain purchasers and prospective purchasers.

Subsection (e) authorizes the Commission, for purposes of carrying out the bill, to purchase any consumer product and to require any manufacturer, distributor, or retailer of a consumer product to sell the product to the Commission at manufacturer's, distributor's, or retailer's cost. Subsection (f) authorizes the Commission to enter into contracts with governmental entities, private organizations, or individuals for the conduct of activities authorized by the bill.

The Commission, under section 27(g), may plan, construct, and operate facilities suitable for research, development, and testing of consumer products in order to carry out the bill; however, appropriations to plan or construct such facilities would not be authorized except as provided in section 32(b) of the bill.

Section 27(h) directs the Commission to prepare and submit to the President and the Congress an annual report which would contain information respecting the Commission's activities, legislative recommendations, and certain other matters, including a log or summary of meetings held between Commission officials and representatives of industry and other interested parties.

Product Safety Advisory Council

Section 28 directs the Commission to establish a Product Safety Advisory Council which it may consult before prescribing consumer product safety rules or taking other action under the bill. The Council is to be appointed by the Commission and to be composed of fifteen members qualified by training and experience in fields related to product safety. Five members are to be selected from governmental agencies; five members are to be selected from consumer product industries (including a small business representative); and five members are to be selected from consumer organizations, community organizations, and recognized consumer leaders. The Council is to meet at the call of the Commission, but not less often than four times during each calendar year. The Council may propose consumer product safety rules to the Commission and may function through subcommittees. Council proceedings (and a record thereof) are to be public. Council members (other than Federal officers or employees) will be compensated on a per diem basis, and receive travel expenses; but such payments will not render Council members officers or employees of the United States for any purpose.

Cooperation With States and Other Federal Agencies

The Commission is directed by section 29(a) to establish a program to promote Federal-State cooperation for the purposes of carrying out the legislation, and it is authorized under such program to—

(1) accept from any State or local authorities assistance in carrying out the legislation, and to pay in advance or otherwise for the reasonable cost of such assistance, and

(2) commission any qualified officer or employee of any State or local agency as an officer of the Commission for the purpose of conducting examinations, investigations, and inspections.

In carrying out subsection (a), the Commission is directed to give favorable consideration to programs which establish separate State and local agencies to consolidate functions relating to product safety and other consumer protection activities.

Section 29(c) authorizes the Commission to obtain from any Federal department or agency such statistics, data, program reports, and other materials it deems necessary to carry out its functions under the bill, and such departments and agencies are authorized to cooperate with the Commission, and, to the extent permitted by law, furnish such materials to it. The Commission and the heads of other departments and agencies which administer programs related to product safety are directed to cooperate to the maximum extent practicable.

Transfers of Functions

Subsections (a) and (b) of section 30 transfer to the Commission all functions of the Secretary of Health, Education, and Welfare under the Federal Hazardous Substances Act and the Poison Prevention Packaging Act of 1970 and all functions of the Secretary of Health, Education, and Welfare, the Secretary of Commerce, and the Federal Trade Commission under the Flammable Fabrics Act. The functions of the Administrator of the Environmental Protection Agency and of the Secretary of Health, Education, and Welfare under the certain acts amended by section 7 of the Poison Prevention Packaging Act of 1970, to the extent such functions relate to the administration and enforcement of the Poison Prevention Packaging Act of 1970, are also transferred to the Commission. In addition, the functions of the Federal Trade Commission under the Federal Trade Commission Act, to the extent such functions relate to the administration and enforcement of the Flammable Fabrics Act, are transferred to the Commission.

Section 30(c) provides that a hazard which is associated with a consumer product and which could be prevented or reduced to a sufficient extent by action taken under the Federal Hazardous Substances Act. the Poison Prevention Packaging Act of 1970, or the Flammable Fabrics Act may be regulated by the Commission only in accordance with the provisions of those acts.

Paragraph (1) of section 30(d) provides that personnel, property, etc., which are used primarily with respect to any function transferred under section 30 (a) or (b) will be transferred to the Commission, but transfer of personnel will be without reduction in classification or compensation for one year after such transfer. The Chairman of the Commission, however, can assign personnel during such one-year period in order to carry out the bill.

The remaining paragraphs of section 30(d) contain savings provisions the principal provisions of which are as follows: Orders, rules, etc., which took effect under functions transferred under section 30 are to continue in effect according to their terms until changed in accordance with law. Section 30 does not affect pending administrative proceedings, except that such proceedings (to the extent that they relate to transferred functions) will be continued before the Commission. Section 30 does not affect suits commenced prior to the date it takes effect, and such suits will proceed as if section 30 had not beeen enacted; except that if, before section 30's effective date, any department or agency (or officer thereof) was a party to a suit involving functions transferred to the Commission, the suit will be continued by the Commission.

Some question has been raised about the interrelationship of the Poison Prevention Packaging Act provisions authorizing special packaging standards for foods, drugs, and cosmetics, and the packaging requirements for these same products under the Food, Drug and Cosmetic Act. In particular, since a new drug application requires approval by FDA of all drug packaging, there would be dual regulation over this particular aspect of the product. The Committee intends that the Commission and the Food and Drug Administration will cooperate fully in coordinating any overlapping statutory requirements. For example, before exercising its authority under the Poison Prevention

Packaging Act to prescribe safety closure standards for drugs which may have been the subject of a new drug application under the Food, Drug and Cosmetic Act, the Commission would be expected to coordinate its activities with FDA to preclude the possibility that a safety closure standard would be inconsistent with requirements imposed by FDA to assure the purity and effectiveness of the drug.

Limitation on Jurisdiction

Section 31 provides that the Commission has no authority under the bill to regulate hazards associated with consumer products which could be prevented or reduced to a sufficient extent by actions taken under the Occupational Safety and Health Act of 1970; the Act of August 2, 1956; the Atomic Energy Act of 1954; or the Clean Air Act. In addition, the Commission has no authority under the bill to regulate any electronic product radiation hazard which may be subjected to regulation under the electronic product radiation control provisions of the Public Health Service Act.

Authorization of Appropriations

Section 32(a) authorizes appropriations to carry out the provisions of the bill (other than the provisions of section 27(g) which authorize the planning and construction of research, development, and testing facilities) and for the purpose of carrying out the Federal Hazardous Substances Act, the Poison Prevention Packaging Act of 1970, and the Flammable Fabrics Act. The authorizations are $55,000.000, $59,000,000, and $64,000,000 for fiscal years 1973, 1974, and 1975, respectively.

Appropriations are authorized, under section 32(b), to plan and construct research, development, and testing facilities described in section 27(g); but no appropriation for planning or construction involving an expenditure in excess of $100,000 may be made unless the planning or construction has been approved by the Committee on Interstate and Foreign Commerce of the House of Representatives and by the Committee on Commerce of the Senate. For the purpose of securing consideration of such approval the Commission is to transmit to Congress a prospectus which would include a description of the facility, its location, and estimated maximum cost. The estimated maximum cost of the facility could be increased in the manner set out in section 32(b)(2).

Effective date

Section 33 provides that the bill will take effect 60 days after the date of its enactment, except that sections 4 and 32 will take effect on the date of enactment of the bill, and section 30 will take effect on the later of (a) 150 days after date of enactment or (b) when at least three members of the Commission first take office.

Cost Estimates

In accordance with Section 252(a) of the Legislative Reorganization Act of 1970 (Public Law 91-510), your committee estimates the following costs will be incurred in carrying out functions under H.R. 15003:

Five-Year Cost Estimate for the Proposed Consumer Product Safety Commission

Fiscal year:	*Millions*
1973	$55
1974	59
1975	64
1976	65
1977	65

NOTE.—Cost estimates do not include appropriations for amounts required in the planning, construction, or operation of research, development and testing facilities authorized under this bill.

* * *

MINORITY VIEWS

The concept that appropriate Federal legislation can result in reducing the risks resulting from the use of some consumer products is generally agreed upon. Any new legislation enacted should, however, build upon programs which have been tried and are known to be effective.

The record shows that the Food and Drug Administration has compiled a record in the past 30 months that can be favorably compared with any other regulatory agency in the Federal Government. The Secretary of Health, Education, and Welfare has testified, and it would be difficult to prove otherwise, that under existing authority the Food and Drug Administration has made the most dramatic progress in the 66 years of the existence of the organization.

In addition to reorganization, which gave FDA full agency status for the first time, the administration has vastly increased its budget. In the fiscal year 1970 the budget for FDA was $76.3 million. For fiscal year 1973 the administration has requested $178.8 million, which represents an increase of 146% over the last four fiscal years. The budget requested by the President for fiscal year 1973 is a 70% increase over 1972, the largest increase requested by any administration in the history of the Food and Drug Administration.

There is no doubt that controls can be more effective and enforcement moves made more quickly if we build upon the experience, capabilities and scientific resources of the existing administration rather than making it necessary to start all over again by creating a new commission.

Although independence from a cabinet department and bipartisan membership of independent regulatory agencies theoretically guarantee even-handed regulation and decision-making, these attributes have in fact resulted in chronic indecision and eternal bickering. Split decision policy-making and case-by-case enforcement have resulted in a mass of lengthy court actions at every turn. This is not to be desired in the field of product safety standard setting.

The very independence of a commission from cabinet affiliation makes it less able to pursue vigorously its purposes. In the matters of funding and competition for scarce personnel allocations, independent agencies have traditionally fared badly. There is no strong cabinet level executive to make the necessary priority decisions and to fight the fight for adequate funding at the highest levels. Chairmen of independent agencies seldom see the President for discussions of their agency needs.

To create a new commission will guarantee that not much of anything will happen in the field of product safety for two or three years. It will take that much time to work out the details, get space and hire the kinds of people needed. Even the commissioners themselves, however competent they may be, will need considerable time to learn to work together. This does not mean there will not be some kind of entity very quickly or that stationery headed "Product Safety Commission" will not appear promptly. It only means that the real business of creating and enforcing product safety standards will not be meaningfully pursued for a long, long time after this legislation is passed.

There is also every reason to believe from a fiscal point of view that the creation of a new commission will cost the taxpayers far more than leaving the product safety effort in an already organized and operating department of government. A new effort will require new forces and new research facilities. HEW has these already. A new commission would of necessity create new and unnecessary costs for the taxpayer. Practically, in the ways of government there is no way to prevent this sort of thing from happening.

The interest of the consumer will clearly be served best by strengthening the present organization (FDA) as a key health and safety related agency within the Department of Health, Eucation, and Welfare.

Samuel L. Devine,
Ancher Nelsen,
James Harvey,
Clarence J. Brown,
James F. Hastings,
John G. Schmitz,
James M. Collins.

APPENDIX H

EXCERPTS FROM DEBATE ON FLOOR OF HOUSE

(from the Congressional Record for September 20, 1972, starting at page H 8565)

CONSUMER PRODUCT SAFETY ACT

* * *

Mr. STAGGERS. Mr. Chairman, I rise in support of H.R. 15003, the Consumer Product Safety Act. This bill proposes to establish an independent regulatory commission with broadly assigned powers to protect the public from hazardous consumer products. This legislation will have an effect in every American household and is important to the safety of every member of our constituency, including our wives, sons, daughters, and grandchildren. Its enactment will be one of the most significant laws written in this Congress.

As most Members will recall, in the 90th Congress we established a National Commission on Product Safety to conduct a comprehensive study of the adequacy of existing laws to protect consumers against unreasonable risks of injury associated with hazardous household products. The seven-member bipartisan commission was appointed in March of 1968. Its final report was submitted to the Congress in June of 1970. This report forms the basis for the legislative proposal which I bring before the committee today.

Most existing Federal safety legislation has been enacted on a piecemeal basis in response to individual tragedies. Thus, the Flammable Fabrics Act was adopted to deal with flame hazards from textile products after several children were killed or disfigured from accidents involving brushed rayon "torch" sweaters. Motor vehicles were subjected to regulation in 1966 after deaths on our highways soared to over 55,000 per year.

In the course of its study, the National Commission listed a large number of products which it found to present unreasonable hazards to consumers. These included "unvented" gas heaters, hot water vaporizers, and infant furniture. Rather than propose individual legislation designed to deal with each of these products, however, the National Commission recommended that we abandon our traditional case-by-case approach and consolidate in a single agency authority sufficient to regulate the full spectrum of products which are sold to or used by consumers.

Toward that end, the National Commission submitted with its final report legislative proposals which recommended the creation of an independent regulatory commission with comprehensive authority to regulate hazardous products. Also, drawing upon the National Commission's report, in the beginning of this Congress the administration proposed legislation which recommended the establishment of omnibus product safety authority in the Federal Government. The administration's bill, however, proposed to vest this authority in the Department of Health, Education, and Welfare rather than create a new agency.

These two proposals formed the focus of 13 days of hearings which extended over a 4-month period. The committee's Subcommittee on Commerce and Finance met eight times in executive session on these proposals. In the end the subcommittee unanimously reported a clean bill representing an accommodation between the legislative recommendations of the National Commission and those of the administration. This bill, H.R. 15003, with certain amendments, was ordered favorably reported on voice vote of the full committee. Seven members of the committee, while not dissenting from the bill, have filed minority views believing that the authority contained in this legislation should be exercised by HEW and not an independent regulatory commission as recommended by the committee.

This bill would authorize spending of $178 million over the first 3 years. These amounts are based upon estimates supplied by HEW. This is, of course, a substantial amount of money. The dimensions of the problem are also substantial, however.

The National Center for Health Statistics estimates that each year 20 million Americans are injured in and around the home. Of this total, 110,000 injuries result in permanent disability and 30,000 in death. The annual dollar cost to the economy of product-related injuries totals over $5 billion. Moreover, home accidents account for more deaths among children under the age of 15 than cancer and heart disease combined.

These statistics have convinced the committee and virtually every witness who testified in the committee's hearings of the substantial need for this legislation.

Many of the major industries in the land have come to me and said they are for this bill, that they think it is needed. There are two points that they say should be changed, and I am going to offer amendments to change those.

The first is to change the manufacturer's date that is required in the bill be placed on each appliance or product that is made so that the consumer might know it. We put it in the bill, but I am going to offer an amendment that it may be done in code. But there are a lot of products put on the market that do not change from year to year, as an automobile does, that has a special model, and so forth. Many people, when they see the date, say that it is an old model because it was manufactured at a certain date, and they do not buy it. A lot of the major retail companies objected to this, and as I say, I think they are rightfully objecting to this, and perhaps it should be changed.

Every precaution, I think, has been taken in this bill to give industry due recognition and a part in making the standards—and this is really unprecedented.

Any industry cannot be convicted, of even a civil penalty or a criminal penalty, if it is shown that they did not knowingly violate the act.

We think it is a good bill and one that has been needed for a long period of years. I know that the gentleman from California said—well, it would be like voting against motherhood to vote against the bill. But I believe it is a bill that is very meritorious and a bill that has been carefully drawn with the precautions taken that not only consumers be protected, but industries of the land be protected as well.

As I have said, I have in my files several letters from large industries saying that they are for the bill, with two changes that I intend to offer.

So I recommend this bill to this House wholeheartedly as one that has been needed for years and one that will prevent a lot of injuries that occur in homes and across the Nation, injuries that are needless.

Mr. LATTA. Mr. Chairman, will the gentleman yield for a question.

Mr. STAGGERS. I yield to the gentleman.

Mr. LATTA. I would like to ask the gentleman a question about the statement he made that industry would be invited to make recommendations as to standards and so forth.

Mr. STAGGERS. That is right.

Mr. LATTA. I would like to have the gentleman refresh my memory as to whether or not the Senate bill contained an amendment which would preclude them from doing this?

Mr. STAGGERS. The Senate does have the so-called Nelson amendment which precludes them from coming in. We definitely put language in our bill that they would have a part in developing standards.

Mr. LATTA. That is your position?

Mr. STAGGERS. That is my position and that is the position of the committee.

Mr. LATTA. I thank the gentleman.

The CHAIRMAN. The Chair recognizes the gentleman from Illinois (Mr. (SPRINGER).

Mr. SPRINGER. Mr. Chairman, I yield myself such time as I may consume.

The idea of creating and enforcing safety standards for consumer products which logically and sensibly lend themselves to such treatment is probably accepted by most consumers and also by most businesses engaged in manufacturing and distributing such items. Considering the complexity of the problem and the issues and technical details which must be resolved to accomplish this purpose it is a wonder that so much agreement exists. There is, however, considerable difference of opinion as to the proper way to administer such an effort.

As reported the bill calls for the creation of yet another independent regulatory agency. I personally doubt that this is either wise or necessary. Past dealings with such commissions indicate serious weaknesses in their operations. Many commissions are fraught with internal bickering which works against the accomplishments expected from the legislation. Most commissions do not have the clout necessary to contend with the budget process nor the access to the White House. It could also be argued that unlike the overall regulation of transportation or communications, safety standard setting is not the kind of activity which lends itself to the regulatory pattern.

Organizing a new administrative entity from scratch is a lengthy affair. Although a skeleton of an organization appears promptly, the real business of the commission cannot be carried out for many moons. What I am saying here as to the disadvantages of a new commission has been said previously in the minority views filed with the committee report. I would commend those remarks to the Members of the House when considering their votes on an amendment to eliminate the commission from the bill and leave the safety standard setting activity in the Food and Drug Administration where it has been for some time now and where it has received high level attention and concern. As pointed out, there will be considerable research and staffing needed in the field. These already exist in FDA but since they do other things as well as safety standards it is not a mere matter of transferring facilities and people to a new entity. If it is the real wish of Congress to see early accomplishments in assuring the safety of consumer products it should opt for leaving the activity where it now rests.

In saying that most people applaud the general idea of standard setting we have grossly oversimplified the problem. There are many features of this bill which seemed correct to the committee which might or might not strike all Members the same. For example, the bill invites and encourages private industry to participate in the creation of safety standards for products which they handle or manufacture. This is traditional. It is also sensible. Maybe it is even necessary. No one knows the processes or the end product characteristics better than those who make the product for public consumption. Now it can be argued that these people have selfish interests and cannot be trusted to have any part in the proceedings except to defend themselves. This, of course, completely overlooks the fact that what expertise exists is in industry, not in government and not in consumer groups. Thousands of standards have been worked out over a long period of years, standards which were aimed at the betterment of consumer products. Most of this was done without any government prodding or assistance. I am not saying that it is improper for government to interject itself—I am only saying that it would be improper to exclude industry as the major resource.

Now and again a consumer product will show up in the market place which presents a clear and imminent hazard to the public. Some toys have fit this category and prompt removal from the shelves was not easy. This bill tries to improve the situation by recognizing that at times fast action is imperative and the full rights of the manufacturer or distributor can only be protected subsequently. This is done by allowing for quick court action rather than peremptory seizure without proceedings of any kind. We should be able to trust the courts to give a realistic interpretation to the term "imminently hazardous consumer product."

Gathering information on injuries arising from use of consumer products and dissemination of such material should work in the best interests of buyers and users of products.

The individual consumer has many courses of action open to him under this bill. He may ask that a standard be promulgated for particular products. This does not force the Government to act but it does give the individual citizen direct access to the machinery. That citizen may also sue directly for damages he may suffer due to failure to meet safety standards. As fair as this may be, it is also very possible for a manufacturer to do everything in his power to turn out a proper item and not do so. The design may be good and the manufacturing process well set up and well supervised and yet a lone defective item can result. If a defendant business can successfully show that all these things obtained it will be considered a defense against losses by reason of the product failure.

Aside from pursuing remedies in court, the consumer is further protected by requirements that discovered defects in a manufacturing run be followed by notification to purchasers and arrangements made for repair or replacement.

Except for the disputed question as to the administrative agency to carry out this program the bill represents a workable system for preventing safety defects in consumer products and a sensible system for redress when they do nonetheless occur.

Mr. STAGGERS. Mr. Chairman, will the gentleman yield?

Mr. SPRINGER. I yield to the gentleman from West Virginia, the chairman of the committee.

Mr. STAGGERS. Mr. Chairman, I would like to point out that under the civil penalty there can be a compromise by the Commission if there are extenuating circumstances which they can take into consideration.

Mr. SPRINGER. I am glad the chairman explained that. If those extenuating circumstances are sufficient, they can waive the civil penalty.

Mr. DENNIS. Mr. Chairman, will the gentleman yield?

Mr. SPRINGER. I yield to the gentleman from Indiana.

Mr. DENNIS. Mr. Chairman, one thing I find, aside from the problem of creating a new regulatory Commission that can set standards for business is something which always personally gives me pause and gives me concern. In this bill there is the provision in section 13 which gives the Commission authority to require the manufacturers of the new consumer product to furnish a notice and a description of the product to the consumer before its distribution in commerce. It seems to me, and I do not think this has been commented on, it is a pretty far-sweeping proposal in a free enterprise economy to say that before a man can manufacture a new product he has got to give notice and a detailed description to some Government bureau before he can even start to sell it.

Mr. SPRINGER. All right. May I say we already in effect have jurisdiction of many products now being produced. Now the question arose as to whether or not if they are going to introduce a new product, we should give certain jurisdiction. In that case we felt it was fair that anybody who introduces a new product on the market ought to give this kind of certification that it falls within this act.

Mr. DENNIS. I can only say to the gentleman it seems to me it would be much more normal to let this Commission do its job and if they find something wrong with a product to call it to their attention rather than having to get a prepermission before they can go into business.

Mr. SPRINGER. Let me say this. I think if the gentleman will talk to his business people who are producing things in his district, he would find they would rather have a submission of an article in substance under this section than they would like to have it come after they have produced the article and put it on the market and then be put out of business. Is it not more reasonable to have certification in the beginning that it is not dangerous? Just as an example, and it is not covered in this act, take automobiles. Maybe 100,000 automobiles have to be recalled by the factory because something is wrong. We do not cover automobiles in this act but I give that as an example of what has been happening. Would it not be far better if we were producing a product to have a precertification rather than put 100,000 on the market around Christmas for example and then have somebody say we cannot sell it?

Mr. DENNIS. Under our system I always thought a man had a certain amount of liberty to take a chance. If we adopt the philosophy that the Government is going to run everything, maybe we should do this. Maybe it would be safe. But I think if I want to put a product on the market I ought to be able to think about it and make up my own mind without running down here and asking some bureau.

I think the gentleman has made a point, but I think this point here is the safety of the product. I repeat, it would be better to do it this way.

Mr. STAGGERS. Mr. Chairman, will the gentleman yield?

Mr. SPRINGER. I yield to the chairman.

Mr. STAGGERS. I should like to answer the gentleman and say that all a manufacturer would be required to do is just give a description and describe the intended use of the article, and it can be put on the market. If you read the report on page 39, it says it does not have to be cleared.

Let me read the bill:

> For purposes of this section, the term "new consumer product" means a consumer product which incorporates a design, material, or form of energy exchange which (1) has not previously been used substantially in consumer products . . .

Then, all they have to do is notify the Commission of the description of what they are going to do, and that is about all. As it says here—

> The Commission may, by rule, prescribe procedures for the purpose of insuring that the manufacturer of any new consumer product furnish notice and a description of such product to the Commission before its distribution in commerce.

That is all he has to do. Then, they take a risk as they do every place else.

Mr. DENNIS. Will the gentleman yield?

Mr. SPRINGER. I yield to the gentleman from Indiana.

Mr. DENNIS. I understand, Mr. Chairman, that you do not have this to the place where a man has to have permission before he can sell; you have not gone that far. You have only taken the first step. He has got to give notice before he sells. I expect that maybe in a year or two from now we will be back here with a bill which makes a precondition. That is what I am worried about, the first step forward.

Mr. BROYHILL of North Carolina. Mr. Chairman, will the gentleman yield?

Mr. SPRINGER. I yield to the gentleman from North Carolina.

Mr. BROYHILL of North Carolina. Mr. Chairman, all I wish to do is agree with what the chairman of the committee has said is the intent of this section. All this section does is provide a means for the Commission to keep informed about what is going on in the area of new products. That is all.

Mr. SPRINGER. I thank the gentleman.

Mr. LLOYD. Mr. Chairman, will the gentleman yield?

Mr. SPRINGER. I yield to the gentleman from Utah.

Mr. LLOYD. Mr. Chairman, did the gentleman support the creation of the independent Commission?

Mr. SPRINGER. No, I did not. I felt it ought to be in HEW from the beginning, but you understand that in these kinds of cases, you often find that the minority does not get out on the floor the exact bill it wants. I see by the seven minority Members who wrote the minority report on this, that this was one of the reasons that they wrote the minority report. They did not agree with the independent Commission idea. I think I have leaned over as far as I can go in this bill in going along with the bill as it is written. I said that I will not go along with anything which changes this bill very much.

Mr. LLOYD. May I ask one question of the gentleman?

Do I understand the provisions of the bill provide that if a manufacturer of a product covered under this act should unknowingly place it on the market without first giving notice to this Commission, he would be subject to a fine of $2,000 and upward?

Mr. SPRINGER. I will have to turn to the chairman. I do not think it does.

Mr. STAGGERS. The bill, I think very clearly, says "knowingly" or "having knowledge of" without due care and so forth; that he has to know what he is doing and so forth.

Mr. LLOYD. Even though he does not know of this new provision requiring that notice be given to the Commission, he will be subject to a civil fine?

Mr. STAGGERS. If he can prove that, I am sure he would not be subjected to the fine, but certainly any man who manufactures products, I think knows the law of the land, what it might be, but if they can prove differently before the Commission or even before the judge, that would be different.

Mr. MOSS. Mr. Chairman, will the gentleman yield?

Mr. SPRINGER. I yield to the gentleman from California.

Mr. MOSS. If you will look under page 101 under Criminal Penalties, section 21(a)—

> Any person who knowingly and willfully violates——

Mr. LLOYD. I was not referring to the criminal penalties.

Mr. MOSS. Then under Civil Penalties it is also "knowingly." I will give you the precise page. It is on page 99:

> Any person who knowingly violates—

Under section 20(a) at page 99 of the bill dealing with civil penalties, so he must knowingly violate.

I thank the gentleman for yielding.

Mr. LLOYD. One of the great problems facing small business in the country today is this continual problem of applying the law and the various regulations that are being passed by this body and the State regulatory bodies. It is becoming very onerous and in many cases almost impossible for small businessmen to remain in business. I believe that is one of the real problems we have to consider.

Mr. SPRINGER. May I say I agree with the gentleman. However, everyone was for a bill. The administration was for a bill and strongly supported a bill.

The question arises as to what the character of the legislation shall be, how far it shall go, who shall determine the standards and enforcement, and how the enforcement shall take place. This is where the great disagreement in the committee arose, over these five particular problems. This was something that was ultimately compromised, as to how this would be done.

Mr. GROSS. Mr. Chairman, will the gentleman yield?

Mr. SPRINGER. I yield to the gentleman from Iowa.

Mr. GROSS. I thank the gentleman for yielding.

Would it be correct to say that this bill is in the nature of an indictment of the present regulatory agencies which deal with the subject matter here being considered?

Mr. SPRINGER. No. I would say it is not an indictment. Actually, we do not have any agency presently covering the matters contained in this bill.

Mr. GROSS. What about the FDA to mention just one?

Mr. SPRINGER. The FDA has some

safety jurisdiction, but not this. For instance, the FDA handles many things having to do with food products, cosmetics, and those types of things. Generally speaking, on the enforcement of that kind, for safety, it has been in the FDA.

The reason why I felt this should be placed there was because I thought this dealt with a product. If we are going to change the character of it, why not leave it in FDA, because these people have had experience in this field? This is why I felt that ought to be done.

They do not cover most of the matters covered in here, but they do cover other products for safety. Those are the others I read, which are not covered; food, drugs, cosmetics, medical devices. Tobacco is covered in FDA. Some of these others are covered in other legislation.

Principally in the past FDA has handled safety or food and drug products, for the most part.

Mr. GROSS. This bill provides, as I undertsand it, for a Commission of five members?

Mr. SPRINGER. That is right.

Mr. GROSS. How many members?

Mr. SPRINGER. Five.

Mr. GROSS. And an advisory board?

Mr. SPRINGER. A council of 15 members.

Mr. GROSS. An advisory council of 15 members. Does not the gentleman believe this is laying still another layer of fat on top of the present regulatory agencies. If the existing agencies have not been doing the job they should in this field, why did the committee not bring out legislation to compel them to assume their responsibilities rather than creating still another Commission and another advisory council in the Federal Government?

Mr. SPRINGER. May I say that the gentleman, having been in the committee process himself, knows that in the minority we do not always get what we want. I believe this was supported very largely by those in the minority.

I am not saying this was partisan. I am saying that there were not sufficient votes to sustain that position we originally wanted. The gentleman is right. Because we come here with another commission, rather than putting it in FDA, a question arises in my mind, "Should I conscientiously oppose this if it is in the public interest merely because I did not get my way in putting it in FDA?"

Mr. GROSS. Will the gentleman yield?

Mr. SPRINGER. I yield to the gentleman.

Mr. GROSS. I was not directing my remarks personally to the gentleman. Those remarks were directed to the majority in the House of Representatives, and since this bill is a House bill and is before the House today, I hope that before this day is over someone on that side of the aisle will tell us why they in the majority brought out this kind of a bill.

Mr. STAGGERS. Will the gentleman yield?

Mr. SPRINGER. Yes; I will yield to the chairman of the committee.

Mr. STAGGERS. I have in my hand here some of the samples of those things that are not covered at all in any regulations that contain unreasonable hazards: Architectural glass, color television sets, floor furnaces, high-rise bicycles, hot water vaporizes, infant furniture, ladders, power tools, protective headgear, rotary lawnmowers and on and on, products that are not under any regulation at all today, products that are hazards around the house.

Now, these have not been covered. In this new agency we cover all of these, and we take the Federal Hazardous Substances Act, the Poison Prevention Packaging Act, and the Flammable Fabrics Act. and place all of them in this agency.

I should point out that this was bipartisan, because both parties did, as I say, cosponsor it.

And may I say this further: This advisory committee is made up of five men from Government, five from industry, and five from the consumers, so that they will know and be able to advise the Commission. We tried to make it as bipartisan and as free as we could, so that industry would have the benefit and the consumers would have the benefit, too.

Mr. SPRINGER. May I ask the Chairman, how much remaining time do I have?

The CHAIRMAN. The gentleman from Illinois has consumed 25 minutes.

Mr. SPRINGER. Mr. Chairman, I cannot yield any further time, since I have at least one Member who wants to speak.

Mr. STAGGERS. I yield 5 minutes to the gentleman from California (Mr. Moss), the subcommittee chairman.

Mr. MOSS. Mr. Chairman, I think the committee is fully aware of the time and effort that has gone into this legislation. Before setting forth the details of that effort, I want to pay my compliments to every member of the subcommittee for the diligence with which they followed this legislation.

Mr. Chairman, the Consumer Product Safety Act is legislation of major importance to every American. It was carefully structured to promote the safety of consumer products, reduce unnecessary deaths and injuries and strengthen consumer confidence in our economic system.

It is cosponsored by every member of the subcommittee, which spent over 5 months in hearings and executive sessions on the bill.

The need for this legislation is documented in literally thousands of pages of testimony before the House and Senate Commerce Committee's and the National Commission on Product Safety. You will recall the National Commission on Product Safety was established by Congress in 1967. It conducted an extensive 2-year investigation of the safety of consumer products. It was a bipartisan commission. Its report was unanimous on all major recommendations. This legislation is based upon that report.

Twenty million Americans are injured every year in accidents associated with consumer products; 110,000 of them permanently; and 30,000 are killed. While not all of these deaths and injuries are caused by consumer products, testimony before the Subcommittee on Commerce and Finance, established that a significant number can be eliminated if proper attention is paid by both Government and industry to accident prevention.

In this connection the National Commission concluded in its report:

> The exposure of consumers to unreasonable consumer product hazards is excessive by any standard of measurements.

Of course, it is easy to talk about statistics, but the real meaning of this legislation lies in the pain and suffering of individual Americans who are unnecessarily maimed by products that can be designed better. For example:

Glass doors and windows that are not made of safety glazing cause 150,000 accidents a year; gas floor furnaces which are not adequately insulated develop temperatures of up to 350° and burn 30,000 a year; unvented gas space heaters which are inadequately designed result in between 350 and 1,000 deaths annually; and rotary power lawnmowers which are not adequately designed result in 140,000 injuries annually.

Should any member think that the list of hazards compiled by the Commission was a final and exhaustive list, I would recommend that he carefully read the hearings of the subcommittee on this legislation. Very serious questions were raised concerning the safety of many products not investigated by the commission, such as children's minibikes, aluminum home wiring and synthetic football turf.

With a little effort by Government and industry and with the assistance of consumers and consumer organizations, these products can be improved and the annual cost of injuries, which may exceed $5 billion, can be reduced.

It should be obvious to anyone familiar with the background of this legislation that the need is clear and present. Every day of delay means more unnecessary injuries. During the month of July alone, the emergency rooms of the 16 California hospitals reporting to the Department of Health, Education, and Welfare treated 2,798 persons for injuries associated with consumer products. And, remember, there are 479 other emergency room facilities in the State which are not in the reporting system.

Now let me briefly describe the manner in which the law will operate.

The bill authorizes the collection of injury statistics and the conduct of medical and engineering studies to assist in determining the causation of accidents. It authorizes the dissemination of educational information to consumers to help them avoid accidents. It provides for the development of safety standards where an unreasonable product hazard is found. These minimum Federal safety standards might relate to the performance, labeling or packaging of a consumer product. They could be promulgated only after fully adequate hearings and judicial review.

The subcommittee and the committee were especially careful to design the act to take into account the legitimate problems of industry. Rarely have I seen legislation dratfed with more awareness of its effect on the industries that will be subject to it. For example:

First, producers and private standards groups are given the opportunity to develop proposed product safety standards for the Commission. So are consumer groups. The Commission may agree to contribute to the developer's costs. I am aware of no comparable provision for industry and consumer participation in the development of other Federal regulations.

Second, product safety standards may be issued only after a hearing pursuant to the Administrative Procedure Act. In addition to the requirements of section 553 of that act the bill requires the agency to afford interested parties an opportunity for oral presentation of arguments and that a transcript of the proceedings be kept for purposes of court review.

Third, under this bill court review of product safety standards will be pursuant to the "substantial evidence" rule rather than the usual standard which sustains an agency's rulemaking action if it is not arbitrary. This is a departure from the normal standard of review in recognition of the importance of commission decisions to the public health and safety, as well as to the industries involved.

Fourth, the agency may proceed against "imminent hazards" solely by court action for injunctive relief. The Federal Hazardous Substances Act, which is already law, allows for an administrative ban of imminently hazardous products.

Fifth, finally, the bill contains careful provisions protecting against the unnecessary disclosure of trade secrets and other confidential business information.

It should be clear, from this description, that the Consumer Product Safety Act is a legislation that will be fair to business—and indispensable to American consumers.

Mr. Chairman, we have heard much discussion about the fact that this legislation creates an independent consumer product safety commission to consolidate existing Federal safety programs and to regulate the many unregulated products that will be subject to it.

I can assure the Members that the subcommittee and the committee weighed carefully the need for a new agency. The original recommendation for the creation of an independent commisison came from the National Commission on Product Safety and it was unanimous.

The Commission stated:

> Statutory regulatory programs buried in agencies with broad and diverse missions have, with few exception, rarely fulfilled their missions . . . the high visibility of a vigorous independent commission would be a constant reminder of Federal presence and would itself stimulate voluntary improvement of safety practices.

The committee was also of the opinion that a bipartisan independent commission would tend to insulate safety decisions from political pressure, speed up the budget process, permit more effective communication with the public and industry, consolidate presently fragmented safety programs and avoid further burdening the already overburdened department of Health, Education, and Welfare.

The subcommittee had 13 days of hearings, spent 8 days in markup, and then took it to the full committee where the work of the subcommittee was reviewed.

At no time in the course of the consideration of this bill was it considered on a partisan basis in the subcommittee. It represents a part of the thinking of each member of the subcommittee. There is not a member who cannot point to something in this legislation and say, "That is my amendment. It is there because that is what I proposed."

I think it is a fine example of the legislative process working most effectively.

But before the legislation ever reached the subcommittee, the Committee on Interstate and Foreign Commerce directed the creation of the National Commission on Product Safety, and that Commission worked for 2½ years at a cost of about $2 million. It had held many hearings, examining into the nature of complaints against products on the American market. The Commission then filed a report. The bill before you represents a significant degree the consensus of the members of that National Commission on Product Safety.

Certainly with respect to the assignment of duties of administration of this act to an independent agency, that was a unanimous recommendation of the special Commission. That Commission reflected rather broadly the commercial interests of this Nation.

I think the success of the legislation offered to you today by the Committee on Interstate and Foreign Commerce in meeting the needs of both industry and business is best brought into focus by looking at some of those who have come forward and said, "We support the House bill."

Sears, Roebuck—the largest merchandising firm not only in this Nation but in the world; the Association of Home Appliance Manufacturers. They are not afraid of the House bill at all; they endorse it. The Consumer Federation of America, the Consumers Union, the American Academy of Pediatrics. There are others, but those are important groups, groups concerned with the problem, as I know every Member of this Congress is.

So we have offered you here good legislation which meets the need for consumer safety that was so amply illustrated in the hearings of the committee and the report made available to every Member of the House as a result of the work of the National Commission on Product Safety.

Mr. Chairman, we are all aware that this legislation affects substantial economic interests. Some of them have not hesitated to remind us of that fact. But I would remind my colleagues consumer safety legislation also affects the public interest. It is an effort to protect the health and safety of all Americans. Most of them still have a deep and abiding confidence in this democracy. The enactment of this legislation will not lessen that confidence.

Mr. HOLIFIELD. Will the gentleman yield?

Mr. MOSS. I am very happy to yield to the gentleman.

Mr. HOLIFIELD. The gentleman knows of my concern for protection of consumers in bringing before the House a bill which was passed by a vote of 300 to 44 on this subject.

The gentleman sees nothing in this bill that would conflict with the establishment of a consumer agency, does he?

Mr. MOSS. I do not. I see nothing at all in here to that effect.

Mr. HOLIFIELD. I have studied this bill, and I think it is a fine piece of legislation. I want to compliment the gentleman from California, the chairman of the subcommittee, and the members of his subcommittee as well as the chairman of the full committee.

This committee, in my opinion, does its work and does it well. It does it carefully and brings to the floor well thought out legislation. Where there are differences among the members of the committee they are logically presented. It is a great comfort to me as a Member of the House to have been able to follow this committee and support it in most of its legislation if not all of it.

I want to compliment the gentleman, the subcommittee chairman, the chairman of the full committee, and all of the members, including the fine members on the minority side, for bringing this bill before the House.

Mr. MOSS. I thank the gentleman.

(Mr. MOSS asked and was given permission to revise and extend his remarks.)

Mr. STAGGERS. Mr. Chairman, I yield 2 minutes to the gentleman from Texas (Mr. ECKHARDT) a member of the subcommittee.

Mr. ECKHARDT. Mr. Chairman, I want to use my time to answer the question that the gentleman from Iowa raised, and I hope it will be to his satisfaction, because many of these same arguments were raised on the subcommittee and ultimately we came out with a unanimous opinion with respect to the independent agency.

It will be noted that the minority report is not signed by any Republican member of the subcommittee.

Let me point out what we were trying to do. Instead of proliferating agencies, we were trying, No. 1, to bring all of the areas of consumer protection against unsafe products under a single agency. For instance, flammable fabrics was controlled by Commerce in establishing standards, by HEW in investigations, and by FTC in enforcement. If you can show me a better model of inefficient administration and of imposing undue loads on the manufacturer by subjecting him to three separate agencies in three different areas, I would like to know it. Hazardous substances, it is true, was under HEW, and the poisonous product packaging was in HEW.

What we felt we ought to do since we were dealing here with an agency that had largely judicial or quasi-judicial powers was to place it in a single agency, a single agency under the surveillance of Congress and not related to any political party.

The CHAIRMAN. The time of the gentleman from Texas has expired.

Mr. STAGGERS. Mr. Chairman, I yield 1 additional minute to the gentleman from Texas.

Mr. ECKHARDT. Mr. Chairman, we wanted to remove it from the departments of Government that move and change with the movement of administration. Ws have activities here that are essentially judicial in function so we provided 7-year overlapping terms that would run outside the terms of administrations. I think we afforded the most effective way of not proliferating agencies, but consolidating in a single agency a quasi-judicial function and of creating an agency that would be most congenial to the due process afforded in this bill.

I know, in the presentation of this bill and in the answers to some of the amendments, you will ultimately see that we have been more sensitive to judicial process than any other drafters of a piece of legislation affecting administrative agencies.

The CHAIRMAN. The time of the gentleman from Texas has again expired.

Mr. STAGGERS. Mr. Chairman, I yield 2 additional minutes to the gentleman from Texas.

Mr. ECKHARDT. Mr. Chairman, I will not take the full 2 additional minutes, because I feel that if there ever was a subcommittee that worked carefully across the aisle on points like these it was our subcommittee.

The question was brought up just a minute ago by the distinguished gentleman from California (Mr. HOLIFIELD) concerning the question of a Consumers' Advocate.

Now, from the other side of the aisle we received the suggestion that the Consumers' Advocate under the other bill should be sufficient, and that we would be proliferating interference with agencies if we created another special

Consumers' Advocate. So we gave that up. They convinced us. We on the other hand convinced them, I believe, and I would invite responses from some of the members of that subcommittee, that since this was essentially a quasi-judicial body it was far better to have it appointed over a long period of time, with long terms, and independent of one of the departments of Government which are really not set up for judicial or quasi-judicial determinations.

Now, essentially that is what we did, and I think it was a fine example of exchange not on the basis of what is in the administration's bill, or what is in somebody else's bill, but what will work.

For instance, we took from the administration bill directly the control of imminent hazards instead of giving the agency any power for an immediate ban. We make them go to court, just as in the administration's bill.

So we have a fine mixture, and I think a very workable total package.

Mr. SPRINGER. Mr. Chairman, I yield 5 minutes to the gentleman from Ohio (Mr. DEVINE).

(Mr. DEVINE asked and was given permission to revise and extend his remarks.)

Mr. DEVINE. Mr. Chairman, we have legislation here today that carries the title "Consumer Product Safety Act." Now who in the world can be opposed to consumer product safety? You know there are those in this Chamber who shudder, shake, and shiver when they think Mr. Nader may take offense at what they do, especially the violation of his code and vote against some title like this. Nader, as you know, is the self-appointed guardian of the people of this country, as well as an "expert" on all subjects.

Now let us take a look at what it does. Let us take a look at this committee report stating the purpose of the legislation.

The bill would create a new independent regulatory commission with comprehensive authority. Now that is all we need in government—another new comprehensive regulatory agency—we do not seem to have enough.

This bill would vest in the consumer product safety commission the authority to collect and to disseminate information on consumer products related injuries; establish mandatory safety standards or to ban a product from the marketplace; obtain equitable relief in the courts and so on.

It provides a system of product certification to compel inclusion of certain safety related information on product labels and so forth.

There are seven of us who attached our signatures to the minority views, in addition to the gentleman currently in the well, the gentleman from Minnesota (Mr. NELSEN), the gentleman from Michigan (Mr. HARVEY), the gentleman from Ohio (Mr. BROWN), the gentleman from New York (Mr. HASTINGS), the gentleman from California (Mr. SCHMITZ), and the gentleman from Texas (Mr. COLLINS).

I will not attempt to go into all the minority views except to point out to you that we deplore the creation of another independent regulatory agency, another commissioner and a five member board with a fifteen member advisory board.

We point this out and I am making reference to the last paragraph on page 69 of the minority views which says the following:

> To create a new commission will guarantee that not much of anything will happen in the field of product safety for two or three years. It will take that much time to work out the details, get space and hire the kinds of people needed. Even the commissioners themselves, however competent they may be, will need considerable time to learn to work together.

It goes on further and says:

> There is also every reason to believe from a fiscal point of view that the creation of a new commission will cost the taxpayers far more than leaving the product safety effort in an already organized and operating department of government. A new effort will require new forces and new research facilities. HEW has these already.

That is why those of us who attached our signatures to the minority views, feel that this should be handled by the existing regulatory agency, the Food and Drug Administration within the Department of Health, Education, and Welfare.

Mr. Chairman, I yield back the balance of my time.

The CHAIRMAN. The gentleman yields back 2 minutes.

Mr. SPRINGER. Mr. Chairman, I yield 5 minutes to the gentleman from North Carolina (Mr. BROYHILL).

(Mr. BROYHILL of North Carolina asked and was given permission to revise and extend his remarks.)

Mr. BROYHILL of North Carolina. Mr. Chairman, that the public is entitled to purchase products without subjecting themselves to the possible risk of injury or death in the operation of these products would appear to be self-evident. And yet, today consumers are not able to confidently rely on the safety of the products they use and should enjoy.

The National Center for Health Statistics estimates that each year 20 million Americans are injured in and around the home. Of this total, 110,000 injuries result in permanent disability and 30,000 in death. The annual cost to the Nation of product-related injuries may exceed $5.5 billion. It is important to note that these figures do not include injuries resulting from automobile accidents, which have been widely reported to total 4 million injuries, 55,000 deaths, and an economic cost of more than $16 billion annually.

And yet, for all these statistics and the assumption that the Federal Government exercises broad authority in the interest of consumer safety, existing Federal authority to curb hazards in a majority of consumer products is virtually nonexistent.

The Congress has attempted to respond to this need by passing a series of acts designed to deal with specific hazards in a piecemeal approach. These acts include the National Traffic and Motor Vehicle Safety Act of 1966, the Gas Pipeline Safety Act of 1968, the Flammable Fabrics Amendments of 1967, the Radiation Control for Health and Safety Act of 1968, the Child Prevention and Toy Safety Act of 1969, and the Poison Prevention Packaging Act of 1970.

In recognition of the problems and the comprehensiveness of the issues involved, the Congress created in 1967 the National Commission on Product Safety with a directive to "conduct a comprehensive study and investigation of the scope and adequacy of measures now employed to protect consumers against unreasonable risks of injuries which may be caused by household products." The Commission, in issuing its report in 1970, recommended two fundamental changes in the Federal Government's approach to product safety. First, it recommended that a single independent agency be given the basic responsibility within the Federal Government for regulation designed to promote the safety of consumer products. Second, the Commission recommended that the new product safety agency have authority over the safety consumer products. The legislation we consider today incorporates these two fundamental changes into the most comprehensive consumer protection legislation ever considered.

It may be asked, "Is new product safety legislation needed?" Consumer spokesmen acknowledge that technological progress, growing affluence, and advances in product distribution have brought great benefits to American consumers over the past half-century. These include widespread availability of electrical appliances, power tools, household chemicals, medicines and countless other products. But accompanying these advances are the new risks to the safety and health of the American public.

There are those who believe that safety begins in the home with behavioral patterns of the family, such as storing chemicals out of the reach of children and providing for steady ladder. Others contend that safety begins with the home itself, the environment where hazardous products find their uses. And still others believe that safety begins in the factory and includes design, construction and hazard analysis, as well as quality control. All three concepts clearly contribute to the overall safety picture. The National Commission attempted to find the weak link in this chain, that area where remedies could best be applied with the assurance of some degree of success. The Commission determined that the greatest promise for reducing risk resides in "energizing the manufacturer's ingenuity." Government stimulation, coupled with this technological know-how could achieve the needed safety controls.

The Congress, in responding to the National Commission on Product Safety, began to study the problems involved in assuring product safety for all consumers. The House Subcommittee on Commerce and Finance of the Interstate and Foreign Commerce Committee held public hearings on a number of national product safety proposals, including the recommendations included in the National Safety Commission's Report and those recommendations contained in the President's consumer message.

As reported from the committee, the legislation we are considering today would vest in an independent regulatory Commission authority to collect and disseminate information on consumer product related injuries; establish mandatory safety standards where necessary to prevent or reduce unreasonable product hazards, or where such standards are not feasible, to ban the product from the marketplace; obtain equitable relief in the courts to protect the public from products which pose imminent hazards to health and safety and administratively order the notification and remedy of products which fail to comply with Commission safety rules or which contain safety-related defects.

The bill also contains a system of product certification and permits the Commission to compel inclusion of certain safety-related information in product labeling. The Commission would be given broad inspection and recordkeeping powers. Enforcement of the provisions contained in this legislation would be obtained through court injunctive process or through imposition by the court of criminal and civil penalties. Private suits for damages are allowed to be brought in Federal courts and consumer suits are permitted to compel compliance with safety rules and certain Commission orders.

All witnesses who testified before the committee including virtually all segments of the manufacturing industry, supported the proposition that the Federal Government should assume a major role in assuring the safety of consumer products. Disagreement among witnesses primarily centered upon the organizational structure for regulating product hazards and the procedures to be employed in the exercise of governmental authority.

The National Commission on Product Safety had recommended that a new independent Federal agency be established; the administration had asked that this authority be given to the Department of Health, Education, and Welfare. The administration planned to build on the activities, personnel, and existing facilities of the Food and Drug Administration and to reorganize the FDA for the purpose of assuming the additional responsibilities of this legislation.

The decision of the committee to create an independent regulatory agency along the lines of the recommendations of the National Commission on Product Safety reflects the committee's belief that an independent agency can better carry out the legislative and judicial functions contained in this bill with the needed neutrality that the public has the right to expect of regulatory agencies formed for its protection. This independent status, bipartisan commissioners with staggered and fixed terms, would form insulation from the political and economic pressures such as exist in the executive branch.

An independent agency can give more objective, single-minded attention to consumer safety. An independent agency has undivided responsibility for product safety and can be more easily held responsible for any failures that occur. Competition for funding has grown more intense and all too frequently funding for needed programs goes unnoticed in the cumbersome budget requests of the superagencies. The authority to publicize budget requests and legislative recommendations by an independent agency without censorship or competition within an agency will enable the product safety function to compete more effectively for money, manpower, and authority. Independent status will help confer greater prestige on the regulation of product safety and make it more visable to the public. This public awareness, it has been argued, is one of the most important factors in stimulating an agency to exercise its full powers in the public interest. Public attention will stimulate consumer viewpoints as well as industry viewpoints.

And significantly, an independent agency would combine existing fragmented programs which are currently dispersed through approximately 30 different Federal organizations. Consolidation would lead to more effective, better coordinated attacks on consumer safety hazards.

Studies have shown the weaknesses and failings of the Food and Drug Administration are unlikely to be remedied from within the overwhelming structure of HEW. Morale problems, inadequate planning and communications problems of long duration have plagued the FDA, as well as insufficient use of its authority in protecting the consumer. The FDA has been dependent on private industry for much of the technical information and expert opinion about the safety of products. Accordingly, this prevents swift action by the FDA where there is controversy and industry opposition.

In addition to the need to establish a comprehensive and effective regulation over the safety of unreasonably hazardous consumer products, there exists the need to insure that procedures relating to consumer products are fair to both industry and consumers. The committee heard witnesses from industry documenting some of the potential difficulties that might be encountered in complying with the proposed regulations.

I believe that the committee has formulated legislation which for the first time affords industry and consumer groups the opportunity to directly participate in the development of safety standards. In other words, it is truly balanced in its approach to solving these important problems of consumer protection without penalizing the manufacturer.

Manufacturers and other interested parties are given the opportunity to develop proposed product safety standards. The Commission may, where appropriate, agree to contribute to the developers' costs. We are aware of no comparable provision for industry participation in the standard-development process in any other safety statute.

In addition, all final product safety standards or proposed bans must be issued after hearings pursuant to section 553 of title 5. The bill further requires the Commission to afford interested parties with an opportunity for oral presentation of arguments, requires that a transcript be kept, and that it be filed as a part of the record upon court review.

In a major departure from normal standards of court review of regulatory actions, this bill would provide court review of any product safety standard or ban, pursuant to the "substantial evidence" rule rather than the usual rule which sustains the agency's action if it is neither arbitrary nor capricious. Procedures under this legislation against "imminent hazards" would be by court action. The Federal Hazardous Substances Act, applicable to many consumer products, provides for administrative banning of imminently hazardous products.

Notification of the public of products presenting "substantial hazards" or products failing to comply with safety standards must be preceded by a hearing pursuant to the Administrative Procedures Act. Any recall order must be preceded by a formal hearing in accordance with section 554 of title 5. Repair, replacement, or refund is at the election of the manufacturer. Refund must be less reasonable allowance for use by the consumer.

This legislation prohibits the public disclosure of trade secrets or other sensitive material. It requires the Commission to notify each manufacturer of its intent to release any information at least 30 days prior to disclosure and offer an opportunity for comment. This provision is not found in any other safety legislation.

Civil penalties for violations of the act apply only where the violation was committed knowingly. Criminal penalties apply only where the violation was committed knowingly and willfully. Other product safety statutes provide for civil penalties regardless of intent.

Current State and local safety standards would be preempted by those included in this act. Exemptions could be obtained only by application to the Commission establishing they are required by compelling local conditions, would not unduly burden interstate commerce, and impose higher levels of performance than Federal standards.

An advisory council would be established, including representatives of industry and the small business community.

An injury information clearinghouse would be established to collect and analyze product-related accident statistics. This function is presently performed to a large extent by industry at its own expense. Such statistical information will better enable the Commission to determine the effectiveness of its programs and determine those areas where further study is needed.

The small retailer would be protected by permitting reliance upon the manufacturer's certification of compliance with a product safety standard or on the manufacturer's representation that the product is not subject to a safety standard.

This legislation clearly creates an atmosphere in which business can operate effectively within the consumer movement. As a lawmaker, my strongest concern is to make sure that when consumer legislation is clearly needed, such legislation provides an environment in which business can flourish under the free enterprise system while providing consumers the protection and information which is their right. This legislation provides that environment and that protection.

Mr. DENNIS. Mr. Chairman, will the gentleman yield?

Mr. BROYHILL of North Carolina. I yield to the gentleman from Indiana.

Mr. DENNIS. I am wondering how much that environment is consistent with the provisions of section 16 which provides that this Commission can require the keeping of whatever records practically that it may desire, and can require admission of the Commission's agents to inspect those records, and when we then turn over to section 20 and section 19, if they have not kept the records the Commission laid down, or they have not let the Commission's agents in to see the records they said they must keep, the businessman can be fined $2,000 to $5,000 for a civil penalty. This is hard lines, and especially for a small business.

The CHAIRMAN. The time of the gentleman has expired.

Mr. SPRINGER. Mr. Chairman, I yield to the gentleman 2 additional minutes.

Mr. BROYHILL of North Carolina. Mr. Chairman, I do not think that anyone who is in business, who has a product safety standard applicable to them, is going to be reluctant to cooperate with this agency. I do not think anyone is going to want to slam the door or bar the door in order to keep one of the agents of this Commission away from his place of business. I think they are going to be willing to cooperate. The business people I have talked to that have been involved in safety legislation or complying with safety legislation that is already on the book, have had good experience with it, and I do not think there would be any more problems with this new Commission.

Mr. SPRINGER. Mr. Chairman, I yield 5 minutes to the gentleman from Minnesota (Mr. NELSEN).

(Mr. NELSEN asked and was given permission to revise and extend his remarks.)

Mr. NELSEN. Mr. Chairman, I want to make the observation that I have received mail, letters from business establishments stating that they feel this is a good bill, but I want to point out that I signed the minority view because the habit around here is to keep on adding new agencies to do more things that ought to be done with existing agencies that are already there. I think Members will recall in our great debate on the cancer bill that the administration recommend a totally new agency, the Senate bill set up a totally new one, but our Subcommittee on Public Health and Environment of the Committee on Interstate and Foreign Commerce felt we should keep what we have and mandate the agency to do a better job by certain guidelines and moneys to be set forth in the bill. So in this case here we had a bill, and the administration recommended that the job stay in HEW, and certainly we have a good place to start, but we start a new agency. This was my feeling and I signed the minority view.

However, we did reach an agreement on parts of the bill, where some of the jobs stayed in the context of the introduced bill, and Food and Drug stayed where it was, so we worked out a little bit of a compromise and I think in the right direction.

But I want to mention again as I did the other day that some of us have experienced that with the passage of a bill in the Congress, with a beautiful title and with all the beautiful objectives, we have found for example in the OSHA situation—the Occupational Health and Safety Act—that the enforcement process went way overboard, to the degree where we had to do an undesirable thing and say we can only make this apply in those situations where they employ above 15 employees, which is not a very good way to legislate, but perhaps there was no other place to turn.

So we need to be aware of the fact that when we set up these agencies to do many things, sometimes they overreact and sometimes we begin to move in the direction of blighting some of the objectives we seek in the bill.

However, I think the committee did do a pretty good job and we do find endorsement for the objectives of the bill and the bill itself.

Mr. STAGGERS. Mr. Chairman, I yield 2 minutes to the gentleman from Ohio (Mr. CARNEY), a member of the committee.

(Mr. CARNEY asked and was given permission to revise and extend his remarks.)

Mr. CARNEY. Mr. Chairman, I am grateful for this opportunity to express my strong support of a bill which I have cosponsored, H.R. 15003, Consumer Product Safety Act. I take this opportunity also to say that the subcommittee worked very hard and to thank the members of the subcommittee and extend my best wishes to all the members of the subcommittee on both sides of the aisle, particularly to our subcommittee chairman, the gentleman from California (Mr. MOSS), and the staff who did such an excellent job in alleviating a great many of the problems that arose between the members.

Mr. Chairman, I hope Members of this body will see fit to adopt this bill.

Mr. Chairman, as we are all too painfully aware, it is only recently that the consumer "has come into his own" in our society and that proper emphasis has been placed on his role in the modern economy.

As evidence of the new interest in the consumer, during the past decade, we in Congress have enacted a broad battery of legislation designed to promote fairness in the marketplace. This bill before us today is a further step in advancing the cause of the consumer.

It is considered self-evident that the public is entitled to purchase products without subjecting themselves to unreasonable risk of injury or death. At the present time, however, consumers are not able to confidently rely on the safety of products which are distributed for their use or enjoyment.

Mr. Chairman, this legislation proposes that the Federal Government assume a major role in protecting the consumers from unreasonable risks of death, injury, or serious or frequent illness associated with the use of or exposure to consumer products. To carry out that objective, this bill would create a new, independent regulatory commission with comprehensive authority to take action across the full range of consumer products to reduce or prevent product-related injuries.

This independent regulatory Commission would have the authority to: First, collect and disseminate information on consumer product-related injuries; second, establish mandatory safety standards where necessary to prevent or reduce unreasonable product hazards, or—where such standards are not feasible—to ban the product from the marketplace; third, obtain equitable relief in the courts to protect the public from products which pose imminent hazards to health and safety; and fourth, administratively order the notification and remedy of products which fail to comply with commission safety rules or which contain safety related defects.

To me what is most important in this legislation is that we can no longer propose individual legislation designed to deal with the product hazards which had been identified. But rather, we must abandon this case-by-case approach to product safety and consolidate in a single agency authority sufficient to regulate the full spectrum of products which are sold to or used by consumers.

I have long supported consumer legislation such as: The Flammable Fabrics Act, Radiation Control for Health and Safety, the National Traffic and Motor Vehcile Safety Act, the Child Protection and Toy Safety Act—to name just a few. But now it is time we move a step further and I feel that H.R. 15003 is that step—this is the type of legislation 1972 calls for.

As a member of the Subcommittee on Commerce and Finance which developed this legislation, I can testify to the careful and extensive deliberations that went into this legislation. Every effort has been made to bring out a bill that will protect the American consumer and at the same time be fair to industry. The need for this legislation is obvious. The Department of Health, Education, and Welfare reports that 30,000 persons are killed, 110,000 permanently disabled, and 585,000 hospitalized every year in accidents associated with consumer products.

Approximately 7,000 of those killed are children under 15 years of age—a death toll higher than that of cancer and heart disease combined. Among the categories of consumer products which were found by the National Commission on Product Safety to include unreasonable hazards were such commonly used products as: architectural glass, color television sets, fireworks, floor furnaces, glass bottles, high-rise bicycles, hot-water vaporizers, household chemicals, infant furniture, ladders, power tools, protective headgear, rotary lawnmowers, toys, unvented gas heaters, and wringer washers.

These hazards are not necessarily the fault of any one individual or group. They are the result of impersonal forces which have trapped producers, sellers and buyers into inability to adequately consider safety in the production and uses of consumer products. This legislation opens a new era of national awareness of the unacceptable toll of home injuries. It is not expensive legislation. The annual economic cost of injuries associated with consumer products may exceed $5 billion according to the National Commission. Many products can be made safer at little expense. For example:

The magnetic latch on refrigerators, to prevent entrapment, adds nothing to the consumer's cost.

A double-insulated drill sells in the same price bracket as other top-line drills without double insulation. The manufacturer says the double insulation added little to his costs.

TV sets whose fire records were below average sold in the same price range as those above the average.

The wringer washer judged to have the safest instinctive release by Consumers Union sells at about the same price as others tested.

Mr. Chairman, the heart of this legislation is the establishment of an independent consumer product safety commission. Since the unanimous action of the subcommittee, many business groups have advised me that they are not as concerned with the structure of a product safety agency as they are with being afforded an adequate administrative hearings, due process and judicial review. These protections the committee has carefully written into the bill.

I urge my colleagues to support the Consumer Product Safety Act as reported. American consumers will thank you.

Mr. BROYHILL of North Carolina. Mr. Chairman, I yield 5 minutes to the gentleman from Nebraska (Mr. McCollister), a member of the committee.

(Mr. McCOLLISTER asked and was given permission to revise and extend his remarks.

Mr. McCOLLISTER. Mr. Chairman, I suppose no Member has any greater concern for the problems of the small businessman than have I, having been one only so recently.

In consideration of this legislation, we were faced with the problem of dealing with that increasing burden of regulation and reporting, and at the same time dealing with a very real problem that exists in product safety. It is my feeling, my strong feeling, that this bill does represent a very good balance between limiting the burden and yet providing the remedy that is needed.

Reference has been made by the subcommittee chairman (Mr. Moss) and by the gentleman from Texas (Mr. ECKHARDT) concerning the high degree of openmindedness and give and take in this committee's action on the bill. Though my view is necessarily more limited in scope than theirs, certainly of all the bills that we have considered in this subcommittee this year and this session. I could not imagine any better attitude existing than what prevailed as we considered this legislation.

There was an openmindedness and the majority was willing often to consider amendments which answered to the concern that the minority expressed. I wish to join in the tribute paid to every Member of that subcommittee in that kind of approach to the problem.

In testimony before the Subcommittee on Commerce and Finance, Mr. Arnold B. Elkind, former chairman of the National Commission on Product Safety, said that:

> * * * the laissez-faire approach to consumer products costs the American public about 20 percent of the overall toll that the public pays in injuries or deaths for the privileges of enjoying consumer products. This translates into 6,000 lives, 22,000 cripples, 4 million injuries, and $1.1 billion in treasure that could be saved each year by an effective system for making products safe to use.

The well-supported conclusion of our committee was that a comprehensive Federal consumer product safety mechanism was needed, to balance the equities between the consumer and the manufacturer. On the one hand, manufacturers are not sufficiently influenced by competitive forces to dedicate themselves to the production of safe products. The Commission and our committee found that self-regulation in the area of product safety just is not enough. On the other hand, the consumer has an ever-increasing appetite for technologically advanced products which he may not understand, which he cannot therefore evaluate in terms of safety and which may pose potential for harm either intrinsically or in a specific application.

Our committee has developed a mechanism in H.R. 15003 that balances the need for safety with the need for fairness to the manufacturer. It impacts on the manufacturing process in a minimal way and yet will be effective to prevent needless injury.

I am likewise enthused about the procedures estabilshed by the committee to carry out the mandate for Federal action. By placing the administration of consumer product safety in an independent regulatory agency, vested with new authority, we are confident that the intent of Congress will be carried out with cold neutrality and be insulated from undue economic and political pressures—more than would be possible or likely if the agency was a part of a Cabinet-level department, and with more dedication to fairness and effectiveness than if the agency was a part of, or if its authority was given to, an already existing regulatory agency. The effectiveness of the regulations is assured because this bill provides that industry and consumer groups will have an opportunity to participate in the standards writing process. We will not have illogical and impractical regulation because the experience and technological expertise of industry and consumer organisations will be utilized to the maximum extent possible, and within a framework of protection for the views of each, since the committee has beefed up the rulewriting procedure by allowing oral presentation of arguments, the keeping of a transcript, and an improved basis for judicial review. The new agency's necessary authority to recall unsafe products likewise has built-in protections for the manufacturer in pre-recall hearings, and these hearings will not unduly delay the removal of unsafe products or repair, replacement or refund.

Mr. BROYHILL of North Carolina. Mr. Chairman, I yield 5 minutes to the gentleman from Iowa (Mr. SCHERLE).

(Mr. SCHERLE asked and was given permission to revise and extend his remarks.)

Mr. SCHERLE. Mr. Chairman, I am concerned. What we have here is another bill to create another Federal bureaucracy. Where the Food and Drug Administration has inspectors across the Nation now responsible for foods, drugs, and product safety, we are going to start a new agency to duplicate that field staff. And, in addition, we are going to have one more new consumer agency. Pretty soon the free enterprise system in this country is going to need a roadmap just to chart its way through all the different official Ralph Naders as well as every overzealous newspaper reporter.

Now obviously I, and every Member here, want to protect the American consumer. The regulatory authority provided in this bill would add an aditional measure of safety particularly with respect to products such as appliances that are now exempt from any form of regulation. The Government Accounting Office has just issued a report outlining other deficiencies in legislative authority which the Congress will have an adequate opportunity to carefully consider in the future. But we do not need to create a new Government agency every time we identify a class of products that somehow escapes regulation. The Secretary of HEW has described these organizational provisions as nothing more than a phony bill of goods.

I have not always agreed with the FDA especially with their administration of the Delaney clause and the regulation of DES in animal feed, but under Commissioner Edwards' capable leadership, I believe FDA has moved effectively to meet the needs of a modern and rapidly changing technological society which is making increasing demands on Government. And I believe FDA is already doing an outstanding job in giving the American public the best protection in the world against harmful consumer products. I don't think we are going to help FDA do a better job by creating a new Federal agency to regulate can openers and tricycles.

The people I represent in Iowa want their food supply to be safe and nutritious. They do not want to buy household products which are hazardous. Parents in Council Bluffs want their children's toys to be safe but no one in the Seventh District of Iowa believes their hard-earned money has to be further taxed to support another new Government agency in Washington.

I am opposed to another layer of expensive and extensive bureaucracy.

This proposal would result in splintering product safety regulation and would also result in serious duplication. A separate field force of inspectors and field laboratories would be required.

An injury information system similar to that of FDA and similar administrative machinery would have to be established by the Commission. The related health expertise of other Departmental agencies would also not be as readily available to a Commission and the Department would be deprived of providing a single direction to health matters.

I think such a move would be counterproductive and would recommend that the needed legislation be assigned to the Department of Health, Education, and Welfare.

Mr. BROYHILL of North Carolina. Mr. Chairman, I yield 3 minutes to the gentleman from North Carolina (Mr. JONAS).

Mr. JONAS. Mr. Chairman, I should like to invite the attention of the Chairman of the Committee and other Members to section 23 on page 102. It strikes me that this section ought to be labeled an act for the relief of lawyers. What you are authorizing here is that any person who claims he has sustained personal injury or illness by reason of the failure of a product to comply with the rule may sue not only the manufacturer of the product or the distributor but also the retailer.

And he can do so in the Federal court regardless of the amount in controversy, and not only obtain damages, but the payment of his legal fees and expenses.

What is to prevent the filing of a multitude of frivolous suits? There is no liability imposed upon the plaintiff if he files a frivolous suit or one that is without merit. Retailers in every municipality and locality in the United States will probably be taken into Federal court even though the claim is a small one. I just cannot imagine how the overcrowded Federal courts are going to be able to handle what I predict will be a multiplicity of suits brought by people who allege that they became ill as a result of the use of some product. Now, may I inquire if this subject was explored by the subcommittee, or was it discussed within the committee? It seems to me that this opens up a wide area for litigation which may or may not be meritorious. I am afraid that this section is going to cause far more than it will provide benefits, and I think it ought to be tightened up.

I just wonder if that subject was explored by the committee or the subcommittee?

Mr. ECKHARDT. Would the gentleman yield?

Mr. JONAS. I will be glad to yield to the gentleman.

Mr. ECKHARDT. The subject was considered by the committee and the subcommittee. The provisions of the bill most directly applicable to the question is the language in section (b) on page 103, at line 19.

We were concerned about the possibility of a great number of suits being brought merely because a product resulted in injury. We did not wish to open that wide a gate, so we placed these limitations:

(b) In the case of an action brought for noncompliance with an applicable consumer product safety rule, no liability shall be imposed under this section upon any manufacturer, distributor, or retailer who establishes (1) that he did not have reason to know in the exercise of due care that such product did not comply * * *

The CHAIRMAN. The time of the gentleman has expired.

(By unanimous consent, at the request of Mr. BROYHILL of North Carolina, Mr. JONAS was allowed to proceed for 2 additional minutes.)

Mr. JONAS. I am familiar with that section, but the trouble is that you require the defendant to come into court and prove that he did not have reasonable notice or was not aware of this; you do not impose the burden upon the plaintiff or any burden, except to prove that he was injured.

I do not believe this section would be subject to much criticism if the suit were restricted as against the manufacturer, but here you are going to open up the Federal courts to suits against every retailer in the United States. And he has to hire counsel. And what if he prevails? Who is going to pay his costs? And what if he wins the suit? Who is going to pay his damage? Nobody.

Mr. ECKHARDT. Will the gentleman yield?

Mr. JONAS. I yield to the gentleman.

Mr. ECKHARDT. The burden would be on the plaintiff first to show that the victim died or sustained personal injury——

Mr. JONAS. Or became ill.

Mr. ECKHARDT. Or became ill because of failure to comply with the applicable consumer standard.

Now, the burden would be on the plaintiff not only to show that the injury resulted, but that it was as a proximate cause of a failure of the product to comply with the consumer product standard. But even if the plaintiff sustained this burden and showed that the product was below the consumer standard—and this is a burden on the plaintiff—then the defendant could come in with an independent defense and could show that even though the product did not comply with the standard, he did not have reason to know in the exercise of due care that such product did not comply.

For instance, he had a very carefully conducted quality control program in his plant, and this managed to slip by.

Mr. JONAS. You are talking about the manufacturer. The retailer and the man who runs the retail store in a little country community does not have any quality control. He is not a manufacturer. How do you justify imposing that burden on him?

Mr. ECKHARDT. It actually would not lie against him, because it would not be by reason of a failure of a consumer product to comply with an applicable standard. This man would not be quilty of any offense.

Mr. JONAS. You allow the retailer to be sued.

Mr. MOSS. Will the gentleman yield to me briefly on that point?

Mr. JONAS. I yield to the gentleman.

Mr. MOSS. In this instance we have to include retailers because there are categories for them. Only in controlling both manufacturer and distributor of the main products.

Mr. JONAS. What about an operator of a country store in a small community? He buys this product in good faith. It is the manufacturer who ought to be held responsible and not the retailer. He should be required to come into court and defend a suit.

Mr. MOSS. I can conceive of no attorney acting on behalf of a plaintiff in those cases not joining the manufacturer and possibly the distributor in the suit.

Mr. JONAS. He may not be able to join the manufacturer who may not have an agent in that district.

The CHAIRMAN. The time of the gentleman has expired.

Mr. BROYHILL of North Carolina. I yield the gentleman 2 additional minutes.

Mr. ECKHARDT. Will the gentleman yield further?

Mr. JONAS. Yes.

Mr. ECKHARDT. It is further provided on page 104:

In the case of an action for noncompliance with an order under section 15, no liability shall be imposed under this section upon any manufacturer, distributor, or retailer who establishes that he took all steps as may be reasonable in the exercise of due care to comply with such order.

The retailer is not under any order, so all he has to show is he was not under an order in order to be completely relieved of any possible liability.

Mr. JONAS. As I read the bill, I think he will be required to go into court and hire a lawyer to establish his defense. I think that is going to be very burdensome to a retailer acting in good faith and who is not responsible for the placement of the product on the market. He did not manufacture it. I think this section might have been all right if it were restricted to the manufacturer.

I have had some little experience in the

practice of law, and I know how crowded the courts are. My prediction is you will have the Federal courts filled up with a multitude of suits involving very small sums of money against retailers all over the United States.

Mr. ECKHARDT. Will the gentleman yield for one comment on this point?

Mr. JONAS. Yes.

Mr. ECKHARDT. Of course, anyone can bring a suit contending that there is product liability because the product was negligently built. It would seem to me a bill of this nature that sets standards and gives relief against those who violate those standards would tend to channel such actions as would be otherwise brought under common law under the statute and against the manufacturer. So I think, if anything, we have protected the retailer by this action.

Mr. STAGGERS. Mr. Chairman, I yield 2 minutes to the gentlewoman from Missouri.

Mrs. SULLIVAN. I thank the gentleman for yielding me this time.

I rise to ask a question of the chairman of the committee or the gentleman from California.

I would like to know whether any consideration was given in the committee to the idea of bringing the Food and Drug Administration under the new independent regulatory commission created by this bill. The bill transfers to the new agency some of the present responsibilities of the FDA in the field of hazardous substances and poisonous product packaging.

I note that the minority report deplores the establishment of an independent agency rather than giving the Food and Drug Administration all the authority that this bill gives to the new commission. And I note also that the Senate bill, on the other hand, transfers FDA, lock, stock, and barrel, to the new independent agency.

Can the gentleman tell me how much consideration was given in committee to doing what the Senate did in transferring FDA to the new agency?

Mr. MOSS. Mr. Chairman, will the gentlewoman yield?

Mrs. SULLIVAN. I will be happy to yield to the gentleman from California.

Mr. MOSS. Consideration was given only to the extent that the committee determined that it would not take that matter under consideration.

It was not part of the recommendations of the Commission on Consumer Product Safety, and it did not lie properly within the jurisdiction of the subcommittee. Our committee did not feel that it had before it either at the time of commencing its hearings, or at the conclusion of them, sufficient evidence to reach a decision. We left that to the Subcommittee on Public Health, which deals with the Food and Drug Administration.

Mrs. SULLIVAN. I thank the gentleman. And if the gentleman will permit, I have one further question: As one who worked with the Food and Drug Administration very closely when I came to the Congress in 1953, and for many years thereafter, I must say that I am far from satisfied with the way its powers within the Department have been limited and restricted so that, it seems to me, decisions are often made at the top in the Department, not on scientific and public safety considerations, so much as they are on political bases.

The CHAIRMAN. The time of the gentlewoman from Missouri has expired.

Mr. STAGGERS. Mr. Chairman, I yield 2 additional minutes to the gentlewoman from Missouri (Mrs. SULLIVAN).

Mrs. SULLIVAN. I thank the gentleman for the additional time.

And if I may continue, we had that situation in the cyclamates; we have it again on the DES issue. I think the Food and Drug Administration has been submerged in HEW. I wonder, does the gentleman agree?

Mr. MOSS. Mr. Chairman, will the gentlewoman yield?

Mrs. SULLIVAN. I will be happy to yield to the gentleman.

Mr. MOSS. For 16 years, as a member of the Committee on Interstate and Foreign Commerce through the administration of both political parties, I must confess to less than enthusiasm over the performance of the Food and Drug Administration. They are not a ball of fire, and they are not an example of one of the most effective or efficient agencies of our Government in my opinion.

Mrs. SULLIVAN. I thank the gentleman.

(Mrs. SULLIVAN asked and was given permission to revise and extend her remarks.)

Mrs. SULLIVAN. Mr. Chairman, as one who has served in the past on two national study commissions created by Congress, the National Commission on Food Marketing, and the National Commission to Study Mortgage Interest Rates, and am currently serving on a third, the National Commission on Consumer Finance. I know how much time and effort can go into the study of a major national problem through the Commission method of approach and how often the hard work done by a Commission is compressed into a final report which is filed and forgotten. Thus, it is a matter of great encouragement to me that the National Commission on Product Safety, which did an outstanding job of spotlighting the gaps in our consumer protections from unsafe household products, has not had its final report relegated to the dusty shelves to be neglected and ignored.

This bill now before the House is a concrete and emphatic consequence of the 2-year study by the Commission on Product Safety made by Chairman Arnold B. Elkind of New York and six associates, including two men whose work in the consumer field have been well known to me for many years—consumer writer Sidney Margolius, who writes a weekly column syndicated by the Machinist newspaper, and Senate Commerce Committee Staff Counsel Michael Pertschuk. I salute all seven members of this fine Commission for a remarkable job in the public interest. It was a personal privilege for me to appear before the Commission on Product Safety at one of its public hearings to discuss the consumer aspects of their work.

Mr. Chairman, I support H.R. 15003 as recommended by the Committee on Interstate and Foreign Commerce to carry out the proposals of the National Commission on Product Safety. It is one of the most important consumer measures to come before Congress in the past 4 years.

LETTER IN 1964 FROM MRS. FLORIS MILLS

It is always hard to pinpoint the origin of any major piece of legislation since, of course, many people become involved independently of each other in the development of an idea for legislation. But it is my belief that a letter I received in April 1964, from a resident of the St. Louis area, Mrs. Floris Mills of Webster Groves, Mo., may very possibly have provided the initial impetus for the proposal which led to the establishment of the National Commission on Product Safety and thus for the eventual development of H.R. 15003. In her letter to me, Mrs. Mills wrote, in part:

DEAR MRS. SULLIVAN: It should be mandatory for all persons responsible for the health of the public to report to a central agency all accidents or diseases clearly related to some product which has been shipped in interstate commerce.

The average person, including many public health officials and doctors, does not know what to do when such a product causes an accident. Usually, each incident "dies" with the patient, or is forgotten if recovery is made. Many such accidents may hapen before someone who cares takes action and brings a report to the proper authority. Therefore, the U.S. Public Health Service, or other designated agency, should place in the hands of all doctors, etc., mandatory reporting forms with adequate provision for the gathering of sample material, and information necessary for the tracing of the source of the material.

Such reports should cover accidents to non-human life as well as human. Such reporting could be provided for under laws now being administered without further Congressional action.

I replied to Mrs. Mills that I would refer her suggestion to the heads of a number of agencies and ask for comments and advice, adding—

It is very possible that the kind of thing you recommend can be carried out without the need for special legislation, but I am going to let them tell me so.

RESPONSES FROM AGENCIES

I thereupon wrote to Surgeon General Luther L. Terry of the U.S. Public Health Service, Commissioner George P. Larrick of the Food and Drug Administration, Administrator Byron T. Shaw of the Agricultural Research Service, and Chief Katherine B. Oettinger of the Children's Bureau. The replies indicated that, first, the proposed project could not be carried out under existing legislation; second, some work of this nature was being done by PHS, however, through its Division of Accident Prevention; third, the Poison Control Centers were making an outstanding contribution to physicians and first-aid centers in saving the lives of children who had ingested dangerous chemicals, but deaths and injuries from these sources were occurring at an alarming rate; and, fourth, flavored baby aspirin for children was the leading cause of death from poisoning of children under 5. This led me to incorporate in all subsequent versions of H.R. 1235, my omnibus bill to rewrite the Food, Drug, and Cosmetic Act of 1938 a section prohibiting the manufacture and sale in interstate commerce of flavored aspirin. This bill in turn led to introduction in 1966 of the Child Safety Act as a counterproposal of the Johnson administration.

In the hearings on that bill I submitted for the printed hearing record about 40 pages of official documentation compiled by Government agencies of the problems cited by Mrs. Mills in her letter of 2 years earlier.

The Product Safety Commission was authorized in the next Congress, to make a thorough study of all of the household hazards which confront the American family. The Commission went on to establish beyond any doubt the need for stronger laws to protect the consumers of this country from the death-dealing, disfiguring, crippling, scarring, and blinding appliances and household products and equipment we are constantly being urged to buy.

THE FOOD AND DRUG ADMINISTRATION

As the work of the Product Safety Commission clearly established, and as the report of the committee on H.R. 15003 amply illustrates, the Food and Drug Administration, despite vast increases in its appropriations over the past 20 years, has not been able to carry out its responsibilities to the public in a manner to give us sufficient assurance the public is adequately protected. When I came to Congress in 1953, the budget for this agency was in the neighborhood of $5 million. Now it is approaching $200 million. In the interval, there has been a tremendous increase in the scope of the agency's responsibilities in the fields of pesticides, 1954; food additives, 1958; color additives, 1960; hazardous substances, 1960; drug efficacy and safety, 1962; child safety, 1966; and toy safety, 1969.

But while the agency's responsibilities and funds were being drastically increased, the FDA itself was being downgraded within the Department of Health, Education, and Welfare in a series of administrative reorganizations which placed it below more and more layers of bureaucratic supervision and policy direction—or interference.

In consequence, decisions of the agency which should have been based entirely on scientific and legal determinations intended to protect the consuming public have been imposed from above, in too many instances, to reflect political judgments, from the cyclamates fiasco to the present indefensible position on diethylstilbestrol—a policy which permits the continued use of a cancer-causing growth hormone in beef cattle feed until present stocks are used up, in disregard of the fact that the law clearly prohibits further use of diethylstilbestrol—DES—in animal feeds now that evidence has finally surfaced that residues of the hormone are apparently impossible to keep out of beef carcasses intended for human food.

As cosponsor with Congressman DELANEY of the 1958 Food Additives Act, including the Delaney clause prohibiting the use in food of any chemical or ingredient which can cause cancer in man or in animal, and as the unsuccessful opponent in 1962 of a provision of the Kefauver-Harris Act modifying the Delaney clause as it related to use of diethylstilbestrol in animal feeds, I see no justification of any kind for the continued use of the hormone now. I was promised in the 1962 battle on the House floor that if residues of DES should ever show up in the meat supply, all animal feeds containing DES would instantly be withdrawn from use. That has not happened.

COSMETICS AMENDMENTS TO SENATE BILL

It has not hapened, I am convinced, because the economic impact on the cattle industry was given greater consideration than the public health in this matter.

The FDA deserves to have enough administrative elbowroom to do its job regardless of political consequences. I believe the Senate was right in placing the functions of FDA, and its personnel, into a new agency set up for one purpose only—to protect the public safety.

Had this been done also in the House bill, I would have tried to amend the bill, as Senator EAGLETON did in the Senate, to tighten the powers of the agency to regulate cosmetics. As it is, such amendments to the House bill would not be germane.

I sincerely hope that when the bill goes to conference, the House conferees will study the Senate provisions with an open mind. If FDA, in the final version of the legislation, is placed under the proposed independent consumer product safety agency, I would like to point out that the Eagleton amendments on cosmetics represent a very limited approach to the problem of cosmetic safety, dealing only with the labeling of cosmetics ingredients. This would be of great importance to millions of Americans who are allergic to various cosmetic chemicals, but it would not get to the basic problem of preclearance of cosmetics for safety before they are sold. The Eagleton amendments deserve support as far as they go. I hope they can be agreed to in conference.

Mr. BROYHILL of North Carolina. Mr. Chairman, I yield 3 minutes to the gentleman from Indiana (Mr. DENNIS).

The CHAIRMAN. The Chair must inform the gentleman from North Carolina that the gentleman has only 3 minutes remaining.

Mr. BROYHILL of North Carolina. I thank the Chairman, and I yield the gentleman from Indiana the remaining time.

Mr. DENNIS. Mr. Chairman, I thank the gentleman for that courtesy, and I will take advantage of it because I think the point made by the gentleman from North Carolina (Mr. JONAS) is a very important one and one that I would like to associate myself with, and I would refer to that point.

This bill not only gives an independent action for damages, regardless of the jurisdictional amount, regardless of the amount of money involved, in Federal court, to the private individual, it also gives him a right to enforce the statute itself by a private suit, and both the Chief Justice of the United States and the president of the American Bar Association, have had occasion to point out the problem of burdening our Federal courts with unnecessary business and additional business that they are not equipped to handle.

Now one way at least which could ameliorate that situation would be an amendment to this section, the section which the gentleman from North Carolina (Mr. JONAS) was talking about, which would at least restore the jurisdictional amount.

As we all know, ordinarily to get in the Federal court in cases of this kind, you have to have in excess of $10,000 involved. Here you could have $15 involved.

I am wondering whether the committee would consider favorably an amendment to the section on page 102 which we have been talking about, section 23, which would reestablish the ordinary jurisdictional amount of $10,000 for these suits in Federal courts.

It seems to me that that would go at least some way to ameliorate the situation which the gentleman from North Carolina (Mr. JONAS) pointed out and which I think is a very real one, if you want this law to operate efficiently and fairly.

I would be glad to know what the view of the committee would be as to such an amendment as that I am now suggesting.

The CHAIRMAN. The time of the gentleman from Indiana has expired.

Mr. STAGGERS. Mr. Chairman, I yield 2 minutes to the gentleman from Indiana.

Mr. DENNIS. Mr. Chairman, I thank the gentleman for yielding me the additional time.

I hope that my time will be used by a response from somebody in management of the bill. I would really like to know, if I or some other Member offers an amendment of the kind that I have indicated, what the position of the committee will be.

It seems to me it would be a very reasonable thing to do here. Just why should we repeal the jurisdictional amount of $10,000 to get into the Federal court for this one type of suit? If it is a good general limit, and I think we mostly think it is—why should it not apply here as it does everywhere else?

Mr. ECKHARDT. Mr. Chairman, will the gentleman yield?

Mr. DENNIS. I yield to the gentleman.

Mr. ECKHARDT. To strike the words "without regard to the amount in controversy," we would not in any way change this statute because as I understand the Federal jurisdictional law, if a right is created under the commerce clause of the Constitution, the $10,000 amount in controversy is not a limitation.

Section 1331 applies to cases arising under diversity of citizenship and not under a Federal right arising under a Federal statute.

So we are not changing the Federal law—we are simply enunciating it. So far as I know, every case which is brought under an act of Congress arising under the commerce clause which does not specifically create a jurisdictional amount may be entertained by a Federal court without respect to the amount in controversy.

The gentleman might want to put in a limitation—but this is not an unusual act—it is a typical act as it stands.

Mr. DENNIS. My memory is that section 1331, and it may not be very clear, of course, is that it applies to civil suits arising under the laws of the United States, which I would have thought would have applied here.

But, assuming for the moment that the gentleman is correct, I call attention to the fact that at least you wrote in here "regardless of the jurisdictional amount," which indicates to me that the committee felt that if they did not write that in there, they would run into the jurisdictional amount.

Pursuing this further, why not, in any case, take up the suggestion that the gentleman just made and propose an amendment here which says—

> This is subject to the provisions of Section 1331 as to the amount in controversy.

Mr. ECKHARDT. Mr. Chairman, if the gentleman will yield, in the first place I did not propose that we write in a jurisdictional limitation.

I was simply pointing out that there would be no jurisdictional limitation if we had not used the words "without regard to the amount in controversy." This case would be governed by section 1337 which says:

> The District Court shall have original jurisdiction of any civil action or proceeding arising under any Act of Congress regulating commerce or protecting trade and commerce against restraints and monopolies.

The CHAIRMAN. The time of the gentleman has expired.

Mr. STAGGERS. Mr. Chairman, I yield the gentleman 1 additional minute.

Mr. DENNIS. I thank the gentleman.

Regardless of whether the jurisdictional provision does or does not apply here in the absence of the language "regardless of the amount in controversy" in the bill as now drawn, I would like to know whether the committee would be inclined to accept an amendment which specifically wrote in that the jurisdictional amount of $10,000 would apply in this particular type of suit.

Mr. LATTA. Mr. Chairman, will the gentleman yield?

Mr. DENNIS. I yield to the gentleman.

Mr. LATTA. Mr. Chairman, I think the gentleman from Indiana and the gentleman from North Carolina have raised a very valid point.

Justice delayed is often justice denied and in our haste to pass this important legislation we might have overlooked its impact on our Federal court system. The Chief Justice of the United States in a speech on August 14, 1972, referred to this matter, and I read it in part——

The CHAIRMAN. The time of the gentleman has expired.

Mr. STAGGERS. Mr. Chairman, I yield to the gentleman 1 additional minute.

Mr. LATTA (reading):

> But there is no escape from constantly enlarging the federal judicial establishment except to adopt new judicial methods and improve performance as we are trying to do, and to have Congress carefully scrutinize all legislation that will create more cases.
>
> In recent years, Congress has required every executive agency to prepare an environmental "impact statement" whenever a new highway, a new bridge, or other federally funded projects are planned. I suggest, with all deference, that every piece of legislation creating new cases be accompanied by a "court impact statement", prepared by the reporting committee and submitted to the Judiciary Committees of the Congress with an estimate of how many more judges and supporting personnel will be needed to handle the new cases.

That is the end of part of the statement by the Chief Justice of the Supreme Court. I think these two gentlemen have raised a very important question with which this Congress should be concerned. If we are going to give all of this additional responsibility to the courts, we should give them the necessary tools to do the job.

The CHAIRMAN. The time of the gentleman has expired.

Mr. STAGGERS. I yield to the gentleman 1 additional minute.

Mr. DENNIS. I thank the chairman. I should like to have the time used for some response to my inquiry as to the view of the committee on the amendment.

Mr. STAGGERS. I just say to the gentleman from Indiana the committee would have to resist the amendment because that would put it in a class for only those who own Rolls-Royces. We are preparing the bill for the protection of all of the people of the land so that they will have recourse.

Mr. DENNIS. I thank the chairman, but I must say I have brought many $10,000 suits for people who never saw a Rolls-Royce.

Mr. STAGGERS. Mr. Chairman, I yield 2 minutes to the gentleman from Texas (Mr. PICKLE).

(Mr. PICKLE asked and was given permission to revise and extend his remarks.)

Mr. PICKLE. I thank the chairman for yielding.

I want to ask two questions of either the chairman or the subcommittee chairman. I notice in section 3(A)(1) there is no language excluding persons covered by the Natural Gas and Pipeline Safety Act, as contained in the Senate version, S. 3419. This was brought up in our committee, and it is my understanding that it was not the intent of the committee to subject this safety program to product safety standards as prescribed in the bill, since the safety aspect on natural gas and its use is presently covered in the Natural Gas and Pipeline Safety Act.

Mr. MOSS. Mr. Chairman, will the gentleman yield?

Mr. PICKLE. I yield to the gentleman from California.

Mr. MOSS. On page 59, line 10, under (A):

> Any article which is not customarily produced or distributed for sale to or use, consumption, or enjoyment of a consumer—

It was the consensus of the committee that a gas pipeline was not sold for that purpose, and we had no intention of including it within the scope of authority of the Commission.

Mr. PICKLE. I thank the gentleman.

May I ask one other question regarding subsection (c) of section 15 which provides that the Commission may call for public notice by the manufacturer of a dangerous product. Would it be possible for this Commission which we are creating by this act to compel a television or radio station to sell or to give time to an offending manufacturer or distributor or retailer for the purpose of complying with the order requiring public notice?

Mr. STAGGERS. No. It is made perfectly clear in the report that this is not the case.

Mr. PICKLE. I thank the gentleman.

Mr. BURKE of Florida. Mr. Chairman, I rise in support of H.R. 15003, the Consumer Product Safety Act.

The appalling dangers that are ever present in the American home compels me to do so. Each year 20 million Americans are injured in and around the home. Of this total, 110,000 injuries result in permanent disability and 30,000 in death. In fact, home accidents reap a death toll among children under the age of 15 higher than that of cancer and heart disease combined.

Perhaps we have been more concerned with chemicals that will clean an oven, remove spots from rugs, keep things from sticking to pans, or clean the bathroom than in the safety of the users. Children cannot always read labels and even the most careful mother cannot always be watching.

Our technology has been geared more with beauty than with safety. Sliding doors to balconies and terraces bring nature to the inside of a home, but, children and pets and even some adults cannot always discern whether the door is open or closed and as a result there are many incidents where people have been badly cut or scarred.

Children who lived years ago in the wild West, or in the wilds of jungles, had only forces of nature to worry about. On the other hand we surround our children and ourselves daily with products that could do us bodily harm.

Regrettably, for various reasons we have been slow, even reluctant, to act to improve product safety. Recently Congress has become more active and exhibited an increasing concern with the safety of the products which consumers buy and use in their daily lives. This concern has been manifested by the passing of a series of acts designed to deal with specific hazards and categories of products for which a substantial regulatory need had been established. These acts include the National Traffic and Motor Vehicle Safety Act of 1966, the Gas Pipeline Safety Act of 1968, the Flammable Fabrics Act Amendments of 1967, the Radiation Control for Health and Safety Act of 1968, the Child Prevention and Toy Safety Act of 1969, and the Poison Prevention Packaging Act of 1970.

The National Commission on Product Safety found after a 2-year study, conducted from 1967 to 1969, that—

> Such limited Federal authority as does exist is scattered among many agencies. Jurisdiction over a single category of products may be shared by as many as four different departments or agencies. Moreover, where it exists, Federal product safety regulation is burdened by unnecessary procedural obstacles, circumscribed investigative powers, inadequate and ill-fitting sanctions, bureaucratic lassitude, timid administration, bargain-basement budgets, distorted priorities and misdirected technical resources.

There are those who will argue that existing Government machinery is presently adequate enough to handle the product safety problem and they suggest that the Food and Drug Administration and HEW be given larger roles. Both of these agencies have done good work in some of their areas of expertise but no agency is perfect. I feel also that it is unfair to saddle several agencies with separate responsibilities to administer consumer safety programs. It is unfair to the consumer and it is unfair to the agency. To do this is being penny wise and pound foolish.

The legislation before us today proposes that the Federal Government assume a major role in protecting the consumers from unreasonable risks of death, injury, or serious or frequent illness associated with the use or exposure to consumer products. To carry out this goal, H.R. 15003 would create a new independent regulatory commission with comprehensive authority to take action across the full range of consumer products to reduce or prevent product-related injuries.

This independent regulatory commission would be vested with authority to:

First, collect and disseminate information on consumer product-related injuries.

Second, establish mandatory safety standards where necessary to prevent or reduce unreasonable product hazards, or—where such standards are not feasible—to ban the product from the marketplace;

Third, obtain equitable relief in the courts to protect the public from products which pose imminent hazards to health and safety; and

Fourth, administratively order the notification and remedy of products which fail to comply with Commission safety rules or which contain safety-related defects.

The bill would also provide a system of product certification and permit the Commission to compel inclusion of certain safety-related information in product labels.

While I am loathe to increase the plethora of Government agencies, and even more loathe to spend the taxpayers money unnecessarily, I feel the time has come when we acknowledge that a man's home, even though it is his castle, is also often his boobytrap, and that strong Federal action must be taken to reverse this trend. The building block of our society is the family, and the family home should b ea happy one, safe from harm so that life in America for all families will be protected against the intrusion of injury from casual purchases made at the grocery store in good faith and in reliance on the manufacturers responsibility to insure safety to all Americans.

Mr. ROYBAL. Mr. Chairman, I rise in support of H.R. 15003 which will protect consumers against unreasonable product hazards.

This bill will establish an independent regulatory commission with plenary authority to prevent and reduce product-related injuries to consumers. The Commission will have the power to collect and disseminate information on consumer product injuries, establish mandatory safety standards, and obtain equitable relief in the courts to protect the public from imminent hazards. At present, there is a lack of a central agency to collect data on product-injury victims, and Federal safety standards for products exist only in a few industries.

Also, the commission will be empowered to administratively order the notification and remedy of products which fail to comply with the safety standards which it proclaims.

Today it is estimated that there are over 30,000 deaths and 20 million injuries every year in and around the house. Product-related injuries cost the economy almost $5 billion every year. The death toll among children under age 15 from product-related accidents is greater than from cancer and heart disease combined. The time has come for Congress to insure that defective and hazardous goods do not find their way into the marketplace.

Prior to this act, the Federal Government has never had a comprehensive program to protect consumers from injuries due to defective products. Rather, Congress has utilized a knee-jerk, hit-and-miss approach which has produced legislation to meet a crisis situation in one area and completely overlooked the larger problem.

Until now, it has been the courts which have been in the forefront developing protection for people injured by defective products. The growth of the doctrine of strict liability under the rubric of "products liability" over the last 15 years is the necessary outgrowth of a society of the mass-produced and multihandled product. The problem with the approach is that it can only aid people after they have suffered injury but it cannot protect them from the initial contact with the improper goods. This bill is the legislative counterpart of the growth of a products liability. It offers the consumer a means of protection from defective goods before they reach the marketplace by providing the Government with effective judicial remedies to deal with defective products. I commend the passage of this legislation to all my colleagues.

Mr. RONCALIO. Mr. Chairman, the Committee on Commerce, in bringing this bill to the Hall of the House, has wisely excluded from the definition of consumer product certain categories which are either now regulated under other safety laws or which it feels may not be amenable to safety regulation as envisioned by this measure. Among the exclusions are firearms and ammunition, which the amendment offered by the gentleman from New York would include in the rather broad coverage of this legislation.

Inclusion of firearms and ammunition in the scope of this bill is viewed by my constituents as a dangerous step toward the type of gun control legislation they adamantly oppose. What it would do is give to Federal agents the authority to establish mandatory safety standards; to conceivably ban those products from the marketplace, even. So, what have we? A back-door approach to gun control which could go far beyond the measure now pending or the bill recently enacted by the other body to control, we have been told, only cheap domestically produced handguns. My views on that measure are well known. It, too, would give too much discretion to the administrators who would enforce it.

Mr. Chairman, the amendment before us would not stop with so-called cheap handguns. It would include the hunting rifles, shotguns, and the components needed by sportsmen and ranchers of my State. Should we agree to this amendment, we would not even know what we were agreeing to in the way of eventual interference with our way of life. Guns and ammunition already are subject to regulation, Mr. Chairman. I believe the committee acted wisely in not including them in the coverage of this bill.

And I certainly hold firmly the belief that, if Congress is to act to broaden the regulation of firearms and ammunition, it must be quite specific in its language, its definitions, and its purpose. It is quite beyond my belief that this body would delegate such responsibility to a new, independent regulatory Commission, such as the one to be created if this bill is enacted. Nor does this bill need the encumbrance this amendment would burden it with. Those Members who support this legislation should realize that and join me in opposing the amendment.

Mr. FOUNTAIN. Mr. Chairman, I am usually extremely hesitant to support new avenues, because, as has been said, we already have too many, but HEW is already big enough and FDA has a big enough job if it protects us from unsafe foods and drugs which it is not adequately doing today. I rise in support of H.R. 15003, a bill to provide better protection for consumers from unreasonably hazardous products.

Ordinarily, I would favor enlarging the consumer protection responsibilities of the Department of Health, Education, and Welfare to include the purposes of this bill. However, because of the inadequate manner in which the Food and Drug Administration is presently administering the food and drug functions entrusted to it by the Congress, I cannot in good conscience support the placement of other consumer product safety responsibilities within the agency. Instead, I believe FDA should be relieved of this administrative burden so that the agency's top management can concentrate on the more effective regulation of foods and drugs.

The Intergovernmental Relations Subcommittee, which I chair, has held hearing after hearing on the FDA's operations. These hearings, and the resulting reports issued by the Government Operations Committee, paint a very unsatisfactory picture of FDA's performance. Not only has the Agency's administrative efficiency been found wanting, but the subcommittee's investigations disclose that FDA officials have repeatedly disregarded the law and their own agency regulations.

To illustrate this point, last week I brought to the attention of the House an opinion by the Comptroller General holding that the FDA Commissioner has acted without legal authority and contrary to law in permitting a "phase out" period for existing stocks of DES premixes used in livestock feeding. The legality of the continued use of the cancer-promoting drug DES in livestock feeding had been thoroughly examined in our subcommittee hearings during the past year and a half. On July 31, 1972, FDA issued an order withdrawing approval of the new drug applications for DES liquid and dry premixes. That order required the immediate cessation of the manufacture of DES premixes, but permitted the continued shipment and use of existing stocks of the premixes until January 1, 1973. It was this latter permission by FDA which I had questioned and which the Comptroller General found to be illegal.

Similarly, FDA is knowingly permitting the continued interstate shipment and sale of the new drug "Sec," despite the fact that the agency has taken final action withdrawing approval of the new drug application for this product. The Intergovernmental Relations Subcommittee will hold a hearing on this matter next Monday.

In a similar vein, only last month, Judge William B. Bryant of the U.S. District Court for the District of Columbia—in American Public Health Association and National Council of Senior Citizens against Acting Secretary of HEW and Commissioner of FDA—also criticized FDA for contravening the law with respect to the efficacy requirments of the Federal Food, Drug, and Cosmetic Act. Judge Bryant said:

> When, as is the case here, the Congress has shown an awareness of a problem and has acted accordingly, it seems inappropriate for any agency to adopt procedures which extend the grace period far beyond that envisioned by the statute, and which effectively stay implementation of the Congressional mandate that drugs in the marketplace be both safe and effective.

I know that some will defend FDA's inadequacies and failures by asserting that the agency has been underfunded and understaffed in the past. However true this argument may be, it does not come to grips with the fact that decisionmaking which violates the law and the intent of Congress has little, if anything, to do with agency funding. Rather, it is principally a function of the quality of top management.

It is for these reasons that I support the establishment of a strong independent regulatory commission, as was recommended by the National Commission on Product Safety and, let me add, a commission which wrote a report which speaks with authority on this subject.

Mr. Chairman, I want to endorse particularly section 5 of the bill, which provides for an injury information clearinghouse to collect, investigate, analyze, and disseminate information relating to the causes and prevention of death, injury, and illness associated with consumer products. I do not have recent figures, but in a hearing before our subcommittee, it was estimated in 1968 that 20 million injuries annually were associated with consumer products.

During the 91st Congress, the Government Operations Subcommittee, which I chair, investigated the adequacy of arrangements by Federal departments and agencies for collecting and utilizing accident and injury data. On the basis of the subcommittee investigation, the committee reached the following conclusions:

1. Adequate information concerning household accidents and injuries is essential for the proper implementation of Federal programs intended to protect the public from hazardous products and substances and to help prevent avoidable accidents. Comprehensive information of this kind is not presently available, nor is there any coordinated system in existence within the Federal Government for collecting, analyzing and disseminating such information.

2. Some potentially useful information about household accidents and injuries is being collected by Federal agencies. However, much of it is not being used advantageously because it has not been sent to or obtained by agencies which should have it or because it is not in usable form.

3. In recent months, steps have been taken by the National Commission on Product Safety and other agencies to obtain additional information on household accidents and injuries. However, although it appears possible to obtain additional data with very litle added cost or effort through minor modifications of existing programs, this has not been done.

4. In too many instances, appropriate corrective action has not been taken by the responsible Federal agency even after sufficient information was available. Fragmented and overlapping jurisdiction has undoubtedly aggravated this problem.

Enactment of this bill should help greatly in correcting deficiencies disclosed by the subcommittee investigation and in accomplishing its recommendation for the establishment of a coordinated system for collection, analysis, and dissemination of data relating to household accidents and injuries.

Mr. GOODLING. Mr. Chairman, as has already been stated by the gentleman from Ohio (Mr. DEVINE) this bill creates another new commission which simply adds to more bureaucracy which is already too vast. The time to stop adding new agencies is now. The time for the Congress to display some sense of fiscal responsibility is now. The time to stop piling bureaucracy upon bureaucracy is now. Each time we do this we add more to budget deficits that are continuing to burst at the seams. There are agencies within the present framework of government that could assume additional responsibilities in a shorter length of time at a lesser cost.

There is another serious potential danger in this type of legislation. I have not heard any Member mention this but this legislation could be one more step down the bureaucratic highway of destroying our free enterprise system. Are we going to stifle the expertise responsible for our inventive genious that brings countless new and improved products to our marketplace? Are we going to, by this legislation, discourage costly research so necessary to the development of any new product when the developer must first secure permission from a government agency to sell his product?

Some time ago, the Congress, in its wisdom or lack of it, set up the Environmental Protective Agency. It has brought out in subsequent hearings that a considerable number of chemical companies would no longer put millions of dollars into research so necessary to produce new and safe chemicals for farm and industrial use when they could not be assured the product could be marketed when compounded.

This appears to be just one more piece of emotional legislation that will probably benefit very few other than those who shall be a part of this bureaucracy.

Mr. PICKLE. Mr. Chairman, I rise in support of the Consumer Product Safety Act.

I realize that some people may feel that this bill would only be a hindrance to the give-and-take of the marketplace. I know that many feel that this bill will only create another agency, which is effective only in meddling.

But, Mr. Chairman, the Members who have worked so diligently on this measure have faced these questions. They have weighed the pros and cons; there has been give and take. The result is a bill that I think meets general accord with Members on both sides of the aisle.

I believe that we can all support this bill in an atmosphere of harmony, resulting from solid accomplishment.

H.R. 15003, Mr. Chairman, is in the best interests of the consumer while not overly burdensome for industry. Thus, I urge Members to vote for the Consumer Product Safety Act.

Mr. CRANE. Mr. Chairman, the bill before us, calling for the creation of a Consumer Product Safety Commission, is an intrinsic part of the growing attack upon private business, and the effort to place business under the control of a huge new Government bureaucracy.

In the name of "protecting the public" we have already seen many interventions by government agencies, a number of which have served only to make it more difficult to do business, thereby harming the Nation's economy and hurting the very people in whose name the action has been taken.

The Federal Trade Commission, acting on the basis of the same need to "protect the public" which motivates the supporters of a Consumer Product Safety Commission, has broadened its power in recent days in an unprecedented manner.

One of the many companies which have felt its wrath has been the Du Pont Co., makers of Zerex antifreeze. I cite this example as only one of many which are available.

The Federal Trade Commission charged that Zerex was falsely advertised in a television commercial, charges which have since been proven to be untrue. The company, nevertheless, lost sales in 1971 and public confidence because of unfavorable publicity.

What the FTC did was to call a press conference in November 1970 and make a "proposed complaint" against Du Pont, alleging, without proof, that the television commercial was misleading, that the antifreeze actually damaged automotive cooling systems, and that it had been inadequately tested. The Federal Agency then publicly threatened to ban the product.

The commercial in question showed a man stabbing a can of Zerex and streams of antifreeze gushing out and then sealing up. After the FTC charged that this demonstration was phony, newspapers across the country carried stories of the Commission's condemnation of Zerex.

Officials at Du Pont were not even informed of the FTC's action before the Washington press conference. Equally important is the fact that the FTC turned out to be wrong. It dropped the charge of false advertising. It dropped the charge that the product could cause damage. The FTC, in fact, found nothing wrong with the product in any way.

The financial damage had, of course, already been done. Du Pont counted 160 newspaper stories after the initial FTC accusation and only 80, half as many, a year later when the Agency admitted it had been wrong. Twenty front-page stories appeared the first time. The FTC's error received no first-page placements a year later.

Discussing the tactics being used by this Federal Agency, Prof. Yale Brozen of the Graduate School of Business of the University of Chicago, declared that—

> The FTC has come up with the technique of unilaterally deciding what is deceptive, conducting a trial by press release, and demanding that the advertiser run ads admitting the deception. The burden of proving innocence is left to the advertiser, if he can survive the trial by accusation and publicity—a complete turnabout from our judicial system in which an accused is regarded as innocent until proved guilty.

The FTC is now calling on advertisers, industry by industry, to file with it documentary proof of all claims. Perhaps, states Professor Brozen:

> The FTC should be forced to substantiate its claims before issuing press releases which greatly mislead consumers.

In the long run, notes Professor Brozen, to advertise at all may become a sin:

> The FTC is leveling a barrage of unsubstantiated claims against advertising which, if it prevails, may well cause a withering of advertising.

There are many other examples of the increasing harassment of private business and industry by Government. The Occupational Safety and Health Act invests authority in the Secretary of Labor for the first time to set job safety standards for the bulk of the Nation's 80 million working men and women.

Among other things, the Secretary is given authority to enforce the safety standards he may issue, and under his broad delegation of power can enter any "factory, plant, establishment, construction site, mine or other area or workplace or environment" to inspect it; close down any operation he finds dangerous; move to cancel Government contracts; and ask courts to impose fines and/or jail sentences for violators of his standards.

One wonders what ever happened to the fourth amendment guarantees against unwarranted search. One wonders what ever happened to fifth amendment guarantees of the security of private property. Our previous system based on State-determined standards, education, and cooperation, produced safety statistics which were the best in the world. This, however, has been abandoned in the interest of a nationalized, bureaucratically run system of harassment of private business.

And now, after the increasing intervention of Government agencies into the economic life of the Nation, making it ever more difficult for American business and industry to compete with those from abroad who are free of such regulation and control, we are told that we need still another Government agency—a Consumer Protection Commission—to regulate business and industry still more, and make it still more difficult to maintain maximum employment, and to compete in world markets.

If the Members of this body seek further to regulate and control business, no new commissions are necessary to implement such a policy. The Secretary of Labor, the Federal Trade Commission, and other governmental bodies have already assumed the powers being called for in this new commission. The Food and Drug Administration is already doing most of the things being urged upon this proposed new body.

What should be remembered, however, is that increasing Government power and control, far from serving the interests of the people, may do serious harm to such interests.

Woodrow Wilson, who was a keen student of history, stated:

> The history of liberty is a history of limitations of governmental power, not the increase of it. When we resist, therefore, the concentration of power, we are resisting the powers of death, because concentration of power is what always precedes the destruction of human liberties.

Today we are witnessing the most unprecedented concentration of such governmental power in our national experience. The bill before us would simply expand such power.

The proposed expansion, we are told, is for a "good purpose"—the safety of consumer products. Freedom, however, is always taken from men for "good purposes." No better warning against expansions of Government power such as is urged in the present legislation has been given than that of Supreme Court Justice Louis Brandeis. He stated:

> Experience should teach us to be most on guard to protect liberty when the government's purposes are beneficient. Men born to freedom are naturally alert to repel invasion of their liberty by evil minded rulers. The greatest dangers to liberty lurk in insidious encroachments of men of zeal. . . .

Our country has been made the most prosperous in the history of the world under a free economy. If we shackle that economy, if we control it and regulate it, we will also impoverish it. The proposed legislation is part of a continuing trend of such regulation and control. As such, it leads in a direction which most Americans, if they understood it properly, would not want to go. On this basis, it must be opposed.

Mr. PODELL. Mr. Chairman, despite the growth of a large consumer movement, not nearly enough effective consumer protection legislation has been passed by Congress. At last, we now have two major bills—H.R. 15003 before the House today and H.R. 4809 in committee—which will create a strong, Federal role in the protection of consumers.

The first bill, H.R. 15003, deals with protection against unsafe products. The bill is based on one simple principle. The buyer has a right to expect that the use of consumer products will not prove injurious or harmful in any way and that the products he buys are safe. He does not have that assurance now.

As early as 1962, President John F. Kennedy in his historic first special message to the Congress on protecting the consumer interest enumerated four consumer rights. What was the first such right? The right to safety—"To be protected against the marketing of goods that are hazardous to health or life."

And how much progress has been made in the area of product safety since then?

Let me quote from a recent statement by Arnold B. Elkind, former chairman of the National Commission on Product Safety. In speaking about the work of the Commission, he stated:

> Our gut estimate was that the current laissez-faire approach to consumer products costs the American public about 20 percent of the overall toll that the public pays in injuries or deaths for the privileges of enjoying consumer products. This translates into 6,000 lives, 22,000 cripples, 4 million injuries, and $1.1 billion in treasure that could be saved each year by an effective system for making products safe to use . . .
>
> Unfortunately it also means that 16 million injuries and 24,000 deaths may occur annually from using consumer products regardless of the care, skill, and best efforts of our society."

The need for legislative action in the field of consumer product safety is immediate and crucial. To quote once again from Mr. Elkind:

> The need of intervention into this problem area by the federal government is generally acknowledged by all men of good will who have considered product safety and its implications to the consumer.

H.R. 15003 goes a long way to satisfying that need. The bill would create an independent Safety Agency. The bill contains important provisions for setting safety standards, for banning unsafe products, and for criminal as well as civil penalties for violations of the law. In addition, the bill transfers the present functions of protecting the public from flammable fabrics, excessive dangerous radiations, dangerous toys, and certain other hazards to the new Safety Agency.

H.R. 15003 should be passed today. But H.R. 15003 deals with only part of the problem.

Consumers also have a right to be protected from false and misleading advertising and product warrantees. The Federal Government, through its Federal Trade Commission, has a duty to help protect consumers in the marketplace. H.R. 4809 gives the FTC the necessary powers to protect the consumer.

All other Federal regulatory agencies already have such powers in their own field. The FAA has such powers to protect airline passengers, the SEC has such powers to protect investors.

Only the FTC, the agency which protects the consumer in the marketplace, is forced to use unreasonably slow and unnecessary procedures.

It is my strong conviction that H.R. 4809 should be considered by the Congress during this session.

Mr. Chairman, the enactment of these twin bills, H.R. 15003 and H.R. 4809, would indicate loud and clear that this Congress is now on the side of the consumer. No special interests, no amount of lobbying should deter us from protecting consumers—because we, as well as our constituents, are the consumers who would suffer if we do nothing.

Mr. HALPERN. Mr. Chairman, I would like to express my enthusiastic support of H.R. 15003, the Consumer Product Safety Act.

Sadly, history shows us that national safety legislation in the United States largely comes about by a reaction to tragedy. Examples of this can be seen in the epidemic food poisoning at the turn of the century and more recently the shocking death toll due to accidents caused by defective automobiles. When faced with these situations, Congress recognized the necessity to provide the appropriate legislation.

Today, living in a space age technology as we do, we constantly come in contact with many new chemical, mechanical, and electronic gadgets. Many of these new marvels are to be found in the home. Strikingly, each year 30 million Americans are injured in and around the home. Of this total, 110,000 injuries result in permanent disability and 30,000 in death. It only takes commonsense to realize that the time has come for us in Congress to come to the aid of the American public.

We must face the fact that unsafe products are being marketed in disturbing numbers. Certainly available statistics show just how harmful they can be. Consumers Union, the independent, nonprofit organization which evaluates products for consumers, prepared a special report at the request of the Senate Commerce Committee several years ago, analyzing the results of their admittedly limited product testing over the past 10 years. During that period their tests and analyses had uncovered 376 products deemed so hazardous as to be unacceptable in the home.

Within the last 6 years, the Congress has exhibited an increasing concern with the safety of the products which consumers encounter in their daily lives. This concern has manifested in the passage of a series of acts designed to deal with specific hazards and categories of products for which a substantial regulatory need had been established.

These acts include the National Traffic and Motor Vehicle Safety Act of 1966, the Gas Pipeline Safety Act of 1968, the Flammable Fabrics Act amendments, the Radiation Control for Health and Safety Act, the Child Prevention and Toy Safety Act of 1969, and the Poison Prevention Packaging Act of 1970. While each of these acts is meritorious in its own right and deserving of enactment, this legislative program has resulted in a patchwork pattern of laws which, in combination, extend to only a small portion of the multitude of consumer products sold in the marketplace.

Mr. Chairman, H.R. 15003 would go a long way toward solving the problem of unsafe consumer products. It would create an independent regulatory commission with the authority to take action across the board on consumer products to reduce or prevent product-related injuries. It would invest authority in an independent regulatory commission to: First, collect and disseminate information on consumer product-related injuries; second, establish mandatory safety standards where necessary to prevent or reduce unreasonable product hazards, or where such standards are not feasible to ban the product from the marketplace; third, obtain equitable relief in the courts to protect the public from products which pose imminent hazards to health and safety; and, fourth, administratively order the notification and remedy of products which fail to comply with Commission safety rules or which contain safety-related defects.

It is considered self-evident that the public is entitled to purchase products without subjecting themselves to unreasonable risk of injury or death. At the present time, consumers are not able to confidently rely on the safety of products which are distributed for their use or enjoyment.

I believe, Mr. Chairman, that H.R. 15003 will remedy this situation and I earnestly hope that my esteemed colleagues will join me in support of this urgently needed piece of legislation.

Mr. DONOHUE. Mr. Chairman, I most earnestly urge and hope that this Consumer Product Safety Act, H.R. 15003, will be overwhelmingly adopted by the House.

In our legislative consideration of this important measure, let us primarily remember that the American public is unequivocably entitled to purchase products without the fear of subjecting themselves to unreasonable risk or injury. Second, Mr. Chairman, let us realize, that unfortunately at the present time, consumers cannot confidently rely on the safety of a tremendous number of products which are distributed for their use or enjoyment. Therefore, I believe the Congress of the United States, must and should legislatively speak out, on behalf of the consumer, through speedy enactment of the Consumer Product Safety Act.

The legislative measure we are considering today is designed to create an independent regulatory commission with comprehensive authority to initiate action to prevent or reduce product-related injuries to consumers. In substance, this legislative measure vests, within an independent regulatory commission, authority to, among other things, collect and disseminate information on consumer product related injuries, establish mandatory safety standards to prevent or substantially reduce unreasonable product hazards, to ban the hazardous product from the marketplace, obtain equitable relief in the courts to protect the public from products which pose imminent hazard to health and safety, and, administratively order the notification and remedy of products which fail to comply with Commission safety rules or which contain safety defects.

Of course, Mr. Chairman, in supporting this legislation, there is no intent whatsoever to inflict extreme and unnecessary hardships on our reputable business community. I think we all recognize and agree that a legitimate business which operates honestly and manufactures and markets safe and dependable goods, stands only to benefit from this legislation creating an independent product safety agency.

However, in spite of congressional concern and our initial legislative response to consumer problems, the evidence clearly reveals that for too long there has been an absence of strong and substantive Federal regulation to adequately protect the American consumer from hazardous consumer products.

Therefore, in simple fairness and equity, let us now act meaningfully to place the consumer on a more equal footing with the seller by the establishment of this regulatory Commission which will serve to effectively reduce and prevent product related injuries to consumers, which will help legitimate business fight the threat of unprincipled and unscrupulous producers, which will establish effective enforcement proceedings regarding consumer product safety and which will serve, in the overall national interest, to restore faith and confidence in the free-enterprise system.

Mr. RODINO. Mr. Chairman, I rise today to express my strong support for the bill before us to establish a new, independent regulatory commission to control consumer products to reduce or prevent product-related injuries.

In 1967 the Congress created the National Commission on Product Safety to conduct a comprehensive study of the scope and adequacy of measures and Federal controls to protect consumers against risks that might be caused by household products.

After a 2-year study, the Commission reported that there is a need for a strong and independent Government agency to protect the public. It concluded that although there are a number of Federal programs to supervise consumer products, these are scattered throughout a number of agencies and departments. In addition, the Commission found that State and local laws are a "hodgepodge of tragedy-inspired responses to challenges" and that self-interest and competitive forces are not sufficient to influence manufacturers to produce safe products.

Obviously, the approach recommended by the Commission and incorporated in the bill before the House today is the best answer to this acute problem. It would establish an independent neutral agency with strong and effective powers. The proposed Commission would be authorized to: First, collect and distribute information on consumer product-related injuries; second, establish mandatory safety standards or even to ban hazardous products from the marketplace; third, obtain relief through court action to protect the public or through the imposition of criminal and civil penalties; and fourth, order the notification and remedy of products that fail to comply with safety rules.

In addition, private suits for damages are allowed to be brought in Federal courts and consumer suits are permitted to compel compliance with safety rules and certain Commission orders.

Mr. Chairman, the National Center for Health Statistics has estimated that each year 20 million Americans are injured in and around the home, and of this 110,000 injuries result in permanent disability and 30,000 in death. It is also estimated that the annual dollar cost to the economy of product-related injuries is over $5 billion. Particularly tragic is the fact that home accidents reap a death toll among children under 15 which is higher than that of cancer and heart disease combined.

The new regulatory agency would have vast authority to regulate all types of consumer products, ranging from color television sets, glass bottles, toys, and infant furniture to household chemicals and such products as rotary lawnmowers.

In my judgment, with enactment of H.R. 15003 we will establish an effective program whereby both the consumer and industry can fairly and directly participate in developing and implementing proper safety standards to protect the public.

Mr. ANNUNZIO. Mr. Chairman, I am grateful for this opportunity to express my strong support for H.R. 15003, the Consumer Product Safety Act.

The purpose of an economy is to produce goods and services, large in quantity, high in quality, reasonable in price for maximum satisfaction in consumer use.

This very apt definition was given by Arch W. Troelstrup, well-known specialist in consumer economics.

But it is only recently that the consumer "has come into his own" and that proper emphasis is placed on the pivotal role of the consumer in the modern economy. To reinforce our recognition of the importance of the consumer, we in Congress must assume a major role in protecting the consumers from unreasonable risks of death, injury, or serious or frequent illness associated with the use or exposure to consumer products.

There are many tragic examples of how dangerous many of our commonplace items can be. For example, every year 125,000 persons are injured by faulty heating devices; 100,000 are hurt and maimed by faulty power mowers or washing machines; 100,000, consisting mostly of children, have their limbs crushed by automatic clothes wringers; 40,000 people are gashed when they fall through a glass door; and another 30,000 are shocked and burned by defective wall sockets and extension cords. These are but a few examples of the possible harm any of us can encounter at any time.

Because this matter of safety in even our most common and familiar products becomes each year more complex, it must be taken seriously by every buyer of appliances and other consumer goods. Safety is a major factor in the value of many things we buy—often unexpected things. We take so much for granted, because not enough information or education for everyday safety has yet gotten through to us as consumers.

In 1967, Congress created the National Commission on Product Safety. The Commission transmitted its final report in July 1970 which confirmed both the absence of and the need for a strong, vigorous Federal presence to protect the public from hazardous consumer products.

Rather than propose individual legislation designed to deal with the product hazards which it had identified, the Commission decided that the Federal Government should abandon its traditional case by case approach to product safety and consolidate in a single agency authority sufficient to regulate the full spectrum of products which are sold to or used by consumers. To this end, the Commission recommended the creation of a new independent regulatory commission with comprehensive powers to minimize or eliminate unreasonably hazardous products.

H.R. 15003 represents these views of the Product Safety Commission and would create a new, independent regulatory Commission with comprehensive authority to take action across the full range of consumer products to reduce or prevent product-related injuries. The powers and procedural requirements contained in H.R. 15003, for the most part, draw and improve upon concepts and practices which the Congress has previously employed in other safety laws.

As a member of the House Banking and Currency Committee, I have fought long and hard for many consumer bills such as the Consumer Credit Protection Act and the Fair Credit Reporting Act. As a member of the committee, I was successful in adding my consumer protection amendment to the Economic Stabilization Act. My amendment is now part of the public law and permits consumers to protect themselves against overpricing during phase II of Government price controls by allowing those who have been overcharged to sue for three times the amount of the overcharge.

As a Member of the House during the past 8 years, I have supported such landmark consumer protection legislation as the National Commission on Product Safety Act; the Traffic Safety Act, which sets performance standards for cars and tires; the Child Protection and Toy Safety Act; the Safe Packaging Act; and the Truth-in-Packaging Act.

Mr. Chairman, I hope my distinguished colleagues will join me in giving their full-hearted support to this, the latest in a series of necessary consumer legislation. I urgently support prompt and affirmative action on H.R. 15003.

Mr. PRICE of Illinois. Mr. Chairman, the Consumer Product Safety Act, H.R. 15003, is one of the most important pieces of legislation the House will consider during this session. The basic purpose of this bill is to have the Federal Government assume a major role in protecting consumers from unreasonable risks associated with the use of exposure to consumer products.

To accomplish this objective this bill creates an independent regulatory Commission, the Product Safety Commission, which brings together under one roof responsibility for regulating household consumer products as to safety. The Commission is authorized to study the causes and prevention of product-related injuries, establish mandatory safety standards for consumer products to reduce potential hazards and, if necessary, ban hazardous products from the marketplace and provide judicial and administrative relief against harmful products.

That this legislation is needed can be understood by the following data. The National Center for Health Statistics estimates that each year 20 million Americans are injured in and around the home. Of this total, 110,000 injuries result in permanent disability and 30,000 in death. One estimate was placed the annual dollar cost to the economy of product-related injuries at over $5 billion.

Moreover, home accidents cause a death tool among children under age 15 which is higher than that of cancer and heart disease combined. Yet the Federal Government is virtually powerless to curb hazards in a majority of consumer products. Also, there is no present central facility for collecting and evaluating injury data to measure the true scope of product-related injuries or to determine with confidence what portion of the annual toll of 30,000 deaths or 20 million injuries at home are actually caused by unsafe products.

This legislation is a culmination of congressional action over the last 6 years dealing with consumer safety. This action includes the National Traffic and Motor Vehicle Safety Act of 1966, the Gas Pipeline Safety Act of 1968, the Flammable Fabrics Act Amendments of 1967, the Radiation Control for Health and Safety Act of 1968, the Child Prevention and Toy Safety Act of 1969 and the Poison Prevention Packaging Act of 1970.

Each of these measures represents an important contribution to consumer safety. However, the resulting patchwork pattern of laws extends to only a small portion of the multitude of products. Moreover, the technological revolution and ever-increasing public demand for consumer products has produced thousands of new products whose impact are less understood and whose use may pose potential harm. Therefore, what is needed rather than the traditional case by case approach is a consolidated effort to promote consumer safety.

In closing, Mr. Chairman, I strongly support this bill and urge my colleagues to join in voting for it.

Mr. HILLIS. Mr. Chairman, I would like to add a word of support for the consumer product safety bill being considered before this body today. I am but one among many Members of the House who have promised their constituents to do a better job of looking after the interests of the consumer—the forgotten American in the past decade. The consumer has been mistreated and cheated far too often in the past. He has not had a voice to speak up for him and usually has not known how to complain if he discovered a faulty product or shoddy business practice. Certainly, a law suit is a possibility, but most consumers have not had either the financial resources nor the desire to undergo a long, unpleasant court battle on the behalf of the consuming public "for the principle" of correcting an unjust situation.

Last year, the House, acting on a mandate from the public, finally enacted a Consumer Protection Act, which sets up an independent agency to represent the interests of consumers in proceedings before Federal agencies and courts, encourages research on consumer products, and disseminate consumer information, as well as establish an Office of Consumer Affairs in the Executive Office. That was a first step beyond what the Food and Drug Administration had offered previously.

But there are many in Congress who have felt we need something more—something that really gets to the heart of the consumer issue and authorizes bold action for effective remedies. We feel the consumer product safety bill is what we have been looking for. It hits at the most crucial issue in consumer affairs—that of safety. Getting a lemon of a sewing machine is a nuisance, or getting a toy for your child which breaks in its first hours of use is annoying—and consumers deserve protection and recourse against such instances.

But a sewing machine with unsafe wiring or a toy which could shatter during play into an object that could poke out your child's eye is far more serious. Often the damage cannot be undone. Here, the consumer generally has little knowledge which qualifies him to determine the future safety quotient of a product. I think the time has come for the consumer to know he can purchase any product without having to worry about the safety factor. That problem simply should not exist in the second half of the 20th century.

Therefore, I am glad to see this bill reported to the House and I am encouraged by its general acceptance here. This is a strong, effective bill, but not so unmanageable or so demanding that it becomes just another bureaucratic irritant. In fact, I am pleased to note that labor and business alike feel this bill is a reasonable approach to the problem. I have received several letters from businessmen in Indiana's Fifth District who recommend its passage as a generally effective means of assuring consumer safety, yet one which will not unreasonably burden businessmen whose products will be subject to inspection by this proposed Product Safety Commission.

I hope my colleagues on the House floor today will agree with those Fifth District constituents and vote to pass the Consumer Product Safety Act. Let us keep our promise to our consumer constituents and enact this piece of tough, but realistic, legislation.

Mr. STAGGERS. Mr. Chairman, I yield myself such time as I may consume.

Just in order to recapitulate what has taken place, I should like to say that in 1967 Congress authorized a commission to make a study throughout the United States on product safety and make a recommendation to the Congress which they have done in the final report of the National Commission on Product Safety. Those men are eminently qualified men. Let me name them for you: Arnold B. Elkind, chairman, attorney, New York; Emory J. Crofoot, attorney, Portland, Oreg.; Henry Aaron Hill, president, Riverside Research Laboratory, Haverhill, Mass.; Sidney Margolius, syndicated columnist, New York City; Michael Pertschuk, Chief Counsel, Senate Commerce Committee, Washington, D.C.; Hugh L. Ray, director, merchandise development and testing laboratory, Sears, Roebuck & Co., Chicago; Dana Young, senior vice president, Southwest Research Institute, San Antonio, Tex.

These gentlemen after 2 years came back with this report. I think most of their recommendations are carried in the bill which is before the House today. They definitely recommend this should be a separate agency.

I would like at this time to pay tribute to all the members of the subcommittee, including the chairman, the gentleman from California (Mr. Moss), and the gentleman from North Carolina (Mr. BROYHILL), and the gentleman from Georgia (Mr. STUCKEY), and the gentleman from Nebraska (Mr. MCCOLLISTER), and the gentleman from Texas (Mr. ECKHARDT), and the gentleman from Pennsylvania (Mr. WARE), and the gentleman from Ohio (Mr. CARNEY).

I might say they have had many jobs and many of them onerous jobs which have been hard to compromise and work out. They have done an exceptional job for America on many of the bills they have brought to this floor.

I want to pay a special tribute to the Members on the other side for their cooperation, and for the hard work of all the men who have worked together, as well as the chairman, the gentleman from California (Mr. Moss), in working out a compromise on bills that seldom met with public approval and on which it is difficult to get a consensus; but they have been able to work out compromises. The chairman has been able to work out compromises on many of the bills which have become the law of the land.

I hope this bill becomes the law of the land because it has been long delayed. Certainly it ought to be passed as the subcommittee recommended. It has been studied as long as any other subject which has been before the committee. They came forth with what I think are good recommendations. The subject was completely gone over by the full committee. It was reviewed and some changes were made, but the full committee thought it was a good bill, and on a voice vote I heard no nays on the bill. The bill was reported out unanimously by the subcommittee to the full committee.

There are those who talk about money and the creation of agencies. Let me say this. In the Commission report they stated there are 20 million accidents in America each year, 110,000 are permanently injured, and 30,000 die as a result of the accidents. We do not measure lives in terms of money. Certainly it is the duty of this Congress to protect as much as we can the welfare of the people of this Nation, and I think this bill does just that. There are many needless accidents that happen from appliances that should not happen. If we read the report we will see that many of these can be prevented, and that is the reason for the creation of the new agency which we hope and pray will carry out the mandates of this Congress to protect the people of this country.

With this, I say this bill ought to be passed overwhelmingly. I recommend it to the Congress as a very important bill.

* * *

AMENDMENT OFFERED BY MR. STAGGERS

Mr. STAGGERS. Mr. Chairman, I offer an amendment.

The Clerk read as follows:

Amendment offered by Mr. STAGGERS: On page 79 of the bill, strike lines 16 through 18 and substitute the following:

"The effective date of a consumer product safety standard under this Act shall be set at a date at least 30 days after the date of promulgation unless the Commission for good cause shown determines that an earlier effective date is in the public interest. In no case may the effective date be set at a date which is earlier than the date of promulgation. A consumer product safety standard shall be applicable only to consumer products manufactured after the effective date."

Mr. STAGGERS. Mr. Chairman, I will just take 1 minute. I think, certainly, this amendment will be agreeable to the Whole Committee of the House. We are just trying to be fair with industry to be sure that they have time in which to amend their practices.

Mr. STEIGER of Wisconsin. Mr. Chairman, will the gentleman yield?

Mr. STAGGERS. I yield to the gentleman from Wisconsin.

Mr. STEIGER of Wisconsin. Mr. Chairman, I appreciate the gentleman yielding. Am I correct in understanding that this amendment to section 9(d) of the bill makes it clear that standards will be applicable only to consumer products manufactured after the effective date of the standard?

Mr. STAGGERS. Yes.

Mr. STEIGER of Wisconsin. I thank the gentleman.

Mr. Chairman, I support the amendment.

The CHAIRMAN. The question is on the amendment offered by the gentleman from West Virginia (Mr. STAGGERS).

The amendment was agreed to.

AMENDMENT OFFERRED BY MR. DENNIS

Mr. DENNIS. Mr. Chairman, I offer an amendment.

The Clerk read as follows:

Amendment offered by Mr. DENNIS: Beginning on page 102, line 23, with the word "If", strike out all down to, but not including, line 11 on page 104, and substitute in lieu thereof the following: "Any person who shall sustain injury by reason of any knowing (including willful) violation of a consumer product safety standard, regulation, or order issued by the Commisisoner may sue therefor in any district court of the United States in the district in which the defendant resides or is found or has an agent, subject to the provisions of section 1331 of title 28, United States Code as to the amount in controversy, and shall recover damages sustained, and the cost of suit, including a reasonable attorney's fee, if considered appropriate in the discretion of the court."

Mr. DENNIS. Mr. Chairman, I have some serious reservations about the basic merits of this bill which spring from my general disinclination to create a new Federal regulatory body to ride herd on American business and from the fact that I personally, at any rate, have not had any great number of complaints from consumers in my own district, but this amendment is not addressed to those general concerns.

This is a legal amendment which is addressed to the question of the proliferation of lawsuits in the Federal courts provided in this measure as it now stands. Section 23 of the bill, which commences on page 102 and runs over to page 104 of the bill, through line 10, provides that any person who suffers or claims to have suffered any injury as a result of the failure of any consumer product to meet the standards which have been laid down under the bill can bring a suit in the Federal court for damages, illness, sickness, anything, regardless of the jurisdictional amount, and recover his damages and a reasonable attorney's fee.

The American Bar Association and the Chief Justice of the United States are both seriously concerned with the Congress loading down the Federal courts unduly with new and additional business. The bill as it is drawn provides for a suit against the retailer, the distributor, the manufacturer, for even as little as $10 or $15 as far as that is concerned. I simply fear that if we pass the bill in that form we are going to have the Federal courts jammed with all types of litigation when they already have plenty to handle.

I have been handed a copy of a telegram which the president of the ABA has sent, I believe, to the Speaker and the chairman of the Rules Committee, as well as other Members. This telegram says:

> While the American Bar Association has taken no position on the substance of H.R. 15003, the proposed Consumer Product Safety Act, we are deeply concerned with any legislation which provides for a substantial increase in the workload of the Federal courts. I am advised that the views of the Judicial Conference of the United States were not sought by the House Committee on Interstate and Foreign Commerce. We recommend that the potential impact on the courts be carefully analyzed before passage of legislation, and in the case of legislation which will substantially add to the burden of the courts, we must oppose it until this has been done.

Chief Justice Burger, in an address to the bar association last August, said:

> . . . . But there is no escape from constantly enlarging the federal judicial establishment except to adopt new judicial methods and improve performance as we are trying to do, and to have Congress carefully scrutinize all legislation that will create more cases.
>
> In recent years, Congress has required every executive agency to prepare an environmental impact statement whenever a new highway, a new bridge or other federally funded projects are planned. I suggest, with all deference, that every piece of legislation creating new cases be accompanied by a "court impact statement", prepared by the reporting committee and submitted to the Judiciary Committees of the Congress with an estimate of how many more judges and supporting personnel will be needed to handle the new cases.

That, of course, in this case has not been done.

So, the thrust of this amendment, very simply, is to strike out the present section and simply provide that any person who sustains an injury——

The CHAIRMAN. The time of the gentleman from Indiana has expired.

Mr. STAGGERS. Mr. Chairman, I ask that the gentleman have 2 additional minutes.

Mr. DENNIS. That any person who has sustained injury may bring suit in the Federal courts under the normal jurisdictional requirements of section 1331, which means the amount in controversy has got to be $10,000 or more. This amendment would hold it down to that, as a means of limiting this proliferating litigation to the more important cases involving the real need for Federal court remedy, relegating others to the State courts.

Mr. Chairman, I yield to the chairman of the committee.

Mr. STAGGERS. The gentleman asked if we had asked the opinion of the Federal courts on this. We did ask the Administrative Office of the U.S. Courts about whether they had made a study. They said no, they had not, and it was not feasible. For that reason, we could not put it into our legislation.

I should like to say this: It seems perfectly clear to me that if we are going to have a Federal law affecting everybody in the United States, they should be dealt with in the Federal courts. This is not mandatory and certainly goes to the other courts as well. How are you going to say a man can only go to Federal court if he has a $10,000 lawsuit? Is a finger worth $10,000? Is a toe worth $10,000? Is an eye worth $10,000? Who is going to be the judge of that? I think the court has to be the judge when they come in as to what kind of damage or injury they have.

Mr. DENNIS. I might say to the chairman that I am only saying that we should treat these damage suits as we treat every other kind of ordinary damage suit in Federal court without giving them preferential status.

Mr. STAGGERS. I think the gentleman is putting the Federal courts ahead of the individual injury. If we need the judges, if this is what we have to have in order to have justice, let us get more judges, but let us give justice in America to the poor people and to the ones who need it.

Mr. ECKHARDT. Mr. Chairman, I rise in opposition to the amendment. I should like to say that the first mistake of the gentleman in assuming that this would overload the Federal courts is the favorable result of reducing danger from products on the market. We presently have authority to go into State courts, and in cases of diversity of citizenship which are frequently available, in Federal courts when damages occur.

The main thrust of this bill is to prevent people from being hurt in the first place. Now, I submit that if this act is passed as written, the offsetting reduction of damages and injuries to people will be at least as great as the additional number of cases brought in Federal court.

Incidentally, the idea of the Federal courts being overloaded is terribly exaggerated. Under this act it would be necessary to show that a rule had been issued with respect to the particular product involved, or that an order had been granted which had been violated.

Rules and orders will be passed as the administrator gets to those matters.

I submit that one should not be permitted to avoid liability in violating a Federal rule merely because the person injured had a finger cut off which is not worth $10,000.

I do not believe we ought to put a price on this type of responsibility. I believe the manufacturer who makes a dangerous product should be subjected to liability as the result of his violation of Federal law without regard to the amount in controversy.

I am tired of hearing this argument that the rights of people, no matter how small they may be, must depend on whether or not we have established enough courts to defend those rights. It seems to me that is putting the horse behind the cart. It seems to me this is entirely wrong thinking in this area.

In the first place, under the present provisions of the law, a person showing that he has a remedy has to show there has been a rule enacted and it has been violated. That cuts down the number of cases.

The rule has to be made. Presumably reasonable public-minded manufacturers will comply with the rule. That will cut down the number of cases.

Why should not a person injured have a right to come in under Federal law regardless of whether the $10,000 is involved? I used to like what Senator Yarborough said, "Let us put the jam on the lower shelf." Why should not the judicial jam be put on the lower shelf. Why should relief only be available to large corporations and to persons with amounts involved of over $10,000? It seems to me the consumers are entitled to have those courts available to them when a manufacturer has violated a rule established under Federal law regardless of the amount in controversy.

I urge a vote of "no" on the amendment.

Mr. WIGGINS. Mr. Chairman, I rise in support of the amendment.

It is important at the outset to understand what the amendment does and what it does not do.

First, Mr. Chairman, it should be understood that a consumer is not denied a right of action simply because he may not have access to a Federal court. He may sue in a State court. He has had that right all along, and it is not denied to him under this amendment.

The pending bill waives the amount in controversy requirement of section 1331 of title 28. At the present time access to the Federal court is not granted in all cases; it is granted only if the amount in controversy for certain specific types of claims is $10,000 or more.

This proposed statute waives that requirement with respect to causes of action arising under the bill.

Why is it necessary that the action be filed in the Federal court? What policy considerations would cause us to impose this added burden on the Federal courts? Certainly the reason cannot be that the Federal court is the only possible forum for the fair resolution of controversies arising under the bill. No one here should impute to the State courts an inability to settle a controversy properly even though it involves an interpretation of Federal law. They do that now. We are heaping a further burden upon the Federal courts for no good cause or reason. We have heard from the Chief Justice and others that it is in the public interest not to further burden the Federal courts.

This amendment would insulate the Federal courts from causes of action that involve lesser sums and would cause the plaintiffs in those cases to seek their relief in the State court.

It is wholly a responsible amendment, Mr. Chairman, and I urge the Members to support it.

The CHAIRMAN. The question is on the amendment offered by the gentleman from Indiana (Mr. DENNIS).

The question was taken; and the Chairman announced that the ayes appeared to have it.

Mr. MOSS. Mr. Chairman, I demand tellers.

Tellers were refused.

So the amendment was agreed to.

AMENDMENT OFFERED BY MR. HENDERSON

Mr. HENDERSON. Mr. Chairman, I offer an amendment.

The Clerk read as follows:

Amendment offered by Mr. HENDERSON: On page 65 of the reported bill, amend section 4—

(1) by striking out all of paragraph (1) of subsection (g), beginning with line 8 down through line 19;

(2) in line 20, strike out "(2)" and insert in lieu thereof "(g)"; and

(3) in line 21, strike out the word "other".

(Mr. HENDERSON asked and was given permission to revise and extend his remarks.)

Mr. HENDERSON. Mr. Chairman, my amendment will delete the provisions of section 4(g)(1), which authorize five political appointments to be made by the Chairman of the Consumer Product Safety Commission.

The provisions my amendment will delete, authorize the Chairman of the Commission, subject to the approval of the Commission, to appoint an Executive Director, a General Counsel, a Director of Engineering Sciences, a Director of Epidemiology, and a Director of Information—

First, without regard to the requirements governing appointments in the competitive civil service;

Second, without regard to the requirements relating to the classification of positions; and

Third, without regard to the General Schedule rates of pay except that the rate of pay fixed by the Chairman for any such appointee may not exceed the rate in effect for GS–18 of the General Schedule.

The provisions have the effect of authorizing five additional supergrades which may be filled by political appointees.

Section 4 of this legislation establishes an independent regulatory commission, the Consumer Product Safety Commission. The Commission will be bipartisan, since no more than three Commissioners may belong to the same political party.

I believe it is proper for the Commission of a regulatory agency, such as this agency, to be bipartisan. I believe it to be more important than the appointees to the five top positions of the new regulatory Commission not be subject to political appointment. They should be appointed under the usual requirements governing appointments to the competitive civil service.

I find no similar provisions or authority for appointments to be made in other regulatory agencies without regard to the competitive civil service. As a matter of fact, the regulatory agencies I have checked, such as the Securities and Exchange Commission, the Civil Aeronautics Board, the Federal Communications Commission, and the Federal Trade Commission, do not have authority proposed to be granted by this legislation.

My amendment, by striking out paragraph (1) of subsection (g), has the effect of subjecting the appointments to the top positions in the new regulatory agency, to the usual competitive civil service requirements. Authority for such appointments is included in other provisions of subsection (g).

Another objectionable feature of the provision which I propose to eliminate, is that it permits the Chairman of the Commission to fix rates of pay for the five positions at the supergrade levels.

As I have stated many times before this House, this is a matter that is strictly within the jurisdiction of the Post Office and Civil Service Committee.

Mr. Chairman, first of all, this matter should have been handled by the Post Office and Civil Service Committee, and second, we are considering legislation which will afford some flexibility in filling supergrade positions. I urge the adoption of my amendment.

Mr. GROSS. Will the gentleman yield?

Mr. HENDERSON. I am delighted to yield to the gentleman from Iowa, the ranking member of the House Committee on Post Office and Civil Service.

Mr. GROSS. I thank the gentleman from North Carolina for yielding, and join in support of his amendment. The House has on several occasions stricken such language from other bills, and I urge the members to approve the amendment.

Mr. MOSS. Mr. Chairman, I move to strike the requisite number of words.

The amendment offered by the gentleman from North Carolina has the effect of striking out not only the authority to appoint outside of the civil service but takes away the specific authority of the director to appoint the designated five officials in effect at a GS–18 level.

After discussion with the chairman, I have been informed that the committee would be agreeable to accepting an amendment which would require that the five enumerated officials at a grade of GS-18 be appointed from the scheduled civil service.

Mr. HENDERSON. Would the gentleman yield for one moment?

Mr. MOSS. I yield to the gentleman.

Mr. HENDERSON. As I understand, it you are suggesting if we would leave in the language of the five, it would be agreeable, but I hope you are not suggesting they have to be GS–18's. That is not your intent, is it?

Mr. MOSS. At an annual basic rate of pay that would not be in excess of GS–18. That would be the sense of the amendment.

Mr. HENDERSON. Mr. Chairman, I ask unanimous consent that my amendment be amended to provide for striking out the language beginning in line 11, on page 65, with the word "individuals," and if that is acceptable, it would leave the enumeration of the five positions in.

Mr. MOSS. That is agreeable to this side.

The CHAIRMAN. The Clerk will report the proposed modification made in the nature of a unanimous-consent request.

Will you please send it to the desk, or would you restate it?

Mr. HENDERSON. I would prefer to restate it.

My amendment would be amended to provide that it should strike out all in paragraph (g)(1), beginning in line 11 on page 65 with the word "individuals." It would have the effect of leaving the first sentence which enumerates the five positions in the bill.

The CHAIRMAN. The Clerk will report the amendment as proposed to be modified.

Mr. STAGGERS. May I clarify the amendment, if I might, before it is being reported?

The CHAIRMAN. The Chair would prefer to have the proposed amendment to the amendment at the desk in writing.

I want to clarify with the gentleman from North Carolina (Mr. HENDERSON) what the intent of his modification is before we reach a general matter of agreement. Will the gentleman from California yield to me further for that purpose?

Mr. MOSS. I yield to the gentleman from West Virginia.

Mr. STAGGERS. Mr. Chairman, I would like to suggest that the first part of this down through "individuals" remain, and then end the amendment before the words "no individual so" on line 17, and then say that they shall not be paid in excess of GS–18.

Mr. HENDERSON. If the gentleman from California will yield——

Mr. MOSS. I yield to the gentleman from North Carolina.

Mr. HENDERSON. Mr. Chairman, I have no objection to that. It is surplusage, because, if you appoint them by designation, they may be appointed at the salary of GS–18, and you say "shall not be in excess of." I have no objection.

If the gentleman will yield further, the effect of my amendment is there could be more than five. This is a limiting amendment to five.

Mr. MOSS. We do desire to limit it to five.

Mr. HENDERSON. Very well.

Mr. MOSS. I thank the gentleman.

Mr. HENDERSON. Mr. Chairman, I ask unanimous consent that my amendment may be so modified, and I would ask that the Clerk read the modification.

The CHAIRMAN. The Clerk will report the proposed modification of the amendment.

The Clerk read as follows:

On page 65, line 11, strike out "Individuals" and all that follows down through line 17, and insert in lieu thereof "No individual so".

The CHAIRMAN. Is there objection to the request of the gentleman from North Carolina (Mr. HENDERSON).

There was no objection.

The CHAIRMAN. The question is on the amendment offered by the gentleman from North Carolina (Mr. HENDERSON) as modified.

The amendment, as modified, was agreed to.

AMENDMENT OFFERED BY MR. STAGGERS

Mr. STAGGERS. Mr. Chairman, I offer an amendment.

The Clerk read as follows:

Amendment offered by Mr. STAGGERS: On page 89 of the bill add after the word "product" the following new sentence: "The Commission may, in appropriate cases, permit information required under paragraph (1) and (2) of this subsection to be coded."

Mr. STAGGERS. Mr. Chairman, this amendment simply allows the commission on such products as perhaps are not changed from year to year, and which are made and put on the shelves of a store for sale, that they do not have to be dated specifically, but that they may have a coded date. It is left up to the commission as to whether or not they think it is essential that a specific manufacturing date be put on, otherwise they may have a coded date. This is a very simple amendment.

Mr. BROYHILL of North Carolina. Mr. Chairman, I move to strike out the last word.

Mr. Chairman, the amendment is acceptable to this side.

The CHAIRMAN. The question is on the amendment offered by the gentleman from West Virginia (Mr. STAGGERS).

The amendment was agreed to.

AMENDMENT OFFERED BY MR. MOSS

Mr. MOSS. Mr. Chairman, I offer an amendment.

The Clerk read as follows:

Amendment offered by Mr. Moss: page 109, insert after line 5 the following:

"(d) No person shall be subject to civil liability to any person (other than the Commission or the United States) for disclosing information at the request of the Comsion."

Page 109, line 6, strike out "(d)" and insert in lieu thereof "(e)".

Page 109, line 15, strike out "(e)" and insert in lieu thereof "(f)".

Page 109, line 20, strike out "(f)" and insert in lieu thereof "(g)".

Page 109, line 24, strike out "(g)" and insert in lieu thereof "(h)".

Page 110, line 3, strike out "(h)" and insert in lieu thereof "(i)".

Page 118, line 18, strike out "section 27(g)" and insert in lieu thereof "section 27(h)".

Page 119, line 8, strike out "section 27(g)" and insert in lieu thereof "section 27(h)".

Mr. STAGGERS (during the reading). Mr. Chairman, I ask unanimous consent that the amendment be considered as read and printed in the RECORD.

The CHAIRMAN. Is there objection to the request of the gentleman from West Virginia?

There was no objection.

The CHAIRMAN. The Chair recognizes the gentleman from California (Mr. Moss).

Mr. MOSS. Mr. Chairman, the purpose of this amendment is to make it very clear that the persons supplying information at the request of the commission, incur no liability because of the supplying of the information.

Mr. BROYHILL of North Carolina. Mr. Chairman, will the gentleman yield?

Mr. MOSS. I yield to the gentleman.

Mr. BROYHILL of North Carolina. Mr. Chairman, the members of the committee have discussed this amendment in some detail and have agreed to it.

Mr. GROSS. Mr. Chairman, will the gentleman yield?

Mr. MOSS. I yield to the gentleman.

Mr. GROSS. Do I understand that the remainder of the amendment—that portion that was not read—simply had to do with renumbering subsections?

Mr. MOSS. That is right.

Mr. GROSS. I thank the gentleman.

Mr. DENNIS. Mr. Chairman, will the gentleman yield?

Mr. MOSS. I am happy to yield to the gentleman from Indiana.

Mr. DENNIS. Mr. Chairman, this is a matter which I had not thought about at all. But I would like to consider with the gentleman for a minute the effect, the possible effect, of his amendment. I assume it changes the law in some respects. In other words, you are addressing yourself to a situation where there might be liability if you did not adopt this amendment—and I am just thinking as I go on—I am just wondering whether or not you want to give complete immunity—if that is what we are doing—to any and all individuals who might, for instance, disclose their employer's trade secrets, or confidential information of a slightly lesser degree, simply because some functionary of this commission demanded it.

Now maybe the man ought to have to make a choice there. I am not so sure he should be blanketed in and given immunity just because some bureaucrat asked for the information.

Mr. MOSS. The understanding of the gentleman from California, on the advice of counsel of the committee, is that it tends to clarify the common law on this matter of requiring in a report the disclosure of certain information which might be otherwise privileged.

Mr. DENNIS. I would say to the gentleman that ordinarily I find the common law pretty good, if you just leave it alone. I would feel a little more comfortable if we would leave them where the common law leaves them, instead of saying that there will not be any common law liability if somebody gives away this information.

Mr. MOSS. Those who have requested this amendment were the hospitals and insurance companies.

Mr. DENNIS. That does not satisfy me particularly.

The CHAIRMAN. The question is on the amendment offered by the gentleman from California (Mr. Moss).

The question was taken; and on a division (demanded by Mr. Moss) there were—ayes 49, noes 10.

So the amendment was agreed to.

AMENDMENT OFFERED BY MR. MOSS

Mr. MOSS. Mr. Chairman, I offer an amendment. The Clerk read as follows:

Amendment offered by Mr. Moss: Page 114, insert after line 14 the following:

"(d) The Commission shall, to the maximum extent practicable, utilize the resources and facilities of the National Bureau of Standards, on a reimbursable basis, to perform research and analyses related to consumer product hazards (including fire and flammability hazards), to develop test methods, to conduct studies and investigations, and to provide technical advice and assistance in connection with the functions of the Commissions."

Mr. MOSS. Mr. Chairman, I offer this amendment in response to a request of the Department of Commerce and the National Bureau of Standards. It was felt that the language here would insure utilizing facilities already existing rather than pressing, perhaps, to duplicate such facilities under some future planning of the agency.

Mr. GROSS. Mr. Chairman, will the gentleman yield?

Mr. MOSS. I yield to the gentleman from Iowa.

Mr. GROSS. Would the gentleman suggest that we might cut a few million dollars out of the authorization contained in the bill in view of the savings he projects?

Mr. MOSS. I believe that the authorization reflects the consensus of the committee to accept this amendment. We believe through the wisdom of those who appropriate, an examination of the needs as they are finally detailed to the Appropriations Committee will be made.

Mr. BROYHILL of North Carolina. Mr. Chairman, will the gentleman yield?

Mr. MOSS. I yield to the gentleman from North Carolina.

Mr. BROYHILL of North Carolina. As the gentleman from California knows, there is in this bill no sizable amount of money for construction, and we just want to make sure that the Commission does use those facilities presently available and if they have need to construct new facilities they have to come back to us and make a formal request.

Mr. MOSS. The gentleman is correct, and I thank the gentleman.

The CHAIRMAN. The question is on the amendment offered by the gentleman from California (Mr. Moss).

The amendment was agreed to.

AMENDMENT OFFERED BY MR. WHITE

Mr. WHITE. Mr. Chairman, I offer an amendment.

The Clerk read as follows:

Amendment offered by Mr. WHITE: Page 81, line 15, by striking the period and adding the following: ", if such petition and reasons for such denial materially differ from any previous petition and subsequent denial."

(Mr. WHITE asked and was given permission to revise and extend his remarks.)

Mr. WHITE. I present this particular amendment to the House in order to prevent a proliferation of petitions and subsequent placements of denials in the Federal Register. The bill provides that any person could petition the Commission, and then the Commission, if denying the petition, must subsequently put in the record their denial of that petition and the reasons for it. What I am saying by this amendment is that the Commissions would not have to continue to put in denials, providing such petition and reasons for such denial do not materially differ from any previous petition and subsequent denial.

In other words, if there are one or two people continually writing in similar complaints, then we are not going to burden the Commission to place in the Register reasons for denials on the same type of petition. I am just trying to save the Government a considerable amount of money by preventing a voluminous Federal Register of Denials, if the Commission has the same denial and reasons for such denial on a similar petition already registered. That is the substance of this amendment.

The CHAIRMAN. The question is on the amendment offered by the gentleman from Texas (Mr. WHITE).

The amendment was agreed to.

AMENDMENT OFFERED BY MR. ECKHARDT

Mr. ECKHARDT. Mr. Chairman, I offer an amendment.

The Clerk read as follows:

Amendment offered by Mr. ECKHARDT: Page 68, line 24, after "therewith" insert the following: (unless the Commission finds that the public health and safety requires a lesser period of notice)".

Page 68, line 25, insert ", to the extent practicable," after "information".

Page 90, beginning on line 7 strike out "the oral presentation of views as well as for written presentations" and insert in lieu thereof "a hearing in accordance with subsection (f) of this section".

Page 91, line 2, strike out "section 554 of title 5, United States Code" and insert "subsection (f)".

Page 92, insert after line 22 the following:

"(f) An order under subsection (c) or (d) may be issued only after an opportunity for a hearing in accordance with section 554 of title 5, United States Code, except that if the Commission determines that any person who wishes to participate in such hearing is a part of a class of participants who share an identity of interest, the Commission may limit such person's participation in such hearing to participation through a single representative designated by such class (or by the Commission if such class fails to designate such a representative).

Mr. ECKHARDT. Mr. Chairman, section (c) that is referred to on page 90 deals with the administrative process which must precede the giving of notice of defect or failure to comply in the case of a product. Section (d) beginning on line 24 on page 90 deals with the ultimate action of the Commission which may order a company to bring a product into conformity or to replace the product or to refund money.

Originally we had provided two separate processes for these two administrative procedures. We had a more or less curtailed process with respect to the giving of public notice of the defect and we afforded the full ramifications of section 554 of title V of the United States Code to the ultimate process of calling for bringing the product into conformity. In other words the ultimate action of holding a product out of conformity and requiring it to be brought into conformity and the money paid back was protected by the full range of the Administrative Procedure Act's adjudicatory processes, but we had thought that a public notice of defect did not necessarily need quite that much protection and might have to be ordered rather summarily.

In discussing the matters with some of the industries that would be affected, they made the point, and I think they made it well, that to notify one's consumers that there may be a defect in one's own product may be very injurious, and that part of the total impact of the proceeding has been sustained by the industry before it has been afforded full process for its defense. Therefore, they said that there should be a fuller adjudicatory process, even preliminary to the defect notice.

They also raised this question: they said there should not be two different hearings. And if we set up merely the standards of section 553 with the additional requirement of the oral hearing as applicable to the defect notice and then we give the full ramifications of the adjudicatory process to the ultimate hearing, this requires two hearings. Why have two under the circumstances?

So, agreeing, we discussed it among the subcommittee and we offer this amendment, which makes the same process available to the notice of defect requirement as that applicable to the process calling for bringing the product into conformity and imposing other penalties or requirements.

Now there is only one thing that falls short of, or one thing somewhat different from, the provisions of 554 of title V of the United States Code. We do recognize that in some of these cases there might be a great number of people involved. This is somewhat like a rulemaking process, but it has adjudicatory aspects.

But it is like rulemaking in that there may be a great number of people distributing the same product, and we simply added the one qualification to the adjudicatory-type procedure that the Commission may require that those who have identical concerns and identical interests choose a single spokesman or else a single spokesman will be chosen and designated. We give the full right of cross-examination in both processes, with that very limited limitation. That is the effect of this amendment.

Now, the amendment to the earlier provisions on page 68 is merely to make it clear that in a proper case, since we are not providing for the quicker means of compelling the manufacturer to give notice of defects that the agency itself may give that notice at an earlier time than after the 30 days ordinarily required as a waiting period.

That is the effect of this amendment.

Mr. BROYHILL of North Carolina. Mr. Chairman, I want the Members of the Committee to know that what you are doing with your amendment is giving a manufacturer whose product is found to be in noncompliance, a greater right to be heard, to have his day in court, as the old saying is, and give him far more protection under this language in the bill. I support the amendment.

The CHAIRMAN. The question is on the amendment offered by the gentleman from Texas (Mr. ECKHARDT).

The amendment was agreed to.

AMENDMENT OFFERED BY MR. BINGHAM

Mr. BINGHAM. Mr. Chairman, I offer an amendment.

The Clerk read as follows:

Amendment offered by Mr. BINGHAM: Page 59, beginning on line 17, strike out "any article" and all that follows down through "any such article, (F)" in line 23.

Page 60, line 2, strike out "(G)" and insert in lieu thereof "(F)".

(Mr. BINGHAM asked and was given permission to revise and extend his remarks.)

Mr. BINGHAM. Mr. Chairman, I would first like to say that I think this is an excellent bill. I compliment the committee for it. I certainly intend to support it whether or not my amendment is adopted.

The purpose of my amendment, very simply, would be to restore to the bill the coverage of firearms. Firearms were covered in the original bill as introduced by the distinguished gentleman from California (Mr. MOSS), for whom I have the greatest admiration, and by other members of the committee. Then, subsequently, during the committee deliberations, the paragraph was inserted in the bill excepting firearms very specifically from the definition of the term "consumer product." It is that paragraph which my amendment would delete.

I would submit to the members of the committee that firearms are an important "consumer product." Some 6 million are sold every year in this country. While firearms are regulated in some respects, they are not regulated with regard to safety. According to the 1969 Eisenhower Commission on Fire Arms and Violence, firearms are the fifth most common cause of accidental deaths in this country, coming after motor vehicles, falls, fires, and drownings. Aside from motor vehicles, firearms are the single consumer item most consistently involved in accidental death.

Moreover, according to the 1970 final report of the National Commission on Product Safety, which appears in full in the committee hearings, 150,000 people are injured in gun accidents every year.

Now, Mr. Chairman and members of the House Committee, do not be alarmed.

I am not bringing out a real pistol to show you at this time, but here is something that I want to show you. Here in my hand is a product that will be covered by this bill. This is a toy pistol. It shoots a little pellet and operates by a spring. This pistol will be covered under the provisions of this bill. But, if this were the real McCoy, if this was something that could blow up in your face and kill you or with which you could kill other people, it would not be covered.

I suggest that this is a topsy-turvy arrangement.

This is not a gun control amendment. It would not affect the question of who might buy guns or under what conditions. It is simply and purely a safety amendment. Hopefully, it would prevent the sale of guns that are unsafe.

I do not always agree with the actions by the other body, but I would call attention to the fact that in the version of this legislation passed by the other body firearms were included within the scope of the legislation.

I hope the Members will support the amendment.

Mr. MOSS. Mr. Chairman, I rise in opposition to the amendment.

(Mr. MOSS asked and was given permission to revise and extend his remarks.)

Mr. MOSS. Mr. Chairman, it pains me somewhat to have to oppose the amendment offered by my distinguished colleague from New York, but I find that I must, for good and sufficient reasons. These are mainly, that neither the Committee on Interstate and Foreign Commerce nor the special Commission on Consumer Product Safety made any kind of an inquiry into firearms. As a matter of fact, it was not included in the original bill, nor was it intended to be.

Out of an abundance of caution, to make clear that it was not to be included, on the redraft we specifically exempted it in order to accord with the instructions given by the Committee on Interstate and Foreign Commerce in the resolution creating the National Commission on Product Safety.

I have here the report of the National Commission of Product Safety, and in the report is included the statutory language creating the Commission. In section 6 of that language, under the definitions, the Commission was specifically excluded from considering the Federal Firearms Act (15 USC 901) and the National Firearms Act was also not within the scope of their activities. It was not within the scope of the hearings.

The distinguished gentleman from New York appeared before the National Commission on Product Safety and gave testimony on other matters but not on firearms.

I have checked carefully the records of the Subcommittee on Commerce and Finance and find no instance of the gentleman requesting the opportunity to come forward and urge the committee to go beyond the scope of the proposals as outlined in the actions of the Congress back in the mid 1960's when we created the National Commission on Product Safety.

This would not necessarily make firearms more safe. We are concerned primarily about the accidental use of firearms. It would not touch that problem. I do not believe we should here attempt to mislead the public. I am afraid that is what would happen if we were to suddenly have a firearms act without any kind of history as to what we intended. I believe it is an important enough subject to be dealt with as a separate subject.

It is being dealt with by the Committee on the Judiciary and I believe the Committee on Ways and Means has jurisdiction also. Neither we in the Committee on Interstate and Foreign Commerce nor in the Subcommittee on Commerce and Finance have at any time undertaken to deal with this subject.

I urge the defeat of the amendment.

Mr. WIGGINS. Mr. Chairman, I rise in opposition to the amendment.

Mr. Chairman, I am not going to take all of the 5 minutes, but I want the Members not to treat this amendment lightly. They ought to recognize what it does.

The present bill defines "consumer products" so as to exclude firearms. The amendment proposed strikes that exclusion and, if adopted, "consumer products" would include firearms.

If consumer products do include firearms, authority is granted to the Commission to set certain standards with respect to consumer products which include, among other things, requirements as to performance, composition, design, construction, and other matters. Failing in meeting those standards subject to certain administrative review provisions, the consumer product can be denied in commerce entirely.

Therefore, what we have, no more nor less, is a gun control bill by administrative rule rather than by act of Congress.

Now, I want to say that I support a regulation of weapons. The House Judiciary Committee is now considering a gun control bill of sorts and I expect to support a reasonable bill. But the Congress ought to consider it, and the Congress ought to adopt the law and not delegate its responsibility to a commission, and that is precisely what would happen if the amendment of the gentleman is adopted.

Mr. HOLIFIELD. Mr. Chairman, will the gentleman from California yield?

Mr. WIGGINS. Yes, of course, I will yield to the gentleman.

Mr. HOLIFIELD. I wish to aline myself with the remarks of the gentleman from California (Mr. MOSS) and the gentleman now in the well (Mr. WIGGINS).

This is a good way to kill this bill. As everybody knows, the gun control issue is a very controversial matter.

Now, they have a good bill; the committee has a good bill here on consumer safety, and regardless of the merit of the gentleman's amendment, from an ideological or theoretical standpoint, the one way to kill this bill is to attach controversial measures to it and have it die over in the other body with months of debate.

Mr. WIGGINS. I agree with the gentleman.

And one further point in conclusion: In the bill now pending before the Judiciary Committee the Secretary of the Treasury is granted very limited authority with respect to promulgating rules and regulations affecting guns. Congress is going to define carefully the authority of the Secretary to promulgate regulations under the legislation pending before the Judiciary Committee.

This legislation, on the other hand, grants almost carte blanche authority to a commission which is not subject to the kind of close legislative scrutiny which would be provided under the bill now pending before the Judiciary Committee.

Ladies and gentlemen, I urge the defeat of this amendment.

The CHAIRMAN. For what purpose does the gentleman from West Virginia, the chairman of the committee, rise?

Mr. STAGGERS. I move to strike the last word.

If I understood the gentleman who just spoke, I understand that he urged the defeat of the amendment; is that right?

Mr. WIGGINS. That is correct.

Mr. STAGGERS. I just wish to say this: We have no jurisdiction in our committee. This would give us jurisdiction in part and would put all the work on the other two committees in what they are doing.

Mr. RANDALL. Mr. Chairman, H.R. 15003 is for the most part a good bill and should be passed by the House. It would be difficult for a Member to oppose a bill which has its title, "A bill to protect consumers against unreasonable product hazards," and then provides in section 1 that the act may be cited as the "Consumer Product Safety Act." To be against objectives or purposes such as these is almost like being against motherhood or the flag.

However, Mr. Chairman, the amendment offered by the gentleman from New York is one that requires a very careful analysis. As you read the amendment, at first there seems to be almost nothing wrong with striking out several lines of the bill commencing at line 17 on page 59 which defines the term "consumer product." The section which is striken out, section E, is one among several listings of exceptions or exemptions to what is defined as a consumer product.

Now I would never attribute to the gentleman from New York anything but the best motives. But I cannot help but be suspicious that this amendment deserves a careful look because while it is innocent appearing, it seems to me that it could be an adroit attempt by the antigun lobby to bring gun control in through the back door in what is otherwise a completely acceptable consumer products safety bill.

We must recall that this bill deals with product hazards or, if turned around in the other direction, product safety. I sense that if this amendment were to be adopted it would remove some exception or some of those exemptions not intended to be included within the definition of consumer products.

In other words, this amendment would permit the inclusion of ammunition and firearms as a consumer product. We all know, of course, that the Consumer Product Safety Commission created by this bill will have the power and authority to lay down standards as to what products are safe and what products are hazardous. If the amendment of the gentleman from New York should pass, there would be nothing to keep the Commission from declaring that all guns of any or every type, and ammunition of all sorts, are dangerous and hazardous products and thereby achieve through indirection what the antigun lobby has never been able to enact directly—their avowed objective to outlaw all guns and ammunition.

Mr. Chairman, I repeat that it is possible this amendment could very well provide for gun control through the back door. It could very well mean that this subtle and rather innocent appearing amendment could result in taking guns away from our sportsmen and law abiding citizens. If the Consumer Commission saw fit it could impair the personal security of all of our citizens by limiting the right they now enjoy to possess firearms to make them secure in their homes.

No, Mr. Chairman, I am willing to face the issue of gun control squarely, either vote it up or down. But let us not do it this way, through the back door. Of course, many of us feel that the best approach to the so-called gun problem is the quick enactment of mandatory penalties for those using firearms in the commission of a crime. We should even get so tough as to deny parole to those using firearms when committing a crime. But today let us not fool ourselves and then later wake up to be surprised at the purpose of this amendment. Then it will be too late to do anything about it. This amendment must be defeated.

The CHAIRMAN. The question is on the amendment offered by the gentleman from New York (Mr. BINGHAM).

The amendment was rejected.

AMENDMENT OFFERED BY MR. ECKHARDT

Mr. ECKHARDT. Mr. Chairman, I offer an amendment.

The Clerk read as follows:

Amendment offered by Mr. ECKHARDT: Page 115, line 2, insert after the period the following: "All functions of the Secretary of Health, Education, and Welfare under subpart 3 of part F of title III of the Public Health Service Act (relating to electronic product radiation), except to the extent that such functions relate to electronic product radiation emitted from electronic products which are devices (as defined in section 201 (h) of the Federal Food, Drug, and Cosmetic Act), are transferred to the Commission."

Page 118, line 7, strike out "The" and all that follows down through line 14 on such page.

(Mr. ECKHARDT asked and was given permission to revise and extend his remarks.)

Mr. ECKHARDT. Mr. Chairman, what this amendment does is transfer authority to the new agency to deal with products which are dangerous because of radiation, except that it does not deal with those products that are used medically, those that are defined under the Food and Drug Act in section 201(h) like X-ray equipment, and so forth, in doctor's offices.

Now, there is no provision in the act as now written that would cover a situation as, for instance, one involving a TV set that emitted radiation. It seems to me utterly ridiculous to put in this authority the control, for instance, of a TV set because it may shock a person and not give authority to the same agency to control the TV set because it emits radiation.

It seems to me legislation which purports to establish in a single agency the authority to protect the public and which protects the public from sustaining a slight shock or cut or injury but which does not protect them from having their children turn out like Mark Twain's Puddin' Head Wilson is rather defective.

For that reason I have tried to bring together in the agency the authority to control all types of dangers to the consumer without trespassing on that very proper jurisdiction of the FDA of controlling that type of equipment relating to medical use. What would be covered by this amendment would be consumer products. They should fall under the product safety agency.

That is all the amendment does.

The CHAIRMAN. The question is on the amendment offered by the gentleman from Texas (Mr. ECKHARDT).

The question was taken; and on a division (demanded by Mr. STAGGERS) there were—ayes 10, noes 46.

So the amendment was rejected.

AMENDMENT OFFERED BY MR. PEPPER

Mr. PEPPER. Mr. Chairman, I offer an amendment.

The Clerk read as follows:

Amendment offered by Mr. PEPPER: Page 104, line 13, after "state", strike out "statutory."

Mr. PEPPER. Mr. Chairman and members of the Committee, those of you who have the bill before you, if you will note, on page 104, line 11, it provides "the remedies provided for in this section shall be in addition to and not in lieu of any other remedies provided by common law or under Federal or State statutory law."

I have conferred with the able members of the committee to call their attention to the fact that the word "statutory" is a limitation here upon the right of the complainant to bring suit in the State court. He should have the right to bring suit under State case law as well as under State statutory law. I am sure the committee did not intend to limit him just to statutory rights.

Mr. STAGGERS. Will the gentleman yield?

Mr. PEPPER. I am glad to yield to the gentleman.

Mr. STAGGERS. Mr. Chairman, I have no objection, and I do not think anyone on this side of the aisle does to the amendment.

The CHAIRMAN. The question is on

the amendment offered by the gentleman from Florida (Mr. PEPPER).

The amendment was agreed to.

AMENDMENTS OFFERED BY MR. RANGEL

Mr. RANGEL. Mr. Chairman, I offer amendments.

The Clerk read as follows:

Amendments offered by Mr. RANGEL: Page 71, line 3, insert after the period the following: "Any labeling warnings or instructions required under a consumer product safety standard shall be printed both in English and Spanish, and shall be printed in any other language which the Commission determines is appropriate."

Page 90, insert after line 23 the following: "Any such notice shall be given both in English and Spanish, and shall be given in any other language which the Commission determines is appropriate."

(Mr. RANGEL asked and was given permission to revise and extend his remarks.)

Mr. RANGEL. Mr. Chairman and Members of the committee, we have before us today a piece of landmark legislation that is dramatic enough to call for congratulations to the drafters of the legislation because it takes into consideration the protection of life and the prevention of injuries.

In this country we have at least 12 million Spanish-speaking people as recorded by the Census Bureau, and for 70 percent of them Spanish is their primary language. We do have a problem in many of our States such as in New York State where we have some 12 million people of Spanish descent which represents 13 percent of our population, and I am certain that there are other States who have the very same problem where the failures of the public school systems have failed many of the people, who have come to this country to improve their political and economic lives, through their inability to deal with the English language.

Mr. STAGGERS. Mr. Chairman, will the gentleman yield?

Mr. RANGEL. I yield to the gentleman.

Mr. STAGGERS. Mr. Chairman, just for clarification, since I do not have a copy of the gentleman's amendments in front of me, would this be mandatory that these be printed both in English and in Spanish?

Mr. RANGEL. No, it is not mandatory.

Mr. STAGGERS. Would the gentleman yield further?

Mr. RANGEL. I yield further to the chairman of the committee.

Mr. STAGGERS. I would say to the gentleman from New York that this is inherent in the law now, and with the commission, that this is permitted, and that they are permitted to have this done wherever it is needed. So I do not think that the amendments are necessary, and I can assure the gentleman from New York that this is the intent of the law.

Mr. RANGEL. Mr. Chairman, in view of the statement by the Chairman, the gentleman from West Virginia (Mr. STAGGERS) and since it is a matter of record, I ask unanimous consent that I may be permitted to withdraw my amendments.

The CHAIRMAN. Is there objection to the request of the gentleman from New York?

There was no objection

Mr. MATSUNAGA. Mr. Chairman, I move to strike the last word.

(By unanimous consent, Mr. MATSUNAGA was allowed to speak out of order.)

GROSSLY EXAGGERATED REPORTS

Mr. MATSUNAGA. Mr. Chairman, late yesterday I returned from Hawaii and rushed from the airport to the floor of the House to cast my vote in favor of the HEW appropriation measure. I then went to my office, handled a few rush matters, and left for my home in Kensington. While I was viewing "Hawaii Five-O" on television with my family, for the special purpose of watching the TV debut of Ed Flood, the son of my good friend Jim Flood, my daughter received a telephone call from a news reporter who was trying to confirm reports that Congressman SPARK MATSUNAGA had suffered a heart attack and had been rushed to the hospital.

To paraphrase Mark Twain, who, upon seeing his name in the obituary column, called the editor and remarked that that news of his demise was slightly exaggerated, let me say loud and clear, here and now, that news reports broadcast over the radio of my having been rushed to the hospital on account of a heart attack have been grossly exaggerated.

Since early this morning I have been receiving telephone calls from concerned friends and colleagues of the Congress, inquiring about my condition and conveying their condolences. I would admit to a slight acceleration of cardiopalpitation on viewing a lovely Hawaiian hula maiden doing a Tahitian dance, but no more—my heart is sound. I have never had a heart attack and certainly am not anticipating any. But to my dear friends who made personal inquiries about my health let me say, "Mahalo nui hoa," which in Hawaiian means thank you very much.

Mr. GROSS. Mr. Chairman, I move to

strike out the necessary number of words.

I should like to ask the chairman or someone knowledgeable about this bill, with respect to section 18. Does this mean products which would otherwise be disqualified under this Consumer Product Safety Act could be exported to foreign countries?

Mr. STAGGERS. If I understand the gentleman's question—that products are excluded?

Mr. GROSS. Products that might not meet the standards established in this bill for domestic use could be exported?

Mr. STAGGERS. No standards have been set on products that are exported.

Mr. GROSS. Why did you put this section in the bill. You are simply calling attention to the fact that you are perfectly willing to permit manufacturers in this country to make unsafe products and to ship them abroad—if I read this right.

Mr. STAGGERS. We are not trying to make the law for any country.

In certain instances certain products might be wrong here, but they might be all right in other countries—we do not know.

But we do know that they have their own laws and they import products and we cannot make the laws for other countries.

Our laws exclude these, of course, and anything else that comes from many of these countries. They import their products from other foreign countries and they do not require any more than may be done in our country. Millions of dollars of merchandise is exported that we would not be able to export from this country because they make their own laws because some would not even be applicable in other countries.

Mr. GROSS. The gentleman is saying, is he not, that we might ship an electrical tool that was dangerous to handle to a foreign country, one that would not meet the standards for sale in this country for sale to consumers? Then what may we expect in return from those who ship products to this country—are they supposed to be safe or unsafe?

Mr. STAGGERS. We require that they be safe in every way. They have to conform to our standards and anything we import from them has to come up to the standards set up by the Commission.

Mr. GROSS. We have a double standard; is that right?

Mr. STAGGERS. No, sir, not for America anyway.

Mr. GROSS. That is the only way I can read section 18 of this bill—that the bill provides two standards.

Mr. MOSS. Mr. Chairman, will the gentleman yield?

Mr. GROSS. I yield to the gentleman.

Mr. MOSS. Yes, it clearly is a double standard because other nations want to have standards lower than ours and open up their markets to products which are nonsafe, as we require for use in our country, and if we deny our manufacturers a right to participate in that market all we are doing is denying them job opportunities because other countries will manufacture and ship into those nations products which conform to their standards. This is not new. We do it under the automobile safety standards and we do it in many cases.

Mr. GROSS. Then I do not know why it has to be written into this bill.

Mr. MOSS. If it is not written into the bill, then they would be prohibited from manufacturing in the United States nonconforming products. This authorizes the manufacturers of nonconforming products for export only.

Mr. GROSS. That is the export of nonconforming products?

Mr. MOSS. As you will, but if we do otherwise we would be working a severe penalty against American manufacturers in worldwide competition.

Mr. ROUSSELOT. Mr. Chairman, will the gentleman yield?

Mr. GROSS. I yield to the gentleman.

Mr. ROUSSELOT. Let me ask the gentleman from California another question. In other words in this section of the bill—section 18—we are perfectly willing to export and sell products to foreign consumers what we are not willing to sell to our own consumers; is that correct?

Mr. MOSS. Would the gentleman from Iowa yield for a reply?

Mr. GROSS. I yield to the gentleman.

Mr. MOSS. I would say, of course, that is not the case. We are willing to export at standards set by the Government receiving the products manufactured in the United States.

Mr. ROUSSELOT. Suppose these are consumer items?

Mr. MOSS. They will be consumer items.

Mr. ROUSSELOT. Then I believe my statement is correct. We are willing to sell so-called defective products to foreign consumers but not willing to sell the same products to our own U.S. consumers.

Mr. MOSS. Would the gentleman propose to amend the bill to require that no product nonconforming to domestic standards be exported and thereby denying a very significant part of the world market to American manufacturers?

Mr. ROUSSELOT. I do not want to deny any proper markets to our manufacturers.

Mr. MOSS. That is exactly what you would do.

Mr. ROUSSELOT. What I am saying is—if we are willing to impose conditions on products to our U.S. consumers, those same conditions ought to be good enough for foreign consumers.

The CHAIRMAN. The time of the gentleman has expired.

(Mr. GROSS asked and was given permission to proceed for 1 additional minute.)

Mr. GROSS. Mr. Chairman, since the gentleman from Texas is on his feet, I would like to ask him where it is proposed to get the $308 million to fund this brandnew super-duper commission and advisory council and all the bureaucrats that are going to go with it? Is there any provision in this bill for raising the taxes to provide the money?

Mr. ECKHARDT. Mr. Chairman, I had not risen for that purpose, but rather to answer the gentleman's first question.

Mr. Chairman, I move to strike the requisite number of words.

Mr. Chairman, the points that the distinguished gentleman from Iowa raises do appear to be serious questitons, but on a little further consideration one can see how impossible it would be for us to impose on our manufacturers standards for foreign export when we have no control over either the economic processes in those countries nor their controls of production of products in their own countries.

Let us suppose, for instance, you have a drill, and our standards require that you have to have a grounding wire and a plug that goes into a three-plug circuit. Let us suppose that in another country they do not use those at all. There is no way you can plug the drill in, but they are manufacturing drills with only two circuit wires and selling them in that country, and they are also receiving the same kind of articles from the Soviet Union. Why conceivably should we not be in a position to compete with other exporters into that country? Quite clearly persons in that country not using plugs for grounding circuit would have no use whatsoever for the third grounding wire and would probably cut it out. Why should not another nation establish its own standards of safety? But if it does not, should we impose our standards upon them and in so doing discriminate against our manufacturers who are in competition with manufacturers in other nations exporting to that same country?

* * *

(H.R. 15003, as amended, was inserted in lieu of the Senate provisions following the enacting clause of S. 3419, and was approved by a vote of 318-50.)

APPENDIX I

TEXT OF BILL AS PASSED BY HOUSE

(September 20, 1972)

SHORT TITLE; TABLE OF CONTENTS

SECTION 1. This Act may be cited as the "Consumer Product Safety Act".

TABLE OF CONTENTS

FINDINGS AND PURPOSES

SEC. 2. (a) The Congress finds that—

(1) an unacceptable number of consumer products which contain unreasonable hazards are distributed in commerce;

(2) complexities of consumer products and the diverse nature and abilities of consumers using them frequently result in an inability of users to anticipate hazards and to safeguard themselves adequately;

(3) the public should be protected against unreasonable hazards associated with consumer products;

(4) control by State and local governments of unreasonable hazards associated with consumer products in inadequate and may be burdensome to manufacturers; and

(5) regulation of consumer products the distribution or use of which affects interstate or foreign commerce is necessary to carry out this Act.

(b) The purposes of this Act are—

(1) to protect the public against unreasonable hazards associated with consumer products;

(2) to assist consumers in evaluating the comparative safety of consumer products;

(3) to develop uniform safety standards for consumer products and to minimize conflicting State and local regulations; and

(4) to promote research and investigation into the causes and prevention of product-related deaths, illnesses, and injuries.

DEFINITIONS

SEC. 3. (a) For purposes of this Act.

(1) The term "consumer product" means any article, or component part thereof, produced or distributed (i) for sale to a consumer for use in or around a household or residence, a school, in recreation, or otherwise, or (ii) for the personal use, consumption or enjoyment of a consumer in or around a household or residence, a school, in recreation, or otherwise; but such term does not include (A) any article which is not customarily produced or distributed for sale to or use, consumption, or enjoyment of a consumer; (B) tobacco and tobacco products, (C) motor vehicles or motor vehicle equipment (as defined by sections 102 (3) and (4) of the National Traffic and Motor Safety Act of 1966), (D) economic poisons (as defined by the Federal Insecticide, Fungicide, and Rodenticide Act), (E) any article which, if sold by the manufacturer, producer, or importer, would be subject to the tax imposed by section 4181 of the Internal Revenue Code of 1954 (determined without regard to any exemptions from such tax provided by section 4182 or 4221, or any other provision of such Code), or any component of any such article, (F) drugs, devices, or cosmetics (as such terms are defined in sections 201 (g), (h), and (i) of the Federal Food, Drug, and Cosmetic Act), or (G) food. The term "food", as used in this paragraph, means all "food", as defined in section 201(f) of the Federal Food, Drug, and Cosmetic Act, including poultry and poultry

products (as defined in sections 4(e) and (f) of the Poultry Products Inspection Act), meat, meat food products (as defined in section 1(j) of the Federal Meat Inspection Act), and eggs and egg products (as defined in section 4 of the Egg Products Inspection Act).

(2) The term "consumer product safety rule" means a consumer product safety standard described in section 7(a), or a rule under this Act declaring a consumer product a banned hazardous product.

(3) The term "hazard" means a risk of death, personal injury, or serious or frequent illness.

(4) The term "manufacturer" means any person who manufactures or imports a consumer product.

(5) The term "distributor" means a person to whom a consumer product is delivered or sold for purposes of distribution in commerce, except that such term does not include a manufacturer or retailer of such product.

(6) The term "retailer" means a person to whom a consumer product is delivered or sold for purposes of sale or distribution by such person to a consumer.

(7)(A) The term "private labeler" means an owner of a brand or trademark on the label of a consumer product which bears a private label.

(B) A consumer product bears a private label if (i) the product (or its container) is labeled with the brand or trademark of a person other than a manufacturer of the product, (ii) the person with whose brand or trademark the product (or container) is labeled has authorized or caused the product to be so labeled, and (iii) the brand or trademark of a manufacturer of such product does not appear on such label.

(8) The term "manufacture" means to manufacture, produce, or assemble.

(9) The term "Commission" means the Consumer Product Safety Commission, established by section 4.

(10) the term "State" means a State, the District of Columbia, the Commonwealth of Puerto Rico, the Virgin Islands, Guam, the Canal Zone, American Samoa, or the Trust Territory of the Pacific Islands.

(11) The terms "to distribute in commerce" and "distribution in commerce" mean to sell in commerce, to introduce or deliver for introduction into commerce, or to hold for sale or distribution after introduction into commerce.

(12) The term "commerce" means trade, traffic, commerce, or transportation—

(A) between a place in a State and any place outside thereof, or

(B) which affects trade, traffic, commerce, or transportation described in subparagraph (A).

(13) The terms "import" and "importation" include reimporting a consumer product manufactured or processed, in whole or in part, in the United States.

(14) The term "United States", when used in the geographic sense, means all of the States (as defined in paragraph (10)).

(b) A common carrier, contract carrier, or freight forwarder shall not, for purposes of this Act, be deemed to be a manufacturer, distributor, or retailer of a consumer product solely by reason of receiving or transporting a consumer product in the ordinary course of its business as such a carrier or forwarder.

CONSUMER PRODUCT SAFETY COMMISSION

SEC. 4. (a) An independent regulatory commission is hereby established, to be known as the Consumer Product Safety Commission, consisting of five Commissioners who shall be appointed by the President, by and with the advice and consent of the Senate, one of whom shall be designated by the President as Chairman. The Chairman, when so designated, shall act as Chairman until the expiration of his term of office as Commissioner. Any member of the Commission may be removed by the President for neglect of duty or malfeasance in office but for no other cause.

(b)(1) Except as provided in paragraph (2), (A) the Commissioners first appointed under this section shall be appointed for terms ending three, four, five, six, and seven years, respectively, after the date of the enactment of this Act, the term of each to be designated by the President at the time of nomination; and (B) each of their successors shall be appointed for a term of seven years from the date of the expiration of the term for which his predecessor was appointed.

(2) Any Commissioner appointed to fill a vacancy occurring prior to the expiration of the term for which his predecessor was appointed shall be appointed only for the remainder of such term. A Commissioner may continue to serve after the expiration of his term until his successor has taken office, except that he may not so continue to serve more than one year after the date on which his term would otherwise expire under this subsection.

(c) Not more than three of the Commissioners shall be appointed from the same political party. No individual in the employ of, or holding any official relation to, any person, engaged in selling or manufacturing consumer products or owning stock or bonds of substantial value in a person so engaged or who is in any other manner pecuniarily interested in such a person, or in a substantial supplier of such a person, shall hold the office of Commissioner. A Commissioner may not engage in any other business, vocation, or employment.

(d) No vacancy in the Commission shall impair the right of the remaining Commissioners to exercise all the powers of the Commission, but three members of the Commission shall constitute a quorum for the transaction of business. The Commission shall have an official seal of which judicial notice shall be taken. The Commission shall annually elect a Vice Chairman to act in the absence or disability of the Chairman or in case of a vacancy in the office of the Chairman.

(e) The Commission shall maintain a principal office and such field offices as it deems necessary and may meet and exercise any of its powers at any other place.

(f)(1) The Chairman of the Commission shall be the principal executive officer of the Commission, and he shall exercise all of the executive and administrative functions of the Commission, including functions of the Commission with respect to (A) the appointment and supervision of personnel employed under the Commission (other than personnel employed regularly and full time in the immediate offices of commissioners other than the Chairman), (B) the distribution of business among personnel appointed and supervised by the Chairman and among administrative units of the Commission, and (C) the use and expenditure of funds.

(2) In carrying out any of his functions under the provisions of this subsection the Chairman shall be governed by general policies of the Commission and by such regulatory decisions, findings, and determinations as the Commission may by law be authorized to make.

(g)(1) The Chairman, subject to the approval of the Commission, shall appoint an Executive Director, a General Counsel, a Director of Engineering Sciences, a Director of Epidemiology, and a Director of Information. No individual so appointed may receive pay in excess of the annual rate of basic pay in effect for grade GS-18 of the General Schedule.

(2) The Chairman, subject to subsection (f)(2), may employ such other officers and employees (including attorneys) as are necessary in the execution of the Commission's functions. No full-time officer or employee of the Commission who was at any time during the 12 months preceding the termination of his employment with the Commission compensated at a rate in excess of the annual rate of basic pay in effect for grade GS-14 of the General Schedule, shall accept employment or compensation from any manufacturer subject to this Act, for a period of 12 months after terminating employment with the Commission.

(h)(1) Section 5314 of title 5, United States Code, is amended by adding at the end thereof the following new paragraph:

"(59) Chairman, Consumer Product Safety Commission."

(2) Section 5315 of such title is amended by adding at the end thereof the following new paragraph:

"(96) Members, Consumer Product Safety Commission (4)."

PRODUCT SAFETY INFORMATION AND RESEARCH

SEC. 5. (a) The Commission shall—

(1) maintain an Injury Information Clearinghouse to collect, investigate, analyze, and disseminate information relating to the causes and prevention of death, injury, and illness associated with consumer products; and

(2) conduct such continuing studies and investigations of deaths, injuries, diseases, other health impairments, and economic losses resulting from accidents involving consumer products as it deems necessary.

(b) The Commission may—

(1) conduct research, studies, and investigations on the safety of consumer products and on improving the safety of such products;

(2) test consumer products and develop product safety test methods and testing devices; and

(3) offer training in product safety investigation and test methods, and assist public and private organizations, administratively and technically, in the development of safety standards and test methods.

(c) In carrying out its functions under this section, the Commission may make grants or enter into contracts for the conduct of such functions with any person (including a governmental entity).

(d) Whenever the Federal contribution for any information, research, or development activity authorized by this Act is more than minimal, the Commission shall include in any contract, grant, or other arrangement for such activity, provisions effective to insure that the rights to all information, uses, processes, patents, and other developments resulting from that activity will be made available to the public without charge on a nonexclusive basis. Nothing in this subsection shall be construed to deprive any person of any right which he may have had, prior to entering into any arrangement referred to in this subsection, to any patent, patent application, or invention.

PUBLIC DISCLOSURE OF INFORMATION

SEC. 6. (a)(1) Nothing contained in this Act shall be deemed to require the release of any information described by subsection (b) of section 552, title 5, United States Code, or which is otherwise protected by law from disclosure to the public.

(2) All information reported to or otherwise obtained by the Commission or its representative under this Act which information contains or relates to a trade secret or other matter referred to in section 1905 of title 18 of the United States Code, shall be considered confidential and shall not be disclosed, except that such information may be disclosed to other officers or employees concerned with carrying out this Act or when relevant in any proceeding under this Act. Nothing in this Act shall authorize the withholding of information by the Commission or any officer or employee under its control from the duly authorized committees of the Congress.

(b)(1) Except as provided by paragraph (2) of this subsection, not less than 30 days prior to its public disclosure of any information obtained under this Act, or to be disclosed to the public in connection therewith (unless the Commission finds that the public health and safety requires a lesser period of notice), the Commission shall provide such information, to the extent practicable, to each manufacturer or private labeler of any consumer product to which such information pertains, if the manner in which such consumer product is to be designated or described in such information will permit the public to ascertain readily the identity of such manufacturer or private labeler, and shall provide such manufacturer or private labeler with a reasonable opportunity to submit comments to the Commission in regard to such information. The Commission shall take reasonable steps to assure, prior to its public disclosure thereof, that information from which the identity of such manufacturer or private labeler may be readily ascertained is accurate, and that such disclosure is fair in the circumstances and reasonably related to effectuating the purposes of this Act. If the Commission finds that, in the administration of this Act, it has made public disclosure of inaccurate or misleading information which reflects adversely upon the safety of any consumer product, or the practices of any manufacturer, private labeler, distributor, or retailer of consumer products, it shall, in a manner similar to that in which such disclosure was made, publish a retraction of such inaccurate or misleading information.

(2) Paragraph (1) (except for the last sentence thereof) shall not apply to the public disclosure of (A) information about any consumer product with respect to which product the Commission has filed an action under section 12 (relating to imminently hazardous products), or which the Commission has reasonable cause to believe is in violation of section 19 (relating to prohibited acts), or (B) information in the course of or concerning any administrative or judicial proceeding under this Act.

(c) The Commission shall communicate to each manufacturer of a consumer product, insofar as may be practicable, information as to any significant hazard associated with such product.

CONSUMER PRODUCT SAFETY STANDARDS

SEC. 7. (a) The Commission may by rule, in accordance with this section and section 9, promulgate consumer product safety standards. A consumer product safety standard shall consist of one or more of any of the following types of requirements:

(1) Requirements as to performance, composition, contents, design, construction, finish, or packaging of a consumer product.

(2) Requirements that a consumer product be marked with or accompanied by clear and adequate warnings or instructions, or requirements respecting the form of warnings or instructions.

Any requirement of such a standard shall be reasonably necessary to prevent or reduce an unreasonable hazard to the public associated with such product. The requirements of such a standard (other than requirements relating to labeling, warnings, or instruction) shall, whenever feasible, be expressed in terms of performance requirements.

(b) A proceeding for the development of a consumer product safety standard under this Act shall be commenced by the publication in the Federal Register of a notice which shall—

(1) identify the product and the nature of the hazard associated with the product;

(2) state the Commission's determination that a consumer product safety standard is necessary to prevent or reduce the hazard;

(3) include information with respect to any existing standard known to the Commission which may be relevant to the proceeding; and

(4) include an invitation for any person, inclduing any State or Federal agency (other than the Commission), within 30 days after the date of publication of the notice (A) to submit to the Commission an existing standard as the proposed consumer product safety standard or (B) to offer to develop the proposed consumer product safety standard.

An invitation under paragraph (4)(B) shall specify a period of time, during which the standard is to be developed, which shall be a period ending 150 days after the publication of the notice, unless the Commission for good cause finds (and includes such finding in the notice) that a different period is appropriate.

(c) If the Commission determines that (1) there exists a standard which has been issued or adopted by any Federal agency or by any other qualified agency, organization, or institution, and (2) such standard if promulgated under this Act would prevent or reduce the unreasonable hazard associated with the product, then it may, in lieu of accepting an offer pursuant to subsection (d) of this section, publish such standard as a proposed consumer product safety rule.

(d)(1) Except as provided by subsection (c), the Commission shall accept one, and may accept more than one, offer to develop a proposed consumer product safety standard pursuant to the invitation prescribed by subsection (b)(4)(B), if it determines that the offeror is technically competent, is likely to develop an appropriate standard within the period specified in the invitation under subsection (b), and will comply with regulations of the Commission under paragraph (3). The Commission shall publish in the Federal Register the name and address of each person whose offer it accepts, and a summary of the terms of such offer as accepted.

(2) If an offer is accepted under this subsection, the Commission may agree to contribute to the offeror's cost in developing a proposed consumer product safety standard, in any case in which the Commission determines that such contribution is likely to result in a more satisfactory standard than would be developed without such contribution, and that the offeror is financially responsible. Regulations of the Commission shall set forth the items of cost in which it may participate, and shall exclude any contribution to the acquisition of land or buildings.

(3) The Commission shall prescribe regulations governing the development of proposed consumer product safety standards by persons whose offers are accepted under paragraph (1). Such regulations shall include requirements—

(A) that standards recommended for promulgation be suitable for promulgation under this Act, be supported by test data or such other documents or materials as the Commission may reasonably require to be developed, and (where appropriate) contain suitable test methods for measurement of compliance with such standards;

(B) for notice and opportunity by interested persons (including representatives of consumers and consumer organizations) to participate in the development of such standards;

(C) for the maintenance of records, which shall be available to the public, to disclose the course of the development of standards recommended for promulgation, the comments and other information submitted by any person in connection with such development (including dissenting views and comments and information with respect to the need for such recommended standards) and such other matters as may be relevant to the evaluation of such recommended standards; and

(D) that the Commission and the Comptroller General of the United States, or any of their duly authorized representatives, have access for the purpose of audit and examination to any books, documents, papers, and records relevant to the development of such recommended standards or to the expenditure of any contribution of the Commission for the development of such standards.

(e)(1) If the Commission has published a notice of proceeding as provided by subsection (b) and has not, within 30 days after the date of publication of such notice, accepted an offer to develop a proposed consumer product safety standard, the Commission may develop a proposed consumer product safety rule and publish such proposed rule.

(2) If the Commission accepts an offer to develop a proposed consumer product safety standard, the Commission may not, during the development period (specified in paragraph (3)) for such standard—

(A) publish a proposed rule applicable to the same hazard associated with such product, or

(B) develop proposals for such standard or contract with third parties for such development, unless the Commission determines that no offeror whose offer was accepted is making satisfactory progress in the development of such standard.

(3) For purposes of paragraph (2), the development period for any standard is a period (A) beginning on the date on which the Commission first accepts an offer under subsection (d)(1) for the development of a proposed standard, and (B) ending on the earlier of—

(i) the end of the period specified in the notice of proceeding (except that the period specified in the notice may be extended if good cause is shown and the reasons for such extension are published in the Federal Register), or

(ii) the date on which it determines (in accordance with such procedures as it may by rule prescribe) that no offeror whose offer was accepted is able and willing to continue satisfactorily the development of the proposed standard which was the subject of the offer, or

(iii) the date on which an offeror whose offer was accepted submits such a recommended standard to the Commission.

(f) Not more than 210 days after its publication of a notice of proceeding pursuant to subsection (b) (which time may be extended by the Commission by a notice published in the Federal Register stating good cause therefor), the Commission shall publish in the Federal Register a notice withdrawing such notice of proceeding or publish a proposed rule which either proposes a product safety standard applicable to any consumer product subject to such notice, or proposes to declare any such subject product a banned hazardous consumer product.

BANNED HAZARDOUS PRODUCTS

SEC. 8. Whenever the Commission finds that—

(1) a consumer product is being, or will be, distributed in commerce and such consumer product presents an unreasonable hazard to the public; and

(2) no feasible consumer product safety standard under this Act would adequately protect the public from the unreasonable hazard associated with such product,

the Commission may propose and, in accordance with section 9, promulgate a rule declaring such product a banned hazardous product.

ADMINISTRATIVE PROCEDURE APPLICABLE TO PROMULGATION OF CONSUMER PRODUCT SAFETY RULES

SEC. 9. (a)(1) Within sixty days after the publication under section 7(c), (e)(1), or (f) or section 8 of a proposed consumer product safety rule respecting a hazard associated with a consumer product, the Commission shall—

(A) promulgate a consumer product safety rule respecting the hazard associated with such product if it makes the findings required under subsection (c), or

(B) withdraw by rule the applicable notice of proceeding if it determines that such rule is not (i) reasonably necessary to prevent or reduce an unreasonable hazard to the public associated with the product, or (ii) in the public interest;

except that the Commission may extend such sixty-day period for good cause shown (if it publishes its reasons therefor in the Federal Register).

(2) Consumer product safety rules which have been proposed under section 7(c), (e)(1), or (f) or section 8 shall be promulgated pursuant to section 553 of title 5, United States Code, except that the Commission shall give interested persons an opportunity for the oral presentation of data, views, or arguments, in addition to an opportunity to make written submissions. A transcript shall be kept of any oral presentation.

(b) A consumer product safety rule shall express in the rule itself the hazard which the standard is designed to prevent or reduce. In promulgating such a rule the Commission shall consider relevant available product data including the results of research, development, testing, and investigation activities conducted generally and pursuant to this Act.

(c)(1) Prior to promulgating a consumer product safety rule, the Commission shall consider, and shall make appropriate findings for inclusion in such rule with respect to—

(A) the degree and nature of the hazard the rule is designed to prevent or reduce, and

(B) the approximate number of consumer products, or types or classes thereof, subject to such rule; and

(C) the need of the public for the consumer products subject to such rule, and the probable effect of such rule upon the utility, cost, tor availability of such products to meet such need.

(2) The Commission shall not promulgate a consumer product safety rule unless it finds (and includes such finding in the rule)—

(A) that the rule (including its effective date) is reasonably necessary to prevent or reduce an unreasonable hazard to the public associated with such product;

(B) that the promulgation of the rule is in the public interest; and

(C) in the case of a rule declaring the product a banned hazardous product, that no feasible consumer product safety standard under this Act would adequately protect the public from the unreasonable hazard associated with such product.

(d) Each consumer product safety rule shall specify the date such rule is to take effect not exceeding 180 days from the date promulgated, unless the Commission finds, for good cause shown, that a later effective date is in the public interest and publishes its reasons for such finding. The effective date of a consumer product safety standard under this Act shall be set at a date at least 30 days after the date of promulgation unless the Commission for good cause shown determines that an earlier effective date is in the public interest. In no case may the effective date be set at a date which is earlier than the date of promulgation. A consumer product safety standard shall be applicable only to consumer products manufactured after the effective date.

(e) The Commission may by rule amend or revoke any consumer product safety rule. Such amendment or revocation shall specify the date on which it is to take effect which shall not exceed 180 days from the date the amendment or revocation is published unless the Commission finds for good cause shown that a later effective date is in the public interest and publishes its reasons for such finding. Where an amendment involves a material change in a consumer product safety rule, sections 7 and 8, and subsections (a) through (d) of this section shall apply. In order to revoke a consumer product safety rule, the Commission shall publish a proposal to revoke such rule in the Federal Register, and allow oral and written presentations in accordance with subsection (a)(2) of this section. It may revoke such rule only if it determines that the rule is not reasonably necessary to prevent or reduce an unreasonable hazard to the public associated with the product. Section 11 shall apply to any amendment of a consumer product safety rule which involves a material change and to any revocation of a consumer product safety rule, in the same manner and to the same extent as such section applies to the Commission's action in promulgating such a rule.

PETITION BY INTERESTED PARTY FOR CONSUMER PRODUCT SAFETY RULE

SEC. 10. (a) Any interested person, including a consumer or consumer organization, may petition the Commission to commence a proceeding for the issuance, amendment, or revocation of a consumer product safety rule.

(b) Such petition shall be filed in the principal office of the Commission and shall set forth—

(1) facts which it is claimed establish that a consumer product safety rule or an amendment or revocation thereof is necessary; and

(2) a brief description of the substance of the consumer product safety rule or amendment thereof which it is claimed should be issued by the Commission.

(c) The Commission may hold a public hearing or may conduct such investigation or proceeding as it deems appropriate in order to determine whether or not such petition should be granted.

(d) If the Commission grants such petition, it shall promptly commence an appropriate proceeding to prescribe a consumer product safety rule, or take such other action as it deems appropriate. If the Commission denies such petition it shall publish in the Federal Register its reasons for such denial, if such petition and reasons for such denial materially differ from any previous petitions and subsequent denial.

JUDICIAL REVIEW OF CONSUMER PRODUCT SAFETY RULES

SEC. 11. (a) Not later than 60 days after a consumer product safety rule is promulgated by the Commission, any person adversely affected by such rule, or any consumer or consumer organization, may file a petition with the United States court of appeals for the District of Columbia or for the circuit in which such person, consumer, or organization resides or has his principal place of business for judicial review of such rule. Copies of the petition shall be forthwith transmitted by the clerk of the court to the Commission or other officer designated by him for that purpose and to the Attorney General. The Commission shall transmit to the Attorney General, who shall file in the court, the record of the proceedings on which the Commission based its rule, as provided in section 2112 of title 28 of the United States Code. For purposes of this section, the term "record" means such consumer product safety rule; any notice or proposal published pursuant to section 7, 8, or 9; the transcript required by section 9(a)(2) of any oral presentation; any written submission of interested parties; and any other information, which the Commission considers relevant to such rule.

(b) If the petitioner applies to the court for leave to adduce additional data, views, or arguments and shows to the satisfaction of the court that such additional data, views, or arguments are material and that there were reasonable grounds for the petitioner's failure to adduce such data, views, or arguments in the proceeding before the Commission, the court may order the Commission to provide additional opportunity for the oral presentation. of data, views, or arguments and for written submissions. The Commission may modify its findings, or make new findings by reason of the additional data, views, or arguments so taken and shall file such modified or new findings, and its recommendation, if any, for the modification or setting aside of its original rule, with the return of such additional data, views, or arguments.

(c) Upon the filing of the petition under subsection (a) of this section the court shall have jurisdiction to review the consumer product safety rule in accordance with chapter 7 of title 5 of the United States Code and to grant appropriate relief, including interim relief, as provided in such chapter. The consumer product safety rule shall not be affirmed unless the Commission's findings under section 9(c) are supported by substantial evidence on the record taken as a whole.

(d) The judgment of the court affirming or setting aside, in whole or in part, any consumer product safety rule shall be final, subject to review by the Supreme Court of the United States upon certiorari or certification, as provided in section 1254 of title 28 of the United States Code.

(e) The remedies provided for in this section shall be in addition to and not in lieu of any other remedies provided by law.

IMMINENT HAZARDS

SEC. 12. (a) The Commission may file in a United States district court an action (1) against an imminently hazardous consumer product for seizure of such product under subsection (b)(2), or (2) against any person who is a manufacturer, distributor, or retailer of such product, or (3) against both. Such an action may be filed notwithstanding the existence of a consumer product safety rule applicable to such product, or the pendency of any administrative or judicial proceedings under any other provision of this Act. As used in this section, and hereinafter in this Act, the term "imminently hazardous consumer product" means a consumer product which presents imminent and unreasonable risk of death, serious illness, or severe personal injury.

(b)(1) The district court in which such action is filed shall have jurisdiction to declare such product an imminently hazardous consumer product, and (in the case of an action under subsection (a)(2)) to grant (as ancillary to such declaration or in lieu thereof) such temporary or permanent relief as may be necessary to protect the public from such risk. Such relief may include a mandatory order requiring the notification of such risk to purchasers of such product known to the defendant, public notice, the recall, the repair or the replacement of, or refund for, such product.

(2) In the case of an action under subsection (a)(1), the consumer product may be proceeded against by process of libel for the seizure and condemnation of such product in any United States district court within the jurisdiction of which such consumer product is found. Proceedings and cases instituted under the authority of the preceding sentence shall conform as nearly as possible to proceedings in rem in admiralty.

(c) Where appropriate, concurrently with the filing of such action or as soon thereafter as may be practicable, the Commission shall initiate a proceeding to promulgate a consumer product safety rule applicable to the consumer product with respect to which such action is filed.

(d)(1) Prior to commencing an action under subsection (a), the Commission may consult the Product Safety Advisory Council (established under section 28) with respect to its determination to commence such action, and request the Council's recommendations as to the type of temporary or permanent relief which may be necessary to protect the public.

(2) The Council shall submit its recommendations to the Commission within one week of such request.

(3) Subject to paragraph (2), the Council may conduct such hearing or offer such opportunity for the presentation of views as it may consider necesary or appropriate.

(e)(1) An action under subsection (a)(2) of this section may be brought in the United States district court for the District of Columbia or in any judicial district in which any of the defendants is found, is an inhabitant or transacts business; and process in such an action may be served on a defendant in any other district in which such defendant resides or may be found. Subpenas requiring attendance of witnesses in such an action may run into any other district. In determining the judicial district in which an action may be brought under this section in instances in which such action may be brought in more than one judicial district, the Commission shall take into account the convenience of the parties.

(2) Whenever proceedings under this section inovlving identical consumer products are pending in courts in two or more judicial districts, they shall be consolidated for trial by order of any such court upon application reasonably made by any party in interest, upon notice to all other parties in interest.

(f) Notwithstanding any other provision of law, in any action under this section, the Commission may direct attorneys employed by it to appear and represent it.

NEW PRODUCTS

SEC. 13. (a) The Commission may, by rule, prescribe procedures for the purpose of insuring that the manufacturer of any new consumer product furnish notice and a description of such product to the Commission before its distribution in commerce.

(b) For purposes of this section, the term "new consumer product" means a consumer product which incorporates a design, material, or form of energy exchange which (1) has not previously been used substantially in consumer products and (2) as to which there exists a lack of information adequate to determine the safety of such product in use by consumers.

PRODUCT CERTIFICATION AND LABELING

SEC. 14. (a) (1) Every manufacturer of a product which is subject to a consumer product safety standard under this Act and which is distributed in commerce (and the private labeler of such product if it bears a private label) shall issue a certificate which shall certify that such product conforms to all applicable consumer product safety standards, and shall specify any standard which is applicable. Such certificate shall accompany the product or shall otherwise be furnished to any distributor or retailer to whom the product is delivered. Any certificate under this subsection shall be based on a test of each product or upon a reasonable testing program; shall state the name of the manufacturer or private labeler issuing the certifiacte; and shall include the date and place of manufacture.

(2) In the case of a consumer product for which there is more than one manufacturer or more than one private labeler, the Commission may be rule designate one or more of such manufacturers or one or more of such private labelers (as the case may be) as the persons who shall issue the certificate required by paragraph (1) of this subsection, and may exempt all other manufacturers of such product or all other private labelers of the product (as the case may be) from the requirement under paragraph (1) to issue a certificate with respect to such product.

(b) The Commission may by rule prescribe reasonable testing programs for consumer products which are subject to consumer product safety standards under this Act and for which a certificate is required under subsection (a). Any test or testing program on the basis of which a certificate is issued under subsection (a) may, at the option of the person required to certify the product, be conducted by an independent third party qualified to perform such tests or testing programs.

(c) The Commission may by rule require the use and prescribe the form and content of labels which contain the following information (or that portion of it specified in the rule)—

(1) The date and place of manufacture of any consumer product.

(2) A suitable identification of the manufacturer of the consumer product, unless the product bears a private label in which case it shall identify the private labeler and shall also contain a code mark which would permit the seller of such product to identify the manufacturer thereof to the purchaser upon his request.

(3) In the case of a consumer product subject to a consumer product safety rule, a certification that the product meets all applicable consumer product safety standards and a specification of the standards which are applicable.

Such labels, where practicable, may be required by the Commission to be permanently marked on or affixed to any such consumer product.

The Commission may, in appropriate cases, permit information required under paragraphs (1) and (2) of this subsection to be coded.

NOTIFICATION AND REPAIR, REPLACEMENT, OR REFUND

SEC. 15. (a) For purposes of this section, the term "substantial product hazard" means—

(1) a failure to comply with an applicable consumer product safety rule which creates a substantial hazard to the public, or

(2) a product defect which (because of the pattern of defect, the number of defective products distributed in commerce, the severity of the risk, or otherwise) creates a substantial hazard to the public.

(b) Every manufacturer of a consumer product distributed in commerce, and every distributor and retailer of such product, who obtains information which reasonably supports the conclusion that such product—

(1) fails to comply with an applicable consumer product safety rule; or

(2) contains a defect which could create a substantial product hazard described in subsection (a) (2), shall immediately inform the Commission of such failure to comply or of such defect, unless such manufacturer, distributor, or retailer has actual knowledge that the Commission has been adequately informed of such defect or failure to comply.

(c) If the Commission determines (after affording interested persons, including consumers and consumer organizations, an opportunity for hearing in accordance with subsection (f) of this that a product distributed in commerce presents a substantial product hazard and that notification is required in order to adequately protect the public from such substantial product hazard, the Commission may order the manufacturer or any distributor or retailer of the product to take any one or more of the following actions:

(1) to give public notice of the defect or failure to comply;

(2) to mail notice to each person who is a manufacturer, distributor, or retailer of such product; or

(3) to mail notice to every person to whom the person required to give notice knows such product was delivered or sold.

Any such order shall specify the form and content of any notice required to be given under such order.

(d) If the Commission determines (after affording interested parties, including consumers and consumer organizations, an opportunity for a hearing in accordance with subsection (f)) that a product distributed in commerce presents a substantial product hazard and that action under this subsection is in the public interest, it may order the manufacturer or any distributor or retailer of such product to take whichever of the following actions the person to whom the order is directed elects—

(1) to bring such product into conformity with the requirements of the applicable consumer product safety rule or to repair the defect in such product;

(2) to replace such product with a like or equivalent product which complies with the applicable consumer product safety rule or which does not contain the defect; or

(3) to refund the purchase price of such product (less a reasonable allowance for use, if such product has been in the possession of a consumer for one year or more (A) at the time of public notice under subsection (c), or (B) at the time the consumer receives actual notice of the defect or noncompliance, whichever first occurs).

An order under this subsection may also require the person to whom it applies to submit a plan, satisfactory to the Commission, for taking action under whichever of the preceding paragraphs of this subsection under which such person has elected to act. The Commission shall specify in the order the persons to whom refunds must be made if the person to whom the order is directed elects to take the action described in paragraph (3). If an order under this subsection is directed to more than one person, the Commission shall specify which person has the election under this subsection.

(e) (1) No charge shall be made to any person (other than a manufacturer, distributor, or retailer) who avails himself of any remedy provided under an order issued under subsection (d), and the person subject to the order shall reimburse each person (other than a manufacturer, distributor, or retailer) who is entitled to such a remedy for any reasonable and foreseeable expenses incurred by such person in availing himself of such remedy.

(2) An order issued under subsection (c) or (d) with respect to a product may require any person who is a manufacturer, distributor, or retailer of the product to reimburse any other person who is a manufacturer, distributor, or retailer of such product for such other person's expenses in connection with carrying out the order, if the Commission determines such reimbursement to be in the public interest.

(f) An order under subsection (c) or (d) may be issued only after an opportunity for a hearing in accordance with section 554 of title 5, United States Code, except that, if the Commission determines that any person who wishes to participate in such hearing is a part of a class of participants who share an identity of interest, the Commission may limit such person's participation in such hearing to participation through a single representative designated by such class (or by the Commission if such class fails to designate such a representative).

INSPECTION AND RECORDKEEPING

SEC. 16. (a) For purposes of implementing this Act, or rules or orders prescribed under this Act, officers or employees duly designated by the Commission, upon presenting appropriate credentials and a written notice from the Commission to the owner, operator, or agent in charge, are authorized—

(1) to enter, at reasonable times, (A) any factory, warehouse, or establishment in which consumer products are manufactured or held, in connection with destribution in commerce, or (B) any conveyance being used to transport consumer products in connection with distribution in commerce; and

(2) to inspect, at reasonable times and in a reasonable manner such conveyance or those areas of such factory, warehouse, or establishment where such products are manufactured, held, or transported and which may relate to the safety of such products. Each such inspection shall be commenced and completed with reasonable promptness.

(b) Every person who is a manufacturer, private labeler, or distributor of a consumer product shall establish and maintain such records, make such reports, and provide such information as the Commission may, by rule, reasonably require for the purposes of implementing this Act, or to determine compliance with rules or orders prescribed under this Act. Upon request of an officer or employee duly designated by the Commission, every such manufacturer, private labeler, or distributor shall permit the inspection of appropriate books, records, and papers relevant to determining whether such manufacturer, private labeler, or distributor has acted or is acting in compliance with this Act and rules under this Act.

IMPORTED PRODUCTS

SEC. 17. (a) Any consumer product offered for importation into the customs territory of the United States (as defined in general headnote 2 to the Tariff Schedules of the United States) shall be refused admission into such customs territory if such product—

(1) fails to comply with an applicable consumer product safety rule;

(2) is not accompanied by a certificate required by section 14, or is not labeled in accordance with regulations under section 14(c);

(3) is or has been determined to be an imminently hazardous consumer product in a proceeding brought under section 12;

(4) has a product defect which constitutes a substantial product hazard (within the meaning of section 15(a)(2)); or

(5) is a product which was manufactured by a person who the Commission has informed the Secretary of the Treasury is in violation of subsection (g).

(b) The Secretary of the Treasury shall obtain without charge and deliver to the Commission, upon the latter's request, a reasonable number of samples of consumer products being offered for import. Except for those owners or consignees who are or have been afforded an opportunity for a hearing in a proceeding under section 12 with respect to an imminently hazardous product, the owner or consignee of the product shall be afforded an opportunity by the Commission for a hearing in accordance with section 554 of title 5 of the United States Code with respect to the importation of such products into the customs territory of the United States. If it appears from examination of such samples or otherwise that a product must be refused admission under the terms of subsection (a), such product shall be refused admission, unless subsection (c) of this section applies and is complied with.

(c) If it appears to the Commission that any consumer product which may be refused admission pursuant to subsection (a) of this section can be so modified that it need not (under the terms of paragraphs (1) through (4) of subsection (a)) be refused admission, the Commission may defer final determination as to the admission of such product and, in accordance with such regulations as the Commission and the Secretary of the Treasury shall jointly agree to permit such product to be delivered from customs custody under bond for the purpose of permitting the owner or consignee an opportunity to so modify such product.

(d) All actions taken by an owner or consignee to modify such product under subsection (c) shall be subject to the supervision of an officer or employee of the Commission and of the Department of the Treasury. If it appears to the Commission that the product cannot be so modified or that the owner or consignee is not proceeding satisfactorily to modify such product it shall be refused admission into the customs territory of the United States, and the Commission may di-direct the Secretary to demand redelivery of the product into customs custody, and to seize the product in accordance with section 22(b) if it is not so redelivered.

(e) Products refused admission into the customs territory of the United States under this section must be exported, except that upon application, the Secretary of the Treasury may permit the destruction of the product in lieu of exportation. If the owner or consignee does not export the product within a reasonable time, the Department of the Treasury may destroy the product.

(f) All expenses (including travel, per diem or subsistence, and salaries of officers or employees of the United States) in connection with the destruction provided for in this section (the amount of such expenses to be determined in accordance with regulations of the Secretary of the Treasury) and all expenses in connection with the storage, cartage, or labor with respect to any consumer product refused admission under this section, shall be paid by the owner or consignee and, in default of such payment, shall constitute a lien against any future importations made by such owner or consignee.

(g) The Commission may, by rule, condition the importation of a consumer product on the manufacturer's compliance with the inspection and recordkeeping requirements of this Act and the Commission's rules with respect to such requirements.

EXPORTS

SEC. 18. This Act shall not apply to any consumer product if (1) it can be shown that such product is manufactured, sold, or held for sale for export from the United States (or that such product was imported for export), unless such consumer product is in fact distributed in commerce for use in the United States, and (2) such consumer product when distributed in commerce, or any container in which it is enclosed when so distributed, bears a stamp or label stating that such consumer product is intended for export; except that this Act shall apply to any consumer product manufactured for sale, offered for sale, or sold for shipment to any installation of the United States located outside of the United States.

PROHIBITED ACTS

SEC. 19. (a) It shall be unlawful for any person to—

(1) manufacture for sale, offer for sale, distribute in commerce, or import into the United States any consumer product which is not in conformity with an applicable consumer product safety standard under this Act;

(2) manufacture for sale, offer for sale, distribute in commerce, or import into the United States any consumer product which has been declared a banned hazardous product by a rule under this Act;

(3) fail or refuse to permit access to or copying of records, or fail or refuse to make reports or provide information, or fail or refuse to permit entry or inspection, as required under this Act or rule thereunder.

(4) fail to furnish information respecting a substantial product defect, as required by section 15(b);

(5) fail to comply with an order issued under section 15 (c) or (d) (relating to notification, and to repair, replacement, and refund);

(6) fail to furnish a certificate required by section 14 or issue a false certificate if such person in the exercise of due care has reason to know that such certificate is false or misleading in any material respect; or to fail to comply with any rule under section 14(c) (relating to labeling).

(b) Paragraphs (1) and (2) of section (a) shall not apply to any person (1) who holds a certificate issued in accordance with section 14(a) to the effect that such consumer product conforms to all applicable consumer product safety rules, unless such person knows that such consumer product does not conform, or (2) who relies in good faith on the representation of the manufacturer or a distributor of such product that the product is not subject to an applicable product safety rule.

CIVIL PENALTIES

SEC. 20. (a)(1) Any person who knowingly violates section 19 of this Act shall be subject to a civil penalty not to exceed $2,000 for each such violation. Subject to paragraph (2), a violation of section 19(a) (1), (2), (4), (5), or (6) shall constitute a separate violation with respect to each consumer product involved, except that the maximum civil penalty shall not exceed $500,000 for any related series of violations. A violation of section 19(a)(3) shall constitute a separate violation with respect to each failure or refusal to allow or perform an act required thereby; and, such violation is a continuing one, each day of such violation shall constitute a separate offense, except that the maximum civil penalty shall not exceed $500,000 for any related series of violations.

(2) The second sentence of paragraph (1) of this subsection shall not apply to violations of paragraph (1) or (2) of section 19(a)—

(A) if the person who violated such paragraphs is not the manufacturer or private labeler or a distributor of the product involved, and

(B) if such person did not have either

(i) actual knowledge that his distribution or sale of the product violated such paragraphs or (ii) notice from the Commission that such distribution or sale would be a violation of such paragraphs.

(b) Any civil penalty under this section may be compromised by the Commission. In determining the amount of such penalty or whether it should be remitted or mitigated and in what amount, the appropriateness of such penalty to the size of the business of the person charged and the gravity of the violation shall be considered. The amount of such penalty when finally determined, or the amount agreed on compromise, may be deducted from any sums owing by the United States to the person charged.

(c) As used in the first sentence of subsection (a)(1) of this section, the term "knowingly" means (1) the having of actual knowledge, or (2) the presumed having of knowledge deemed to be possessed by a reasonable man who acts in the circumstances, including knowledge obtainable upon the exercise of due care to ascertain the truth of representations.

CRIMINAL PENALTIES

SEC. 21. (a) Any person who knowingly and willfully violates section 19 of this Act after having received notice of noncompliance from the Commission shall be fined not more than $50,000 or be imprisoned not more than one year, or both.

(b) Whenever any corporation knowingly and willfully violates section 19 of this Act after having received notice of noncompliance from the Commission, any individual director, officer, or agent of such corporation who knowingly and willfully authorized, ordered, or performed any of the acts or practices constituting in whole or in part such violation and who had knowledge of such notice from the Commission shall be subject to penalties under this section in addition to the corporation.

INJUNCTION ENFORCEMENT AND SEIZURE

SEC. 22. (a) The United States district courts shall have jurisdiction to restrain any violation of section 19, or to restrain any person from distributing in commerce a product which does not comply with a consumer product safety rule, or both. Such actions may be brought by the Attorney General, on request of the Commission, in any United States district court for a district wherein any act, omission, or transaction constituting the violation occurred, or in such court for the district wherein the defendant is found or transacts business. In any action under this section process may be served on a defendant in any other district in which the defendant resides or may be found.

(b) Any consumer product which fails to conform to an applicable consumer product safety rule when introduced into or while in commerce or while held for sale after shipment in commerce shall be liable to be proceeded against on libel of information and condemned in any United States district court within the jurisdiction of which such consumer product is found. Proceedings in cases instituted under the authority of this subsection shall conform as nearly as possible to proceedings in rem in admiralty. Whenever such proceedings involving identical consumer products are pending in courts of two or more judicial districts they shall be consolidated for trial by order of any such court upon application reasonably made by any party in interest upon notice to all other parties in interest.

SUITS FOR DAMAGES BY PERSONS INJURED

SEC. 23. (a)(1) Any person ·ho shall sustain injury by reason of any knowing (including willful) violation of a consumer product safety standard, regulation, or order issued by the Commissioner may sue therefor in any district court of the United States in the district in which the defendant resides or is found or has an agent, subject to the provisions of section 1331 of title 28, United States Code as to the amount in controversy, and shall recover damages sustained, and the cost of suit, including a reasonable attorney's fee, if considered appropriate in the discretion of the court.

(c) The remedies provided for in this section shall be in addition to and not in lieu of any other remedies provided by common law or under Federal or State law.

PRIVATE ENFORCEMENT OF PRODUCT SAFETY RULES AND OF SECTION 15 ORDERS

SEC. 24. Any interested person may bring an action in any United States district court for the district in which the defendant is found or transacts business to enforce a consumer product safety rule or an order under section 15, and to obtain appropriate injunctive relief. Not less than thirty days prior to the commencement of such action, such interested person shall give notice by registered mail to the Commission, to the Attorney General, and to the person against whom such action is directed. Such notice shall state the nature of the alleged violation of any such standard or order, the relief to be requested, and the court in which the action will be brought. No separate suit shall be brought under this section if at the time the suit is brought the same alleged violation is the subject of a pending civil or criminal action by the United States under this Act. In any action under this section, such interested person may elect, by a demand for such relief in his complaint, to recover reasonable attorney's fees, in which case the court shall award the costs of suit, including a reasonable attorney's fee, to the prevailing party.

EFFECT ON PRIVATE REMEDIES

SEC. 25. (a) Compliance with consumer product safety rules or other rules or orders under this Act shall not relieve any person from liability at common law or under State statutory law to any other person.

(b) The failure of the Commission to take any action or commence a proceeding with respect to the safety of a consumer product shall not be admissible in evidence in litigation at common law or under State statutory law relating to such consumer product.

(c)(1) Subject to section 6(a)(2) but notwithstanding section 6(a)(1), (A) accident and investigation reports made under this

Act by any officer, employee, or agent of the Commission shall be available for use in any civil, criminal, or other judicial proceeding arising out of such accident, and (B) any such officer, employee, or agent may be required to testify in such proceedings as to the facts developed in such investigations.

(2) Subject to sections 6(a)(2) and 6(b) but notwithstanding section 6(a)(1), (A) any accident or investigation report made under this Act by an officer or employee of the Commission shall be made available to the public in a manner which will not identify any injured person or any person treating him, without the consent of the person so identified, and (B) all reports on research projects, demonstration projects, and other related activities shall be public information.

EFFECT ON STATE STANDARDS

SEC. 26. (a) Whenever a consumer product safety standard under this Act is in effect and applies to a hazard associated with a consumer product, no State or political subdivision of a State shall have any authority either to establish or to continue in effect any provision of a safety standard or regulation which prescribes any requirements as to the performance, composition, contents, design, finish, construction, packaging, or labeling of such product which are designed to deal with the same hazard associated with such consumer product; unless such requirements are identical to the requirements of the Federal standard.

(b) Nothing in this section shall be construed to prevent the Federal Government or the government of any State or political subdivision thereof from establishing a safety requirement applicable to a consumer product or its own use if such requirement imposes a higher standard of performance than that required to comply with the otherwise applicable Federal standard.

(c) Upon application of a State or political subdivision thereof, the Commission may by rule, after notice and opportunity for oral presentation of views, exempt from the provisions of subsection (a) (under such conditions as it may impose) a proposed safety standard or regulation described in such application, where the proposed standard or regulation (1) imposes a higher level of performance than the Federal standard, (2) is required by compelling local conditions, and (3) does not unduly burden interstate commerce.

ADDITIONAL FUNCTIONS OF COMMISSION

SEC. 27. (a) The Commission may, by one or more of its members or by such agents or agency as it may designate, conduct any hearing or other inquiry necessary or appropriate to its functions anywhere in the United States. A Commissioner who participates in such a hearing or other inquiry shall not be disqualified solely by reason of such participation from subsequently participating in a decision of the Commission in the same matter. The Commission shall publish notice of any proposed hearing in the Federal Register and shall afford a reasonable opportunity for interested persons to present relevant testimony and data.

(b) The Commission shall also have the power—

(1) to require, by special or general orders, any person to submit in writing such reports and answers to questions as the Commission may prescribe; and such submission shall be made within such reasonable period and under oath or otherwise as the Commission may determine;

(2) to administer oaths;

(3) to require by subpena the attendance and testimony of witnesses and the production of all documentary evidence relating to the execution of its duties;

(4) in any proceeding or investigation to order testimony to be taken by deposition before any person who is designated by the Commission and has the power to administer oaths and, in such instances, to compel testimony and the production of evidence in the same manner as authorized under paragraph (3) of this subsection; and

(5) to pay witnesses the same fees and mileage as are paid in like circumstances in the courts of the United States.

(c) Any United States district court within the jurisdiction of which any inquiry is carried on may, upon petition by the Attorney General, in case of refusal to obey a subpena or order of the Commission issued under subsection (b) of this section, issue an order requiring compliance therewith; and any failure to obey the order of the court may be punished by the court as a contempt thereof.

(d) No person shall be subject to civil liability to any person (other than the Commission or the United States) for disclosing information at the request of the Commission.

(e) The Commission may by rule require any manufacturer of consumer products to provide to the Commission such performance and technical data related to performance and safety as may be required to carry out the purposes of the Act, and to give such notification of such performance and technical data at the time of original purchase to prospective purchasers and to the first purchaser of such product for purposes other than resale, as it determines necessary to carry out the purposes of this Act.

(f) For purposes of carrying out this Act, the Commission may purchase any consumer product and it may require any manufacturer, distributor, or retailer of a consumer product to sell the product to the Commission at manufacturer's, distributor's, or retailer's cost.

(g) The Commission is authorized to enter into contracts with governmental entities, private organizations, or individuals for the conduct of activities authorized by this Act.

(h) The Commission may plan, construct, and operate a facility or facilities suitable for research, development, and testing of consumer products in order to carry out this Act.

(i) The Commission shall prepare and submit to the President and the Congress on or before October 1 of each year a comprehensive report on the administration of this Act for the preceding fiscal year. Such report shall include—

(1) a thorough appraisal, including statistical analyses, estimates, and long-term projections, of the incidence of injury and effects to the population resulting from consumer products, with a breakdown, insofar as practicable, among the various sources of such injury;

(2) a list of consumer product safety rules prescribed or in effect during such year;

(3) an evaluation of the degree of observance of consumer product safety rules, including a list of enforcement actions, court decisions, and compromises of alleged violations, by location and company name;

(4) a summary of outstanding problems confronting the administration of this Act in order of priority;

(5) an analysis and evaluation of public and private consumer product safety research activities:

(6) a list, with a brief statement of the issues, of completed or pending judicial actions under this Act:

(7) the extent to which technical information was disseminated to the scientific and commercial communities and consumer information was made available to the public;

(8) the extent of cooperation between Commission officials and representatives of industry and other interested parties in the implementation of this Act, including a log or summary of meetings held between Commission officials and representatives of industry and other interested parties;

(9) an appraisal of significant actions of State and local governments relating to the responsibilities of the Commission; and

(10) such recommendations for additional legislation as the Commission deems necessary to carry out the purposes of this Act.

PRODUCT SAFETY ADVISORY COUNCIL

SEC. 28. (a) The Commission shall establish a Product Safety Advisory Council which it may consult before prescribing a consumer product safety rule or taking other action under this Act. The Council shall be appointed by the Commission and shall be composed of fifteen members, each of whom shall be qualified by training and experience in one or more of the fields applicable to the safety of products within the jurisdiction of the Commission. The Council shall be constituted as follows:

(1) five members shall be selected from governmental agencies including Federal, State, and local governments;

(2) five members shall be selected from consumer product industries including at least one representative of small business; and

(3) five members shall be selected from among consumer organizations, community organizations, and recognized consumer leaders.

(b) The Council shall meet at the call of the Commission, but not less often than four times during each calendar year.

(c) The Council may propose consumer product safety rules to the Commission for its consideration and may function through subcommittees of its members. All proceedings of the Council shall be public, and a record of each proceeding shall be available for public inspection.

(d) Members of the Council who are not officers or employees of the United States shall, while attending meetings or conferences of the Council or while otherwise engaged in the business of the Council, be entitled to receive compensation at a rate fixed by the Commission, not exceeding the daily equivalent of the annual rate of basic pay in effect for grade GS–18 of the General Schedule, including traveltime, and while away from their homes or regular places of business they may be allowed travel expenses, including per diem in lieu of subsistence, as authorized by section 5703 of title 5, United States Code. Payments under this subsection shall not render members of the Council officers or employees of the United States for any purpose.

COOPERATION WITH STATES AND WITH OTHER FEDERAL AGENCIES

SEC. 29. (a) The Commission shall establish a program to promote Federal-State cooperation for the purposes of carrying out this Act. In implementing such program the Commission may—

(1) accept from any State or local authorities engaged in activities relating to health, safety, or consumer protection assistance in such functions as injury data collection, investigation, and educational programs, as well as other assistance in the administration and enforcement of this Act which such States or localities may be able and willing to provide and, if so agreed, may pay in advance or otherwise for the reasonable cost of such assistance, and

(2) commission any qualified officer or employee of any State or local agency as an officer of the Commission for the purpose of conducting examinations, investigations, and inspections.

(b) In determining whether such proposed State and local programs are appropriate in implementing the purposes of this Act the Commission shall give favorable consideration to programs which establish separate State and local agencies to consolidate functions relating to product safety and other consumer protection activities.

(c) The Commission may obtain from any Federal department or agency such statistics, data, program reports, and other materials as it may deem necessary to carry out its functions under this Act. Each such department or agency may cooperate with the Commission and, to the extent permitted by law, furnish such materials to it. The Commission and the heads of other departments and agencies engaged in administering programs related to product safety shall, to the maximum extent practicable, cooperate and consult in order to insure fully coordinated efforts.

(d) The Commission shall, to the maximum extent practicable, utilize the resources and facilities of the National Bureau of Standards, on a reimbursable basis, to perform research and analyses related to consumer product hazards (including fire and flammability hazards), to develop test methods, to conduct studies and investigations, and to provide technical advice and assistance in connection with the functions of the Commission.

TRANSFERS OF FUNCTIONS

SEC. 30. (a) The functions of the Secretary of Health, Education, and Welfare under the Federal Hazardous Substances Act (15 U.S.C. 1261 et seq.) and the Poison Prevention Packaging Act of 1970 are trnasferred to the Commission. The functions of the Administrator of the Environmental Protection Agency and of the Secretary of Health, Education, and Welfare under the Acts amended by subsections (b) through (f) of section 7 of the Poison Prevention Packaging Act of 1970, to the extent such functions relate to the administration and enforcement of the Poison Prevention Packaging Act of 1970, are transferred to the Commission.

(b) The functions of the Secretary of Health, Education, and Welfare, the Secretary of Commerce, and the Federal Trade Commission under the Flammable Fabrics Act (15 U.S.C. 1191 et seq.) are transferred to the Commission. The functions of the Federal Trade Commission under the Federal Trade Commission Act, to the extent such functions relate to the administration and enforcement of the Flammable Fabrics Act, are transferred to the Commission.

(c) A hazard which is associated with consumer products and which could be prevented or reduced to a sufficient extent by action taken under the Federal Hazardous Substances Act, the Poison Prevention Packaging Act of 1970, or the Flammable Fabrics Act may be regulated by the Commission only in accordance with the provisions of those Acts.

(d) (1) All personnel, property, records, obligations, and commitments, which are used primarily with respect to any function transferred under the provisions of subsections (a) and (b) of this section shall be transferred to the Commission. The transfer of personnel pursuant to this paragraph shall be without reduction in classification or compensation for one year after such transfer, except that the Chairman of the Commission shall have full authority to assign personnel during such one-year period in order to efficiently carry out functions transferred to the Commission under this section.

(2) All orders, determinations, rules, regulations, permits, contracts, certificates, licenses, and privileges (A) which have been issued, made, granted, or allowed to become effective in the exercise of functions which are transferred under this section by any department or agency, any functions of which are transferred by this section, and (B) which are in effect at the time this section takes effect, shall continue in effect according to their terms until modified, terminated, superseded, set aside, or repealed by the Commission, by any court of competent jurisdiction, or by operation of law.

(3) The provisions of this section shall not affect any proceedings pending at the time this section takes effect before any department or agency, functions of which are transfered by this section; except that such proceedings, to the extent that they relate to functions so transferred, shall be continued before the Commission. Orders shall be issued in such proceedings, appeals shall be taken therefrom, and payments shall be made pursuant to such orders, as if this section had not been enacted; and orders issued in any such proceedings shall continue in effect until modified, terminated, superseded, or repealed by the Commission, by a court of competent jurisdiction, or by operation of law.

(4) The provisions of this section shall not affect suits commenced prior to the date this section takes effect and in all such suits proceedings shall be had, appeals taken, and judgments rendered, in the same manner and effect as if this section had not been enacted; except that if before the date on which this section takes effect, any department or agency (or officer thereof in his official capacity) is a party to a suit involving functions transferred to the Commission, then such suit shall be continued by the Commission. No cause of action, and no suit, action, or other proceeding, by or agaihst any department or agency (or officer thereof in his official capacity) functions of which are transferred by this section, shall abate by reason of the enactment of this section. Causes of actions, suits, actions, or other proceedings may be asserted by or against the United States or the Commission as may be appropriate and, in any litigation pending when this section takes effect, the court may at any time, on its own motion or that of any party, enter an order which will give effect to the provisions of this paragraph.

(e) For purposes of this section, (1) the term "function" includes power and duty, and (2) the transfer of a function, under any provision of law, of an agency or the head of a department shall also be a transfer of a function, under any provision of law, of an agency or the head of a department shall also be a transfer of all functions under such law which are exercised by any office of officer of such agency or department.

LIMITATION ON JURISDICTION

SEC. 31. The Commission shall have no authority under this Act to regulate hazards associated with consumer porducts which could be prevented or reduced to a sufficient extent by actions taken under the Occupational Safety and Health Act of 1970; the Act of August 2, 1956 (70 Stat. 953); the Atomic Energy Act of 1954; or the Clean Air Act. The Commission shall have no authority under this Act to regulate any hazard associated with electronic product radiation emitted from an electronic product (as such terms are defined by sections 355 (1) and (2) of the Public Health Service Act) if such hazard of such product may be subjected to regulation under subpart 3 of part F of title III of the Public Health Service Act.

AUTHORIZATION OF APPROPRIATIONS

SEC. 32. (a) There are hereby authorized to be appropriated for the purpose of carrying out the provisions of this Act (other than the provisions of section 27(h) which authorize the planning and construction of research, development, and testing facilities) and for the purpose of carrying out the functions, powers, and duties transferred to the Commission under section 30—

(1) $55,000,000 for the fiscal year ending June 30, 1973;

(2) $59,000,000 for the fiscal year ending June 30, 1974; and

(3) $64,000,000 for the fiscal year ending June 30, 1975.

(b)(1) There are authorized to be appropriated such sums as may be necessary for the planning and construction of research, development and testing facilities described in section 27(h); except that no appropriation shall be made for any such planning or construction involving an expenditure in excess of $100,000 if such planning or construction has not been approved by resolutions adopted in substantially the same form by the Committee on Interstate and Foreign Commerce of the House of Representatives, and by the Committee on Commerce of the Senate. For the purpose of securing consideration of such approval the Commission shall transmit to Congress a prospectus of the proposed facility including (but not limited to)—

(A) a brief description of the facility to be planned or constructed;

(B) the location of the facility, and an estimate of the maximum cost of the facility;

(C) a statement of those agencies, private and public, which will use such facility, together with the contribution to be made by each such agency toward the cost of such facility; and

(D) a statement of justification of the need for such facility.

(2) The estimated maximum cost of any facility approved under this subsection as set forth in the prospectus may be increased by the amount equal to the percentage increase, if any, as determined by the Commission, in construction costs, from the date of the transmittal of such prospectus to Congress, but in no event shall the increase authorized by this paragraph exceed 10 per centum of such estimated maximum cost.

EFFECTIVE DATE

SEC. 33. This Act shall take effect on the sixtieth day following the date of its enactment, except—

(1) sections 4 and 32 shall take effect on the date of enactment of this Act, and

(2) section 30 shall take effect on the later of (A) 150 days after the date of enactment of this Act, or (B) the date on which at least three members of the Commission first take office.

APPENDIX J

REPORT OF CONFERENCE COMMITTEE

92D CONGRESS, *2d Session* } HOUSE OF REPRESENTATIVES { REPORT No. 92–1593

CONSUMER PRODUCT SAFETY ACT

OCTOBER 12, 1972.—Ordered to be printed

Mr. STAGGERS, from the committee of conference, submitted the following

CONFERENCE REPORT

[To accompany S. 3419]

The committee of conference on the disagreeing votes of the two Houses on the amendment of the House to the bill (S. 3419) to protect consumers against unreasonable risk of injury from hazardous products, and for other purposes, having met, after full and free conference, have agreed to recommend and do recommend to their respective Houses as follows:

* * *

(Here follows the text of the bill as reported by the Conference Committee and ultimately enacted.)

JOINT EXPLANATORY STATEMENT OF THE COMMITTEE OF CONFERENCE

The managers on the part of the House and the Senate at the conference on the disagreeing votes of the two Houses on the amendment of the House to the bill (S. 3419) to protect consumers against unreasonable risk of injury from hazardous products, and for other purposes, submit the following joint statement to the House and the Senate in explanation of the effect of the action agreed upon by the managers and recommended in the accompanying conference report:

The House amendment struck out all of the Senate bill after the enacting clause and inserted a substitute text.

The Senate recedes from its disagreement to the amendment of the House, with an amendment which is a substitute for both the Senate bill and the House amendment. The differences between the Senate bill, the House amendment, and the substitute agreed to in conference are noted below, except for clerical corrections, conforming changes made necessary by reason of agreements reached by the conferees, and minor drafting and clarifying changes.

Establishment of Federal Agency To Regulate Consumer Product Safety

structure of agency

Both the Senate bill and the House amendment established a new Federal agency to carry out the product safety functions dealt with in the legislation.

Senate.—The Senate bill provided for the establishment of an independent Food, Drug, and Consumer Product Agency. The Agency was to be headed by an Administrator, appointed by the President (with Senate confirmation) for a 5-year term. He could be reappointed as Administrator only once in succession. Within the Agency there would be established a Commission of Food and Nutrition, a Commission of Drugs, a Commission of Veterinary Medicine, and a Commission of Consumer Products, each to be headed by a Commissioner, appointed by the Administrator. In addition, the Senate bill directed the Administrator to appoint a Director of the Office of Consumer Information, to establish a Consumer Information Center and a Public Information Room, and to set up a National Injury Information Clearing House. The Administrator would be compensated at level III of the Executive Schedule, and the Directors and General Counsel would be compensated at level IV. The Senate bill authorized the Administrator to place twenty-five "supergrade" positions (grades GS 16–18).

House.—The House amendment provided for the establishment of an independent regulatory Commission—the Consumer Product Safety Commission—consisting of five Commissioners appointed by the President (with Senate confirmation), one of whom would be designated by the President as Chairman (and when so designated would act as Chairman until the expiration of his term of office as Commissioner). A member of the Commission could be removed by the President only for neglect of duty or malfeasance in office. Commissioners would be appointed for staggered seven-year terms. Not more than three Commissioners could be appointed from the same political party. Commissioners were prohibited from having certain specified financial interests in the manufacturers or sellers of consumer products, or their suppliers.

The Chairman would be the principal executive officer of the Commission, and would exercise all of the executive and administrative functions of the Commission, subject to general policies of the Commission and its regulatory decisions, findings, and determinations. The Chairman would be authorized, subject to the approval of the Commission, to appoint an Executive Director, a General Counsel, a Director of Engineering Sciences, a Director of Epidemiology, and a Director of Information.

The House amendment prohibited any full-time officer or employee of the Commission who was at any time during 12 months preceding termination of employment with the Commission paid at a rate in excess of that for grade GS-14 or above from accepting employment or compensation from any manufacturer subject to the bill for a period of 12 months after terminating employment with the Commission.

Under the House amendment the Chairman of the Commission is compensated at level III of the Executive Schedule, and the other Commissioners are compensated at level IV.

Conference substitute (§ 4).—The Senate recedes.

GENERAL POWERS AND DUTIES OF NEW FEDERAL AGENCY

In addition to functions specifically relating to safety regulation of consumer products and functions transferred from other agencies, both the Senate and House versions confer certain general powers and duties on the new agency.

Senate.—Under the Senate bill, the Administrator of the new Agency is authorized to employ experts and consultants, appoint advisory committees and a Joint Scientific Advisory Committee, prescribe regulations to carry out his functions, issue subpenas and order persons to respond to written questions, utilize other public and private agencies, enter into contracts and other arrangements with other public agencies or with any person, accept gifts, maintain liaison with public agencies and independent standard-setting bodies carrying out consumer safety activities, construct research and testing facilities (if subsequently authorized by Congress), conduct public hearings after publishing public notice thereof, submit budget estimates directly to the President for review and transmittal to the Congress and receive appropriations directly from the President and the Office of Management and Budget, submit legislative recommendations, etc., without prior clearance, initiate and direct all litigation of the agency, and delegate within the agency any of his functions (other than issuance of subpenas). The Agency was directed to submit an annual report, which would include, among other matters, the Administrator's budget requests, and the budget recommendations of the Commissioners.

The Senate bill directed each of the Commissioners of the Agency to attempt to eliminate products presenting unreasonable risk of injury; and to establish certain analytic and investigatory capabilities, including a capability to engage in risk-based analysis.

House.—The House amendment authorized the Commission to conduct hearings (after publishing public notice thereof) and to conduct other inquiries, to issue subpenas and to order persons to respond to written questions, to take depositions, to enter into contracts with public agencies or any person, to construct a research and test facility (if the prospectus therefor is approved by the House Interstate and Foreign Commerce Committee and the Senate Commerce Committee), to require manufacturers of consumer products to provide performance and technical data to the Commission and to retail purchasers. The Commission is directed to submit an annual report, which would include, among other matters, a log or summary of meetings held between Commission officials and representatives of industry and other interested parties.

Conference substitute (§ 27).—The conference substitute follows the provisions of the House amendment with the following additions:

(1) The Commission is authorized to accept gifts and voluntary and

uncompensated services, notwithstanding the provisions of section 3679 of the Revised Statutes (31 U.S.C. 665(b)).

(2) The Commission is authorized to initiate, prosecute, defend, or appeal any court action in the name of the Commission for the purpose of enforcing the laws subject to its jurisdiction, through its own legal representative with the concurrence of the Attorney General or through the Attorney General.

(3) Section 27(k) of the conference substitute provides that, whenever the Commission submits any budget estimate or request to the President or the Office of Management and Budget, it shall concurrently transmit a copy of that estimate or request to the Congress; and that no Federal officer or agency may require the Commission to submit its legislative recommendations, etc., to any such officer or agency for approval, comment, or review prior to the submission of such recommendations, etc., to the Congress. A copy of such recommendations would have to be concurrently transmitted to the President.

(4) The Commission may delegate any of its functions (other than the function of issuing subpenas) to any of its officers or employees.

The committee of conference decided not to include the detailed provisions of the Senate bill regarding risk-based analysis and decided instead to rely on the provisions of the House amendment relating to the Commission's research and test capabilities [section 5(b)(2)].

COOPERATION WITH STATE AND FEDERAL AGENCIES

Senate.—The Senate bill authorized each Federal agency, on request of the Administrator, to make its services, etc., available with or without reimbursement to the greatest practicable extent to the new Agency to furnish information, and to allow the new Agency access to information; directed the Agency, to the maximum practical extent, to utilize the personnel, facilities, and other technical support available in other Federal agencies; and authorized the Agency to utilize the National Bureau of Standards, with or without reimbursement, for purposes related to carrying out the responsibilities of the Agency under the bill. Technical research support for fire safety projects undertaken by the new Agency was required to be provided by the National Bureau of Standards on a reimbursable basis.

In addition, the Agency was generally authorized to use the services and facilities of, and enter into contracts and maintain liaison with, State agencies.

House.—The House amendment required the Commission, to the maximum extent practicable, to utilize the National Bureau of Standards, on a reimbursable basis, to perform research and analyses related to consumer product hazards, to develop test methods, to conduct studies and investigations, and to provide technical assistance relating to the Commission's functions. In addition, the Commission was authorized to obtain information and other materials from any Federal agency. Such agencies were authorized to cooperate with the Commission and, to the extent permitted by law, furnish such materials to it.

The House amendment also authorized the Commission to establish a program to promote Federal-State cooperation for the purposes of carrying out the bill, in which it could accept assistance from any

State or local authorities in the administration and enforcement of the bill, to pay for the reasonable cost of such assistance, and to use State or local officials to conduct examinations, investigations, and inspections for the Commission.

Conference substitute (§ *29*).—The Senate recedes.

OBLIGATIONS OF AGENCY CONTRACTORS

Senate.—The Senate bill required certain recipients of financial assistance under the bill to keep specified records and to allow the Administrator and the Comptroller General access to those records.

House.—No comparable provision.

Conference substitute (§ *27(i)*).—The House recedes.

SCOPE OF REGULATORY AUTHORITY

Both the Senate bill and House amendment transferred certain existing Federal agency functions relating to product safety regulation to the new agency, and also provided the agency with new legal authority which, in general, was designed to permit it to regulate consumer products which are not subject to adequate Federal safety regulation under existing law.

TRANSFERS OF FUNCTIONS

Senate.—The Senate bill transferred to the Administrator of the new Agency all functions of—

(1) the Secretary of Health, Education, and Welfare administered through the Food and Drug Administration;

(2) the Secretary of Health, Education, and Welfare relating to licensing of clinical laboratories and to regulation of biological products; and

(3) the Secretary of Commerce and the Federal Trade Commission under the Flammable Fabrics Act and under the Act of August 2, 1956 (refrigerator safety).

The Senate bill also made provision for delegation by the Administrator of these transferred functions to appropriate Commissioners within the new Agency, and permitted certain Public Health Service officers to acquire competitive service status in the new Agency.

House.—The House amendment transferred to the Commission all functions of—

(1) the Secretary of Health, Education, and Welfare under the Federal Hazardous Substances Act, and the Poison Prevention Packaging Act of 1970, and of the Administrator of the Environmental Protection Agency and the Secretary of Health, Education, and Welfare under the Acts amended by subsections (b) through (f) of section 7 of the Poison Prevention Packaging Act of 1970, to the extent such functions relate to the administration and enforcement of such Act, and

(2) the Secretary of Health, Education, and Welfare, the Secretary of Commerce, and the Federal Trade Commission under the Flammable Fabrics Act, and of the Federal Trade Commission under the Federal Trade Commission Act, to the extent such functions relates to the administration and enforcement of

the Flammable Fabrics Act.

The House amendment also provided that a product hazard which could be prevented or reduced to a sufficient extent by action taken under the Federal Hazardous Substances Act, the Poison Prevention Packaging Act, or the Flammable Fabrics Act could be regulated by the Commission only in accordance with the provisions of those Acts.

Conference substitute (§ *30*).—The conferees adopted the provisions of the House amendment with the following changes:

(1) The functions of the Secretary of Commerce and the Federal Trade Commission under the Act of August 2, 1956 (15 U.S.C. 1211), are transferred to the Commission.

(2) Personnel, property, obligations, etc., associated with fire and flammability research in the National Bureau of Standards are not transferred to the Commission.

(3) The Senate provision permitting Public Health Service officers to acquire competitive service status was included.

In determining whether a risk of injury can be reduced to a sufficient extent under one of the Acts referred to in this section, it is anticipated that the Commission will consider all aspects of the risk, together with the remedial powers available to it under both the bill and the other Acts.

DEFINITION OF CONSUMER PRODUCT

Senate.—The Senate bill authorized safety regulation by the new Agency of any "consumer product". Consumer product was defined as a product, or a component thereof, produced for or distributed to an individual for his personal use, consumption, or enjoyment in or around a household or residence, a school, in recreation, or otherwise. Specifically excluded from the definition were:

(1) Tobacco and tobacco products.

(2) Products subject to safety regulation under the National Traffic and Motor Vehicle Safety Act of 1966.

(3) Aircraft or other aeronautical products subject to safety regulation by the Federal Aviation Administration.

(4) Food or drugs as defined in the Federal Food, Drug, and Cosmetic Act.

(5) Products subject to safety regulation under the Federal Insecticide, Fungicide, and Rodenticide Act.

(6) Products subject to safety regulation under the Occupational Safety and Health Act of 1970, insofar as such products are regulated for use in employment.

(7) Products subject to safety regulation under the Gas Pipeline Safety Act.

(8) Products subject to safety regulation under authority of the Atomic Energy Act of 1954.

(9) Vessels, appurtenances, and equipment subject to safety regulation under title 52 of the Revised Statutes, the Federal Boat Safety Act of 1971, or other marine safety statutes administered by the Coast Guard.

The Senate bill treated firearms as consumer products, but prohibited the new agency from administratively banning them.

House.—The House amendment defined "consumer product" as any article, or component part thereof, produced or distributed for sale to, (or for the personal use, consumption, or enjoyment of) a consumer in or around a household or residence, a school, in recreation, or otherwise; unless the article is not customarily produced or distributed for sale to or use, consumption, or enjoyment of a consumer. The exclusions from the House's definition were the same as those from the Senate's with the following exceptions:

(1) The House did not exempt aircraft or vessels (including boats), nor did it specifically exempt products subject to regulation under the Gas Pipeline Safety Act.

(2) The House added exemptions for firearms and ammunition, medical devices, and cosmetics. It also provided (under section 31) a qualified exemption for product hazards which could be prevented or reduced to a sufficient extent under the Clean Air Act, the Act of August 2, 1956, and for product hazards which could be regulated under the electronic product radiation provisions of the Public Health Service Act.

Conference substitute (§3(1), 31).—The conference substitute follows the House amendment but adds exemptions for aircraft and vessels including boats. The latter exemption is for boats which could be subjected to safety regulation under the Federal Boat Safety Act of 1971, vessels, and certain appurtenances thereto which could be subjected to safety regulation under title 52 of the Revised Statutes or other marine safety statutes administered by the department in which the Coast Guard is operating; and certain boat and vessel equipment to the extent that a risk of injury associated with the use of such equipment on boats or vessels could be eliminated or reduced by actions taken under any of the above statutes. It is not intended by this provision to in any way detract from the authority of the Coast Guard with respect to seaworthiness or operational capabilities concerning vessels, boats, or marine equipment.

TREATMENT OF CERTAIN PRODUCTS REGULATED UNDER OTHER LAWS

Senate.—All products excluded from the definition of "consumer product" (other than tobacco, foods, and drugs) were excluded only to the extent that they were subject to safety regulation under specified Federal laws. ("Subject to safety regulation" was defined as authorized to be regulated for the purpose of eliminating any unreasonable risk of injury or death, as determined by the Administrator through consultation with appropriate Federal officials.) However with respect to any of the specifically exempted products, the new Agency was authorized to petition any Federal agency which had jurisdiction over the products to establish and enforce appropriate safety regulations for the product; to participate in the establishment of such regulations; and upon request of such agency, to establish and enforce such regulations in accordance with the Consumer Safety Agency's authority under the bill. Upon such request, the product would no longer be excluded from the definition of "consumer product".

House.—The House (under section 31 of the bill) provided for an exemption from the Commission's authority for product hazards which could be "prevented or reduced to a sufficient extent" under the Occupational Safety and Health Act, the Act of August 2, 1956, the Atomic Energy Act, and the Clean Air Act. An exemption was also provided for electronic product radiation hazards which could be subjected to regulation under the electronic product radiation provisions of the Public Health Service Act. (See explanation of *transfers of functions* for similar House provisions applicable to product hazards which can be regulated under the Flammable Fabrics Act, the Federal Hazardous Substances Act, and the Poison Prevention Packaging Act.)

Conference substitute (*§ 31*).—The conference substitute incorporates the provisions of the House bill with an amendment which deletes the reference to the Refrigerator Safety Act (the Act of August 2, 1956) which is transferred to the Commission. In determining whether a risk of injury can be reduced to a sufficient extent under one of the Acts referred to in this section, it is anticipated that the Commission will consider all aspects of the risk, together with the remedial powers available to it under both the bill and the remedial powers under the other law available to the agency administering the law.

Consumer Product Safety Information and Research; Disclosure of Information

Senate.—Under the Senate bill, the Office of Consumer Information, the National Injury Information Clearinghouse, and the Commissioner of Product Safety all were to participate in gathering and making available to the public information concerning consumer product safety.

(1) Office of Consumer Information

The Office of Consumer Information had the basic responsibility of informing the public concerning consumer product hazards. The Office was to make available to the public through its Consumer Information Center, subject to the limitations on the disclosure of information contained in the bill, information concerning consumer product safety hazards, copies of any communications, documents, reports, or other information received or sent by the Administrator or any Commissioner, and communications received by the Agency from any person outside the Agency concerning any matter under consideration by the Agency in a rulemaking or adjudicatory proceeding.

The Consumer Information Center was to respond to written inquiries from consumers and to conduct consumer education programs designed to inform the public about specific consumer product safety hazards.

The Director of the Office was to establish a Consumer Information Library and a Public Information Room in which the public would have access to Agency information and to a copying machine.

(2) National Injury Information Clearinghouse

The National Injury Information Clearinghouse would carry out a program under which a system of nationwide reporting centers would monitor injuries associated with foods, drugs, and consumer products. The system would identify causes of injury from such products, investigate the manner in which the injury occurred, and ascertain the severity of the injury. In carrying out his functions, the Director of the Clearinghouse would obtain injury data from both governmental and private sources and require persons engaged in the manufacture, distribution, or sale of foods, drugs, or consumer products (and their insurors) to provide information to him concerning injuries from such products which have come to their attention.

(3) COMMISSIONER OF PRODUCT SAFETY

The Commissioner of Product Safety was to collect, evaluate, and disseminate information on the types, frequency, severity, and causes of injury associated with the use of consumer products and on means to test, measure, or evaluate the risks of such injury. The Commissioner was authorized to undertake studies and research and otherwise to collect data to provide a basis for establishing consumer product safety standards in reducing the risk of injury; to form special study teams to gather information concerning injuries from consumer products; to provide assistance to persons and agencies engaged in research designed to minimize consumer product injury risks or designed to develop means of testing, measuring, and evaluating such risks; to secure information on consumer product injury risks from other government agencies and from private sources; to publish or otherwise make available information concerning consumer product injury risks (including recommendations for reducing such risks and for testing products for such risks); and to obtain products for research and testing and dispose of such products. The Commissioner was authorized to obtain information relating to consumer product injuries by subpena from any person. Information disclosed by the Commissioner was subject to the limitations on public disclosure of information. The Commissioner was directed to inform any manufacturer of any unreasonable or significant risk to health or safety determined to be associated with any product of that manufacturer. The Commissioner was authorized to make recommendations to building, electrical, or other similar household environment code-making authorities with respect to any matter subject to such code which he determines to present an unreasonable risk of personal injury or death, without regard to whether that matter is a consumer product.

(4) LIMITATIONS ON DISCLOSURE OF INFORMATION

Information related to trade secrets or other confidential business information described in section 1905, title 18, United States Code, could not be released to the public unless it related to a consumer product in such a way as to indicate the presence of an unreasonable risk or injury or death or unless its release was necessary to protect the health and safety of the public. Before any such information could be made public, the manufacturer of the product to which the information related was entitled to notice and an opportunity to comment in writing, or in a closed session, on the information unless it was determined that the delay inherent in this procedure would be detrimental to the public health and safety. Such information could be disclosed to other Federal agencies for official use upon request, to appropriate Congressional committees, in any judicial proceeding under court order, or in any proceeding under the bill.

Information was not required to be publicly disclosed if it is information described in section 552(b), title 5, United States Code (relating to information protected from public access under the Freedom of Information Act), or which is otherwise protected by law from disclosure to the public.

No information could be made public which identified any individual injured by a consumer product or any person treating him for his injury without the express written consent of the individual or person involved.

House.—The House amendment provided for an Injury Information Clearing House which was charged with the duties of collecting, investigating, analyzing, and disseminating information related to the causes and prevention of illness, injury, or death associated with consumer products and with the duty of conducting such studies and investigations of deaths, injuries, diseases, the impairment of health, and economic loss resulting from accidents involving consumer products as it deemed necessary.

(1) LIMITATIONS ON DISCLOSURE OF INFORMATION

Information obtained by the Commission which contained or related to a trade secret or other matter referred to in section 1905, title 18, United States Code, could not be publicly disclosed. Such information could be disclosed to agency officers or employees carrying out the provisions of the House amendment or, when relevant, in any proceeding under the provisions of the House amendment. Not less than 30 days before the public disclosure of information obtained under the provisions of the House amendment (or sooner if necessary to protect the public health and safety), the Commission was to the extent practicable to give notice and a summary of the information to each manufacturer or private labeler of any consumer product to which that information related, if the information to be disclosed would permit the public to identify that manufacturer or distributor, and to permit the manufacturer or distributor to submit comments to the Commission on that information. The Commission was directed to take steps to assure that publicly disclosed information from which specific manufacturers or distributors could be identified was accurate and that the disclosure was fair in the circumstances and reasonably related to carrying out its duties. No information would be required to be publicly disclosed if it is information described in section 552(b), title 5, United States Code (relating to information which is entitled to be protected from public access under the Freedom of Information Act), or which is otherwise protected by law from disclosure to the public.

The limitations on the disclosure of information did not apply to imminently hazardous consumer products against which the Commission had instituted a seizure action or to products which failed to conform with applicable product safety standards or which were banned hazardous consumer products, or to information in the course of, or concerning any, administrative or judicial proceeding under the provisions of the bill.

The Commission was to publish a retraction of any inaccurate or misleading information disclosed to the public.

(2) PRODUCT SAFETY RESEARCH

The Commission was authorized to conduct research studies and investigations concerning the safety of consumer products and means of improving the safety of such products, to test consumer products and develop product safety testing methods and devices, and to offer product safety investigation and testing training and otherwise assist public and private organizations in the development of safety standards and testing methods. The Commission could make grants or enter into contracts with any person, including a government agency, to carry out such functions. Whenever a person, other than the Commission, carried out any information, research, or development activity under contract with the Commission or with the aid of a grant from the Commission, provision was to be made for the availability to the public, without charge, on a nonexclusive basis, of the rights to information, uses, processes, patents and other developments resulting from that activity.

Conference substitute (*§ 5, 6*).—The conference substitute incorporates the House provisions respecting consumer product safety information and research, and disclosure of information.

Safety Regulation of Consumer Products

DEFINITIONS

Both bills contained definitions applicable to the entire bill. The principal definitions in the bills are described below with the exception of the definitions of "consumer product" and "subject to safety regulation" (discussed under *scope of regulatory authority*) and "risk based analysis" (mentioned under *general powers and duties of agency*).

Senate.—The Senate bill included the following definitions:

(1) "Consumer product safety standard" was defined as a minimum standard promulgated under the bill which prevents such product from presenting an unreasonable risk of injury or death.

(2) "Injury" was defined as harm (including adverse reactions and illness) produced by biologic, chemical, thermal, mechanical, electrical, radiological, or other natural or manmade agents.

(3) "State" was defined as a State, the District of Columbia, Puerto Rico, the Virgin Islands, American Samoa, Guam, Wake Island, Midway Island, Kingman Reef, Johnston Island, the Trust Territory of the Pacific Islands, or the Canal Zone.

(4) "Unreasonable risk of injury presented by a consumer product" was defined as that degree of risk which the Commissioner determines is incompatible with the public health and safety because the degree of anticipated injury or the frequency of such injury, or both, is unwarranted because the degree of anticipated injury or the frequency of such injury either (A) can be reduced without affecting the performance or availability of the consumer product or (B) cannot be reduced without affecting the performance or availability of the consumer product but the effect on such performance or availability is justified when measured against the degree of anticipated injury or the frequency of such injury.

(5) "Use" meant (A) exposure to, and (B) normal use or reasonably foreseeable misuse.

(6) "Commerce" was defined to include commerce within a State.

House.—The House amendment definitions of "State" and "commerce" were comparable to the Senate's definitions, except that the House did not treat certain possessions of the United States as States.

The House did not require consumer product safety standards to be "minimum" standards, and did not define "unreasonable risk of injury presented by a consumer product" or "use". The House defined the term "hazard" (which is used comparably to "injury" in the Senate bill) as a risk of death, personal injury, or serious or frequent illness.

The House amendment contained the following definitions not present in the Senate bill:

(1) "Manufacturer" was any person who manufactures or imports a consumer product.

(2) "Distributor" meant a person to whom a consumer product is delivered or sold for purposes of distribution in commerce, except that the term did not include a manufacturer or retailer of such product.

(3) "Retailer" was defined as a person to whom a consumer product is delivered or sold for purposes of sale or distribution by such person to a consumer.

(4) "Private labeler" was defined as the owner of a brand or trademark on the label of a consumer product which bears a private label. (A consumer product bears a private label under the House amendment if the product (or its container) is labeled with the brand or trademark of a person other than a manufacturer of the product, the person with whose brand or trademark the product (or container) is labeled has authorized or caused the product to be so labeled, and the brand or trademark of a manufacturer of such product does not appear on such label).

(5) "To distribute in commerce" and "distribution in commerce" meant to sell in commerce, to introduce or deliver for introduction into commerce, or to hold for sale or distribution after introduction into commerce.

(6) A common carrier, contract carrier, or freight forwarder was not, for purposes of the bill, deemed to be a manufacturer, distributor, or retailer of a consumer product solely by reason of receiving or transporting a consumer product in the ordinary course of its business as such a carrier or forwarder.

Conference substitute.—The Senate recedes with an amendment treating certain possessions of the United States as States.

CONSUMER PRODUCT SAFETY RULES

(1) Authority to prescribe consumer product safety standards

Senate.—The Senate bill authorized the Commissioner of the new Agency, whenever he found a need for action to eliminate unreasonable risk of injury or death associated with the use of a consumer product (or type or class thereof), to promulgate a consumer product safety standard for such product (or type or class). The Senate bill provided that standards, insofar as practicable, must be compatible with any Federal environmental standards established for the product. A standard must, where feasible, pertain to the safety performance characteristics of the product (or type or class), and it must, to the extent practicable, set forth test procedures to measure such performance characteristics, except that any such standard may apply to the composition, design, construction, or finish of the consumer product (or type or class) if the Commissioner determines that it is not feasible to protect the public health or safety by development of a performance standard or any other consumer product safety standard authorized by the foregoing provisions.

The Senate bill provided, in addition, that a consumer product safety standard may require that a consumer product (or type or class) be marked, tagged, or accompanied by clear and adequate warnings or instructions, or be subject to safety precautions related to physical distribution.

House.—Under the House amendment the Commission was authorized to prescribe consumer product safety standards containing the same type of performance, design, and labeling requirements as were envisaged by the Senate bill (except that there is no House provision for safety precautions relating to physical distribution). Any requirement of such standards had to be reasonably necessary to prevent or reduce an unreasonable hazard to the public associated with the product. Requirements (other than requirements relating to labeling, warnings, or instructions), whenever feasible, had to be expressed in terms of performance requirements.

Conference substitute (§ 7(*a*)).—The Senate recedes. The committee of conference is of the opinion that any safety problems created by methods of physical distribution can be met by a product safety standard related to the performance, composition, design, construction, or finish of a consumer product including packaging or, in appropriate cases, may be dealt with under the provisions of the substitute concerning imminent hazards [sec. 12].

(2) Commencement of standard-setting proceeding

Both the House and Senate versions provided that a proceeding to develop a consumer product safety standard be commenced by publication of a notice in the Federal Register containing certain information concerning the product hazard and an invitation to the public to participate in the standard-setting process.

Senate.—The Senate required the notice of proceeding to contain an invitation to the public to submit information challenging the need for the standard.

House.—The House amendment did not require the notice of proceeding to invite submission of information challenging the need for the standard, but did require the notice to specify a period during which public or private standard-setting organizations would be given an opportunity to develop a proposed standard. The period would be 150 days unless the Commission found a different period was appropriate.

Conference substitute (§ 7(*b*)).—The Senate recedes.

(3) Development of proposed standard

Senate.—The Senate bill provided that, unless he accepts an existing safety standard, the Administrator of the new agency could accept one or more offers from qualified offerors to develop a proposed standard. An offer could not be accepted if the offeror is a manufacturer, distributor, or retailer of a product to which the standard applies, or an employee of such a manufacturer, distributor, or retailer. The Senate permitted the Agency to proceed with development of a proposed standard whenever a notice of proceeding is published, even though the Agency accepted an offer to develop a standard.

House.—The House amendment differed from the Senate bill in that unless the Commission accepted an existing standard it was required to accept one or more offers from qualified offerors. The House did not prohibit acceptance of offers of offerors who were manufacturers, distributors, or retailers, or employees thereof.

The House also provided that if the Commission accepted an offer to develop a proposed consumer product safety standard, it could not, during the "development period" for the standard publish a proposed rule applicable to the same product hazard, or develop (or contract for the development of) proposals for the standard unless no offeror was making satisfactory progress. The "development period" was defined as a period beginning with the acceptance of an offer to develop the standard and ending (1) with the expiration of the period specified in the notice of proceeding (which period could be extended), (2) the date the Commission determines no offeror is able and willing to continue satisfactory development of the standard, or (3) on the date on which an offeror submits a recommended standard, whichever of the three first occurs.

Conference substitute (§ 7(*d*)).—The conference substitute is identical to the House amendment except that the Commission is permitted during the development period to proceed independently to develop proposals for a standard in any case in which the sole offeror whose offer is accepted is the manufacturer, distributor, or retailer of a consumer product proposed to be regulated by the consumer product safety standard. These provisions should not be interpreted, however, as preventing the Commission or its staff—while awaiting the submission of recommended standards—from developing or acquiring the technical capability necessary to properly evaluate the standards recommended to it.

(4) *Regulations governing offerors' development of standards*

Senate.—The provisions in the Senate bill relating to regulations applicable to offeror's development of proposed standards included requirements that interested persons be given an opportunity to participate in the development of the standard "in accordance with accepted standards of due process".

House.—No comparable provision.

Conference substitute (§ 7*d*)).—The Senate recedes.

(5) *Proposed consumer product safety rules*

Senate.—The Senate bill required the Agency, within 180 days after publication of a notice of proceeding (which period could be extended), to publish a proposed consumer product safety rule or withdraw the notice of proceedings. The Agency was specifically authorized to publish proposed rules in the alternative. The Agency was given authority to conduct a hearing on the proposed standard subject to conditions or limitations imposed by the Agency.

House.—The House amendment required publication of the proposed standard or withdrawal of notice of proceedings within 210 days (unless extended). The Commission was not specifically authorized to publish proposed rules in the alternative and was required to provide for an opportunity for oral and written presentation of views respecting the proposed rule.

Conference substitute (§ 7(*f*)).—The Senate recedes.

(6) Findings

Both the Senate bill and the House amendment required the new agency to make generally similar findings before finally promulgating a consumer product safety rule.

Senate.—The Senate bill required a finding respecting means of achieving the objective of the rule while minimizing adverse effects on competition or disruption or dislocation of manufacturing and other commercial practices consistent with the public health and safety.

House.—The House amendment required no comparable finding, but did require an additional finding that the rule be in the public interest.

Conference substitute (§ *9(c)*).—The conference substitute requires both the Senate finding, respecting competition and commercial practices, and the House finding that the rule be in the public interest.

(7) Effective date of standard

House.—The House amendment added a provision requiring that the effective date of a consumer product safety standard be set at least 30 days after the date of promulgation unless the Commission for good cause shown determines that an earlier effective date is in the public interest. In no case could the effective date be set at a date which is earlier than the date of promulgation. A consumer product safety standard could apply only to consumer products manufactured after the effective date of the standard. The provision described above did not apply to rules banning a product.

Senate.—No comparable provision.

Conference substitute (§ *9(d)* *(1)*.—The Senate recedes.

(8) Stockpiling

Senate.—The Senate bill prohibited any manufacturer or importer, in an effort to stockpile a consumer product, from producing or importing such product, between the time a final order establishing a consumer product safety standard is issued and the time the order becomes effective, in quantities significantly greater than quantities he had produced for a base period established by the new Agency prior to the promulgation of the final order establishing the standard.

House.—No comparable provision.

Conference substitute (§ *9(d)* *(2)*).—This provision of the Senate bill is incorporated in the conference report with technical and conforming changes. As so changed, it authorizes the Commission by rule to prohibit a manufacturer (including an importer) of a consumer product from stockpiling any product to which a consumer product safety rule applies so as to prevent the circumvention of the purpose of that rule. "Stockpiling" is defined as manufacturing or importing a product between the date of promulgation of the consumer product safety rule and its effective date at a rate which is significantly greater than the rate at which such product was produced or imported during a base period ending before the date of promulgation of the consumer product safety rule.

(9) Banned hazardous products

Both bills gave the new agency administrative authority to ban a consumer product if no feasible consumer product safety standard would adequately protect the public.

Senate.—The Senate bill included a provision requiring a person in the distribution chain to repurchase any product sold by him after a proposed rule banning a product was published. The obligation to repurchase was subject to certain limitations if notice of the proposed banning rule was given down the distribution chain.

House.—The House amendment contained no provision applicable only to repurchase of banned hazardous products. However, the notification and remedy provisions of the House amendment (sec. 15(d)) gave the Commission authority to impose somewhat similar requirements in the case of substantial product hazard. The House amendment also authorized a court, upon application of the Commission, to require repurchase of a banned hazardous product if the court found it to be an imminently hazardous product.

Conference substitute (§8).—The Senate provision on repurchase is not included in the conference report.

COMMISSION RESPONSIBILITY—PETITION BY INTERESTED PERSON

Senate.—The Senate bill contained two provisions permitting the public to seek initiation of agency action. The first provision generally permitted any individual or class of individuals who alleged that he or they have been exposed by an act or omission of the Agency to a food, drug, or consumer product presenting an unreasonable risk of injury or death, to petition the Agency to take specific action sufficient to eliminate the alleged unreasonable risk. After opportunity for comment, the Agency was required to determine whether an unreasonable risk of injury or death existed as a result of an act or omission of the Agency and issue a decision either refusing to take any action or taking action designed to eliminate any unreasonable risk of injury or death. If the Agency refused to take sufficient action to eliminate the alleged risk, the petitioner could bring a civil action in a United States Court of Appeals. If the court found, based upon a preponderance of the evidence in the Agency's record, that the Agency, by an act or omission, had exposed the petitioner to a food, drug, or consumer product presenting unreasonable risk of injury or death, the court was directed to remand the matter to the Agency for appropriate action. A civil action under this provision would not have been available for the purpose of requiring the Agency to permit the distribution, etc., of any food, drug, or consumer product, or to obtain money damages. Costs of the petition and civil action (including reasonable attorney's fees) would be apportioned to the parties as the interests of justice require.

The second provision of the Senate bill permitted any consumer or other interested party to petition the Commissioner of the new Agency to commence a proceeding for the issuance, amendment, or revocation of a consumer product safety standard or other action. The Commissioner was required to publish petitions in the Federal Register, to allow opportunity for comment, and, if he denied the petition, to publish his reasons therefor.

House.—The House amendment did not have a provision comparable to the first Senate provision described above, but did have one comparable to the second. However, this House provision permitted petitions only for consumer product safety rules (defined as safety standards or banning rules). The Commission was not required to allow opportunity for comment unless it decided to commence a rulemaking proceeding under the bill.

Conference substitute (§ *10*).—The conference substitute permits any interested person (including a consumer or consumer organization) to petition the Commission to commence a proceeding for the issuance, amendment, or revocation of a consumer product safety rule. The petition must be filed in the principal office of the Commission and must set forth (1) facts which it is claimed establish that a consumer product safety rule or an amendment or revocation thereof is necessary, and (2) a brief description of the substance of the rule or amendment thereof which it is claimed should be issued by the Commission. The Commission may hold a public hearing or may conduct such investigation or proceeding as it deems appropriate in order to determine whether or not the petition should be granted.

The Commission is required, within 120 days after filing of a petition described above to either grant or deny the petition. If the Commission grants such petition, it must promptly commence an appropriate proceeding under section 7 or 8 of the bill. If the Commission denies such petition it must publish in the Federal Register its reasons for such denial.

Subsection (e) of section 10 of the conference substitute provides that if the Commission denies a petition made under this section (or if it fails to grant or deny the petition within the 120 day period) the petitioner may commence a civil action in a United States District Court to compel the Commission to initiate a proceeding to take the action requested. Any such action must be filed within 60 days after the Commission's denial of the petition, or (if the Commission fails to grant or deny the petition within 120 days after filing the petition) within 60 days after the expiration of the 120 day period. If the petitioner can demonstrate to the satisfaction of the court, by a preponderance of evidence in a de novo proceeding before the court, that the consumer product presents an unreasonable risk of injury, and that the failure of the Commission to initiate a rulemaking proceeding under section 7 or 8 of the bill unreasonably exposes the petitioner or other consumers to a risk of injury presented by the consumer product, the court is required to order the Commission to initiate the action requested by the petitioner. In a civil action authorized by subsection (e), the court will have no authority to compel the Commission to take any action other than the initiation of a rulemaking proceeding in accordance with section 7 or 8 of the bill. The judicial remedy under subsection (e) applies only with respect to petitions filed more than 3 years after the date of enactment of the bill.

The remedies under section 10 of the conference substitute are in addition to, and not in lieu of, other administrative and judicial remedies provided by law. Section 10 does not authorize the petitioner to recover damages from the Commission or any of its employees.

JUDICIAL REVIEW

Both bills had a provision for pre-enforcement judicial review, under the "substantial evidence" rule, of certain regulations prescribed under the bill.

Senate.—The Senate's provision applied to the following types of rules: consumer product safety standards, banning rules, rules applicable to standards development, rules requiring manufacturers to conduct safety analyses, and rules relating to compliance testing.

The Senate bill permitted the court in its discretion to award the manufacturer of a product declared a banned hazardous consumer product, damages, interest, and the cost of suit, including reasonable attorney fees, for actual damages suffered by him as a result of any banning order of the new Agency if the court determined that the order constituted an abuse of the discretion granted under the bill.

House.—The House judicial review provision applied only to consumer product safety rules. It contained no provision for awarding damages and attorneys fees to manufacturers. It contained a provision, not present in the Senate bill, authorizing the court under certain circumstances to order the Commission to conduct proceedings for additional presentations of data, views, or arguments.

Conference substitute (§ *11*).—The Senate recedes.

IMMINENT HAZARDS

Senate.—The Senate bill provided for initiation of judicial proceedings against any imminently hazardous consumer product, and against any manufacturer, importer, or seller of such a product. "Immediately hazardous consumer product" was defined as a consumer product presenting an unreasonable risk of injury or death which requires action to protect adequately the public health and safety prior to the completion of administrative proceedings under the bill. The Senate provision had no specific provision for seizure of an imminently hazardous product.

House.—The House amendment provided for initiation of judicial proceedings against any imminently hazardous consumer product and against any manufacturer (including importer), distributor, or retailer of the product. "Imminently hazardous consumer product" was defined as a consumer product which persents imminent and unreasonable risk of death, serious illness, or severe personal injury. The House provision specifically authorized the court to order seizure of such a product, and also contained provisions relating to venue, process and subpenas, and to multidistrict litigation. The Commission was authorized (but not required) to request the recommendations of the Product Safety Advisory Council (established under the bill) before commencing an action under the imminent hazard provision.

Conference substitute (§ *12*).—The Senate recedes.

SAFETY ANALYSIS; NEW PRODUCTS

Senate.—The Senate bill authorized the new Agency (where applicable) to require by regulation that a consumer product not subject to a consumer product safety standard (or type, class, or component thereof) be subjected to a detailed safety analysis in accordance with regulations of the Agency.

House.—The House amendment had no provision specifically authorizing the Commission to require a safety analysis. However, the House version contained a provision not present in the Senate bill requiring notification to the Commission respecting new products. The Commission could, by rule, prescribe procedures for the purpose of insuring that the manufacturer of any new consumer product furnish notice and a description of such product to the Commission before its distribution in commerce. "New consumer product" was defined as a consumer product which incorporates a design, material, or form of energy exchange which (1) has not previously been used substantially in consumer products and (2) as to which there exists a lack of information adequate to determine the safety of such product in use by consumers. The House amendment also authorized the Commission to require any manufacturer to provide to the Commission such performance and technical data related to performance and safety as may be required to carry out the purposes of the Act.

Conference substitute (§ *13*, *27*(*e*)).—The Senate recedes.

PRODUCT CERTIFICATION

Senate.—The Senate bill required any manufacturer, importer, or distributor of a consumer product subject to a consumer product safety standard to furnish to the distributor or dealer at the time of delivery of such consumer product certification that each such consumer product conforms to all applicable consumer product safety standards. Any certification had to be based upon test procedures prescribed in the standards or (if none are prescribed) upon a reasonable testing program approved by the Agency.

The Senate bill directed the new Agency to conduct (or contract for) compliance testing of consumer products subject to consumer product safety standards. Manufacturers and importers of consumer products subject to standards were required to furnish a reasonable number of such products (drawn from regular production runs) without cost to the Agency upon request. The product tested would be returned to the manufacturer or importer upon the completion of any compliance testing, but the manufacturer or importer, in any subsequent sale or lease of the product, would have to disclose that it had been subjected to compliance testing.

The Senate bill also provided that whenever the new Agency had good cause to believe that a particular manufacturer was producing a consumer product with a significant incidence of noncompliance with a particular consumer product safety standard; it could require the manufacturer to submit a description of his relevant quality control procedures; and if the Agency determined that the noncompliance was attributable to the inadequacy of the manufacturer's control procedures, it could, after an adjudicatory hearing, order the manufacturer to revise his quality control procedures to the extent necessary to remedy the inadequacy.

House.—The House's certification provision was generally similar to the Senate's, except that the requirement to provide the certificate applied only to manufacturers and private labelers. The certificate was required to accompany the product and to be based on a test of each product or upon a reasonable testing program. In cases where more than one person was required to certify any given product, the Commission could designate one or more of them as subject to the requirement and relieve the others of the requirement. The Commission could by rule prescribe reasonable testing programs for products subject to a standard.

The House amendment authorized the Commission, for purposes of carrying out the bill, to purchase any consumer product and to require any manufacturer, distributor, or retailer of a consumer product to sell the product to the Commission at manufacturer's, distributor's, or retailer's cost.

The House amendment authorized product testing, but did not *require* the Commission to conduct compliance testing activities and did not expressly authorize it to order manufacturers to revise their quality control procedures.

Conference substitute (*§ 14*).—The Senate recedes.

PRODUCT LABELING

House.—The House amendment authorized the Commission by rule to require the use and prescribe the form and content of labels containing the date and place of manufacture of a consumer product, and a suitable identification of the manufacturer of the consumer product (unless the product bears a private label in which case the label must identify the manufacturer by code and also identify the private labeler). If the product is subject to a consumer product safety rule, the rule under this provision may require the label to certify that the product meets all applicable standards and to specify the applicable standards. These labels, where practicable, could be required by the Commission to be permanently marked on or affixed to the consumer product. The Commission could permit any information as to date and place of manufacture and name of manufacturer to be coded.

Senate.—The Senate bill contained no comparable provision.

Conference substitute (*§ 14*).—The Senate recedes.

NOTIFICATION AND REPAIR, REPLACEMENT, OR REFUND

(*1*) *Notification by manufacturer to agency*

Senate.—The Senate bill required every manufacturer, importer, or distributor of, or dealer in, a consumer product who discovers that such product has a defect which relates to the safety of use of such product or that such product fails to comply with an applicable consumer safety standard to immediately notify the new Agency of the defect or failure to comply if such product has left the place of manufacture.

House.—The House amendment required every manufacturer of a consumer product distributed in commerce, and every distributor and retailer of such product, who obtains information which reasonably supports the conclusion that the product fails to comply with an applicable consumer product safety rule, or contains a product defect which could create a substantial hazard to the public, to immediately inform the Commission of such failure to comply or of such defect, unless such manufacturer, distributor, or retailer has actual knowledge that the Commission has been adequately informed of such defect of failure to comply.

Conference substitute (*§ 15*(*b*)).—The Senate recedes.

(*2*) *Notification by manufacturer to public*

Senate.—The Senate bill provided that if a consumer product fails to comply with an applicable order issued under the regulatory provisions of the bill and thereby presents an unreasonable risk or injury or death or has a defect which causes it to present an unreasonable risk of injury or death, the manufacturer, importer, or distributor of, or dealer in, such product could be required by the Agency (by order after an adjudicatory hearing) to give public notice and to mail to consumers and certain persons in the distribution chain notification containing information required by the Agency.

House.—The House amendment authorized the Commission, if it determined (after affording an opportunity for a hearing) that a product distributed in commerce presents a substantial product hazard and that notification is required in order to adequately protect the public from such substantial product hazard, to order the manufacturer or any distributor or retailer of the product to take any one or more of the following actions:

(A) To give public notice of the defect or failure to comply.

(B) To mail notice to each person who is a manufacturer, distributor, or retailer of such product.

(C) To mail notice to every person to whom the person required to give notice knows such product was delivered or sold.

Any such order shall specify the form and content of the notice.

The House bill defined "substantial product hazard" for purposes of the notification and remedy provision of the bill as a failure to comply with an applicable consumer product safety rule which creates a substantial hazard to the public, or a product defect which (because of the pattern of defect, the number of defective products distributed in commerce, the severity of the risk, or otherwise) creates a substantial hazard to the public.

Conference substitute (§ *15*(*a*) *and* (*c*)).—The Senate recedes.

(*3*) *Repair, replacement, or refund*

Senate.—The Senate bill provided that in any case in which the Agency could order the manufacturer, importer, dealer, or distributor to notify the public of a defect or failure to comply, it could also require him to bring such product into conformity with the requirements of such order without charge to the consumer, or to either replace such product with a like or equivalent consumer product which complies with such order without charge to the consumer or to refund the purchase price of such product upon its tender, whichever option is elected by the manufacturer, importer, distributor, or dealer whose product fails to comply. If an election is made to refund the purchase price, the price shall be less a reasonable allowance for use, if such product has been in the possession of the consumer for more than one year at the time of tender.

House.—The comparable provision of the House amendment authorized the Commission, if it determined (after affording an opportunity for a hearing) that a product distributed in commerce presents a substantial product hazard and that action under this provision would be in the public interest, to order the manufacturer or any distributor or retailer of such product to take whichever of the following actions the person to whom the order is directed elects—

(1) to bring the product into conformity with the requirements of the applicable consumer product safety rule or to repair the defect in such product;

(2) to replace the product with a like or equivalent product which complies with the applicable consumer product safety rule or which does not contain the defect; or

(3) to refund the purchase price of the product (less a reasonable allowance for use, if such product has been in the possession of a consumer for one year or more (A) at the time of public

notice under subsection (c), or (B) at the time the consumer receives actual notice of the defect or noncompliance, whichever first occurs).

An order under this provision could also require the person to whom it applies to submit a plan, satisfactory to the Commission, for taking action under whichever of the foregoing paragraphs the person elected. The Commission would specify in the order the persons to whom refunds must be made if the person to whom the order is directed elects to take the action described in paragraph (3). If an order under this provision is directed to more than one person, the Commission shall specify which person has the election under this provision.

Conference substitute (§ *15(d)*).—The Senate recedes.

(4) *Reimbursement*

Senate.—The Senate required any manufacturer, importer, distributor, or dealer against whom an order is issued under the provisions relating to repair, replacement, etc., to reimburse each consumer of the product which is the subject of such order for any reasonable and foreseeable expenses (including transportation expenses) incurred by such consumer in availing himself of the remedies provided by the order.

House.—The House amendment provided that no charge shall be made to any person (other than a manufacturer, distributor, or retailer) who avails himself of any remedy provided under a repair, replacement, or refund order, and the person subject to the order shall reimburse each person (other than a manufacturer, distributor, or retailer) who is entitled to such a remedy for any reasonable and foreseeable expenses incurred by such person in availing himself of such remedy. In addition, the House provided that any order issued under the notification, and repair, replacement, or refund section may require any person who is a manufacturer, distributor, or retailer of the product to reimburse any other person who is a manufacturer, distributor, or retailer of such product for such other person's expenses in connection with carrying out the order, if the Commission determines such reimbursement to be in the public interest.

Conference substitute (§ *15(e)*).—The Senate recedes.

(5) *Hearings*

Senate.—The Senate bill required full adjudicatory hearings under section 554 of title 5, United States Code in proceeding to order notification or replacement, refund, or repair.

House.—The House provided that a notification order or a replacement, refund, or repair order may be issued only after an opportunity for a hearing in accordance with section 554 of title 5, United States Code, except that, if the Commission determines that any person who wishes to participate in such hearing is a part of a class of participants who share an identity of interest, the Commission may limit such person's participation in such hearing to participation through a single representative designated by such class (or by the Commission if such class fails to designate such a representative).

Conference substitute (§ *15(f)*).—The Senate recedes.

Inspection and Recordkeeping

Both bills had provisions dealing with inspection and recordkeeping.

Senate.—The Senate bill provided that a separate written notice was to be given for each inspection, but a notice was not required for each entry made during the period of inspection set forth in the notice. If the officer or employee who made the inspection obtained any sample in the course thereof, he was, prior to leaving the premises, to give to the owner, operator, or agent in charge, a receipt therefor describing the sample.

The Senate bill further provided that the district courts of the United States were to have jurisdiction to issue any warrant in aid of an inspection or investigation, if the warrant was required by the Constitution or laws of the United States, upon a finding that the inspection or investigation was for the purpose of enforcing the bill's provisions.

The Senate bill also authorized the Commissioner to establish, by order at any time, procedures to be followed by manufacturers or importers of a consumer product required to conform to a consumer product safety standard, including procedures to be followed by distributors, dealers and consumers to assist manufacturers or importers in securing and maintaining the names and addresses of the first purchasers (other than dealers or distributors) of consumer products for which consumer product safety standards had been promulgated. These procedures were to be reasonable for the particular type or class of consumer products for which they were prescribed. In determining whether to require the maintenance of the names and addresses of the first purchasers, the Commissioner was to consider the severity of the injury that could have resulted if a consumer product had not been manufactured in compliance with an applicable consumer product safety standard, the likelihood that a particular type or class of consumer products would not have been manufactured in compliance with an applicable consumer product safety standard, and the burden imposed upon the manufacturer or importer by requiring the maintenance of the names and addresses of the first purchasers (including the cost to consumers of the maintenance).

House.—The House inspection and recordkeeping provisions did not contain any specific provisions similar to the above Senate provisions and its recordkeeping provision was applicable to every manufacturer, private labeler, or distributor of a consumer product, whether or not required to conform to a consumer public safety standard. However, the House amendment did authorize the Commission to require by rule manufacturers, private labelers, and distributors to establish and maintain such records as may be required to implement the Act.

Conference substitute (§ *16*).—The Senate recedes.

IMPORTED PRODUCTS

Senate.—The Senate bill provided that any consumer product imported into the United States to which a consumer product safety standard applied or which was declared a banned or imminently hazardous consumer product, was not to be delivered from Customs custody except as provided in section 499 of the Tariff Act of 1930. In the event an imported consumer product was delivered from Customs custody under bond, as provided in section 499 of the Tariff Act of 1930, and was declared a banned or imminently hazardous consumer product or failed to conform with a consumer product safety standard in effect on the date of entry of the merchandise, the Administrator was to inform the Secretary of the Treasury, and unless it appeared to the Administrator that the product could have been brought into compliance with all applicable requirements was to request the Secretary of the Treasury to demand redelivery. Upon a failure to redeliver, the Secretary of the Treasury was to assert a claim for liquidated damages for breach of a condition of the bond arising out of the failure to conform or redeliver in accordance with regulations prescribed by the Secretary of the Treasury or his delegate. When asserting a claim for liquidated damages against an importer for failure to redeliver such nonconforming goods, the liquidated damages were not to be less than 10 per centum of the value of the nonconforming merchandise if, within five years prior thereto, the importer had previously been assessed liquidated damages for failure to redeliver nonconforming goods in response to a demand from the Secretary of the Treasury.

Destruction of products which failed to comply to regulations under this bill took place within ninety days after notice to the importer or consignee.

House.—The House amendment provided that any consumer product offered for importation into the customs territory of the United States (as defined in general headnote 2 to the Tariff Schedules of the United States) was to be refused admission into this customs territory if the product failed to comply with an applicable consumer product safety rule, was not accompanied by a certificate labeled in accordance with regulations under section 14 of the House amendment, was or had been determined to be an imminently hazardous consumer product in a proceeding brought under section 12 of the House amendment, had a product defect which constituted a substantial product hazard, or was a product which was manufactured by a person who the Commission has informed the Secretary of the Treasury is in violation of the inspection or recordkeeping requirements of the House amendment.

All actions taken by an owner or consignee to modify the product were subject to the supervision of an officer or employee of the Commission and of the Department of the Treasury and if it appeared to the Commission that the product could not be modified or that the owner or consignee was not proceeding satisfactorily to modify the product it was to be refused admission into the customs territory of the United States, and the Commission could direct the Secretary to demand redelivery of the product into customs custody, and to seize the product if was not redelivered.

The House amendment further provided that products refused admission into the customs territory of the United States had to be exported, except that upon application, the Secretary of the Treasury could have permitted the destruction of the product in lieu of exportation. If the owner or consignee did not export the product within a reasonable time, the Department of the Treasury could have destroyed the product.

Under the House amendment, the Commission was allowed to, by rule, condition the importation of a consumer product on the manufacturer's compliance with inspection and recordkeeping requirements and rules of the Commission with respect to these requirements.

Conference substitute (§ *17*).—The Senate recedes.

PROHIBITED ACTS

Both bills contained similar provisions dealing with prohibited acts, and, in particular, they prohibited manufacture, distribution, etc. of consumer products which do not comply with a consumer product safety rule.

Senate.—The Senate bill contained provisions making it unlawful for any person engaged in the business of making consumer products available to consumers, either directly or indirectly, to fail or refuse to comply with any requirement as to the Senate bill's compliance section (dealing with quality control procedures, names of first purchases, compliance testing, and certification) and stockpiling section, to alter, modify, destroy, or remove any poition of, or do any other act with respect to, a consumer product or labeling thereon or attached thereto, if the act is done while the product is being held or transported for sale, and results in the consumer product or its labeling failing to conform to a consumer product safety standard, or renders the product a banned or imminently hazardous consumer product, to fail to provide to the Director of the National Injury Information Clearinghouse the information concerning injuries, or to fail to provide any required safety analysis.

House.—The House amendment made it unlawful for any person to fail or refuse to permit access to or copying of records, fail to furnish information respecting a substantial product defect, fail to furnish a certificate or issue a false certificate if the person in the exercise of due care has reason to know that the certificate is false or misleading in any material respect, or fail to comply with any rule relating to labeling.

The House amendment further provided that the unlawful acts of manufacturing for sale, offering for sale, distributing in commerce, or importing into the United States any consumer product which was not in conformity with an applicable consumer product safety standard or manufacturing for sale, offering for sale, distributing in commerce, or importing into the United States any consumer product which had been declared a banned hazardous product by a rule were not to apply to any person who held a certificate to the effect that the consumer product conformed to all applicable consumer product safety rules, unless the person knew that the consumer product did not conform, or relied in good faith on the representation of the manufacturer or a distributor of the product that the product was not subject to an applicable product safety rule.

Conference substitute (*§ 19*).—The conference substitute incorporates the provisions of the House bill with a conforming amendment making violations of the Commission's stockpiling rules under section 9(d)(2) a prohibited act.

CIVIL PENALTIES

Senate.—The Senate bill stated that whoever knowingly committed any act prohibited in its prohibited acts section, or, in case of commission of any act so enumerated in the Senate bill's prohibited act section by a corporation, the corporation and any individual director, officer, or agent of the corporation who knowingly caused in whole or in part the corporation to commit the act, were to be subject to a civil penalty of not more than $10,000 for each act which was to accrue to the United States and could have been recovered in a civil action brought by the United States or the Agency in its own name by any of its attorneys designated by the Administrator for that purpose. "Knowingly" was defined in the Senate bill to include knowledge of the probable consequences of action taken in disregard of reasonable safeguards.

House.—The House amendment provided that any person who knowingly violated the prohibited acts section of the House amendment was to be subject to a civil penalty not to exceed $2,000 for each violation. A violation of section 19(a) (1), (2), (4), (5), or (6) was to constitute a separate violation with respect to each consumer product involved, except that the maximum civil penalty was not to exceed $500,000 for any related series of violations. A violation of section 19 (a) (3) was to constitute a separate violation with respect to each failure or refusal to allow or perform an act required; and this violation was a continuing one, each day of the violation was to constitute a separate offense, except that the maximum civil penalty was not to exceed $500,000 for any related series of violations.

The House amendment further provided that the second sentence of the above paragraph did not apply to violations of paragraph (1) or (2) of section 19(a) of the House amendment if the person who violated these paragraphs was not the manufacturer or private labeler or a distributor of the product involved, and if the person did not have either actual knowledge that his distribution or sale of the product violated these paragraphs or notice from the Commission that the distribution or sale would have been a violation of these paragraphs.

Any civil penalty under the House amendment was authorized to be compromised by the Commission. In determining the amount of the penalty or whether it should have been remitted or mitigated and in what amount, the appropriateness of the penalty to the size of the business of the person charged and the gravity of the violation were to be considered. The amount of the penalty when finally determined, or the amount agreed on compromise, could have been deducted from any sums owing by the United States to the person charged.

Conference substitute (*§ 20*).—The Senate recedes.

CRIMINAL PENALTIES

Senate.—The Senate bill provided that whoever knowingly committed any act prohibited by the prohibited acts section of the Senate bill, or, in case of commission of any prohibited act described in the prohibited act section of the Senate bill by a corporation, the corporation and any individual director, officer, or agent of a corporation who knowingly caused in whole or in part the corporation to commit the act, and, if the act had been willfully committed, was to be guilty of a misdemeanor and, upon conviction, fined not more than $10,000 for each such act or imprisoned not more than one year, or both. "Knowingly" was defined to include knowledge of the probable consequences of action taken in disregard of reasonable safeguards.

House.—The House amendment provided that any person who knowingly and willfully violated the prohibited acts section of the House amendment after having received notice of noncompliance from the Commission was to be fined not more than $50,000 or be imprisoned not more than one year, or both. Any individual director, officer, or agent of the corporation who knowingly and willfully authorized, ordered, or performed any of the acts or practices constituting in whole or in part a violation of the prohibited acts section and who had knowledge of notice of noncompliance received by the corporation from the Commission would be subject to criminal penalties under this section.

Conference substitute (§ *21*).—The Senate recedes.

INJUNCTIONS

Senate.—The Senate bill provided that upon application by the Administrator or the Attorney General, the district courts of the United States were to have jurisdiction to enjoin the commission of acts prohibited by prohibited acts section of the Senate bill, and to compel the taking of any action required by the Senate bill.

House.—The House amendment provided that the United States district courts were to have jurisdiction to restrain any violation of the prohibited acts section of the House amendment, or to restrain any person from distributing in commerce a product which does not comply with a consumer product safety rule, or both. These actions were authorized to be brought by the Attorney General, on request of the Commission, in any United States district court for a district wherein any act, omission, or transaction constituting the violation had occurred, or in the court for the district wherein the defendant was found or transacted business. In any injunctive action process could have been served on a defendant in any other district in which the defendant resided or could have been found.

Conference substitute (§ *21*(*a*)).—The Senate recedes with a conforming amendment.

SEIZURE

Senate.—The Senate bill provided that any consumer product which was not manufactured in compliance with an applicable consumer product safety standard, or which was not in compliance with such a standard as the result of altering, modifying, destroying, or removing any portion of, or doing any other act with respect to, a consumer product or labeling thereon or attached thereto, if the act was done while the product was being held or transported for sale, and resulted in the consumer product or its labeling failing to conform to a consumer product safety standard, or rendered the product a banned or imminently hazardous consumer product, or which was declared a banned or imminently hazardous consumer product, was to be liable to be proceeded against while in commerce or at any time thereafter, on complaint for forfeiture by the Administrator, and condemned in any district court of the United States within whose district the consumer product was found.

House.—The House amendment provided that any consumer product which failed to conform to an applicable consumer product safety rule when introduced into or while in commerce or while held for sale after shipment in commerce was to be liable to be proceeded against on libel of information and condemned in any United States district court within the jurisdiction of which the consumer product was found. Proceedings in cases instituted under this authority was to conform as nearly as possible to proceedings in rem in admiralty. Whenever these proceedings involving identical consumer products were pending in courts of two or more judicial districts they were to be consolidated for trial by order of any of these courts upon application reasonably made by any party in interest upon notice to all other parties in interest.

Conference substitute (§ *21*(*b*)).—The Senate recedes with amendments permitting the commission's attorneys with the concurrence of the Attorney General to represent the Commission in seizure proceedings, and allowing consolidation where proceedings involved "substantially similar" products, rather than "identical" products as in the House amendment.

PRIVATE ENFORCEMENT OF PRODUCT SAFETY RULES AND OTHER PROVISIONS

Both the Senate and the House bills had similar provisions for private suits for enforcement of consumer product safety rules and certain other requirements.

Senate.—The Senate bill provided that any person who could have been exposed to unreasonable risk of injury or death presented by a consumer product was authorized to bring an action to enforce a consumer product safety standard, or to enforce any order with respect to a banned hazardous consumer product under section 306(f) of the Senate bill, to enforce any order with respect to an imminently hazardous product under section 311 of the Senate bill, and to obtain the appropriate injunctive relief. The court could have awarded reasonable attorney's fees to the prevailing party.

House.—The House amendment provided that any interested person may bring an action to enforce a consumer product safety rule or to enforce any order relating to notification and repair, replacement, or refund under section 15 of the House amendment, and to obtain appropriate injunctive relief. The court could under certain conditions award costs of the suit, including reasonable attorney's fees, to the prevailing party.

Conference substitute.—The Senate recedes.

EFFECT ON PRIVATE REMEDIES

Senate.—The Senate bill contained a provision stating that compliance with any consumer product safety standard did not exempt any person from any liability under common law.

House.—The House bill contained a provision stating that compliance with consumer product safety rules or other rules or orders were not to relieve any person from liability at common law or under State law to any other person, and the failure of the Commission to take any action or commence a proceeding with respect to the safety of a consumer product was not to be admissible in evidence in litigation at common law or under State law relating to such consumer product.

The House bill further provided that—

(1) subject to the confidentiality requirements of section 6(a)(2) of the House amendment but notwithstanding 6(a)(1), accident and investigation reports made by any officer, employee, or agent of the Commission were to be available for use in any civil, criminal, or other judicial proceeding arising out of the accident,

and any officer, employee, or agent could have been required to testify in proceedings as to the facts developed in the investigations, and

(2) subject to section 6(a)(2) and 6(b) but notwithstanding section 6(a)(1), any accident or investigation report made by an officer or employee of the Commission was to be made available to the public in a manner which will not identify any injured person or any person treating him, without the consent of the person so identified, and all reports on research projects, demonstration projects, and other related activities were to be public information.

Conference substitute. (§ *25*).—The House provisions, other than the provisions described in paragraph (1) above are included in the conference substitute.

EFFECT ON STATE LAW

House.—The House amendment provided that whenever a Federal consumer product safety standard is in effect and applies to a hazard associated with a consumer product, no State or political subdivision of a State could either establish or continue in effect any provision of a safety standard or regulation which prescribes any requirements as to the performance, composition, contents, design, finish, construction, packaging, or labeling of such product which are designed to deal with the same hazard associated with such consumer product; unless such requirements are identical to the requirements of the Federal standards. This provision also provided that it should not be construed to prevent the Federal Government or the government of any State or political subdivision thereof from establishing a safety requirement applicable to a consumer product for its own use if such requirement imposes a higher standard of performance than that required to comply with the otherwise applicable Federal standard.

This provision also provided that upon application of a State or political subdivision thereof, the Commission by rule, after notice and opportunity for oral presentation of views, could exempt these preemption provisions (under such conditions as it may impose) a proposed safety standard or regulation described in the application, where the proposed standard or regulation (1) imposes a higher level of performance than the Federal standard, (2) is required by compelling local conditions, and (3) does not unduly burden interstate commerce.

Senate.—The Senate bill was generally similar except that the exemptive authority was not required to be exercised by rule, and a State or political subdivision to qualify for an exemption and to adopt its standard pursuant to procedures and requirements which in the judgment of the Agency were substantially comparable to those prescribed for Federal consumer product safety standards.

Conference substitute. The Senate recedes.

PRODUCT SAFETY ADVISORY COUNCIL

House.—The House bill provided that the Commission would establish a Product Safety Advisory Council which it could have consulted before prescribing a consumer product safety rule or taking other action under the House bill. The Council was to be appointed by the Commission and was to be composed of fifteen members, each of whom was to be qualified by training and experience in one or more of the fields applicable to the safety of products within the jurisdiction of the Commission. The Council was to be constituted of five members selected from governmental agencies including Federal, State, and local governments, five members selected from consumer product industries including at least one representative of small business, and five members selected from among consumer organizations, community organizations, and recognized consumer leaders. The Council was to meet at the call of the Commission, but not less often than four times during each calendar year.

The House bill gave the Council authority to propose consumer product safety rules to the Commission for its consideration and to function through subcommittees of its members. All proceedings of the Council were to be public, and a record of each proceeding was to be available for public inspection.

The House bill further provided that members of the Council who were not officers or employees of the United States were, while attending meetings or conferences of the Council or while otherwise engaged in the business of the Council, to be entitled to receive compensation at a rate fixed by the Commission, not exceeding the daily equivalent of the annual rate of basic pay in effect for grade GS–18 of the General Schedule, including traveltime, and while away from their homes or regular places of business they would have been allowed travel expenses, including per diem in lieu of subsistence, as authorized by section 5703 of title 5, United States Code. These payments were not to render members of the Council officers or employees of the United States for any purpose.

Senate.—The Senate bill had general authority to establish advisory committees.

Conference substitute (§ 28).—The House provision is incorporated in the conference report.

AMENDMENTS TO OTHER LAWS

FEDERAL FOOD, DRUG, AND COSMETIC ACT AMENDMENTS

Senate.—The Senate bill amended section 602 of the Federal Food, Drug, and Cosmetic Act to provide that a cosmetic is to be considered misbranded unless its label conspicuously sets forth the common or usual name of the cosmetic substance and that of each of its ingredients, subject to exemptions which may be prescribed by the Secretary of Health, Education, and Welfare, and sets forth adequate warnings against use where its use might be dangerous to health. Section 201 of that Act was also amended so as to include "soap" within the definition of cosmetics, and thereby subject soap to the provisions of that Act.

House.—No comparable provision.

Conference substitute.—The Senate recedes.

FEDERAL HAZARDOUS SUBSTANCES ACT

Senate.—The Senate bill amended the Federal Hazardous Substances Act to establish a new procedure under which possibly toxic or corrosive substances to be used around a household or by children would be subjected to screening tests for toxicity and corrosiveness before being distributed commercially. Those substances which the tests indicated were toxic or corrosive were to be registered with the Secretary of Health, Education, and Welfare, together with a description of the substance, the results of the tests, and the proper antidote or treatment for any injury or illness which might result from contact or use. Such substances were to be assigned a registration number which was to appear on the label of any container of the toxic or corrosive substances. The Secretary of Health, Education, and Welfare was to establish an office through which the registered information would be available at all times for medical treatment purposes. In other amendments to that Act, the Senate bill provided that any substance registered with the Secretary under the Act, which failed to bear its registration number on the label of its container, was a misbranded hazardous substance; that foods, drugs, and cosmetics regulated under the Federal Food, Drug and Cosmetic Act and fuels in containers, used around a house in heating, cooking, or refrigeration, were to be covered under the Federal Hazardous Substances Act (present law explicitly excludes them from the definition of hazardous substances) that failure to conduct the required screening tests was a prohibited act under the Federal Hazardous Substances Act; and that employees of the Department of Health, Education, and Welfare were authorized to enter factories, warehouses, and other establishments to inspect and copy screening test results.

House.—No similar specific provision.

Conference substitute.—The Senate recedes.

FEDERAL CAUSTIC POISON ACT

Senate.—The Senate bill repealed the Federal Caustic Poison Act.

House.—No comparable provision.

Conference substitute.—The Senate recedes.

AUTHORIZATION OF APPROPRIATIONS

Senate.—The Senate bill authorized the appropriation of $250,000,000 for fiscal 1973, $300,000,000 for fiscal 1974, and $350,000,000 for fiscal 1975. The authorization limited the expenditure of appropriated funds by providing that no funds appropriated to carry out the bill could be expended to plan, design, or construct any research or testing facility unless that expenditure was specifically authorized by law. The Senate authorization included sums necessary to carry out the Agency's regulation of foods, drugs, medical devices, and cosmetics, as well as consumer products.

House.—The House amendment authorized the appropriation of $55,000,000 for fiscal 1973, $59,000,000 for fiscal 1974, and $64,000,000 for fiscal 1975. No amount appropriated under that authorization could be expended for the planning or construction of research, development, or testing facilities. A separate provision authorized the appropriation of such sums as might be necessary for the planning and construction of such facilities, subject to the limitation that no appropriation might be made for any such planning or construction involving an expenditure of more than $100,000 unless that planning or construction had been approved by resolutions adopted by the

House Interstate and Foreign Commerce Committee and the Senate Commerce Committee.

Conference substitute.—The Senate recedes.

Effective Dates

Senate.—Section 119 of the Senate bill provided a general effective date of 90 days after the date on which the Administrator of the Agency first took office, or on such earlier date as the President might prescribe. Officers could be appointed at any time after the date of enactment of the proposed Act. Section 401 of the bill provided that the amendments made by that section to section 602 of the Federal Food, Drug, and Cosmetic Act were to take effect 1 year after the date of enactment of the proposed Act. Section 508 of the bill provided that the provisions in title V, amending the Federal Hazardous Substances Act, and repealing the Federal Caustic Poison Act, were to take effect 180 days after the date of enactment of the proposed Act. The Secretary of Health, Education, and Welfare was authorized to delay the applicability of the changes in law, made by the amendments to the Federal Hazardous Substances Act, to any person in any case in which he determined that the delay was necessary to allow sufficient time for testing and registration of the hazardous substances manufactured, compounded, or processed by that person.

House.—The House amendment provided that the proposed Act would become effective on the sixtieth day after the date of enactment, except for sections 4 (relating to the establishment of the Consumer Product Safety Commission) and 32 (relating to the authorization of appropriations) which were to take effect on the date of enactment of the proposed Act, and section 30 (relating to transfers of functions) which was to take effect 150 days after the date of enactment of the proposed Act or on the date on which at least 3 members of the Commission first took office, whichever was later.

Conference substitute (§ 34).—The Senate recedes.

Harley O. Staggers,
John E. Moss,
W. S. (Bill) Stuckey, Jr.,
Bob Eckhardt,
William L. Springer,
James T. Broyhill,
John Ware,
Managers on the Part of the House.

Warren G. Magnuson,
John O. Pastore,
Frank E. Moss,
Abraham Ribicoff,
Edward M. Kennedy,
Norris Cotton,
Marlow W. Cook,
Charles H. Percy,
Jacob K. Javits,
Managers on the Part of the Senate.

APPENDIX K

STATEMENT OF HOUSE CONFEREES

(from the Congressional Record for October 13, 1972, starting at page H 9908)

CONFERENCE REPORT ON S. 3419, CONSUMER PRODUCT SAFETY ACT

Mr. STAGGERS. Mr. Speaker, I call up the conference report on the Senate bill (S. 3419) to protect consumers against unreasonable risk of injury from hazardous products, and for other purposes, and ask unanimous consent that the statement of the managers be read in lieu of the report.

The Clerk read the title of the bill.

The SPEAKER. Is there objection to the request of the gentleman from West Virginia?

There was no objection.

The Clerk read the statement.

(For conference report and statement, see proceedings of the House of October 12, 1972.)

Mr. STAGGERS (during the reading). Mr. Speaker, I ask unanimous consent that further reading of the statement of the managers be dispensed with.

The SPEAKER. Is there objection to the request of the gentleman from West Virginia?

There was no objection.

Mr. STAGGERS. Mr. Speaker, with relatively few substantive amendments, the committee of conference has agreed to accept the House bill. Let me comment briefly on the most significant matters agreed to in conference.

As the Members will recall, the House bill proposed to establish a new independent regulatory commission with comprehensive authority to protect consumers from hazardous products. The House bill did not disturb the Food and Drug Administration's authority over foods, drugs, medical devices, or cosmetics. The Senate bill went much further. Under its terms the Food and Drug Administration would have been abolished and its responsibilities entirely transferred to a new safety agency. The committee of conference has agreed to the more limited purposes and scope of the House bill.

Two amendments to the House bill agreed to by your conferees require special mention. First, we have accepted a Senate amendment which adds to the provisions in the House bill which allowed interested persons to petition the Product Safety Commission to initiate a rulemaking proceeding for the development of a consumer product safety standard or to ban a hazardous product. The House provisions required the Commission to publish in the Federal Register its reasons for denying any such petition. The Senate amendment agreed to by the conferees will allow a petitioner whose request is denied to apply to district court for review of the Commission's denial. If the petitioner is able to convince the court by a preponderance of evidence that the product presents an unreasonable risk of injury and that the Commission's failure to initiate a rulemaking proceeding unreasonably exposes the petitioner or other consumers to a risk of injury, the court may compel the Commission to begin a proceeding. Two important limitations are placed on this authority.

First, the court may not order the Commission to take any action beyond the initiation of a proceeding. It could not, for example, order the Commission to adopt a particular standard. Second, we have decided to delay the effective date of this provision until 3 years after enactment. Several members of the conference expressed concern that the Commission should have an opportunity in the first years of its existence to properly order its priorities.

The National Commission on Product Safety has identified over 40 products which may require mandatory safety standards. Accordingly, the committee felt that the Commission should be given 3 years in which to act before allowing interested persons to bring a proceeding to compel action.

The second substantive addition to the House bill which I want to mention relates to stockpiling. In the past, under other safety laws, unscrupulous manufacturers have taken advantage of the lag between the date on which a safety standard is promulgated and the date on which it takes effect to produce non conforming products in great quantity. This practice obviously defeats the purpose of the safety standard. Accordingly, the Committee on Conference has agreed to accept a provision from the Senate bill which would allow the Commission to prohibit stockpiling in order to prevent circumvention of a consumer product safety rule.

Mr. Speaker, I believe the committee of Conference has reported a good bill. As I noted, it departs in only minor ways from the House passed bill and I strongly urge the House to agree to the conference report.

Mr. BROYHILL of North Carolina. Mr. Speaker, I rise in support of the conference report and the following is a brief discussion of the major differences.

The House bill was used as the vehicle for conference and came out essentially unchanged although numerous language changes were involved.

When the bill was before the House many members were concerned about a provision called the Nelson amendment which did not appear in the House bill but which had been inserted in the Senate bill.

The Nelson amendment prohibited manufacturers and other business interests from participating in the standard-setting process. This was diametrically opposed to the philosophy of the House bill which encouraged such participation.

The conference version retains a very limited portion of the Nelson amendment providing that in the very limited situation wherein a manufacturer of a product is the one and only offeror in a bid to create a product standard, the Commission may concurrently investigate and develop a similar standard.

Such a provision is justified in that the Commission should have independent knowledge of the subject matter where only one outfit is working up a standard which will apply to its product and similar products of possible competitors. In all other cases the Commission is foreclosed from duplicating the work of offerors to avoid unnecessary double expense.

The House bill allowed for individuals or groups to request action by the Commission on products not already subject to safety standards. If the Commission did not see fit to start such a proceeding it was required to state its reasons in the Federal Register. The Senate bill provided for a court appeal and a forcing of Commission action.

The conference version adds to the House version a provision for appeal to a district court with the petitioner bearing the burden of showing by a preponderance of the evidence that a safety standard is needed for the particular product. If the court agrees it must remand the case to Commission which is then required only to commence a rule making proceeding. Thereafter the matter goes along in the same manner as a proceeding initiated by the Commission. Persons unhappy with the resulting standard may appeal under the provisions of the Administrative Procedures Act.

In addition to the safeguards insisted upon by the House it was also agreed that the right to so petition would be delayed for 3 years. A new entity such as this Commission must first of all get organized. When it has done so there will be many obvious products needing attention. These should be handled before the Commission is beleagured by everyone's pet peeve.

A Senate provision set penalties for producing inventories of noncomplying items between the time a standard is set and it becomes effective. Many circumstances may inflenuce a decision to continue or step up production at any given time. To avoid injustice from such an automatic offense, language was inserted to make clear that the so-called stockpiling had to be done to circumvent or flout the new safety standard.

Except as to injunction proceedings for imminent hazards, a power which exists in the other regulatory agencies, the basic control of litigation was left with the Department of Justice.

Mr. STAGGERS. Mr. Speaker, I move the previous question on the conference report.

The previous question was ordered.

The conference report was agreed to.

A motion to reconsider was laid on the table.

APPENDIX L

STATEMENT OF SENATE CONFEREES

(from the Congressional Record for October 14, 1972, starting at page S 18198)

CONSUMER PRODUCT SAFETY ACT—CONFERENCE REPORT

Mr. MOSS. Mr. President, I submit a report of the committee of conference on S. 3419, and ask for its immediate consideration.

The PRESIDING OFFICER. The report will be stated by title.

The legislative clerk read as follows:

The committee of conference on the disagreeing votes of the two houses on the amendment to the bill (S. 3419) to protect consumers against unreasonable risk of injury from hazardous products, and for other purposes, having met, after full and free conference, have agreed to recommend and do recommend to their respective Houses this report, signed by a majority of the conferees.

The PRESIDING OFFICER. Is there objection to the consideration of the conference report?

There being no objection, the Senate proceeded to consider the report.

(The conference report is printed in the House proceedings of the CONGRESSIONAL RECORD of October 12, 1972, at pp. H9844–H9853).

Mr. MOSS. Mr. President, I move that the Senate agree to the conference report on S. 3419.

This bill represents the culmination of 10 years of legislative effort to secure the consumer's right to safety in the marketplace. The bill creates an independent regulatory agency composed of five Commissioners who would have the authority to set product safety standards for consumer products of all types. The Commission would also be empowered to ban certain products which could not be made safe by the establishment of a safety standard. Consumer products which were imminently hazardous could be removed immediately without administrative proceedings through court action initiated by the Commission.

This bill provides the Federal Government with the weaponry to make significant inroads against unsafe consumer products in the marketplace thereby preventing many of the 20 million product associated injuries that occur each year. The bill also contains safeguards against bureaucratic indifference. Congress for the first time has created a mechanism whereby private citizens can compel, through petition court preceedings, an agency to initiate action to protect the public health and safety. The Commission responsibility provisions agreed to by the conference committee will guarantee that the promises of safety made by the sponsors of this legislation will be met in subsequent years.

Mr. President, while the bill agreed to by the conference committee is a great step forward for the American consumer, I cannot help but express my regret that the Senate was not able to prevail in its efforts to upgrade the quality of Government regulation of foods and drugs by transferring the Food and Drug Administration to this new, independent regulatory agency. Those of us concerned about the safety of products in the marketplace realize that we have more work to do with respect to the safety of foods, drugs, cosmetics, and medical devices. I share the frustration expressed by Senator PERCY that we have created a new, independent regulatory agency to watch out over consumer products but have done nothing to upgrade the performance of the agency responsible for the safety of foods and drugs. We must fight that battle again next year.

I understand the distinguished Senator from New Hampshire (Mr. COTTON) will be on the floor shortly and would like to be present before final action is taken on the conference report.

I also intend to insert a floor statement by the chairman of the Commerce Committee (Mr. MAGNUSON).

Mr. President, I would like to offer the following remarks concerning specific provisions of the product safety bill agreed to by the committee of conference. My comments will expand the joint statement of managers in those areas where I believe greater comment is appropriate:

First. Establishment of Federal agency to regulate consumer product safety: The Senate bill would have established a comprehensive program to regulate foods, drugs, cosmetics, medical devices, and other consumer products. The House bill provided only for the regulation of consumer products. In the Senate bill proper staffing of the agency was assured by a provision authorizing the appointment of 25 supergrades. In agreeing to the House amendment which contained no similar provision, the Senate did not in any way recede from its commitment to a properly staffed agency. It is my hope that sufficient supergrade positions will be allocated to this important new regulatory agency.

Second. Consumer information: The Senate bill provided for the establishment of a "public information room" designed to insure all interested parties access to consumer safety information. The House amendment had no specific provision requiring the establishment of a public information room. Although the Senate conferees agreed to the general language of the House bill, I am hopeful that the new independent regulatory agency will take appropriate steps to assure the public access to consumer safety information so as to prevent injury and make consumer participation in agency proceedings meaningful.

Third. Meaning of phrase "Unreasonable risk of injury associated with a consumer product": The Senate bill defined the phrase "unreasonable risk of injury presented by a consumer product." The definition set forth a balancing test which emphasized the primacy of health and safety over other factors. Two particular measures of public health and safety were to be considered: the degree of anticipated injury and the frequency of such injury. In those situations where either the degree of anticipated injury or the frequency of such injury could be reduced without affecting the "performance" or "availability" of that class of consumer product, then almost any risk capable of producing injury would become unwarranted. When "performance" or "availability" were affected, then a balancing of competing interests would have to be undertaken. The House bill did not contain a specific definition of "unreasonable hazard." Note that the House bill defined "hazard" as "risk of injury." The report accompanying the House amendment to S. 3419 set forth the same kind of balancing test which was incorporated in the definition of "unreasonable risk of injury presented by a consumer product" in the Senate bill.

While the full reach of the term "unreasonable risk" will be left for the courts to decide, it is my hope that they will be guided by this important legislative history which sets forth an important balancing test. It is also my hope that the courts will take notice of the fact that the word "associated" was chosen so as to convey the fact that the risk of injury did not have to result from "normal use" of the consumer product but could also result from such things as "exposure to or reasonable foreseeable misuse of the consumer product." See, for example. the definition of "use" in the Senate bill.

Fourth. Title V of the Senate bill: Title V of the Senate bill amended the Federal Hazardous Substances Act to strengthen that act by requiring submission of product formulas, the results of screening tests for hazards, and antidote and treatment information. Title V also deleted the present exemption from the Federal Hazardous Substances Act for food, drugs, and cosmetics in certain fields. The House amendment did not contain an express provision for the collection of this information. But under section 27(e), the House amendment authorized the Commission to require any manufacturer—

> To provide to the Commission such performance and technical data related to performance of safety as may be required to carry out the purposes of the Act.

In agreeing to the deletion of title V, the Senate conferees were hopeful that the Commission under authority of section 27(e) would obtain formulation, information and toxicological test data on consumer products so as to aid the poison prevention activities of the Consumer Product Safety Commission.

Fifth. Safety analysis: The Senate bill authorized the Commissioner of Product Safety to require the manufacturer of a consumer product to subject such product to a detailed safety analysis. The purpose of the safety analysis study was to identify and thereby eliminate risks associated with the use of consumer products short of promulgating a consumer product safety standard. The House amendment did not contain specific provisions relating to safety analysis. However, a House provision agreed to in conference—section 27(e)—does authorize the Commission to obtain information to the same extent as if the safety analysis provisions of the Senate bill had been included.

Sixth. Retention of the names of first purchasers: The Senate bill authorized the Product Safety Commissioner to establish procedures to be followed by those persons in the distribution chain and consumers themselves in securing and maintaining the names and addresses of first purchasers of consumer products. In determining whether or not to require the maintenance of the names and addresses of first purchasers, the Commissioner would be required to consider the severity of the injury that could result if the consumer product was manufactured not in compliance with an applicable standard, the likelihood that a particular type or class of consumer product would be manufactured not in compliance, and the burden imposed upon the manufacturer, and ultimately the consumer, in requiring the maintenance of the names. Although the names of first purchasers would not be required to be maintained for all consumer products subject to consumer product safety standards, the recall of noncomplying consumer products would be very difficult without the names of the first purchasers.

The House amendment did not contain a specific provision relating to the maintenance of the names and addresses of first purchasers. However, in section 16(d) of the House amendment, which was accepted by the committee of conference, the Commission is authorized to require any manufacturer, private labeler, or distributor—but not retailer—to establish and maintain such records as may be reasonably required for the purpose of implementing the act. Therefore, there is authority to require the maintenance of the names and addresses of first purchasers within the bill as reported by the committee of conference. It is my hope that retailers will cooperate with manufacturers, private labelers, or distributors who are requested by the Commission to maintain the names and addresses of first purchasers. It is also my hope that the Commission looks to the guidelines set forth in the Senate bill in order to determine which manufacturers, private labelers, or distributors should be required to retain such information.

Seventh. Submission of Legislative Recommendations: The Senate bill authorized and directed the Admiinstrator of the Food, Drug, and Consumer Product Agency to submit legislative recommendations directly to the Congress without prior review of the Office of Management and Budget or any other Federal officer or Agency. The House amendment contained no comparable provision. The committee of conference agreed to the Senate provision authorizing and directing the direct submission of legislative recommendations. One might ask: "Why is this necessary?"

A recent situation involving administration proposed amendments to the Auto Safety Act illustrates the need for this provision. The agency responsible for implementing the Auto Safety Act, namely, the National Highway Traffic Safety Administration, submitted to the Secretary of Transportation, which in turn submitted to the Office of Management and Budget, a proposed amendment to the auto safety law to require automobile manufacturers to repair without charge vehicles which had been recalled because they contained a safety-related defect. The Department of Commerce communicated to the Office of Management and Budget their opposition to this amendment to the auto safety law. The Office of Management and Budget refused to submit the legislative recommendations for free repair of safety-related defects. In other words, the agency charged with responsibility of preventing death and carnage on our Nation's highways was precluded from communicating to Congress its desires concerning improvement of this legislation.

Only good fortune enabled the Congress to find out that there had been a difference of opinion and that, in fact, the National Highway Traffic Safety Administration endorsed legislation authorizing them to require the free repair of defective automobiles subject to recall. On the basis of this experience and similar experiences, those of us interested in a viable safety program want to know what the agency responsible for implementing the safety program thinks they need in the way of new authority to protect the health and safety of the American consumer. Therefore, we have required submissions of legislative recommendations to Congress, without prior review of OMB or anyone else.

Eighth. Private remedies: Both the Senate bill and the House amendment authorize an individual who has been injured by a consumer product that has been produced by a manufacturer who knows that the product does not meet an applicable product safety standard to sue such manufacturer in Federal court if the person's injuries were alleged to be greater than $10,000. In creating this Federal right but limiting the access to the Federal courts to injuries causing damage alleged to be greater than $10,-

000, the Senate and House conferees did not mean to preclude State courts from concurrent jurisdiction in enforcing the Federal right in those situations where the extent of injury was less than $10,000.

Ninth. Legal action by Commission: The Senate bill authorized the Administrator of the Food, Drug, and Product Safety Agency to "initiate, prosecute, defend, or appeal any court action in the name of the Agency for the purpose of enforcing the laws subject to its jurisdiction, through his own legal representative or through the Attorney General, and direct the course of all litigation." The House amendment had no similar authorization. The committee of conference agreed to a provision which gives the Commission the authority to initiate, prosecute, defend, or appeal any court action in the name of the Commission for the purpose of enforcing the laws subject to its jurisdiction. But the Commission may not use its own legal representatives if the Attorney General notifies him that he does not concur. In the event of such notice the action would be handled by the Attorney General in the name of the Commission.

Mr. President, this concludes my detailed remarks concerning S. 3419. I urge my colleagues to report its passage in the Senate and I urge the President to sign this important consumer measure into law as soon as possible.

Mr. President, I ask unanimous consent to have printed in the RECORD a statement by the chairman of the Committee on Commerce (Mr. MAGNUSON).

There being no objection, the statement was ordered to be printed in the RECORD, as follows:

STATEMENT OF SENATOR MAGNUSON

Mr. President, today is truly a momentuous day for the American consumer. The enactment of the Consumer Product Safety Act will mark the culmination of five very long and intensive years of study and analysis of the problem of safety presented by the growing number of consumer products in the marketplace. The formulation of this bill is the result of work by many segments of the society: engineers, lawyers, businessmen, consumers, economists, statisticians and medical personnel, just to name a few.

The bill which the Senate and House conferees have agreed upon is an adequate start towards protecting the American consumer from unsafe products. The new Consumer Product Safety Commission has been given a strong mandate from Congress to drastically reduce losses from product-related injuries. We have armed the Commission with an administrative procedure which will enable it to act "before the bodies stack up" while at the same time, insuring affected industries due process. Finally, we have afforded consumers an opportunity to actively become involved in the regulatory process.

The great disappointment of the bill which the Conference Committee has produced is its failure to effect any change in the federal regulatory structure of foods, drugs, cosmetics and medical devices. It is a well known fact that the American people have lost faith in the Food and Drug Administration's ability to provide the required measure of protection against adulterated foods and drugs.

A recent G.A.O. report revealed that 40 per cent of the food plants in the United States operate under unsanitary conditions and that only 3 of every 10 plants are in compliance with existing sanitary standards. It was also of little comfort to learn of the totally inadequate "filth tolerance standards" that F.D.A. has adopted for the food industry.

The Senate adopted by a vote of 69–10 the recommendation of three Committees that responsibility for foods and drugs should be transferred to the new Product Safety Agency. Even when that provision was defeated in Conference, Senators Kennedy, Percy, Ribicoff and Javits persisted in attempting to create a more functionally independent F.D.A. within H.E.W. It was only when the entire product safety bill was threatened, that they receded in their efforts. To these colleagues, and to the American people, I pledge that next year we shall begin the badly needed work of revitalizing food and drug regulation in the federal government.

With the enactment of S. 3419, we begin a new era in the cause of the consumer. In 1962, President Kennedy told consumers that they had an inalienable "Right to Safety" in the products they purchase in the marketplace. Today, one decade later, we have finally crafted the machinery to begin insuring that right.

Mr. MOSS. I am very happy to yield to the ranking Republican member of the committee, the Senator from New Hampshire (Mr. COTTON).

Mr. COTTON. Mr. President, S. 3419—the Food, Drug and Consumer Product Safety Act of 1972—was considered and passed by the Senate this past June. At that time I voted against passage of the bill because:

First, there was no demonstrated need for the establishment of an independent food, drug, and product safety agency which would have had transferred to it the Food and Drug Administration now lodged within the Department of Health, Education, and Welfare;

Second, the impact of including "an electronic product" in the definition of "consumer product," coupled with the repeal of the Radiation Control for Health and Safety Act, was not clear; and

Third, the confusion arising out of the legislative interpretation given to the term "subject to regulation."

Mr. President, although there still exists opposition to the establishment of an independent product safety regulatory agency, I am pleased to note that my three principal concerns have, in large measure, been met by the conference report on S. 3419 now pending before the Senate.

The conference report on S. 3419 does establish an independent Consumer Product Safety Commission. But, it does not transfer to that Commission the functions of the Food and Drug Administration within the Department of HEW. The conference report in section 31 also provides that "the Commission shall have no authority under this act to regulate any risk of injury associated with electronic product radiation emitted from an electronic product—if such risk of injury may be subjected to regulation under" the Radiation Control for Health and Safety Act. The matter of the legislative interpretation of "subject to regulation," the exclusions from the definition of "consumer product," has been met, in large measure, by following the format of the House provision.

I am pleased to note, also, that as far as cost is concerned the 3-year appropriation authorization provided for the conference substitute is approximately one-fifth that which passed the Senate. It therefore represents a more reasonable and less costly approach.

Finally, Mr. President, the conference substitute in section 10 does provide for interested persons to petition the Product Safety Commission to commence a proceeding for the issuance, amendment, or revocation of a consumer product safety rule. Quite frankly, I did have some initial concern that such an action against the Commission there might involve money damages to be recovered from the Commission. However, I am pleased to note that the joint explanatory statement of the Committee of Conference makes clear that this is not possible with the following language:

> Section 10 does not authorize the petitioner to recover damages from the Commission or any of its employees.

Mr. President, I fought long and hard last June in this very Chamber attempting to structure this organization within the Department of HEW. While I still feel that my proposal represents a more logical first step in approaching the problem of consumer product safety regulation, both this body and the House felt otherwise and, although not agreeing entirely, I can accept that result. If there is to be such an independent Product Safety Commission, then I believe the conference report, which is the result largely of the efforts of the distinguished chairman of our Committee on Commerce (Mr. MAGNUSON), represents a commendable approach.

Mr. President, I therefore urge the adoption by the Senate of the conference report on S. 3419—the Consumer Product Safety Act.

The PRESIDING OFFICER. The question is on agreeing to the conference report.

Mr. MOSS. Mr. President, may I say just one further word? I wish to commend the Senator from New Hampshire for his very constructive and able assistance on this matter. It required a great deal of time and committee consideration. He was always very magnanimous during the consideration of the bill; he did not agree with all of it, and stated his position very clearly, but never at any time did he use any restraint on our going ahead. And when the committee finally acted, he cooperated, as he always does, fully and completely, in the presentation of the matter to the Senate for its action.

Mr. COTTON. Mr. President, I thank the distinguished Senator from Utah for his very generous words. We did have rather strong disagreements about the independent agency. As the Senator knows, when the bill passed the Senate I struggled to keep it within the HEW. But I do think the result of the conference is a very constructive one, and I am happy to join in advocating the passage of this measure. I am grateful to the distinguished Senator from Utah for his constant fairmindedness and courtesy throughout the consideration of this long and rather controversial measure.

The PRESIDING OFFICER. The question is on agreeing to the conference report.

The report was agreed to.

APPENDIX M

WHITE HOUSE ANNOUNCEMENTS ON SIGNING OF BILL

THE WHITE HOUSE

(October 28, 1972)

STATEMENT BY THE PRESIDENT

The Consumer Product Safety Act

I am pleased to sign into law S. 3419, the Consumer Product Safety Act. This legislation is the outgrowth of a proposal which I submitted to Congress in February of 1971. It is the most significant consumer protection legislation passed by the 92nd Congress.

S. 3419 creates a new independent Consumer Product Safety Commission to develop consumer product safety standards and to enforce these standards, in court if necessary. In addition, the commission will have authority to ban outright the sale of hazardous products which cannot be adequately regulated.

As beneficial as this legislation is for the consumer, the act contains certain language which will tend to weaken budget control – and a coordinated, unified budget is the consumer's ally in keeping inflation and taxes down. These provisions are unfortunate and should not be regarded as precedent for the future legislation.

The most important thing about this bill, however, is its recognition that a defective lawnmower or electric heater can be just as dangerous to the consumer and his family as contaminated food or improperly packaged drugs. It is high time that the Government provided for comprehensive regulation of the many potentially dangerous products commonly used in and around American households. While the Consumer Product Safety Act differs in several ways from the legislation I proposed, it answers a long-felt need and I am happy to give it my approval.

* * *

WHITE HOUSE ANNOUNCEMENT

The President has signed S. 3419 which establishes an independent Consumer Product Safety Commission and provides it with new regulatory authority over consumer products to prevent or reduce product hazards to health and safety.

The principal features of the bill follow:

Organization and Jurisdiction

– It creates a new independent Consumer Product Safety Commission to issue and enforce safety standards for products customarily used by consumers in the home, the school, or in recreation.

– The new Commission will consist of five Commissioners appointed by the President (one of whom he will designate as Chairman) serving staggered seven-year terms.

– Commissioners could be removed by the President only for neglect of duty or malfeasance in office.

– Establishes statutory fifteen-member Product Safety Advisory Council to assist the Commission.

– Transfers to the new Commission the functions, budget, and personnel of several agencies relating to the Hazardous Substances Act, the Poison Prevention Packaging Act, the Flammable Fabrics Act, and the Refrigerator Door Safety act.

Regulatory Provisions

– Gives the Commission broad authority to promulgate and supervise compliance with mandatory safety standards; ban or seize hazardous products from the marketplace; and obtain enforcement through court injunctions or criminal and civil penalties.

– Permits private suits for damages, for injunctive relief, and for compelling initiation of standard proceedings or compliance with Commission rules and orders.

Other Provisions

– All budget estimates or legislative proposals submitted by the Commission to the President or the Office of Management and Budget are to be concurrently transmitted to the Congress.

– The bill authorizes appropriations of $55 million, $59 million, and $65 million to carry out the Commission's functions in fiscal years 1973, 1974, and 1975, respectively.

– Provides that the Act would become effective 60 days after enactment except that the establishment of the Commission and the appropriation authorization would be effective upon enactment.

APPENDIX N

REVISED CONSUMER PRODUCT LIST

(prepared by National Commission on Product Safety)

I. GENERAL HOUSEHOLD APPLIANCES

Clothes washers without wringers or other dryers
Washing machines with wringers
Washing machines with spin dryers without thermal dryers
Washing machines with electric dryers
Washing machines with gas dryers
Electric dryers without washing machines attached
Ironers
Electric blankets and electric sheets
Electric heating pads
Electric fans
Sewing machines
Floor buffers and waxers
Electric rug cleaners
Vacuum cleaners
Electric sweepers
Automatic door openers and closers
Gas water heaters
Electric water heaters
Oil water heaters
Incinerators without gas or electric heat supply
Electric incinerators
Gas incinerators
Water fountains, with or without cooling or heating units
Water softeners and conditioners
Washing machines not otherwise specified
Clothes dryers, not otherwise specified
Water heaters, not otherwise specified
Incinerators, not otherwise specified

II. KITCHEN APPLIANCES

Electric ranges with ovens, except self-cleaning ovens
Electric ranges without ovens
Gas ranges with ovens, except self-cleaning ovens
Gas ranges without ovens
Electric ovens separate from ranges
Gas ovens separate from ranges
Electric refrigerators
Gas refrigerators
Electric freezers
Gas freezers
Automatic corn poppers
Can openers, powered
Dishwashers
Electric blenders
Electric broilers
Electric coffeemakers and teapots
Cutlery, powered
Electric deep fryers
Electric defroster devices
Electric food warmers and hot trays
Electric fry pans and skillets
Electric griddles
Electric hot plates and grills
Electric ice-cream makers
Electric ice crushers
Electric ice makers, separate from refrigerators
Electric juicers
Electric kettles
Electric meat grinders
Electric mixers
Electric scissors
Electric slicers
Toasters
Electric waffle irons
Faucet water heaters
Garbage disposers
Irons with dry heat
Steam irons
Knife sharpeners
Rotisseries
Electric immersion heaters
Ranges, not otherwise specified
Ovens, not otherwise specified
Refrigerators, not otherwise specified
Freezers, not otherwise specified
Irons, not otherwise specified
Electric ovens, self-cleaning
Gas ovens, self-cleaning
Range and oven accessories (including racks, broiler pans, etc.)

III. SPACE HEATING, COOLING, AND VENTILATING APPLIANCES

Electric air conditioners
Gas air conditioners
Fans, water cooled
Humidifiers
Vaporizers
Dehumidifiers
Ionizers
Broilers
Coal furnaces, including floor furnaces
Gas furnaces, including floor furnaces
Oil furnaces, including floor furnaces
Panel and cable electric radiant heat units
Electric space heaters
Gas space heaters and gas heating stoves, attached.
Note: For portable heaters see category XII, sports and recreation equipment
Kerosene space heaters and kerosene heating stoves, attached.
Fireplaces and wood or coal stoves, factory built
Chimneys, factory built
Electric furnaces, including floor furnaces
Other heating systems, including heat pumps
Radiators and hot water or steam pipes
Air conditioners, not otherwise specified
Furnaces, not otherwise specified
Space heaters, not otherwise specified
Heating stoves, not otherwise specified
Water heaters, not otherwise specified
Floor furnaces, not otherwise specified

IV. HOUSEWARES

Can openers, unpowered
Chafing dish with open flame heaters
Table stoves - open flame
Non-electric coffee grinders
Coffee makers and teapots, unpowered
Cooking utensils and ovenware including glass
Cutlery, unpowered
Ironing boards and covers
Manual ice crusher
Manual juicers
Manual heat grinders
Pressure cookers and canners
Waste containers
Cutting and chopping devices including scissors
Candles and candleholders, including butane candles
Corkscrews and other opening devices
Flatware, except cutlery
Tableware, including insulated design

1/In the case of certain product categories (primarily IX and XVI), some products may be subject to limited Federal regulations under existing laws. In each case, such products are listed here because all potential hazards are not subject to regulation or because some remedial means (such as labeling) are covered, while others (such as performance standards) are not.

V. HOME COMMUNICATIONS AND ENTERTAINMENT APPLIANCES AND EQUIPMENT

Television sets
Radios, and record players, including Hi-Fi and Stereo equipment
Sound and video recording and reproducing equipment (tape recorders and players)
Musical instruments including electric musical instruments
Motion picture and still cameras
Other photographic equipment and accessories
Movie projectors
Slide projectors
Intercommunication devices
Telephone and telephone accessories
Typewriters, electric and manual
TV and radio antennas
Art supplies and equipment
Clay, pottery and ceramic supplies and equipment
Printing presses

VI. HOME FURNISHING AND FIXTURES

Beds, springs, mattresses, covers and pads
Chairs
Tables
Other furniture including multiple use and lawn furniture
Electrical outlets, built-in wiring devices, and distribution systems for use in or around the household
Electric power plants
Gas pipes, fittings and distribution systems
Plumbing fixtures and pipes, including sinks and toilets
Structural glass and glass doors, including bathtub and shower enclosures
Bathtub and shower enclosures of materials other than glass
Bathtub and shower structures other than doors and panels, including the tub, walls, handgrips, etc.
Runners and throw rugs
Carpeting including outdoor carpeting but excluding runners
Sheets and pillow cases
Pillows
Blankets, except electric and baby blankets
Drapes, curtains including plastic curtains and shower curtains
Step ladders
Straight ladders
Stepstools
Appliance cords, extension cords and replacement wire
Gas meters
Meters for LP gas
Electric meters
Gas lamps
Electric table lamps and floor lamps
Light bulbs
Electric light fixtures, attached
Electric clocks
Medicine cabinets
Gun cabinets, ammunition cabinets and racks
Other cabinets, shelves and storage areas
Sump pumps
Furniture, not otherwise specified
Fabrics not otherwise specified
Ladders or stepstools, not otherwise specified
Meters, not otherwise specified
Window shades and venetian blinds
Flashlights and electric lanterns
Mirrors and mirror glass
Glass - unknown origin

VII. HOME ALARM, ESCAPE, AND PROTECTION DEVICES

Fire extinguishers
Fire and smoke alarms
Fire excape devices, including chain ladders
Burglar alarms
Ground fault circuit interrupters
Lighting arrestors, rods and grounding devices
Locks and padlocks

VIII. HOME WORKSHOR APPARATUS, TOOLS, AND ATTACHMENTS

Power saws
Power drills
Power sanders
Power routers
Power lathes
Power grinders
Power jointers
Power shapers
Other portable and stationary power tools
Workshop manual tools and accessories
Torches
Welding equipment
Soldering guns and irons
Hoists, lifts, jacks and chains
Test equipment
Battery chargers
Batteries
Extension work lights and continuous use flood lights
Separate electric motors
Internal combustion engines, for use in or around the household
Automotive tools and accessories
Paint sprayers
Air compressors, separate

IX. HOME AND FAMILY MAINTENANCE PRODUCTS

Cleaning agents and compounds
Bleaches and dyes
Solvent based cleaning and sanitizing compounds
Waxes
Polishes
Fumigants
Paints, paint removers, brushes and rollers
Thinners
Adhesives and adhesive products including glues and tapes
Gasoline
Kerosene
Anti freeze
Lubricants
Alcohol
Caustics
Charcoal
Caulking compounds
Other chemicals, including photographic chemicals
Wallpaper cleaners and removers, including steamers
Other cleaning equipment

X. FARM EQUIPMENT

Electric fences
Home pasteurizers
Cream Separaters

XI. PACKAGING AND CONTAINERS FOR HOUSEHOLD PRODUCTS

Pressurized containers
Vacuum containers
Self-contained openers
Resealable closures
Child resistant closures
Glass bottles and containers
Containers made of materials other than glass, except vacuum or pressure containers
Plastic wrapping products, including plastic trash and garden bags
Paper and cardboard products, and other paper objects, including magazines, newspapers, books, etc.

XII. SPORTS AND RECREATIONAL EQUIPMENT

Playground equipment, swings, slides and associated hardware.
Bicycles and bicycle equipment
Boats, motors and accessories for recreational use
Baseball equipment
Basketball and volleyball equipment.
Bowling equipment
Boxing and wrestling equipment
Croquet equipment
Exercise equipment
Fishing equipment
Football equipment
Golf equipment except golf carts
Golf carts
Hockey equipment, including ice skates
Lacrosse equipment
Skiing equipment, including skiis, poles, boots and bindings
Sleds and toboggans
Snowmobiles
Tennis equipment, including badminton and table tennis
Swimming and underwater sports equipment, including scuba accessories and spear guns

Headgear for cycling
Beach equipment
Stationary and portable grills, kerosene, charcoal and gas
Portable gasoline and kerosene stoves
Portable gasoline, alcohol, and gas heating equipment
Note: For attached heating devices see category III.
Gasoline, kerosene and propane lanterns and lamps
Battery powered cooking devices
Picnic equipment including coolers
Camping equipment including tents, cots, and sleeping bags
Camping trailers, other than mobile homes
Swimming and wading pools and associated equipment
Charcoal igniters, electrical or chemical
Rebound tumbling devices
Play houses and tree houses
Archery equipment and darts
Unlicensed motor scooters and go-karts
Gas, air and spring operated guns
Other special sports and camping clothing
Horseback riding equipment
Aquariums, including pumps, heaters and accessories

XIII. TOYS

Wheeled toys - carrying the child, powered and unpowered including wagons, tricycles, stand-up scooters, pedal cars, sit-in airplanes, sit-in trucks
Non-mechanical dolls and toy animals
Mechanical dolls and toy animals including keywind and battery operated
Other windup and battery operated toys
Wheeled toys not carrying the child, powered and unpowered including toy cars, electric trains, and non-flying airplanes
Gasoline powered toys, including model airplanes
Electric games
Skates and skateboards
Kites and kite string
Pogo sticks and stilts
Toy guns and other toy weapons without projectiles
Toy guns and other toy weapons with projectiles
Fireworks, explosives and caps
Rocketry sets
Chemistry sets
Other science kits and toys
Flying devices, not gasoline or rocket powered
Other models and their construction materials. For glues see category IX.
Metal and plastic molding sets
Games, other than electric
Toy home equipment, including ovens, stoves, sinks, irons, sewing machines, washing machines, etc.
Children play tents, play tunnels and other enclosures
Toy balls and balloons
Inflated toys other than balloons
Blocks, pull toys, and similar items

XIV. YARD AND GARDEN EQUIPMENT

Power mowers of all types
Hand mowers
Hand garden tools
Power trimmers and edgers
Garden tractors
Snow throwers and snow plows
Garden sprayers
Power tillers and cultivators
Other power garden tools
Outdoor lighting equipment
Chain saws
Pumps including electric submersible fountain pumps
Greenhouse equipment
Garden hose, nozzles, and sprinklers
Winter manual yardtools
Insect traps and insecticide vaporizers, electrically operated
Yard decorative equipment including fish ponds, bird baths, planters, bird houses, etc.

XV. CHILD NURSERY EQUIPMENT AND SUPPLIES

Highchairs
Changing tables
Infant seats
Cribs, including springs and mattresses
Carriages
Gates
Baby blankets, sheets, pads, pillows, etc. and other baby bedding equipment
Walkers
Bottles, nipples and related items
Bottle warmers
Sterilizers
Diapers and diaper pins, including disposable diapers
Playpens
Baby baths
Baby scales
Other nursery furniture and equipment, including baby rattles

XVI. PERSONAL USE ITEMS

Razors and shavers
Hair dryers
Hair curlers
Cigarette, cigar and pipe lighters, and lighter fluid
Wigs
Eyeglasses, not including contact lenses
Eye protection devices, including light shields, sunglasses
Powered tooth brushes and picks
Sun lamps
Massage devices
Manicure devices
Saunas including facial saunas
Electric shoe polishers
Clothing
Footwear except for sports footwear
Other beauty aids, and jewelry
Ear protection devices, including noise plugs
Respiratory protection devices
Personal protection devices, including tear gas pens and tear gas guns
Hearing aids
Umbrellas
Wrist watches, wrist compasses, pendant watches, pocket watches, etc.
Luggage
Contact lenses

XVII. HOME STRUCTURES, CONSTRUCTION MATERIALS,

Stairs, ramps and handrails, indoors and outdoord
Fireplaces, individually built
Insulation materials
Siding materials, including aluminum siding
Doors, trap doors, hatches and other ingress-egress devices
Note: Glass doors and automatic door openers are listed elsewhere.
Roofs and roofing materials
Floors and flooring materials, including patios
Awnings and shutters
Patio and porch covers
Outside structures, including retaining walls, fences and separate enclosures
Elevators and other lifts
Windows and window glass
Scaffolding
Landings, porches, balconies, open side floors and floor openings
Cisterns, cesspools, and septic tanks
Nails, carpettacks and construction materials
Hardware including doorknobs, hinges, cabinet pulls, door springs, etc.

XVIII. OTHER PRODUCTS

Christmas and other seasonal decorations, including trees
Switchblade and gravity knives
Mobile homes and related equipment including campers
Matches
Ash trays
Crutches and canes
Wheelchairs
Special beds
Other special equipment for the injured or aged
Home first-aid and health equipment including hot water bottles, thermometers, etc.

TOPICAL INDEX

D

E

F

G

H

I

J

K

L

M

N

O

P

R

S

T

U

V

W